In the Province of History

In the Province

of

HISTORY

The Making of the Public Past in
Twentieth-Century Nova Scotia

———◆———

Ian McKay *and* Robin Bates

McGill-Queen's University Press • Montreal & Kingston • London • Ithaca

© McGill-Queen's University Press 2010

ISBN 978-0-7735-3703-3 (cloth)
ISBN 978-0-7735-3704-0 (paper)

Legal deposit second quarter 2010
Bibliothèque nationale du Québec

Printed in Canada on acid-free paper that is 100% ancient forest free (100% post-consumer recycled), processed chlorine free.

This book has been published with the help of a grant from the Canadian Federation for the Humanities and Social Sciences, through the Aid to Scholarly Publications Programme, using funds provided by the Social Sciences and Humanities Research Council of Canada.

McGill-Queen's University Press acknowledges the support of the Canada Council for the Arts for our publishing program. We also acknowledge the financial support of the Government of Canada through the Canada Book Fund for our publishing activities.

Library and Archives Canada Cataloguing in Publication

McKay, Ian, 1953–
In the province of history : the making of the public past in twentieth-century Nova Scotia / Ian McKay and Robin Bates.

Includes bibliographical references and index.
ISBN 978-0-7735-3703-3 (bnd)
ISBN 978-0-7735-3704-0 (pbk)

1. Tourism–Social aspects—Nova Scotia. 2. Heritage tourism—Nova Scotia—History—20th century. 3. Tourism—Nova Scotia—History—20th century. 4. Tourism—Government policy—Nova Scotia. 5. Culture and tourism—Nova Scotia. 6. Collective memory—Nova Scotia. 7. Nova Scotia—Historiography. I. Bates, Robin, 1979— II. Title.

FC2311.M337 2010   971.6'03   C2010-901920-2

This book was designed and typeset by studio oneonone in Bembo 10.7/13.

Contents

Illustrations ◆ vii

Acknowledgments ◆ ix

A Note on Usage ◆ xi

Prologue: The People of "Canada's Ocean Playground" ◆ 3

1 How a Land without Antiquities Became the Province
of History ◆ 18

2 This Is the Province Primeval: Evangeline and the
Beginnings of Tourism/History ◆ 71

3 "All the world was safe and happy": The Innocence
of Will R. Bird ◆ 130

4 Down the Twisting Path of Destiny: The Impossible
Liberalism of Thomas Raddall ◆ 200

5 Marketing Race: Angus L. Macdonald, Tartanism, and the
Cultural Politics of Whiteness ◆ 253

6 Of Runic Stones and Lockean Dreams: The Triumvirate
and Its Treasures, 1935–1964 ◆ 317

Conclusion: Is the Romance Ended? ◆ 369

Notes ◆ 381

Index ◆ 457

Illustrations

Inside back cover of *Nova Scotia, Canada's Ocean Playground*
  (caption omitted) ◆ 4
"Native Types," inside back cover of *Nova Scotia, Canada's Ocean Playground*
  (caption included) ◆ 10
"Louisbourg, Near Sydney, Cape Breton, N.S." ◆ 39
"Baptism of Indians at Port Royal" ◆ 41
Visions of civilized Halifax ◆ 55
Halifax parks ◆ 56
The home of Evangeline as imagined by Currier & Ives illustrator Frances
  Flora (Bond) Palmer ◆ 82–3
The Dominion Atlantic Railway's Land of Evangeline network ◆ 105
Cover of *High Lights of Nova Scotia History* ◆ 106
Image of Evangeline ◆ 106
Marketing Acadians ◆ 108
The park at Grand Pré, also known as "The Heart of Evangeline Land" ◆ 109
Map of Land of Evangeline Route ◆ 110
Evangeline and A.L. Hardy, and "A Modern Conception of the
  Maid Evangeline" ◆ 116
"Playground with a History" ◆ 120
Highly stylized tourist map of Nova Scotia from the early 1970s ◆ 125
Contemporary *Hectoriana* from the town of Pictou ◆ 274
Kilted Cape Breton Scots ◆ 293
"Keltic Lodge, Cape Breton" ◆ 293
"Highland dancing at Antigonish" ◆ 305
The provincial coat of arms ◆ 313
Historical tartanism ◆ 314
Twenty-first-century tartanism ◆ 314

The famous (or infamous) runic stone ◆ 318
The arrival of New England Planters in 1760 ◆ 340
The provincial flag on the cover of Will R. Bird's *Historic Nova Scotia* ◆ 341
"Order of the Good Time, Nova Scotia" ◆ 343
Port Royal habitation ◆ 344
Frost Monument, Yarmouth ◆ 361
Promotional painting by Franklin Arbuckle for the Dominion Atlantic
  Railway, c. 1950 ◆ 370

Acknowledgments

In the Province of History has emerged from six years of intensive collaboration between the co-authors. Earlier versions of some discussions, such as that on Angus L. Macdonald and the Scottish tradition in chapter 5 and on historic sites and monuments in chapter 6, appeared in 1992 and 1993 articles by Ian McKay in *Acadiensis*, whose editors are thanked for permitting their inclusion in this book.[1]

As our prologue suggests, the present work can legitimately be read as a sequel to the investigation into the cultural contradictions of capitalism in Nova Scotia initiated in *Quest of the Folk* (1994). All the remaining material, incorporating radical revision of the earlier work, was prepared by both authors together, and this book not only continues, but in many ways transforms the argument of its 1994 predecessor. In particular, it analyses at greater depth the relations between tourism/history, liberal order, and the logic of commodification in capitalist society.

Robin Bates would like to thank J.F. Acevedo, Barbara Duffin-Bates, Arvind Elangovan, Tyson Leuchter, Gregory Malandrucco, Carolyn Purnell, Paul Reale, and Dwaipayan Sen for reading and commenting on portions of the manuscript, as well as Ted Cook and the British Studies Workshop at the University of Chicago for hosting a round table discussion on chapter 4.

Ian McKay would like to thank Barry Cahill and Nova Scotia Archives and Records Management for facilitating his research in Halifax; Ross Cameron, Susan Jodrey, Jeremy Morrison, Kate Shaughnessy, and Tena Vanderheyden for their research assistance; and the late George Rawlyk, Brian Osborne, and participants in York University's graduate symposium for their comments and advice. He also gratefully acknowledges the assistance of the Social Sciences and Humanities Research Council, whose standard research grant #410-02-1549 allowed him to undertake this project, and Queen's University, which administered the grant on his behalf. And many thanks to Robert Vanderheyden, who is owed a special debt of gratitude for his patience and understanding.

A Note on Usage

As far as possible, we have sought to retain the spelling and punctuation found in original documents. On those rare cases when we have felt it necessary to correct or comment on an original source, we have placed our additions in square brackets.

In 1997 the Public Archives of Nova Scotia (PANS) in Halifax was renamed Nova Scotia Archives and Records Management (NSARM). In the company of many other scholars, and in line with a convention then established, we have retained "PANS" as our short form in references to papers held by this institution.

In the Province of History

Prologue: The People of "Canada's Ocean Playground"

Before we begin in earnest, let us offer you a little iconology as an aperitif for the feast to follow. The inside back cover of *Nova Scotia, Canada's Ocean Playground* (1936) – published under the authority of the Honourable A.S. MacMillan, minister of highways in the provincial Liberal government of Angus L. Macdonald – presents an arresting montage of seven photographic portraits. The top two are circular (with diameters of 2.25"). The lower four are rectangular, ranging in size from (centre right) 2" by 2.75" to (bottom right) 2.25" by 1.75". Finally, in the centre we see a much larger image, 3" by 4.75". None of the six smaller images touch, but they all touch the half-inch frame of the central figure. The boundaries of the two circular images overlap this frame and even intrude on the central photograph itself.

The images appear in an official tourist publication issued by a government unlikely to leave much to chance where tourism was concerned. Hence we may assume the montage means to tell us something important about Nova Scotia. Yet, without the guiding explanatory assistance of the title and caption (which, in our first run through this illustration, we have deliberately suppressed), we might feel perplexed about what could possibly unite this smorgasbord of portraits. Each photo portrays an individual, none of whom has an intrinsic connection with any of the others. The two top figures, for example, offer a study in contrasts. She is young, smooth-faced, and dressed in immaculate white. He is middle-aged, weather-beaten, dressed in a fisherman's sou'wester and work clothes. The middle figures, both seated, are more of an age, but they

Inside back cover of Nova Scotia, Department of Highways, *Nova Scotia, Canada's Ocean Playground* (Halifax, n.d. [1936]) (caption omitted).

too seem to hail from different worlds. She sits in a cozy room, eyes on her spinning wheel. He stands outside, a rock-bound coast behind him, gripping his net with a brawny, swollen, possibly damaged (isn't he missing a finger?) hand. And the bottom two portraits could hardly be more different. In one, a woman surrounded by quilts gazes confidently down at us from her porch, cutting rather an elegant figure with her white collar and dotted blouse. Yet her male counterpart, dressed in homespun, barely meets our gaze as he plays his fiddle.

These people seem not to share any collective way of life. By implication, they inhabit distinctly separate gendered spheres: women on the left, men standing to the right. All the men are outdoors, whereas the women, with the ambiguous exception of the bottom-left quilt-maker (occupying the liminal area of the porch), are indoors. Though paired in male-female duos, they seem not to be positioned as three heterosexual couples, for their eyes do not meet. Moreover, the milieus where we encounter these individuals look starkly different. Of the lower four, we seemingly glimpse three in the midst of their everyday working lives. The top two, on the other hand, have obviously posed for the occasion so as to eliminate the contextual detail of rock bound cliffs, rolling hills, and cozy homes that situate the others. We get a much closer look at their faces – the smooth complexion and gentle smile of the one, the weathered lines and resolute expression of the other. What, apart from the mere happenstance of living in Nova Scotia, could explain their togetherness?

When we look more closely at the arrangement of the seven portraits, we begin to notice some formally unifying patterns. Women and men seem to occupy separate places on the page, but these spheres relate to each other as left does to right. If the man and the woman in the small photographs at the bottom of the page seem to be looking away from each other, then the next two figures, both seated and engaged in their separate (but, we imagine, complementary) tasks are seen face-on, but in ways that subtly obscure their eyes from us – his are shadowed and seem fixed on a distant spot, while she has lowered her eyes, attending to her work. Finally, the woman and man in the top two images – captured in profile and looking in opposite directions – seem (on the page) to gaze in each other's direction, he more directly at her than she at him. Their faces are aglow with light. As we work our way *up* the photograph, in short, we seem to confront imagined individuals in closer and closer contact with each other.

On a purely formal level, this montage playfully balances informality and order. The distribution of the photographs recalls the carelessly spontaneous arrangement of snapshots in a tourist's photo album. Contrasted with, say, a template that imposed a standard shape and size on the photographs and then arranged them in rectilinear columns, this one plays with the borders of the portraits, allowing the circular images at the top to overlap the central image and accommodating slightly different-sized images in the centre of the page. At the same time, rules evidently govern this play. The images are arranged symmetrically so as to approximately balance each other. And the layout of the title and text furthers the overall impression of balance and harmony, for together they form an upside-down "T" formation reminiscent of a historical monument standing upright or a column arising from a plinth.

Moreover, the large (3″ by 4.75″), centrally located seventh photograph, of a kilted man, connects all six smaller images. Not only does he stand at the centre of the group, but his face – the palest of all those represented – seems (by symbolic implication) like the source of the transfiguring glow that enlivens the striking faces of the top two figures. Furthermore, these two both gaze, not at each other, but at him – like moons made radiant by his wan visage. And, while the others gaze out with downcast, shadowed, or distanced eyes, he alone confronts us directly with a look of power and confidence. Moreover, and obviously, he has dressed for the part. His stature, his air of decisiveness, and of course his costume – all give the appearance of command. He wears full-dress Scottish costume, including a most striking military-style horsehair sporran (an article useful in daily life for stashing keys, money, and so on, but here, located at the montage's dead centre, functioning as the phallic centre of a symbolic micro-cosmos). Finally, in contrast to the others, who occupy rustic environs, this dashing Scot stands at the foot of a large staircase, whose urbanity we can surmise from the elegant banister post beside him and the attractive stonework of the building in the background. At the very centre of his image is his plaid, a tartan piece worn over his shoulder and secured with a splendid brooch. He confronts us as the image of male potency, surrounded but hardly overpowered by the six marginal figures in the other photographs.

If we can go this far in deciphering the play of informality/formality, dispersion/concentration, margin/centre in this montage, what can we say about what it means? In an earlier work, *The Quest of the Folk* (1994; 2006), one of us suggests a way of approaching such images. As McKay remarked then, "The sense that we can make of a given photograph ... depends very much on the relationship between the photograph and the 'frame work' performed by those who, working in a particular context, develop implicit or explicit stories within which a given representation makes sense."[1] We go some distance towards understanding this montage if we pay attention to its formal characteristics. Yet, to grasp this montage's message more fully, we need to combine structure and context. What is the designer trying to tell us about these people? Here, of course, we have the advantage of the reader, for in our initial reproduction of this montage we have repressed the two-word main title and the 165-word text that establish its official meaning. We will get to this in a moment. But play along with us, because a small experiment will illustrate the core thesis of the book that follows.

Study the montage. Now insert, in the solemn textual centre of the title and caption – the latter shaped so much like a historical monument – the following:

PROGRESSIVE PEOPLE.
We Nova Scotians are an active, energetic and progressive people: men and women, young and old, rural and urban, all push our society to new frontiers of knowledge, culture and industry. Harold Boutilier, top right, and

his father Joseph, centre right, are two of the modern fishermen who have made Lunenburg County world famous for its mastery of the seas. James Martin, bottom right, has won an international reputation among musicians for his excellent fiddles. On the left, from bottom to top, home handicraft workers Molly McGuire, Jennie McPherson and Bonita Landry demonstrate the skills they bring to an innovative program that has transformed the province's countryside. How has it all been possible? "Hope, resolution, and courage," explains Captain William McPherson, centre, of Pictou County, seen here in his full ceremonial dress. "We returned from the Great War with a big job to do. No turning back." Their very faces seem to glow with that light of the better future which awaits dynamic Nova Scotia.

Here is one prevalent way of framing Nova Scotia's history: as a story of progress, growth, and liberty. It was both applied to the province by visitors and affirmed with gusto by Nova Scotians themselves. Down to the 1920s, when they looked at themselves and when others looked at them, Nova Scotians saw a land living the dream of inspired individualism, applied industry, and scientific improvement. In the sleek smokestacks of the steel mills, the bustling bankheads of the coal mines, the well-ordered farms and electrified rural towns, the technical institute and the agricultural college, not to mention the new insane asylum, they perceived the tangible signs of a new order. This way of framing the past did not disappear – indeed, we expect that any reader of the daily press could document its presence ad infinitum even now – and, arguably, it will persist so long as the capitalist social relations of a liberal order structure the lives and the politics of Nova Scotians. In this first framing, even images recalling a distant, primitive past flatter the present day: the more backward our supposed past, the more impressive is our bustling modern world.

Now return to the montage and insert a different title and message:

HISTORICAL PROVINCE.
Nova Scotia is blessed with a rich history – and one with a happy ending! Left, Jeanne-Marie Landry, her mother Josephine, and her aunt Marie, of Clare County, remember many childhood tales about the French Shore in the troubled 1750s. "Those were fighting days," says Jeanne-Marie, "but now we live in peace." Right, Harold Boutilier, his father Samuel, and his brother George, all of Lunenburg County, remember their Foreign Protestant families, brought here to rival the French Catholics. "Our forefathers came from Europe to build a new life," says George, who plays at many of the county's square dances. "We feel proud to carry on their work." This

achievement of peace, harmony and order could only have happened in the British Empire, which since 1710 has given Nova Scotia stability through good government. "We should celebrate our accomplishments," says Captain William McPherson, centre, dressed in the tartan that brought civilization to the world. "Nova Scotia has shown the world that freedom can wear a crown."

Here we encounter a second way to frame the past. It resembles the first – history still inspires and progress still triumphs – but this time we look back upon the past, not as the distant source of a better future, but as a series of specific inspirational happenings that we should recollect in some detail even today. Our ancestors and their deeds, remembered with specificity, legitimize our own identities in the present. Here is a history fascinated by character and circumstance, by named forebears and well-remembered locations, a historical practice that collected family trees and erected monuments to the heroes of a glorious tradition. This way of framing the past did not disappear either – as anyone familiar with local historical societies, with discussions of naming streets and buildings, and with the writing of memoirs can attest. Arguably it too will persist so long as individuals feel a need to identify ancestors, admire characters, and locate themselves, somehow or other, in their own time. It is not so much the story of *progress* as the story of *people*, grasped in at least some of their particularities.

We have supplied two plausible captions whose imposition on the montage does not grossly violate the expectations many twenty-first-century people bring to history. This book will document a third, and very different, strategy of history-making. Although it bears some resemblance to these earlier frameworks, and certainly draws upon the same pool of events and characters, it does so in a radically different way. This third way involves the transposition onto the past of the more general mythic framework of *Innocence*. *The Quest of the Folk* defines the concept: "Innocence discerned the essence of the society. The province was essentially innocent of the complications and anxieties of twentieth-century modernity. Nova Scotia's heart, its true essence, resided in the primitive, the rustic, the unspoiled, the picturesque, the quaint, the unchanging: in all those pre-modern things and traditions that seemed outside the rapid flow of change in the twentieth century."[2]

In this third dispensation, history grinds to a halt. Rather than an ongoing, complicated, unrepeatable process (like a river into which one can never step twice, to echo Heraclitus), it becomes something more like a treasure house of static *things* – images, objects, ideas – all frozen in time. Rather than giving us ancestors whose ideals and lives offer a counterpoint to our own, it gives us *particular properties* — units of exchange, discrete experiences, decontextualized images.

While the content of Innocence — which we capitalize to stress its status as a framework — denies modernity, its form incarnates it. These decontextualized properties and images function as so many units in a liberal political economy. Incommensurable objects are construed as having an abstract essence that differs in magnitude but never in kind. The logic of commodification works to restructure them, to make them units of exchange within a common myth. For all their elaborately cultivated differences in surface detail, the objects that developed within this framework are equivalent to one another as bearers of exchange value whose social function (as opposed to their concrete use value, which is personal rather than social) is to mediate human contacts by their production, sale, and distribution. If this seems conjectural, abstract, and counterintuitive, we hope it will become clearer as we proceed.

With this third framework of "tourism/history" in mind, let us turn now to the actual text from 1936:

NATIVE TYPES.

Five distinct white races are represented in Nova Scotia: English, Scotch, French Acadian, Irish and Hanoverian, all holding to many traits of their forefathers. The Acadians, first white settlers, from Normandy and Brittany, cling to their own customs and traditions thus making a contact with the long ago. The Hanoverians settled largely in Lunenburg and today their descendants, skilled sailors and fishermen, possess one of the finest fishing fleets in the world. The Highland Scots settled in Cape Breton Island, Pictou and Antigonish counties, and their descendants reserve the kilt and plaid for ceremonial occasions and cherish the Gaelic language of their forefathers. The English came from the New England States or direct from England, and their descendants are notably friendly and undemonstrative people. The Irish settlers came over from Ireland or the New England States, and their descendants are noted for their enterprise, generosity and sociability. Home handicrafts — including hooked rugs, spinning and weaving — are a feature of rural life in the Province.

Though framed by the same number of words, the montage suddenly takes on a vastly different meaning than those we had earlier imagined for it.

Our two imaginary texts unify the montage on the basis of concrete relationships between the individuals, binding them by ties of kinship, locality, and occupation, and even (to some limited extent) by common visions of the past and present. Such individuals bore names and dates, markers that placed them

Five distinct white races are represented in Nova Scotia: English, Scotch, French Acadian, Irish and Hanoverian, all holding to many traits of their forefathers. The Acadians, first white settlers, from Normandy and Brittany, cling to their own customs and traditions thus making a contact with the long ago. The Hanoverians settled largely in Lunenburg and today their descendants, skilled sailors and fishermen, possess one of the finest fishing fleets in the world. The Highland Scots settled in Cape Breton Island, Pictou and Antigonish counties, and their descendants reserve the kilt and plaid for ceremonial occasions and cherish the Gaelic language of their forefathers. The English came from the New England States or direct from England, and their descendants are a notably friendly and undemonstrative people. The Irish settlers came over from Ireland or the New England States, and their descendants are noted for their enterprise, generosity and sociability. Home handicrafts— including hooked rugs, spinning and weaving—are a feature of rural life in the Province.

"Native Types," from Nova Scotia, Department of Highways, *Nova Scotia, Canada's Ocean Playground* (Halifax, n.d. [1936]), inside back cover (caption included).

historically and would also allow them to debate the veracity of the story in which they would find themselves included. (For instance, if our imaginary Captain McPherson had been an antimonarchist Bolshevik in real life, he could have written an angry letter to demand a retraction and express dismay over the unauthorized appropriation of his picturesque likeness.) The imaginary texts allude, even if very generally, to specifiable conflicts and events (the Great War of 1914–18 in the first instance, as a springboard for progress and achievement; the complicated conflicts and adjustments of the 1750s in the second case, as a foil to subsequent imperial tranquility). But these historical details disappear in the actual text. As it turns out, no such verifiable historical or personal ties as kinship, locality, or ideas bind these seven individuals together. What unifies them is *whiteness.*

The master concept of "five distinct white races" is simultaneously definitive yet perplexing. We have seven individuals. Each must belong to a race.[3] Otherwise, why would they appear in this montage? Yet most of them do not obviously belong to any race in particular. Because she sports raiment conventionally associated with Acadian women, we guess that the top-left figure has to be the Acadian. Our kilted gentleman is at least dressing up as a Highland Scot, whatever his actual ancestry, so presumably that is his racial pigeonhole. The others present certain interpretive challenges, especially because we must apportion seven individuals to only five races. But in some sense the cultural identity of each individual hardly signifies – not enough, in any case, to belabour the text with such unnecessary details. It matters less that we can tie each individual to a "race" than that each one is "raced." The common theme is whiteness, with each specific identity merely elaborating its characteristics.

Moreover, if we turn to the title "Native Types," pondering its deeper resonances, we might wonder who would constitute a "Non-Native Type." In this connection, we may note that the montage omits at least three large groups: recent immigrants from Europe and Newfoundland, numerous indeed in industrial Cape Breton; Afro–Nova Scotians, the longest-settled black population in Canada; and the Mi'kmaq, who had lived in Nova Scotia since approximately ten thousand years before the arrival of Europeans. Representatives of the first two groups appear nowhere in the montage or in the publication as a whole. The third group does receive some notice elsewhere in the pamphlet: "The original inhabitants, Micmac Indians,[4] are a colorful folk on their reservations where they make baskets and beadwork to sell to visitors. Each year, on St. Ann's Day, they have an annual gathering at Mission Island in Cape Breton when a special procession and services are held. Bear River, in Annapolis County, has another reservation where the characteristics of the Micmacs are maintained to a high degree, and each year a typical Indian Carnival is held at Annapolis and Digby."[5]

Rather than mitigating the exclusion of the actual natives from the imagined "Native Types," this textual reference accentuates their absence. They do not function as one of the "distinct races," but as a source of souvenirs and entertainment for the travelling public. Indeed, no people of colour figure among the "Native Types," even if, in other contexts, some of them did count as "Natives."

The montage implicitly lays out a coherent doctrine whereby whiteness supplies the criterion of the true "native type." Moreover, this is a particular kind of whiteness. Formally, as we have seen, the montage is dominated by its largest single portrait – cynosure of the people we may now call the Acadian Woman and the Fisherman. In a representation of the races that leaves many of its represented individuals with an uncertain status, he stands front and centre in this montage (and, by implication, the society it represents). The boundaries of this figure at the centre are clear; the boundaries of many of those around him are fuzzier, literally and figuratively. If native types are drawn from all five distinct white races, only one occupies centre stage, defining the places and the functions of the other types around him. No wonder he alone confidently returns our gaze without qualification. As would become the norm in Nova Scotia between the wars, the white races are equal but one white race is more equal than the others. The Scots centre this imagined universe, while the others gravitate to its margins.

Looking more carefully at the "Native Types" text, we discern a history that returns obsessively to themes of stasis, retention, maintenance, and preservation. The Acadians "cling," the Hanoverians "possess," the Highland Scots "preserve" the kilt and "cherish" the Gaelic. Each character stays true to *type*. "Type" is a polyvalent word, but in this context – and especially when combined with the word "native" – one feels drawn to its biological acceptation, as designating "a plant or animal that represents its genus by having the main qualities that define it." When linked so clearly to "race," it also brings to mind "pheno*type*": "the visible characteristics of an organism resulting from the interaction between its genetic makeup and the environment."[6] "Native Types" suggests that a racial logic quietly structures the tangible world around us, encompassing not only ethnically appropriate items such as kilts and sporrans, but also moral qualities like enterprise, generosity, sociability, and so on. Beneath the visible world, and directly affecting its events, course unfathomably deep forces of race that generate the "types" of people we encounter and the particular things these people treasure. One reason to come to Nova Scotia is to purchase units – of things, experiences, atmospheres – that endow their possessor with a more direct and vivid encounter with these white races. Divided by their evident dissimilarities, then, the people in this illustration are all implicitly united by their status as *objects* of consumption. They are located in this text in order to draw its reader into an implied (and, it is to be hoped, realized) relationship in which the reader will proceed from one (indirect and passive) form of acquiring these units to another – one that involves passage to the province and profits for its promoters. And they are explicitly united to their exemplars through race.

In twenty-first-century critical thought, race (often encased in scare quotes, viz., "race"), along with its cognates racism, racialism, and racialization, has become perhaps the most contested term in the theoretical lexicon. Most contemporary scholars would agree with Susan Smith when she writes that "race is not a biological fact – it exists only as an ideological and historical construction. Separate human races do not exist even if human variation does. Instead race is something created in our language, laws, and science."[7] As a "biological fact," race has lost credibility among natural and social scientists. Yet this has not diminished its popularity, as a category and an explanation, in the wider world.

As Michael Banton notes, the use of the word "race" has pervaded Western European languages for perhaps five centuries. Originally used to "denote lineage, a line of descent, as in 'the race of Abraham,'" it tended to loosely define what we would now call nations – such as the Gauls and the Saxons in France and Britain, respectively. By the end of the eighteenth century, race had also come to delineate "a class of creatures with common characteristics, making it synonymous with either species or subspecies in modern classifications." Over the nineteenth century, this delineation became more and more elaborate, positing "different capacities and inherent antagonisms" for each race. By the 1850s, the master category of race could underpin an entire historical narrative that "offered a general explanation of the unequal development of the world's peoples." In the United States, biblical descriptions of human beings as descendants of Adam and Eve were contrasted with views holding that blacks and whites were "distinct types or species descended from different ancestors over a longer time period than was allowed for by the Bible." From the perspective of those holding this typological theory,

[t]o say that Gauls and Franks, or blacks and whites, were different races, was to equate their differences with those between lions, tigers, and leopards, different species within the genus *Panthera*, each with its peculiar capacities and behaviour patterns. The species maintain their distinctiveness of weight and body mass, not because the animals formulate and observe their own rules, but because nature keeps them distinctive through genetic inheritance. If the differences between Gauls and Franks, and blacks and whites, were permanent, political programmes needed to allow for them, either by compensatory measures or by acknowledging the limits to equality. For example, some deduced from such premises that in Ireland the descendants of seventeenth-century Protestant settlers from Scotland could never live in harmony with the indigenous Irish as members of one political unit.

… The typologists presented their notion of a racial type as an analytical concept that explained the underlying determinants of human grouping.

"Race science," based in part on a spurious appeal to Charles Darwin's writings, lent credence to pervasively influential contentions that races actually existed, that they formed a hierarchy from the more backward to the more advanced, and that, in the interests of social and political order, their separate and unequal existence should continue.[8] Nor has this view gone away, though the *bien pensant* now shun association with it. Bob Carter remarks that "sociologists have been confronted by the paradox that whilst science may have recognized the inutility of the concept, many human beings continue to employ it as a means of making sense of their lives and many political movements continue to exploit it as a means of gaining power."[9]

Our montage, though designed to sell twentieth-century tourists on Nova Scotia, offers almost a visual homage to nineteenth-century concepts of race that touted the creation of races by God or Nature. It hails from an era when it was generally accepted that the "best races in the world" not only could be readily identified, but, providentially, had populated Nova Scotia.[10] Races that regularly produced certain types – body types, character types, even (as here) distinctive costumes – formed the essences that lay beneath the appearances, explaining much more than biological distinctiveness. The montage would have race explain the "traits of the forefathers," from the material (kilts) to the spiritual (generosity), that groups in the present now manifest.

The montage may not be racist, for it does not communicate the savage derision that the word connotes. But it is at least racializing. *Racialization* is a practice whereby social actors apply the idea of race to a slew of social relationships and practices. "Native Types" easily fulfils these criteria. But is it racist? That depends on the definition. If "racist" names someone who consciously maintains that races actually exist, that they can be ranked, and that they should be kept separate so as to perpetuate themselves, then this montage falls short of racism. It proposes no practical program of segregation, exclusion, or denigration. A society may retain race in its "cultural register" without necessarily implying a move to outright racism in this sense.[11] Perhaps, though, this sets the definitional bar too high. What if, once a field is racialized, the tasks of placing races in a hierarchy, arguing for their separate and unequal development and discouraging racial mixing, go on quietly, between the lines and behind the scenes – as in the case of this montage, where absences and silences explain why some are included and some are excluded?[12] In other words, racism might occupy a middle ground between a consciously held idea and an unconscious predisposition – a notion that, implicitly and without announcing itself, accords recognition to some but not to others. The montage, for example, subliminally suggests not only a hierarchy, but also a sense of separateness and superiority. The other races are centred by the pivotal Scot, whose white light (in two cases) symbolically casts a transfiguring glow upon their faces. He alone occupies a position of command. Moreover, the montage's conspicuous silences and gaps – no Eastern Europeans, Afro–Nova Scotians, or Mi'kmaq – conduce to racial separateness.

More generally, this third framing of the history of Nova Scotia evidences a transition from history – preoccupied with verifiable details and specifics – to heritage, a form far better suited to the requirements of commodification. As memorably defined by David Lowenthal, "heritage" differs radically from history. If both draw on the actual events of the past, history as such necessarily upholds a notion (however nuanced and qualified) that some stories about the past are better – more accurate, complex, verifiable, ethical – than others. Heritage, he argues, "is not like this at all. It is not a testable or even a reasonably plausible account of some past, but a *declaration of faith* in that past." Unlike history, heritage does not advance falsifiable positions, not even when it comes to us arrayed in the forms of a history: "It uses historical traces and tells historical tales, but these tales and traces are stitched into fables that are open neither to critical analysis nor to comparative scrutiny."[13]

This book traces the emergence of a "new kind of history," or *tourism/ history,* as a forerunner of today's full-blown "heritage." Tourism/history ended up creating a fictive province – a "Province of History" in large measure conjured up from concepts of race and liberal order. It consciously reordered representations of the past as it catered to (real or imagined) tourists. One went so far as to reshape nature itself, so it would live up to tourist expectations – expectations themselves shaped by provincial tourism promotion. The resulting tourism/history feedback loop allowed for very few empirical objections. Instead of an active and detailed engagement with the past, tourism/history encouraged the passive reception of images. Instead of opening itself up to dialogue with alternative readings of evidence, it forcefully imposed an authoritative reading (backed by state resources) that made any such dialogue difficult if not impossible.

The 1936 montage offers a fine example. Almost every single "fact" cited in its text presents us with an oversimplification or an error. The description of the Highland Scots overlooks the numerous Lowlanders who emigrated to Nova Scotia, omits such counties as Victoria and Inverness where the Scots also settled in numbers, and (as we shall discover in chapter 5) erroneously implies widespread Gaelic fluency. The Acadians were the "first white settlers" – if one discounts the Norse – but most came not from Normandy or Brittany but from regions of central-western France (by one estimate, 55 per cent from

Poitou-Charentes).[14] The most egregious misinformation concerns the Hanoverians. Precious few Hanoverians emigrated with Lunenburg's "Foreign Protestants," of whom most came from small states in southwest Germany (except for those who were Swiss and French Calvinists). Furthermore, by treating these fictitious Hanoverians as a race, the text occludes the religious reasons for their emigration.[15] Is this nitpicking? Not if plaques, staged events, employment opportunities, and countless other state-sanctioned myths and symbols come to be regulated by assumptions that, factually, are *not the case*. Nor, again, if this process of cultural selection is complemented by the marginalization and exclusion of others. This book will contend that tourism/history helped to make both of these circumstances pervasive throughout twentieth-century Nova Scotia.

We locate three men as the crucial intellectuals of this new tourism/history: Will R. Bird, Thomas H. Raddall, and Angus L. Macdonald. We call them intellectuals insofar as their creative endeavours, organizational skills, and leadership capacity made a whole cohort aware of its own identity and function, in a way that altered the terms of social and cultural life.[16] The new kind of tourism/history opened social possibilities whose realization nonetheless required intellectual elaboration and persuasive presentation. The men and women who undertook this great work over two or three generations represent a cadre of intellectuals who, though often unsung today, helped change their world into our own.

From the late nineteenth century, particular people worked on the Nova Scotia past to develop saleable commodities for tourists – not just souvenirs, but also aesthetic experiences and romantic emotions. They developed what we might call a "mnemonic apparatus" – that is, a network of words and things that convey an impression of *pastness*, even if important elements of that represented past never actually existed (as we saw in our opening montage). This entailed not only the elaboration of tourism/history, but also the construction of an extensive network within which that sort of history made sense. From the 1930s on, this fledgling entrepreneurial mnemonic apparatus was largely supplanted by a bigger state-centric complex that organized, certified, and marketed the public past. This decisive shift not only affected the content of the province's tourism/history, so that it became more and more suited to consumer tastes, but also led to its structural transformation. Twentieth-century tourism/history transmitted a new kind of history geared to the commodification of decontextualized elements from the past. It transformed a restricted tourism *trade* into a much more thoroughgoing tourism *industry*, in which the provincial government and local entrepreneurs assiduously commodified the past (after the fashion of liberal political economy). Moreover, these ambitious projects issued in a form of cultural politics according to which highly partic-

ular readings of the past became reified as stable markers of Nova Scotian identity. Despite their often quite recent provenance, these markers of identity
became widely accepted as extending back into the unplumbed depths of the
most primeval past.

The point we want to make about the montage extends far beyond the
issue of race, important as that is. In essence, this book argues that Innocence
applied to history – in the form we call tourism/history – precluded any sense
of movement over time. History became more and more backward looking.
It was a question of saving remnants from a process of decay, of forestalling
entropy by isolating and preserving objects.[17] Even as it became increasingly
objectified in this way, history also became more abstract, especially suited to
the commemoration of decontextualized moments and experiences. This
process of abstraction made history more amenable to consumerism, easy to
access quickly, momentarily enjoy, and then discard. Tourism/history did not
really concern itself with speaking to a community or honouring the dead,
but with generating profits. Undertaken largely by men and women who
probably would not have identified themselves as intellectuals, this transformation nonetheless entailed an intellectual revolution – the instantiation in
countless state-sponsored sights and sounds of a new philosophy of history.
That philosophy of history was inevitably turned back onto Nova Scotia itself,
made to interpret its past and its present in terms of tourism/history. The
result of this interpretation we call "The Province of History" and the present
volume will map its contours.

I

How a Land without Antiquities Became
the Province of History

In his instant classic *The Heritage Crusade and the Spoils of History*, David Lowenthal distinguishes "heritage" from "history." Heritage, as we mentioned in the Prologue, is "not a testable or even a reasonably plausible account of some past, but a *declaration of faith* in that past. Critics castigate heritage as a travesty of history. But heritage is not history, even when it mimics history. It uses historical traces and tells historical tales, but these tales and traces are stitched into fables that are open neither to critical analysis nor to comparative scrutiny." He goes on:

> Heritage and history rely on antithetical modes of persuasion. History seeks to convince by truth and succumbs to falsehood. Heritage exaggerates and omits, candidly invents and frankly forgets, and thrives on ignorance and error. Historians' pasts, too, are always altered by time and hindsight. To be taken seriously by other historians, however, these revisions must conform with accepted tenets of evidence. Heritage is far more flexibly emended … Heritage is immune to critical reappraisal because it is not erudition but catechism; what counts is not checkable fact but credulous allegiance. Commitment and bonding demand uncritical endorsement and preclude dissenting voices.

The history-versus-heritage distinction might apply to our discussion here. Recall our two hypothetical explanations of the photo montage that began this book. Both of these brief texts commemorate the past, yet also engage with evidence. They are to some degree vulnerable to factual critique. Historians aim (however imperfectly) to reduce bias, whereas tourism/history "sanctions and strengthens it." What counts in tourism/history is not checkable fact but "credulous allegiance." History "tells all who will listen what has happened and how things came to be as they are." On the other hand, like Lowenthal's heritage, our tourism/history "passes on exclusive myths of origin and continuance, endowing a select group with prestige and common purpose." The legacies of heritage underwrite the exclusive purpose of group identity: "Those who seek a past as sound as a bell forget that bells *need* built-in imperfections to bring out their all-important individual resonances."[1]

While benefiting from Lowenthal's famous distinction, we wonder whether history and heritage can be separated so sharply in practice as he separates them in theory. His analysis almost assumes some impermeable barrier dividing heritage from history. The division, however, has more heuristic than empirical value. In our research, we find history and heritage constantly shading into each other. Many of the same people using the same conceptual tools to produce similar narratives produced both history and heritage in twentieth-century Nova Scotia. Popular historical pastiches often proudly display the imprimatur of the archives, for instance, to give them an appearance of historical grounding that makes them all the more persuasive as heritage objects. On the other side of the coin, apparent histories often proceed according to a narrative template previously set by novels or tourist literature. Heritage might well have implications for history and vice versa.

From a chronological rather than analytical standpoint, meanwhile, Lowenthal posits a dramatic explosion of heritage since the 1970s, whereas we document an earlier efflorescence in the 1930s–1950s. In Nova Scotia, a decisive shift in representational strategies took place during the second quarter of the twentieth century, connected both to the province's profound socio-economic crisis and to the correlative rise of a new consumer capitalism exemplified above all by the advent of tourism. This historical context has important theoretical implications. "Tourism/history" and "history" in twentieth-century Nova Scotia never existed as autonomous discourses floating free of social structures. They confirmed pre-existing power relations and forestalled challenges to them.[2] Nor did they merely endorse a social form; they incarnated and furthered it. Tourism/history was part and parcel of the rampant commodification of history during the interwar period. More and more, the traces of the past were enlisted to make money – whether profits for entrepreneurs, wages for skilled employees, or tax revenues for government. Since we find it implicated in certain social transformations and political programs, tourism/history deserves sustained interrogation in a way that Lowenthal's analysis of heritage seems to preclude. His discussion might lead to the quietist conclusion that at best one mythical construction could replace another, with all of them partaking of the same fundamental nature as heritage. Without overstating the extent to which one might attain epistemological trans- parency and unqualified objectivity, however, we consider it both desirable and feasible to subject existing official stories about the past to critical analysis.[3] To privilege a sphere of state-sanctioned myths and symbols as above and beyond evaluation and critique is a dubious position both epistemologically and ethically.

J.E. Tunbridge and G.J. Ashworth argue that, as a form, heritage creates insiders and outsiders. It acclaims some members of a society while dismissing others: "all heritage is someone's heritage and therefore logically not some- one else's." Some people are more essential than others to the narrative that tells all the citizens what their society is like. (The "Native Types" montage, for instance, obviously makes Scots seem more essential than Mi'kmaq, but it applies equally to all of Nova Scotia.) Hence "the shaping of any heritage product is by definition prone to disinherit non-participating social, ethnic or regional groups, as their distinctive historical experiences may be discounted, marginalised, distorted or ignored." Since heritage always requires "selectivity," it inevitably involves politics.[4]

Does its ardent embrace of tourism/history make Nova Scotia unique? On the one hand, we should exercise caution when advancing any strong claims for priority because what we might think of as original Nova Scotia develop- ments often turn out to merely extend earlier British or New England proto- types. This should come as no surprise. Until the confederation of Canada in 1867, Nova Scotia was a British colony. Informally and culturally, it remained one long after. Meanwhile, many Nova Scotians have come from New Eng- land (and vice versa). Salient features of twentieth-century public history in the province can seem uncannily similar to those found in New England two or three decades earlier.[5] In short, much of Nova Scotia's tourism/history derives from its status as a hinterland of London and Boston.

Yet, at the same time, we can see something happening in Nova Scotia that exceeds anything reported from these metropolitan centres. Perhaps as a con- sequence of its geopolitical location – an underdeveloped province on the margins of the world's most dynamic capitalist economy – Nova Scotia was extraordinarily precocious in commodifying its past. Assiduous commodifica- tion would issue in a virtual history whose themes, to a great extent, became pervasively accepted among residents as well as tourists. Nova Scotia seemingly pioneered forms of tourism/history that suggest just how drastically a given place could reinvent itself in the interests of tourism revenues. While the record of tourism/history in this relatively small province – as of this writing, its population still does not top one million – is of obvious interest to its residents, it thus also offers rich material for reflection to anyone interested in how history and tourism can mesh. While not pressing any risky case for absolute originality, we are struck time and again by the all-embracing radicalism of tourism/history in Nova Scotia. "Let's cash in on antiquity," a prominent politician and tourism planner urged in 1946 – and by *cashing in* he meant the concoction of historical attractions for the tourist marketplace.[6] "History is what gives the flavour to any tourist area," proclaimed a path-breaking brief of the Historical and Cultural Committee of the Canadian Tourist Association in 1953.[7] It was preaching to the long-converted in Nova Scotia, a province unusual in having at its helm people who since the 1930s had so clearly grasped the bottom-line implications of the new dispensation.

It will hardly come as news to anyone who has followed the international "history-making" literature that public history meant a politics of the past – inventing traditions, imposing interpretations that suited the ruling order, marginalizing alternative accounts, and highlighting the continuous national traditions that supposedly shaped every citizen.[8] In the 1970s and 1980s, scholarship on tourism frequently outlined the ways in which the "golden hordes" of tourists subverted local culture.[9] More recent work in the 1990s and 2000s has wondered whether some of this important work did not err on the side of hypercriticism, elitism, and reductionism. In more recent writing, "while tourism and vacations were increasingly enmeshed within cultures of consumption, mechanically produced images, and various political and economic agendas, tourism and vacations have enabled a persistent quest for experiences of the self and its pleasures, and for education and knowledge."[10] A rather mechanical "hypodermic needle" model of the culture of tourism, in which cunning corporate villains manipulate a brainwashed travelling public and an equally pliant host society, is replaced by a subtler, more dialogical understanding, in which the sites of tourism are interpreted as zones of contact between the visitor and the visited. Much the same movement away from implicitly social-control readings – a move, one might say, away from Talcott Parsons and towards Antonio Gramsci – can be discerned in work on the public past. Over the past decade, Canadianists have joined an international army of scholars pursuing both tourism[11] and history-making[12] with many of these ideas in mind. This study locates itself within this second, more dialogical problematic. It dwells on evidence suggesting that although the external demand for a pre- or antimodern Nova Scotia was significant, it had to be articulated to provincial realities by local cultural elites and (especially after the 1930s) by an ambitious provincial government. Throughout the writing of this book, we have been impressed by the extent to which forms of history that were seemingly generated from *without* came also to be articulated and developed from *within*. Tourism/history not only blurred the line between fact and fiction, but also between insider and outsider.

At the same time, the Nova Scotia case flashes a caution light about pushing the contemporary dialogical models of tourism in too benignly pluralist a direction. One might almost imagine, to follow some accounts, that we have arrived at a utopia of unconstrained consumer preferences and uninhibited cultural identities – a veritable playground of difference. But the "contact zone" where tourists encountered the toured-upon, to cite a useful term from Mary Louise Pratt, was no such place.[13] As we shall see, it has been all too obviously structured by pre-existing inequalities. Nowhere could be so inhospitable for the free play of identities, ideas, bodies, &c. than this contact zone we have named the Province of History.

◆

Nova Scotia is a small province on Canada's Atlantic coast.[14] Since the complexity of its past can sometimes bewilder any but the most learned of sages, we present a brief synopsis here, accentuating the period from 1604 to 1867 – that is, the period that tourism/history most avidly exploited. Any such succinct description must come with the caveat that, as one leading historian complained, Nova Scotia has tended to be "so unintegrated a province" that generalizations about it are bound to be hazardous.[15] Furthermore, many foundational historical facts remain subject to debate. Bookshelves groan beneath the weight of studies detailing the province's constituent communities, pivotal events, and prominent personalities, but they are far less crowded with studies offering general interpretations and analytical frameworks. Even our short outline must often venture into interpretive territories at which scholarly literature gestures but does not fully explore. And, with that, we had best begin.

For many years, present-day Nova Scotia was part of Mi'kma'ki, the land of the Mi'kmaq. People have lived here for at least ten thousand years. Nevertheless, most history books focus narrowly upon the last four hundred of them. This seemingly arbitrary choice proceeds from an initial error: when Europeans landed on these shores, they fancied themselves occupiers of a virtually uninhabited land. They could scarcely *see* the very different aboriginal society. Neither, for many years, could the historians and writers who inherited their outlook. Exacerbating the neglect of indigenous Nova Scotia, environmental changes have destroyed a significant portion of the archaeological record. Because the seas have since submerged the ancient coastal areas found at the end of the last Ice Age, much evidence from seven to four thousand years ago has vanished (fishing nets occasionally capture fragments of it). On land, meanwhile, the province's acidic soils have not helped matters.

Despite all, sufficient evidence (such as large burial mounds suggesting Ohio Valley influences and goods drawn from deep in the continental interior) has emerged to suggest "a level of cultural complexity well beyond a mere hand-to-mouth existence" and to dispel any notion of the First Nations as static, unchanging peoples.[16] Their lands evidently included present-day Cape Breton Island, mainland Nova Scotia, Prince Edward Island, northeastern New Brunswick, and part of the Gaspé Peninsula. Well before the arrival of French explorer Jacques Cartier in 1534, they appear to have traded with Europeans. These trade goods had lasting effects on the Mi'kmaq, but we should not overstate their initial impact. Although anxious to obtain certain select European trading goods, especially metal cookware, much of their own material culture – canoes, snowshoes, toboggans, wigwams – suited local conditions better. By 1600, "the Micmac had learned how to sail and were taking European-made shallops over impressive distances." They had become intermediaries trading in furs or European goods over a large area extending from Massachusetts Bay to Quebec's north shore.

Commercial advantage aside, contact with Europeans presented many challenges. European diseases – deadly visitors throughout much of indigenous North America – may have arrived rather late in Mi'kma'ki, but when they did strike (on the evidence of one cleric's account, c. 1616), they wiped out a large percentage of a pre-contact population estimated at around twelve thousand. It appears likely that under the new conditions a once-pervasive native egalitarianism waned as "certain individuals, because of their relationship to Europeans or their differential acquisition of European goods, had come to have a degree of prestige and authority greater than they would have in pre-contact bands of hunter-gatherers." By the seventeenth century, the Mi'kmaq had a complex political system. They evidently divided themselves into seven districts, each governed by a district chief who in turn presided over other chiefs drawn from local communities. The chiefs met in a grand council headed by a grand chief.

The Mi'kmaq would exert a powerful force in Nova Scotia at least until the 1760s – perhaps, John Reid has argued, even until the massive Loyalist influx of the early 1780s. Europeans could establish settlements on the shores of Mi'kma'ki only insofar as the more numerous indigenous inhabitants tolerated it. Furthermore, European settlers benefited from the strength, not the weakness, of indigenous society. As Geoffrey Plank notes, the linguistic and political unity of Mi'kmaq in the Wabanaki Confederacy (which had kept the peace since the seventeenth century) created an auspicious environment for well-disposed colonists. Unlike the *habitants* of Quebec, these settlers did not stumble into an arduous struggle between contending aboriginal nations. William Wicken observes that the Mi'kmaq and their Abenaki neighbours may both have regarded access to European goods and French military support as useful counterweights to Iroquois power, which both groups had resisted since the 1500s. Their acceptance of missionaries into their midst, which presaged widespread conversion to Catholicism, represented commercial and political alliance with the French.[17] Now, in the reverse of the St Lawrence pattern, the Mi'kmaq had themselves stumbled into an arduous struggle between contending Europeans.

In the early seventeenth century, Mi'kma'ki became the object of intense imperial rivalry. Europeans felt entitled to claim it, though they obviously had to deal with the possibility that its inhabitants might resist them.[18] In these early years of colonialism, incipient capitalism brought merchants and the states into close (if sometimes fractious) relationships. Elizabeth Mancke and John Reid explain that the New World offered "new, unknown and unstable arenas" that rulers, merchants, and aristocrats all hoped to exploit to their own advantage. Kings dispensed rights and privileges to well-placed subjects in return for certain considerations (financial, defensive, and otherwise), balancing immediate need for revenue with the long-term interests of statecraft.[19] This situation repeated itself in several distinct cases in Nova Scotia history. Six competing transatlantic powers – Spain, Portugal, the Dutch Republic, France, Scotland, and England – had designs on the region, though only the last three proved enduringly significant. As a result, rightful possession of Acadia/Nova Scotia was fraught even by colonial North American standards. J.B. Brebner, perhaps the greatest historian of the colonial Maritimes, remarked that sovereignty "was debated on the grounds of prior discovery, prior settlement, and, with greatest futility of all, on the basis of limits defined in those royal charters whose authors concealed their ignorance of geography in the magnificent generosity of their concessions."[20] At any given sixteenth- or seventeenth-century moment, several sovereigns could claim a territory generally (though not universally) denominated "Acadia." Success in pressing any particular claim came as the complex outcome of many mutually interacting demographic, economic, political, military, religious, and other factors.

In the early going, the French succeeded best. By 1700, "Acadia" – roughly corresponding to the current Maritime provinces, along with (perhaps) some of the Gaspé Peninsula and the state of Maine – held a French-speaking population of about two thousand, mainly settled on the salt-marsh shores of the Bay of Fundy. This population slowly began regarding itself as "Acadian," equally distinct from the European French and the *Canadiens* on the banks of the St Lawrence. The variability of French imperial fortunes in the region abetted the Acadian sense of distinctness. From 1604 to the turn of the eighteenth century, Acadia, though usually recognized as a French possession, was repeatedly seized by rival powers: Scotland (1629–32), the Dutch Republic

(1674), and England (1613, 1654, and 1690). Samuel Argall of Virginia would raze Port Royal in 1613, the first of many such seventeenth-century changings of the guard.[21] Only with the commissioning of Isaac de Razilly as governor over Acadie on 10 May 1632, and his subsequent recruitment of over a hundred permanent settlers, did the colony acquire an on-the-ground reality that corresponded to the notional "Acadia" of diplomatic imagination. The British again seized the colony in 1654, ushering in a period of Bostonian rule that some historians credit with loosening the hold of metropolitan French institutions such as the seigneurial system. With the reassertion of French control in 1670, Acadia became a jurisdiction of New France. One might have expected Acadia finally to become like the St Lawrence colony, with a strong governor representing the king, seigneurs presiding over their estates, and a formidable institutional church. Wrong on all three counts: governors came and went in rapid succession; seigneuries never attained in reality the magnificent dimensions they had on paper; and, while the Acadians retained their Catholic faith, the Church in Acadia paled before its mighty counterpart in Quebec (upon which it abjectly depended). The workaday reality of a population capable of conducting its affairs on its own contradicted the appearance of top-down monarchical, seigneurial, and clerical control from France.[22]

From the perspective of European colonial powers, the Acadians were from the 1630s on an *awkward* people. Their territory remained devilishly difficult to define in diplomatic terms, since they lived on the borderlands of two rival empires. Were they French? Yes, in their language and culture. Then again, no: their intimate relations with the Mi'kmaq led some to qualify their status as fully European.[23] Were they British? Yes, in that after 1710 they lived on land claimed by the British sovereign – to whom some had sworn an oath of allegiance. Were they "American"? Yes, in that from the 1670s to the 1750s they profited handsomely from New England trade, some established long-standing relations with Boston, and in a more general sense they all felt entitled to occupy new lands whether or not a monarch sanctioned such migrations. Were they a conquered people? Yes: after the fall of Port Royal in 1710 (and confirmed by the Treaty of Utrecht in 1713), they lived on British territory. But also no: during an occupation lasting from the 1710s to the 1740s, the Acadians entered their period of maximum demographic and economic growth, in practice only intermittently subject to rule from the renamed capital Annapolis Royal, and even formulated a kind of informal foreign policy. They adopted a policy of active neutrality – meaning that the neutral party, though inextricably involved in the dispute, would maintain communications with both sides, would help or hinder each equally, and would refrain from favouring one side at the expense of the other. Their stance required "a sound understanding of the issues at hand, and the character of the combatants." It would become a core political idea of the 1720s–1750s, and beyond that – as Brebner would note – into the era of the American Revolution.[24] Whoever says "Acadia" says "complexity" too.

The same goes for the "British" who eventually would replace Acadian society with something very different. The British definitively assumed control over much of the territory, which they dubbed "Nova Scotia," in 1710 (France retained Île Royale, the present-day Cape Breton Island). Yet these British comprised at least three distinct major groups, each heterogeneous in itself: the Scots, the English, and the New Englanders. The relative importance of each remains a matter of some dispute. Although enshrined in the name "Nova Scotia," Latin for "New Scotland," in other respects the Scots had the least significance. From 1621 on, the Scottish monarchy had sought to colonize the territory, even to the point of establishing "knights-baronetcies" as a lure to potential colonizers and actually establishing a colony in 1629. But soon they had to cede it back to the French.[25]

England held more sway than Scotland, but even this remained something of a legal fiction. Even after the 1707 Act of Union united Scotland with England, even after the aforementioned Treaty of Utrecht in 1713, London's predominance remained contested, uneven, and relative. Strong at Annapolis Royal on the Bay of Fundy, it weakened precipitously once one ventured beyond that fort's palisades. In reality, it was the American Thirteen Colonies to the south – especially the New England ones – whose demographic expansion and growing sense of their own autonomous interests transformed the British presence in Nova Scotia. Historian George Rawlyk pointed out that the emergent Massachusetts–Nova Scotia relationship was sharply unequal, in line with their relative demography: in 1670, Massachusetts had 30,000 settlers to Nova Scotia's sub-500 total; by 1750, Massachusetts could boast 190,000 British colonists to Nova Scotia's "estimated 10,000 Acadians."[26] Fuelled by cash crops, the "sheer weight of numbers," and their distinctive political theology, which bestowed upon them a distinctive role as a "chosen people," New Englanders loomed large in the minds of those who pondered the fate of the territory after 1670. As they increasingly saw the Acadians as enemies, united with the native peoples who on occasion raided their farms, New Englanders came to play a decisive role in launching reprisals on (and subsequently full-scale invasions of) the northerly French Catholic colony.

Looking more closely at these New Englanders, we can see that they themselves offered a study in contrasts. Take their seizure of Port Royal in 1690 – a deft sally that, duly accomplished, immediately collapsed in disarray. What went wrong? Geoffrey Plank suggests that the New England camp was divided against itself: "Some of the promoters of the expedition wanted to lay the groundwork for profitable postwar relations with the Mi'kmaq and the Acadians, while others sought only to punish them for their alleged complicity in recent attacks against New England." Many of the New Englanders – almost solipsistic in their focus on their farms, their faith, and their families – just wanted to keep the "French and Indians" at a distance. Driven by an eye-for-an-eye philosophy of reprisal against aboriginal incursions, these New Englanders raided the Acadians, whom they (mistakenly) perceived as complicit in native attacks. Others, who had traded profitably with the Acadians for decades, wanted to oust the French colonial government but retain contacts with the Acadians by bringing them within the Empire. Still others (disregarding divines who warned against any permanent occupation of a land so reminiscent of biblical Babylon) felt motivated by the sermons of preachers like Cotton Mather, who "at his most effusive ... suggested that destroying the French presence in North America would defeat the devil forever and usher in the 'Chiliad' – the thousand-year reign of Christ."[27] Was "Nova Scotia" (and this name, attached by the Scottish crown to a vaguely defined area of the Atlantic seaboard, had attained popularity in New England) really a colony of the more populous New England all along? Brebner argued as much. The official military expeditions undertaken by New England in 1654, 1690, 1704, 1707, 1710, 1745, 1746, and 1755 – as well as unofficial confrontations at Canso in the 1720s – do present an impression of a rather persistent New England interest. Rawlyk, however, cautioned that Acadia preoccupied New Englanders only episodically. Complicating the issue, the overlapping Anglo-American identities of many leading figures, the indistinct and at times contradictory articulations of colonial policy, and the myriad of contingencies structuring each local context, all make it extremely difficult to disentangle "British" from "New England" interests.

In short, colonial Nova Scotia offered a stubbornly liminal situation. The ultimate location of hegemony, the actual identity of the most culturally and economically dominant state power, remained in profound obscurity throughout the first half of the eighteenth century. The romance of history loves two-sided conflicts with clear turning points that presage dramatic declines and falls. Early modern Nova Scotia looks more like a five-sided conundrum. True, two sides confronted each other at Annapolis Royal in 1710, but both sides were descended from, and embroiled in, far more complicated and less dualistic realities. For example, had the Mi'kmaq intervened massively on the side of the French during the Conquest of 1710, it is hard to imagine the British holding the province, outnumbered as they would have been. Nor did the French go away after renouncing lawful possession. Though they lost Annapolis Royal, they retained Île Royale and built there the mighty Fortress Louisbourg, a towering symbol of their military might that put Annapolis Royal absolutely in the shade. The British had undoubtedly won the battle, but they had fallen short of winning any war on the peninsula that would con-clusively settle its future. They proceeded to neglect the colony, as they proved unable to settle it with a British population or, failing that, reliable Protestants from the Continent. To muddy the picture completely, nobody was entirely clear on the boundaries of the Acadia that the British had taken.

Although the Treaty of Utrecht sealed the first durable victory of British arms against the French Empire in what has become Canada, it is easy to see why it has never taken on the mythic proportions of the Plains of Abraham (where Wolfe bested Montcalm in 1759, thereby sealing the fate of New France). The British wanted to settle Nova Scotia with Protestants but seemingly lacked the capacity to do so. They sought to administer Nova Scotia cheaply under a series of pacific and frugal governors. Annapolis Royal, though the capital of the colony, amounted to a ramshackle garrison beyond whose perimeter British control rarely extended; in the 1720s and 1740s, the Mi'kmaq (with Acadian support on the second occasion) almost overwhelmed it. Barry Moody sums up the situation: "[F]or a period of nearly forty years, [the British] presented an image of great weakness, a message that was not lost on Mi'kmaq, Acadian, or French, and all responded, in their own way, to the failure to provide for the adequate defence of the colony."[28] The British faced a hostile population. Nor did they manage to import a loyal base of their own supporters until the 1750s, by which time simmering conflicts had already boiled over.

After the French ceded Acadia to Britain, they reasserted their presence in the region with a grand gesture on the Atlantic shore of Cape Breton Island: Fortress Louisbourg. The fortress was simultaneously a gauntlet thrown down to the British, a thriving fisheries *entrepôt*, and an attractive alternative mart for some Acadians.[29] It testified to the resources at the command of a powerful monarchy – magnificent, munificent, and militarily misconceived (since nei-ther its fogbound coastal location nor its failure to command the high ground boded well for its future). Louisbourg troubled many New Englanders who considered Nova Scotia their backyard. Their fishers were waging an unofficial war against the Mi'kmaq, their traders came and went from Acadia at will (British authorities notwithstanding), and they warily eyed the new French military counterweight to their regional influence.

The British, overshadowed militarily by the Mi'kmaq and Louisbourg and demographically by the Acadians, pursued a policy of simultaneous appease-ment and encroachment. They allowed the Catholic Church freedoms unpre-cedented in a British context and effectively left the Acadians to regulate themselves, on the realistic assumption that mass Acadian disaffection would jeopardize their own hold on the peninsula. In the meantime, they plotted to strengthen their hand in the region. As for the Acadians, having seen power change hands so often before, they were unlikely to overlook the possibility that it might do so again. Thus, their pragmatic policy of active neutrality was not the pigheaded obstinacy that some have since considered it. The Mi'kmaq found it more difficult to maintain neutrality. Nevertheless, although they did end up as enemies of the British – fighting a series of wars with Anglo-Americans between the 1720s and the 1760s – this was by no means inevitable. Whether or not the Treaty of Utrecht unsettled the Mi'kmaq – who likely felt it imposed no obligations on them – it is highly suggestive (as William Wicken observes) that they obviously did not rush to the defence of Port Royal, perhaps because doing so would have conflicted with more immediate interests, such as taking advantage of the fishing season. In fact, it would be the fishery that brought the Mi'kmaq into open conflict with Britain when they rebuffed New Englanders' encroachment on their age-old control of the Atlantic coast-line – especially at the fishing station of Canso. Between 25 June and 24 September 1722, Boston's three newspapers printed thirteen separate stories describing violent altercations along the east coast of mainland Mi'kma'ki; this war between New Englanders and natives would last until 1725.[30] Although these reports invariably blamed the natives, it is worth pointing out that at least since the 1630s New Englanders had embraced terror and exemplary violence (even mutilating the bodies of the dead) as appropriate revenge against aboriginal "savagery."[31] On one occasion in 1720, Geoffrey Plank notes, "two vessels manned by New Englanders engaged in a two-hour naval battle with a group of Mi'kmaw warriors who were sailing in captured ships. The fishermen tossed bombs and set fire to the Mi'kmaw vessels. The warriors tried to swim to land, but the New England men fired on them in the water. They reported killing twenty-two, though only five bodies washed ashore. As a warning to the survivors the New Englanders decapitated the corpses and set the severed heads on pikes surrounding Canso's new fort."[32] The conflicts between Mi'kmaq and New Englanders that engulfed Canso would claim far more lives than did the far better known Siege of Port Royal.

The treaties and agreements of 1726 finally settled these bloody disputes. The documents that declared the (ambiguous) submission of the Mi'kmaw signatories also implied and specified aboriginal rights to hunt, fish, and plant – rights that unavoidably circumscribed those of British subjects in the territory. In signing the treaty, the British treated the Mi'kmaq as "a political and legal entity that existed independently of the colonial and imperial order," which in effect acknowledged that their community "was governed by customs over which British colonial society did not exercise authority." It followed from both the written text and the oral understandings surrounding it that the Mi'kmaq would have regarded the unilateral establishment of major new British settlements as a violation of their agreement. Yet the British authorities, especially after Edward Cornwallis's fleet landed in 1749 to establish Halifax, tendentiously misrepresented the treaties as ratifying an absolute dominion of British law.[33]

Even as British conflicts with the Mi'kmaq were subsiding, another conflict was brewing with the Acadians over their allegiance to the British sovereign. Adapting the doctrine of active neutrality with considerable subtlety, the Acadians made their compliance with the British Empire contingent upon a conditional oath relieving them of the duty to bear arms for either the British or the French.[34] The official written record of 1729 and 1730 did not include oath-taking ceremonies or the oral promises accompanying them, but the Acadians believed they amounted to British agreement with their position. The British, however, could not trust Acadian neutrality because of the company they kept. Acadians maintained their historic alliance with the Mi'kmaq, much to the discomfort of colonial officials. After the prominent Acadian merchant Prudent Robichaud entertained a group of aboriginals, British soldiers clapped him in irons and "displayed" him. French Catholic priests presented another problem. The Treaty of Utrecht guaranteed priestly access to the Acadian populace, but the colonial government considered them (sometimes with reason) conniving agents of the French connection. In 1725 the Bishop of Quebec and Nova Scotia governor Lawrence Armstrong agreed that the Church would not station its clergy in Nova Scotia without British consent, but this by no means settled the controversy.

This pentagonal eighteenth-century contest – French colonial authorities, British colonial authorities, New Englanders, Acadians, and Mi'kmaq – might have lasted many more decades but for the outbreak of war between France and Britain in 1744. In the emergent new world order, antique European conundrums – in this case, a war from 1740 to 1748 over the "Austrian Succession" (of Maria Theresa of Austria to the Habsburg dominions of her father Emperor Charles VI) – could have far-reaching colonial consequences. Britain's war with France began in 1744. French forces at Louisbourg and their Mi'kmaw allies seized the opportunity to attack their old *bête noir,* Canso. They badly miscalculated, because threatening Canso brought New England directly into the conflict. Led by Governor William Shirley, a wide cross-section of Massachusetts society came to identify generally with the British cause and particularly with the conquest of Louisbourg, which a ragtag army of tough volunteers surprisingly seized in 1745.

The war had grave consequences for the peoples who since 1710 had skilfully manoeuvred over the perilous landscape of so contested a terrain. Long-running ambiguities were about to be settled for good. Just where was the point of no return? Perhaps it came in 1744, when the government of Massachusetts formally declared war on the Mi'kmaq and the Massachusetts

General Court promptly placed a bounty of £100 on the scalp of any adult male Mi'kmaq (£50 for scalps of women and children). On 2 November, Shirley extended this policy by offering a reward for any Indian killed or captured east of the St Croix River (exempting only those serving under Anglo-American command). In January 1744, Acadian deputies asked the provincial council if the scalp bounty applied to those of mixed ancestry.[35] After due deliberation, the council officially exempted those who lived as Acadians – though the magistrates did not specify how to determine this identity by examining a scalp. On the other side, the renowned Abbé Le Loutre, vicar-general of Acadia and resident missionary at Shubenacadie, rallied the Mi'kmaq against the British. At the same time, France proved its commitment to reoccupying Nova Scotia by sending a massive armada of seventy vessels and about thirteen thousand men across the Atlantic. Unfortunately for the French, this massive effort under Jean-Baptiste-Louis Frédéric de la Rochefoucauld de Roye le duc d'Anville was defeated by storms, disease, and disorganization. D'Anville himself did not survive even a week in Acadia. As one might have predicted in this paradoxically complex region, the Mi'kmaq sustained the most grievous loss because of the French armada's debacle: smallpox carried by French sailors would kill perhaps half their warriors.[36]

Although the Treaty of Aix-la-Chapelle in 1748 ended the European conflict, it provided only the briefest respite in Nova Scotia. To the dismay of New Englanders, the treaty returned Louisbourg to France. To counterbalance the repatriated fortress, the British founded Halifax in June 1749 with twenty-five hundred settlers. Lest they think Halifax had mastered the mainland, though, the Mi'kmaq promptly testified to their continued military effectiveness by mounting a formidable attack upon a settlement they likely believed to infringe their treaty rights. The governor and council responded with a proclamation ordering British subjects to "destroy the savages commonly called Micmacs wherever they are found." For their part, native warriors raided Dartmouth in May of 1751, causing eight British fatalities.[37]

This "Anglo-Mi'kmaw War" continued on and off from 1749 until 1760, sometimes overlapping with the more widespread and renowned Seven Years' War (1756–1763), which involved all the major European powers and spelled the end of New France.[38] There was a lot to fight over. The Treaty of Utrecht had left the boundaries of Acadia unsettled. The French thought they controlled the Isthmus of Chignecto. In 1751 they accordingly erected Fort Beauséjour as a riposte to Britain's nearby Fort Lawrence, built the previous year. Meanwhile, French authorities instructed Le Loutre, now in Louisbourg, to move to Beauséjour with his Mi'kmaw allies and as many Acadians as he could cajole into settling north of the Missaguash River (which now divides Nova Scotia from New Brunswick). One might qualify it as an attempt to re-establish Acadia in a new northerly setting. Acting in accordance with his own reading of the Treaty of Utrecht, Le Loutre also visualized a native buffer state that would have left the Mi'kmaq secure in their traditional hunting and fishing grounds throughout much of peninsular Nova Scotia. This new entity would separate a repositioned Acadia (encompassing all of present-day New Brunswick, Prince Edward Island, and Cape Breton) from a severely abbreviated British Nova Scotia. The British, for their part, were also attempting to secure geopolitical objectives via large-scale population movements. They augmented Halifax in 1753 by founding Lunenburg with a population of (mostly) German-speaking "Foreign Protestants" from continental Europe. They also worked to isolate and starve Beauséjour and Louisbourg. On 2 June 1755, about two thousand British regulars and New England militiamen arrived at Fort Lawrence. Beauséjour fell to the British and colonial forces after a two-week siege later that month.

Acadian neutrality ended that summer. Their Catholicism and ambiguous allegiance had long incensed Anglo-American opinion. Plans to expel the Acadians had floated about since the 1710s, but the proposition attained a new immediacy in wartime. In 1754, Surveyor-General Charles Morris had presented the Governor's Council in Halifax with an operational plan for their expulsion. His scheme found favour with Colonel Charles Lawrence, lieutenant-governor of Nova Scotia since 21 October 1754, who considered the Acadians complicit in Mi'kmaw attacks and resented their provisioning of Beauséjour and Louisbourg. After the capture of Beauséjour and nearby Fort Gaspereau, the British demanded that the Acadians surrender all their firearms on pain of being branded as rebels. When Acadian delegates went to Halifax to request the return of their guns, the authorities demanded that they sign an unconditional oath of allegiance that would force them to take up arms against Mi'kmaq and the French. Upon refusing, they were imprisoned. A second group of delegates met the same fate. The council made the final decision to remove the "French inhabitants" on 27 July 1755. That August, many Chignecto Acadians were rounded up and imprisoned at Fort Beauséjour (by then renamed Fort Cumberland). In September, the deportation commenced at Grand Pré. The British took care to destroy Acadian houses and barns so as to preclude their return. Overall, about six thousand Acadians were deported from Nova Scotia in 1755; a high but unknown percentage of them died aboard the transport ships. Their captors consigned them to divers Anglo-American colonies, many harshly unwelcoming. Some returned to France, which proved little more accepting. Some made their way to Louisiana, where their descendants became the "Cajuns." No written testimony survives from the Acadians who underwent this ordeal, but other evidence testifies to disease, near-starvation, and the breaking up of families.

The death toll attributed to this policy likely outweighed that associated with any earlier military engagement in Nova Scotia on the part of any of the parties contesting for supremacy within it, with the exception of d'Anville's ill-fated naval expedition.

Despite the deportations, Acadian and Mi'kmaw resistance continued. Indeed, British fears of native resistance predisposed them to renew their long-neglected treaty negotiations. John Reid explains that after the Seven Years' War there followed a decade-long interregnum "during which aboriginal and British pacification strategies competed, followed by a partial reconciliation which was finally swept away only by the sudden force of numbers brought by the Loyalist migration [in the 1780s]."[39] The British ultimately succeeded because waves of Anglo-American immigration completely changed the local demography. "Planters" from New England in the 1760s, Loyalist refugees from the American Revolution in the 1780s, Yorkshiremen and Scots from the late eighteenth century to the 1820s, and large numbers of Irish immigrants down to the 1840s, all transformed "Acadie" and "Mi'kma'ki" into "Nova Scotia."

Now with a free hand, the British attempted to revive in the New World a host of traditions and institutions threatened in the Old. They granted vast tracts of land to absentee proprietors, in hopes they would entrench a landed aristocracy in America. (The most famous case, perhaps, was that of the cartographer and future governor of Cape Breton and of Prince Edward Island, J.F.W. DesBarres, who created large estates at Castle Frederick and Minudie, managed by his mistress Mary Cannon.) Successive territorial reorganizations proceeded partly from an imperial concern with providing land for various claimants, whether the winners of a state land lottery in the case of Prince Edward Island or Loyalist refugees in the cases of New Brunswick and Cape Breton. This land redistribution helped shape the political geography we know today. "Nova Scotia" at first encompassed all three present-day Maritime provinces, parts of which gradually separated into independent jurisdictions: the Island of St John (now P.E.I.) in 1769 and New Brunswick and Cape Breton in 1784 (the latter to be rejoined to Nova Scotia in 1820).

Nova Scotia's fortunes would henceforth be conjoined with those of the British Empire. The Crown directly employed hundreds of people in dockyards and indirectly supported many others in the staple trades that supplied naval stores – especially masts – to the Royal Navy. Fortunes established in war would come to bankroll shipping, as Nova Scotia became home to one of the largest merchant marines in the world. Halifax would remain, down to the 1870s, a city vitally dependent upon British military spending. Through an unusual use of the royal prerogative, the Duke of York came to hold a monopoly on many of the colony's mineral rights, including all of its coal; he eventually sold his lease rights to settle a jewellery bill.

Vast social and economic transformations were sweeping the North Atlantic world. They did not spare Nova Scotia. The American Revolution (in essence that country's first major civil war) brought some Nova Scotians to the point of rebellion. Yet the "fourteenth colony" did not go over to George Washington's side, arguably because of its relative isolation from American events, the deep British connections of the Haligonian elite, the diffuseness of its settlement patterns, the immediately obvious power of the British military, the outrageous depredations of American privateers, and (perhaps) the coincident occurrence of a major religious revival. The war brought the region about thirty-five thousand Loyalists, who briefly transformed the lightly settled area around Shelburne into one of the largest cities on the Atlantic seaboard (until its lack of either an agricultural hinterland or a competitive harbour caught up with it). It also brought Nova Scotia its first large population of free blacks, who coexisted with the slaves accompanying the Loyalists.

In a less obvious but nonetheless profound consequence of the continued British connection, the province came into direct contact with the massive socio-economic transformations sweeping Britain itself. Thousands dispossessed by capitalist development – whether Scots cleared from their ancient crofts or unsettled by modern manufacturing, or the Irish emigrating from colonial poverty and servitude, or the English themselves in quest of land and prosperity – made Nova Scotia their destination. Between 1800 and 1803 alone, more than thirty-five hundred Scots settled in Nova Scotia, mostly in Pictou County. The immigrants brought with them the British political and cultural movements that responded to these changes. As the nineteenth century proceeded, a fascination with British political events, reverence for the Common Law and English constitution, and close attention to religious and cultural currents in the motherland, all marked Nova Scotia society, especially in Halifax.

By the mid-nineteenth century, Halifax was by many measures the most politically sophisticated of Her Majesty's North American possessions. Nova Scotia was the first serious testing ground of responsible government, its polity now strikingly influenced by the ideas and precepts of British liberalism – exemplified above all by Joseph Howe, whose passionate advocacy of civic freedoms made him a great popular hero. He became even more popular in the 1860s when he opposed the Confederation Agreement. This document, against the clearly expressed wishes of the Nova Scotian public, annexed the province to Canada – a development discussed in a public sphere sufficiently liberal to allow for a free and vigorous debate on such a fundamental constitutional change, yet also sufficiently elitist that London simply overruled the will of the voters. By the first decade of Confederation in the 1870s, we have exited the period that most interested the architects of tourism/history, whose eyes turned insistently back to the "glorious days" of eighteenth-century imperial conflict.[40] Despite what academics have subsequently had to say about the matter, this post-Confederation period held only limited interest from the standpoint of the organic intellectuals of the new kind of history.

Even this very brief précis should establish that Nova Scotia's history is more complicated than commonly supposed. Its implications confute at least five commonplace historical narratives of its key events, namely: (1) narratives that trace a path of improvement through inevitable stages that lead from barbarism to civilization; (2) narratives that tell a story of good versus evil in which the two are easily distinguished and the first prevails over the second; (3) narratives that show how Europeans, upon encountering the boundless forests of the continent, became democratic yeomen as the effete elitism of the old continent yielded to the energetic egalitarianism of the new; (4) narratives that celebrate the achievement of national liberation from the iron hand of empire; and (5) narratives that reveal how white settlers brought order and progress to the primitive aboriginal residents of the New World.

We might start with the developmental "stadial" narrative beloved of the Scottish Enlightenment, which traced linear ascents from savagery to culture, ignorance to knowledge, and primitivism to civility. Such stages, if at all useful in this context, overlap to such an extent that any sense of one inevitably and definitively succeeding another seems forced. Rather than a steady, unstoppable line of development, the Nova Scotia pattern was often one of forced growth at the behest of distant states, as in the case of those imposing artificial communities named Louisbourg and Halifax. Moreover, instead of ascent from benighted disorder to beneficent order, the province was by many measures far more chaotic in the 1750s than it had been in the 1600s.

Second, any narrative seeking to develop clear-cut heroes and villains and align them on the progressive and regressive sides of "history" would capture but one possible reading of a five-sided situation. With the partial exception of the Acadians (some of whom disavowed violence), all of the major antagonists committed horrific atrocities, often against non-combatants. We cannot lay the blame for these atrocities at just one door. This holds true for the most famous case of violence against a civilian population, the Acadian Expulsion of 1755–63. A cloud of moral ambiguity surrounds the responsibility of the British colonial administrators, the various New Englanders very active at the time in settling the affairs of the colony, and the French authorities – whom some blame for manipulating the Acadians without considering the high price they would likely pay for flouting British authority. Furthermore, the many catastrophes that beset colonizers in this period – from d'Anville's fatal expedition to the Acadians' tragic deportation – pale before the quieter but more lethal assault of Europeans upon the Mi'kmaq, whose population was devastated by a combination of European disease, alcohol, and warfare.

Third, frontier narratives, beloved of historical romance, do not correspond very well with Nova Scotia evidence. An interpretation *à la* Frederick Jackson Turner that stresses isolated yeomen carving out little homesteads from the forest, fending off "Indians," and bringing raw but vibrant democratic ideas into their public assemblies, would become immensely popular in tourism/history. The examples of state-imposed Louisbourg and Halifax, and even, in their own curious way, Annapolis Royal and Lunenburg, tell against this interpretation. So does a consideration of Acadian salt-marsh agriculture, which characteristically made Acadians dependent less upon individual efforts at clearing forests than upon the sophisticated communal management of the sea and its bordering marshlands. The Acadians *did* quietly exemplify some "Turnerian" qualities, as suggested by their independence from seigneurial and clerical institutions. As time went on, however, this independence waned. Their position of neutrality vis-à-vis British and French colonial authorities became untenable. State power impinged on them more and more often, ultimately casting them out. After the Expulsion, the imposition of vast estates in the region, to a point, made the post-1770s *ancien régime* on the land a much more tangible regional reality than it had been a century beforehand, suggesting a Turner thesis working, disconcertingly, in reverse gear.

Which leads to the fourth popular narrative structure: national liberation from the iron hand of empire, presented as a step on an onwards-and-upwards path to liberal freedom and rationality. Yet if we reflect that, on good Lockean liberal grounds, the Acadian farmers had undoubtedly mixed their labour in with their land, thereby acquiring sound property claims, then the state-orchestrated destruction of their farms cannot quite meet the demands of the Whig interpretation of history. Acadia *circa* 1670 may have enjoyed more commercial and civil freedoms, in this classical liberal sense, than Nova Scotia *circa* 1790, when imperial mercantilism, an imposed Established Church, and top-down rule from Halifax presented structural barriers to such freedom – barriers of a sort little known in the benignly neglected French colony. Moreover, Acadian standards of living – which archaeological and demographic evidence suggests afforded them a considerable margin above subsistence – compare favourably to the poverty pervading much of mid-nineteenth-century Nova Scotia, beset by crop blights, economic panics and epidemic diseases.[41] The notion of a path from servitude to independence cannot stand much scrutiny if Acadia's inadvertent de facto independence from the French metropole is juxtaposed with the aggressive assertion of imperial interests after 1755 (as suggested by the construction in Halifax of a massive citadel that cemented the city's position as a crucial bastion of British sea-power).[42] Moreover, as we have seen, it is highly treacherous to read present-day nationalisms back into the eighteenth century, since nation-states (in any recognizable modern sense of the term) existed in only a very restricted sense.

Finally, all the previous four narratives might cohere into a master narrative of how superior Europeans gradually brought a benighted province into the white light of reason, civility, and order. In such a history, the primitive (Acadians, Mi'kmaq, and sometimes even the Highland Scots) yield before the inevitable progress of the civilized (encompassing the New Englanders and the British). Yet this approach also fails, and not only in confrontation with the widespread evidence of British scalping and New England atrocities. It also fails in the face of Mi'kmaw and Acadian interests and identities enduring long past 1755. Such a narrative would invest the colonizers with an exclusive power to make history that is not only ethically problematical but conflicts with the historical record. Yet the master narrative of civilization and whiteness, as we suggested in the Prologue, has enjoyed tremendous staying power even as race as an analytic category has suffered a steep decline. Metaphors of lightness and darkness repeatedly served to make British colonial rule seem enlightened and heavenly, and alternatives to it dark and devilish. The obvious crudity of this rhetorical strategy does not lessen its persistent appeal. On the contrary, the substantial difficulties attending attempts to impose upon this history a liberal narrative of growing private property, enlightened public opinion, and civility offer an opening for much more reductive racial narratives in which the "white races of Nova Scotia" founded the province – and, implicitly, rescued it from some notional non-white opposition. The white races filled a mythic role that enlightened sages, noble heroes, yeomen farmers, and freedom-loving liberals could never really play. In the twentieth century, such mythologizing forestalled the nuanced appreciation of Nova Scotia's complicated and partially understood history, substituting ahistorical narratives of inevitability and essentialism.

◆

Critical historiography has repeatedly qualified, questioned and subverted these narrative patterns. Tourism/history has not so much avoided contact with such work as it has imposed upon it a rigorous politics of selection. It has in essence frozen the present-day imagined past in a Victorian framework and marginalized or ignored much of the more critical and realistic work of subsequent periods.

For the sake of convenience, one might divide Nova Scotia historiography into three major periods. From the 1820s to the 1920s, nationalism pervaded history with a particular intensity. History-writing in Nova Scotia reached its first significant milestone in 1829 with Thomas Chandler Haliburton's *An Historical and Statistical Account of Nova Scotia.* (Although M. Brook Taylor estimates that "approximately 70 per cent of the narrative in volume one was copied," what we would today regard as plagiarism did not raise many eyebrows at the time.)[43] As we shall see in chapter 2, Haliburton would indirectly have an enormous impact on the tourism/history complex in the province via the Evangeline Phenomenon because his book included details on the Expulsion of the Acadians. Haliburton struck an emphatically upbeat note in his study. Nova Scotia was progressing because of its sturdy yeomen. He looked with a jaundiced eye upon the aristocrats who had ventured to the colony, as well as upon the Shelburne Loyalists, who received from him one of the first of their many harsh reviews as profligate and dissipated. He also harboured grave doubts about the Highland Scots of Cape Breton and about the Acadians, believing that neither group really knew how to farm. He preferred the New Englanders, the Foreign Protestants, and the Scottish Lowlanders, who had enclosed the land and improved it. These true Nova Scotians combined Yankee knowhow and independence with British balance and maturity. The notion that the races were arranged in a hierarchy – determined, at bottom, by how they supposedly developed their properties – was thus already entrenched in the 1820s.

For nineteenth-century Anglo-Canadians like Haliburton, most of whom proudly identified with the civilizing mission of the British Empire, the real history of Nova Scotia began in 1749 when the Empire made its first substantial investment in the colony by founding Halifax. Imperialists presented the French regime as a bleak period whose absolutism, superstition, and ignorance warranted their general neglect of it. Virtually no one paid it serious attention until the publication of Francis Parkman's majestic *France and England in North America* (1865–92). Parkman wrote beautifully turned, smoothly flowing sentences that recall the fulsome sonorities and elegant periods of Edward Gibbon. His volumes transported many a Victorian back to the romantic battlefields of eighteenth-century North America. As Taylor remarks, "the very quality of Parkman's work, at the same time as it attracted readers, discouraged would-be imitators. In effect, after Parkman what was there left to say?" This was especially so since the eminent Bostonian had essentially confirmed what Anglo-Canadians had always thought: the struggle between France and Britain had been a "conflict between the forces of light and the forces of darkness, between the nation of Progress and the nation that stood opposed to it; between Anglo-Saxon Protestant liberty – which was the hallmark of Progress – and French Roman Catholic absolutism."[44] Parkman also allowed some Nova Scotians to develop a new sensibility about the history of their province. If the sheer complexity and intractability of the seventeenth and eighteenth

"Louisbourg, Near Sydney, Cape Breton, N.S.," from J. Wesley Swan, *Through the Maritime Provinces (New Brunswick and Nova Scotia): including the Gaspé Coast, Cape Breton, Prince Edward Island and a portion of the Province of Quebec* (Montreal: Canadian Railway News Company, n.d. [c. 1903]). The haunting ruins of Fortress Louisbourg drew a variety of history-seeking visitors in the early twentieth century, many of them inspired by the extraordinarily popular works of Francis Parkman, the most renowned North American historian of the nineteenth century.

centuries seemingly defied dualistic constructions, if only for the mind-boggling number of treaties and territorial transfers, thereafter "France and England in America" would serve as a tidy simplification allowing readers to cheer for one side or the other. Would one select superstitious, priest-ridden France or enlightened, liberty-loving England? In these satisfying (if ultimately propagandistic) formulations, Parkman's readers could find reassurance that the British triumph over the French constituted the triumph of enlightenment over backwardness.

One should never underrate Parkman's enduring power over the construction of Nova Scotia's public history. As we shall see in chapters 3 and 4, both of the province's great public historians, Bird and Raddall, betrayed his profound influence. For one thing, they shared his calm certitude in passing judgment upon other cultures. Of the Acadians, Parkman would write:

> Their mental horizon was of the narrowest, their wants were few, no military service was asked of them by the English authorities, and they paid no taxes to the government. They could even indulge their strong appetite

for litigation free of cost; for when, as often happened, they brought their land disputes before the Council at Annapolis, the cases were settled and the litigants paid no fees. Their communication with the English officials was carried on through deputies chosen by themselves, and often as ignorant as their constituents, for a remarkable equality prevailed through this primitive little society.[45]

We should note here how Parkman illustrates the vulnerability of the facts to the interpretive schemes that order them. After all, these facts could be related very differently. Could we not cite the supposed "litigiousness" of the Acadians as evidence of their progressive, materialistic, practical initiative in defending what was theirs by asking the courts to uphold their sacrosanct rights to property? Yet here in Parkman, merely by virtue of the fact that they did not have to pay out of pocket to take cases to court – and what real liberal individuals would volunteer to subsidize an unelected monarchy with taxes levied on their industry by the biggest government around? – these enterprising qualities are subsumed into his general portrait of Acadian fecklessness and isolation.[46]

Throughout Canada, the 1920s initiated a second, more professional, period in historiography. We can see this new professionalism exemplified in Nova Scotia by the work of J.B. Brebner and D.C. Harvey, as well as in the foundation in 1931 of the Public Archives of Nova Scotia, which became in the 1930s and 1940s the nucleus of a remarkable cohort of scholars and heritage activists. For the first time, and with an intensity unparalleled in most other Canadian provinces, a dedicated team of professional historians wrestled with the province's vast record holdings. D.C. Harvey, the archivist, never managed to produce the major synthesis that his many provocative articles seemed to portend. Nevertheless, the cumulative impact of his work shifted much scholarly attention to the 1820s–50s, a period during which he insisted that Nova Scotia underwent an intellectual awakening – finally, one might say, achieving a veritable liberal enlightenment that brought scholarship, industry, and agricultural improvement to a sluggish colony.[47] Once again, however, the implied narrative was confounded by the province's frustratingly nonlinear history: this nineteenth-century enlightenment did not (at least by most conventional measures) eventuate in a twentieth-century liberal society of contented and prosperous individuals, but in a de-industrializing province scarred by mass unemployment, poverty and out-migration.[48]

One of those who watched developments at the new Public Archives of Nova Scotia (PANS) with interest was J.B. Brebner. Brebner, educated at the University of Toronto and Oxford, was for many years a professor at Columbia University in New York. In his first major Nova Scotia study, *New England's*

"Baptism of Indians at Port Royal," in Hezekiah Butterworth, *Zigzag Journeys in Acadia and New France. A Summer's Journey of the Zigzag Club through the historic fields of the early French settlements of America* (Boston: Estes and Lavriat, 1885), 157. Butterworth's youthful readers were expected to immerse themselves in Parkman's works, and his vision of beneficent European colonization is evident in the book's visual treatment of the native peoples.

Outpost: Acadia before the Conquest of Canada (1927), the focus on "the great conflict between England and France and between their North American colonies" might have been standard fare, but not his emphasis upon "geographical conditions" and "the foreign policy of New England." In particular, he wanted to bring "good historiography" to bear on the Acadians, rather than letting political allegiance determine his views of them. Accordingly, he attended carefully to their mores, to the role New England played, to the nature of British administration, and most of all to "how the wars of the mid-eighteenth century and the expedient policies of Great Britain and France fatally and selfishly involved the simple Acadians and brought about their expulsion." He thus sought to "provide an accurate and dispassionate account of a most complicated experiment, rather than to argue the virtues and vices of the Acadians or debate the policies of Great Britain, New England, France, and New France, which involved them." In essence, he attempted to differentiate between the organic (or structural) and the contingent (or conjunctural) components of a historical situation. He generally construed the first as geographical and the second as political, military, social, and even cultural.

41

Later, forced readings of Brebner notwithstanding, he never overlooked the "evil fruit" of New England's involvement in Nova Scotia. He referred often enough to the "great tragedy of the Acadian people," the "cruel, pitiless affair" of their expulsion, and the qualities of the French and English in Europe and America that, when "brought to bear on Nova Scotia, so easily triumphed over common sense and humanity." Few have equalled his sharp characterization of the London Board of Trade's apathetic response to news of Lawrence's drastic action:

> They did not pause to think of the agony of those who perished slowly and miserably or whose bodies and minds were bruised and broken by their persecutors. They had no adequate conception of the transformation of pleasant farms, green meadows, comely orchards, and primitive homesteads, into a barren waste scarred by fire and destruction. Lawrence, who could have described the tragedy, spoke instead of "perfidy" or "treachery" or "ingratitude." These generalizations permitted the elimination of the details of human misery in favor of the "larger issues" of international politics. To the authorities in England the expulsion of the Acadians was merely an incident in one small campaign in a bitter, dangerous and expensive war, something already accomplished and therefore beyond useful discussion.

Brebner could sometimes sound like Parkman when characterizing the victims of the deportation. His Acadians too were "essentially" simple-minded, apolitical, reclusive inhabitants of a backwater outside the mainstream of American life, "content to live for generations much as their fathers had done." Yet Brebner also concedes them a moral status as individuals – "self-reliant ... pioneers," "truly a self-made people" – warm commendations indeed coming from a liberal like himself. He contrasted these Acadian virtues with the unfeeling and unimaginative moral midgets who orchestrated their deportation. Brebner's Acadians also came off well in comparison to his representations of a Halifax elite soaked in patronage, complacency, and alcohol.[49] In many respects, his Haligonians would consistently stand as the antitheses of the freestanding, pioneering Acadians: "At bottom, and they were well aware of it, the people of Halifax in 1760 were pensioners of the British Government."[50]

Brebner's most original contribution was to explode Parkman's facile "France and Britain" dichotomy by revealing the distinctive role of New England. "If one is tempted to seek a single and therefore incomplete explanation of why the Acadians suffered as they did," he remarked – and this tentative bow to causality typifies his scholarly caution – "it is far more likely to be found in the expanding energies of New England than in the character of Charles Lawrence." New Englanders played a more determinative role than a

London preoccupied with a far-flung *imperium*: they spent much of their time and energy dominating their "section of the long Anglo-French frontier in America."[51] Despite the moniker "Nova Scotia" (an "undeserved seventeenth-century name"), not to mention its reputation as "the Land of Evangeline" (the "product of a nineteenth-century poet's legend"), the basic fact of Nova Scotia's eighteenth-century history was New England influence. New England "repeatedly fought for the region in the seventeenth century, gradually drew it into her marine and mercantile domain, finally conquered it in 1710, supplanted the immigrants from England after the founding of Halifax in 1749, stimulated and carried out the expulsion of the Acadians in 1755, and planted twice as many settlers in the Province in their place." Brebner exceeded the evidence a bit – personifying New England as "she," then attributing to this "she" the almost undivided responsibility for having "stimulated and carried out the expulsion of the Acadians in 1755."[52] But he had a point.

Brebner's second major study, *The Neutral Yankees of Nova Scotia: A Marginal Colony during the Revolution Years* (1937) picked up where *New England's Outpost* left off by focusing on Nova Scotia's lukewarm response to the American Revolution. Why did the transplanted New Englanders who preponderated within the population of Nova Scotia take such an ambivalent stance on the revolution animating their erstwhile compatriots? In answer to this question, Brebner advanced a multi-causal explanation. He had to. As he took pains to point out, Nova Scotians were sufficiently diverse that "no summary phrase can be adequate to explain the behaviour of so unintegrated a province." Disunity persisted in default of credible leadership from "[p]ensioned Halifax," a capital city separated from the rest of the province "by more than geographical factors. Her habitual subservience to London … had been crystallized by war prosperity, by the presence of the navy and the army, and by the stories of the Loyalist refugees." How could Haligonians rebel against the Empire that paid the bills? Nor would sympathizers of the revolution make headway elsewhere "because their friends in the rebellious Colonies had no navy and because they themselves could not assemble from the scattered settlements an effective force for unassisted revolt." The hard-pressed populace, impoverished, apathetic, and isolated, could not even afford proper representation in its own assembly.

Nova Scotia thus went from abject dependence upon New England to an equally colonial relationship with Great Britain. The Americans had stopped paying much attention anyway: "The general North American tide of migration had turned west. New England, having received what she thought she wanted most at the peace settlement in the St. Croix boundary and in access to the North Atlantic fisheries, released her already weakened grip." In summary, "to use a generalization so broad as to be almost meaningless without

43

corroborative detail" – another practised Brebnerian nod to the perils of causal analysis – "Nova Scotia had insulated and neutralized the New England migrants so thoroughly that as Nova Scotians they had henceforth to look eastward to London for direction and help rather than southwestward to Boston as they had done in the past."[53] New England had provided the geo-historical framework of the Expulsion and the basic political assumptions guiding Nova Scotia thereafter; now, through the achievement of its diplomatic and trading demands, it thrust the province into the arms of the Mother Country. Meanwhile, the Nova Scotians' very individualism brought forth a divisiveness that played into the hands of the pensioners of the British state in Halifax. Brebner brought structural and conjunctural levels of analysis to bear upon the three most famous moments in the region's eighteenth-century history – the Expulsion of the Acadians, the founding of Halifax, and Nova Scotia's puzzling inattention to the call of revolution – in a way that stressed the many consequences of the province's position on the northern margins of New England.

The rise of social and cultural history during the 1960s and 1970s (a development spanning the Anglosphere) inaugurated a third moment in Nova Scotia's historiography. When it came to the eighteenth century, the new breed of historians renovated and modified Brebner's framework – without, perhaps, completely replacing it. Perhaps most importantly they followed Brebner in his masterful deconstruction of any Parkmanesque notion that the French/English duality held *the* key to eighteenth-century history. Yet his position on New England came in for new scrutiny. Brebner's most memorable historiographical innovation had been to treat the New Englanders as paramount shapers of Nova Scotia's history from the 1690s to the 1780s and to represent their situational neutrality during the American Revolution as a stance that ironically resembled that of the very Acadians they had displaced. Brebner sometimes marshalled persuasive evidence, as when he looked at those who decided to expel the Acadians:

> The men who reached this momentous decision were Charles Lawrence, Benjamin Green (son of a Harvard graduate who was rector of Salem, and a Boston merchant who had transferred his activity to Louisbourg and then to Halifax), John Collier (retired army officer and 1749 settler), William Cotterell (Provincial Secretary in succession to Davidson, ex-captain, probably English, first Provost Marshal), John Rous (master of a Boston privateer in 1744, messenger of victory from Louisbourg 1745, Captain R.N., and chief naval officer in Nova Scotia), and Jonathan Belcher (son of Governor Belcher of Massachusetts, Harvard graduate and member of

the Middle Temple, first Chief Justice of Nova Scotia). The fatal fruition of New England's interest and policy thus emerged from the hands of men who were either New Englanders or who, without exception, had been fairly saturated with that policy for years.[54]

At other moments, though, his judgments seem unsupported and partial. When *Neutral Yankees of Nova Scotia* came out, the archivist Jim Martell remarked that by giving the Bay of Fundy–Boston axis such weight Brebner implicitly downgraded other groups in ways that he had perhaps not fully examined.[55] Barry Moody has in essence recently seconded this early critique: "Nova Scotia did not turn out to be Massachusetts writ small in the wilderness, not merely the outer frontier of New England, even if some greatly desired it to be so."[56] For his part, George Rawlyk, while accepting much of Brebner's emphasis on New England, nonetheless argued that the New Englanders only focused on their northern margins at moments when they were especially worried about their security or their fisheries.[57] Along with Gordon Stewart, he would also object that Brebner implicitly disregarded the impact of the religious "Great Awakening" that accompanied the revolutionary years in Nova Scotia.[58] In the late 1980s, the emergence of "Planter Studies" refocused attention on the eight thousand New Englanders who immigrated to Nova Scotia (then encompassing the whole Maritimes) between 1759 and 1768. While building on Brebner's "mighty labours," Planter Studies also pursued research into a wide diversity of social and cultural topics, including many important initiatives in the history of, among others, blacks, women, and religion.[59]

Brebner also had an obvious tendency to view the history of eighteenth-century Nova Scotia through the narrow focus of pan-Canadian developments.[60] Historians of the third moment of Nova Scotia historiography have tended to argue that the eventful period initiated by the Conquest of 1710 (even this nomenclature is new) and concluded with the Acadian deportation should come in for analysis in its own right, not simply as a prelude to or parallel with Canadian developments – always Brebner's starting point.

From a conceptual point of view, Brebner can seem so convinced of historical inevitability that he seems to leave little scope for contingency, chance, or choice. Rawlyk may have deeply admired Brebner but nonetheless also thought he had imposed his "environmental deterministic framework" upon the "complex overlapping of names, events and personalities."[61] One might develop this point by observing that Brebner's mode of historical explanation is bound to generate contradictions because of his simultaneous commitments to geographical determinism and individualist voluntarism. He often cannot reconcile a liberal epistemology and ontology with post-liberal insights into the centrality of structures. Doing so would have required him to work much more intensively with concepts of mediation that could bring together structural and agential concepts of history.

If few would now agree with Brebner in every particular, he nonetheless opened the door – very early in the Canadian context – to a critical realist methodology far removed from the antiquarianism and jingoism of previous historians. He stands among the first Canadian historians whose work, by emphasizing the New Englanders, implicitly signalled the hazards of reading back into the past the national categories of the present. Observing the case of early Acadia, he remarks on how French actors could suddenly don Scottish honours, all the while aligning themselves with New England interests. Admitting that such "Frenchmen" showed more versatility "than would be considered reputable today," as they hopped from allegiance to allegiance, he asked his readers to take "the temper of the times" into account: "Not only were there then many soldiers of fortune, but European nations were torn by internal civil and religious dissensions. There were abundant grounds not only for profound differences of party opinion, but for transferences of allegiance … It seems useless to estimate it by our own standards."[62] We could consider contemporary historians who fiercely critique Brebner as nonetheless neo-Brebnerian in their willingness to reconstruct eighteenth-century history as something far more complex than "A Half-Century of (Anglo-French) Conflict," emphatically distancing themselves from the fife-and-drum history of Parkman.

The recovery of First Nations voices and agency has, however, gone well beyond anything Brebner did. John Reid has recently shown the potential of this approach in his pioneering article "*Pax Britannica* or *Pax Indigena*? Planter Nova Scotia (1760–1782)." He indicates the richness of the Gramscian concept of hegemony, applied in an unanticipated context. Rather than looking for unqualified evidence of British control, he evaluates the quotidian struggle of the colony's British rulers to understand, influence, and dominate the society around them through a flexible repertoire of coercion, consent, and corruption. Even the casual use of the word "control" may lead to the mistaken impression that there was a single nucleus of authority in what seems plainly to have been, down to at least 1815, a sharply contested terrain with no certainty about the permanence of the power or powers claiming sovereignty over it. Reid concludes that British hegemony was far from a finished project in the early 1760s, and hence the treaties between the First Nations and the conquering British did not represent the liquidation of Mi'kma'ki and Wulstukwik by Nova Scotia, but rather their ongoing interactions. These documents spoke not of surrender but of the pragmatics of mutual coexistence.[63]

Reid does not aim at the easy target of Brebner's stereotypical characterizations of the "savages" but at his grasp of geopolitical realities. Indigenous peoples' continuing military and diplomatic strength down to the early 1780s fundamentally qualifies both Brebner's characterization of their supposed "helplessness" after the 1760s and, more generally, the adequacy of Brebner's main theses about Yankee Nova Scotia. Fears of imminent native warfare, for example, may have conditioned the Nova Scotia Yankees' reluctance to embark upon a revolutionary venture as much as did their proverbial dispersion, marginality, and vulnerability to British coercion.

What goes for the First Nations has gone double for the Acadians. Brebner's texts unreflectively echo Parkman in representing Acadians as ignorant, isolated, and politically myopic. Most historians would have trouble agreeing now. New work on the Acadian *aboiteaux*, highlighting their engineering prowess, calls these characterizations sharply into question – a point Brebner himself might have developed as he pondered why the Acadians he thought of as primitive nonetheless proved crucial to the New Englanders struggling to preserve their predecessors' achievement of creating fertile fields from tidal marshes.[64] A more pointed challenge has come from a new generation of Acadian historians, impatient with the "Golden Age" antimodernism that patently suffuses representations of the colony. By recovering evidence of Acadian merchants, power elites, divided loyalties, and generation gaps, they have seriously qualified Brebner's interpretation of a pre-modern *Gemeinschaft* suddenly thrust into the modern world by events far beyond its control. Robert Sauvageau has emphasized the figure of the Acadian warrior, questioning the influential myth of an entirely tranquil people who "never bore arms with or against the French, British, or Mi'kmaq." Rather than being hounded by the fanatical Le Loutre, perhaps many willingly joined him in an armed resistance movement. Jean Daigle, meanwhile, has given us the Acadian merchant profiting from exchanges with his counterparts in New England. Maurice Basque has creatively appropriated a suggestive comment of Brebner's: "There were, in effect, two Acadies, each important in its own way. The one was the Acadie of the international conflict, the other the land settled and developed by the Acadians. They were almost separate geographical entities as well, and as such involved separate populations." Extending this idea a little, Basque posits a "Third Acadie" of "influential families and individuals who utilized – sometimes very cleverly – accommodation, neutrality, and/or open support for French or British crowns as a means to promote and protect their own interests." These elite arbiters, "calling upon older European traditions in dealing with troubled times," mobilized a much wider community of Acadians through their moral authority and control over access to trade.[65] Largely shunted aside is the old picture of an undifferentiated community of equals who faced simple problems of local dimensions (we shall, however, come back to it in chapter 2). Our understanding of eighteenth-century Acadia has been transformed just as completely as our understanding of the First Nations has. Historians no longer think of Acadians as the childlike innocents or frustratingly obtuse peasants of Parkman and (to a considerable extent) Brebner. Instead, Acadians appear as a small agrarian people in early modern times, driving hard bargains with an emergent British hegemony while appeasing the French authorities who might have returned in force at any moment.

One could make similar points about the New Englanders (now more commonly called "the Planters"), the blacks, the Loyalists, and the Scots among others. Planters disagreed vociferously with one another about subjects ranging from religion to revolution. Some "blacks" were their slaves, some were free; some joined a remarkable turn-of-the-nineteenth-century back-to-Africa movement, some remained in Nova Scotia. Loyalists, although mythically elite and Tory, often arrived with attitudes seemingly as democratic and republican as those of the revolutionaries whom they fled.[66] Scots – proverbially divided between Lowlanders and Highlanders – also differed according to religion, class, and language. One should refrain from reading back national and political identities that would only (and precariously) take shape in the following century.[67]

The province was just more complex than commonly supposed. For instance, European colonizers found seventeenth-century Nova Scotia an unclear entity indeed. Should it be settled – or be traded away at the bargaining table? Was it a giant wharf with handy access to the North Atlantic fisheries? Or was it a potential treasure trove (as the eighteenth-century British royals hoped when they secured monopoly rights not only to its coal, but also to its hypothesized lapis lazuli)? As one of the earliest North American sites of intensive European colonization (long predating the consolidation of the nation-state system and its accompanying nationalism) the province was, for many powerful people, a token in European dynastic politics. No one knew until 1763 which European monarch would predominate in the region, though New Englanders were increasingly exploiting it as a resource-rich hinterland. Simplifying this situation – for instance, construing the province *only* as a supplement to Europe – probably means misunderstanding it.

We can nonetheless arrange many elements of this flux in meaningful patterns, without eliding their particularities. Perhaps we should follow Reid to invoke "hegemony," not as a general theory for allocating social control but as a method of investigation. "Hegemony" typically names the process whereby a group comes to power, effectively (if always provisionally) unifying a territory under its rule. It makes sense only within an "eventful" concept of temporal-ity, which assumes (to cite Bill Sewell) that "what has happened at an earlier point in time will affect the possible outcomes of a sequence of events occurring at a later point in time."[68] Out of the manifold contradictory identities and interests evident in eighteenth-century Nova Scotia, the British Empire would construct a workable hegemony that by the mid-nineteenth century commanded the loyalty of a sufficient number of inhabitants as to permit the colony's integration into a transnational imperial order. This hegemonic project would usher Nova Scotians into a project of colonial state formation whose early roots can be discerned in that unusual mid-eighteenth-century statist experiment, the city of Halifax.

Used with discrimination, the concept of hegemony allows us to appreciate both the distinctiveness of each particular community and the pragmatics by which an overarching political order sought to secure their cooperation. Hegemony in this reading seeks to uncover how and why *this* regime change, *this* Conquest, *this* Confederation came to elaborate a social and political common sense that, over time, most people began taking for granted. It denotes not a *thing* or even a *relationship* (whether of coercion or consent) but a *historical process*. Rather than encapsulating a specific model, it condenses a powerful narrative about the emergence, the consolidation, and (potentially) the downfall of a ruling group. Arguably, then, hegemony helps to make sense of this remarkably heterogeneous territory without recourse to determinism or teleology.

It is important to insist on this because Nova Scotia's historiography has conventionally proceeded according to categories of nation-states (England versus France) that are saturated with determinism and teleology. Reading back the nation-state onto Nova Scotia history — translating the "Acadians" and "*canadiens*" into "the French," for example — distorts the truth. Before the nation-state became a dominant form of geopolitical organization, many people may have had more salient alternative foci of allegiance, as suggested by the arduous struggles of both British and French monarchs to overcome domestic enemies as they slowly unified their notional realms. Furthermore, an indeterminate but certainly non-zero number of such a monarch's most loyal retainers would have identified far more closely with the royal house than with any putative abstraction like "France" or "England," considered as a political space on a map (which helps explain how Germans with imperfect command of English came to rule the United Kingdom during the eighteenth century). Seventeenth-century France and Britain were not yet "nation-states." The boundaries and meanings of the respective claims these kingdoms staked in Nova Scotia remained sufficiently unclear as to leave many people in the dark about such basic issues as when one's sovereignty stopped and the other started. Most seriously of all, to talk in terms of state actors would ignore other significant collectivities – the Mi'kmaq, Acadians, and New Englanders most prominently – which, while obviously not nation-states, often proceeded with cohesive strategic purpose. Yet after the nation-state did become the dominant model, the boundaries and identities we associate with states became ever more definite and the almost inescapable temptation arose of projecting them back into the past. For people faced with this temptation, trumpeting the "five white races" provided an escape from the fluidity and complexity of this context, allowing twentieth-century historical romanticists confronted with a liminal terrain of such irksome complexity a way to retain their constitutive binaries, animating teleologies, decisive battles, turning points, noble heroes, and despicable villains.

◆

Twentieth-century tourism/history has, under the aegis of liberal order, largely recapitulated nineteenth-century romances of history. It found much of Parkman entirely to its taste, as evidenced by a string of battlefield restorations and commemorations from the 1890s to the 1940s. Post-Parkman historiography posed more of a problem. From the 1930s on, the characteristic fate of historians was to feebly protest the dangers of romanticized tourism/history without feeling any capacity or perhaps even obligation to contest it. The Province of History would be, and to a certain extent still is, the Province of Parkman. Why does it remain so? The tourism/history complex constitutes a vast system generating ideas about the past. Because investment in its sites of memory costs money, its direction is not readily reversed – even when the "heritage" conveyed comports uneasily with the values and interests of, for example, a twenty-first-century public committed to liberal multiculturalism and impatient with talk of racial destiny. Not all representations of the past in the public sphere are elements of tourism/history – cemeteries and other personal commemorative sites, for instance, have generally resisted absorption within it. Yet, insofar as it merged into tourism/history, the public past generated representations that bear only a tangential relationship with the history we have summarized or the historiographies that seek to describe and analyse it.

The construction of the Province of History in the period that stretches from the 1920s to the 1960s had almost nothing to do with historical investigations, whether by the newly accredited university-based professionals or the local amateurs. Such people were called upon periodically to look up a date, reread a text for historical accuracy, and validate a given interpretation. Yet overall their representations of the past are categorically different than those incarnated by tourism/history. Tourism/history determinedly insulates itself from most forms of historical knowledge and critique. Rather than a public sphere of open, democratic debate about history, tourism/history creates a closed commercial sphere in which the significance of any given historical issue boils down to its capacity to generate saleable commodities. If we think back to the "Native Types" who exemplified the "white races" in 1936, we remember that there was no way these individuals could actually have contested the terms under which the promotion represented their supposed essence. Although the public past was *public* in one sense – massively distributed by and sustained by the state – it was *private* in another – that is, outside the cut-and-thrust of public debate.

The key decisions furthering tourism/history occurred without public scrutiny and discussion. Responsibility for factual research fell to the traditional intellectuals (professors, archivists, librarians, etc). Much of the responsibility for specific acts of commemoration fell to the purely local intellectuals (family historians, rank-and-file preservationists, local-history columnists in the provincial press). But such people were increasingly overshadowed by a third, more powerful breed – the organic intellectuals of a new commodified history – that is, those organic to the systemic changes in the province's symbolic economy. Wielding new powers within the state, organic intellectuals could craft a new form of history and make that history believable across a broad swath of the public. They brought forth a kind of anti-history, a way of thinking about the past that was often viscerally hostile to the concept of change itself. We might think of the province's adoption of this form of public history as itself a form of hegemony, one acutely responsive to the province's social and economic crisis of the 1920s and 1930s.

These interwar years saw a significant departure from earlier ways of conceptualizing the past. M. Brook Taylor has furnished signposts for any discussion of attitudes towards history in English Canada in his discussion of British North America's (and subsequently Canada's) nineteenth-century historians, whom he alliteratively dubs "promoters, patriots and partisans." At first, a somewhat rootless cohort of *promoters* touted the possibilities of British North America for investors and settlers in Britain. Most of them "wanted to talk about the future. Indeed, initially, there was little else to discuss." As the decades passed, the promoters gave way to the more settled *patriots,* who shared the promoters' optimism about economic growth but more realistically discussed obstacles on the road to prosperity. Rather than seeing British North America as fulfilling the requirements of the colonizers, they would talk in terms of how settlers themselves needed to live up to the land: "The wilderness was a forge that fired a hardy and industrious society of independent yeomen, men and women who represented the best of the British heritage." Their ideal found expression in all the colonies; Nova Scotia in particular conjoined it to a "smug cosmopolitanism" prompted by the colony's undoubted strategic significance and by the tranquil advent of responsible government. Slowly, the central Canadian historians, bent on nurturing powerfully cohesive national sentiments, began playing to audiences not from Britain but from Canada itself: "Pleased with present achievement, they were confident of future success if past habits of conciliation, consolidation, and assimilation were imitated and reinforced and remnants of radicalism, regionalism, and racism permitted to fade." Yet this nation-building vision conflicted with that of Maritime historians, who, "confident in futures that did not include the Canadas, saw little reason to merge with the past of their continental brethren." After Confederation, "their future suddenly stolen from them," they agonizingly reconciled with the new pan-Canadian reality. Indeed, "[m]any retreated into nostalgia." At the same time, central Canadians confronted the disappointing record of Confederation itself, which made them a little pessimistic too: "After a century of looking for a Golden Age in the future, Canadian historians now suddenly found it in the past." Although the nascent historical profession subsequently disparaged them as dilettantes, it actually preserved many touchstones of the nineteenth-century amateurs: "The basic premise, for instance, that the history of Canada was held together and co-ordinated by geographic expansion and constitutional growth still stood. Competing identities of region, race, and religion remained subordinated and in some ways illegitimate."[69] As Taylor's last observation might suggest, this literature abounded in paeans to progress and eulogies for the lost Golden Age.

These guidelines can preliminarily orient us to the turn-of-the-century public past in Nova Scotia on the eve of its transformation by tourism/history (we discuss the one glaring exception in chapter 2). With local variations and different accents, historians articulated progressive visions, whether blatantly as promoters, more discretely as patriots, or yet more subtly as covertly partisan local historians weaving together accounts of stalwart pioneers with anticipations of their future success. All these articulations of Canadian history bespoke deep confidence in liberal order, broadly conceived with reference to Lockean ideals of liberty, property, and improvement. This orientation required not only the marginalization of such competing identities as emerged from regional, racial, and religious differences, but also the erasure of non- or antiliberal conceptions of property and person. The deeper ideological structure of the three forms of Victorian historical consciousness discerned by Taylor was possessive individualism – a consistent theme throughout Nova Scotia historiography, from Haliburton and Howe in the early nineteenth century to R.R. McLeod and Beckles Willson in the early twentieth. This was a historiography of liberal *improvement*, defined quite clearly in terms of clearing forests, enclosing farms, British parliamentarianism, attachment to the Empire, and the inspiring growth of cities, industries, and transportation systems. Contemporaries celebrated such things when they encountered them or lamented their absence when they did not.

◆

To ground these abstract observations, let us look at one particular instance: the representations of the city of Halifax in travel literature and tourism brochures from the late eighteenth century to the eve of the Great War. As we shall further show in chapter 4, Halifax's history can be framed in strikingly different ways. An admirer of Parkman might well present the city as an imperial garrison that owed its most notable physical features – the Citadel, the dockyard, the Grand Parade – to the legacies of empire and whose world-historical importance owed everything to its imperial function. With a slightly different emphasis, one might plausibly depict Halifax as an outpost of British civilization, an exemplar of that "Greater Britain Beyond the Seas." After all, its Georgian architecture testifies to this living cultural link: St Paul's Church (1750), Prince's Lodge (c. 1795), and Government House (1805) – not to mention, from the later Victorian period, the Halifax Public Gardens (1867) and the ubiquitous Union Jacks that still flew from public buildings well into the twentieth century. Equally, Halifax might appear as a bustling city of business – a hub of merchants and, later, industrialists, as evidenced by its lively waterfront and its smoke-belching factories (so proudly displayed in many late-Victorian illustrations of the thoroughly modern capital). In all three different cases, however, visitors and locals alike determined the success or failure of the city according to reasonably fixed ideas about propriety, property, and progress. All of these ideals ultimately cohered into a consistent way of seeing the world.

These pre–Great War representations of Halifax give no real sense that the city could become a *therapeutic space*, a welcome and quaint retreat from the stresses and strains of modernity. The supposed Old World charm of Halifax, a fixture of later tourist literature, remained stubbornly inaccessible to nineteenth-century visitors. In short, this historical Halifax had yet to become "Historic Halifax." Local boosters considered it an up-and-coming city whose minor flaws presented only minor obstacles on the ever-upward path of improvement. Cynical detractors, on the other hand, considered it a sleepy, deficient, and shabby city that improvement had bypassed. For neither group did Halifax offer a wholesome refuge from deracinating modernity.

During the nineteenth century, just about everyone agreed that neither Halifax nor Nova Scotia had much history to offer tourists. Whatever the incidental pleasures the province might hold, history was not among them. As early as 1821, Howe lamented that Nova Scotia's scenery, while attractive, lacked the historical associations necessary for consideration as truly picturesque.[70] The traveller Andrew Learmont Spedon remarked of all Canada in 1863 that "though in many parts beautiful and picturesque, [it] is destitute of much of that romantic antiquity characteristic of older countries, which excites the traveler with admiration; and is a magnet to the poet's fancy, and a mirror to the painter's eye."[71] Not everyone lamented this fact. Herbert Crosskill, in his boosterish 1872 emigrant tract *Nova Scotia: Its Climate, Resources and Advantages*, writes, "Emigrants from Europe care but little whether this Province possesses a history the most remarkable and extraordinary of any country in the world, or, comparatively, no history at all."[72] Whatever immigrants might have thought, having "no history at all" presented certain challenges for tourism promotion. At the turn of the twentieth century, local historian R.R. McLeod, wonderfully eccentric in his firm opinions, bluntly asserted, "For a certain class of tourists, *Nova Scotia has no attractions*. It is destitute of such human antiquities as may be found in most other portions of the globe. Here are no buried cities, nor feudal castles, and blood-stained battlefields. Professional globe-trotters will find here but little to tickle their jaded appetite for wonderful things."[73] In vivid contrast to many writers and promoters of the interwar period, these authorities, both visiting and local, felt convinced that Nova Scotia, far from being the Province of History, pretty much entirely lacked it. They would have heard the later slogan "Cashing in on Antiquity" with considerable befuddlement, since for the life of them they saw no antiquity to cash in.

The nineteenth and early twentieth century featured a number of revealing debates between outsiders and insiders about how to characterize Nova Scotia. Though sharp disagreements cropped up, all commentators framed their arguments in terms of the classic liberalism shared by most mainstream Victorians. Richard Dashwood's 1872 guide to the province for sportsmen, *Chiploquorgan*, portrays a wild land inhabited by "very ignorant and rather lawless" people[74] – a portrayal that at the very least marked its author as a fool in Crosskill's eyes. The local writer and politician indignantly rubbished Dashwood's descriptions as "perfect nonsense, and calculated to give to the intending emigrant an erroneous impression of the country."[75] An irate reader (perhaps Crosskill himself) splattered outrage, in the form of protesting marginalia, across the copy of Dashwood's book at the Public Archives of Nova Scotia: "false," "rot," "bosh," and "again bosh," culminating – when Dashwood goes so far as to suggest that local girls were rather "fast" at skating rinks – with the startled reproach "What sort of company he must have kept!"[76] The visitor who implied that Nova Scotians lagged in the fields of progress or respectability could expect to have his or her opinions challenged. Beckles Willson's 1913 opus *Nova Scotia: The Province That Has Been Passed By* prompted

Visions of civilized Halifax, from Nova Scotia, Department of Highways, *Nova Scotia, Canada's Ocean Playground* (Halifax, n.d. [1931], 27). The Memorial Tower, built to honour the granting of representative government to Nova Scotia, looms over the city's Northwest Arm. Other attractions in the city include the Old Town Clock and the gateway to Ordnance Wharf – historic sites not widely publicized in "progressive" accounts.

a debate in the House of Assembly, driven by the Halifax *Herald*'s outrage that Willson had included descriptions of prostitutes. Perhaps more seriously, he had even indulged in a "vile slander" of the local architecture.[77]

This flashpoint suggests not only the contentiousness of travel descriptions and the tourism with which they were associated, but reveals a widespread local common sense – at least among the affluent white men whose opinions counted most – about the province. Nova Scotians in a position to pronounce on such questions believed they lived in a rapidly industrializing and socially progressive province, integrated into a great dominion that in turn belonged to

the world's largest and most successful empire. Nova Scotians were Britons across the sea, more progressive and forward-looking than their cousins in the Mother Country, yet more civilized and orderly than Americans.[78] Nova Scotia's destiny flowed from its advancing and intrinsic British civilization.

The geographer Paul Williams has brought out the spirit of the imperial public history in his work on the Halifax Memorial Tower, which opened in 1912. (The next four paragraphs owe everything to him.) The building of the tower probably stands out as the most noteworthy act of public history-making in Nova Scotia before the Great War. Located on the western bank of the Northwest Arm, a narrow inlet of the sea that forms the southwest boundary of the peninsula on which the nineteenth-century city was located, the tower sits on the former estate of Sir Sandford Fleming. Fleming, the inventor of Universal Standard Time, was the engineering colossus behind the Intercolonial and the Canadian Pacific Railways, the chancellor of Queen's University, and an ardent imperialist. Having retired to Halifax, he was deeply inspired by the unveiling of a plaque at Province House on 19 August 1908 to honour the sesquicentennial of the first meeting of the Assembly of Representatives on 2 October 1758. He felt that the simple plaque understated the significance of the occasion, so he offered the city of Halifax land for a municipal park where the province could erect a far more grandiose commemoration.

Sir Sandford, never short of visionary ideas, quickly planned "an Italian tower, probably 25 feet square and 100 or more feet in height." From a granite base, it would "gradually increase in architectural beauty until crowned by the finale." The architecture would form an allegory of constitutionalism: a massive and simple lower portion conveyed the plain beginnings of representative government; a somewhat finer middle portion incarnated the years of

---

Opposite: Halifax parks: "In Point Pleasant Park, Halifax, N.S." and "Public Park, Halifax, N.S.," from J. Wesley Swan, *Through the Maritime Provinces (New Brunswick and Nova Scotia): including the Gaspé Coast, Cape Breton, Prince Edward Island and a portion of the Province of Quebec* (Montreal: Canadian Railway News Company, n.d. [c. 1903]). Did Halifax stand in bleak contrast to turn-of-the-century ideals of progress and improvement – or did it triumphantly live up to them? Its partisans often claimed that the city's majestic parks, especially the Public Gardens, were among the finest in the entire Dominion. As A.L. Hardy remarks, "Halifax has very many attractions for the tourist; among the most important are her parks. In proportion to their size they are not second to any in the cities of America. With their cool and shady walks, gurgling streams and flowing fountains, placid lakes and fragrant flower beds they afford a charming spot for the weary traveler to while away a few hours enjoying the beauties of nature, made doubly beautiful by the taste of an artistic designer."

colonial responsible government; and a much more elaborate upper structure captured the splendour of Canadian political achievement from 1867 to 1908. A viewing gallery and a flagpole bearing the Union Jack would cap it all off. Williams explains that "[f]or Fleming, the Tower would serve as 'an instructive object lesson ... to foster in the minds of the youth and future generations a worthy pride in their past, and lead them to a correct knowledge of the basal elements of national greatness.'" It took quite literally the concept of an evolutionary political ascent from base simplicity to lofty refinement, a beneficent process crowned (both metaphorically and actually) by the proud flag of a triumphant empire.

The actual tower only faintly echoed Fleming's grand, if perhaps unworkable, design. Still, although much of its planned baroque complexity fell by the wayside – including the memorial galleries celebrating Joseph Howe and Sir John A. Macdonald – the imperial narrative stood out unmistakably. The final version, as the Duke of Connaught would point out, was "carved from so many different portions of the empire" and included

> slate bearing the Red Dragon of Wales; a black granite slab from the Giant's Causeway in Ireland; a stone from the Indian subcontinent; a two-ton block of Melbourne freestone with the arms of the Commonwealth of Australia; the arms of the Union of South Africa on a slab of brown free-stone; those of the Dominion of New Zealand were painted in heraldic colours on native granite; the Colony of Newfoundland's were incised on red granite; and those of the Dominion of Canada on white marble. Local stones also bore the arms of the nine provinces of Canada. Plaques were also supplied by the cities of London and Edinburgh, by various Canadian universities, by the Royal Society of Canada, and by the Canadian Institute, Toronto. Of particular significance were a Bronze plaque from the City of Bristol, depicting John Cabot's voyage to the New World, and a stone from Brouage in France, the birthplace of Samuel de Champlain.

At its official opening on 14 August 1912, Canada's governor-general proclaimed the Halifax Memorial Tower the "Canadian Statue of Liberty." The *Times* of London echoed the Statue of Liberty suggestion, remarking that the tower would inform visitors to the Dominion that they were entering a land of liberty "not less real, though perhaps a little less declamatory, than that which is celebrated by the famous statue that meets him as he enters a harbour farther south."

The Halifax Memorial Tower contributes to a decidedly imperial memory-scape. Fleming even liked to call it the "imperial tower." He wanted to awaken in those who viewed it a reverence for the Empire and its constitution, unfolding majestically through time. As Dougald Macgillivray, one of its key promoters, remarked on the tower's opening day, "It will, we hope, awaken the widest patriotism. It will foster loyalty to the empire which as a common heritage we call our own, and which we are assured is the greatest secular agency for good in the world today."[79] From the "monarch-of-all-I-survey" vistas afforded by its viewing gallery down to the Trafalgar Square lions guarding its portals, the tower offered a stunning monument to an imperial vision of the city and the province. Yet, Williams concludes, it has declined to a "mere curiosity, defaced and crumbling," encoding a text that few can read and that, if they could, even fewer would identify with.[80] It is a prime example of Tunbridge and Ashworth's "dissonance" in that it unself-consciously celebrates a narrative that is now irremediably dated. It probably brings to mind Shelley's statue of Ozymandias crumbling in the desert more than it does the Statue of Liberty presiding over New York Harbor.

In its heyday, the tower fit into a British, liberal, improving province. Tourists who visited Nova Scotia ought to have come away impressed by the splendid redcoats in Halifax, the attractive LaHave River (inevitably, as with so many of the continent's riparian vistas, "the Rhine" of North America), the urbanity and new electric light system in Liverpool, not to mention that town's "tramway, fine churches, school house buildings, social life, each of which would interest the visitor as his tastes dictate."[81] In the 1870s, the governor-general's wife, Lady Aberdeen, was introduced to the scientific wonders of the lunatic asylum in Halifax, as well as to the "very interesting reformatory for boys."[82] Travel guides down to the 1920s urged visitors to take in steel mills, coal mines, and quarries. As late as 1931, the Halifax *Herald* – in a publication revealingly titled *Nova Scotia, the Atlantic Pier of America* – enticed tourists and investors to the province with lavish photographs of "Steel Making at the great Sydney Mills."[83] What visitor to Yarmouth would want to miss the town's "unique feature" – that is, "the Freshest, most Splendid Evergreen Hedges in the World"?[84] Rave reviews of pastoral scenery reminiscent of the British home counties did not contradict equally enthusiastic endorsements of industry. Both testified to peace, order, and good British government – civilization, in a word.

Disgruntled visitors to the province – a numerous company indeed – operated within much the same universe of assumptions about history and progress. They repeatedly condemned Halifax as a drab, dismal disappointment. "Halifax wears an air of poverty," complained Robert Everest in 1855. Admitting its military centrality, he could not help noticing how small and unprepossessing its houses were. Despite the prevalence of British stock, no one kept gardens – "even in the suburbs." Children were "ragged" ("particularly among the coloured race"). Regrettably influenced by a dissolute officer class, the populace abandoned itself to "drunkenness and prostitution." Salutary economic development might have saved the situation, but it looked unlikely, what with the "poor and rocky" soil, inadequate communications with "the interior," and the unfortunate puniness of nearby timber.[85] "But oh! what a slow place it is," exclaimed an exasperated Frederic S. Cozzens in a travel book of 1859, carping, "Even two Crimean regiments with medals and decorations could not wake it up. The little old houses seem to look with wondrous apathy as these pass by, as though they had given each other a quiet nudge with their quaint old gables, and whispered: 'Keep still!'" Hoping for "something picturesque," he wandered up and down the old streets, but saw "scarcely any thing remarkable to arrest or interest a stranger." The broadminded Cozzens did make an effort to warm up to the city, and found mild interest in its "queer little streets, its quaint, mouldy old gables, its soldiers and sailors, its fogs, cabs, penny and half-penny token, and all its little, odd, outlandish peculiarities." He could thus bring himself to damn it with faint praise: "Peace be with it! after all, it has a quiet charm for an invalid!"[86]

Such critiques of Halifax were gallingly evident when the Prince of Wales visited North America in 1860. As shown by Ian Radforth, visiting journalists found the city dusty, drab, and dissolute. *Harper's Weekly* of New York thought Halifax had "an old and decrepit look, as if blight had fallen upon its energies somewhere about the close of the last American war," found the town's public buildings "few and shabby," and speculated that it would be a "dreary" place to grow up. More painful still were the harsh assessments from the *Times* of London. Its correspondent Nathan Woods found the "quaint, rickety little village" as dull as an old English cathedral town. He wrote vividly of its sex trade and its drunks, ending his report by observing that Halifax was "less like a town itself than the *debris* of an old one for sale, with its dusty old streets – stagnant and lethargic without being quiet – noisy without being busy." Such charges sparked responses whose very fire and energy demonstrated that the spirit of enterprise was alive in Halifax. Yet fault-finding outsiders also prompted self-critical assessments of the town's inability to measure up to imperial standards. The *Acadian Recorder* freely admitted Halifax's shortcomings: "It is useless to deny that Halifax really has not a hotel in it ... that its streets are not paved and are in danger, almost any day in the year, of holding the passenger fast in the mud, or suffocating him with dust; and that, architecturally speaking, Halifax is the meanest city, for its population in North America." "These extended and elaborate replies," Radforth argues, "make it obvious that the local press took strong exception to affronts to the city's self-image. In the mid-Victorian period, when industry and enterprise were the hallmarks of the age, these comments about lethargy cut deeply indeed."[87]

So it went, decade after Victorian decade. "The houses are chiefly built of wood," regretted Alexander Heatherington in 1868, in a guidebook mainly intended for people interested in the province's goldmines, "and some of the older ones are not much better than wigwams." Only the South End had a few tolerable dwellings. Even here, Heatherington saw garbage strewn about the yards, "gathered up in a heap under the back parlour window for the winter, and in summer it is put into boxes or barrels in front of the house until cleared away by the wind, or the city scavenger." The city's hotels were second-rate, its gardens untended, its dirty omnibuses overcrowded, and its officials indolent, blundering, and insufferable.[88] In 1912, Beckles Willson remarked on the glaring contradiction between Halifax's imperial pretensions and its slovenly architecture: "Wooden houses may be cheap, wooden houses may be easy to build, wooden houses may be painted to look like stone or brick, but wooden houses are not for men, but children. People who live in glass houses, we are told, shouldn't throw stones; and people who live in wooden can't care for posterity, for it is certain that posterity won't care for them."[89] Halifax "is a disappointment, – one might even say a shock," exclaimed Margaret Morley, also in 1912. She found it "a mere huddle of narrow gloomy streets and cheap buildings."[90]

Such criticism provoked rebuttals. Revealingly, these counterblasts accepted precisely the same progressive standards of improvement and progress as the critics. Their authors merely argued that these universal standards had been misapplied. In a pamphlet aimed at potential immigrants, eloquently titled *Nova Scotia Canada: The Country and Its People and the Opportunity It Offers to Other People* (1907), the Ministry of the Interior declared Halifax a hive of industry and a hub of civilization. Forty churches, active charities, a lending library, numerous clubs, innovative entrepreneurs, public parks, electrified trams, all bolstered civic culture in a city that offered a perfect "combination of urban and rural advantages." Come-from-aways might blanch at the inclement weather, but "the people forgive the ocean at their door for such climatic vicissitudes as the Atlantic thinks fit to bestow, because it is this very Atlantic that secures to their city its commercial supremacy."[91] Halifax held still more attractions, advised a further ministry pamphlet of 1914, marvellously titled *Nova Scotia Canada: Fertile, Productive Lands, Free School System, Contented and Law-Abiding People*. How about the "principles of democratic government" as introduced by Joe Howe, or what of the chance to become a self-made man in an open society? "Many of the leading statesmen and professional men of high standing in the Province have risen from humble beginnings and from country homes, where the means of living were scanty." Nova Scotians were cultured, progressive folk: "The people are fond of reading, and keep abreast of the leading social, political and religious movements of the day, and take a deep interest in social and moral reforms."[92]

Locals bristled when called backward. "In coming to Nova Scotia," Crosskill lectured potential visitors, with more than a touch of asperity,

> emigrants do not leave a civilized country to reside among savages, or in a wilderness. They must bear in mind that they are coming amongst a people who are quite as far advanced in the arts of civilization as they are themselves, and who, owing chiefly to our system of free schools, are bet-ter educated than are, on an average, the people of England. The inhabitants of this country are mostly descended from British settlers, are governed by the same laws, animated by the same feelings and sentiments, and speak the same language as their British ancestors; and in point of intelligence, in morality and religion they are second to no people in the world.[93]

Put that in your pipe and smoke it! This British-imperial progressive motif persisted well into the twentieth century. It came as no accident that one of the two great hotels that opened in Halifax in the 1920s bore the name of Lord Nelson, evoking the empire-building feats of the great British admiral, the cul-tured gentility of Europe, and the naval role of the city. In this ambitious era, the Nova Scotia Tourist Association sought to justify its decision to drop the tainted word "Tourist" from its name by advising the province that "one of the main incentives to the encouragement of tourist travel lies in the justifiable expectations of interesting moneyed visitors in industrial projects."[94] From this perspective, the most appropriate tourist came with investment capital in tow – at the ready to plant an industry or take up farming.[95]

◆

Prior to the 1920s, tourism/history existed only in the Annapolis Valley, which a truly precocious tourist gaze had refigured as "the Land of Evangeline" (about which more in chapter 2). Elsewhere, few Nova Scotians considered that they might profit from the public past. If (as we have seen) one common-sense nineteenth-century objection to the notion of cashing in on antiquity might have been that Nova Scotia (as a young province) simply had no antiq-uity to speak of, another might have been to ask, "Whose cash?" Relatively few tourists chose Nova Scotia as a destination. Furthermore, down to the

1920s, the very word "tourist" connoted the tawdry exploitation of credulous foreigners. It was in better taste to speak of "summer visitors."[96]

Summer visitors (i.e., tourists) began arriving in noticeable numbers in the early 1870s, when new railroads made it possible to travel from New York to Halifax in just thirty-six hours.[97] The pseudo-aristocratic "sports" attached to the garrison, who had established a few hunting and fishing traditions of their own, started complaining about uncouth out-of-towners typified by "the town loafer and the cock-tail sportsman."[98] Such books as *The Fishing Tourist* by Charles Hallock, editor of the New York magazine *Forest and Stream*, had perhaps drawn such interlopers to the province. By the turn of the twentieth century, one could fill a considerable bookshelf with guides to provincial hunting, fishing, and camping.

Yet such swallows did not a tourism springtime make. Only in the interwar years would mass tourism debut in Nova Scotia. The province lagged far behind New England. As late as 1922, according to the first impressionistic statistics compiled by the provincial government, 49,000 tourists came to the province in the tourist season (generally defined as June to September). It sounded impressive, until one reflected that about three times as many had travelled to less-populous New Hampshire twenty-three years earlier. Since the Nova Scotia figures included recent émigrés returning to visit friends and family, the statistic diminishes still further. Given a Nova Scotia population of about 523,000, this represents an approximate resident/tourist ratio of 10.7:1. Soon, though, the number of tourists would skyrocket to a pre–Second World War high of 322,723 in 1938. They now came by motorcar, not train. Tourists arriving in automobiles would constitute 56 per cent of the 165,906 summer visitors in 1928 and 63 per cent of the 168,844 who arrived in 1933. Of these automobile tourists, 47,000 hailed from the United States.[99] A new tourist infrastructure welcomed them.

Down to the mid-1930s, Nova Scotia had nothing that compared with Nantucket in Massachusetts or Litchfield in Connecticut as sites deliberately designed for tourists. "By 1900, the tourist industry had penetrated almost every corner of New England, from the coast of Maine to the hill towns of Connecticut," writes Dona Brown in her history of New England tourism.[100] The Nova Scotia historian, on the other hand, would have to write, "By 1900, the tourist industry had penetrated almost no corners of Nova Scotia, excepting only the Annapolis Valley and the resort towns of Chester on the South Shore and Baddeck in Cape Breton. And even these last two, elite resorts of long-term American summer people rather than tourists as such, relied on gentlemanly vacationing rather than mass tourism." Nova Scotia lay on the furthest extremity of New England's therapeutic frontier.[101] That was about to change.

Many interwar Nova Scotians believed tourism offered the province a ticket out of the economic doldrums. There was more truth than fiction in the Halifax *Chronicle*'s observation that Nova Scotia's tourist industry was "Depression-born" – especially if one remembers that, in much of Nova Scotia, the Depression started in 1921.[102] Private business efforts were soon supplemented by the Nova Scotia Tourist Association – renamed the Nova Scotia Publicity Bureau in 1924 – which promoted the province and collected tourism statistics (initially haphazard and down to the 1960s fraught with inconsistency).[103] By 1923, the Nova Scotia Motor League had organized a variety of "trail markings" to guide the motoring public. The provincial government embarked on a program of highway construction, yielding sixty-five hundred miles of improved roads by 1938.[104] Outside investors also got into the act. Canada's two major railways, the Canadian Pacific Railway and the Canadian National Railways, erected no fewer than five major hotels and resorts from 1927 to 1930.

The new tourist economy wrought dramatic changes in the public history of the province. Instead of coming to Halifax to see the Memorial Tower, whose very masonry had once taught an object lesson in the indispensability of Nova Scotia to a liberal North Atlantic order, one now went there to regain contact with an older, better time. For the first time, but from then on, Nova Scotia abounded in distinctively Nova Scotian essences: a rock-bound coast, a primordial Scottishness, a Golden Age of Sail, the whole panoply of signifiers that redefined the province as a temporally displaced realm of Innocence essentially exempt from modernity – with a folk, not a citizenry; a way of life, not an economy; an authentic mode of being, not a complex of social relations.

Four general contexts can explain these discursive and material shifts. First, the interwar depression eviscerated Nova Scotia's industrial economy, which never fully recovered. Coal and steel had once symbolized modernity, but these industries now plunged into a demoralizing series of wage cuts, strikes, and bankruptcies.[105] Like inhabitants of post-whaling Nantucket in the 1870s,[106] increasingly post-industrial Nova Scotians saw tourism as an alternative – perhaps the *only* alternative – to economic collapse. Second, if severe local depression *pushed* the province, Nova Scotia was also *pulled* by the new prospect of a travelling public in North America, which, to an unprecedented extent, enjoyed paid vacations and ownership of newly affordable motorcars.[107] Third, geopolitical changes – the slow decline of the British Empire, the meteoric ascent of the United States as a world power, Canada's own attainment of self-government – attenuated local identification with British imperialism.

Imperialism imperceptibly changed from a matter of celebrating one's partic-ipation in the pre-eminent world power to waxing nostalgic over the loss of its supposed civility and elegance. Fourth, a dynamic corps of organic intellectu-als emerged to self-consciously adapt the province's culture to the demands of the travelling public. The rest of this book tells their story.

We can discern this momentous shift in public culture by attending to the dramatic transformation of symbolic landscapes. Nineteenth- and early twentieth-century observers praised industrial and pastoral landscapes. They discreetly averted their eyes from the rocky coast of the South Shore – con-sidered a desolate, even deformed, region. This way of seeing changed dramatically in the 1920s. Automobiles and mass tourism (along with, by the early 1930s, Halifax-bound cruise ships for elite tourists) brought more and more of the province within the tourist gaze. The general economic crisis prompted middle-class interest in back-to-the-land movements, primitivist aes-thetics, and a reappraisal of pre-capitalist traditions and values. Nova Scotia's rocky coastline with its fisherfolk, once condemned as unsightly, uncivilized, and (physically and socially) dangerous, rapidly gained symbolic currency. Peggy's Cove, a little fishing village on St Margaret's Bay, almost entirely absent from tourist geography before 1920, became central within it after *circa* 1928. Photographers and painters celebrated its rocks and wharves, travel writers the homespun simplicity of its people.[108] If nineteenth-century intellectuals laboured to present local landscapes as somehow European and their early twentieth-century counterparts struggled to summarize the greatness of the British Empire in a lofty tower, they now proclaimed an essential Nova Sco-tia that was Western civilization's polar opposite. Here one met the *real* Nova Scotians – raw, vital, shorn of pretensions, primitive, stripped to the bedrock. Both fictional and touristic representations focused on rocky coastlines and the many rocky islands lying off Nova Scotia's coast. They became the truest harbours of provincial essence. There, it seemed, one could cash in on not just antiquity, but eternity.

The changes in symbolic geography correlated with a second great transi-tion in the idiom of Nova Scotia tourism: the rise of the "folk." As throughout much of the West, celebrating the folk involved upper-middle-class urbanites appropriating the songs, sayings, and dress of nearby country people. In the Nova Scotia case, it meant not so much an appreciation of local cultural expression as a reverence for surviving British "Childe ballads." Funded by institutions like the Canadian Pacific Railway and by American philan-thropists, folklorists argued that folk culture was foundational to the entire province. In the case of handicrafts (which in so industrialized a province had predictably languished since the mid-nineteenth century), it meant reinventing rural crafts and teaching Acadians, who would insist on using bright colours in their rugs and tapestries, to tone down their palates for the New England market.[109]

As we shall explore in chapter 5, this new folk dispensation also had a racial dimension. It was Scottish. To trumpet Nova Scotia's supposedly deep Scottishness demanded that one overcome the objection that persons of Scottish descent constituted less than 30 per cent of the population listed in the 1931 federal census. It was also a message completely at odds with the work of the leading interwar historians, such as Brebner, who had little time for such romanticism. It was even distanced from many of the actually existing traits of Nova Scotians of Scottish descent, requiring them to perform their ethnicity in a new manner. A new language of "tartanism" encouraged them to set aside their specific practical or symbolic interests – such as a deep emotional investment in Calvinist doctrinal debates, a concern to maintain the vanishing Gaelic language, an interest in Scottish autonomy back home – in order to develop a stylized Scottishness easily marketed to tourists.

The new Scottishness was accompanied by, and ultimately subordinated to, a new Canadian nationalism. Nova Scotians took note of the touristic possibilities offered by the larger national economy. The 1934 Senate Report, out of which would emerge the Canadian Government Travel Bureau, was inspired in large measure by Maritimers, William Dennis of the Halifax *Herald* prominent among them.[110] Intra-dominion traffic mattered to this strategy every bit as much as did the more-celebrated American tourist trade. From the 1930s to the 1950s, at least as many Canadian as American tourists motored to Nova Scotia. Nova Scotia officially became "Canada's Ocean Playground" in 1935. Canadian tourists excitedly filled their newspapers back home with accounts of this newly accessible vacationland, travel to which could be rationalized as a form of economic nationalism. The history of colonial Nova Scotia was interpreted as a series of anticipations of what would come later in Canada. Ethnic themes were repositioned so that they reassuringly confirmed Canadian nationalism.[111]

A final theme added to the provincial tourism repertoire was what we might call "maritimicity" – the bold claim that, in Nova Scotia, a seafaring population carried on the proud traditions of the romantic Golden Age of Sail. As with all the historical themes articulated within tourist discourse, this one pushed well beyond an empirical observation applicable to a minority of Nova Scotians in order to make a statement about the essence of the entire society. The Grand Banks schooners had an especially important role to play. One of them, the *Bluenose*, today features on every provincial licence plate in honour of its victories over American competitors in the International Fishermen's Races of the 1920s and 1930s. (The Canadian dime displays a very similar vessel too.) This schooner bore a symbolic freight far weightier than codfish. One might say that it transformed the "poor relations of the poor relations" into proud people with a noble past everyone could enjoy in the present. Within antimodern gender typologies, the *Bluenose* provided a record of stalwart heroes, the rugged individuals of a maritime frontier (its Captain Angus Walters even got his own comic strip). Within a liberal narrative starved for much in the way of successes traceable to actually existing local capitalism, it provided inspiring images of a self-made man. Within folk discourse, the schooner's victories stood for those of simple traditional people against decadent big-city yachtsmen ("the rich man's toys of the Gloucester [Massachusetts] boys with their token bit of cod," as Stan Rogers would later sing, as opposed to a bona fide working schooner manned by real men).[112] Within Canadian nationalism, moreover, the *Bluenose* could stand for a victory over the United States.

Everything symbolizing Nova Scotia – the windswept coast, the ballad-singing fisherfolk, the Scottish clans, the heroic skipper of Canada's own schooner – seemed to speak not of a modern industrializing province but of a land innocent of modernity. After the mid-1920s, Nova Scotia became an Old World province, primordial in its beauty and primeval in its customs – such a welcome respite from the harried, sweltering cities of New England and central Canada. We might return to Halifax for a moment to watch this transformation take place. If the city can provide a good example of "British progressive tourism," it can also suggest how radically the new tourism framework could clarify a complex community. The transition to the new way of seeing goes back to the years immediately before the Great War. Professor Archibald MacMechan, a substantial figure in the Nova Scotia Historical Society, acknowledged that the city *looked* drab: "[A]s a hasty tourist, you may dash through Halifax, and put yourself on record as having seen only a certain number of buildings much in need of paint and the scrubbing-brush." But once tourists realized they were in fact in *storied Halifax*, once they took the time "to study and learn her past," her special charm would come to the fore. They had only to imagine the magic of an earlier time, because "the balls, parties, levees, dinners, the Sunday reviews on the Common, the illuminations for great victories by sea and land, the feasting, the fighting, the raids of the press-gang, the constant military bustle in the streets, the coming and going of ships in the harbour, the prizes sold at the wharf has made life in this demure old town a brilliant, stirring spectacle down to the dramatic close of the great Napoleonic wars."[113] A city routinely denounced in the 1860s as a bedraggled and backward disgrace was now promoted precisely because it preserved the colour and romance of the olden days.

Promoters of the Halifax Hotel proudly wrote that to visit their city was to savour quaintness, notably on market days, for "peasant life of France or Italy is not more interesting than those groups of French Canadians, Jamaicans, Micmac Indians and the Hardy Fisher folk from along the shore, who offered their wares, old-fashioned flowers, berries and baskets, lobsters, scallops, fruit and game to the tourist or householder."[114] It was, as *Nova Scotia by the Sea* (c. 1928) proclaimed, a "city of glamour." History lived on in the "Old World atmosphere" of the streets, in the "crowning majesty of the citadel" (such a "monument to the glories and the tragedies of the past"), in the marvellous ships that "whisper queer messages of strange worlds," in "its gardens, stately with beauty, and the dahlias, glowing things with faces like happy humans."[115] But, then, all of Nova Scotia was, in the words of Emma-Lindsay Squier, "an old-world land that civilization has not yet robbed of its charm."[116] "Historic ruins, the remains of old fortifications and of bygone cities, are always fascinating," the *Sydney Post-Record* remarked in 1936. "But why go to the Old World to see them – when you can find them in the New?"[117]

Betty D. Thornley, writing in the 1920s, acutely observed, "The visitor to-day can get the soul-taste of all these phases of history, mingled with the brine of the sea and hazed with that faint dimness that adds the final touch of haunting beauty to the thoughts of yesterday."[118] It took work to organize this "soul-taste" so as to make it readily available for sale to the travelling public. Addressing a Halifax meeting of the Canadian Authors Association, Thomas H. Raddall exhorted his colleagues to mine the rich vein of cultural meaning that lay just beneath the surface of Nova Scotia, land of living traditions and famous ghosts: "Life! That's it! Life, back there in the shouting past or life here and now ... and all awaiting an ear, an eye and a pen."[119] A canny operator with a head for figures and a world-beating historical romancer to boot, Raddall saw that, for tourism/history to succeed, discerning pens would need to work up the "shouting past" into an array of consumable experiences. Tourism/history needed a committed cohort of organizers and publicists.

The provincial state provided a locus for these tourism/history intellectuals. The small and vestigial state organs of the 1920s were replaced by a much more vigorous, cabinet-level representation in the 1930s. Rhetorically committed to a New Deal–style "new liberalism" but fiscally cautious in practice, the Liberal Party that dominated political life from 1933 to 1956 embraced tourism as a highly visible, seemingly low-cost investment in the provincial economy. (T. Stephen Henderson has nicely dubbed the governing ideology "infrastructure liberalism.")[120] Paving roads, promoting new national parks, organizing a handicrafts bureau (in part inspired by New Hampshire), employing a New York advertising agency to coordinate the mass distribution of images, all suggested a province determined to grasp the most modern, mass-market means of promoting its pre-modern Innocence.

The rudimentary nineteenth-century tourism/history complex had operated, in a sense, by remote control. Local amateurs had put forward a miscellany of attractions, from hedgerows to lunatic asylums, which they hoped might get people to open their wallets. (The Evangeline Phenomenon, which we will explore in chapter 2, was better organized.) In the twentieth century, things became more planned and systematic. The organic intellectuals of the new tourism/history – those who most clearly sensed what the new society and economy of Nova Scotia demanded, and had the breadth of vision and political clout to do something about it – could institute wide-ranging official interpretations that, instantiated in historic sites, rituals of commemoration, new public landscapes, novels and even mass spectaculars, attained the status of a new "common sense" in the province.

At the heart of this process we locate three men. The first two were historical novelists who doubled as promoters of tourism/history. Will R. Bird and Thomas H. Raddall both wrote historical romances set in Nova Scotia. Bird, the focus of chapter 3, was perhaps the most widely read Nova Scotia author of his time. He first gained renown as a Great War writer. In fact, his harrowing wartime experiences played directly into his immensely popular representations of an innocent, pure, simple Nova Scotia. Although born in England in 1903, Raddall, the subject of chapter 4, would be identified as the archetypal Nova Scotia "Bluenose" because of a series of historical novels set in Nova Scotia, some of which, unlike those of Bird, have joined the canon of Canadian literature. Raddall's Nova Scotia strongly resembled Bird's in being the true homeland of the valiant Anglo-Americans. Both writers were especially significant because they naturalized the concept of the foundational white races of Nova Scotia and made it seem a matter of common sense. Tourism/history's third organic intellectual, and arguably the most important, was Premier Angus L. Macdonald, the focus of chapter 5. His detailed interest in the commercial possibilities of tourism found its perfect complement in his intensely antimodern Scottish sensibility. It was largely thanks to Macdonald that Nova Scotia was branded as Scottish, acquiring a tourist slogan, a bagpiper at the border, and – evidently for the first time in the world for any political jurisdiction – its own distinctive tartan. As these three organic intellectuals – a veritable tourism/history triumvirate – came together in the Historic Sites Advisory Council and other venues, as discussed in chapter 6, it was as if the entire province had become a novel whose actually existing sites and commemorative events were plotted out in accordance with Parkman's vision of history.

Thanks to this alert and well-connected cadre, who mediated underlying structural shifts in the province's economic position, what had been somewhat ad hoc acts of official commemoration before 1935 became elements within a consistent state policy to develop Nova Scotia's "historical resources" in the interests of promoting tourism. The provincial government became so enamoured of mass media that it seems possible to speak of a "promotional state" that, over two decades, ventured into film production (including avowedly "racial" films), the startlingly early use of television, mass newspaper campaigns, the organization of artificial sporting events, the hiring of publicity agents – anything and everything to keep the brand name "Nova Scotia" in the public eye. Nova Scotia, once considered by both locals and visitors to have no history worth talking about, had become a storied playground, a refuge for seekers after historical romance – verily, the Province of History.

This Is the Province Primeval:
Evangeline and the Beginnings
of Tourism/History

THIS is the forest primeval. The murmuring pines and the hemlocks,
Bearded with moss, and in garments green, indistinct in the twilight,
Stand like Druids of eld, with voices sad and prophetic,
Stand like harpers hoar, with beards that rest on their bosoms.

List to the mournful tradition still sung by the pines of the forest;
List to a Tale of Love in Acadie, home of the happy.[1]

It all started at a Boston dinner party on the evening of 5 April 1840. Henry Wadsworth Longfellow – already a poet of considerable renown – had invited his fellow writer Nathaniel Hawthorne and the Reverend Lorenzo Conolly, rector of St Matthew's Episcopal Church. Hawthorne prompted the clergyman to tell Longfellow a tale he had heard from a parishioner, Mrs George Mordaunt Haliburton. It concerned a young Acadian woman separated from her beloved, Gabriel, when the British expelled her people from Grand Pré. The lovers vainly sought each other for years, until a final bittersweet reunion at the hospital where he lay dying. The story so captivated Longfellow that he asked Hawthorne for the first opportunity to make use of it. Longfellow struggled to versify the tale, a task he would not complete until the morning of 27 February 1847. On October 20th of that year, Ticknor published the

poem in Boston under the title *Evangeline: A Tale of Acadie*.[2] It became a publishing sensation, selling out five editions of a thousand copies each. So began
one of the odder, but also more important, episodes in the cultural history of
Nova Scotia.

Had Longfellow not held his dinner party, Conolly not told his story, and
Hawthorne not permitted his friend to write it up, who knows what might
have happened? At the very least, many details of tourism/history in Nova
Scotia would have looked rather different. Without *Evangeline,* Nova Scotia
never could have become the Land of Evangeline. In the event, however, the
publication of Longfellow's masterwork ushered in a wholesale reorganization
of an actual landscape in order to make it conform to a bestselling historical
romance. This Evangeline Phenomenon would offer a practical demonstration
of tourism/history that served as a template for later developments. As we have
seen, much of the public past in Nova Scotia from the 1880s onward celebrated
the march of improvement in a progressive quadrant of the British Empire. In
an apparently glaring exception to this optimistic imperialism, the Evangeline
counter-model positioned the province as New England's therapeutic outpost,
offering stressed-out American urbanites a chance to relive the romance of
older and better times, recover their vital energies, and derive inspiration from
tranquil landscapes bathed in the transfiguring glow of history. Would it ever
have come to pass without Longfellow?

The most revered American poet of his time, Henry Wadsworth Longfellow
(1807–1882) found enormous audiences for such poems as *The Song of Hiawatha*
(1855), *The Courtship of Miles Standish* (1858), and *Tales of a Wayside Inn* (1863).
Christopher Irmscher pronounces him the man "who pretty much invented
poetry as a public idiom in the United States and abroad." He made himself
remarkably accessible to his public. Despite his lofty position at Harvard, he not
only responded to his mountains of fan mail but even politely handled those
who, having read his poems, felt entitled to invade his privacy. Irmscher argues
that Longfellow's immense cultural influence – evidenced by thousands of letters sent to him by admirers both eminent and humble – stemmed from his
ability to craft accessible works with which millions of his contemporaries could
identify. Dealing simply, effectively, and affectingly in "generalized emotions"
("Longfellow said himself that his antislavery poems were 'so mild that even a
Slaveholder might read them without losing his appetite for breakfast'"), he
offered broadly consensual sentiments as "empty vessels to be filled with the
readers' own feelings." Readers believed themselves his intimate friends, having
shared with him the joy and – more powerfully – the grief of life. At a time of
massive social and economic disruption, punctuated by the Civil War and marked
by widespread industrialization, Longfellow's epics (especially *Hiawatha* and
Evangeline) spoke of communities on the brink of upheaval and destruction,

wherein individuals courageously found the inner strength to persevere in the face of crushing odds. In a sense, he served as a universal grief counsellor offering consolation and insight to a storm-tossed generation.

More than this, Longfellow's immense following rested on his reputation as the first American poetic genius – the only American commemorated in the Poet's Corner of Westminster Abbey, the protean creator who could link his readers with the best of European culture without merely aping it. He gave readers "a chance to imagine themselves, vicariously, as more than just citizens of one country, namely as inhabitants of the world and participants in traditions other than their own." The Europe he called so vividly to American minds was truly the Old World, a "Land beyond the Sea" bathed in a dreamy atmosphere of (invariably mystical) Catholicism, "a world in which mumbled Latin prayers resound in the deep, dark interior of decaying churches." Although a pacifist Unitarian with little patience or sympathy for the institutional church, Longfellow delighted in the splendour of a cosmopolitan Catholicism suffused with the smell of incense, the sounds of bells summoning the faithful to prayer, and the notion of a kind of "global community with porous, indistinct boundaries that, in a way, becomes synonymous with humankind itself." Thus, the "nostalgic impulse in Longfellow's poetry" inspired in his many readers a complex mélange of longings – for their own lost loved ones, for a more settled world, and for the compassionate and colourful culture of old Catholic Europe, replete with chants, spires, prayers, and piety. In this exotic world, "closer in spirit to the Middle Ages than anything they'd previously known," Longfellow's readers could also encounter an antimodern emphasis on community, tradition, and social harmony.[3]

Even more than his other works, *Evangeline* induced in many readers an almost obsessive need to experience Longfellow's imagined world. That the poet had never visited Nova Scotia, that his heroine Evangeline never existed, or that the historical event he described was still deeply controversial – none of it mattered. *Evangeline* offered escape to a better, more European, more settled world, the "Home of the Happy," yet one tinged with that delicious nostalgia that came from knowing the transience of all such happiness. Though critics today may deprecate it as pandering or maudlin, the poem has more subtlety than it might initially seem to. By reviving hexameter (rarely used in English), Longfellow simultaneously gestured towards antiquity, hinted at his belletristic sophistication, and lent his poem a driving, onward intensity, as if Fate itself were setting the pace. Thematically he drew upon notions of a harmonious state of nature, derived in part from the Abbé Raynal, whose *L'Histoire philosophique et politique des établissements et du commerce des Européens dans les deux Indes* (1770) depicted an Arcadian Acadia inhabited by a simple, noble peasant folk. Their honest lives reproached the over-civilized, avaricious

Europeans who ended their idyllic existence. Much of Longfellow's ode to the Acadia he had never seen thus stems from the social philosophy of the French Enlightenment, which created such noble savages as a foil for the oppressive artificiality of the *ancien régime*. What appears as a straightforward moment of antimodern cultural nostalgia paradoxically re-enacts, on North American soil, a seminal trope of Enlightenment modernity – the hypothetical, harmonious, and inescapably normative "state of nature," a timeless past without events that disclosed the true human condition before history and its attendant moral complexities sullied it.[4]

Longfellow actually handled historical meaning and its allied cultural resonances with considerable deftness. Though he lacked first-hand experience of Acadia, he grounded its hypothesized Golden Age in historical evidence. This he derived in large part from Thomas Chandler Haliburton's 1829 *Historical and Statistical Account of Nova Scotia*, whose description of events in 1755 – right down to the appearance of the burned-out cottages and wandering animals – the poet closely followed.[5] The proverbially ancient rhythm of the hexameters, evoking Golden Age harmonies, presented the poem in a mythical light. But the abundance of precise detail – the dykes, moss-dripping trees, thatched roofs, dormers, and projecting gables – stakes a claim to historical truth. Generations staunchly believed in it. This fictional Acadia would live in far more North American minds than any drably factual reconstruction put forward by scholars. In that sense, it became more historically significant than the real thing.

Skeptics keen to expose the inaccuracies committed in the name of romance have had a field day with this poem. Had the Acadians followed Longfellow's directions for their *aboiteaux*, whereby they periodically opened the floodgates to allow the "sea to wander at will o'er the meadows," they would have suffered many a lean winter.[6] Generations would learn that the Acadians were Normans, as evidenced by their architecture, whereas most of them hailed from quite different parts of France. In his turn-of-the-century guidebook to Grand Pré, John Herbin published a detailed list of other discrepancies: misplaced meadows, nonexistent plains, and phantom primeval forests.[7] Moving to another level of abstraction, contemporary analysts will find Longfellow's description of childlike people content in their simplicity and isolation radically misleading. Archaeological work on Acadia suggests extensive trading networks, a popular yen for luxuries, and the economic surpluses to buy them. Furthermore, people who lived as the Acadians had done for more than a century on the ill-defined borderland separating the North American claims of two warring powers could pretend to neither simplicity nor isolation.

Naomi Griffiths sagely remarks, "Had the Acadians been a society of simple and devout peasantry, who were ignorant victims of imperial policies they were too naïve to understand, their community would never have survived the attempt to destroy it between 1755 and 1764."[8] After 1710, these francophone Catholic British subjects caught between rival imperial designs carefully developed a nuanced communal policy of neutrality. Their *aboiteaux* were marvels of early modern engineering. Their litigiousness suggests their legal savvy and keen appreciation of property rights. *Evangeline* suggests their artlessness and traditionalism, but many alternative stories drawn from the annals of Acadian history would imply complication and instability instead. Take, for instance, Joseph Broussard *dit* "Beausoleil," the future founder of "New Acadia" in Louisiana (and, as we shall later see, a figure mythologized in the late twentieth century as a "resistance fighter"). Before he became a guerrilla leader against the British occupation, Broussard was a scandalous figure in Acadia. He fathered an illegitimate daughter and fought a case in the council at Annapolis Royal over child support. Or take the prosecution of Francis Raymond and Francis Meuse for theft and obstruction of the highways with trees, actions apparently linked with a wood-haulers' riot.[9] Or the tense, anguished debates within families over the Abbé Le Loutre's policy of militant resistance to the British, or that fascinating priest's own conflicted relationship with the Mi'kmaq, whom he seems to have both used as pawns and respected as allies. Rather than the Victorian "home of the happy," this re-imagined *Acadie* would be the "precarious homeland" whose early modern populace confronted moral dilemmas and political quandaries quite as complicated as any today. In losing their innocence, these Acadians would gain not only the dramatic plausibility that comes of having some relationship with historical realities, but also the politico-ethical status that pertains not to passive simpletons but to resourceful agents.

Yet any such representation would face resistance, for *Evangeline* has informed many scholarly as well as popular representations of the past.[10] It perfectly suited the purposes of what John Reid has usefully called the "ideological juggernauts" eager to conscript the eighteenth-century French/English rivalry for rival political projects in the twentieth century.[11] More than this, *Evangeline* would become the *locus classicus* of tourism/history. The Evangeline Phenomenon marks the first real indication of the uncanny power of this kind of history to generate a counterfactual force field, to construct internally many of the purportedly external objects of its own discourses, and to give its shapers and consumers the palpable and unanswerable sense of knowing how it was. As has so often been the case, the historical representations associated with tourism and pressed into service as commodities cannot be neatly isolated from the lived experiences of the host community. It is foolhardy to think of tourism/history as a set of inert sights, sounds, and experiences for tourists, whose production and distribution bear no implications for producers themselves who can manipulate them at will. Within the force field that tourism/ history generates, an unstoppable logic simplifies, isolates, freezes, decontextualizes, and reifies the historical events and patterns upon which it draws, blurring all these constructions in swirling, all-encompassing, and promethean processes of accumulation and exchange. As tourism/history extends its reach, the lines between fact and fantasy, reality and illusion, evidence and experience, fade into nebulous indistinctness. The past increasingly becomes inaccessible as anything other than a series of radically decontextualized but marketable stimuli. The specificities vary from author to author and place to place, but the promise – that we can be delivered from the vicissitudes of modern times through a re-engagement with a mythologized past that we access through the consumption of commodified experiences – stays the same.

Evangeline itself, however, so beguiles us with its rhetorical force that we find it difficult to deny its veracity. While the poem certainly offers a paean to Innocence, it also appears to give us an on-the-ground report about actual people. Naomi Griffiths captures this when she describes the immediacy with which Longfellow conveys the destruction of Grand Pré: "One has the impression of being there, and of being forced to witness suffering, caught involuntarily in this unforeseen event, that unimaginable moment: the children running to the shore with toys in their hands by the side of wagons piled high with household goods, the sudden flare of flame and smoke as the village catches fire."[12] Something like these scenes (which echo Colonel John Winslow's account as reported in one of Longfellow's key sources, Haliburton's *History*) did transpire. Longfellow himself believed he had written a realistic account of "the tragedy enacted in the little Acadian village, not one feature of which have I darkened or deepened."[13] *Evangeline* secured its claims to truth in a way that rendered these inaccessible to reason or evidence. Longfellow's Acadia became true in the very specific sense that claims and statements within tourism/history were true – that is, they accomplished useful, profitable, and edifying things in the world. *Evangeline* even disclosed the true, inalterable essence of the entire province.

This calls out for some explanation. As we have seen, nineteenth-century Nova Scotia lagged in developing tourism in general and heritage sites in particular. Local journalists, politicians, and travel writers presented it as a young, forward-looking community and spiritedly rebutted anyone who said otherwise. Yet, thanks to Longfellow, part of the province successfully branded itself as a Land of Evangeline, an Old World site peopled by quaint peasants. Entrepreneurs developed a formidable infrastructure around this brand, complete with advertising copy, postcards, railway coaches, steamships, and pseudo-events. With only slight exaggeration, one could acclaim the nineteenth-century Land of Evangeline as the very early beginnings of the twentieth-century theme park.

To explain the Evangeline Phenomenon, we might turn to the odd couple of J.B. Brebner and L.D. Trotsky. Brebner, as we have seen, consistently argued for Nova Scotia as a de facto outpost of New England, profoundly shaped by its geo-historical situation at the margins of the fast-developing American society to its south. The Land of Evangeline offered yet another variation on the theme of "New England's outpost." The rise of industrial capitalism in New England supplied its crucial precondition. Advanced capitalism had a complex impact upon a burgeoning northeastern middle class that, amid the tumult and disorder of the economy that sustained them, longed for the tranquil and orderly existence of an earlier time. Their eighteenth-century ancestors had often looked north to see their own fascinating symbolic antithesis – fanatical papists, menacing fortresses, the slyly ambiguous and elementally menacing "French and Indians." Their nineteenth- and twentieth-century descendants still looked north, but now they saw a quasi-medieval Catholicism and quaint countryside redolent of the pleasantly comforting traditions and memories of a more settled agrarian epoch. In both cases, New Englanders projected dreams and fantasies rooted in their own social and political conflicts onto Acadia.

The structural preconditions of the Evangeline Phenomenon lay in what Leon Trotsky called patterns of "uneven and combined development." He posited a developmental pattern according to which a core area of developed capitalism projected its wealth and power into a periphery of regional economic dependencies, but did not exactly remake them in its own image. Rather, capitalism tended to generate lopsided developments in the periphery – "odd mutations" combining the latest forms of urbanism and technology with far more archaic social relations, which, contrary to many Marxist expectations, it did not rapidly transform.[14] Transposing this meta-theory of political and economic development onto the case of Nova Scotia tourism/history usefully highlights the paradoxes of the Evangeline Phenomenon. Rather like the Scottish Highlands, once feared and hated as England's foe and then, once militantly subdued, fondly patronized as a centre of folklore, tradition, and quaintness, French Acadia, once dreaded and violently repressed as New England's nemesis, could – once drawn forcibly into its commercial and industrial nexus – be put to further use as a site of therapeutic renewal, Boston's greatly extended playground. At the very moment when industrial capitalists based in London, Montreal, and Boston were investing in the province's coalfields and steel mills, they were also developing a tertiary economy of tourist-oriented resorts, railways, steamship lines, and sites of history. The anomalous result was the appearance in Nova Scotia of a well-developed tertiary sector that had somehow sprouted up before the expected antecedent forms of capitalism. The Land of Evangeline only made sense within a context imported from the financial world of British capital hungry for overseas investment opportunities and from the cultural world of Boston Brahmins looking for relaxation and edification. Like harried Londoners repairing to the Lake District and the Highlands, frazzled Bostonians could decamp to Nova Scotia in quest of the very Acadians whose society their ancestors had so proudly demolished. Nova Scotia's development as a premodern, historic, picturesque zone was organically related to the industrial capitalist revolution transforming London, Montreal and, especially in this case, Boston.

Local peculiarities assisted this development. Acadia lent itself to metropolitan re-description as a *paradis perdu* because it had seen epic events, but these had left few traces. On the one hand, the conquest of Acadia was a foundational moment in the history of the Canadian state – a precondition of British conquests in Louisbourg and Quebec, portending the end of French power in North America more generally. Yet we have remarkably little original documentation of Acadia. The destruction of Acadian architecture, the absence of visual representations of Acadians, and the lack of any literature offering eyewitness Acadian testimony about the events of 1755 allowed Longfellow and his successors to project whatever they imagined onto the relatively blank screen of the past. Such projections would raise few common-sense objections, because they did not obviously contradict a pre-existing historical consensus. Yet plainly the *content* as well as the *context* of these projections must have mattered. After all, laments for a lost Golden Age had already become passé in Socratic Athens. The human mind often calls up such fantasies as inspiration and consolation in the face of incomprehension and dislocation. So why was this Golden Age fantasy so potent? We think it drew upon five powerful sets of ideas that were deeply important to the nineteenth-century North Americans who encountered them.

There was, first, *pastoralism*. We might define this as the depiction of beautiful relationships between people that mirror their harmonious lives within the natural, generally bucolic, world.[15] Although the characters in Longfellow's Acadia sometimes disagree about this or that, we never doubt their profound unity secured by their place in a natural order. *Evangeline* appeared in the 1840s, when the North Atlantic world was rocked by revolutionary upheaval out of which the distinctive forms of liberal order and capitalist modernity would emerge. It would be hard to imagine a world further removed from the Arcadian order described (and then so eloquently lamented) in the poem – which is precisely the point. Longfellow presented Acadia as an alternative social world where each stalwart peasant rejoiced in a free and abundant life, the antithesis of the intractable social antagonisms characteristic of the capitalist modernity already so evident in Massachusetts. *Evangeline* is the contemporary of the *Communist Manifesto* (published a year later) and takes its place amid an outpouring of utopianism. Longfellow's utopia has a certain kinship with the romantic socialism that Marx's manifesto skewers.[16] Although keen-eyed readers will remember that some of the imagined Acadians are richer than others (Evangeline's father is "the wealthiest farmer of Grand-Pre"), they all luxuriate in an organic and egalitarian order characterized by authenticity, warmth, solidarity, simplicity, and piety:

> Alike were they free from
> Fear, that reigns with the tyrant, and envy, the vice of republics.
> Neither locks had they to their doors, nor bars to their windows;
> But their dwellings were open as day and the hearts of the owners;
> There the richest was poor, and the poorest lived in abundance.[17]

Furthermore, the poem even shows us how to use this confection of Grand Pré as an antidote to less congenial modern circumstances. When she ends up in diseased and fractious Philadelphia, Evangeline wistfully recalls "the old Acadian country, / Where all men were equal, and all were brothers and sisters." For her, as for her creator, Acadia stands as the utopian antithesis of everything wrong with stressful, strife-torn conurbations.

Longfellow's ideas soon became common sense. As Marx and Engels remarked in 1848, these "duodecimo editions of the New Jerusalem" were castles in the air that appealed deeply "to the feelings and purses of the bourgeois."[18] When Frederic S. Cozzens visited Nova Scotia in 1859, he asked his travelling companion, "[W]hat is the moral condition of the Acadians?" His comrade assured him it was quite good: "I do not think an Acadian would cheat, lie, or steal; I know that the women are virtuous, and if I had a thousand pounds in my pocket I could sleep with confidence in any of their houses, although all the doors were unlocked and everybody in the village knew it." It all reminded Cozzens of a certain poem. "Neither locks had they to their doors, nor bars to their windows," he could not help but repeat after Longfellow, "But their dwellings were open as day and the hearts of their owners / There the richest was poor, and the poorest lived in abundance."[19] Would he have let anything he saw tell him otherwise?

Though many could quote the poem by heart like Cozzens, images inspired by *Evangeline* almost overshadowed its text. To some extent, these images came into a vacuum, given the dearth of visual evidence about Acadia. From pre-deportation Acadia, we have, in essence, hundreds of pages of texts and several dozen maps, but no illustrations of Acadians and only a few of the colony's buildings. Longfellow himself only gives somewhat skimpy details of Grand Pré houses, and these – with their thatched roofs, dormer windows, and projecting gables – plausibly if whimsically elaborate on the plain structures archaeologists have since uncovered. On the other hand, illustrators (often people who, like Longfellow, had never seen Nova Scotia) could depict anything suitably pastoral without fear of contradiction. The forty-five illustrations in the 1850 edition, for example, present Grand Pré as a quaint English village, providing readers with an experience radically different than that afforded by the text itself. In the 1860s, Currier & Ives – Philadelphia's formidably productive lithographers – asked one of their premier illustrators, the English-born Frances Flora (Bond) Palmer, to depict "The Home of Evangeline." She delivered a stunning depiction of Acadia as a sort of Switzerland or Bavaria. Moreover, because the quaint homesteads of the Acadians had been carved out of the "forest primeval," as required by frontier myth and legend (if not exactly in historical fact, since so many were located on the edges of the marshes), looming forests could tower over these quasi-Alpine habitations like so many props from a Brothers Grimm fairy-tale book.

Such illustrations reinforced the impression that Longfellow's Evangeline was more than fiction. A.J.B. Johnston observes that the illustrations generated a sense of the poem "as a creative presentation of a specific historical time, place, and event. By implication, to most readers the 45 supporting illustrations showed how the different people, places, and events actually appeared." A torrent of visual representations would follow, making Acadia into a storybook land in the manner of the "Wild West" or the "Mysterious East." In both 1908 and 1911, Evangeline would be depicted in short films. By 1913, it was the subject of the first feature film ever produced in Canada, tinted and toned to give it the atmosphere people had come to expect from Acadia. Hollywood followed suit in 1919 and 1929, with Mexican actress Dolores del Rio in the lead role.[20]

Visitors arrived in Nova Scotia yearning to see the landscapes they remembered from Evangeline. Remarkably, they did. Although Nova Scotia boasted relatively little extant "forest primeval" – especially not in the Evangeline-related areas of the Annapolis Valley frequented by tourists – it nonetheless was seen. Sometimes people simply applied the phrase to other, more heavily forested, parts of the province, and sometimes they would see the forest even in the absence of the trees. Cozzens found the forest primeval beside the hilly roads leading from Halifax to Chezzetcook on the Atlantic coast. After he repeats "this is the forest primeval," he remarks, "The distinct and characteristic feature of the forest is conveyed in that one line of the poet."[21] The evergreen forest described by Cozzens was, to his eye, entirely free of Longfellow's elm, chestnut, beech, cedar, or maple. A resolute realist might ask, if the "forest primeval" is exactly as presented by Cozzens, whence came the "frames of oak and chestnut" Longfellow so eloquently described in the houses of the Acadians? This skeptic might wonder why, given that the Acadians had relied far more upon salt-marsh agriculture and fishing than upon the establishment of "clearings in the forest" (primeval or otherwise), so much attention should be paid to the towering pines that *weren't* a fact of life in Grand Pré. No matter. Whether they arrived on fishing trips, cultural explorations, or just to escape the city, tourists could be counted upon, when they wrote up their travels, to exclaim, "This is the forest primeval."

Of course, the pastoral landscape was only one element within a phenomenon that would eventually encompass even Dolores del Rio. It would be remiss to overlook a second major strength of the Evangeline Phenomenon: *romance.* The steadfast loyalty of Evangeline for her beloved Gabriel drew Longfellow to the story and, in turn, countless readers to Longfellow. The relationship of Gabriel and Evangeline achieved its renown because, even more than that of Romeo and Juliet, it went unfulfilled. Thanks to the cataclysm of 1755, Gabriel and Evangeline grow old separately, and consequently Longfellow can spare us the sobering details of their raising ten children, maintaining storm-battered dikes, or juggling the demands of marketing the harvest to Fortress Louisbourg with maintaining politically judicious ties with Annapolis Royal – the couple remains forever in the undiminished bliss of young love. The poem is, after all, aimed at those who "believe in the beauty and strength of woman's devotion," and the greater part of it takes place outside Acadie, as Evangeline pursues Gabriel over vast stretches of North America before finally settling down as a Sister of Mercy in Philadelphia. She is, writes Barbara Le Blanc, "all that is loyal, demure, selfless, kind, patient, and religious" – the ideal Victorian woman.[22]

As Evangeline made her transition from poem to visual representation, she became ever more frozen as a perpetual seventeen-year-old. As would so often be the case throughout the entire tourism/history complex of which the Evangeline Phenomenon was the prototype, physical attractiveness equated to moral excellence. After all, had Evangeline been plain, she nonetheless could have been as constant, enduring, and steadfast. It mattered to Longfellow, however, that on the contrary she be "[f]air ... to behold," with eyes as black "as the berry that grows on the thorn by the way-side," gleaming softly beneath "the brown shade of her tresses." In one remarkable scene (whose suggestiveness was unlikely to have escaped the millions of high school students required to read the poem from the 1870s to the 1940s), she actually stands at least partly unclothed in her bedroom, exposed to the desiring gaze of Gabriel:

The rather Black Forest–like home of Evangeline, reminiscent of the fairy tales of the Brothers Grimm, as imagined by Currier & Ives illustrator Frances Flora (Bond) Palmer.

Ah! she was fair, exceeding fair to behold, as she stood with
Naked snow-white feet on the gleaming floor of her chamber!
Little she dreamed that below, among the trees of the orchard,
Waited her lover and watched for the gleam of her lamp and her shadow.

In the poem and subsequently in medallions, statues, paintings, etchings, advertisements, and even candy containers, Evangeline is indeed a sight for sore (male) eyes. Better yet, unlike the somewhat unpredictable Juliet, she promises to remain entirely happy as her father settles her dowry and her priest attends to her spirit. Although the "Sunshine of Saint Eulalie" had grown into "a woman now, with the heart and hopes of a woman," these hopes seem confined to bringing "delight and abundance" to her husband's house and "filling it full of love and the ruddy faces of children." What more could a man ask? Looking back on the imagined Acadians from the vantage point of a *fin-de-siècle* troubled by such complications as contraception and divorce, travel writer Morel de la Durantaye would argue that, as to Acadian morality, "no other proof is needed than that of the fecundity of their families."[23] From Evangeline to Anne of Green Gables – and parallels between the two heroines did occur to some early twentieth-century commentators – regional tourism/history has taken it upon itself to produce representations of young women as accessible blends of purity and beauty.

Popular representations invariably present Evangeline as the epitome of young womanhood – an *almost available* young womanhood, if one assumes in imagination the eyes of Gabriel. Many of her male fans did. Nathaniel Hawthorne felt so incensed about Evangeline's insufficiently comely appearance in the illustrations of artist Jane E. Benham that he wrote the publisher in protest: "[R]epresentations of the heroine have suggested to me a new theory about the poem: 'Evangeline is so infernally awkward and ugly … that Gabriel was all the time running away from her … when she at last caught him, it was naturally and inevitably the instant death of the poor fellow.'"[24] Writing five decades later about a "Sister to Evangeline," Charles G.D. Roberts would itemize a list of the attractions that Longfellow had generated more artfully:

Her wide white lids downcast over her great eyes, her long lashes almost sweeping the rondure of her cheek, she looked a Madonna. The broad, low forehead; the finely chiselled nose, not too small for strength of purpose; the full, firm chin – all added to this sweet dignity, which was of a kind to compel a lover's worship. There was enough breadth to the gracious curve below the ear to make me feel that this girl would be a strong man's mate. But the mouth, a bow of tenderness, with a wilful dimple at either delectable corner always lurking, spoke her all woman, too laughing and loving to spend her days in sainthood. Her hair – very thick and of a purply-bronze, near to black – lay in a careless fulness over her little ears. On her head, though in all else she affected the dress of the Grand Pré maids, she wore not the Acadian linen cap, but a fine shawl of black Spanish lace, which became her mightily. Her bodice was of linen homespun, coarse, but bleached to a creamy whiteness; and her skirt, of the same simple stuff, was short after the Acadian fashion, so that I could see her slim ankles, and feet of that exceeding smallness and daintiness which may somehow tread right heavily upon a man's heart.[25]

Tourists arrived in fervent quest of women who looked like the Evangeline whom they remembered from the poem and from her visual representations by the Scottish brothers Faed – the painter Thomas (1826–1900) and the engraver James (1821–1911), who adapted his brother's paintings for reproduction in books. After these Faed images debuted in the mid-1850s, they would inevitably reappear in Evangeline promotions.[26] With the Faed images fresh in his mind, Cozzens would actually find two living analogues of Evangeline in nineteenth-century Acadia, with "eyes so lustrous, and teeth so white, and cheeks so right with brown and blush, that if one were a painter and not an invalid, he might pray for canvas and pallet as the very things most wanted in the critical moment of his life. Faed's picture does not convey the Acadian face. The mouth and chin are more delicate in the real than in the ideal Evangeline."[27]

Evangeline itself does not necessarily support such a tendentious reading of its heroine. Longfellow gives us many important scenes of Evangeline as a senior Sister of Mercy, scenes conspicuously absent from subsequent representations, which eternalize her youth. The poem commemorates womanly devotion (almost) overcoming time, space, and fortune. Subjected to a process of cultural selection, however, the poem could generate the more marketable figure of the perpetually attractive, disarmingly submissive, temptingly available young woman. Acadia abounded in such women, many observers insisted, as borne out by the wonderfully high birth rates there – an indication of natural Acadian morality. Abbé Casgrain remarked of the Acadians, agreeing with Morel de la Durantaye, "As to their morality, it needs no more proof than the astonishing fecundity of their families, which has not been equalled save by the Boer shepherds of Transvaal."[28]

As the abbé suggests, in the Evangeline complex one could vicariously savour the beauty of a seventeen-year-old girl without any guilty thoughts of voyeurism because, in this Arcadia, faith permeated life as a fail-safe against carnality. Nonetheless, Longfellow remained tactfully diplomatic about the substance of this faith (though details about Evangeline's joyous return from the confessional might have jarred a few New England ears). The poet espoused an ideal-typical quasi-medieval Catholicism short on doctrine and long on romance. As Jackson Lears suggests, and as Longfellow so vividly demonstrated, an abridged version of Catholicism – attuned more to its scents, sights, and sounds than to its theological or institutional legacy – transfixed many a nineteenth-century writer at odds with modernity.[29] Evangeline's very name, unknown among actual Acadians until Longfellow invented it, made his heroine implicitly a bearer of "evangel" or the Christian gospel. Accordingly, her life would embody Christian faith, resignation, and service. Father Felicien, the "[p]riest and pedagogue" beloved of all, likewise exemplifies these ideals. When Basil the Blacksmith and his compatriots get angry about their impending deportation, Father Felicien recalls them to their Christian duty. They must forgive. Gesturing to the crucifix on the wall of the church where the redcoats have immured them, he exhorts,

> See! in those sorrowful eyes what meekness and holy compassion!
> Hark! how those lips still repeat the prayer, "O Father, forgive them!"
> Let us repeat that prayer in the hour when the wicked assail us,
> Let us repeat it now, and say, "O Father, forgive them!"

Not exactly a man after the warrior heart of Abbé Le Loutre. Nor, in fact, anything like any actual figure in September 1755, for the British had apprehended both the local *curé* and priest early in August. Indeed, one might wonder if Felicien would have lasted for five minutes in the actual Acadia, where mediating village disputes, troubleshooting relations between the locals and the government in Annapolis Royal, handling the archbishop and his emissaries in Quebec, seeing to the run-of-the-mill regulation of moral and religious life, and the less predictable management of the ongoing relations with the Mi'kmaq were all part of the job. From all accounts, the Church found its position in Acadia very complicated. Priests were answerable to the British Protestant authorities (who actually assisted in the collection of tithes), but were also beholden to the ecclesiastical higher-ups in Quebec while also being influenced by France and always necessarily attentive to the opinions and actions of the Mi'kmaq.

Then there were the parishioners themselves. Their simple-hearted, uncomplicated faith became a staple feature of tourism/history, but pre-deportation Acadians, though profoundly Catholic in culture, maintained a rather independent stance towards the Church. They resisted tithing and proved reluctant either to invest in imposing ecclesiastical buildings or to join religious orders.[30] News of their innate and perpetual obedience to the Church probably would have surprised Abbé Jean-Mandé Sigogne of Ste Marie in Clare, a refugee from revolutionary France and one of the outstanding figures of post-deportation Acadian history who laboured mightily to preserve their communities in southwestern Nova Scotia. His biographer, Bernard Pothier, suggests that his hopes of finding "idyllic, God-fearing communities" when he arrived in 1799 ran up against the obdurate realities of hardscrabble Acadian life. Sigogne pronounced them "a benighted people … [steeped] in crass ignorance … infected with ideas of equality [and] liberty, or rather license and libertinism … and the most foolish [of them] is often the most stubbornly determined to set his wishes as the standard." The same rustic republicanism that Longfellow would later turn to his purposes revolted Sigogne, for whom it smacked of the Jacobin excesses he had fled. Too late did he come to heed the warning given him by British official James Jones: "[I]n regard to ecclesiastical regulations they are true Americans." To his death, having suffered "incessant rebuffs, suits, and petitions, all of which he faithfully reported to his bishop," Sigogne would find the Acadians "hard to satisfy and quarrelsome." A young couple denied his sanction to marry in 1826 brazenly got married by a Protestant pastor, for which they were assigned the public penance to advance "no farther than the church entrance, and to wear white kerchiefs, so as to be recognized by all as fomenters of scandal." They would not have done Longfellow much good as prototypes.[31]

All such moments of complexity and resistance progressively disappeared from the clerico-nationalist appropriation of Acadian suffering. The reactionary Count Gobineau reported that the "sufferings of the martyrs of Grand-Pré" had become "the common glory of all the faithful."[32] Abbé H.R. Casgrain, reporting on his "pilgrimage" to the Land of Evangeline in 1887, presented a history of pre-deportation Acadia that focused on the selfless ministry of Catholic missionaries sent by the Archbishop of Quebec. Admittedly some ("abbé Leloutre" among them) had gone overboard in their patriotism, but in general the Catholics had distinguished themselves by civilizing the Mi'kmaq and giving the Acadians sound values. Casgrain found the common anglophone attacks on the missionaries as enemy agents ridiculous, given the harsh British tyranny under which they worked (made so much worse by such as that "maniac" Armstrong). And although he made a show of reminding us how "*Acadia* was never *Arcadia*," long passages strayed into reverie worthy of Longfellow himself:

The population of Grand-Pré had formed into little gaggles throughout the village, or appeared at open windows and by the doors of their houses. Here and there rang out the joyous cries of children gathered beneath the trees of orchards filled with fruit, or the voices of women who sang to lull their newborns to sleep. Several elders, sitting on fences, tranquilly smoked their pipes while conversing about the future. Groups of boys and young girls, dressed in their Sunday clothes, chatted as they passed by the church-yard; the young boys clad in fabrics woven at home; the young girls with petticoats and mantelets, wearing straw hats which they had woven with their own hands. Many a couple who, in that moment, were pledging their troth and making plans to wed, were far from suspecting that they were on the verge of being separated, never to see each other again.

As for the Acadians of the 1880s, Casgrain would insist on their continued devout Catholicism. He admitted that some had strayed, fallout from the veri-table mania for anglicization sweeping parts of the French Shore, where he found young ladies who bore the ancient names of Acadie speaking English while dressed in the latest American styles. But when a priest overhears two women answering to this description making fun of traditionally costumed Acadian women, he brings them to order: "What! he says to them, have you no shame? You, who are Acadians? You are ashamed of your nationality! What's more, I know you; you are far from being the equals of those two good women whom you mock. I know them too, they are excellent mothers of families, an example to their parish; and you!" Casgrain reported that some of those who strayed farther still, after listening to Protestant preaching and even marrying Protestants, had logically advanced to the next level: prostitution. Yet such delin-quent exceptions proved the Catholic rule; the heart of Acadia, its enduring legacy to the future, lay in the excellent morals instilled in its young by way of Catholic schools: "All the races and all the sects in North America agree in regarding the Acadians as an honest, peaceable and law-abiding people. Here is the school in which all their generations have been raised."[33] As Jean-Paul Hautecoeur would argue in 1975, the nostrum that "primitive Christianity" defined notional Acadia would help entrench a clerical-nationalist leadership among actually existing Acadians. And this idealization played a role in the devel-opment of the "providential interpretation" of Acadian history, according to which the Acadians were God's chosen people, with the Catholic priests their collective Moses. Their heroic martyrdom for their faith was rewarded by God by their return from exile and their flourishing under the aegis of the Church.[34]

Clerical enthusiasm for a romanticized rendition of Acadian history har-monized with a Quebec nationalism that, from the 1870s onward, entwined itself with ultramontane Catholicism. Along with other francophone Catholics in the rest of Canada, Acadians had an important but sometimes odd part to play within this emergent nationalism. A.I. Silver argues that it was by no means inevitable for French Quebeckers to identify with French and Catholic minorities outside Quebec. They knew little about them. Confederation had appealed to many Quebec patriots because it meant a divorce from the remainder of British North America, dominated by anglophone Protestants. Gradually, however, extra-provincial outrages forced their way into Quebec consciousness: "the harassment of Métis in the North-West, the dismantling of Catholic separate school systems in New Brunswick, Prince Edward Island, and the prairie provinces, the disestablishment of the French language on the prairies, the attempt to eliminate French from Ontario schools." A bicultural vision of Canada emerged as French-speaking Quebeckers began to identify with francophone minorities elsewhere.[35]

Though written by a New England Unitarian, *Evangeline* fit right into this emergent French-Canadian nationalism. It made its first French appearance in Quebec in 1865, as translated by the poet Pamphile Lemay (1837–1912) in the *Essais poétiques,* which also included other poems by Longfellow as well as fifty of Lemay's own. (Ironically, as Naomi Griffiths remarks, it translated awkwardly: "This is the forest primeval" lost something when it became "C'est l'antique forêt ..."[36]). Nonetheless, Evangeline would soon become a great heroine of the French Canadians, outranking – so thought historian Robert Rumilly – even Maria Chapedelaine. A bit like Louis Riel (although happily without his disconcerting religious heterodoxy), Evangeline had fallen victim to perfidious Albion, that diabolic entity that perpetually schemed to draw French Canadians into foreign wars, convert them to Protestantism, and make them speak English.

In her French-Canadian nationalist incarnation, Evangeline became militantly and newly anti-British. Longfellow's poem, though it suggests servants of His Majesty did bad things, never focuses on their atrocities and instead recommends Acadian forgiveness of the past (indeed, as we have seen, Felicien even counsels a doctrine of pre-emptive forgiveness before any atrocities have been committed). The translator Lemay reinvented the poem for a francophone readership. The hexameters became alexandrines, the invading soldiers were simply "les Anglais," and – to Longfellow's chagrin – Evangeline transformed from a survivor to a dying martyr at the end of the poem. (Perhaps, as Irmscher remarks, Lemay understood that his nationalist audience would prefer Evangeline "the unhappy victim of British imperialism" to Evangeline "the pale icon of saintly endurance.")[37] Even more strikingly, Lemay rewrote passages describing Basil the Blacksmith's success in the United States. In the original, Basil welcomes the wandering Acadians to Louisiana with an upbeat description of his new home:

Welcome once more, my friends, who so long have been friendless and
  homeless,
Welcome once more to a home, that is better perchance than the old
  one!

Here no hungry winter congeals our blood like the rivers;
Here no stony ground provokes the wrath of the farmer.

If once more we must recall that Longfellow knew less than he let on about salt-marsh agriculture, in which "stony ground" did not quite pose the problem it did in Massachusetts, the passage is even more interesting for showing how rigorously the poem had to be edited in order to become a hymn to *la survivance*. In fact, most of *Evangeline* (8,160 of its 15,758 words) concerns things that happen outside Acadia.[38] This part of the poem tells a very American story of how plucky young newcomers to the great republic made their way in a land of boundless opportunity. As Evangeline seeks Gabriel from the Ozarks to the Great Lakes, *Evangeline* becomes a stirring travelogue for the emergent American West. Basil can barely restrain his enthusiasm: "No King George of England shall drive you away from your homesteads," he assures his visitors.[39]

Evangeline thus offers two futures. One, especially esteemed by the author, involves inscribing on the New World many of the charmingly medieval customs of the Old. The other entails shooting rapids, blazing trails, and winning the West. For about five generations, young North American students had to memorize great stretches of this long, long poem. One can easily imagine how some of them might have preferred the latter future to the former. Dynamism, health, *and* wealth all array on the side of those who embrace the American Manifest Destiny, like Basil, whereas quaint inward-looking passivity awaits those who stand back from it. No wonder Lemay the Quebec nationalist exercised his translator's prerogative to excise passages with just such a connotation. When Basil blurts out that their new home might be "better perchance than the old one," Lemay's translation has him express his continued commitment to his ancestral homeland.[40]

In this altered form, *Evangeline* won many French-Canadian hearts. To a Quebec swimming in clerical nationalism, the poem extolled Catholicism in a refreshingly down-to-earth manner. Casgrain would repeatedly reference the poem as a basically truthful account of Acadia in the eighteenth century.[41] Robert Rumilly, Quebec's historian laureate of clerical nationalism, in describing what he reckoned was the Acadian response to Evangeline, surely spoke from his own heart as well when he wrote, "Evangeline is becoming the national heroine, not only the most touching, but also the most lively, girl of her race." Henri Bourassa, the province's leading nationalist politician, became so enthusiastic a promoter of Evangeline that he was sometimes called "the second discoverer of Acadia."[42] If one could forget that she sprang from the pen of a Bostonian heretic who had not visited the Acadia he commemorated, Evangeline had much to offer clerical nationalism as a North American virgin who heeded her father, her church, and *L'Appel de la Race*.

On the face of it, nothing might seem less likely to have appealed to Americans, many of whom (if they thought about it at all) might have agreed with generations of New Englanders that the persistence of a peculiar pocket of francophone Catholics on their northern borders promised more tribulation than inspiration. As it happened, however, Evangeline had much to offer nascent U.S. nationalism. From the outbreak of the War of Independence in 1776 until the Great War of 1914–1918, U.S.-British relations were frequently strained and even bellicose. In this jingoistic climate, a patriotic American could ask for no more gratifyingly vivid demonstration of the monstrosity of the British than that offered by their tyrannical treatment of a somewhat republican-sounding community in Acadia. Already, in 1841, in a book that Longfellow stoutly denied ever having read (contemporaries said otherwise), American writer Catherine A. Williams had used the Acadians to demonize the British. The British had persecuted the Acadians "in open and shameless violation of treaties, most solemnly guaranteeing to them protection, their liberties as freemen, the free exercise of their religion, and the protection of their property." The "nefarious and dark transaction" in 1755 came as merely the latest instalment of Britain's evil designs on the continent. Even the actions of New Englanders, if superficially reminiscent of those of the British, only arose because of the contagious influence of this profoundly evil empire: "They had learnt that every outrage perpetrated against their French neighbors was more than tolerated, generally rewarded, and they were unwilling to look on and see so profitable a business going on, and not be sharers in the enterprise." Williams thought that the British treatment of the Acadians cast in the shade such U.S. phenomena as the forcible relocation of Indians to the West or even slavery.[43] When Frederic Cozzens visited Grand Pré, he repeated Daniel Webster's piety: "Thank God! I too am an American."[44]

Above and beyond reinforcing clichéd critiques of the redcoats, the poem also proved that Americans could write world-class poetry. Often acutely conscious of their European reputation as crude upstarts, the American elite could hail Longfellow as a man worthy of recognition by Oxford and Cambridge. Despite his highbrow reputation, moreover, the average middlebrow reader could appreciate his "relentlessly accessible texts."[45] Millions of American students would memorize his poems. A good number of those who could afford to travel yearned to see first-hand the landscapes and people Longfellow had described. And *this* poem, so much of which concerned American places and events, also spoke to Americans about their country. Indeed, it sparked a cult of remembrance in Louisiana, including an entrenched folk belief in the *real* Evangeline whose story allegedly inspired that of Longfellow.[46] American visitors could reflect that the Acadians victimized by the English king had found a refuge in the beneficent republic. "Acadia is still to be found in Louisiana, with its traditional homes of simple religious faith and true affections," one writer claimed in 1885. "The Acadians have had little to disturb their quiet habits in the lands beneath the warm, sunny skies of the South."[47]

Conversely, unlikely as it might seem, the Evangeline Phenomenon could even welcome local Nova Scotia patriots. A tale of an event that (as one reviewer of Longfellow remarked) combined "more of cruelty and suffering, more of perfidy and foul wrong, more of deliberate, premeditated atrocity, than any single act which we can call to mind" would not seem a particularly auspicious inspiration for Nova Scotians proud of their British ancestry.[48] That the poem reflected badly on the formative years of the English-speaking community in Nova Scotia created interpretive dilemmas – of which more in a moment – but it could also play nicely into *bonne ententisme* in ways that paralleled the Saint John and Annapolis Royal celebrations studied by Ronald Rudin and Gregory Marquis, and the Quebec tercentenary celebrations studied by Viv Nelles.[49] Nationalism's "reassurance of fratricide" (to follow Benedict Anderson) meant that the very ability to recollect past conflicts and to incorporate them into official sites of remembrance not only symbolically consigned such disturbances safely to the past, but also reassured the polity that even such unfortunate events had not dislodged a more fundamental underlying unity. (The modal case in nationalism studies is Ernest Renan's comment that every true Frenchman must learn how to forget "la Saint-Barthélemy," the notorious 1572 sectarian massacre.)[50] A semblance of this was already evident in Thomas Chandler Haliburton, who maintained close relations with his Acadian constituents and with Father Sigogne as he struggled for a balanced appraisal of the Expulsion, one which, in the end, accepted the progress and order promised by the British Empire, while regretting the costs of its imposition. Haliburton's account, of course, would inspire Longfellow.

It became *de rigueur* to grace every public commemoration of the Expulsion with reflections on the biracial liberal order that had blessedly overcome it (while spending virtually no time on the hardship, deprivation, and marginalization that many Acadians continued to suffer). H.P. Emerson, member of Parliament for Westmorland, New Brunswick, articulated Renan's proposition perfectly for a Canadian context at the unveiling of Henry Beau's painting *La dispersion des Acadiens* in 1901 when he said he wished he could erase this "sad moment" from history and place beside Beau's painting another one "representing the Acadians and the English walking hand in hand with common interests and goals."[51] Even the hardnosed J.B. Brebner, doyen of a more critical realist appraisal of eighteenth-century Nova Scotia, felt obliged to close *New England's Outpost* with a curiously anachronistic homage to Governor James Murray, who so wisely forbore to replay the Expulsion in Quebec. The Empire, Brebner piously concluded, should value its new French-Canadian subjects.[52] By 1930, "fratricide" had become so "reassuring" that Canada's Post Office could issue a fifty-cent commemorative stamp depicting Grand Pré, its church, "Evangeline's Well," and so on, to mark the Expulsion's one hundred and seventy fifth anniversary.[53]

Canadian governments have tended to argue that no one local really bore any responsibility for this tragedy, authored as it was by ruthless external interests who manipulated the Acadians as pawns in their game. At the same time, in a country whose intelligentsia has always looked anxiously to London, Paris, and New York for approval, any event putting Canada on a map noticeable in such important places had its value. Nova Scotians could not help but be flattered to have Longfellow call their province the "Home of the Happy." This Province of History was most provincial in its yearning for significance in the eyes of the imperious, imperial metropole. Its cultural leaders felt sensitive about the negative images of Nova Scotia that reportedly circulated in the mid-nineteenth-century United States. "[W]hen some poor, houseless vagabond is seen to pass," Catherine Williams remarks, it was said "that 'he looks as though he were *bound to Nova Scotia*;'" while of some "hardened villain, who is a nuisance to the community," one might say that "he ought to be banished to Nova Scotia."[54] To associate Nova Scotia with a romantic narrative beloved by millions of Americans could only have seemed an improvement.

Of all the nationalistic adoptions of Evangeline, however, perhaps the most perplexing was that of Acadians themselves. Here we have a poem written by an anglophone Protestant American. He had never seen Nova Scotia. He knew next to nothing of Acadian life. As we have seen, the very name of his heroine was un-Acadian. *Evangeline* was only very enigmatically and indirectly a poem about *la survivance acadienne*.[55] Acadians may have followed the standard script for romantic nationalism by adopting a poetically remembered national hero – Robert the Bruce (Scotland) and William Tell (Switzerland) come to mind – but they diverged from it radically by embracing as their epic a foreigner's poem about their cataclysmic defeat, more than half of which narrates the history of a completely different country.[56] Still, it happened. Among the Acadians, as Barbara Le Blanc reports in her immensely useful study, the poem became popular between 1864 and 1887. Collège St-Joseph adopted *Evangeline* for its students almost as soon as Lemay's translation appeared. *Le Moniteur Acadien* serialized it. "Evangeline" became common currency – first applied to fishing vessels and then to baby girls. In 1887, Valentin Landry named his new Acadian newspaper *L'Évangéline*, explaining that this name would ensure his New Brunswick–based publication a welcome in Nova Scotian homes.[57]

Why this surprising development? We would point to the liminal status of Acadia itself, a homeland that, because it emerged before the abstract, fixed-and-firm boundaries of contemporary nation-states, always resisted a conclusive definition (whence much of the mayhem inadvertently unleashed by the 1713 Treaty of Utrecht). Acadians undoubtedly compose a nation, principally because, united by language, religion, and a common myth-symbol complex centred on 1755, they feel themselves to be one. But they lack a contiguous, internationally recognized, potentially sovereign territory that could generate conventional national forms such as frontiers, a currency, and a passport. This lack of sovereignty made Acadians even more disposed to seize upon *Evangeline* as a protean medium whereby their disparate communities could develop a network of communication and solidarity. Conveniently for people living in predominantly anglophone countries, Acadians could laud Evangeline without necessarily attacking her persecutors. After all, she sprang from the pen of the premier English-speaking poet in mid-nineteenth-century North America. We might think of Evangeline as a "weapon of the weak," a novel form of resistance adopted by a subaltern people with a vivid collective memory of what might happen if they pushed their independence too far.[58] She allowed Acadians to expose the perfidy of the oppressor while seeming merely to express admiration for a widely praised romantic poem.

Moreover, the poem's themes supply a serviceable basis for group cohesion. As a minimalist statement about Acadian virtues, ardently celebrating their (admittedly chimerical) homogeneity and simplicity, it rarely strays into territory a nineteenth-century nationalist would find questionable – at least not in stanzas dealing with Acadia. Like many iconic poems of nineteenth-century nationalism, *Evangeline* conjures up a shared memory of a better time, evokes a historically significant landscape, refers loosely to legendary events, romanticizes a shared religiosity, and portrays a heroic female character who, like "Britannia" or "Marianne," could figure as an instantly recognizable symbol of a people.[59] Romantic distortions aside, *Evangeline* conveys an underlying truth. An act of appalling collective cruelty perpetrated in the mid-eighteenth century had turned a flourishing community into a diaspora. In a way that would surely have surprised Longfellow, *Evangeline* gave the Acadian renaissance a shrine at Grand Pré, a hero-martyr in Evangeline, and an image capable of uniting a scattered people.

This brings us to the fifth great thematic element of the Evangeline Phenomenon. The poem enshrines the Acadians, often condemned for intermarrying with the Mi'kmaq, among the prestigious white races of Nova Scotia. Bernard Pothier reminds us how sensitive an issue this had been in the post-deportation Acadian communities of Clare, citing Father Sigogne's wry remark with respect to the contempt loaded upon persons of Acadian/Mi'kmaw heritage: "[I]t is the only area in which their rule of equality does not apply."[60] Anglophone commentators, meanwhile, repeatedly argued that the Acadians had forfeited their racial prerogatives by mixing with the Mi'kmaq. (They almost invariably forgot that the British themselves had proposed subsidizing inter-marriage between their colonists and the natives.)[61] Racist denigrations of the Acadians melded into a more generalized repertoire of contempt. "The French settlers are a lower order of people than either the British or Germans," judged the ever-authoritative Richard Dashwood in 1872.[62] In the early twentieth century, one could bring out for the tourists poems that made coarse fun of the supposedly crude speech of the primitive Acadians.[63] Even scrupulous Brebner repeated attributions of laziness and slipshod farming, stupidity, and stubborn-ness.[64] Such dismissive condescension went hand in hand with an anglophone definition of "Nova Scotia" that implicitly erased "Acadia." Some of the most powerful shapers of public history in the twentieth-century province effectively denied that the Acadians could really be Nova Scotians, since the Acadians had compromised their whiteness through interracial marriage.

The story of Evangeline offered an inadvertent but powerful set of images that worked against such damaging racial categorizations. The poem estab-lished the Acadians not as "people in between" but as *Europeans*, whose only crime had been that they were *too* Old World.[65] Through a somewhat awk-ward appropriation of Samuel de Champlain and Pierre Dugua, Sieur de Monts, as honorary compeers, Acadians could even claim to be *the* founding white race.[66] Paulette Chiasson remarks that travellers to Nova Scotia often rated the Acadians far above not only the Mi'kmaq and blacks, but also the Scots and Irish.[67] Not only did Longfellow give the Acadians a flawless Euro-pean pedigree, but he bestowed upon them the profound gift of a *Northern* European background, thereby removing them from the "Latin" races of the Mediterranean whom mid-nineteenth-century race science already associated with ineradicable character flaws.[68] By imagining the Acadians as Normans, he even gave them standing within British narratives, since Normans had arrived in 1066 to make England a stronger nation. "The Acadians ... practically all from Normandy, were almost entirely soldiers or farmers," Gobineau pro-nounced, with the same impressive certainty with which he had deemed the aboriginal peoples in Cape Breton "Esquimaux." "Being a strong and active race, they are well suited to intermarriage with Anglo-Saxons, all of whose qualities they possessed, though without their rather vulgar coarseness," he reasoned.[69] Were one to work on the basis of Le Loutre's combined Mi'kmaw and Acadian activism, and of at least some demographic evidence,[70] one could have assigned some Acadians to a Métis racial category, with lastingly dire implications for their position in an age of emphatic white supremacy. But this never caught on. Well into the 1960s, Nova Scotians would cherish the notion that each of its white races had maintained its pure and distinct character.

All in all, the Acadians ingeniously appropriated from the dominant Anglo-American culture an inspiring heroine developed for one purpose and put her to work for quite another. While seeming to accede to the terms of their oppression and marginality, Acadians also subtly and persistently contested them. If perhaps one cannot quite *dismantle* the master's house with his own tools, as the poet Audre Lorde famously said,[71] one can at least use them to carve out a habitable apartment in his basement and fortify this precarious and temporary homestead against some of his more disagreeable incursions. This, we submit, is more or less what the Acadians did.

Thus, the Evangeline Phenomenon was never simply a device for luring tourists to the province. Its symbolism was rich enough to sustain different readings to suit the different purposes of different people – sometimes conflicting things for one and the same person. An American could come to Nova Scotia to honour an illustrious countryman and experience the landscape he had brought to life – and, with that, also to commune with Old Europe, whose folkways and spirituality the Acadians had so miraculously preserved in the New World. A French-Canadian nationalist might go to Nova Scotia to appreciate the enduring wisdom of the Catholic Church, visit sites important to its *mission civilisatrice*, or, more combatively, to hear the "call of the race" and to confront those hateful heretics who (symbolically or directly) had committed a crime against it.[72] Especially after the 1920s, an Anglo-Canadian traveller might well be drawn by the notion that Canada had begun in Acadia, and learn there a lesson about its early conflicts. In doing so, these Anglo-Canadians might also feel themselves contributing to a liberal *bonne entente* between the "founding races" that might prevent the recurrence of any such unpleasantness – not to speak of the collapse of Confederation. Similarly, an Acadian nationalist (not necessarily from Canada) might visit the Land of Evangeline to pay homage to the "Bethlehem" of her people, celebrating its noble persistence in the face of adversity. None of these readings were wildly implausible, but neither were they easily reconciled, as the ensuing record of the Evangeline Phenomenon shows us.

In its initial iteration from the 1860s to the late 1880s, the Evangeline Phenomenon was both unpredictable and unorganized. The poem burst upon the local coterie of historians with all the subtlety of a bombshell, permanently altering at least a few of their reputations. At the same time, the poem drew a crowd of well-heeled visitors to the province in quest of the folk it immortalized. With the unsettling certainty proper to amateur Victorian aficionados of physiognomy, they would scan Nova Scotia for evidence of *true* Acadians, alternately expressing delight or disappointment with those they encountered. Did they measure up? Were they the real thing? Or had they diverged from their true character (as Longfellow had disclosed it)? "It was a little disappointment not to find an Acadian priest at Meteghan; it would have been more in harmony with people and place, and – *more like the poem*," wrote one such visitor.[73]

As historians M. Brook Taylor and Brian Cuthbertson have both discovered, the publication of *Evangeline* set off a heated local debate. Taylor remarks (and the following four paragraphs lean very heavily on his pioneering work, references to which are placed in parentheses)[74] that *Evangeline* suggested that the province was founded upon a crime, "an act of immorality which tainted all subsequent achievements." Prior to 1847, chronicles of Nova Scotia history had emphasized the establishment of Halifax in 1749 as the birth of the province. This one event "established the rule of British law and banished the chaos of native and Acadian custom, replac[ing] an era of exciting romance with one of stolid achievement" (47). Now this history confronted an alternative reading that turned on the collective wrong the Acadians suffered in 1755. Although drawing directly upon Haliburton's foundational *Historical and Statistical Account of Nova-Scotia* (1828), Longfellow inadvertently challenged a ruling historical consensus that justified the expulsion of the Acadians on two grounds. Firstly, their supposed sloth and their dalliances with the Indians had prevented them from adequately developing the provincial economy: "they were therefore fated to be superseded by a more energetic race of Anglo-Americans." Secondly, in thrall to nefarious emissaries of Quebec and its church, they launched "terrorizing assaults on peaceful British settlements; they were therefore expelled of military, if admittedly cruel, necessity" (49). *Evangeline* confounded both arguments. In doing so, it troubled many well-placed nineteenth-century Haligonians. Intently focused on 1755, Longfellow implicitly questioned not only the justice and inevitability of British rule, but also the patriotic bona fides of the members of the heritage elite as organized in the "Old Nova Society" (63n8). They felt that Longfellow had libelled "the honour of the province" (51). Beamish Murdoch put it this way in 1869 while reflecting on the impulses that had spurred him to write his recent history of Nova Scotia: "I was led into the labor & execution of my book, by a desire to throw the light of truth, if possible, upon the merits & demerits of the expulsion of the French Acadians from this country in 1755 – The abbé Raynal, – [George] Bancroft, – Longfellow, &c. had given popularity to a view of this transaction so disgraceful to the British name and nation, that we of Nova Scotia, who knew traditionally something of the truth, were annoyed at the reiteration of such severe charges against our nation" (54).

The poem stirred this somewhat complacent community of historians and antiquarians to activism. Murdoch's cousin Thomas Beamish Akins, who had assisted Haliburton with the *Statistical Account* and authored his own authoritative history of Halifax, pressed the provincial government to establish a commission of public records in order to "explain the reasons for the expulsion of the Acadians, and in large measure exculpate the imperial and provincial administrators of the day" (53). Defending the honour of the province thus figured directly in the establishment of the office of the commissioner of public records, the first of whom would be Akins himself. It came partly as an unintended consequence of Longfellow's poem (though also the example of historical record preservation in New England) that the Nova Scotia Assembly on 30 April 1857 unanimously passed a resolution directing the governor "to cause the ancient records and documents illustrative of the history and progress of society in this province to be examined, preserved and arranged." The creation of these provincial archives preceded those of the dominion by fifteen years. Only in the twentieth century would other provinces follow suit. The long-term consequences of this development for the culture of the province would be enormous.[75]

Akins would serve as keeper of the records until his death thirty-four years later. In the long light of posterity, we remember him for the collection and organization of books and papers that formed the nucleus of the subsequent Public Archives of Nova Scotia. In his own day, though, Akins's most public accomplishment was publishing a selection of documents relating to "the removal of the Acadian French from this country in 1755," in the belief that "papers that may in any way discover the motives, views and conduct of those engaged at the period in the settlement of the country, and which may tend to contradict or explain partial statements, or put in a new light, transactions hitherto considered harsh and cruel, should be given to the public."[76] His *Selections from the Public Documents of the Province of Nova Scotia*, published in one thousand copies at public expense, appeared in 1869. The first two parts focused particularly on the Expulsion, because when it came to the Acadians "the necessity for their removal has not been clearly perceived and the motives which led to its enforcement have been often misunderstood."[77]

Much seminal historiography in Nova Scotia, then, was prompted by a felt need to change international opinion on the Expulsion. In his *History of Nova-Scotia,* Akins's cousin Murdoch argued that, far from being the simple pastoral people imagined by Raynal, the Acadians intrigued with French officials and significant numbers had abetted French incursions at Grand Pré in 1747 and Fort Beauséjour in 1755 (55). As for the deportation itself, Murdoch ingeniously pinned blame for the "dismal affair" on "the likes of Governor William Shirley of Massachusetts, Colonel Winslow, and Chief Justice Jonathan Belcher – New Englanders all" (56). By the late 1860s this concerted effort to restore the honour of the province had borne fruit. Influential historians – among them the authoritative Justin Winsor, in the fifth volume of his *Narrative and*

Critical History of America, and even more impressively Francis Parkman, the most noted historian of North America – aligned themselves with the Akins-Murdoch position. The 1884 publication of Parkman's *Montcalm and Wolfe* not only set the master's seal of approval on the Akins-Murdoch settlement, but established a narrative framework within which many shapers of historical memory in Nova Scotia would work down to the 1970s. Parkman's commentary on Acadians and Longfellow would long be repeated in the Province of History. "In fact," he adjudged, "the Acadians, while calling themselves neutrals, were an enemy encamped in the heart of the province. These are the reasons which explain and palliate a measure too harsh and indiscriminate to be wholly justified." As for Longfellow, Parkman implicitly criticized him in one of those thunderously conclusive passages that established his reputation as America's answer to Edward Gibbon:

> New England humanitarianism, melting into sentimentality at a tale of woe, has been unjust to its own. Whatever judgment may be passed on the cruel measure of wholesale expatriation, it was not put in execution till every resource of patience and persuasion had been tried in vain. The agents of the French Court, civil, military, and ecclesiastical, had made some act of force a necessity. We have seen by what vile practices they produced in Acadia a state of things intolerable, and impossible of continuance. They conjured up the tempest; and when it burst on the heads of the unhappy people, they gave no help. The Government of Louis XV began with making the Acadians its tools, and ended with making them its victims.[78]

There it was. It had been said. The French were to blame for their own expulsion.

Just as many English-speaking Nova Scotians had felt obliged to rise to the defence of British actions in 1755, so French Canadians now felt obliged to answer "a challenge to their conception of their own race as pastoral, simple, and God-fearing" (57). Foremost among them was Casgrain, who as we have seen brought out *Un Pèlerinage au pays d'Évangéline* [A pilgrimage to the Land of Evangeline] in 1887. Chided via correspondence by Parkman for his lack of objectivity, he spent 1887–88 in London and Paris examining new materials. In 1888, he startled a meeting of the Royal Society of Canada with the revelation that the British had illegally prevented the Acadians from exercising their treaty right to remove themselves and their property from Nova Scotia. Even more explosively, he then alleged that the Nova Scotia government, in cahoots with Akins, had doctored the evidence, deliberately omitting documents favouring the Acadians from the archives. The charge was unfair. The missing documents came primarily from enclosures not sent to Halifax, and thus Akins had no reason to know of their existence. But it blotted his escutcheon. Even Parkman deserted the beleaguered archivist.

Furthermore, Casgrain sparked an incendiary debate in the press that quickly degenerated into shallow ad hominem polemics. This was an era of heightened religious and ethnic tension in Canada, inflamed by the second Riel Rebellion and about to confront such venomous issues as Jesuit Estates, Manitoba Schools, and (later) the anti-French and anti-Catholic Regulation 17 in Ontario. Casgrain saw his struggle as a campaign against Protestant heretics, or "Saracens" (61). Pascal Poirier, a major figure in the Acadian ren-aissance, thought Akins's "suppression" of evidence made him "still more odious, perhaps, than [Col. Charles] Lawrence" (who had actually organized the Expulsion!). In 1908, Poirier prevailed upon the Acadian Convention to demand that the government "set up a commission to examine the records of the provincial archives and expose all documents relevant to the expulsion pre-viously suppressed" (62). On the other side, as Cuthbertson tells us, a defence of the Expulsion of the Acadians became obligatory among the Haligonian bourgeoisie who dominated the Nova Scotia Historical Society.[79] By this point, Longfellow skeptics were by implication racist, anti-Acadian, and anti-Catholic; Longfellow enthusiasts were by implication racist, anti-British, and anti-Protestant. In the far more complex and subtle work of recent scholars, the old questions – Were the Acadians really loyal? Should "we" have expelled them? – have transformed into new ones – Of the parties struggling for hegemony in this territory, which were predominating, and why? How can this struggle be realistically measured in all its complexity and fluidity? What dynamic drove these events? These questions were seldom raised in the Province of History, which would remain, down to the 1970s, essentially the Province of Parkman.

Of course, many more visitors knew it as the Province of Longfellow. Fred-eric Cozzens, who visited in the 1850s, unleashed the deluge of Evangeliniana with *Acadia; or, A Month with the Blue Noses* in 1859. Right from the start, we get lithographs of Evangeline lookalikes: "This, with the antique kirtle and picturesque petticoat is an Acadian portrait," proclaimed one caption; "There is nothing modern in the face or drapery of this figure," claimed another; "She might have stepped out of Normandy a century ago," went a third. Lest any-one doubt the accuracy of the portraits, Cozzens touted their credentials:

> These are literal ambrotypes, to which Sarony [the artist] has added a few touches of his artistic crayon. It may interest the reader to know that these are the first, the only likenesses of the real Evangelines of Acadia. The women of Chezzetcook appear at daybreak in the city of Halifax, and as

soon as the sun is up vanish like the dew. They have usually a basket of fresh eggs, a brace or two of worsted socks, a bottle of fir-balsam to sell. These comprise their simple commerce. When the market-bell rings you find them not. To catch such fleeting phantoms, and to transfer them to the frontispiece of a book published here, is like painting the burnished wings of a humming-bird.[80]

From Cozzens forward, tourists hunted for Acadians. They carefully jotted down details of their dress and described their physiognomies. They collected them with an intensity of folklorists recording ballads or of phrenologists studying skulls.

Cozzens began his "Evangeliad" proper with a eulogy to Longfellow's "intuitive perception," which had somehow allowed a man who had never visited the province to capture its landscape with breathtaking accuracy: "As we travel on this hilly road to the Acadian settlement, we look up and say, 'This is the forest primeval,' but it is the forest of the poem, not that of our childhood ... The distinct and characteristic feature of the forest is conveyed in that one line of the poet."[81] But are we dealing with the same forest? Longfellow, in his description of the "forest primeval," meant the landscape near Grand Pré. Cozzens first transports this (itself quite misleading) description to Chezzetcook, on the other side of the province, then uses it to argue for Longfellow's magical powers of intuition. Yet the two locales look nothing alike. When Cozzens meets two Chezzetcook Acadians, such perplexities only proliferate. One of these "Acadian peasants" comes clad in disappointingly standard-issue workingmen's garb. Luckily, "the pretty brown-skinned girl beside him, with lustrous eyes, and soft black hair under her hood, with kirtle of antique form, and petticoat of holiday homespun, is true to tradition" – not to *their own* tradition, but to the *poem*. The Acadian man has unwittingly relinquished his poetic essence by dressing the wrong way. When Cozzens visits Grand Pré, he exhibits an almost palpable sense of letdown. He did spot a few "weeping willows" and a smithy vaguely reminiscent of Basil's, but on closer inspection "[t]he face of the smith was of the genuine New England type, and just such faces as I saw everywhere in the village." Of the poor Acadians, "not one remains now in the ancient village."[82]

Perhaps the oddest contribution to Evangeliniana was Hezekiah Butterworth's *Zigzag Journeys in Acadia and New France* (1885), aimed at the young reader with a penchant for historical romance. Butterworth inundated his readers with romantic tales, sumptuously dressed European monarchs, and tomahawk-wielding "savages," in a decidedly down-market rendition of Parkman. Yet, characteristically of this period, the visitor was expected to wrestle with the details. He counselled his young readers to study more broadly – Haliburton's

Nova Scotia, plus *all* of Parkman, not to mention volumes by other eminent historians – before enthusiastically diving into the map collection at the Boston Public Library, Le Moine's *Picturesque Quebec*, and, of course, Longfellow's *Evangeline*. The romance of history was there for the taking, for if the "tales of the St Lawrence" were as pleasing as "those of the Rhine," those emanating from Acadia were, if anything, more diverting. Even the brief train ride from Halifax to Windsor was charged with romance: "The traveller is charmed by the poetic names of places as well as by the pleasing views. Romance is in the air. He hears of Gold River and Gaspereaux Lake. One of the towns is called Paradise." And little Wolfville, notwithstanding its "forbidding name," could also claim three hotels with "lovely names – 'Village Hotel,' 'Acadia,' and 'The American'" – amid an "atmosphere of refinement." Yet nothing could compare to the "idyllic meadows" of nearby Grand Pré, supposedly a considerable town of no less than "eighteen thousand souls" (the hamlet had grown considerably since Evangeline's day, evidently): "It was one of the most lovely settlements of New France, with its hundreds of thatched roofed houses and white chapels. Its inhabitants were peaceful, light-hearted, and pure minded people, and, like the patriarchs of old, lived by pastoral occupations. Having no ambitions beyond the cultivation of their fields and the care of their families, religion was their life, – a religion free from the selfishness and barbarism of their English neighbors of the time."

The humble religiosity of the Acadians contrasted favourably with the vengeful fanaticism of Benjamin Church, the New England raider whose conscience "never seems to have told him that selfishness and cruelty were wrong, that even savages have feelings, and that peaceful Catholics were entitled to his love and respect." The flagitious New Englander "burst upon the settlement like a beast upon its prey; and the simple cottages of the Acadians vanished into smoke, and blackness and desolation wrapped the land." How could he have preyed upon such a charming village? "Nearly all of them owned houses, thatched by their own hands. They pastured some sixty thousand head of cattle. They had little or no money, and needed none. Poverty was unknown. If one were unfortunate, he had a common home with the whole community. Instead of being an outcast, he was adopted by all. There were no crimes. The priests settled the few difficulties that arose. The churches were supported by all the people, who contributed for the purpose one twenty-seventh of their harvests."

Without "any false poetic colorings," Grand Pré came near to realizing an Edenic holism. Certainly it represented "one of the purest and most unselfish communities that has had even a temporary existence … there were not one Gabriel and one Evangeline; there were thousands." So, in essence, the visitor to Grand Pré was returning to a place "colored with romance," a veritable Paradise Lost (indeed Paradise Regained for the tourist, if not for the Acadians) whose "tragedy" only lent an edifying melancholic tinge to its "superlative beauty."[83]

The Evangeline Phenomenon underwent a transformation in its second major version, from the late 1880s to the early 1920s. No longer just the preoccupation of historians and cultured visitors, it became an organized campaign mounted by corporate interests and entrepreneurs. The Land of Evangeline became one more front on New England's therapeutic frontier, offering a variety of attractions to well-heeled East Coast folk as a respite from their stressful urban lives. This development coincided with the rise of high-class summer resorts, such as Chester, Digby, and Baddeck (the latter associated most famously with Alexander Graham Bell, inventor of the telephone, who built a palatial retreat nearby at Beinn Bhreagh).

Businesspeople sensed a golden opportunity to enhance the experiences of such visitors. As early as 1869, the opening of the Annapolis–Grand Pré railway connection was hailed with a banner welcoming visitors "to the land of Evangeline and Gabriel." They promoted the Land of Evangeline with such zeal that Charles G.D. Roberts worried that tourists might arrive with unrealistic expectations. "Few countries could live up to a standard so exacting as that which has been set for this peninsula of Old Acadie," he fretted (but also boasted): "The heritage of a romantic and mysterious past is in itself no small responsibility. The tourist, moreover, escaping to this cool atmosphere from the tropic fervors of Washington or Broadway, has smothered the land with indiscriminate ecstasies; while persuasive handbooks have praised it in language that might make the Garden of Eden feel diffident. Beyond all this, one of the most tender and human of poets has stepped in, and cast over the Acadian landscape the consecration and purple light of his imaginings. It is through such a transfiguring glow that our hills, our streams, our fields, appear to him who views us from a distance."[84] This romantic "transfiguring glow" had behind it the rapidly consolidating capitalism of the *fin-de-siècle*. Notwithstanding the gap in the rail network between Annapolis Royal and Digby, which prevented continuous travel from Yarmouth to Halifax, the Yarmouth Steamship Company (formed by the Hon. L.E. Baker in 1885) and the Windsor and Annapolis Railway had already launched an Evangeline promotion in the American northeast. Tourists arrived by the thousands. Investors saw that the novel trade offered substantial profits. As capital poured in, a rail line finally connected Digby to Annapolis in 1891. The Yarmouth Steamship Company upgraded to the magnificent (and aptly named) Clyde-built *Boston*, "largest and most up-to-date steel screw steamer leaving Boston." Having decisively committed itself, the steamship company orchestrated a massive press campaign to promote the Land of Evangeline across New England. There would be no looking back. Evangeline – already the name of a navigation company and its little ferry – had become a tourism phenomenon as well as a heroine.

As would so often be the case in the turn-of-the-century Maritimes, a foreign enterprise soon engulfed and devoured the local businesses. The London-based Dominion Atlantic Railway (DAR), capitalized at £500,000 in 1894, snapped up the old Windsor and Annapolis Railway. The DAR aimed not only to improve this venerable line but to integrate it more completely with steamship services, especially those linking Boston to Yarmouth. The ascendant DAR touted its state-of-the-art steamship *Prince Edward,* a $250,000 Hull-built beauty, white with a black hull resembling Her Majesty's men-of-war, with teakwood fittings appropriate for its intended passengers. Lounges, cabins, a smoking room and a dining room, elegant silverware and dishes, an ample supply of wine, and "even 'a bugle with a silken cord' for the steward" awaited travellers on the vessel's first twenty-three-hour Yarmouth-to-Boston voyage on 8 September 1897. The DAR drummed up business by establishing its own New England agency on Washington Street in Boston, spending a fortune in newspaper publicity and even commissioning Charles G. D. Roberts to expatiate on the company's behalf in his inimitably breathless fashion. The company could thus profit both from the thousands of Maritime workers leaving home to pursue jobs in the "Boston states" and from the thousands of Bostonians leaving home to pursue a therapeutic historic interlude. They were fleeing, one might say, the very modernity the London capitalists engineered and their glistening steamship exemplified.

A cutthroat business war ensued, pitting the DAR network against the local steamship company. Rumours circulated about the seaworthiness of the pretty *Prince Edward,* whose yacht-like lines befit the short English Channel crossings more than the gruelling twenty-four-hour voyage across the Bay of Fundy. The DAR responded by commissioning another costly vessel, the *Prince George,* more suited to local conditions. In desperation, the Yarmouth Steamship Company cut the rates on its smaller, inferior boats – "[d]uring 1899–1900 when the rate war was at its height," historian Margaret Woodworth remarks, "a ticket to Boston could be had for 75 cents." Unsurprisingly, the local firm soon had to liquidate. The DAR reigned supreme. It would continue to draw hordes of tourists, marking, in 1907, the biggest tourist traffic it had recorded to date.[85]

The Dominion Atlantic Railway integrated the local tourism economy directly into the North Atlantic triangle. In this new form of triangular trade, New Englanders purchased experiences of Nova Scotia from a British company. To succeed in this business, the DAR had to stay on the cutting edge of

S. S. PRINCESS HELENE
Operating between Digby, N. S. and Saint John, N. B.

Land of Evangeline Route

Between NEW YORK, BOSTON and
Points in NOVA SCOTIA, PRINCE EDWARD ISLAND
and NEWFOUNDLAND

The direct line to the noted Summer Resorts of Nova Scotia.

CLARE and ST. MARY'S BAY SHORE
    (Where Evangeline's people dwell today.)
DIGBY the Delightful
    (Summer Hotels and Golf Course, Mountains and Sea.)
BEAR RIVER of THE CHERRY CARNIVALS
ANNAPOLIS ROYAL, Historic and Lovely
    (Settled by the French in 1604.)
KEDGEMAKOOGE and SOUTH MILFORD
    (Fishing, Hunting and Canoe Cruising with 'Clubhouses
    and Log Cabins by lakes and rivers in the deep woods.)
THE VALLEY OF RED APPLES
    (A hundred-mile valley fragrant with apple blossoms in
    June.)
GRAND PRE and THE LAND OF EVANGELINE
CAPE BLOMIDON and THE MAGIC MINAS REGION
CAPE SPLIT, Abode of Sea Birds
WINDSOR and the Tides of Avon
HALIFAX, the Historic Capital

For full information in respect to any of these apply to:—

DOMINION ATLANTIC RAILWAY

Room 506, Little Bldg.,   379 Barrington Street,
80 Boylston Street,   Halifax, N.S.
Boston, Mass.   A. A. DUNPHY,
                                    Manager,
                                KENTVILLE, N. S.

The Dominion Atlantic Railway's Land of Evangeline network, from Dominion Atlantic Railway, *Evangeline Land in Nova Scotia* (Kentville: DAR, n.d. [c. 1938]), 29. Tourists in quest of the simpler life of an older and better day were provided with the most modern steamships, hotels, and "historical" experiences.

publicity and marketing. It understood how to appeal to a lucrative, almost untapped market – that vast northeastern U.S. population, undergoing one of the world's most spectacular socio-economic transformations – in search of carefree vacations. From Nova Scotia, it sent out an irresistible appeal: bring us your weary, culturally starved, aesthetically crippled, and hay-fever–afflicted middle-class multitudes, and we shall send them back to you revived, historically richer, sensually alert, and nasally uncongested.

It would only exaggerate the truth slightly to call this newly configured Province of History by an anachronistic but telling name: "theme park." The DAR promotion would entail a thematization of landscape in line with a hypothetical tourist gaze. Prepared for what they would see by lavishly illustrated guidebooks read ahead of time in New England, tourists would then board those regally named steamships. Once in Nova Scotia, they would alight upon DAR trains drawn by locomotives bearing a name from the history of French

Left: Cover of Dominion Atlantic Railway, *High Lights of Nova Scotia History* (Kentville: DAR, 1936). "The visitor … cannot help but recapture some of the spirit of the long ago. The old Fort Anne at Annapolis Royal, a gnarled apple tree here and there in the Happy Valley, dating from the French occupation, the shrine of the exiled Evangeline, at Grand Pré, The Grand Pré Memorial Park, all help to transport him to the heroic past." By naming each of its locomotives "after some historic figure of the past," the Dominion Atlantic Railway hoped to keep history alive: "Step on board with us and go thundering through the centuries to 1604" (2). Apart from this slight reference to Evangeline's exile, the Expulsion of the Acadians itself did not merit inclusion as a "High Light of Nova Scotia History."

Right: Image of Evangeline: Dominion Atlantic Railway, *Evangeline Land in Nova Scotia* (Kentville: DAR, n.d. [c. 1938]), back cover, 4. Evangeline's image became the corporate logo of the Dominion Atlantic Railway, principal twentieth-century promoter of the "Land of Evangeline." Travellers were enticed by the prospect of "Old Acadia in Nova Scotia. History and Romance, Cradled in Scenic Charm." The booklet glosses over the actual events of the Expulsion: "… it is no purpose of this booklet to revive the bitterness of history. It has, instead, the happier aim of revealing how all schools of opinion have united in the noble task of establishing at Grand Pré a shrine worthy of its surroundings, scenic and historic."

colonization (Engine No. 42 was named after De Monts; No. 520 honoured Champlain). Tourists could read DAR historic guides that explained the significance of the sights they could – if they but exercised their imaginations – catch sight of from their train windows.[86] Upon arrival in Grand Pré, they would glimpse Evangeline's well (where, were she alive today, she could no doubt be found at work).

And what else could the Dominion Atlantic Railway possibly adopt as its pivotal symbol – reproduced on hundreds of thousands of pamphlets, medallions, and menus – but the profile of Evangeline, as interpreted so famously by the brothers Faed? The DAR tirelessly reproduced Thomas Faed's famous 1859 image of the *acadienne* on stationery and menus, advertisements and pamphlets. When we see this image of Evangeline on DAR ephemera, we begin to understand the Evangeline Phenomenon. We are rediscovering a decisive moment in capitalist culture, when more and more aspects of quotidian life were commodified and everyday sensory experiences overlaid with a patina of marketing. The reality that the brand name bespoke was less and less distinguishable from the brand itself. In fact, the image on the pamphlet was six steps removed from history: it was (1) based upon the lithograph of James Faed, (2) based in turn upon his brother's painting of Evangeline, (3) inspired by Longfellow's fictional heroine, (4) inspired in turn by a compound impression of Haliburton's and Raynal's, (5) which found its ultimate basis, finally, upon a memory of a story, (6) which may or may not have been true. Evangeline had become, like Aunt Jemima or Mr Clean, an icon – in her case, of femininity, romance, and cultural heritage. One would have been as off the mark to complain that the Land of Evangeline lacked factual substance as a contemporary visitor would be to complain that the depiction of Caribbean pirates at Disney World lacks annotated references to the latest scholarship on early modern capitalism.

Branding worked. The tourists came by the boatload, eyes aglow, ready to see Acadians. Nothing could persuade them that Nova Scotia wasn't really the Land of Longfellow. "The American poet, who transmuted into an exquisite idyll the story that Hawthorne cast aside, never visited the Land of Acadie, 'home of the happy,'" the railway candidly advised its potential customers in 1928. "He was content to draw all the familiar Cuyp-like pictures, whose mellow radiance is so well-known to us in the pages of the poem, from his imagination. They are pictures of a poetic land."[87] They could well afford such warnings, for they mostly fell on deaf ears. Visions of Longfellow dancing in their heads, most tourists refused to assimilate contrary information. As late as the 1940s, when even the most romantic of tourists could hardly have ignored evidence that the Annapolis Valley had long since outgrown its primeval period, the railway reassured potential customers that "[i]t is still

A resident of one of the interesting Acadian villages of Nova Scotia with her old French spinning wheel

Well-matched ox teams, picturesque and powerful, add a pleasant touch of novelty to the highways of Nova Scotia

Marketing Acadians, from Nova Scotia, Department of Highways, *Nova Scotia, The Ocean Playground* (Halifax, 1930). Elsewhere the same publication advises us that "[t]hey speak the French of Louis Fourteenth and have preserved unchanged many of the interesting seventeenth century customs" (3).

ACADIA; the mists, the soft lights, the grateful shades are the same, the call of the wild goose still comes over the meadows, the forests and streams are still the sportsman's paradise, and, as in the older days, the land is beloved and favoured above all other American lands for its natural beauty and the romance of its history."[88]

The park at Grand Pré, also known as "The Heart of Evangeline Land," from Department of Industry and Publicity, *Sea-Conditioned Nova Scotia* (n.p. [Halifax], n.d. [1949]), 5. "There is no historical spot on the continent as loved by all, both north and south of the Border, as the Memorial Park at Grand Pré," the pamphlet remarks. "The old French willows, Evangeline's well and the chapel of Norman architecture are enclosed in a lovely garden of flowers and hedges ... In 1755 the English expelled the Acadians from the country. Longfellow's metrical story of this exodus tells history in memorable form, but the emphasis on British guilt in this tragedy is more the poet's than history's." Such was the official version in the 1940s.

In the increasingly serious business of beauty, when big money rode on where a landscape fit into a hierarchy of aesthetic significance,[89] the DAR unceasingly trumpeted the Annapolis Valley. Some Americans felt disillusioned by scenery that was pleasant but not, for most consumers, awe-inspiring. "'Where is Grand Pré, anyway?'" asked the proverbial man from Michigan. He was actually standing right in the middle of it. Once informed of this fact, he found it hard to believe. He had expected so much more. "'Never!'" he exclaimed, while "glancing suspiciously around as though under the belief that some one [had] hidden Minas under a bushel on purpose to defraud him of his right as an American citizen." When someone pointed out the Minas Basin to him, he remained entirely unimpressed: "'Umph! You could drop it in one corner of Lake Michigan and never know it was there.'" Stonily unmoved by

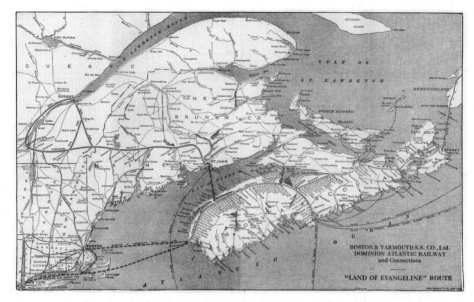

Map of Land of Evangeline Route, from Boston and Yarmouth Steamship Co. and Dominion Atlantic Railway, *Vacation Days in Nova Scotia: The Playground with a History. The Land of Evangeline Route* (New York: Rand McNally, n.d. [1929]). As this map suggests, Evangeline-centred and railway-oriented tourism was highly localized, in contrast to its post-1930s automobile-dominated successor.

the beauties of Blomidon, he was also left cold by the meadows of Grand Pré: "'I've got meadows at home that can knock the spots off any I see here.'"[90] Clearly, the "transfiguring glow" was not going to work for everybody.

Nor would it work everywhere. "As all roads led to Rome, so all descriptions of Nova Scotia inevitably lead to Grand Pré – and Evangeline," proclaimed the Boston and Yarmouth Steamship Company.[91] Maybe so, but the Land of Evangeline could not easily accommodate landscapes without any tie to Longfellow, especially not those obviously reshaped by industrial capitalism. Tourists who tried to evade the often stomach-turning Boston-to-Yarmouth route by travelling overland to Nova Scotia via train sometimes felt shock at what they saw. The Amherst-Springhill leg of the journey traversed a bleak "coal and lumber district, where only an occasional log house relieves the monotony of the scene, – log huts which look as if they have strayed away from the far South and dropped down in this wilderness." It had to be asked: "Do you think the poet who longed for 'a lodge in some vast wilderness,' would have been satisfied with this?"[92] Frank Bolles, reporting on his trip to the Land of Evangeline in 1894, had a similarly "unpoetic" experience. He found the supposedly enchanting scenery overrated: "So much of Nova Scotia between Yarmouth and Halifax, and so nearly the whole of the country between Halifax and Grand Narrows, had been of a kind which every one sleeps through or scowls at in the States," he sniffed. Worse, his train got stranded at Springhill Junction. When he asked the conductor about the place, the man levelled with him: "A coal-mining town, with thousands of miners, pits, shafts, dirt, poverty, and the memory of the horror of three years ago, when scores of widows and hundreds of fatherless children wept and wailed round the pit mouths after the explosion which suffocated their bread-winning husbands and fathers." This information gave the journalist pause: "A whisper came in my ear, – 'Better to ride to Parrsboro on the engine than to spend a night here'; and my heart assented."[93] The Evangeline Phenomenon, in short, would work only for those who had learned the Evangeline script beforehand and stuck to it no matter what. Sights and sounds outside the script were discordant and disappointing. But where the phenomenon *did* work, it constructed a new kind of relationship between the consumer of history and – what, exactly?

The old debates that had rocked the nineteenth-century historical community, though unpleasant and otiose at times, were at least about something – for instance, collective guilt, stern necessity, loyalty to empire, and the imperative call of the race. In the second iteration of the Evangeline Phenomenon, only tiresome cranks worried overmuch about the accuracy of *Evangeline* or the morality of the Expulsion. Such issues made little sense within this new framework. In his day, Butterworth had expected young tourists (perhaps unreasonably) to master a daunting library of historical literature before savouring the romance of history. But what could he have said to the newer tourists in the 1890s? What was the Land of Evangeline about for them? The passing pleasures of watching a landscape through the secure frame of the Pullman car window – the gorgeous shape of a seventeen-year-old girl; exquisite incense-filled churches with quaint priests murmuring Latin; a land magically forgotten by time, with its oxcarts and peasant folk – never connected to any way of understanding the modern world. The Evangeline Phenomenon pioneered, in Canada and perhaps much more generally, a new relationship to history: distanced objectification.[94] This new form of history generated, in its turn, countless products to be sold in the marketplace – not just souvenirs, postcards, and crafts, but also sights, experiences, and memories. In the Land of Evangeline, one could remember – vividly – a person who had never existed, as imagined by artists who never saw her. The commodity bought and sold was the experience of a generic *pastness*, a generalized tender nostalgia.

The Evangeline Phenomenon stood out at the time as an innovative, and possibly unique, way of linking culture to tourism.[95] It was narrated not only by the anonymous voice of the Ministry of the Interior, but also by novelists and poets whose works still resonate within Canadian literature.[96] As D.M.R. Bentley remarks, poet Charles G.D. Roberts combined the "medicinal value" of the local scenery "for Americans suffering the consequences of monotony, cacophony and pollution of cities such as New York," with the therapeutic benefits of luxuriating in landscapes rich in "the heritage of a romantic and mysterious past." All in all, Nova Scotia would bring content to "o'er-wrought nerves" and fill with "healing breath" the "troubled lungs" of urbanites.[97] Writers like Roberts did the indispensable intellectual work of repositioning the recalcitrant topography of Nova Scotia within an imaginative framework, the Land of Evangeline, whose romantic suasion could ensure that the public would see it as part and parcel of the phenomenon. A pleasant if relatively unremarkable valley, not really the "forest primeval" demanded by the poem, could come to seem saturated with Evangeline.

The boundaries between factual and fictional representations, in this case somewhat blurry to begin with, virtually disappeared in the full-blown Evangeline Phenomenon. In 1900, the *Canadian Magazine* suggested an almost complete fusion of the landscape imagined by Longfellow and that which tourists might reasonably expect to see, in what amounted to a reverie of Evangeline, her house, and her village. "We see old Benedict Bellefontaine's house with its thatched roof, its gables, and its dormer windows, and we see the big hale Benedict in the doorway," the magazine enthused:

> He has a pride in his harvest ripening for the sickle, in his flocks and his herds, but ah, so much more in the maiden beside him! How well you know her, the maiden of seventeen summers. You can see her at her wheel, singing to herself, and turning her dark eyes often toward the village, for may not Basil's son be coming for the long talk in soft grey twilight? You see her going from one thirsty harvester to another with her foaming pitcher. You see her in the early morning, the pails in her hands waiting for the cows to come up from the pasture land – such a pretty bustling house-wife, this week-day Evangeline. The Sabbath Evangeline is sweeter, though. There she goes, in her blue kirtle, as the church bells ring. Is she or is she not a trifle conscious that she is fair to look upon in her Norman cap, ear-rings in her ears, kerchief over her bosom, as she walks onward with God's benediction upon her? Yonder is Basil's forge, and Basil at it with his leather apron on.[98]

One could, the federal minister of the interior advised prospective visitors in 1907, even visit the well "from which Evangeline is supposed to have drawn water."[99]

"It is one of the wonders of literature," a British travel writer would later exclaim, "how Longfellow's hexameters have fenced in this Acadian Valley, and even peopled it with poetic ghosts. Thither in their thousands come the living twentieth-century flesh-and-blood to pay their tributes to the genius loci." These pilgrims came "almost without exception" from New England, not Old England.[100] Why were Americans so taken with this stuff? We have many descriptions of them arriving in "the Longfellow spirit," convinced that the most implausible landscape features had some connection with Evangeline. Nova Scotians sometimes poked gentle fun at such Americans, like the man from Worcester, Massachusetts, full of "Longfellow sentiment," who was supposedly persuaded that he was about to see the actual heifer that had once belonged to Evangeline.[101] These were *active* tourists, seeking out the notional landscape of the poem, peopling it (so they fervently hoped) with Acadians and perhaps with fond memories of the childhoods when they had first read the wondrous words of Longfellow.

The "tourist gaze" refers not merely to the commonplace notion that tourists objectify what they see. Beyond this, both the tourists and the sights they take in are systematically constructed within a framework of significance that provides them with the categories and hierarchies through which to organize sensory impressions.[102] Listen to Elizabeth B. Chase in *Over the Border* (1884) describing a place she has yet to see: "The Basin of Minas! What a flood of thoughts rise at the name. Fancy paints dreamy and fascinating pictures of the fruitful and verdant meadow land, the hills, the woods, the simple-hearted, childlike peasants; upright, faithful, devout, leading blameless lives of placid serenity: 'At peace with God and the world.'"[103] If we consider her fantasy of what she *hopes* to see when she sees the valley, the workings of the gaze become evident. Yet to do so, we must enter a discursive construct five times removed from any reality outside what the Gaze has already reshaped. It is a question of our take on her anticipatory take based on Longfellow's take based on his informant's take on the Acadians' story of 1755. Betty Thornley playfully conceded the ambiguous epistemological status of Longfellow's heroine: "To be sure, she never lived, in the mere concreteness of seventeenhood." She could admit it because Evangeline's "concreteness" scarcely mattered anymore.[104] Those with a serious *political* investment in Evangeline continued to argue their positions, but on the periphery of their vision, those with a substantial *economic* investment in her were reaching a far wider audience. Not for the first time did the dry-as-dust historians, with their perplexing questions of evidence and ethics, find themselves outrun by the gleeful popularizers who were so much more entertaining.

When G.H. Gerrard arrived in the woods of southwestern Nova Scotia on a four-week hunting trip, he said what almost no one seemed able to refrain saying when he encountered his destination: "We were now in the wilderness, without doubt, and I was reminded of the opening words of Longfellow's Evangeline, 'This is the forest primeval.'"[105] When Arthur P. Silver explored the hunting possibilities of Nova Scotia, he tipped his hat to the notion of a primeval racial essence: "Every normal Anglo-Saxon has in his nature, however deeply hidden, some latent reminiscence of primitive instincts not quite eliminated by the habits of civilized life."[106] Even the hopelessly bleak rock-bound topography of much of the South Shore – which had not yet become picturesque – might interest Americans, it was fondly hoped, because there they could discover the kind of Nature that had made for their Manifest Destiny.[107] When visiting the "Acadian coast" of Nova Scotia, Charles G.D. Roberts remarked in 1899, "[T]he tourist will [presumably have] ... an open volume of 'Evangeline' in his hand, or at least ... a copy of Longfellow in his pocket."[108] *Evangeline* is even used to frame the sight of Digby-area fishermen, busy with their nets along the coast of the Bay of Fundy, "crossing themselves devoutly" and "giving thanks for the sunshine of St. Eulalie, which 'Filled their orchards with apples.'"[109] It seemed anywhere could become an Acadian landscape redolent of Evangeline. It was all thanks to the DAR, said the inevitable Roberts: "To the tourist it seems to have its *raison d'être* in a poem ... The atmosphere of Longfellow pervades it; its great red-and-black engines bear such names as Gabriel, St. Eulalie, Basil, Minnehaha; and the staunch little steamer that traverses the historic waters of Minas is called 'Evangeline.'"[110]

One of the most widely distributed of the turn-of-the-century publications associated with the Evangeline Phenomenon was A.L. Hardy's *The Evangeline Land* (c. 1902) – or, to give it its full title, *The Evangeline Land. Made famous by the expulsion of the Acadian farmers by the British Government on account of their fidelity to their French King, and afterward immortalized by Longfellow, an American poet.*[111] Graeme Wynn tells us that as a commercial photographer Hardy was one of the many Nova Scotians who made modest careers out of the new tourism economy. With a studio located a short distance from the Kentville railway station, he devoted himself to photographing landscapes that might interest the travelling public. In June of 1901, he displayed more than a hundred "highly coloured" views to illustrate a local lecture on Evangeline in the Kentville Music Hall. These Grand Pré photographs "skilfully created an illusion of historical authenticity by including local people dressed in 'Acadian' garb,' and elicited great admiration from his audience." Shortly afterwards, similar (or possibly even the very same) photographs appeared in *The Evangeline Land*, a collection that covered the length of the Dominion Atlantic Railway from Yarmouth to Halifax. It was, says Wynn, "clearly intended to appeal to tastes of contemporary travellers on the Flying Bluenose." Hardy provided Longfellow's "transformation of harsh fact into romantic legend" with a photographic record. Nova Scotia really was the Land of Evangeline whose well, heifer, and even visage could still be seen.[112] So interlinked were the fates of the heroine and the photographer that Faed's engraving, reproduced under the misleading caption "Longfellow's conception of Evangeline," was placed right beside that of A.L. Hardy himself. They worked as a team.

Hardy's photographs did not present a Nova Scotia that uniformly lagged behind the onward march of improvement. In general, promoters did not tempt foreign visitors with the prospect of unmediated confrontations with "the province primeval." They offered them all the comfort and civility of modern life, with some intriguing forays to islands of quaint tradition.[113] Hardy strove to display modern, progressive Nova Scotia. Yarmouth and Kentville appeared as busy hubs of civilization and modernity, with (in the latter case) the headquarters of the DAR and "modern, well painted, bright and cheerful houses," inhabited by "[m]any families of wealth and culture." On the other hand, tourists in Nova Scotia could touch base with living history. Real "Indians" lived near Yarmouth. Annapolis Royal had a real fort. Cape Blomidon featured real buried treasure. Indeed, the Annapolis Valley boasted a real Evangeline, in a "Modern Concept," whose photograph was captioned with a line from Longfellow's poem: "Homeward serenely she walked with God's benediction upon her."[114]

Moving pictures could even improve on Hardy's rather static ones. With the release of Canada's first feature film, *Evangeline,* which premiered in Halifax on 2 February 1914, pastoral tranquillity had conquered the most exciting new medium of the day. "Have you seen *Evangeline?*" potential consumers of this spectacle were asked. "All scenes were photographed in the Land of Evangeline, including Annapolis Valley, Port Royal, and Grand-Pré. A Pure, Sweet, Sympathetic Pastoral of French Acadian Life in ACADIA, HOME OF THE HAPPY." When the time came to erect a statue to Evangeline in St Martinville, Louisiana, it only made sense to model it on Dolores del Rio, who played the heroine in the 1929 re-make.[115] The Mexican actress's costume, although bearing no resemblance to the garb worn by most past or contemporary Acadians, then became the template for innumerable local re-enactments of "Evangeline and Gabriel" from the 1940s on. Acadians turned to Hollywood for guidance in dressing up as Acadians.[116]

We have now entered the third, even more complex, period, extending from the early 1920s to the mid-1950s, when the Evangeline Phenomenon attained its greatest prominence but also betrayed signs of ideological wear and tear, as radically contrasting frameworks vied to definitively fix the meaning of Acadia, especially Grand Pré itself. Only now did Grand Pré begin to assume its present dimensions as a direct response to touristic expectations. The tourism/history framework developed by the Dominion Atlantic Railway and

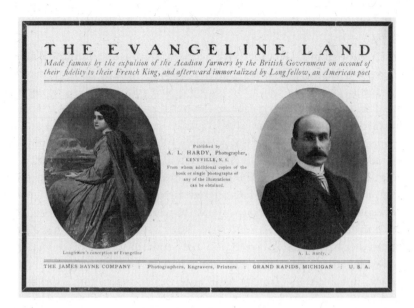

THE EVANGELINE LAND

*Made famous by the expulsion of the Acadian farmers by the British Government on account of
their fidelity to their French King, and afterward immortalized by Longfellow, an American poet*

Published by
A. L. HARDY, Photographer,
KENTVILLE, N. S.
From whom additional copies of the
book or single photographs of
any of the illustrations
can be obtained.

Longfellow's conception of Evangeline

A. L. Hardy.

THE JAMES BAYNE COMPANY : Photographers, Engravers, Printers : GRAND RAPIDS, MICHIGAN : U. S. A.

Title page showing Evangeline and A.L. Hardy and "A Modern Conception of the Maid Evangeline," from A.L. Hardy, *The Evangeline Land. Made
famous by the expulsion of the Acadian farmers by the British Government on
account of their fidelity to their French King, and afterwards immortalized by
Longfellow, an American poet* (Grand Rapids, Mich.: James Bayne Co., n.d.
[c. 1900]). A.L. Hardy brings the "Maid Evangeline" to life c. 1900 on a
country road near Wolfville, Nova Scotia. By this point, "Longfellow's
conception of Evangeline" has come to be equated with Faed's visual
interpretation of her – an interpretation of the poem focused on the
Acadienne's girlhood rather than on her old age in Philadelphia.

sustained by such local entrepreneurs as Hardy and Herbin never quite imposed a single commanding destination to hold the attention of the visitor. All the company's efforts to sell tourists on Evangeline might dissipate if, at the end of their travels, they wound up in an unprepossessing cow pasture. Herbin's turn-of-the-century guidebook had already sounded a note of despondency over the state of the relics from the old days of Grand Pré. For all that visitors were *told* about the historical significance of the site, there was precious little they could actually *see* – and this posed serious drawbacks in an age increasingly oriented to visuality.

John Frederic Herbin, who resolved this dilemma, ranks among the foremost developers of the Land of Evangeline. Like Hardy, he was an Annapolis Valley small businessman – proprietor of a jewellery store and subsequently Mayor of Wolfville, just down the road from Grand Pré itself. In some respects, Herbin was among the most complicated figures within the Evangeline Phenomenon. His books strove for a degree of critical balance unusual in the field. He cared about the actual landscape of Grand Pré, well beyond any mercenary interest in selling it. Yet, much like Angus L. Macdonald in his advocacy of the Scots (discussed in chapter 5), Herbin could not make an unqualified claim on the identity he championed so vigorously. His mother, Marie-Marguerite Robichaud, was indeed an Acadian from Meteghan, but his father, John Herbin, was a French immigrant goldsmith. Moreover, at a time when French-Canadian nationalists were positioning the Acadians as collective martyrs of Catholicism and "the race," Herbin was a Protestant.[117] He was also, effectively, an anglophone with a limited capacity for French conversation. Within the prevailing white races typology, he could have counted as a Foreign Protestant as easily as an Acadian. On the other hand, he claimed repeatedly to be the sole Acadian in the Grand Pré area and wrote eloquently about the sorrows of the Acadian "stranger" shut out from the new homes in a land "[w]here speech is strange and this new people free."[118] From the 1890s on, he crusaded for proper commemoration of the Grand Pré site – which he came to own. Partly as a result of his campaign, Nova Scotia passed an act in 1908 to protect the site for the general public.[119] In 1917, he sold his land to the Dominion Atlantic Railway. Although he died in 1923, Herbin influenced the interpretation of the site long afterwards. His *History of Grand-Pré* went through five editions. As late as 1969, tourists were still buying it, although some of them must have felt mystified by a guidebook that made no mention of the many attractions and sites added during the seven intervening decades.

Notwithstanding some elements of down-to-earth realism in his outlook in 1921's *The Land of Evangeline: The Authentic Story of Her Country and Her People* (he compiled a refreshingly candid list of Longfellow's factual errors), Herbin consistently leavens fact with fiction. Many of his depictions of Acadian life take direct inspiration from Longfellow and seem radically under-referenced. Acadians are as usual essentialized as a "home-loving people," notwithstanding their quite substantial voluntary migrations to Louisbourg, Île St Jean, and Beaubassin in the pre-deportation days. Having told us that, Herbin cannot restrain himself from quoting the poem: "Their dwellings were open as day, and the hearts of the owners; / Where the richest was poor, and the poorest lived in abundance." Herbin effectively converts the imagined Golden Age of the poem into an actual, tangible past.[120]

On 28 May 1919, the Société mutuelle l'Assomption (SMA) – a second Acadian national organization organized by émigrés in Waltham, Massachusetts, that also operated as a mutual aid society and would eventually grow into Assomption Vie, a Moncton financial institution – signed an agreement with the DAR stipulating that the Société "would obtain a 9000-square-foot piece of land upon which they would build a commemorative church near the site of the historic St. Charles Church of Grand Pré." The Acadians would bear the construction costs. The Société mutuelle l'Assomption and the Comité de l'Église-Souvenir launched a subscription fund to attract contributions from Acadians throughout North America. In 1922, the Memorial Church at Grand Pré began its complicated career.[121] The Acadians would pay for the upkeep of the church and maintenance of the land; they would share the maintenance costs of the cross and the well with the DAR. If this was a legally complicated arrangement sure to cause trouble, it was also symbolically intricate: it intertwined the romantic public history associated with the DAR, the sacred traditions associated with the Church, and the nationalist narratives developed by Quebec and Acadian activists. Who owned the site – and, beyond it, Evangeline? If it belonged to the DAR and commemorated Longfellow, then it made sense to make the poet the man of the hour. (Longfellow, opined tourism impresario Leo Dolan, had been the "best publicist" the province ever had.)[122] On the other hand, if Grand Pré commemorated the Acadians and they owned it, then it made sense to make it a site of memory where the wrongs of the eighteenth century would be recollected and twentieth-century remedies for them rehearsed. If the local community had a claim to the site, then it made sense for it to reflect the histories and interests of the area's current inhabitants, primarily anglophone descendants of the eighteenth-century Planters who had taken up residence on the Acadians' old farms a few years after the Expulsion. If the (unconsecrated) church was a religious shrine, it made sense to erect stone crosses outside and stations of the cross within.[123] This was a site that could mean many different things, and, after the company bought it from Herbin in 1917, it became the answer to the DAR's own objective of provisioning its fare-paying public with a touristic focal point. Cutting this Gordian knot would take at least until the 1980s.

Especially between the 1930s and 1950s, Grand Pré thus became a truly conflicted terrain of memory. For Acadians, mobilizing as a nation since the second half of the nineteenth century, the site had rich historical significance. From 1921, Grand Pré would host many gatherings highlighted by the unfurling of the Acadian tricolour flag as patriotic addresses summoned up the heroism and sacrifice of past generations.[124] The 1919 contract between the DAR and the SMA gave the Acadians the right to construct other buildings and to beautify and improve the site, which they did. The site's most memorable single feature was its new statue to Evangeline by Philippe Hébert, who claimed descent from the first French settlers at Port Royal. Interestingly echoing the Faeds' Evangeline, Hébert imagines the heroine with her head turned in profile, as though wistfully taking leave of her homeland. The viewer who stands before her is thus invited to take part in her mourning (but not challenged to rise up against the oppressor or reflect guiltily upon his implication in the tragedy).

This non-confrontational "Evangeline" was suggestive of the complex economic and cultural colonial context within which it was erected. The outcome of the third attempt to commemorate Evangeline with a Grand Pré statue – earlier attempts in 1882 and 1895 had come to nothing – the statue was the joint inspiration of J. Murray Gibbon, the British-born railway publicist who would later popularize the idea of the "Canadian Mosaic"; Henri Hébert, fellow member of the Montreal Arts Club; and Hébert's father Louis-Philippe (d. 1917), who designed it. The actual object was cast in Paris. Although the Héberts were of Acadian descent, no Acadians were present when Louis-Philippe's statue was unveiled in 1920 – the DAR having decided to take maximum publicity advantage of the Canadian visit of the Imperial Press Conference. Even in 1920, the clash between "History as Remembrance" and "History as Commodity" favoured the latter. Yet this decision was not uncontested – *L'Évangéline* lamented the Acadians' exclusion from a ceremony marking their own history in an incendiary editorial titled "Une Évangéline Impérialisée" – and the 1920s would be marked with emphatically *nationaliste* markings of the site, including the erection of the "Deportation Cross" in 1924 to mark and mourn the tragedy of 1755.[125]

Evangeline also joined in Henri Bourassa's *nationaliste* agitations of the 1920s, becoming the object of *Le Devoir* pilgrimages in 1924 and 1927. (His father had brought out his own love story about the deportation, *Jacques et Marie*.)[126] The agitations played a major role in the development of Bourrassa's French-Canadian nationalism, which attracted support from many francophone organizations throughout North America, including Action catholique jeunesse and Action française. Bourassa himself had taken an interest in the right-wing French intellectual Charles Maurras, until warned against his heterodoxy by the Church. But both Bourassa and many of his supporters

Late-1920s Nova Scotia as the "Playground with a History," with Evangeline brooding over a Longfellowish and rather art-nouveau "forest primeval," from Boston and Yarmouth Steamship Co. and Dominion Atlantic Railway, *Vacation Days in Nova Scotia: The Playground with a History. The Land of Evangeline Route* (New York: Rand McNally, n.d. [1929]), cover. Nova Scotia would become "Canada's Ocean Playground" in 1931.

felt drawn to blood-and-soil versions of nationalism, pervasive in the 1920s. Reverence for the blood and soil of Acadia could easily fit within a French-Canadian nationalism that hearkened ever more attentively to the call of the race. Certainly, the "pilgrimages" received massive publicity in Quebec and sparked a remarkable commemoration movement, linked to Louisiana politician Dudley J. LeBlanc, that not only erected a statue and renamed highways and parks in the southern state, but sent a delegation of "Evangeline girls" to Canada, who were received with almost "delirious enthusiasm" in Quebec

City and Montreal in 1930.[127] They also roused anglophone interest. Some commentators welcomed the pilgrimages as evidence that such touchy topics no longer needed to be avoided, for "we have reached a mood in which we can re-discuss them together."[128] Others, such as Rev. Dr H.J. Cody of the University of Toronto, worried that *Evangeline* gave the "wrong impression" as to British "justice, chivalry and administration."[129] Like-minded local history activists mobilized to commemorate moments that (if spun a certain way) cast a harsh light on the French or at least mitigate the impression of British wrong-doing. Mr Nova Scotia himself, Will R. Bird (whom we shall meet again in the next chapter), marked the 1955 bicentennial of the Expulsion by publishing *Done at Grand Pré*,[130] wherein he dwelt upon the perfidious French raiding the blameless English in the Grand Pré Massacre of 1747 – a crime held to explain the Acadians' expulsion eight years later by a rather tardy British Army.

Such attempts to establish moral equivalence between a massive act of ethnic cleansing and one local battle notwithstanding, the Evangeline Phenomenon reached its apex in the years leading up to and including the bicentennial commemoration in the summer of 1955. Writing to her aunt, archivist Phyllis Blakeley marvelled at the number of projected visitors: "This weekend 6,000 tourists are expected in Halifax from Quebec, Louisiana etc and on Monday they are having High Pontifical Mass and other celebrations at Grand Pre and expect about 15,000 people." Would the "Baptist Founding Fathers" of Wolfville's Acadia University roll in their graves, she wondered whimsically, if they knew that their institution would serve meals to the predominantly Catholic pilgrims? "I hope they warn the people to take box lunches to Grand Pre and to Port Royal," she wrote solicitously, "because both places are only tiny villages and can't cope with providing meals for thousands of people."[131] Thousands congregated from across North America – Quebec, Louisiana, New Brunswick, and other regions of Nova Scotia. Urged on by Dr Pierre Belliveau, member of the Legislative Assembly for Clare, the provincial House of Assembly even officially commemorated Longfellow (partly for the benefit of tourists). The bicentennial coincided with the emergence of schemes to draw the Atlantic heritage sites into a federal apparatus, in part to address wrenching economic and social problems but also to show the federal government's attunement to the French fact in North America. If the reconstructed Fortress Louisbourg on Cape Breton Island served as the lynchpin of this twofold federal agenda, the nationalization of the Grand Pré site supplied its more modest mainland analogue. At the 1955 bicentennial commemoration, Jean Lesage – a new force on the political scene who would soon lead Quebec's remarkable Quiet Revolution – announced that the federal government would acquire and develop the site. If the Dominion Atlantic Railway and the Société nationale l'Assomption assented, he would recommend that the park join the

Canadian national historic parks system. In 1961, Grand-Pré National Historic Park was an accomplished fact.[132]

The 1955 commemoration apotheosized the Land of Evangeline. Yet it also revealed its inner contradictions and attenuated influence. From the 1950s to the 1980s, the Evangeline Phenomenon began showing its age. Even the province's official guidebook of 1950, *Nova Scotia, Canada's Ocean Playground*, gave the Evangeline theme just three of sixty-two pages.[133] Maritime tourist locales still retailed *Evangeline*, but the number of Americans who arrived in Nova Scotia full of the "Longfellow mood" declined precipitately. What explains this fall-off? The changing fortunes of Longfellow himself have something to do with it. His stock among literati had sharply declined. "Who, except wretched schoolchildren, now reads Longfellow?" demanded one acerbic critic as early as 1932. Another depicted him as "a tattered and ridiculous relic from the past, an unpleasant reminder of a time when America hadn't yet come into her own." A banal versifier of gushy sentimentality, Longfellow stood only a small step above the writers of saccharine birthday cards. Few poets exemplified more plainly the mawkish melodrama that the new critics of the 1950s routinely denounced. As Christopher Irmscher remarks, "When Robert Graves first met Ezra Pound from Idaho, 'plump, hunched, soft-spoken and ill at ease,' he asked T.E. Lawrence: 'What's wrong with that man?' Lawrence's answer was: 'Pound has spent his life trying to live down a family scandal: he's Longfellow's grand-nephew.'" The low point probably came in 1998 when that middlebrow bellwether the *New York Times* (in the course, ironically enough, of castigating Canadians for *their* "historical amnesia") misattributed *Evangeline* to the English romantic William Wordsworth.[134]

If criticism had changed, then so had historiography. As early as the 1850s, Cozzens had already warned his fellow Americans that, while they might enjoy citing the Expulsion as another instance of redcoat villainy, they should keep in mind that there was still plenty of blame left to go around.[135] In the 1920s and '30s, Brebner made this theme of American complicity in the Expulsion impossible to ignore. From his strategic position in New York, he directly attributed the Expulsion to "New England's expanding energies," after which time Nova Scotians would insist ever more adamantly that Americans themselves bore the brunt of responsibility for the tragedy. Subsequent scholars have qualified his thesis but never chased it from the field. However much historians will plumb the psychology of Lieutenant-Governor Charles Lawrence and review the rationales of Chief Justice Jonathan Belcher, the fact remains that without two thousand–odd New England troops the deportation would have been a logistical impossibility. U.S. historians who accepted Brebner's argument could no longer comfortably describe the Expulsion as a "British outrage" when it seemed to clearly implicate Americans. If "perfidious New

England" had as much to do with the Expulsion as did "perfidious Albion," then Longfellow's moving epic came as a critique of his own society rather than as a pretext for nationalistic attacks on Britain.[136]

Both French-Canadian (by now Québécois) and Acadian nationalists were also growing impatient with Evangeline. Having so indelibly incarnated clerical nationalism in the 1920s and 1930s, Evangeline inevitably suffered when that ideology languished in the 1960s and 1970s. Moreover, those nationalists who wished to stand up as francophone increasingly identified themselves not with a diffuse French Canada but with a self-determining Quebec wherein sovereigntists of various descriptions would define the terms of political culture for three decades. Meanwhile, in the 1970s, many young articulate Acadians expressed a marked distaste for clerical nationalism. In his eloquent 1975 book *L'Acadie du discours*, Jean-Paul Hautecoeur critiqued not only the conservative politics underlying nationalism, but also went after many of the historical assumptions underlying such phenomena as Evangeline, which he considered an aspect of an Acadian myth.[137] Many others felt no affinity for a construct so obviously imbued with the elite culture of New England and the high romanticism of the Victorians. Evangeline had little to do with the working-class lives of many francophones in the Maritimes. Antonine Maillet's *La Sagouine* introduced a very different character, more down-to-earth and practical than her Victorian predecessor.[138] Her popularity has risen as Evangeline's has declined. Nowadays, if one wants to visit a theme park constructed around an *acadienne*, one might go not to the Land of Evangeline but to the Pays de la Sagouine, opened in 1992. The Congrès mondial acadien of 1994 drew approximately seventy-five thousand people, not mainly to Grand Pré and the Land of Evangeline, but primarily to New Brunswick (with its much larger Acadian population). Acadian nationalism has become increasingly global and, at the same time, ever more focused on the New Brunswick heartland of present-day Acadian culture. Nor, one might add, does "Acadian" as a unitary lyrical category necessarily capture the fullness of francophone culture in the Maritimes.[139]

Anglo-Canadian nationalism no longer had much use for the Evangeline Phenomenon either. Following the Second World War, such nationalism focused on the St Lawrence River system – acclaimed as the crucial fact of Canadian historical geography by an entire Toronto-based school of nationalist intellectuals. From their perspective, the Evangeline Phenomenon raised an awkward reminder of past ethnic animosity and, moreover, amounted to a trivial episode in a marginal region. Nova Scotians often told such haughty Upper Canadians that their nation's birthplace lay along the Fundy shore, but most of the Upper Canadians steadfastly refused to believe it, as evidenced by the contrast between the rapt attention they lavished on commemorating Quebec and their casual disinterest in Port Royal or Grand Pré. Insofar as the Canadian Broadcasting Corporation's recent *People's History of Canada* and the televised "Heritage Moments" indicate the mainstream of Canadian history, it is suggestive how both reconstructions accord the Acadian deportation a minor significance at best.[140]

Meanwhile, the Evangeline Phenomenon continued to barely conceal substantial unresolved tensions. Some of these resurfaced in the 1980s when Parks Canada held public consultations about a "Management Plan" for Grand Pré. Over the years, the Memorial Church, established by the Acadians to commemorate the deportation, had come to reflect the history of the Planters who had displaced their ancestors. After intense debate, the church morphed into a "meditative space" housing "an impressive exhibit, including a stained-glass window, six oil paintings by Acadian artist Claude Picard, two sculptures outside the church and a list of 300 families who lived in Acadia until the 1755 deportation."[141] As it has (in effect) made a transition from a local museum to a site of mourning, its governing narrative has been rewritten once again, this time according to the new official culture of the federal, bilingual, and bicultural Canadian state.

And no longer only bicultural – the rise of First Nations consciousness has put the identity politics of both French and English colonizing projects in question. The claims made for either in terms of progress, reason, civilizing missions, and so on, seem less credible in the face of the chronic suffering that both inflicted on the indigenous inhabitants. Internationally, the global revolution of decolonization set in motion after the Second World War has for many disqualified claims of imperial beneficence, whether British, French, American, or, for that matter, Canadian. As John Reid points out, the loss of life the Mi'kmaq suffered as a result of European colonization dwarfed the number of fatalities caused by the Expulsion.[142] Against this new historiographical backdrop, Acadian dalliances with the Mi'kmaq appear in a fresh light. Elite commentators once adduced intermarriage and alliances as racial criteria for dismissing the Acadians as a founding white race comparable to the conquering British, but in a multicultural Canada, they are now conversely sometimes touted to valorize Acadians.[143] As a result, few now seek out *Evangeline*'s discursive magic to elevate the Acadians to the status of pure-blooded Normans.

Gender politics had changed as much as ethnic politics. The *fin-de-siècle* saw a few valiant attempts to give Evangeline some feminist credentials. Margaret Marshall Saunders, for a time the country's bestselling novelist, even essayed a new improved Evangeline-like character, Bidiane Le Noir, who rode a bicycle, engaged in political agitation, and freely spoke her mind to all and sundry, in sharp contrast to Rose à Charlitte, whose saintliness, devotion, and passivity are more in keeping with the Evangeline prototype.[144] Yet this binary division of

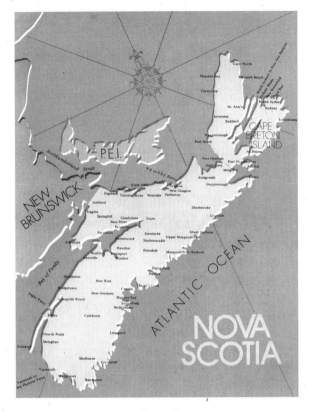

This highly stylized tourist map of Nova Scotia from the early 1970s suggests the spatial expansion of tourism from its railway-oriented days to the era of automobility. From Nova Scotia, Department of Tourism, *Annual Report 1971/72*, inside back cover.

Evangeline only underlined the unsuitability of Longfellow's original heroine for a new era of sexual politics. "It is the best illustration of the faithfulness and constancy of woman that I have ever heard," Longfellow reportedly said of the story that inspired *Evangeline*. A feminist rereading might describe it as a vintage example of how men fantasize women according to their own specifications. Feminists might also raise the awkward point that, while the nationalist movement created a veritable cult of an etherealized Evangeline, it made virtually no room for flesh-and-blood women. "[A]ctual Acadian women played no major role at the national conventions," Le Blanc points out. "Some may have accompanied their husbands; many worked in the kitchen preparing meals for the delegates and their male guests."[145] Conceived as an uncomplaining helpmeet to patriarchy, Evangeline might have been invented to illustrate the straitening limitations of Victorian gender roles.

As though wholesale cultural change were not enough, even technological progress told against a myth symbol so dependent upon a series of widely separated sites orchestrated by romantically named railway coaches and luxury liners. Railway tourists might dally at a grand hotel for weeks as they absorbed the atmosphere of a specially designated site; their automobile postwar successors were more apt to spread far beyond any specially demarcated Land of Evangeline. By then, however, a whole Province of History awaited them.

The first major moment of tourism/history in Nova Scotia, the precocious Evangeline Phenomenon would serve as a template for other historically oriented promotions. Rather like the early-modern states of Europe that jealously eyed the extraordinary metallic windfall garnered by the Spanish conquistadores in the New World, the other potential tourism promoters in Nova Scotia enviously contemplated the riches the entrepreneurs of the Evangeline Phenomenon had harvested for themselves. They paid attention and took notes. Beginning at least in the 1920s, there were repeated calls to emulate Evangeline in other settings. If an Evangeline-themed Grand Pré could succeed within tourism/history, then why couldn't a Highland village in Cape Breton?[146]

The Evangeline Phenomenon set important precedents for subsequent provincial developments in tourism/history. It demonstrated that such forms of historical consciousness and activism were not easily isolated or manipulated. In the haunting words of Barbara Le Blanc, the development of Grand Pré (and allied acts of history-making) left many Acadians as "tourists of their own culture."[147] The same point can be made for many other Nova Scotians. In essence, they risked becoming consumers rather than producers of their own history, a history decanted into a set of static and decontextualized artifacts and experiences. The products of tourism/history took on a weird life of their own. As in the Evangeline case, they often initially arose from the local politics of history, complexly reflecting its debates and contradictions. Yet, once fully assimilated into a logic of commodification, they came to seem like inert things, as so many products (usually manufactured elsewhere) to arrange in the provincial shop window. Because of the substantial investments involved and the development of brand loyalty (here we think of the DAR and Evangeline), once a myth or a symbol has become an element of tourism/history, it becomes very difficult to dislodge, no matter whether it is true or false, so long as it should prove remunerative.

Tourism/history demands a herculean suspension of disbelief. Only a few gullible tourists really believed that Evangeline and Gabriel had actually walked the earth or bequeathed to posterity their heifers and water wells. Many more, however, did think that there had once been, in Nova Scotia, a *paradis perdu*, a Golden Age, a "Home of the Happy." Repeated again and again, such motifs transmogrified into commonsensical propositions that oriented (or disoriented) people to their world. Insofar as these motifs attracted throngs of tourists in quest of the better and simpler life, they became economic mainstays and thus local culture had to accommodate them. If, as we have seen, Nova Scotia at first represented itself as a young progressive land without much history to speak of, from the 1850s onward at least a significant part of the province was constructed as an Old World land that moved to a different, slower rhythm. It would now be Nova Scotia's fate to serve as the accessible and happy Old World that one could reach within twenty-four hours from Boston – or, later, on two tanks of gas. The Evangeline Phenomenon showed how Nova Scotia, notwithstanding its partially deserved post-Confederation reputation as a have-not province, was – thanks largely to its geopolitical position as an outpost of *both* New England and Great Britain (a position that unleashed the logic of combined and uneven development) – precocious in its early development of a tourism/history complex fully adapted to the needs of capitalist accumulation on a transatlantic scale.

The most important lesson of the Evangeline Phenomenon was that tourism/history would work very differently than other relationships with the past. Longfellow's poem described a chilling premonition of ethnic cleansing. It was then repositioned as an advertising icon for a carefree, romantic vacation. Perhaps the most revealing thing about the Evangeline Phenomenon was how the record of a brutal atrocity could be marketed as a portal to placid happiness. Within a general therapeutic logic that designed the Province of History according to the emotional and spiritual requirements of harried émigrés from modernity, no event was too tragic, no ethnic tradition too exotic, no local politics too opaque, and no history too ambiguous to successfully resist its translation into the upbeat language of improvement through consumption. History in this new key offered a sensuous experience, not a rational argument or even a coherent story. Facts were for pedantic historians. The fictions of tourism/history were for everyone. So profound was the collapse of these boundaries that, just as many writers once presented the Province of History as a place where Evangeline and Gabriel had actually existed, now some argue that there *never* was a Grand Pré, Longfellow himself having invented it.[148]

Despite their blatantly fictive character, there was nothing inherently frivolous or trivial about the forms of historical education provided by the new forms of history. They functioned concretely as foci of hegemony, colonizing carefully selected aspects of the past in order to generate revenues, instil bourgeois values, and justify a hierarchical social order. Exposure to supposedly less-evolved races and to decontextualized historical artifacts provided reassurance about one's own advanced and sophisticated position in life.

It perhaps bears repeating that the need to establish imaginative connections with generations past and future is a very general human trait. It is difficult to imagine any coherent form of social or political thought that lacks such a dimension. *Evangeline*, for all its factual inconsistencies and aesthetic lapses, helped people forge such links. The poem has an "almost symphonic impact," Naomi Griffiths writes, and in it we find a "framed and completed vision."[149] It led generations of anglophones to sympathize with the plight of a people victimized in part because of their ethnicity. It also helped Protestants empathize, even if only in a rudimentary fashion, with a people they had often demonized and persecuted because of their faith. And, as we have hypothesized, the story provided a safe symbolic space for Acadians to develop arguments for more recognition and respect from their social and cultural superiors. We might rehabilitate it as a fascinating attempt to explore human sufferings and personal relationships in time of war – given the context of its time and as one statement among many.

But *Evangeline* was not "one statement among many." Taken up by tourism and made authoritative within its structures of significance, it became in many public contexts *the* statement about Nova Scotia's past. It generated a formidable symbolic and material framework composed of unexamined categories. There was a lot at stake – in terms of racial position, economic well-being, professional status, nationalist politics, and forms of class and gender power – in the development of the new kind of history that arose in such close collaboration with tourism. And after the 1920s, this new kind of history overflowed the Annapolis Valley and the Land of Evangeline to inundate more and more of the province.

The 1920s never roared in Nova Scotia, afflicted with precipitous declines in all its key industries, high levels of out-migration, industrial wars in the coalfields, and political turmoil. In such a setting, the development of a tourism economy became increasingly attractive. Now the Evangeline Phenomenon, which for all its eerie anticipations of postwar theme parks was still very limited in geographical scope and cultural range, played a catalytic role as a working model for the development of tourism/history. It had proved that history held treasures for investors, possibly even for the state. In a context in which the dominant progressive historical narrative no longer held up and the revolutionary changes advocated by a minority were unthinkable for most, the new kind of history became both possible and necessary. The Land of Evangeline framework of tourism/history had emerged from and was applied to a tourist *trade* – so marginal that the state could not be bothered to measure its volume or impact – and not to a fully-fledged tourism *industry*. Now, in a province with foundering steel and coal sectors, crippled staples trades, and few alternatives, tourism gradually came to be seen as the last, best hope. The remainder of this book will trace the particular ways in which a new politics of the past came to prevail in what some started calling "The Playground with a History."

The Evangeline Phenomenon exemplifies the enclave pattern typically associated with combined and uneven development. It entailed an island of advanced consumerism in a province struggling to industrialize. After many decades, the provincial government championed the tourism/history matrix that had developed within this export-oriented enclave, transposing it more generally to the Province of History. After the Second World War, this complex was transformed once again, as the federal government invested massively in tourism/history, both to counter the social and economic consequences of regional underdevelopment and to further certain core ideological objectives (i.e., defending the legitimacy of the Canadian state against its various critics). Although the underlying message of Innocence persisted over these transformations, it was turned to very different purposes depending on the mnemonic framework within which it functioned at a given moment. In the Land of Evangeline, we see the first instalment of what was to become a decades-long transformation of Nova Scotia into the Province of History.

3

"All the world was safe and happy": The Innocence of Will R. Bird

Spare a thought for Will Bird. Although almost forgotten today, even in his natal province that he served so well, he was undoubtedly Nova Scotia's single most influential promoter of tourism-oriented romantic history. He stands at the forefront of a generation that took the structure of the Evangeline Phenomenon and suffused it with Anglo-Saxon, rather than Acadian, content. We would do well to get reacquainted with him. Born on 11 May 1891 in East Mapleton, Cumberland County, Bird came from a humble background that provided no literary encouragement. His childhood effectively came to an end following the death of his father, Stephen, in December 1895, a tragedy that left Will's mother, Augusta (née Bird), widowed and four months pregnant. Five months later, she gave birth to her third son, named Stephen ("Steve") in honour of her late husband. Unable to run the family farm, Augusta migrated with her children to Amherst when Will was twelve. The boy worked through much of his childhood, as a helper on a dairy farm and a delivery boy for a grocery store. Twice he travelled West on harvest excursions.[1]

He started writing to relieve boredom. Stricken with a "bad case of blood poisoning" during his service in the First World War, he had to sit for a week with his right hand in a solution. To pass the time, he read everything he could. He eventually came across a Halifax *Sunday Leader* contest offering a prize for the best fish story. He not only won the prize with his submission but actually secured a job with the paper. His contract committed him to produce a boy's story ("ghost stories, shipwrecks, Indian sagas and what have you") every week.

"I sat night after night at my ancient typewriter," he later recalled, "sweating blood, but developed a hero and put him through a series of adventures that lasted fifty-two weeks … [L]ife for me was a nightmare of deadlines, double spacing and word diarrhoea."[2] Like so many other major cultural figures of interwar Nova Scotia – Helen Creighton, J.W. Regan, and Thomas Raddall also come to mind – Bird paid his dues on Grub Street, writing hastily for cash.

When he sent an extra story to the *Western Home Monthly,* Bird was surprised to get a cheque four times larger than what the *Leader* paid him. He took note. Always a fast writer who often mailed stories to publishers unrevised, he sought a market with the likes of the *Family Herald*, the *Canadian Countryman,* and the *Canadian National Railways* magazine, labouring over his typewriter every night. Success did not come easily. "*Maclean's* first stories came back so fast that I wondered if they kept an official at the post office to take out my offerings and reject them," he later recalled. "The next sale was to *Sweetheart Stories.*"[3] By his own count, he sold a whopping 552 short stories to Canadian, American, and European publications. The archivist Phyllis Blakeley would later sum up Bird's credo: "[I]t paid him better to have 30 stories in the mail all the time than to work longer over each one. He has written 600 stories and only failed to sell 6 of them. Be very leery of editors – if one refuses send your story along to another magazine. Don't be discouraged."[4] Hard work paid off. Soon he owned a nice house in Halifax's tony South End, with (Blakeley reported) a living room that could comfortably hold thirty people. In his prime, he became a publishing titan both in Nova Scotia (where his books were enormously popular) and in Canada as a whole (where his work earned him an honorary degree from Mount Allison University and presidency of the Canadian Authors Association). There was a time when, if the literary marketplace could speak, it might have sounded a lot like Will R. Bird.

Three major themes stand out in the collected works of Bird: the Great War, the history of Yorkshire emigrants in Nova Scotia, and the Maritimes as a travel destination. Bird's first book, *A Century at Chignecto* (1928), traces the history of the narrow isthmus connecting Nova Scotia to New Brunswick, focusing on eighteenth-century military conflicts between the French and the English. *And We Go On* (1930), *Thirteen Years After* (1931), and *The Communication Trench* (1933) chronicle Bird's experiences in the Great War and convey his postwar impressions of war zones where Canadians had fought. Then, between 1936 and 1944, he took a hiatus from book publishing. During this time, he devoted himself to writing articles and short stories, as well as to promoting the province's fledgling tourist trade (as exemplified by *Historic Nova Scotia* [1935], an innovative attempt to link history with tourism). In the mid-1940s, Bird started writing fiction in earnest, bringing out thirteen novels and short-story collections, of which the most famous are *Here Stays Good Yorkshire* (1945), *Judgment Glen*

(1947), *The Passionate Pilgrim* (1949), *So Much to Record* (1951), *To Love and to Cherish* (1954), *The Shy Yorkshireman* (1955), *Despite the Distance* (1961), and *An Earl Must Have a Wife* (1969). Meanwhile, he won specialized audiences for his military histories – *The Nova Scotia Highlanders: No Retreating Footsteps* (1955) and *The North Shore Regiment* (1963) – and a broader constituency for *Ghosts Have Warm Hands* (1968), which revisited many of the themes of *And We Go On*. His fastest-selling books, however, were travel accounts of the Maritimes – *This Is Nova Scotia* (1950), *Off-Trail in Nova Scotia* (1956), and *These Are the Maritimes* (1959). He was "with Ryerson" for most of a writing career, which saw the press bringing out no fewer than thirteen of his books.[5]

Bird wrote to put food on the table as much as to express himself. He was keenly aware of the aesthetic tradeoffs he made to further his career, fretting, for instance, that scholars might deprecate his pamphlet *Historic Nova Scotia* as "tourist propaganda."[6] Indeed, his methods did not produce masterpieces. Of the twenty-seven books he published between 1928 and 1975, almost none have secured a place within the Canadian literary canon. His present-day low status in Canadian letters (which contrasts with the considerable renown his novels won in their own time) may make a detailed investigation of his corpus seem like overkill. Yet, in fact, few worked harder, or to greater effect, at shaping the twentieth-century Nova Scotian identity in general and its practices of public history in particular. Ironically, he is not himself widely remembered today. He deserves to be. Much of the historical common sense expounded in the province's tourism-oriented sites of memory can be best explored through his work.

To put the matter in the most conceptually direct way, Bird set the stamp of a radical form of childlike innocence upon the public past in Nova Scotia. Far from constituting the unpremeditated and unreflecting simplicity of a homespun autodidact (as he presented himself), Bird's Innocence was the calculated construction of a highly skilled professional who knew what would sell. (Insofar as it was a consciously adopted stance towards the world, we will capitalize "Innocence" in order to differentiate it from the simple absence of experience that the word usually signifies in lowercase). It is vital to keep in mind the artfulness of Bird's artlessness. His work restates the abiding value of truisms against the lures of sophistication, because he has made a moral choice to do so – not because that is all he knows. One's actual degree of experience has nothing to do with it. The real issue is a principled decision to reject analytic reasoning as an illicit temptation, in order to instead uphold a categorical imperative to live by unexamined nostrums that are represented as in keeping with transcendent truths inaccessible to human understanding.[7]

This does not preclude his work from having political and philosophical commitments. Bird, this ardently anti-intellectual intellectual, provided, in his fiction, his histories, and his bureaucratic work, compelling and vivid evidence of the truth of liberalism – namely, the ontological and epistemological primacy of the individual. Far from representing the natural result of the province's supposed primitive isolation, Bird's Innocence was the conscious stance of a writer whose vision of the world proceeded directly from that turning point in the history of modernity, the Great War of 1914–1918. This faux "Innocent Abroad" worked the theme of childlike simplicity into the leitmotif of an entire tourism apparatus within which he functioned as the organic intellectual in chief.[8]

◆

Although at first glance Bird's experience of the Great War may seem irrelevant to a study of his historical writings and activism, in fact it provides the key to understanding his entire career. The physically unprepossessing Bird first tried to enlist in August 1914, but the recruiting sergeant told him, "We can get enough good men ... without taking them we've got to repair."[9] He would not succeed until his third attempt. In April of 1916, he joined the 193rd Battalion, Nova Scotia Highlanders, raised primarily from the Amherst area. They sailed for England in October and were broken up to reinforce other battalions. Bird (aka Service Man No. 901552) was sent to the 42nd Battalion, the celebrated Black Watch of Canada. The 5,500 soldiers in the Black Watch would fight many of the fiercest battles of the war, sustaining about 800 fatalities and 2,000 wounded. On 5 January 1917, Bird joined the kilted soldiers in the trenches of Vimy Ridge. His bravery during the capture of Mons on 10–11 November 1918, the very last night of the war, won him a Military Medal. Demobilized in March 1919, he went home to Nova Scotia.[10]

After the war, Bird became (in the words of Norm Christie) a "one man remembrance program."[11] The war changed Bird's life. Most obviously, his wounds hospitalized him and his beloved brother Steve (of the 25th Battalion) was killed.[12] Furthermore, many of his writings resound with battle cries. In articles for *Maclean's* and in public appearances, he stirred veterans to demand public recognition of their sacrifices. Veterans found in him an accessible, trustworthy voice. His later success in becoming "Mr Nova Scotia" was in large measure prepared by his earlier career as a sort of "Mr Great War." The war gave Bird a vast fund of stories and a constituency of veterans eager to hear them. Christie observes, "The men were hungry to share their wartime experiences, and Will Bird gave them their chance."[13] Bird claimed to have received as many as five thousand letters in response to his war journalism and to have given slide presentations at no fewer than 106 branches of the Canadian Legion.[14]

Especially in *And We Go On*, a lost classic, Bird was an *engagé* writer bent on countering an emergent fashionable skepticism about the Great War. The subtitle on its front cover pugnaciously declared its mission: to offer "A story of the War by a Private in the Canadian Black Watch; a Story Without Filth or Favor." "We are being deluged now, a decade after the war, by books that are putrid with so-called 'realism,'" Bird complained. Realist war-writing reduced the soldier to "a coarse-minded, profane creature, seeking only the solace of loose women or the courage of strong liquor." Bird objected to those authors, often without combat experience, for whom "vulgar language and indelicacy of incident are often their substitute for lack of knowledge." Their books offered "an irrevocable insult to those gallant men who lie in French or Belgian graves." To counter this outrage, Bird proposed to "show that the private in the trenches had other thoughts than of the flesh, had often finer vision and strength of soul than those who would fit him to their sordid, sensation-seeking fiction."[15]

Though sharply critical of "sordid" realism about the war and resentful of pacifist critics, Bird nonetheless also resisted what might be called the Great War mystique – what historian Jonathan Vance has influentially described as "Canada's myth." Vance suggests that Canadians confront a stark dichotomy with respect to the public history of the Great War. On the one hand, shallow (generally anonymous) skeptics drew on simplistic social-control theories to deprecate Great War commemoration as nothing more than elite manipulation. On the other hand, profound (often intensely religious) believers in a myth of Canada saw the war dead as heroic martyrs whose sacrifices had redeemed Canadian democracy. On one side, a whiny klatch of "neutralists, non-interventionists, and isolationists" raised their "faint voices" against the supposed futility of war; on the other side stood a majestic chorus of true believers, whom Vance summons up in his closing passage as a veritable all-Canadian celestial choir:

> To dismiss the dominant memory as elite manipulation is to do a disservice to the uneducated veteran from northern Alberta who wistfully recalled the *estaminets* of France, the penurious spinster in Vancouver who sent a dollar to the war memorial fund, or the schoolgirl who marched proudly in a Nova Scotia Armistice Day parade. People like this embraced the myth, not because their social betters drilled it into their minds by sheer repetition, but because it answered a need, explained the past, or offered the promise of a better future. But they did more than simply embrace the myth: they helped to create it. By their very actions, each of these people played a role in nurturing the nation's memory of the war and of giving it life within their consciousness as Canadians. That memory was not con-

ferred on them from above; it sprouted from the grief, the hope, and the search for meaning of a thousand Canadian communities.

Canada's myth revered the sanctity of the fallen. Canada's citizen-soldiers, in their "stubborn individuality," not only "represented Canada" but actually personified it. Rather than exposing the flaws of imperialism and the futility of armed conflict, the mythic Great War confirmed the justice of the pre-existing social hierarchy: "The imagined community that the myth would forge was not a new Canada at all, but a Canada in which the old power structures were bolstered." To stand outside this imagined community is to stand outside the nation.[16] It is to spurn a grieving people by denigrating the uplifting national memory that delivered them from despair. It is to reject a High Tory notion of the holistic, harmonious, hierarchical community and a High Anglican marriage of church and state, politics and religion, which likens the body of the people to the body of Christ. It is to declare oneself against Canada and perhaps God too.

Leaving aside the reactionary irrationalism evoked by Vance's dichotomous characterization of public memory, we must observe that its symbolic reach exceeds its analytic grasp. If he is right, then the whining neutralists and limp-wristed secular pacifists who rejected the myth of Canada must surely have been isolated figures of contempt. Yet unbelievers in the myth like Agnes Macphail, J.S. Woodsworth, and William Lyon Mackenzie King actually rose to prominence in spite of – sometimes even on the basis of – their pacifist tendencies.[17] All three, true, had to face opponents who used war memory in the manner Vance suggests. Nevertheless, one wonders if such figures disloyally resisted something as fundamental as the "myth of Canada."

Bird presents us with a good case for why a mythic dichotomy cannot grasp Canada's response to the Great War. It is important to stress this, because, on Vance's reading, Bird (misidentified as a "renowned Maritime folklorist" – Vance has presumably confused Bird with Helen Creighton) contributed directly to the conservative myth. Vance particularly admires *And We Go On*. "The tone is different from his other books and short stories," he writes. "There is little humour, except of a grim kind, and an abundance of tragedy. Indeed, Bird's narrative is filled with incidents that might not be out of place in *Generals Die in Bed* [Charles Yale Harrison's harrowing bestseller of 1930]." Vance notes that, "despite this grim record," the book won many positive reviews. *Saturday Night*'s reviewer found it "in many respects a fine book; clean, unusually temperate and packed with action." Vance expands upon the word "clean," which he glosses: "Not clean in the literal sense, for it has every bit as much mud and grime as any war book, but clean in a metaphorical sense." The cleanliness here was spiritual, connoting (mark well) innocence: "Bird's soldiers remain pure. They may gripe about their officers, their food, and the war in general, but Doggy, Waterbottle, Sambro, and the rest of Bird's comrades retain an innate goodness ... Whatever misdeeds they occasionally commit, they are not brutalized or dehumanized by the war." Conceding that Bird writes a few brutal passages that recall the militantly anti-war Harrison or Remarque, Vance insists that Bird satisfied his readers with a concluding passage on the "equalizing treasure in memories" that the Great War had bequeathed him.[18]

As Vance points out, the crucial issue for Bird was how soldiers could keep from being "brutalized" or "dehumanized." Jay Winter has proposed that, confronted with the unprecedented slaughter of the Great War, most men and women could "reach back into their 'traditional' cultural heritage to express amazement and anger, bewilderment and compassion." The catastrophe was encoded in several ways: visually, "through images of the dead and their return"; in prose and poetry, which sought to visualize the dead among the living; through the reconfiguration of sacred images and icons; with a more secular tendency to *see* the dead among the living and even in spiritualism; and, socially, through commemorative rites, mutual assistance, reunions, and other measures attesting to the meaning of the war for the great majority of people. "The cutting edge of 'modern memory,' its multi-faceted sense of dislocation, paradox, and the ironic, could express anger and despair, and did so in enduring ways; it was melancholic, but it could not heal," Winter argues.[19] In general, commemoration sustained traditional forms, not cultural innovations.

Yet to follow Vance in conceiving these "traditional forms" as organically conservative, even High Tory, misses their potential to sustain multiple readings. In Canada, a pervasively reverent and generically traditional tone of commemoration coexisted, without a sense of contradiction, with spirited denunciations of wartime excesses and cruelties. Faced with this human catastrophe, many middle-most Canadians turned to the hegemonic language of politics with which they were most familiar: liberalism. As they shaped the interwar cultural world, they would fortify themselves with positive thinking. They sought to transcend the memory of war by focusing on the future – not in an iconoclastic, ironical, or radical way, but by firmly insisting that strong people should get over it. Against the destructive memories of war, they upheld idealized images of bustling communities composed of indomitable individuals.

Bird must figure as a pioneering organizer of battlefields tourism and one of the most compelling memoirists of the war, but he also devoted much of his adult life to actively resisting its corrosive and destabilizing memory. His war writings anticipate a protean theme that will extend throughout all his cultural work: an active and self-aware resistance to negativity and realism – a refusal of the war that entailed a retreat into childlike innocence and simplicity, as if recoiling from the adult horrors and historical complexities that unfolded between 1914 and 1918. Vance's description of *And We Go On* accurately captures some of its tone and valuably points out how it is meant to rebut sordid realism. Bird, who clearly wanted his readers to admire and respect the soldiers, sets aside discussions of their sex lives and (most of the time) resists the notion that the fallen had died in vain. Yet Bird creates unavoidable difficulties for any dominant, homogenizing, organic, and conservative myth of Canada. In attempting to make *And We Go On* fit his model of the myth of Canada, Vance highlights only one voice in Bird's complex text. An alternative reading would bring out the plurality of voices and, more particularly, would focus on another theme in Bird's representation of the war: the psychological and moral danger of realism.

Those who approach Bird's memoir expecting to find the myth of Canada are in for a shock. The myth supposedly precluded divisive critiques about the purpose and conduct of the war. Yet Bird stridently insists on stark divisions and unpardonable inequalities, often in the course of savagely denouncing officers. The myth cannot encompass such an account, certainly not from a popular pro-war writer. In terms of the high diction analysed by Vance, the "imagined community" remembering the war was a "Canada in which the old power structures were bolstered" by drawing upon a unifying, sanctifying sense of the sacrifices of the fallen.[20] On the contrary, however, much of Bird's writing demystifies the war. He dwells at such length on injustices and imbecilities that worsened soldiers' suffering that it is hard to imagine the average reader finishing his book convinced that all was right with the world. Bird does not really fit into either of Vance's camps. His case constitutes an anomaly of some national importance, then, given his immense stature among the veterans who struggled for remembrance of their sacrifices despite his belligerent refusal to respect High Tory protocols.

Bird sharply rebuked the elites who had run the war and then set the terms of its remembrance. He savaged the military record-keepers who continued to guard bits of information "more closely than the gold of the Mint," even from veterans. "We, the men who served, want them NOW, have wanted them for years," Bird exclaimed. "Within twenty years the veterans will have gone to their last roll-call – then they can bury for ever, with the spiders and stale tobacco, everything regarding the Great War. It will then be of no interest to the existing generations." With respect to the crop of battalion histories emerging in the 1930s, he acidly remarked that those of the 16th and 42nd should have come bearing the disclaimer "For Officers Only." What about the hundreds of "incidents along the trenches at night," almost completely ignored by official histories? Most ordinary soldiers, no matter their valour, appeared only as "names in the Nominal Roll."[21] No passive consumer of a myth that patriotically ironed out the differences in sacrifice and commitment between officers and men, Bird bucked what he perceived as a consolidating establishment line on the war. He spoke with the authority of one who had been there.

"Fourteen years have not removed the rancor that bit my whole being," he writes of the "mosquito-brained recruiting officers" who rejected him – along with so many others – the first time he tried to enlist. With only a few exceptions, the officers Bird describes deserve only contempt. Their bullying soon convinced every soldier of that. One week of "bull-throated sergeants" yelling at him sufficed to make the recruit "more or less a sceptic" with a "vastly weakened" patriotism. Absurd martinets forced men weighed down with gear to march back and forth pointlessly – "and these men who had left good jobs and home and had come, as the orators said, to fight for right and loved ones."[22] Bird's own punishment for stealing a chicken changed him "from a soldier proud to be in uniform" to "one knowing there was no justice whatever in the army."[23]

For all his populist vitriol, Bird never doubted the cause. While he resented his officers, he fervently believed that the Allied fight against the Central Powers was unequivocally justified. Vance argues that when H.G. Wells coined the phrase "the war that will end war," he used "war" as a "euphemism for Prussianism or militarism" rather than as an exact description of "war." "In this sense," Vance adds, editorializing rather freely, "he was *entirely correct*, and Canadians never lost sight of the fact that November 1918 marked *a victory over the forces of barbarism*."[24] Leaving aside the problematic status of this claim about the history of civilization, one can still say that Bird would have broadly agreed that the sides fighting in the Great War were not morally equivalent. He denounced the "German mind" that had brutalized Belgium and France, as "proven" by pictures painted on the walls of an abandoned concert hall in Lewarde that depicted an enslaved and conquered people dominated by a "giant Prussian soldier, as repulsive as an animal."[25]

Bird, however, would have resisted any suggestion that "Prussianism" was only the fault of Germans and had been decisively vanquished with their defeat. The Canadian Corps harboured officers "with the same mentality and regard for their fellow men as their counterparts in the Prussian divisions." They treated the men like criminals for failing to salute any officer in the general vicinity. Two such infractions earned soldiers a sentence to Camp Aldershot's "Glass House," "staffed by very large ruffians who lacked all qualities of decency."[26] Years later, he still burned with indignation over the "authority-crazed, over-fed, routine-bound staffs, old fogies with a tragic lack of imagination and a criminal ignorance of actual warfare."[27] If the war was all about resisting Prussian militarism, in Bird's view many Prussian militarists wore British uniforms.

He would never forgive the insulting treatment he had received from a Canadian officer in Boulogne. Even into the 1960s, he would retell the story with undiminished bitterness. As he walked along, en route for leave in England, he amused himself with a lighthearted book. Completely preoccupied, he did not see a passing officer. Suddenly a "squeaky" voice hailed him: "Drop that damn book and salute an officer!" A "smirking, pip-squeak in officer's uniform," in the company of "a female in atrocious hat and gown," confronted him. Bird complied, but "my blood boiled every time I thought of the incident during my leave."[28] In his 1930 account, Bird staged an improbable second encounter with this officious "peacock of Boulogne" late in the war. Bird came upon the officer, who had lost his way in the trenches. The "bewildered and craven" little man directed an ill-considered outburst at Bird, who coolly told the ridiculous twerp "just what his kind were doing to hurt the army, and just what would happen to him at the front." Bird had never seen "a more spineless creature than that shaking, fear-stricken lieutenant."[29] The story, which had likely lost nothing in the retelling, concretized a consistent critique of brainless officialdom that provides *And We Go On* with many of its most memorable passages.

Bird probably took special satisfaction in contemplating the smarmy officer lost in the trenches. It infuriated him that the arrogant higher-ups were shielded from the war in a way other soldiers were not. They saw only a third as much of the "raw, undiluted war" as those whom they commanded. The men stayed at their posts – six hours on, six hours off. Officers put in just two hours a day, "a hurried tour of the trench." The men did the lousy jobs, hauling rations, barbed wire, and ammunition in all kinds of weather. They endured near-starvation. It fell to them to dig out their dead or wounded comrades. Where were the officers? Bird saw just one during the two worst days of Passchendale.[30] For Bird, how the war was remembered depended to a considerable extent on whose war one was talking about – the officers' war or the men's war.

Villers-au-Bois might, Bird wrote, seem like a miserable little spot to officers, who had the luxury of such aesthetic judgment. Indeed, it was "quite the dirtiest little place" on the day Bird re-encountered it in 1931. Yet years before it had seemed different to the men "who did six on and six off in the crater posts, and went down to sleep or shiver in clammy, dripping dugouts, with no warm food to put inside them, no chance for dry socks for their feet, or hope of anything but a return to the miserable half-frozen mud they had just quitted." To them, Villers-au-Bois offered a "glimpse of heaven itself" after the "long black and white dominos" of the seemingly endless days in the trenches, a haven where the frozen soldier could toast himself by a stove until thawed. He freely admitted, "It was, and is, a third-rate little place with dirty, narrow winding streets, and huge walls jumping in front of you, and barns opening on the street, the whole an awful jumble without sanitation or system, but it was a perfect home to us when we came back from Vimy."[31] It stands as a central complicating problem for the Vance interpretation that officers and men would look at the same battlefield landscapes with different eyes.

Bird dramatizes this perceptual difference when he discusses medals. The most tangible, cherished, personal mementos of the Great War were the medals bestowed upon its bravest combatants. Yet – explosively, one must imagine, in the context of a military culture kept fresh in Canadian Legions and on Remembrance Days – Bird viewed them suspiciously. (Remember he had one.) Medals went disproportionately to "conspicuous lads fresh from training camps, without a year of hard days of trench routine, and shell fire and Death's flutter about them." Medals seldom went to those who displayed the sterner courage demanded by long periods of fighting. Although he conceded that few won Victoria Crosses without "exhibiting extraordinary courage," he insisted many equally courageous men had gone "unadorned, in every company on the western front."[32] To illustrate the transparent unfairness of the process, he described how a Dane serving with the MacLean Highlanders had received the Victoria Cross. Even before the award became official, canny sergeants had placed bets on the likelihood of the Dane getting the VC. The reasons were obvious: "the Dane was a blueblood, received mail with a family crest, owned a hotel in New York City, and had a private yacht. He was a private in the ranks and yet each night he ate in the officers' mess."[33] When the officers looked at the Dane, they saw themselves. By recognizing his bravery, they vicariously lauded their own.

The affair of the Dane's medal (like so many other seemingly trivial wartime incidents) made Bird implacably angry because it revealed a pervasive, priggish elitism. Officers held themselves aloof from their men. When the men sat down at their long tables, eating nauseating food with their fingers in a place so dirty it was "hardly fit for a stable," an officer and a sergeant might drop by their hut, ask "Any complaints, men?" then vanish before anyone could reply. Many officers lost their lives in the war, but Bird suggested that all too often their own stupid unwillingness to heed their men did them in. The first combat death Bird witnessed was that of an officer who ignored a warning that he should not stick his head up over the trench walls: "Clang! His steel helmet flew back over the rear wall and lodged in the wire, and brains and blood were spilled all over the front of my overcoat and on my arms as the officer sank down at my feet."[34] According to the myth of Canada, transcendent patriotism and reverence for the fallen should have effaced memories of injustice and inequality. In contrast, Bird vividly remembered for half a century everything that had made him rebel against the authorities who had presided over his war experiences.

In fact, he felt only disillusionment for the "platform patriots" who propagated the myth of Canada – those many clergymen, politicians, and editorialists who honoured the Great War as a crusade for decency and humanity. He felt sure that most ordinary soldiers would have shared his skepticism. A "7th Battalion man" informed him that "patriotism" was not a "password" in his company, "that loyalty was a word they sneered at; discipline, with the death penalty behind it, a canker we could not cure. Then he derided the caste of the nation and cursed the propaganda passed out by preachers, editors, staff officers and platform patriots of both sexes." Not only were platform-patriot sentiments insincere, sanctimonious, and unearned, but they were even delusive and dangerous to believe. "The first Germans in the war were brutes, I think," reflects one of Bird's fellow soldiers, "but the last crowd were just like we are, and their papers and preachers told them the same twaddle ours told us." It gave his friend pause: "I've got so that I don't believe anything, and I'll have to go back and pretend I do because I could never make my mother understand that the Germans aren't horned devils, and that the British weren't haloed champions of Christianity."[35]

In fact, not even clergymen were haloed champions of Christianity. Bird reports that padres, irredeemably identified with the officer class, were "scorned." He softens the blow a little by adding, "Our own padre was not disliked," before damning him with faint praise: "Sometimes on the crater line he came at night with cigarettes and warm drinks and talked with a private, but he was apart from the men, and usually with, perhaps through circumstance, an officer whom the majority cordially hated." Soldiers declined to heartily sing the compulsory church parade hymns. Yet, offered the chance to go to the YMCA hut and sing voluntarily, the men would "fairly bring down the roof with singing that throbbed with fervour." *And We Go On* stages a debate between a padre and Tommy, Bird's friend whom he means us to admire. When the padre brashly promises that after the war the churches will return to the real gospel, revealing to the people that the war has been a "horrible crime," Tommy stops him with this objection: "Don't do that ... You'll lose the few you've still got if you turn hypocrite. The war hasn't changed. If it's wrong now it was wrong in '14, and what did you shout then?"[36] The padre's eyes fill with tears. He cannot speak. The authentic voice of the soldier silences religious authority.

For Bird, the most authentically valuable part of the war – perhaps its only redeeming feature – was the remembered solidarity of the men under fire: their shared humour, their dogged camaraderie, their sheer determination to pull through. If this placed him at odds with those who would soften memories of injustice with sweet words of piety and harmony, it also set him against those "modernists" who would reduce the average soldier to a suffering animal. The spontaneity, simplicity, and goodness of ordinary people, which Bird would later celebrate in Nova Scotia, first appeared in his war writings. In the "trench at zero hour," "insincerity" and "the superficial" dissolved. Combat revealed the truth of men, removing their pretences, destroying their snobbishness, for "[n]o artificial imposition could survive in the ranks where inherent value automatically found its level … a man's endurance under that which he most dreads was something we could not gauge."[37]

"Endurance under that which he most dreads" is a hard-won, bittersweet kind of virtue. It is not sublimely transcendent or morally unquestionable. Vance concedes almost in passing, en route to his more general characterization of the book's ostensible upbeat optimism, that *And We Go On* reports much of the dirt and confusion of the war. This misrepresents the overall balance of the book. *And We Go On* derives its very title from the last words of Bird's fellow soldier, the innocent young Mickey. Bird cradles the mortally wounded Mickey as he lies dying:

[H]e nestled to me like a child, his white face upturned to mine.
"At last," he murmured, "I'm through." Then his whisper was shrill and harsh. "I never had a white tunic or a red one," he said. "I didn't want – to kill people. I hate war – and everything. Why did they do it – why – did – they?"
He seemed delirious and I tried to soothe him, but he would not listen. He talked about what we had read in my little guide book, the way boys trained for fighting, the soldiers killed in France and Belgium, the other wars that had been fought, the futility of the endless repetition. "And we just go on and on," he finished. "Doing things because – because – "
His voice sank so low I could not hear but his lips still moved. Little white-faced Mickey! I held him there, held him tight, and tried to comfort him as he grew weaker and weaker. Then he twisted, strained in my arms, "… and we go on – on – on – on," he shrilled, and stiffened.
I laid him there by the roadside with his rifle upright at his head, and took his belongings from his pockets.[38]

Perhaps Bird is (in Vance's words) "the quintessential articulator of Canada's war," but it is difficult to discern a straightforward optimism in his book.[39] Bird makes the dying words of a confused, delirious, and terrified young man into the volume's very title – symbolically framing all of its contents.[40] His optimism is a choice he makes in the face of a wrenching acknowledgment of dehumanizing horror, a horror that could at any moment overwhelm the human capacity to endure.

And We Go On suggests that anyone who had not lived through the war could never even imagine it. Bird hauntingly describes his introduction to trench warfare. The officers dispatch the green Bird and a fellow soldier to an emplacement recently hit by mortar fire. A stench hung thick in the air, over-powering even the miasma "of decay and slime" that pervaded the battlefield as a whole. Something had died. A corporal stepped in, ordering the men to clean up whatever it was. "A flying pig [a heavy mortar shell] had exploded as it left the gun and three men had been shredded to fragments. We were to pick up legs and bits of flesh from underfoot and from the muddy walls, place all in the bags and then bury them in one grave. It was a harsh breaking in."[41] So it went, hour after hour, day after day, for years. No one else could ever understand.

Nothing brought home the sheer incommensurability of the war experi-ence so much as "that Passchendale horror."[42] What horrified him most about Passchendale was the pervasive smell of death that "seemed to penetrate one's inmost being, that awful stench of death, a foul thing, a filthy thing, its reek was sickening." Passchendale undermined individuals, devouring their bodies and destroying their reason. In the dead of the night, Bird twice awoke to find "a man on his hands and knees, gazing about him, wakened by the horrors of his own mind." An admiring Briton advised Bird, on leave, that as a soldier in the famous battle the Canadian had "lived in a great day." "I don't think so," Bird replied. Then he added, with words that marked a striking departure from the myth of Canada, "This war is wrong." "War – I hated it, despised it, loathed it," Bird later wrote, before adding, "yet felt I was part of it."[43] Thir-teen years later, surveying landscapes ravaged by war, he cried, "Ruins, ruins, ruins! … Desolation, wreckage, disaster – war!"[44] Time had done little to heal his psychic wounds.

The great theme of *And We Go On* is how trench warfare permanently changed the mentality of the ordinary soldiers who most directly bore its bur-den. Language could never express what they had witnessed. No veteran of Passchendale, Bird wrote, "would talk about it at all." After a soldier had undergone this shattering experience, he could never again claim to under-stand life or even himself: "[E]very man who had endured Passchendale would never be the same again, was more or less a stranger to himself." Visions of its scenes would hold men on a rack, tortured by memories of screams and shouts – "I knew that years would not entirely remove such remembrances." In the "competition of life," the returned soldiers would struggle under the psychic assaults of "overshadowing visions and phantoms."[45] Just to get along, to be normal, a veteran would have to live in a state of permanent alienation against a part of himself, against a chapter of his own biography. To survive, he would have to deny what he knew.

Reflecting on the war would actually work against the survival of those fighting it. Moreover, thinking things through could yield no real insights: the "Master Knot of Human Fate" so bound the lives of individual soldiers that the war simply lay beyond explanation. Bird remembered a soldier called the "Professor," a cultivated man who (according to Bird) should have been spared the front lines. Unable to sleep, he "unloaded his mind" upon Bird. The agitated man implored Bird that surely someone had to tell the world about the malefic futility of the war. Surely "the few sane men left on earth should combine their efforts to stop the carnage." Wracked by trauma and insomnia, unable to stem the onrushing tide of his own thoughts, he fell into hysterical despair: "Our existence was, he said, an ugly nightmare, and Heaven must shudder in protest."[46]

Later, while travelling on a coach, the Professor resumes his critique of the war, that "ghastly paroxysm of civilization." Bird sees that the Professor is upsetting his young friend and fellow soldier Mickey but does not contradict him. Indeed, he can see what the Professor means. Yet he viscerally opposes the Professor's step beyond description towards analysis. His words are worse than untimely; they are categorically wrong. They imply the possibility of critique and even (implicitly) that of alternatives. They suggest that experiences are comprehensible through reflection, that soldiers can step back to analyse their predicament. What could Bird do? In a move that foreshadowed his future career as an organic intellectual of tourism/history, Bird dove into a handy guidebook for tales of "coaches of crystal and gold, horses draped in cloth of gold, courtiers and conquerors dazzling with diamonds, ladies in silks and plumes and laces." History here becomes a form of therapy, a healthful diversion from harsh reality. Bird was trying to divert his comrades-in-arms with entertaining historical details and, perhaps, to reassure them that nothing in the years 1914 to 1918 was terribly unusual given the many battles that had previously been fought over the same countryside. Yet the hypercritical Professor, along with another soldier, was unimpressed: "We were simply civilians in soldier's clothing, and war was a mess of grotesque murder," one retorted. Poor Mickey "absorbed every word." He sat, "staring at us and through us, seeing things, fearful things." The Professor shuts up when he notices what is happening to Mickey, but – too late. Analysis has done its worst to undermine innocence.[47] In this cultural clash between the Professor and "the innocent," Bird's sympathies lie entirely with the latter.

Those who had suffered most in the war would never be able to explain it. Those at home could never understand. They would get impatient with the mute soldiers who refused to mention it, "the boys who would be surly, taciturn, moody, resenting good intentions, perhaps taking to hard liquor and aim-less drifting." Even the other veterans could only do so much: "We, of the brotherhood, could understand the soldier, but never explain him. All of us would remain a separate, definite people, as if branded by a monstrous des-potism."[48] All across the interwar world, many of these "separate, definite people" would be thorns in the side of their rulers. In Canada, as the Win-nipeg General Strike revealed, some would turn to the radical left. Bird's abrasive denunciations of authoritarianism suggest at least some rapproche-ment between his egalitarianism and their position. Yet he would not go that route. With some dexterity, Bird salvaged liberal individualism from the very war that many others saw as its erasure.

Character is the fundamental category through which Bird accomplished this feat. In the end, what determined one's fate in the battlefields of Belgium and France was character – the moral qualities composing the essence of an individual. Some might come to understand such innate dispositions, seeking to maintain them in the face of temptation and danger. Yet, in truth, such efforts could only go so far. In the heat of battle, character emerged no matter what. If soldiers turned to drink (as, heretically, the abstaining Bird suggested many did), they merely exposed themselves as those "weak-kneed ones [who] used S.R.D. [Service Rum Diluted] to fortify them[selves]," a condition allegedly endemic among officers.[49] Drink made men "flushed, unnatural," undermining the nerve of the impressionable. Yet their alcoholism represented the manner, not the cause, of their downfall. Drinkers simply confirmed their weak characters, for which they bore no intrinsic responsibility. Strength or weakness existed as essences apart from the conscious self. In battle, some pre-viously considered timid proved themselves heroes. Some once thought brave crumbled under pressure. Some instinctive dreamers faced the cruel dilemma of experiencing every danger twice, once in their imagination and again in reality.[50] The lived experience of war was incomprehensible, so much so that no one could steel himself for it. How one fared depended upon a character deeply constitutive of oneself yet beyond one's conscious grasp.

Character belonged to free-standing male individuals. It did not pertain to women. Bird scrupulously catalogued their physical attributes as so many signs of the underlying spirit of a given place, not as expressions of a personal char-acter that conferred agency. "We returned to Aix-Noulette, which is but another 'war' village – corrugated iron galore, gardens, children and dogs, with four sloppy estaminets and several enormous women," writes Bird in *Thirteen Years After*. At Hersin-Coupigny, "Madame was just as fat and moist as when I last saw her, and seemed to have on the same dress and the same black shoes. She was very genial until we showed no desire to leave more money with her, then suddenly became busy." In his description of "[e]very village on the

Somme," the "barns are established with the same haphazard method of location … Here and there the big doors are open and you view a spongy midden crowded with pigs and fowl, and get a glimpse of a bony female clumping around the brick or cobbled ledge of the yard. She will be carrying a bush broom or spade or pitchfork, her feet in clumsy sabots and a scarf around her neck. In the corner of the yard there will be an accumulation of tools and poles and various buckets and tubs, and a yapping dog will be straining at his chain as you go by." The hypothetical woman in this generalized landscape description serves to reinforce an overpowering impression of disorder in a world that has imperfectly recovered from the war. She has no persona of her own.[51] In company with many turn-of-the-century liberals, Bird does not view women as real individuals.

Character belongs to men, but only to certain men. One such man was Will Bird's brother Steve. Will rhapsodized about the brotherly love they shared. In fact, they were "more like David and Jonathan than brothers."[52] They followed the same sports teams, had the same likes and dislikes, and could read each other's minds. Steve's death in 1915 drew Bird into the military. These brothers-in-arms, separated by the mere technicality of death, epitomized the uplifting fraternity of the Great War. Despite his own earlier descriptions of grim mayhem, Bird would maintain in 1968 that the war was, in this specific sense of a *fraternal contract between individuals*, a wonderful experience – because "life in the trenches forced men to know each other in a manner that is impossible in civilian life."[53] The remembrance of deep male comradeship consoles Bird at the very end of *And We Go On* when he confronts the nihilistic thought that remembered wartime horrors will torment the returned soldiers forever: "I warmed as I thought of all that the brotherhood had meant, the sharing of blankets and bread and hardships, the binding of each other's wounds, the talks we had had of intimate things, of the dogged simple faith that men had shown, flashes of their inner selves that strengthened one's own soul."[54]

The war almost miraculously delivered male individuals of their isolation from one another. Among the ordinary soldiers, excluding the privileged officer class, war abolished artificial divisions to create a true egalitarianism: "Down in dugouts where there was hardly room to breathe, men who had come from comfortable homes moved without complaints to their fellows. All grousing was reserved for the higher-ups, the 'brass-hats' and the 'big bugs' responsible for everything. The men were unselfish among themselves." The trenches provided an unexpected place where men could forge lasting bonds. Among the deepest intimacies such men had experienced was a common fear – in a sense, a shared openness to their own limitations. Some of the most moving passages in Bird's remarkable war writings reflect on men convinced of their cowardice who nonetheless face up to the ordeal of war. The "bravest men in France" were not those who did "great deeds when officers were watching them," but the often sensitive, generally unnoticed souls for whom every hour on "sentry go" or trench duty "held the agony of a torture rack."[55]

The male bonding on the front, though intense, had nothing to do with homosexuality. Again and again, Bird shows an anxious concern to demarcate the manly love of the trenches from the effeminate love that could not be named. In *Ghosts Have Warm Hands,* Bird tells a story about a man from the 8th Winnipeg Black Devils concerning a "wild spree" at Arras. The Canadians captured a young German. On closer inspection, "he was extremely handsome, with quite feminine features." They decided not to take their captive to headquarters. "It was very late when they arrived in Arras," Bird relates, "so they kept the German with them in billets till the morning." The soldiers had requisitioned a once-grand residence, stocked with many fine clothes. Faced with such a profusion of "French feminine finery," they accordingly "stripped off the young German's uniform and arrayed him wondrously in a flowing skirt and waist, putting an attractive bonnet on his head and [took] him down into the street. He was very afraid of what might happen to him when they let him loose and indicated he was to walk up the street ahead of them." The soldiers hoped their "lady" would attract some "army buck," but instead the group ran into a fat and pompous major – whereupon the captive fled for his/her life (and, we imagine, masculine honour) accompanied by the major.[56] Much in the story remains unsaid. Cross-dressing the enemy undermined his gender identity; the potential of an "army buck" picking him up would add, by implication, further fun to the enemy's sexual transformation. The humour of his humiliation, fear, and emasculation lies in its unexpected contravention of the established sexual order.

Some effete officers more conclusively fail the test of male individuality. In *Private Timothy Fergus Clancy* (a novel based on Bird's dear friend Timothy Flinn of County Cork, killed at Passchendale in November 1917), Clancy – the stereotypical tough-talking, hard-fisted Paddy – finds himself appointed as batman to a Lieutenant Biggar. Something is quite amiss with Biggar, something well beyond his aristocratic background and officer status. His body, with its "small pink face and serious blue eyes, small hands and feet and a bird-like voice," discloses disquieting signs. Then we have Lieutenant Biggar's nickname, "Lucy." Finally, there is the question of his "equipment," which Clancy is invited to inspect. The tent is in "apple-pie order" and "'Lucy's' leather and brass were glistening. On the table was a wondrous array of hair-oil, tooth-powder, mouth-wash, and various bottles, with French names, that were horribly like perfume containers." Clancy is "speechless" before the sheer volume of Lucy's equipage. "'Now Clancy, I wish you would tell me what is really necessary for the trenches,' said 'Lucy,' beaming again. 'You see, I know nothing whatever about this war and I want you to tell me everything. You be my instructor, won't you?' Here was a "dapper canary bird," a "wistful little fellow." Or, to use the more direct vocabulary of Clancy's sergeant, "that sissy" and "that mama's boy."[57] "Lucy" – the effeminate man who (not coincidentally) is also an officer – serves to underscore the truth of inherent hierarchies, the sovereign general rule of character. Under the stress of war, Bird suggests, a man like Biggar could never hope to evade the unalterable truths of his bioethical constitution. Such sissies are congenitally unfit as soldiers, yet – in the comedy of a mismanaged war effort pervaded by British elitism – must perform as officers.

Race joins gender and sexuality as a fundamental building block of character. *Timothy Clancy* makes many appeals to whiteness as an ideal, as when Clancy explains that for all his peculiarities Lucy was his charge and the boys must "treat him 'white.'"[58] Non-white people, meanwhile, come in for ridicule, dismissal, or exoticism. In *The Communication Trench*, one finds a long poem in pseudo-Chinese doggerel – "Welly good flend to Chinamen, Chinky Pincky Pak ah pu."[59] Black people appear in *And We Go On* as remarkably exotic casualties of war: "Sengalese [Senegalese]" corpses intrigue him, with "rotting, rat-picked bones, with fezzes, faded red sashes and brass-studded belts among the skeletons."[60] Their living counterparts combine racial and gendered defects: they are "strange, soft-eyed fellows with their hair done up in black buns."[61] Elsewhere, people of colour come in for mockery as "niggers"[62] and "coons."[63]

Character inheres pre-eminently in sober, self-possessed Anglo-Celtic males. Other ethnicities, by virtue of characterological defects, are other kinds of people. Bird's major representations of French Canadians suggest instability, eccentricity, and irresponsibility. "They lagged in the trench, talking loudly, making much noise, and one man even played a mouth organ," Bird writes of the legendary Van Doos. Describing two inseparable soldiers, Slim and Joe, Bird remarks, "Joe, [Slim's] mate, was a French-Canadian, who also was uneducated, and who had no dependents. They did not get any mail, were very slovenly in dress and drill, and would not wash or shave unless forced to do so." Their racially determined character deficiencies are plain for all to see. "The French-Canadians would not be hurried and their officers humored them like children."[64] Like children, they deserved forbearance because they could not help lacking the capacity to do things properly.

In addition to the inborn forces of character, the role of chance also made rational analysis of war risible. Luck (sometimes with supernatural assistance) could determine whether one lived or died, so any search for coherent patterns in the world was foredoomed to fail. War could not be – more crucially *should* not be – explained. It could only be experienced and remembered personally, never rendered in an inter-subjectively accessible manner. Bird felt that history should represent a struggle, not to understand the war, but rather to resurrect it – reliving the moment privately, putting one's individual character through its boundary-defining tests once again. Yet throughout *And We Go On* we hear credible voices saying that the war confirms the decline of human civilization. War was simply wrong. For those who had reached this stark conclusion, remembering the war might have involved reconstructing its social, economic, and political preconditions – transcending their personal experiences to reach a more general framework of explanation. In Bird's remembered war, though, the principal vector for this reading is the Professor (whose denunciation of "our existence" as an "ugly nightmare" interestingly extends to the tourism sector itself – to the souvenir-sellers selling their "gaily-woven silk souvenirs and postcards"). First of all, Bird unmistakably infers that the Professor's elucidations do not represent real understanding but express his nervous disposition and indeed exacerbate his inherent psychic instability. Bird all but acknowledged the truth of the Professor's indictment – "This war is wrong," we remember Bird bluntly declaring – but he also thinks one should refrain from speaking this truth too loudly in front of innocents such as Mickey. Even the most tentative beginnings of analytical reason dangerously compromise innocence. Yet, given the incommensurable setting of the trenches, how could one keep from seeking the reasons underlying such remarkable events? And how, in that "land of topsy turvy," could one keep sane?[65]

For Bird, the answer lies in the supernatural. Faith was a necessity: "Never on earth was there a like place where a man's support, often his sole support, was his faith in some mighty Power." His belief in a "mighty Power" bore little apparent resemblance either to his childhood Methodist faith or to the High Anglicanism that enshrined the myth of Canada. As he surveyed a service in a beautiful English church with the sun's rays falling on the altar and the choir stalls, flooding the sanctuary with a wash of colour, as the vicar, in white surplice and crimson stole, implored God to intercede for British arms on the Western Front, Bird even allowed that he felt like "a rank outsider." He reflected afterwards that in his own haversack he carried a similar entreaty, inscribed on a belt buckle he had taken off a dead German: "Gott Mitt Uns."[66] In this moment of insight, Bird came close to implying a moral equivalence between the two sides of the European conflict.

Bird's wartime belief in a "mighty Power" drew from innovative forms of faith as much as traditional Christianity. During the Great War, many soldiers embraced spiritualism. Jay Winter has shown that wartime horrors led "to the deepening of well-established Victorian sentiments and conjectures concerning the nature of the spiritual world."[67] Certainly they did so in Bird's case. *And We Go On* promises to reveal the "psychic effect" of the war on combatants: "There existed before all battles and even in the calms of the trench

149

routine, a condition before which all natural explanations failed, and no super-natural explanations were established." He maintains that unseen forces guided him through the war. "Every case of premonition I have described is actual fact," he insists, going on to admonish his readers: "[E]ach of my own psychic experiences were exactly as recorded. The reader may term them fantasies, the results of overstrained emotion, what he will; there were many who know he cannot explain them."[68] Most crucially, a tangible manifestation of Steve's spirit guided Bird through the conflict.

It is wholly typical of Bird that, rather than massed armies of eerie spirits, or luminous mists, or battlefield visitations of angels (as at Mons in 1914), he calls up the pragmatic, functional figure of his brother. Steve returns from the afterlife not to convey his deep thoughts about the meaning of it all to Will, but to rescue his brother from one scrape or another. Moreover, Steve does not reappear as an intangible spectre, but as a real resurrected human being – as Bird would affirm decades later in the very title of *Ghosts Have Warm Hands*. Steve "literally" pulled Will to a stairway and spoke to him with a completely natural voice. "His legs had been just in front of me up the cellar stair," Bird remembered. "The more I thought of it, the more certain I became that there is much in the world we do not understand, that the next phase of life to which we pass is in close communication with those left behind. Some day the connection will be discovered."[69]

Steve is not Bird's only visitor from beyond. Steve's English girlfriend, Phyllis, possessed of "the gift," also makes two strategic appearances. The first time, Bird, without any foreknowledge of where he is going or who he is meeting, has a premonition that mystically guides him to meet Phyllis at a small inn called the Black Boar near Maidenhead in England. "Something gripped me, held me," he says of his impulsive decision to go there. He felt a chill come upon him in the dusky twilight, "as if an unseen door had opened." Turning, he saw a girl who "appeared like a phantom, but she was very warm and real, for she took my hand and welcomed me to the village." The phantom turns out to be Phyllis, whom Bird had never met. The older Will would remember, "It seemed, all at once, as if I had entered a different sphere of exis-tence, that such a coincidence were natural and that it was not mine to either doubt or query." Phyllis, who strikes up a correspondence with Will, makes a second appearance in the narrative when Bird returns to the Black Boar. Phyllis had been expecting him, announced the old man who answered the door of a little cottage:

> I interrupted to tell him I had not written her, but he shook his head again and said, in an almost reverent way, that Phyllis had "gifts," had no need of letters, she knew by some mysterious sixth sense.

"Where is she at now?" I broke in. "I'll look her up in London."

Again the slow shake of the head. "'E be too late," he said, and thrust me a crumpled paper. It was a wire from London. Phyllis had been killed by a bomb dropped by the German raiders.[70]

Did Phyllis actually exist? Did Bird really go to the Black Boar? Both the pub's name and the wispy spectre seem somehow formulaic. Nor do we have any way of corroborating the story. It is suggestive that several decades later Steve is once again haunting Europe in *Ghosts Have Warm Hands*, while Phyllis has mysteriously vanished from the narrative.

Few readers who envision Passchendale with Bird will begrudge him a ghostly guardian or two. Nonetheless, both in his wartime writings and his subsequent career, the turn to irrationalism had consequences far exceeding Bird's own handling of his particular situation. His move foreclosed any possibility of critical engagement. If the world of experience only exists as the distant echo of what transpires in the spirit world, why try to change it? Debate can achieve little if in fact ethereal forces of fate and character that we cannot see, much less comprehend, predetermine worldly events. Spiritualism clinches Bird's successful circumvention of any burden of proof. Bird could explain much of the Great War in terms of character traits. He could attribute any residuum to unseen forces, supernatural intuition, and the hand of fate. Moreover, spiritualism served character. Faith in the supernatural reassures the soldier that a timeless sphere of spirits who can help him in adversity presides over the apparent chaos of events. Thus fortified, he can keep at bay the negativity and skepticism of the sardonic Professor and his sophistical ilk. Just as Bird escaped the sordid realities of war-torn France with his trip down memory lane, so soldiers could find positive therapeutic responses to the trenches in the spirit world. Whatever might befall them, they could always cast their minds into an unseen dimension where death held no dominion.

History, too, can play a limited but valuable part in the survival of a positive thinker, providing a helpful diversion in times of trouble. Bird used guidebook tales of romanticized medieval warfare to reassure his fellow soldiers on the Western Front that they played parts in a well-established, even colourful, drama of Western civilization. Filling in a cold drizzly interval with his friend Tommy, near Ypres, Bird regales him with tales of how "in 1382 the Bishop of Norwich had landed at Calais with sixty thousand men and marched to take Ypres – and failed." The guidebook told him many interesting facts about the surrounding Belgian countryside, a land of "white villages [glistening] in warm sunshine, orchards teeming with golden fruit, here and there a gleam of water." How odd to think that this bucolic scene, "so lovely in an aspect of repose, has been the theatre of almost all the sanguinary wars which from time to time have desolated Europe; that luxuriated crop has been manured with the best blood of the brave, the gay, the virtuous; those sleeping groves have responded to the storm of slaughter – and may yet again."[71] (At this point, long-suffering Tommy tells him to shut up.)

Similarly, when Bird later surveys the postwar landscape, he believes that the ghosts of history might play a useful role – so long as one does not allow them to run the show. The ruins of the war usefully provide benchmarks for the wondrous progress that has taken place all around them. They demonstrate that, as a matter of course, things just keep getting better. In the same way that soldiers with strong characters know they should not bother dwelling on unfairness and injustice, so too effective communities understand that history is not something to mope about but something to use. *Thirteen Years After*, Bird's contribution to the genre of European battlefields travel-writing, gives both a traveller's impressions of the old Great War battlegrounds of Europe and a positive thinker's critique of the communities that have somehow not realized that they have to *get over it*. A few ravaged villages have gotten with the program, but many delinquent towns have not shaped up. The dour, taciturn folk who cling to such places remain glumly trapped in the past. Perhaps they are just too lazy or fearful to grasp the future.

The Belgian village of Verbrandenmolen offered much evidence of such deficient characters. "At the mill I tried to talk with the old man there," Bird remarks, "but he was an unfriendly sort. The war, he said, was nothing to him. He hated such months as August and the country would suffer because the crops were not good. I told him he was lucky to have a farm after such a war, and he spat at a wall and vanished into his house." Regrettably, this sad sack typified the entire village: "All the inhabitants of that place seemed of the same ilk. One notices that the peasants are either small-faced folk with furtive manners, or a stolid people with huge, broad faces and unwinking stares."[72] Whether broad- or narrow-faced, whether furtive or stolid, the Belgian "peasants" did not measure up. They wore their degenerate characters on their faces. To expect Bird to sympathize with the pain of their bereavement is to ask the wrong thing of the wrong man.

Everywhere in the Salient, Bird the battlefields tourist comes across more dispiriting "types." "There is a dreadful, solemn depression that engulfs one," Bird says of Messines. Living amidst an "enormous graveyard" has taken its toll: "All year long they see people coming to visit the dead; all year they work their ground with careful touch, never knowing when they will uncover a corpse or a live shell. It has made them the dour, dead-eyed race they are." Contrary pieces of evidence, such as the parties held by young people – which could have been described as zestful if hard-drinking manifestations of high spirits – are instead psychoanalysed as manifestations of the same dread spirit of racial failure: "They are but trying to defy that hovering something that is over every acre of the Salient."[73]

Character flaws implacably express themselves in the physical appearance of actual places. Consider the case of Cherisy, "a dirty town" where "the street is vile and there are no walks." Barn doors, duck puddles, crows, magpies, peasants, and pigeons all blend into the slough of despond. "Even the people seem different in this war region," Bird reports, describing them as "duller," "almost stupid." He relates a conversation with an old man who "told me of losing a fine colt down an old dugout shaft, of his son being killed by the exploding of a shell in the garden, and how another of his family died from blood poisoning, a scratch from old barbed wire. They hate the war, loathe it; don't want to talk about it at all." Of the Arras area, Bird remarks, "All the streets are a mass of chalky clay and water, and barn doors open on them, spreading straw and filth. Corrugated iron, red and rusty, is used conspicuously, and the village looks as if its inhabitants were making a 'civil resistance' against anything orderly or clean." Hendecourt, meanwhile, "is another spiritless village, dirty and ill-favoured, with more corrugated iron, more bony, apathetic women, drab estaminets, and ducks." At Ploegsteert, Bird associates the country's "flat unhealthy" look with the fact that "the workmen seem affected by sleeping sickness."[74] Failed individuals sink into the mire of their surroundings. By the same token, ugliness, both in buildings and in facial features, testifies to the presence of defective characters – "grouches" and "growlers."

Contrariwise, prosperity and attractiveness signalled good, forward-looking optimists. Occasionally, even in blighted Belgium, Bird found "intelligent" and "very friendly" people. Orderly and clean Cambrai featured less corrugated iron and fewer wooden huts: "Here you see signs warning motorists about schools near by, and the walks and streets are clean, and there are clean curtains in the windows, often flowers, and gardens and bowers worthy of Picardy." Armentières impressed him as "another world" compared to the towns of the Salient: "Every place had a flag flying, all the population seemed in holiday attire. Such a contrast, the faces, to those we had left. Everyone seemed cheerful[,] happy, responsive."[75] Any feature of any landscape or person presents an epiphenomenal manifestation of an underlying essence that Bird never fails to grasp.

Bird had not come back to the front looking for corrugated iron, dirty farm animals, and the incorrigibly bereaved. No tourist would want to go to those dingy Belgian towns with their "endless glare of red brick and painted concrete," nor take in "powdered and smashed" remnants of war in the Salient. Rather, they would want to see the low-roofed, white-walled quaintness of the villages down Amiens way, where the well-maintained war ruins were "more poignant." Tourists would appreciate the "wonderful, marvellous" concrete trenches of Vimy, and the exactitude of the restoration would leave any soldier, like Bird, "thrilled beyond words."[76]

Historical tourism à la Bird rendered definitive judgments aplenty, but abjured even a preliminary analytical grasp of the landscapes through which one travelled. Visitors should not ponder the structuring patterns – social, cultural, religious, geographical, historical – that might account for the visible differences between one place and the next. That would broach forbidden subjects like analysis, categorization, and abstraction. Bird has no wish to follow the Professor into the treacherous realm of realism. In his European travels, he saw an uneven process of recovery that others might have explored in terms of differential patterns of economic development, population displacement, and state investment, but he resolutely placed them within his governing framework of character traits.

Bird felt that history should establish contact with *personal* experiences. These experiences should be pleasant, not disturbing. He feared that contested memory brought in its wake a "monstrous despotism" that would come to dominate the core of one's individuality. History exists, one might say, as those circumstances that real characterful individuals are put on earth to rise above. Its memory has a purpose (as in the example of Bird's guidebook) only as a therapeutic diversion from harsh reality. Tourism/history required exactly the right mix of friendly natives, a pretty landscape, and the tourist's own positivity, plus homeopathic doses of tidily restored ruins. Individuals who grasped what tourism/history could offer might well succeed in the competition of life. Years earlier and in Europe, Bird had already hammered out much of the framework that would reposition Nova Scotia as "The Playground with a History" during the 1930s and 1940s.

Bird's wartime writings stand out for their unflinching candour. In contrast to his saccharine Nova Scotia works, where he tends to airbrush conflict and turmoil, Bird often strikes a bracingly critical note when he writes about the Great War. *And We Go On* has far more psychological complexity than anything else he wrote. Even the style of this book, with its visceral descriptions and carefully structured sentences, sets it apart. It stands among the most powerful Canadian reactions to the Great War, almost launching a pre-emptive strike against any attempt to assimilate all enduring responses to the cataclysm into the high diction of the supposed "Myth of Canada." This book offers an unusually explicit jeremiad against the irrational autocracy of the men who organized the war, escorting readers to the very outskirts of a critique of the established order. Bird sometimes allows voices within his narrative, though seldom his own, to recognize the agonizing existential crisis that the Great War posed for many who lived through it and who found no way to assimilate it into the commonsensical nostrums of their culture. In the crucible of war, conventional Victorian liberal categories proved painfully inadequate for interpreting human experience.

Paradoxically, though, the crisis of liberalism brought on by the war would ultimately issue in a magical rescue operation whereby all social phenomena irreducible to the inevitable unfolding of individual character are set aside as unexplainable. Bird wanted people to remember this history, but only in a certain way – as a strictly personal encounter with the unfathomable and the uncontrollable. This provided the means to establish benchmarks for the sure and steady march of progress. Experiences should be recalled but not examined. In default of such a critical examination, an unexamined classic liberalism remains the ruling cultural politics by default.

Bird, then, wrote as a liberal rather than a Tory, and he probably would not have appreciated attempts to Anglicanize the war experience to develop a myth of Canada that surely would have excluded him. Nor would he have identified with modernist or socialist critics who took the Great War as proof that a crisis-ridden social order had run its course. And he rejected this option not because he was an unsophisticated innocent, but because he rejected any critical or theoretical stance as dangerous. Apart from an agreeably amorphous concept of progress, Bird actually had no theories at all. Indeed, there could be no such thing. There was only, on the one hand, the individual who accessed particular memories and assessed particular sights, while, on the other hand, the unseen forces of the spirit world made unfathomable interventions into temporal events. Individual character and occult forces determined whether one survived history to enjoy the fruits of progress or whether history left one behind as a failure, a grouch, or a corpse.

◆

Bird had a good run as a war writer. In the early 1930s, though, he noticed unmistakable signs that the market was drying up. H. Napier Moore of *Maclean's* ominously informed Bird in 1930, "Sometime ago I decided not to run any more war stories."[77] A fellow freelancer commiserated in 1932: "Adventure is now a nearly hopeless market ... Short stories is [*sic*] more open, but a very dangerous market to play with."[78] Faced with the choice of adaptation or extinction, Bird adapted. He transposed many plot lines from his Great War writings onto the relatively undeveloped theme of Nova Scotia history. In this new configuration, they sold like hotcakes.

For many regional writers, the interwar years were golden years. A boom in romantic Nova Scotiana would last until the late 1950s. Bird prospered as a novelist specializing in romantic historical fiction, as a state-employed tourism promoter, and as a travel writer. In all three interrelated spheres, he developed compelling variants of the radical Innocence that had sustained him in the Great War. Prima facie, Bird's muddy-and-bloody Europe seems to have nothing in common with his quaint-and-cosy Nova Scotia (call it "Bird-land"). A pleasantly pastoral symphony of sights and sounds in Nova Scotia soothes Bird's aggrieved sense of a world out of joint in Northern Europe. Though he doughtily struggles to keep at bay the despair that seeps through passages of *And We Go On*, he unceremoniously ushers it out the door in his Nova Scotia writings. Bird's Nova Scotia is simultaneously both wonderfully historical and splendidly modern. If (as Marshall Berman famously urged) modernity should adopt Marx's "All That Is Solid Melts into Air" as its slogan, Birdland might trumpet the slogan "All That Has Melted Away Can Be Made Solid Again."[79] In this idyllic Nova Scotia, fantastically popular in Canada during the 1940s and 1950s, no one oppresses anyone and everyone (apart from a few defective characters) lives pleasantly. Its history amounts to a series of amusing anecdotes, colourful tales told by salty schooner captains down by the blue salt sea.

Yet, in other respects, Birdland actually develops themes first discernible in Bird's treatment of the trenches. In Europe, history had functioned as a health-ful tonic for too much reality. In Nova Scotia, history would also serve as a tonic, a healthful respite from too much trouble. Paul Fussell has usefully remarked that "pastoral" is instinct with elegy so that literary travel between the wars constituted an "implicit rejection of industrialism and everything implied by the concept of modern northern Europe." Cultivated interwar travellers sought the Golden Age, an imagined time that many placed in the middle of the preceding century. The point of travelling was to regain the past; thus, travel was an "adventure in time" as well as in distance.[80] In Bird's case, history is about travelling to an older, better time and travel is primarily a way to access history. Just as Bird personally found that writing gave him a form of occupational therapy as a wounded soldier, his stories take on the dimensions of communal therapy for an entire generation wounded by the Great War.

This communal therapy was in some respects Bird's own venture, but in other respects it resembled a government program. An unusual aspect of Bird's career was the extent to which – ironically for one who so strenuously cele-brated the classic virtues of the true individual – it took place within contexts constructed by the state. Bird became a civil servant. He worked for the new Nova Scotia Bureau of Information for three years in the 1920s, later resum-ing work for the province in 1933 after a seven-year absence. From 1933 to 1965, he comported himself as a semi-official "Mr Nova Scotia" whose appearances and publications bore the (oft-concealed but nonetheless quite real) imprimatur of the state. When he made speeches as the national president of the Canadian Authors Association, Bird was regularly introduced with the phrase "*This* is Nova Scotia."[81]

In no less than nineteen books written while he was in government employ, Bird helped tourists and Nova Scotians alike to see the province from his romantic perspective. Erasing the boundary between fact and fiction was part of his job. This becomes a little troublesome in a book like *An Earl Must Have a Wife*. This account of eighteenth-century Governor J.F.W. DesBarres may have been largely fictional, but it nevertheless incorporated (somewhat controversially) months of research paid for out of the provincial treasury.[82] Many of his historical novels use archival resources to heighten the verisimilitude of their imagined pasts, some of which are recycled from one product to another.[83] As Thomas Raddall does in his work, Bird uses specific historic details as reassuring reminders that the author has a total command of the milieus in which he sets his novels.

And We Go On hints at the psychological dilemmas of the soldier struggling to endure a horrifying reality, eventually to return home a "stranger to himself." Such introspection is foreign to the historical novels, which send dozens upon dozens of their characters hurtling through time and space while supplying only the barest indications of their subjectivities. As in the *Diamond Dick* dime novels, Bird's typical protagonist lives in a world inhabited by a cast of instantly identifiable heroes and villains who face black-and-white moral choices. The author relates their stories in short sentences stacked up on each other. It is as if the adult author of *And We Go On*, a book abounding in well-turned paragraphs expressing complicated sentiments, had regressed to writing, perpetually, for the *Boy's Own Annual*. A rather accomplished passage such as this one, from *And We Go On* −

> One came down from his post, chilled, half-dazed from lack of sleep, and pushed his way into the crowded underground to his chicken-wire bunk. There he could lay on his elbows and eat his rations, and consider himself lucky if there were any lukewarm tea to drink. The warmth of the men thawed the earthy walls enough to cause them to ooze water. Rats were everywhere, great, podgy brutes with fiendish, ghoulishly-gleaming eyes. They came at night on the parapets and startled one so that he thrust at them with his bayonet, or crawled over him as he lay under his blanket in his bunk trying to "shiver himself warm."[84]

− might translate into the language of Birdland as follows:

I left my post. I was cold and tired. I lay on my elbows and ate my rations. I was lucky to have cold tea. Rats were everywhere. They were big. They came at night. Sometimes they scared me. It was hard to keep warm.

Perhaps in part because of this style of writing, Bird's books found a huge audience. They could be appreciated by people with little formal education, by Maritimers impressed by Bird's attention to local detail, or by Canadians in search of a simpler and more innocent way of life, conveyed as much through Bird's childlike prose as through their content.

Bird won glowing accolades for his work – prizes (the Ryerson Press All-Canada Fiction Award in 1945 for *Here Stays Good Yorkshire* and in 1947 for *Judgment Glen*), positions (the presidency of the Canadian Authors Association), and even academic recognition (the University of Alberta Award for Literature and his treasured honorary doctorate from Mount Allison University). Most importantly, he also reached large audiences of ordinary readers. This was especially true with his travel books. Their narratives register pure, unrelated presents, connected to each other by only the slim thread of the author's itinerary. They are deceptively complicated productions, for he wrote with a directness and simplicity that tempt one to overlook the subtlety and power with which his way of seeing contours Nova Scotia. *This Is Nova Scotia* (1950) – which, at over five hundred thousand copies sold in North America, was Bird's all-time bestseller – is a study of happy primitives, written by a local trying to see with the tourist's eye.[85] He does not let on, for example, that he himself had written the text for many of the commemorative plaques he encountered on his tour. Birdland was not reality, but neither was it the imaginary world of a hopeless romantic.

Bird's brilliantly re-described Nova Scotia earned praise from reviewers and travellers alike. A critic from the Prairies claimed that "[w]hen one reads *This is Nova Scotia*, one knows the whole of Nova Scotia – the history, the geography, the people, the climate, the economy."[86] An Ontario journalist, perhaps in unconscious homage to Bird, expressed his approval with a list of the pleasantly quaint: "With Mr. Bird, we talk to the shad fishermen, see oxen in the hayfields, watch wooden ships being built, see the fishermen at Indian Harbor mending nets in the sun on the shore, climb the granite ledges of Peggy's Cove, visit old forts and churches, ramble through some of the last-remaining covered bridges, see the lobster traps piled high up at Sandford, and travel the Cabot Trail."[87] The fourth estate clearly grasped the therapeutic value of travelling the Bird way. "Mr. Bird has reproduced for a harried age the timeless beauty and color of Canada's most storied province," the *Winnipeg Tribune* exclaimed. The book offered a tour in itself: "The near-sacred legends, the characters and picturesque villages of Nova Scotia are adequately prepared for the arm-chair traveler."[88]

Bird presents his readers with a Nova Scotia devoid of all the noisy, confusing, and unfamiliar features of the 1950s – no "crowds and honking horns and the smell of gas and hot tires" here, as Bird reports a Vermont couple enthusing in *This Is Nova Scotia*'s very successful sequel.[89] Our tourist-narrator bumps into scores of rustic locals who, at a moment's notice, recite folksy stories in colourful dialects. The book's tone of drowsy serenity is sustained by a veritable chorus of Nova Scotians, salty old characters whose lives are open books awaiting the tourist-as-reader. Anyone weary of urban formality and anomic detachment might find a ready supply of warmth and understanding among these preternaturally chatty Nova Scotians.[90] Unlike the gloomy postwar Belgians, they are unmarked by the twentieth century. The quaint Cape Breton community of Sydney, for example, has so cleverly situated its steel mill that the prevailing winds carry "all smoke and odour" away from the city; the dumped slag paints "crimson sunsets on a skyline dotted with fine brick structures." The town echoes with tales of the colourful eighteenth century (not with the cries of the defiant strikers, unemployed workers, or raucous radicals that others reported having heard there).[91]

Bird offered his touristic sensibility to everyone. For the benefit of the locals, he recommended tourism as an economic salvation for a backward region. In *So Much to Record* (1951), set in "Carrsboro" (a thinly fictionalized version of Parrsboro, Cumberland County), he demonstrated how tourism had helped Nova Scotians regain the dignity they had supposedly lost following the Golden Age of Sail. Set between the 1890s and the 1910s, the novel portrays the arrival of American vacationers who spur a great construction boom as they build their summer cottages. The declining old seaport might just have a future as a great summer resort.

Such new economic circumstances present a test of character. Rather like the doomed weaklings in the trenches, the weaker Nova Scotians complained about the tourists. Carrsboro's ineffectual complainer Elaine, for example, whines about summer people who have "fine cottages and plenty of money but they were rotten inside." Other weak-willed Carrsboronians think the summer people have "no more religion than [a] cat."[92] Unperturbed by these grouches, our strong and effective hero John Winstill sets his own independent course. Scion of an old Carrsboro shipping family embodying the community's true values, he is master of his fate and skipper of his own vessel. He can face down adversity – a triple whammy of shipwreck, suicide, and insolvency (briskly delivered in the first fifty pages). Revealingly, he will restore his family's shipping fortune by making, not ships, but *model ships*. Tourists snap them up. John prospers. The Age of Sail returns, albeit in miniature. While many around him bemoan their fates, he gets rich. He wins back the old family mansion, earlier seized by a pasty-faced and loose-living banker. It is all thanks to tourism. The weak will flee the province, disgusted by the fickleness and economic instability of the tourist trade. The strong will wisely realize that they can use the new culture of consumption to redeem the values and traditions of the venerable Age of Sail. Just like Bird, they could answer carping critics of their inauthentic products or shallow worldview by pointing proudly to the bottom line.

Bird's 1950s travel books endorse the cultural logic of the new age of tourism even more directly. They rather obviously de-emphasize or simply avoid unpleasant realities, but – more subtly – they insinuate a fully-formed Province of History through Bird's tone of voice. In earlier writings on the province, Bird had flat-out declared Nova Scotia pre-industrial and romantic. In these later works, he implies Innocence more effectively by filtering all perceptions of Nova Scotia through the persona of the Bird-the-naive-narrator. Here he describes his accommodations in Bridgetown:

> The room she [the innkeeper] gave us was large, and the wallpaper was cheerful. A large engraving of the Twelve Apostles gazed at us from the space beside the closet door. An angel in blue outlines with a rather heavy-looking harp watched us from the far side, and a calendar of a little girl patting a dog was over the head of the bed.
>
> We made up our notes for the day and descended the stairs, thinking to go out for a stroll and an ice cream somewhere. The prim lady appeared at her parlour door and invited us to join her. "I took you in for company, much as anything," she said. "It isn't easy for me to talk with some of the people around here, but I always get on well with strangers."
>
> It wasn't an impressive beginning, but we entered and sat on big chairs that were very comfortable. The black cat came in and curled up on a horsehair sofa. The prim woman sat beside it and folded her hands limply, then began to talk.[93]

He presents us with one thing after another, portraying each just as it comes, leaving us awash in a flood of sensory impressions. Each thing means just what it seems to mean. The wallpaper, the cat, and the engraving – each object completely fills the absolute present of the moment. Tourists who read the book could imagine a timeless land of wide-eyed childhood. A perpetual golden glow suffuses these Maritimes.

To demand anything beyond immediate experience is to bring adult criteria into a realm of fairy-tale enchantment. There is no risk here of the professorial negativity that so threatened all concerned in *And We Go On*. Visitors to Birdland will find themselves in an unexplainable world, but will be the happier for it. Bird's old-fashioned storytellers inhabit a serene realm of parlour organs, gentle barnyard animals, and bucolic scenery. What about the rest of us? How can we moderns regain innocent and unproblematic happiness? Bird genially tutors his readers in how to refashion themselves by means of numerous vignettes in which he encounters American tourists. Everything is wonderful for them. A smiling family man from Massachusetts typifies their elation as he tells Bird of his unadulterated joy at visiting a Williamsdale fish hatchery: "Boy! Say, I never saw a fish hatchery before. And we saw a rabbit on the road. And we're going to picnic somewhere on a logging road in here. These country roads are wonderful!" Just about all Bird's tourists are of the same mind.[94]

Tourists in Birdland prove themselves adept at spitting out little speeches that amount to perfectly modulated product-satisfaction testimonials on behalf of the bureau that employed their newfound friend Will Bird. They share a uniform propensity to confirm their contentment by making a list of pleasant things. A Vermont couple excitedly tells Bird, "We love the salt water ... and we saw it at Windsor but we're going to find your Noel Shore and watch that tide come in two miles. That's the sort of thing we want, and we can hardly wait till morning to get over to Bear River and have a treat of those cherries. We stopped at Uniacke House on the way, and at Haliburton House at Windsor, and we were to Grand Pre Park."[95] Salt water, Windsor, high tides, cherries, historic houses, and parks are all very nice things for the Vermonters, just as fish, rabbits, and picnics are very nice things for the man from Massachusetts. These items, one after another, do not just summarize a travelogue – they define a whole form of consciousness. One need not actually be a tourist to enjoy it. Maritimers could too, as Bird shows us by his own example. He summons up New Brunswick with a list of his favourite things: "Oysters – lobsters – pulpwood – shore line – forest – waterfalls – handcraft – covered bridge – pottery – park – tree-shaded streets."[96] In this passage, which he writes in his own voice rather than ventriloquizing a tourist, he is freed from the necessity of fashioning his list into plausible dialogue that someone might have spoken to him unbidden over the course of a chance encounter. Through list-making, Bird resolves his society into tasty seafood, attractive scenery, and quaint byways.

When social relations (particularly unequal ones) threaten to obtrude such that they call to mind certain connections between all of these isolated things, Bird can always drive away. Motoring through Cape Breton, "it was as if a spell descended on us, the spell of seascape and great reaches of wild beauty, of sparsely settled country and a different atmosphere." In Inverness, however, the spell lifted. Instead of ghost stories and moose-hunting yarns, the Bird family heard some frank talk (reminiscent of glum Belgian peasants) "about closed mines and hardship and lack of co-operation by authorities and hard times and some families with little to eat. But the youngsters we saw looked happy enough and hardy enough and we hoped that some day coal mining would start again."[97] Having assuaged their consciences with their good wishes, they continued down the road to see the memorial to John Cabot at Cape North. The spell obligingly descended again.

Bird ingeniously converted a mode of conveyance – the automobile – into a way of mediating one's relations with the world. Motorists could easily insinuate themselves into a locale where they were complete strangers, then just as easily leave again without having contracted any particular obligation towards the people whom they encountered. One could resurrect the innocence of childhood – the ever-repeated excitement of meeting new grown-ups with great stories – then tootle away when the stories ended or stopped being fun. The province becomes a series of experiences to consume quickly, then to casually discard. In this idealized childhood, reality consists of overwhelmingly vivid sights and sounds that defeat any attempt at contextualization because one still lacks any analytic categories. Yet, at the same time, the sine qua non of this perpetual childhood is the sophisticated automotive infrastructure of mass tourism. The road to perpetual Innocence runs through consumer culture.

Bird consciously chose Innocence as a strategy, in adulthood, for grown-up reasons. In certain places, he made a return to childhood very literal. Contemplating an abandoned farm near Amherst (the countryside where he grew up), his family "stopped … and wondered if some man in a remote part had been a boy around the place." Now they proceeded to imagine a childhood for the hypothetical boy. They saw him "enjoying a feeling of security as he tended sleek horses and placid cows, jumping from the scaffold to piles of hay pitched to the barn floor for supper feeding." Captivated, they get out of the car to walk around the yard. They find an old cellar, the sight of which fills Bird with nostalgic longing: "If you have any feeling for history, there is poignant meaning in old cellars that tell of yesteryear."[98] Bird prizes a sort of communion with an array of objects that may have lost their immediate utility but can thereby, because they seem to have lost contact with the present day, act as portals to a blessed state of Innocence that has by their felicitous agency been vested in a homogenized past – a past devoid of events and lit but softly.

One such object is the parlour organ. Bird makes great claims for its affective properties. "In these days a man can watch television and see lady wrestlers pull hair and kick and scratch until he has no qualms about the pioneering qualities of modern womanhood," he claims, in a rare moment of explicit cultural criticism. "The parlour organ belongs to a quieter and more flavourful era of our history." The mere sight of such an instrument in the home of a sweet old lady brings back that elusive era when "on a cold, starlit winter evening it was heart-warming as friends and family gathered around the organ and mother played old familiar home songs and cherished hymns. Voices were not trained, but were rich and true ... The last piece was always 'God Be with You till We Meet Again.' Then the boy took his lamp and climbed the stairs and all the world was safe and happy."[99]

Insensibly, over the course of this reverie, the "man" watching television, confused about the gender roles enacted before him, becomes a "boy" going to bed with a sleepy head, secure in the knowledge that everyone was just as they ought to be. It is the child, not the man, who finds himself beside the parlour organ. An adult would have come to this situation lumbered with too many memories, afflicted with too acute an awareness of how contingent and insecure were all of the elements of the scene. As so often with imagined pasts, the whole point of evoking them is to access "a time when folk did not feel fragmented, when doubt was either absent or patent, when thought fused with action, when aspiration achieved consummation, when life was whole-hearted."[100] What Bird knew so well was that such a state of mind is incompatible with adulthood. He knew that (as was the case with young Mickey in the trenches) sequential thought inevitably punctures childlike contentment. Innocence can only survive in the way adults imagine childhood might have been like, now that they are no longer children.

Bird leveraged this profound insight into his long, profitable tenure as Mr Nova Scotia. To market his province, he tantalized his readers with the proposition that Innocence lay just within reach as soon as they sighted the piper at the border. Having entered Canada's ocean playground, one could insert oneself into Bird's "narrative that breathes and throbs with the good life." One could recover from the strain of living in a conflicted world, whose solid components had long since melted into air, by inserting oneself into the holism that flourished "where salty little villages are spaced in unexpected places along a jigsaw coastline, where mellowed inland clearings offer drowsy summer afternoons and wild berries for the hiker ... where memories have gathered giving depth and meaning to the lives of a people who always had leisure to be kind."[101]

However, only certain kinds of interaction with the people possessed of the "leisure to be kind" were advisable. Hoping for good stories in Fredericton, Bird instead found himself accosted by a crank who pressed him to use his book to talk about regional underdevelopment – to decry the way federal economic policies systematically marginalized the region. The whole vacation was suddenly imperilled. As Bird tells it, "[W]e had to leave him as such ideas could become headaches and we wanted to be fresh for Highway 9 the next day." "Ideas could become headaches" and ought to be avoided. Thus did the Birds earlier fly away from another politically inclined interlocutor in Woodstock, New Brunswick, since "it was easy to see he carried a heavy grouch, and he was still shaking his head as we drove away and inhaled a beautiful morning, one with no room for a growler."[102] Public affairs were just a lot of growling. People interested in them were just grouchy. Could they not see that the sun was shining? Their discussions were unpleasant and, ultimately, pointless. Grouches would always growl about something. That was what grouches did. Bird wrote off discontent as a bad mood or an incurable debility inherent to congenital killjoys. Given the terms of Bird's discussion, it could have been no other way. Birdland lacks any means for analysis, abstraction, or explanation. Neither the social, nor economic, nor philosophical can exist there. Instead, Innocence becomes a form of consciousness fulfilling a particular ideological function – one it performs all the better because its vocabulary rules out any systematic thinking capable of discerning ideology or function. It is a fine addition to the repertoire of liberal political styles, all of which seek to efface their politico-economic origins by making talk about social relations impossible in their terms.

This Is Nova Scotia might seem like the spontaneous production of a charmingly ingenuous man. In fact, a state functionary with an exquisitely sensitive marketing nose for the North American culture of consumption had manufactured this picturesque portrait at public expense. Bird was no innocent. Acquainted with the North American cultural marketplace for three decades, he knew which sales pitch would work. The shrewd merchant of romance felt sure his books brought business to Nova Scotia. He even advised Premier Angus L. Macdonald that one commercial establishment he had mentioned in his book viewed Bird's recommendation as better than any amount of conventional advertising.[103]

Bird's modus operandi as a tourism professional was to disaggregate the context of Nova Scotian society into a series of easily digested experiences. Rather like John Winstill in *So Much to Record* (Winstill earned big bucks by returning in adulthood to the childlike occupation of model-building), Bird creates a vast array of diminutive historical vignettes that will appeal to the American and Canadian tourist. They will be enticed, not by the prospect of recognizing a grand narrative in which they themselves might be implicated (such as revolution, slavery, capitalism), but by many little stories whose very charm lies in their remoteness from any contemporary issue – their message of ingratiating reassurance summed up in dollhouses, miniature golf courses, and lawn ornaments.

In their foreword to Bird's *Historic Nova Scotia*, Percy C. Black (minister of highways) and L.W. Fraser (director of information) sound almost like Bird himself as they wax poetically: "There is hardly a hill or a valley, a lake, an island or a headland within [Nova Scotia's] boundaries which does not hold some tradition or legend, some story of sacrifice, of heroism or of devotion."[104] As well as ship's models, one might sell "first things" and "splendid sights" to the tourists – small, anodyne, unthreatening replicas of long-gone romantic experiences. One could come to the Land of Evangeline and imagine the "First Gardener" (Samuel de Champlain), the first permanent settlement in North America (Port Royal), and so on.[105]

Bird's histories, like his tourist literature, identify complexity, controversy, and revisionism with the mean-spirited. A grouch might represent the eighteenth-century invasion of Acadia by New Englanders as a hostile act of war. A true Birdian would realize that it also, and more crucially, anticipated the tourism industry. When the invaders relax at a serene Fort Cumberland, it is as if they had come to Nova Scotia, not to trouble the Acadians, but to drink in lovely Chignecto's scenery. They gaze upon the "wealth of beauty" encircling the hill. The Chignecto Basin glimmers in the sunshine, with "silvery ribbons" of rivers splitting the marshes. "Hazy in the heat, dark blue in the distance, the forest-crowned mountains of Shepbody and Cobequid rimmed the horizon. And across in distant Minudie and at Tantramar the white-washed homes of the Acadians were enbosomed in scenes of plenty." We can imagine the American leaders of the invasion strolling over the ridge, "drinking in the rich aroma of the marsh grass freshened by salty tangs from the sea."[106] With a little repackaging, every incident in provincial history can become a marketable costume drama.

In the Acadia of 1755, one finds "a perfect 'Indian summer'" – a clime that "made the venture of the English a very pleasant outing. All the gorgeous colourings of our hardwoods enhanced the beauty of the hillsides as they skirted lakes, crossed rivers and paralleled the trail their quarry had taken." Everyone is a tourist. There is no experience beyond the tourist gaze. A grouch might harp on Acadian suffering during the English "venture" of 1755. A Birdian would imagine that even the many fleeing Acadians would pause to drink in the simply breathtaking scenery of the land, which many of them would never see again. After a brisk paragraph acknowledging that their deportation entailed some unpleasantness, Bird devotes many more lines to the more urgent question of the pots of gold the Acadians might have buried in the scenic countryside. They even left behind an enigmatic stone, on which are chiselled "quaint characters that have entertained visitors ever since the fall of Beausejour." Might these weird petroglyphs hold the key to their buried treasure? "There must be scores of hiding places never yet revealed," Bird remarks breathlessly. He adds, as further enticement to the tourist motivated by money as much as memory, the tale of a local farmer who found so much gold "that he moved to the States and lived comfortably without working for the remainder of his days."[107]

If hunting for treasure got boring, one could turn to the many romantic tales of the 1750s. A grouch might insist that the Missiquash, a short river along the border of New Brunswick and Nova Scotia, lacks those qualifications (waterfalls, Riesling, castles, even much of a current) expected in riparian applicants for the title "The Rhine of North America." For all its tidal peculiarities, the Missiquash (aka Missaguash) looks to the skeptical eye like a forgettable muddy stream.[108] Bird would instantly point out that the bog-fed Missiquash sparkles with the romance of a bygone day, for here, in the latter days of September 1754, a little band of Acadians defied the mad priest Le Loutre's orders, deciding to move to the British side of the river. Alas, they drowned. Fortunately, their ghosts remain, adding allure to a romantically challenged river.

Similarly, when tourists glimpsed an otherwise generic red-stone chasm of the Tantramar, they could thrill to "another tale of Micmac horror." The typically diabolic Indians had captured "an officer and his sweetheart," brought them by canoe to the river, and tied them to stakes, there to await the coming tide. The "red men" even fastened the girl to a post "purposely set higher so that she might witness the death of her lover." If these details had failed to endow the scene with sufficient romance, one could add another: on the verge of rescue, the girl (in accordance with the laws of love, if not physiology) thrust her head beneath the lapping waters "and died before they could release her." Only after we have become entranced by the tale do we encounter the discrete caveat, "Charles G.D. Roberts has put the episode, be it tradition or fact, into a vivid and poignant tale." Setting aside the tedious "facts of the matter," here was a tale to enliven tourist journeys – much as it had once provided the garrison with "much material with which to wile away dull hours."[109] Star-crossed lovers, bloodthirsty "savages," selfless heroines – who could ask for anything more? So what if some growler demanded evidence?

These examples typify Bird's relentless promotion of Chignecto, site of heavy state investments in heritage during the 1920s and 1930s. Bird christened Fort Monckton the "Gateway to the Land of Evangeline." In 1927 alone, over a thousand tourists had tarried by the old fortifications. Once the government had completed its work of restoration, "it will soon become a Mecca for tourists," whom Bird thought would come from distant parts to imagine "the intrigue of Pichon, the spy clerk, exchanging French confidences for English coin." They could fancy "the chapel bell of the Acadians, see candles gleaming in their cottages, and watch Acadian lovers in the moonlight among the old orchards of Beausejour." Or they could walk through the picturesque ruins, whose "very atmosphere carries one back to those days when all disputes were settled by the sword, when torch and tomahawk were rampant in the night, when romance was entangled with all frontier history and spying played its part in every struggle."[110]

We will not come to understand Birdland by trying to distinguish fact from fiction, since Bird shades them into each other. Bird self-consciously presents the "factual" *A Century at Chignecto* as an "entertaining" antidote to dry-as-dust history whose "jumbled dates and lists of rulers" so quickly bored us in "our youth."[111] Bird's history does not ask us to learn anything we do not already know. Instead, it transports us to a perpetual time of adventure – war as imagined by a little boy, with the occasional selfless hero's death, abounding in fierce "Indians" and even treasure-burying pirates constructed on the template of *Peter Pan*. Chignecto becomes Neverland. Tourists real and notional could now savour, in the words of Fred W. Munroe (quoted *in extenso* by Bird), an evening at Fort Monckton: "There is a low moon adrift on a cloudless sky, and a glint of pale gold on Baie Verte's still water. As we wander about the barrack-square, it seems to us that a high palisade marks its bounds again. Look through this loophole. Over there looms a dark forest of fir trees – haunt of warlike redskins once more."[112] A bit like the nicely restored trenches of Belgium, and even more like a summer camp, the playground with a history did not demand that its visitors understand anything. It merely laid out the details of romantic scenes they could pleasurably imagine.

Even when he is not avowedly spinning a yarn, we cannot be entirely easy about whether Bird is telling us the truth. Suspiciously, his nonfictional Nova Scotians all tell much the same kinds of stories in the same tone of voice using Bird-like singsong sentence structures. One story in particular arouses nagging doubts. Nor was it just any old anecdote. In a classic instance of putting a dollar value on folk romanticism, Bird told one audience that eleven hundred visitors had come to the province in direct response to the story of shy Willie Anderson. Willie built himself a house with four trees as corner posts. As the trees grew, they lifted the house off the ground. The story's success proved, Bird said, the "importance of romance" in the promotion of tourism. In *This Is Nova Scotia,* the tale comes from the mouth of a colourful rustic (complete with a "stubble chin" and a stalk of timothy in his mouth). Bird's after-dinner speech, however, attributed this same tale to the Cape Breton author and journalist Dawn Fraser. If Bird got the story from a timothy-chewing hayseed, he got it second-hand.[113] But that hardly mattered. Marshalling eleven hundred visitors trumped recourse to empirical evidence.

This Is Nova Scotia recounts a new kind of history bathed in a serene, sunlit atemporality. Indeed, so timeless was Bird's pastoral vision that McGraw-Hill Ryerson decided that it could put the book through its eighth printing as late as 1972. Even its author balked at the idea of reissuing a book for tourists of the 1970s that omitted the Trans-Canada Highway, boosted an expired tuna festival, and promoted defunct hotels.[114] The publishers brought it out anyway, arguing cogently (as they proclaimed on the dust jacket) that *This Is Nova Scotia* had captured "the true flavour of Nova Scotia – aged in wood and salt water, with a tang all its own."[115] They sensed even better than Bird himself that the facts mattered less than the feelings – above all, the recaptured feeling of the child hearing one story after another, safe and secure in a cozy province that held no disquieting histories to keep one up after bedtime.

Bird offered his uniquely attuned sensibilities to the state. In his position as assistant director of publicity with the Bureau of Information, he churned out copy. "Would you care for an article on Oak Island, our 'buried treasure' mystery?" he asked a publisher. "Or a story of Peggy's Cove? Of our quaint old churches? Of our annual Gaelic Mod? Of the founding of Halifax?"[116] In 1955, after Bird had left the bureau, the government brought him back as a writer on the strength of his excellent publishing record. In 1957, Bird wrote Premier Robert Stanfield that he had had stories either published in or accepted by twenty publications (ranging from the *Canadian Geographic Magazine* to the *Springfield Republican*). He boasted that it would have cost the province more than nine thousand dollars to purchase as advertising space the coverage he had obtained gratis.[117] Accordingly, he asked for a raise.[118]

As important as his writing was, it does not represent the sum of Bird's service in popularizing tourism in Nova Scotia. Just as important were his efforts as a public speaker, almost as a travelling pitchman. By the 1950s, having polished his craft in many Legion presentations on the Great War, Bird had become a gifted and indefatigable public-relations man. In 1972, he estimated that he had given 1,552 speeches at dinners, luncheons, and graduations.[119] An undated note lists some of his engagements in 1949 and 1959. He spoke to the Halifax Rotary, the Bank of Nova Scotia, the Gyros and Gyrettes of Windsor, the Musquodoboit Board of Trade, the Wolfville Lions Club, the Rotary Convention in Yarmouth, the Chemical Institute of Canada, the Regina Gyros, the Canadian Manufacturers Association, the Y's Men's Club of Yarmouth, the Commercial Club Ladies' Night, etcetera, etcetera, ad infinitum.[120]

In his tourist work, Bird was simultaneously an insider who claimed privileged access to the innermost secrets of Nova Scotia history and an outsider who connected the locals to circuits of capital and technology. When Nova Scotians opened their monthly telephone bills, out might pop a Birdian missive – also included in *Telephone Lines*, a promotional magazine distributed free by the Maritime Telegraph and Telephone Company, Limited (MT&T). Bird's telephone tales were folksy and direct. In 1953's "Keep Your Powder Dry,"

Bird told a funny story about the simple people of Arichat who had tried to fire their cannon – the pride of their community – only to find that the damp powder would not light. A "fish hand" and his friends chanced upon the scene. This fish hand tapped out his pipe at the breech of the gun, whereupon "[t]he gun rocked on its ancient platform and it is legend in Arichat that the poor fellow who had been seated on it came down to earth with his feet going and never stopped running until he was in Grand Anse."[121] In the same issue that carried Bird's story, MT&T announced yet another takeover of a local company's telephone territory (serendipitously, the one in Arichat itself). Why complain about a company with monopoly powers buying up its competitors when it was so obviously down with the Folk?

MT&T was a centralized node of monopoly capital, developing a new industrial plant. It proudly touted its "New Halifax–Saint John Radio System" that extended 134 miles direct, eliminating tedious local go-rounds: "The radio beam … travels in line of sight so 5 relay towers located between 20 to 30 miles apart at high vantage points, are needed to clear obstructions and to compensate for the curvature of the earth."[122] Bird and MT&T came bundled in one convenient package. He could remind Nova Scotians of the extraordinary role that coincidence and luck played in their lives –

> During World War I a man from Kings County was going on leave and wondered whether or not his cousin, serving in another division, had survived the Vimy show. He had not heard from him in a year. In the last mail he received before going on leave was a newspaper clipping from an aunt. The clipping described Nelson's Monument in London and stated some observers declared the stone face of Nelson lighted on a Friday, the day of his greatest victory. So the soldier on leave went to view the statue on a Friday – and there stood his cousin, holding in his hands a clipping he, too, had received from the same aunt!

– while the phone company reminded its customers what a wonderful bargain it was giving them in terms of "value and dependability."[123] Mr Nova Scotia and MT&T were clearly a team.

Bird's career suggests the widening scope for state cultural intervention, which aimed not at hindering but at hastening the commodification of culture. He was working in essence as an organic intellectual of a new type, one who combined promotional activities with creative writing in the interests of enhancing the state-supported service sector. Yet he did not view himself that way. He longed for professional status of a more traditional sort. An autodidact without a university education, he cherished the honorary doctorate bestowed upon him by Mount Allison University; *This Is Nova Scotia* was the work of Will R. Bird, "Litt.D." Although he may have written many books, it was left to Bird himself to plead his own case for official honours (perhaps an Order of Canada?).[124] In the uncertainty of his professional status, Bird paid the price of his otherwise rewarding career in public relations and local history.

◆

Bird practised a strange kind of history that never historicized. The social, political, and economic disappear from all his texts. Society is organized by everything except organization. Character can more than compensate for this analytical paucity as it powerfully (if tacitly) structures this imagined terrain. Inborn moral dispositions – as articulated by gender, race, and ethnicity – order the world by virtue of their irrepressible determination of what is possible for different people. Events, however alarming or even deadly, lack the force to alter this timeless natural order. Yet events proliferate. As the Montreal *Gazette* noted, Bird's *The Passionate Pilgrim* had everything: "hangings and scalpings and buried treasure, Indians and friendship, told with such a gusto you can't put it down." Dorothy Dumbrille (who would do for Ontario's Glengarry County what Bird had done for Chignecto) found the book "packed with incident and drama. The courage and endurance of the pioneers dominate a story that thrills with passion and romance."[125] Bird, critics agreed, was a master of historical fiction.

Widely considered Bird's greatest novel, *Here Stays Good Yorkshire* (Joint Winner of the Ryerson Fiction Award in 1945) narrates the arrival of the Yorkshiremen who settled Cumberland County in the 1770s. As the jacket enthuses, "into the writing of this story has gone a life-time of research. Every detail is etched with fidelity and affectionate care."[126] Bird proudly announced that he had consulted the eminences of Maritime historical scholarship, including D.C. Harvey and J.S. Martell at the Public Archives of Nova Scotia, Muriel Kinnear at the Public Archives of Canada, J.C. Webster at the New Brunswick Museum, and J.B. Brebner at Columbia University. The truth is a little more complicated. The book occupies that hinterland between fiction and nonfiction that its author made his stomping grounds. Bird himself rhetorically disclaimed pretensions to historical realism: "This novel is not written as authentic history. It is, rather, an attempt to tell of the rooting of Yorkshire settlements in Cumberland, Nova Scotia."[127]

Here Stays Good Yorkshire is many things: a history and a fiction, a product for the marketplace, and an intensely personal homage to Bird's own family.[128] To its publisher, however, it was primarily a study in character – and one for which Ryerson made bold claims. "When you have read this book," claims the promotional blurb, "you will have a vivid and unforgettable picture of the founding of one of the most interesting parts of Canada. You will also have added to your portrait gallery of the great characters in Canadian fiction Tristram Crabtree."[129] Tristram – whose adventures would fill two more books (*Despite the Distance* and *Tristram's Salvation*) and whose descendants in the twentieth century would take up another (*The Shy Yorkshireman*) – seems to be Bird's game stab at the sort of hard-edged anti-hero who was something of a specialty of his friend Thomas Raddall.

Most of Bird's Yorkshiremen are wholesome folk imbued with an apple-cheeked vitality and instinctive decency. Tristram is not. He is "a heavy man with immense shoulders and arms, swarthy, with thick hairs on the backs of his hands and wrists, with small tufts in his ears, and black shaggy brows." His rough exterior conceals a rough interior. He is a bull of a man. When he and his brother Matthew (a bully of Tristram's dark and brutal ilk) fight, "their struggle was like that of yoked oxen, a tremendous straining and wrenching."[130] A deep-seated, uncontrollable aggression impels them.

Melody, Patience, Jonathan, and Lancelot, the other Crabtree siblings, just cannot understand their two dark-haired brothers, who seem so unlike themselves. Discussing Tristram's latest outburst of unreasonable anger, Melody asks Jonathan, "What makes him so? ... Thear's times, Jonty, when he don't seem oor brother."[131] Lo and behold, it is true. A little more than a hundred pages into the book, we learn that Tristram and Matthew are not really their brothers. They have different paternity. When Tristram learns that he and Matthew are the children, not of gentle Asa Crabtree, but of vicious Barney Scurr, it suddenly all makes sense. Why are he and Matthew knuckle-dragging brutes? They were born to it. They simply cannot be any other way. In contrast, their siblings – made of better stuff – are constitutionally incapable of the casual brutality and absolute selfishness that actuate their illegitimate half-brothers.

All of the seeming misfortunes that befall Tristram in fact come as the inescapable consequences of inherited moral turpitude. Although a skilled farmer who works with superhuman determination, he sees all of his ventures fail. He works an abandoned homestead, but then its owners return to claim it. He marries an apparent widow, but then her missing husband resurfaces. He fights bravely for the king, but then his gangrenous foot has to be amputated. Recuperating from this wound in a remote farmhouse, he broods about how "life did not add up. It did not seem worth while." On the wall across the room from his bed there hangs a sampler whose text "bothered him" (and which provides the reader with the moral of the whole story): "If your heart is wrong the world is against you."[132] His trials and tribulations are not really misfortunes at all. Chance and contingency had nothing to do with them. His own bioeth-ical constitution leads him to act in ways that invite disasters a thoughtful reader can easily foresee, but which Tristram, the son of Barney Scurr, never does.

Tristram buys a menacing black bull, an animal he loves but which terrifies everyone else. "Yon's an ugly devil," a neighbour warns him. The oblivious Tristram, seeming not to hear him, "watched with pride as the powerful ani-mal, disdaining the yearling nearby, pawed the earth and shattered the silences with mad bellowing." He loves the animal because it is exactly like himself. The usually callous man genuinely cares for it as he seems not to care for any-one else. One blazing hot summer day, the tethered beast becomes maddened with discomfort, its eyes "shot with changing lights" that "seemed to emanate a smouldering temper."[133] With misplaced charity, Tristram frees the bull of its bothersome chain. It proceeds to vent its wrath on its would-be comforter, nearly killing him. Perhaps reminiscent of the "bull-throated" officers Bird met in the trenches, Tristram loves violence and belligerence, believing them strength. He cannot understand their dangers any more than the bull can. What appears to be bad luck— being gored by one's own bull on one's own farm — results from a character flaw.

This book invites us to judge Tristram (and in so doing teaches its readers to avoid spite, greed, and bullying), but it also renders such moral judgments beside the point. Tristram is the perpetrator of his misdeeds, but hardly their author. He cannot help being what he is. Moral choices do not really exist for him, since in order to make them differently he would have to be somebody else, to have had different parents, to be well bred and not the spawn of a sub-human. The other characters know this. His good brother Lancelot makes a pet of an orphaned bear cub. In a spasm of wanton violence, Tristram kills it one morning and hides the corpse. Later, tormented by his conscience, he admits what he has done. Lancelot remains calm, for the news has come as no surprise. "I reckoned it wur. Jonty would not do t' like," he explains impas-sively.[134] Lancelot has no reason to reprimand Tristram, because there is no real possibility that he could modify his behaviour. The promptings of his con-science cannot actually produce anything other than remorse in Tristram, nor will that last long.

In a dramatic moment late in the novel, a guilty Tristram confesses his sins before the whole community. "I'm cursed wi' sin," he sobs. "I've worked harder than most o' thee know, all wi' thinking of nowt but gain. It's bigger fields I've wanted, more cattle, bigger barns — to gloat over like a merchant wi' his money." The townsfolk, too kind-hearted to hold a grudge, readily for-give him. In that moment, Tristram reverts to type. Now "a sense of triumph seized him. He was being admired. He would be admired in the settlement, pointed to with pride." Self-congratulation sabotages salvation. Soon he loses himself in daydreams of omnipotence. In his blessed state, his neighbours will admire him "for his possessions, respecting him as a Christian."[135] He cannot repent even when he confesses. He lacks any capability for appreciating the dignity and value of others, so he can envisage no relationship with them other than domination. Even when he bares his soul, his base nature keeps him from having a religious experience.

The Yorkshire novels bring to the fore a theme dear to Bird's heart: the persistence, in generation after generation and in defiance of all circumstances that might alter it, of character. The call of the blood is strong. Resistance is futile. Bird seldom dwelt upon this theme specifically, being a man who studiously avoided clear-cut declarations of principle. Adopting a bemused tone, he wrote to one admirer, "Of The Shy Yorkshireman, one critic said I was wrong in having heredity make the characters act as they did, as such stuff was a myth, and another said I had ignored heredity, which governed such types as I wrote about."[136] To say Bird ignored heredity in *The Shy Yorkshireman* – the fourth and final Yorkshire novel – does the man a gross injustice. He filled this book up with mysterious, intractable tensions that can only resolve themselves once it comes to light in the last chapter just what parentage everyone actually has. As his response itself suggested, his characters are often "reverting to type."[137]

Ryerson Press promoted *The Shy Yorkshireman*, starring a cast of Crabtree descendants in early twentieth-century Cumberland County, as "a moving tale of unusual emotional impact, a tender, bittersweet tale of love." Chapter titles like "You're Not a Very Good Liar, Alicia!", "Didn't Grandfather Leave Any Will?", and "No, Robin, No! It Isn't Right!" all suggest the book's atmosphere of secret guilt, manipulative intrigue, and imperilled innocence. The character in the middle of this highly charged milieu, Robin Crabtree, resembles his author insofar as he too grows up on a rural farm near Amherst, serves bravely in the First World War, and takes up an Alberta homestead only to heed the call of home again. Most importantly, early in life, he also loses his father (who dies selflessly saving people from a burning building). The father's death hits his son hard: "Robin's head throbbed and he felt sick all over. Each time he started to think he broke out in new sobbing. It was the end of everything."[138]

The rest of Robin's family members seem curiously unmoved by Tom Crabtree's heroic demise. Particularly diffident is Robin's eldest sister, Esther, who seems to have nothing in common with either Robin or his middle sister, Alicia. Where the two of them are fair, Esther is dark. Where they are generous, she is greedy. Where they are kind, she is cruel. Alicia submits to their unnatural home life, surrendering her will to her sister and mother. Robin cannot stand it, however. The little blond boy screams at his distant mother and wicked sister Esther, "I hate you! I hate both of you! I always will! I hate you!

I hate you!" And once again, emphatically (if somewhat superfluously), "I hate you!"[139] Precociously recognizing that he is not the same as they are, Robin renounces kinship with them.

Robin's declaration of independence notwithstanding, his family stymies and stifles him at every turn. Most gravely, they keep him from his true love Nellie Jack. Nellie is surely beautiful and talented, but regrettably cursed with the misfortune of having as her mother the degenerate alcoholic and loose woman Mary Jack. That the daughter of such a creature should marry into a respectable family simply cannot bear thinking about. The trio of censorious Crabtree women will do everything possible to keep her away from Robin. The boy's wise grandfather, however, knows that since Robin has "stubborn blood," he will overcome any possible obstacle barring him from the woman he loves. Furthermore, there is nothing to worry about where Nellie is concerned. She is nothing like her dissolute parent. As the poor but honest cousin Burdy explains to Alicia, Nellie has "got good stuff in her and she's got on in spite of what people have said about her. Today she's just as good-looking as you, she's dressed just as good, and she's every bit as smart as you are."[140] Alicia does not understand how it could possibly happen that Nellie could have so unaccountably risen above her origins. Nor does she understand how Robin could always find himself so at odds with the rest of the family, nor why her sister and her mother seem not to love her and Robin as much as they ought. Sadly, she falls ill and dies before she can learn the truth.

The truth comes out after the grandfather's death when Robin and Nellie discover some of his closely guarded personal papers in a locked chest. Nellie is really the lovechild of the kind-hearted Susan Mallow and a distinguished lawyer, placed with the execrable Mary Jack by her college student mother because she had no other options. No wonder she has been good all along, as her good breeding has proven impervious to any environmental influence. The conniving Esther, meanwhile, was also conceived out of wedlock – her mother had her by an English "wastrel" whom the grandfather paid off to leave town. All of a sudden, Robin can see everything clearly. Heredity is destiny. As he notes, "[W]e can't blame Esther in any way," since her greed and irresponsibility have been with her since the moment of her conception.[141] How right Burdy has been. All the characters in the novel have simply recapitulated the capacities and character traits bequeathed them by dint of their parentage.

As the Crabtree family saga demonstrates, Bird credits even the slightest variances in heredity with drastic implications. What is true on a familial level is also true on a racial level. Thousands of years can suddenly erupt into the present, as the accumulated characteristics of one's stock powerfully assert themselves. Lancelot Crabtree, one of Tristram's good brothers in *Here Stays*

Good Yorkshire, negotiates the Nova Scotia woods with such aplomb because "some inherited strain in Lancelot's blood gave him a true hunter's instinct. Ancestors with brass-studded leather shields and inadequate spears, relying on their wits as they pursued a stag or wild boar, had passed along an instinctive understanding of creatures in the wild and an inherent love of the forest."[142] Lancelot exemplifies Bird's efforts to idealize certain virile men, particularly Highlanders and Yorkshiremen. (After all, as a kilted soldier of Yorkshire descent, Bird himself had combined the essential characteristics of both.)

As it was in fiction, so it was in fact. In *Off-Trail in Nova Scotia*, Bird treats us to many, many stories concerning feats of strength. He eagerly sought them out. Arriving in a Cape Breton hamlet, his family ask the locals, "'Were there any big fellows?' thinking of strong men." The chatty locals treat them to a tale of "Maggie's Bill" – a three hundred–pound farmer who, having broken his plough because he did not know his own strength, walks to town to buy a replacement. Blithely slinging the new plough over one shoulder, he starts home, stopping only to buy a great sack of bran to cushion his arm whilst he toted the great implement. Then there was Archie Minnis, the Nova Scotia sailor who, during a stay in Turkey, boxed with a seven-foot-tall eunuch bodyguard to the Ottoman sultan, knocking the poor slave down five or six times "until he had the right chance and then put him down to stay." Or mighty John Orpin, a usually peaceful man spurred to uncharacteristic action by his outrage at seeing two Irish bullyboys fighting in church. He grabbed both combatants, one with each hand, before proceeding to bump their heads together to get their attention. "Stop your fighting," he warned, "or I'll spank the two of you in turn." Suitably chastened, the two rowdies slunk away. These strongman stories have the cumulative effect of establishing the genetic fitness of Nova Scotia's British settlers. They prevail – over native peoples, Acadians, floods, wild beasts, and toffee-nosed aristocrats – because they deserve to. While relating tales of nineteenth-century Pictou County, Bird exclaims, "There were giants in those days, as it was the best and brawniest of the Highlanders who crossed the Atlantic to make new homes in New Scotland."[143] The men had not grown taller as tall tales were told and retold. No, human thoroughbreds had come to their promised land in Nova Scotia.

Such renditions of Nova Scotia history naturalize an Anglo ascendancy in the present day as the obvious outcome of certain inborn tendencies that by their very character rule out historically specific accounts of imperialism. This aim becomes even clearer when Bird comes to deal with people who are not components of that Anglo ascendancy. Bird remembers no French or aboriginal strongmen. His "Indians" win some battles because they are so savage they will do things that the Britons have too much common decency even to contemplate. His "Frenchmen" might score fleeting victories because they lack the compunctions that so hem in their British adversaries. But, in the end, neither of these other groups can ever win. They are weak.

Acadians are unavoidably part of Birdland. It would be hard to perpetuate the Land of Evangeline without them. Yet their inclusion entails much awkwardness. On the one hand, to be at all suitable as an atmosphere conducive to childlike enchantment, *Acadia* has to be a kind of *Arcadia* – a peaceable rural Eden. In glistening, prospering Beaubassin, Bird explains, "The children sang gaily under the apple trees and their merry shouts echoed over the fields as they clapped hands to frighten the wild pigeons from the crops." Everywhere in this Longfellowish domain is peace and plenty: "The wood of the interior of the home was usually rubbed to a bright polish of many homespun backs leaned there on jovial evenings ... Rough crockery shone from dresser shelves and the logs crackled in the huge fireplace." Even the sheep know they live in paradise ("great flocks of sheep nibbled daintily in luxurious feeding"). Nor is the chatter of the happily gossiping women quelled by the sight of a peaceful Mi'kmaw party, in quest of buttermilk and cider. Bird credits a contemporary visitor with remarking of the Acadians, "I have never heard of marital infidelity among them. Their long cold winters were spent in the pleasures of joyous hospitality. As they had plenty of firewood, their houses were always comfortable. Rustic songs and dancing were their principal amusements."[144]

So what serpent had infiltrated this Eden to upset Heaven on Earth? One might plausibly gesture to the Anglo-American invaders. After all, they orchestrated the Expulsion. Moreover, even in Birdland, they were closely associated, not with the idyllic countryside, but with such corrupt, morally vicious cities as Boston and Halifax. As we learn in *Despite the Distance*, eighteenth-century Halifax was a disgusting, garbage-strewn place. It was afflicted with innumerable stray cats, fowl foraging for garbage in ditches and lanes, idle and dissolute sailors "sullenly indifferent to passers-by," taverns, bad language, and women standing in the doorways of shabby dwellings.[145] Paralleling (as we shall explore in the following chapter) novelist-historian Thomas Raddall's depictions, Bird's imagined Halifax is to Acadian Minudie as sin is to purity, maturity to childhood, and guilt to innocence.

Bird would have balked at portraying Britons as villains, however. If he knew anything, he knew that British liberal ideals had freed the individual from medievalism, tyranny, and wickedness. Questioning that verity might obviate a sense of history as romance, with its admirable heroes and despicable villains engaged in their thrilling adventures, to give way instead to a sense of history as a morally ambiguous, highly complex, intensely conflictive process. Within Birdland, bad things happen because bad people with bad blood make them happen. Since the British are basically good, somebody else must have made the bad things happen. Therefore, the snake in Eden, aka Acadia, was not, all appearances to the contrary, the British. They were just doing their job of civilizing the planet. Bad things had happened because of one insidious individual, Abbé Louis-Joseph Le Loutre.

If you want to understand the fall of Acadia and the Expulsion, look no further. Here, in Le Loutre (sometimes "La Loutre" for Bird), we can identify "the chief author of it all." Following in Parkman's footsteps, Bird scripts Le Loutre as the diabolically powerful villain whose arrival at Louisbourg in autumn 1737 set the stage for his deadly career as the eighteenth-century region's number-one terrorist. He is almost a caricature of anti-Catholic denunciation: fanatical yet fiendishly clever, cruel and Jesuitically subtle, flitting about the countryside fomenting dissension, yet never man enough to stand up and fight fair and square. He is the "fiery black-robed Le Loutre," a Snidely Whiplash of colonial history. He moves restlessly about the Chignecto isthmus, "escorted by his half-tamed savages, with crucifix and scalping knife as their chief possessions." Le Loutre bore responsibility for Acadia's tragedy, "was answerable for the miseries that overwhelmed it."[146]

Here we find Bird once again echoing Parkman while discounting Brebner (see chapter 1). Parkman paints Le Loutre as "a fiery and enterprising zealot, inclined by temperament to methods of violence, detesting the English, and restrained neither by pity nor scruple from using threats of damnation and the Micmac tomahawk to frighten the Acadians into doing his bidding." Parkman attributes the influence of Le Loutre to the extreme ignorance and simplicity of the Acadians, "trained in profound love and awe of their Church and its ministers, who were used by the representatives of Louis XV as agents to alienate the Acadians from England."[147] Brebner, on the other hand, argues that Le Loutre's association with military matters had obscured his basic religious motivation: "Convinced that the Acadians and Indians were about to be exposed to an Anglicization which would include direct or indirect proselytism and perhaps the exclusion of their former spiritual ministrants, he decided that the most effective counter-move would be assistance to the French forces in the hope of a re-conquest of Acadie or, failing that, the creation of a new Acadie protected by French arms, in which the persecuted might find sanctuary and to which he might by argument or less pacific means urge others for their souls' salvation."[148]

J.C. Webster argues that Le Loutre "made the unfortunate mistake of subordinating the functions of a missionary to those of a political intriguer, and, thereby, became an important factor in disturbing the peace of a foreign province, of which he was not a citizen, and in determining the course of events which culminated in the Acadian tragedy of 1755."[149] Norman McLeod Rogers pleas for a more balanced treatment of Le Loutre as early as 1930, arguing that both English and French had made warlike use of their native allies and that "[a]s a Frenchman he caught a vision of a new Acadia, secure in its allegiance to his king and firm in its fidelity to his church."[150] In the light of contemporary work on the "First Way of War" in eighteenth-century North America, Le Loutre seems not to have diverged much from the general conviction among all belligerents that attacks on the enemy's civilian populations and infrastructure were entirely appropriate. The companies of American rangers sent to wage war in Minas and Chignecto certainly adopted such an approach.[151] From the standpoint of contemporary historical interest in the First Nations, meanwhile, Le Loutre might receive sympathetic treatment as a liminal figure, at once native and French, whose project of a native buffer state between a much-reduced English Nova Scotia and a still-flourishing French Acadia suggested both considerable political sophistication and a shrewd grasp of Mi'kmaw military power. Many facts about his career still remain obscure. With regard to his supposedly crucial involvement in the murder of merchant Edward How in 1750, one measured academic account suggests that his "participation, direct or indirect, in this affair" can be neither confirmed nor denied.[152] Bird, however, insists that "[t]here was not the least doubt that the murder was plotted by La Loutre."[153] No amount of contrary evidence would likely ever have budged him.

Had he lacked Le Loutre, Bird surely would have had to invent him. The "black-gowned disturber" performs three useful functions. Most obviously, he resolves the problem of evil. Since the Acadians were good-hearted, God-fearing, and hardworking, Bird can hardly call them the authors of their own misfortune (though he would later come close in *Done at Grand Pré*). Since the British were also on the side of the angels (bearing as they did the torch of liberal freedom, of Protestant religion, and of all the values that would make the Dominion great), evil can hardly reside in them. And even in Birdland, which had to bear at least some relation to historical realities, one could hardly place the blame for the deportation on the natives.

Le Loutre solves the problem. He lets everyone off the hook. "The Acadians were in the main a simple-minded folk," writes Bird, "who had from infancy depended on their priest for all their guidance ... It was surely natural that at such a crisis they should still have open ears for his counsel, even if his methods were much harsher than usual." When it came to the Mi'kmaq, Le Loutre works his evil magic on a credulous people, acting as their "black-gowned supervisor" while they rush from one building to another, "with blazing birch bark torches, spreading destruction with a wanton hand." Faced with such mayhem, the British have no alternative but to expunge the terrorist and the childlike innocents he has mesmerized. Bird acknowledges that some episodes of the Expulsion were a mite excessive – "The attack on Minudie is omitted in many accounts of the deportation, probably for shame's sake," he candidly admits[154] – but the reader of *A Century at Chignecto* comes away with the sense that such atrocities were merely the overzealous applications of a fundamentally sound policy.

Not only does Le Loutre's elevation to the prime mover of the Acadian tragedy seemingly account for it, but it also allows us to indulge in some guilty, if delicious, gothic romanticism. Whether Le Loutre wore a black robe or a white jumpsuit is somewhat beside the point in a sober assessment of the eighteenth century's tangled diplomatic and military affairs. Yet his supposed costume and accoutrements, the scalping knife and the crucifix, work splendidly to create a gothic atmosphere. A mass murderer and terrorist really ought to wear black, especially since it handily links him with the horrors of the Inquisition, the dangers of irrational superstition, and other popular themes of conventional anti-Catholicism. Perhaps most crucially, Le Loutre facilitates a circumlocution of geopolitical phenomena that defy explanation at the individual level, where Bird operated most comfortably. If we can believe that one man and one man alone did this damage, then there is no need to bother with profuse treaty dates, mind-bogglingly complicated trade patterns, shifting allegiances, or liminal (at times indecipherable) identities.[155] No, it all came down to the character of one man who no doubt acted much as his blood prompted him.

Bird does not always focus quite so intently on one villain, but he does consistently blame the French for what happened in 1755. In *This Is Nova Scotia,* he blames the Expulsion on Quebec agents as well as on Le Loutre.[156] In *Done at Grand Pré* (published in 1955 to coincide with the bicentennial of the Expulsion), Bird shifts the focus away from the Expulsion to an earlier military engagement in which he could represent Acadians as the aggressors. He further argues, after examining all the relevant evidence with the utmost objectivity, that the Acadians had likely brought the Expulsion upon themselves by failing to behave "as British citizens" in 1747.[157] Bird thus deftly transforms Longfellow's image of Acadian-as-victim into that of Acadian-as-delinquent. Finally, whatever responsibility did not fall on the shoulders of the Acadians and French seems to rest with the New Englanders, whose "expanding ambitions" had "produced the situation."[158] Despite Bird's assuming an air of disinterested neutrality, his study was unmistakably a brief for the defence, popularizing an interpretation of 1755 developed earlier by T.B. Akins, R.G. Haliburton, and Beamish Murdoch (and shared by Thomas Raddall).[159] On the one hand, there was Bird's "objective truth" – "based on *all* records available" – and, on the other, the "biased diatribes" of "bigots" and "extremists."[160]

Turning to other peoples whom Bird considered unsuited by heredity to win the day, we first should mention the blacks. Bird could marginalize them with near impunity, no event in their history having forced itself into the master narrative with the force of the Acadian Expulsion. In his historical writing, Bird treats slavery as so much period scenery in the wonderful pageantry of Chignecto history. "Slaves were bought and sold, the prevailing price being forty dollars," notes Bird of Fort Cumberland, moving on briskly to discuss the markets for rum, fish, and fur.[161] Tristram Crabtree has a "strong dislike of slavery," but tactfully minds his own business when he visits Carolina. Obtusely unaware of the economic realities of plantation agriculture, Tristram plans to "oust the whole grinning tribe of blacks and hire whites in their place," although – characteristically – we never really learn why.[162] *An Earl Must Have a Wife* paints a portrait of freed blacks in Halifax who (having become citizens) were naturally inclined to "swagger a bit," fought with each other over prime locations in Hammonds Plains and Preston, and were ill-clad for a Nova Scotia winter.[163] That many Afro–Nova Scotians built the fortifications of Halifax, suffered severely from discrimination, and left en masse for Sierra Leone escapes his notice.

Even master/slave relationships can be smoothed over in Birdland. In *Judgment Glen*, the black slaves Moses and Aaron appear in a score of passages. We learn that they are "big, powerful fellows," that the headstrong Helger unsuccessfully attempts to place irons on their ankles when they retire at night, that they sleep in a snug little cabin, build a prison house for Helger's son and then help him escape from it, find the winter difficult, and are "pitifully eager" to hear if the white hero Dugald is going to return to take charge of the farm, which has gone to seed in his absence.[164] The raison d'être of the slaves is to move the white characters forward in the narrative. How they felt about their bondage, how long they worked, what they believed, even whether the removal of the leg irons was their act of resistance or orchestrated by someone else – all are topics left unexplored.

Even more striking is the treatment of slavery in *The Passionate Pilgrim*, another Cumberland County epic set in the 1750s. Here the key slave character is Adam, who has escaped from his master, Colonel Thomas Longreed, "a brute with both humans and animals when he was drunk." We brace ourselves for a description of the hardships endured by slaves and their struggle for freedom as Adam unburdens himself to our hero, Steeley. Instead, we find this: "It was pleasant to sit by the fire and talk. Adam had quaint ideas and a long memory. He talked about his childhood, his being sold on the market in New York. He talked about the different masters he had had, and the way he had been taken away from his mother and brothers." Only a growler would want to dwell overlong on the conditions of slaves. Adam suffers from no such negativity. In fact, he seems completely unworried about enslavement – either of himself or of anybody else. Once he hears of the death of his vicious former master Longreed, he does not rejoice. Instead, "Adam's jaw dropped when he heard the news. He stood on the bank and wavered like a winter-darkened reed. 'Reckon I'se got to go back,' he pronounced. 'Ain't nobody 'round dis earth good as Missus Cunnel [i.e., Col. Longreed's widow]. She need a man for plantin' her garden.'"[165] Adam re-enters servitude chez Longreed with a happy heart. His mistress's niceness outweighs any dreams of freedom he might harbour. If he fails to become a true individual, it is because he does not truly want something for which he is unsuited.

Native peoples posed a more difficult challenge. Bird felt uncomfortable with them. At least with his New England and Yorkshire characters, all know where they stand in the ledgers of good and evil, kindness and cruelty, honesty and deceit. But with "Indians," you just cannot tell. Their very faces are inscrutable masks. Their eyes are unreadable. Their actions are unpredictable and often irrational. They steal babies for fun, start fires because they are careless, and when they are not behaving as animals, often act like cruel children. Bird, assuming for once a tone of resolute realism, will not countenance romantic misunderstandings of their incalculable, menacing, ominous otherness. Natives are not native to Birdland.

In "The Original Nova Scotians," published in the Halifax *Sunday Leader* in July 1925, Bird explains for contemporary readers why he believed that "romantic writers" had "given the redskin a prestige to which he is not entitled." He first delineates the physical traits that distinguish "true natives." They had ("and have") "lank, black hair, brown or copper-colored skin, dull eyes till they are aroused, full, compressed lips, dilated nostrils and high cheek bones. They rarely displayed emotion, were haughty and taciturn, in temperament poetic and imaginative, and in speech making very eloquent, using picturesque and extravagant language." Bird was struck by the contrast between the "ragged, smoky-tinted family that comes off the blueberry plains at dusk" and "the red terrors that haunted the trails of those hardy pioneers, of isolated families awakened in the night by fearsome yells and the smell of burning torches." The "dull-eyed basket and handle maker of today" was "yesterday arrayed in bright paint and feathers," as he harassed the white settlers and "took a keen delight in assisting in the torture of captives." Even in this short journalistic text, Bird oscillates between characterizing natives as simple, fun-loving people ("Their days were spent in hunting and fishing, travelling and visiting, and having a general good time") or as "red terrors."[166]

At the same time, though, Bird prided himself on his friendly relations with aboriginal peoples. When interviewed by Rosemary Bauchman in the 1980s, he made a point of drawing her attention to the "Indian war club" he had been given by a grateful troupe of performing Indians in Connecticut. One of them had fallen ill, so Bird had offered to fill in. When the big moment came, "there was Will Bird in feathered head-dress and appropriate regalia, whooping, dancing and brandishing an axe as realistically as any of them, doubtless getting a great kick out of an opportunity to indulge in 'hamming it up.'" Because he had helped them out of an awkward situation, the troupe gave him the war club as a token of their appreciation.[167] There is a logic to the coexistence of Bird's seemingly opposed positions of affection and revulsion vis-à-vis native peoples. He could fondly appreciate twentieth-century "Indians" so long as they appeared quaintly costumed. Playing Indian meant taking part in a costume drama that raised no difficult questions for him. He could prize the war club as a colourful curio because white people had long since won the war. Meanwhile, he consistently demonized natives and their conduct in other periods of history when they had seriously rivalled British power in the region. Like Highland Scottish customs that the English first fiercely repressed, then patronizingly indulged, aboriginal customs – once feared and detested – could be taken up again as entertaining spectacles once it seemed certain that Native peoples were dying out.[168]

A Century at Chignecto offers an even sharper articulation of Bird's dichotomous view of First Nations peoples, juxtaposing – without missing a beat – "Noble Savages" with "bloodthirsty redskins." The "Micmac race" comes in for praise as a superior breed "far above the majority of American red men," whose (supposedly vague) religious beliefs brought them "nearer to Christianity than any other form of uncivilized worship." In fact, their morals "were far better than our own." They were honest, hospitable, and truthful, kind to children and the aged. Moreover, they had bequeathed the province beautifully musical place-names: "'Stream of the Hills,' 'Battle of Rainbows,' 'Lake of the Morning,' 'Sleeping River,' 'Pool of Nights,' etc." The great explorers, Bird remarks, found the Mi'kmaq "well-fed, light-footed, swarthy, beardless, pleasing specimens, with tall, slender, agile forms, high cheek bones and lustrous hazel eyes, with the five bodily senses trained to most exquisite keenness."

Bird credits contemporary accounts that describe them as "a thinking and civilized people," speaking a musical and refined language, living amidst peace, order, and good government.[169] Yet, on the other hand – and largely without explanation (although he invokes the demon rum at one point) – he reports that they transformed into skulking "savages." Their deceitfulness evidenced itself in the "cowardly" 1755 murder of one New Englander out looking for milk. After the deportation of the Acadians, the Mi'kmaq became "tigers in their vengeance" (though rather chicken-hearted tigers who "lurked outside the range of the fort guns"). Five soldiers leaving Fort Cumberland, perhaps merely out on a harmless expedition, found themselves set upon by Indians as they crossed a small bridge. The gallant New Englanders, "though their case was hopeless, fought as only white men can, and before they crumbled under

the red men's hatchets the stream below ran red." Bird acknowledges in passing that New Englanders had placed a bounty of £100 on the scalp of each
male Indian over twelve years of age and £50 for those of women and small
children, but his history of Chignecto recounts the conflict in terms of native
atrocities against white settlers.[170] Bird's major historical novels do not contain
one graphic description of suffering that the British inflicted on native peoples,
whereas the body count of scalped, drowned, and kidnapped settlers mounts
up rapidly.

Along with their supposed cruelty, Bird obsessively underlines the dirtiness
and disarray of the imagined Mi'kmaq. Again and again, in terms reminiscent
of his earlier disgust at slovenly Belgian villages, he links Mi'kmaw encampments with loose dogs, foul smells, and other physical symptoms of moral
disorder. In *Judgment Glen*, a "greasy-looking Indian" sits by the entrance to a
wigwam as she waves a greeting at Dugald, a handsome young Yorkshire emigrant with whom Bird means us to identify. "They walked shyly past another
wigwam. Two dogs growled over bones at the back. An iron pot hung from a
lug pole, untended, the fire below fast dying to gray ash. An Indian slept in the
shade of a tree, a cap of rabbit skins pulled over his face his feet bare." Our
hero disapproves: "He had not liked the smells of the Indian camp. He was not
sure that he wanted to visit redskins again." Later, under the threat of starva-
tion and rescued by a nice Mi'kmaw named Harry (predictably "an outcast
from his tribe"), Dugald overcomes his squeamishness long enough to eat disgusting aboriginal food, cope manfully with the "rank ... Indian smell," even
accept instruction in the art of constructing a quick shelter of boughs to with-
stand the rain. When Harry dies, Dugald remembers how "the old redskin had
been kind and instructive on days when he had felt well."[171]

Perhaps the figure in Bird's work who best represents native/white reconciliation is the son of Tristram Crabtree who figures prominently in *Despite
the Distance*. Tristram Jr may be unusual in his mixed native-white parentage,
the result of the notorious elder Tristram's "moral lapse" with a native woman,
but he fits comfortably into the Birdian universe. His "memories of a mother
who was very kind to him, of Indians who were not," and his youthful pledge
"to love God and never to drink a drop of rum" mark him out as a man after
Bird's own heart. Through a series of coincidences remarkable even by Bird's
standards, Tristram Jr arrives in Halifax, flees a press gang, and is saved from a
fatal bullet by Tristram Sr, his repentant father, who in death achieves a peace
that had eluded him in life: "His strength had left him. He had such great happiness that he did not worry in the least. He had saved his son. And his son
had forgiven him. Nothing else mattered."[172] The white man has taken a bullet for his Métis son. Tristram Sr's self-sacrifice brings him peace and salvation,

but it also allows Tristram Jr – a lapsed, perhaps even former, native in his cultural identity – salvation as a probationary Nova Scotian. Cut off from his unkind tribe, he might regain his standing in Birdland.

Yet if Tristram Jr had perversely persisted in being Mi'kmaw, he would thereby have thrown his Nova Scotianness into doubt. Writing in 1925, Bird regards with undisguised irritation the claims the Mi'kmaq might make on a province to which they scarcely belonged. That they argued for a "right to cut down or bark a tree in any unfenced or uncultivated wilderness," that they claimed an "inherited … right to hunt fowl or fish at any season on any territory" if they needed food, jarringly reminded twentieth-century Nova Scotia of their continued presence. It was not entirely welcome. They had a "decided aversion to manual labor." They frequently trespassed on private property, where they showed "little or no regard for our fishing or hunting regulations." By implication, they had become skulking lowlifes rather than the Noble Savages of the romantic tradition. Such did Bird contend in 1925. We have no reason to think that, when it came to rights rather than quaint rituals, he ever changed his mind.[173]

Almost a quarter century later, in *The Passionate Pilgrim* (1949), Bird's Indians are almost exclusively bloodthirsty savages. The novel relates the quest of Steeley Bonsel, a young frontiersman from Pennsylvania, to avenge the death of his parents, indirectly caused by his cowardly cousin Winky Bonsel, who had inconveniently absconded with the family musket just as the Indians arrived. "Them devils has the paint on," exclaims Steeley's father before his untimely demise. Over the course of the next 324 pages, as Steeley pursues Winky through Pennsylvania, Massachusetts, and Nova Scotia, Bird treats us to many more graphic scenes that reveal an almost unlimited aboriginal capacity for atrocity.

Fleeting episodes of bonhomie – epitomized by the polite demeanour and solemnity of Chief Gray Moose, whom Steeley rescued in Nova Scotia's Cumberland County, and who attains a certain dignity as a Noble Savage after being dressed appropriately in European-style clothing – hardly make up for aboriginal savagery. Chief Gray Moose cannot prevent the (completely unexplained) Mi'kmaq kidnapping of a child dear to Steeley. Even the Acadians rescued by the natives find their deliverance a mixed blessing: "the filthy wigwams, the incredible chill, the persistent smoke that blinded them, the meat that was their only diet, half-cooked, nauseating" – it was all just too much for the Acadian refugees.[174] Even when natives *intended* kindness, their bioethical makeup generally prevented them from *being* kind. This novel never directly shows us an Acadian meeting a bad end at the hands of a British or New England soldier, even though the Expulsion would in fact ultimately cost hundreds of Acadian lives. But it does graphically if enigmatically describe Acadian deaths through the agency of the natives' intrinsic animality, expressed in their smells, filthiness, and bad cooking. How exactly the dubious odours and dodgy cuisine killed the guests never becomes clear.

In truth, Bird inveighs more against the general nature of Indians than against their specific misdeeds, their alleged crimes serving him only as an index for measuring the incurable savagery that defines their racial essence. "The Indians were pitiful cowards, as always," Bird writes to one correspondent who wanted information on events in Nova Scotia and at Fort Cumberland in 1775–76.[175] "There is much we do not understand," says the wise Margot, destined after many twists and turns to become Steeley's wife. "We don't know why some Indians are bad, and why good people are killed." "The Injuns is like the measles," expounds another wise white person, insofar as "[y]e can't tell you're havin' 'em till you see 'em, and then it's too late." For Steeley's Pa, who even after death provides his son with almost too many words of posthumous wisdom, most of the "Injuns" are "careless devils." Another character adds his emphasis: "Injuns! … Bloody sneekin' devils! … Injuns … " "Injuns is bad," chimes in the eager-to-please slave Adam. Strengthening an association already firmly established in *Judgment Glen*, Bird finds numerous parallels between the Mi'kmaq and dogs: "The squaw had followed him … Suddenly she raised a howl like a dog with its paw under a wheel."[176]

"Squaws" are barely human. *The Passionate Pilgrim* contains a scene – with no ethnographic foundation – in which Bird uses the trope of the savage aboriginal to dispatch the detestable Winky, without compromising our identification with the avenging Steeley. He accomplishes this by projecting all of Steeley's violence and hatred of his enemy onto a group of "squaws" who torture the vile Winky: "She [the leading native woman] went to Winky and held him as he made a feeble squirming. She tugged his shirt from inside his breeches and raised it. Winky whimpered aloud. His back was a livid mass of old welts, many still scabbed with slow healing. The squaw released him and he put his shirt back in place, edging away from them. No one checked him and he went over to a sandy spot and sat down. Three of the dogs trotted over and nuzzled down beside him. 'You want him?' The squaw picked her nose." This last graphic detail, as much as the cruel fate awaiting Winky, confirms the woman's inhumanity. Her every gesture confirms her baseness as she lives out the inner truth of her character. Steeley leaves the native encampment, picturing Winky, "when the winter came, perpetually troubled with chilblains, tortured by his unhealed hurts, beaten by every squaw in the camp, yet fed enough and warmed enough to be kept alive and in working condition. The crafty and merciless squaws would see to it that he did a big day's work every day and every day."[177] This novel, which went through two Canadian printings in 1947 alone, generally won acclaim.

As the skin-crawling descriptions of "squaws" might suggest, as non-white was to white, so women were to men. To understand the true deficiency of woman, we first must understand the splendidly virile character of the real (as opposed to corrupt) man. To be a man in Bird's cosmos was to live according to the natural laws of character. True men – always excepting effeminate aristocrats and officers – were transparent, to themselves and others. In neither his histories nor his fiction do they call out for any analysis. The successful ones are resourceful, propertied, and proud. Their bodies faithfully reveal their characters. Rupert in *Judgment Glen*, for example, is a Yorkshire lad well suited by nature to the tough environment of Nova Scotia: "He moved with surprising ease and vigour possessed him. He was good to look at, blond of hair and brown of skin. His rough dress and ruddy cheeks proclaimed him an outdoors man and when he smiled little wind lines crinkled at the corners of his blue eyes, making him look curiously boyish." On his "sun-bronzed body," the "muscles bulged and crawled in his back. Muscles rippled from shoulder to wrist, and cables of muscle ridged stomach and chest under his amber skin." All in all this hunky Yorkshireman is a far cry from his drunken, dissolute, snivelling, title-obsessed father Helger. Another settler warns this pathetic patriarch that the frontier makes demands to which only a special kind of man will be adequate: "A new country needed a stubborn breed. Farming was a gamble and a man needed stiff-necked faith in his judgments to stand against the wilderness. Once he began to be uncertain he was a failure." Helger is the very model of a limp-wristed elitist who cannot adapt to the frontier. Yearning for a title he thinks has been promised to him, he savours the thought of how all those who disrespect him will think twice once he is *Sir* Helger Fallydown. He consoles himself with drinking binges during which he slips into a private world of privilege. His very last words will be "Sir … Helger … Fallydown!" and he dies without realizing he has been the victim of a practical joke.[178] Incapable of masculine honour, deceitful to his family, priggish with his mates, Helger is a fictionalized version of the British officers with whom Bird sparred in the trenches of Belgium.

One unerring indication of whether or not a man had character was whether or not he drank liquor. Bird (who swore a childhood pledge never to imbibe, which he apparently kept even in the hard-drinking milieu of the trenches) believed that drink universally undermines reason and corrupts families. Many of his novels echo earlier works of moral uplift mass-produced by writers such as Marshall Saunders, striking notes of outraged innocence familiar to anyone who has frequented a Sunday school. Drinkers lose their masculinity and independence. As Rev. Meracious Admore advises Tristram Crabtree in *Despite the Distance*, "Let no man tell you that drink is not the tool of the devil. It is so easy to acquire the taste." The poor pastor's own clueless parishioners had plied him with the stuff by way of being sociable. Before he knew it, "I had to have a glass before starting my day's work. My dear wife begged with me to leave it alone, but I had the argument of the devil that drinking was condoned in the Scriptures."[179] A drinker's weakness is perceptible even before he opens his mouth, as we learn from *The Passionate Pilgrim*: "The major scanned them one by one. He looked … like a hard drinker."[180] Drinking is just the most obvious manifestation of a fundamentally compromised character structure.

Character is destiny. Men are not born equal. They are inheritors of different bloodlines that assign them their place in creation. Such a metaphysical conception of human individuality removes any need for a concept of society. Even in descriptions of processes that seemingly require a social analysis – such as the replacement of the old mercantile economy of Carrsboro with a tertiary economy based on tourism – Bird simply refuses to go beyond the level of the individual. In Carrsboro, the predatory banker who holds a mortgage on the Winstill property is appropriately named Deker Tight – "a parasite" in the harsh verdict of John Winstill's father: "His kind grow nothing, build nothing, invent nothing. They sit by and profit from the troubles of the workers. But it is the system we have and we may as well keep our thoughts to ourselves. Now what notice have they put up at the store?" The pasty Deker fears John, whose mild demeanour conceals his he-man instinct to punch out his adversaries. John is a constant reader of *The Book of Job* – meaning not the Biblical text, but the family history that started with the swashbuckling iron man John Winstill in 1811 and suggests the trials and tribulations experienced by this august lineage since the Age of Sail ended. "Promise me," his mother commands, "that, God being your helper, you will never forget you are a gentleman and, above all, a Winstill, no matter what happens." John spends night after night reading his family saga, convinced that "if he did right as he saw it, held to his respect, was tolerant with those temporarily his equals, his full rights would be restored." The Winstill name carries cachet. John can tell his new love Judy, when she worries whether she will be received by Carrsboro society, "I don't think … that you understand about the Winstills. The people would not dare be mean to you."[181] Even after his death, Judy, who comes from the hardscrabble hamlet of Purple Rocks, is rocketed by the force of the Winstill family name to the presidency of a prestigious women's club. A strong man, defending a proud tradition, can elevate those around him.

Conversely, one bad man can poison a whole community. The explanation for the desperate poverty of Judy's Purple Rocks (the name would likely call to many minds the South Shore's Blue Rocks, a quaint fishing village discovered by visiting artists in the interwar period) lies mainly in the poisonous influence of one Jigger Loney, Judy's supposed father. The Rocks are a bleak and awful place, with stray dogs, a noticeable smell (never a good sign in Bird-land), and a jumble of tumbledown shacks, "each with mean little windows and the doors like those in sawmill camps." What caused this wretched deso-lation? Not the price of fish, not the marginal livelihood of rural woodsmen, not any such abstraction, but the personality of Jigger, who, "black-whiskered, big, evil-looking and incredibly dirty," was "the personified evil of the sur-roundings." The obvious first step to redress the situation is to knock Jigger down, laying him flat out in the mud.[182] Men in Birdland understand that two strong fists often supply a straightforward solution to tough problems. "Men were really men in those days," remarked Bird of the 1780s in Nova Scotia, a purportedly factual observation that his fiction tirelessly reconfirms.[183]

If men are transparent, women in Birdland are infinitely mysterious. As the authoritative Pa Bonsel explains in *The Passionate Pilgrim*, the dichotomous cat-egorization of men (bad or good) ran into conceptual difficulties when applied *pari passu* to women, for they "came in so many kinds that nobody could list them." This typological complexity arose from the specific character of women's feelings. "Their feelings always carried them further and stronger, Pa said, and the best of them could not explain some things they did." Yet if their essence is radically fungible, their lot in life nonetheless proves amenable to catego-rization. Bird's women confront, with only a few variations, a set of standard career paths. One may (rather unusually) become a sensible, virtuous woman, with a calm demeanour, culinary proficiency, and a willingness to please a lov-ing husband and pleasant children. Then again one may, and one rather more commonly does, surrender to the wild blood surging in one's veins, that call of the female wild that sends many into the depths of irrationality, promiscu-ity, poor housekeeping, nude dancing on the dykes, illegitimate pregnancy, and, perhaps worst of all, rum. Two intermediate positions are that of the calculat-ing, manipulative wench, twisting men to one's hidden purpose, and that of the purse-lipped society lady, hell-bent on social domination. At the end of many of these trajectories lies a rather dismal stint as a crone. The grave difficulty fac-ing male heroes is that these categories are not airtight. Pa Bonsel elucidates this analytical problem: "There ain't nothin' finer on God's earth than a good woman, but most men's too blind or crazy to tell which is the good ones."[184]

Good women are almost always (actual or prospective) mothers. Often the mothers are deceased, but they impart posthumous words of wisdom that echo on in the minds of our heroes. Perhaps the best of the Birdian women is Mar-got in *The Passionate Pilgrim*, an Acadian whose charming efforts at learning English, fetching cool drinking water for our hero as he ploughs the field, and cooking delectable meals, all testify to her qualities as Steeley's best choice for his wife. (That she seems a carbon copy of Evangeline, but this time in love with an anglophone, is an added attraction.) Steeley considers Margot the epitome of purity and innocence, the antithesis of the strumpets and wild women who have beset him for hundreds of pages. She has the great advantage of coolness and even temper – "as if there were no heat in her veins, nor ever would be."[185]

As Steeley can testify only too well, however, the trouble for men lies in the determination of the *differentia specifica* through which to demarcate the good woman from the wild woman. Wild women proliferate in Birdland. *An Earl Must Have a Wife* gives us Martha Williams, who strikes J.F.W. DesBarres as "the nearest to an animal in heat of anything he had ever seen." Once this creature has worn out poor J.F.W., she turns to a series of more vigorous men on Charlottetown's noisome Collins Street. She makes a rather unlikely addition to high society in Prince Edward Island. "You are nothing – a liar and cheat and, who knows, a harlot," cries J.F.W., himself a serial adulterer.[186] Such is the price of mixing with wild women.

Hetty Holder is another wild woman, "born to be friendly, it seemed, and no one wanted to change her." She dogs Steeley through much of *The Passionate Pilgrim*, sometimes appearing to be really in love with him, yet invariably proving to be in league with someone else. Steeley finds it increasingly hard to forgive her duplicitous lapses: "No matter how he tried to convince himself, he was not sure that Hetty was sincere in everything she said." Furthermore, Hetty's disconcerting forwardness drives our hero to look to the Holy Word itself for reassurance: "He knew that if he were a woman he would never seek a mate but let a man come seeking a wife. He was not sure that such things were written in the Bible but it seemed to him that it was likely they were."[187]

The Passionate Pilgrim presents another such troubling figure, Hagar Potter. She is, in the words of her husband, "skittered in her mind." Her appearance tends to give this away, for her white hair "stuck out from her head like a witch's dream, ragged and coarse, free of pins or combs or hampering ribbons, presenting every evidence of being trimmed by shears operated by Hagar herself. Her eyes were large and dark, seeming to dilate with intensity as she spoke." An indication of Hagar's somewhat idiosyncratic approach to the eighteenth-century concept of marriage is her offer to Steeley, made notwithstanding the proximity of her husband, that she sleep with him as his Christmas treat.[188]

A worrisome sign that a woman who seems good might in fact be wild is poor housekeeping. We discover such a "slattern" in *The Passionate Pilgrim*: "She had been doing some washing beside a slimy water hole, and she looked as if she had long forgotten any ambition. Her hair straggled down over her eyes. A tub in the yard held water and garbage that had scummed over greenly. Flies hovered in clouds about some fish heads and bones that had been thrown on the ground. The cabin roof was made of poles covered with bark, and long strings of fibre dangled over the eaves like the woman's untidy hair."[189] As Bird's description makes clear, physical disorderliness connotes mental derangement.

Wild women have overrun Purple Rocks in *So Much to Record*. As one resident puts it, "'Polly and Dolly are twins. They chew tobacco and drink like a man. Maggie Bones is nineteen and she's had three babies. There's Nell and Sue Critter, too. They'd just about take your clothes off if you went around the Rocks.' She paused. 'I don't like any of them,' she added fiercely."[190] Men should give these sexual predators a wide berth. Their presence in large numbers could only augur the dissolution of all normative standards, from the socio-economic to the moral.

Men must also take care around the manipulative wench. Some women transgress the civilized boundaries that circumscribe gender identity through the calculated wielding of their sexuality to control people who should rightfully be the stronger. A noteworthy manipulative wench is Bella Bonsel in *The Passionate Pilgrim*. As the local constable describes her, "That woman's a power in this settlement … She twists the Major round her thumb."[191] Another such woman is the "tall and thin and censorious" Abigail Danthorne in *Despite the Distance*, who (according to gossip) "ruled her husband, Ahab, like a child, as well as their dwarfed son Saul."[192] In some respects, wenches pose an even graver threat than their wild sisters do. The wench's refusal of womanly goodness does not manifest itself in her own degradation, but in that of certain unfortunates whom she wishes to control.

At the other end of the spectrum from wild women and manipulative wenches are society ladies, who function in Birdland as figures of fun and also as foils for the sincerity and authenticity of good characters. They are too cultivated for their own good. Perhaps the best examples of society ladies are the Carrsboro matrons in *So Much to Record*. Here we find Elizabeth, Esther, and Theresa, whom everyone calls Bessie, Essie, and Tessie: "They were fat, stodgy women, corset-conscious and incapable of emotion, paying their respects because Boniface had told them it was their duty. John perspired with uneasiness when his mother suggested with a sugary tone that they have a cup of tea, and the three sisters nodded in agreement. She brought a plate of biscuits and jam, and the ladies ate and licked their fingers, sipping their tea with obvious enjoyment."[193] These women do not radiate the goodness that so crucially upholds the social order. Rather, they abide by its strictures only of necessity and take advantage of its forms whenever the opportunity presents itself.

Finally, in a class all by themselves in Birdland, we have old women. They tend to be grotesque and unbalanced. Bird interrupts his memoirs of trench warfare to bring us the urgent (if physiologically improbable) news that he had spotted a "very skinny grey-haired" Belgian grandmother who "proudly showed us she could lay her extremely long breasts over her shoulders and they would stay there."[194] In one of his novels, Bird leaves us with this portrait of an old Acadian woman struggling to answer those who are searching for her kin to deport: "When the question was repeated she grinned with a dull silly look, reminding Steeley of the leer of a no-account dog."[195] The obviously post-menopausal forfeit dignity and respect, a condition only intensified by the fact we tend to see them through the eyes of rather macho young men. An alternative non-Birdian perspective might credit *Judgment Glen*'s Mercy Gooding for performing an invaluable service as the local midwife; as a denizen of Birdland, however, Mercy knows herself to be nothing but a gossipy "old hag" – as she self-identifies. The male narrator sees her as a "shriveled old woman a foot shorter than himself. Her hair stood out from her head like dried weeds. Her dress was ragged and her skinny feet were bare." His incomparably sensitive Birdian nose picks up from her "a pervading odour of shut-in cats."[196] The whole demeanour of this batty old woman has become viscerally repellent because she has lived long enough to show her age.

Despite the Distance actually gives us a character called "The Witch." A "half-witted derelict left in the area by a New England family," she unsurprisingly had a propensity to get "drunk at every opportunity and [make] a nuisance of herself." Fittingly, she finds herself in Halifax caring for other women of her age and station, which means she must endure "endless days filled with complaint and old-woman prattle." Sly and cunning as well as dipsomaniacal, she falls out with her charges, gets drunk, stabs one Sleepy Jones, and is hanged: "[T]he drayman lashed his horse and the rig tore down the street leaving The Witch revolving at the end of the rope, twisting and turning in convulsive struggles. The Witch's patched shoes were kicked clear of her feet and one stocking dangled until it, too, was kicked free."[197]

Given the hazards with which this treacherous feminine diversity confronts any man, it is unsurprising that Birdland resounds to the cries of domestic conflict. Women are to blame. On their own, as evidenced so powerfully by the Great War books, men can form deep friendships. In Bird's fiction, we also encounter men who cannot bear to be apart. In *The Passionate Pilgrim*, Steeley and his pal Mike are so tied to each other that Mike is inspired to exclaim, "We sound like a pair of wimmen ... but it don't matter a damn. I couldn't bear ye leavin' me."[198] Women are another matter. In *So Much to Record*, John Winstill reflects that Carrsboro holds not a single girl he would want to marry, because "none of them were good enough for him ... He was realizing the power the Winstill name had carried, one generation to another."[199] "Don't it beat hell what kin happen to wimmen?" muses Steeley, who runs through a veritable army of female types before he finally finds his docile Acadian helpmeet. "It beat all how a woman could upset a man's brain," he later elaborates.[200] Women seem almost as out of place in Birdland as they would have been in the trenches.

Having sex is usually a mistake. Sexuality encompasses a realm of almost incalculable danger, because it erodes the clear and firm boundaries of the self-restrained and self-contained individual. Men pay the highest price. For reasons never entirely explained, they cannot help wanting sex, but, as with rum (a parallel drawn by one of J.F.W. DesBarres's daughters as she indicts him for his dissipation at the conclusion of *An Earl Must Have a Wife*), a strong man should just say no. If he cannot, he runs DesBarres's risk of having his entire life damningly summed up by his peers as one big disappointment: "It is sufficient to say you had the ability and the opportunity to become one of the most famous men of the Empire. Had you been a Christian gentleman you would have been an earl at least." Alas, "you fouled your life with the conduct of a guttersnipe."[201]

One novel after another tells the sorry tale of men tempted, seduced, and betrayed by lustful, impure Jezebels. *Despite the Distance* shows us Tristram "set … tingling" by the touch of "man-crazy" Thora, whose affliction commenced at the age of ten and, by her adolescence, was full-blown. Now she has grown into a femme fatale who is too much for him: "He felt they were moving now under the control of a shared need, which can bring strangers into a closer communion than blood kin can ever know. His conscience cried a warning, but he put an arm around her and kissed her warmly, thinking it was what she wanted." She will repay Tristram by deceiving him, then breaking his heart. Too late does he realize the terrible truth about her: "He had glimpsed a Thora Gidney that made him shudder. She was suddenly revealed as a woman who would stop at nothing to get her way."[202] Much like Thora Gidney, Hetty Holder works her wiles on Steeley. He almost succumbs: "A suspicion of her intentions flashed into his thinking too late. Her lips were soft against his suddenly and the night was something warm and full, spreading through him, down through him into his boots, in a way no night had ever done before." A close call – but he manages to push her away. He even wrestles with the idea of taking Hagar up on her idea of their sleeping together as his Christmas present. Once he turns away, "burning with remembrance of Hagar's hands, and her urgings," a "great guilt" descends upon him, a boundless contrition that "brought thoughts of his mother. He hurried as if he could escape his conscience, but despite all he could do it was as if he could hear Hagar's coaxing voice again and a new fear forced him into scalding sweat. Perhaps Hagar was really in love with him."[203]

Even the stalwart John Winstill of *So Much to Record* nearly gives himself over to Molly, a young woman who seems good but is really wild. Operating on the first premise, John (as is his wont) discourses at length upon "his people," the illustrious Winstills of Carrsboro. Molly responds by biting his cheek and (metaphorically, one gathers) setting him "on fire." They go to bed. Then the "enormity" of it all startles John "with the force of a great shout": "He knew the only honest thing to do was for him to marry Molly but he was only eighteen and had not a cent to his name. The fact that stunned him, left him unable to think at all for moments at a time, was that he had ruined the Winstill name." Soon he comes to a more mature perspective on the tryst. It was all her fault: "Molly had tricked him. She had had her way with him. She had made a complete fool and wreck of him, and he was sure she had planned it from the first."[204] Sex, this inexplicable and unwelcome eruption into the proper order of things, creeps over characters like an identity-challenging fever and as quickly recedes, leaving them sad and blue. They feel so because, chances are, they have gone against the order of the world. This order is good. It should not be tampered with.

Bird illustrates the world's fundamental goodness in his treatment of physical force. Force is always on the side of the honest and the true. If there are sometimes a few scares on the way to their ultimate triumph, these white-knuckle moments only underscore its inevitability and desirability. Bird loves to dramatize this alliance of force and goodness in the most direct fashion he can. He enjoyed a reputation as a "master of the psychology of physical violence" for his practice of punctuating every chapter or so with "a slugging match or a moose hunt or a run with a Halifax press gang."[205] These incidents tell a larger moral story. The first chapter of Bird's paean to the Loyalists, *To Love and to Cherish*, finds the colonial New England farmboy Heber Marrack recalling, in all its gory details, a vicious slugfest with the would-be cattle thief Joe Denter: "I drove my fist into Joe's face. He tried to shout and to let go of the rein at the same time, but my knuckles closed his mouth and rocked him backward and I pressed in on him, hitting with both hands. He was as big a man as I, but he was a coward and wanted to get away, not to fight." Joe tried to run, but "as he started to dodge I hit him with all my weight, turning on one foot. The blow almost broke my wrist but he went down like a poled steer."[206] There is something undeniably satisfying about the way handsome, honest, loyal Heber teaches gross, thieving, treacherous Joe a lesson – but good.

Most of Bird's fistfights and brawls pit a good man deserving our unqualified approval against a bad man deserving our unqualified disapproval. In *Here Stays Good Yorkshire*, Patience Crabtree (one of the good blond siblings) confronts her brother Matthew (one of the bad dark siblings) after discovering he has tried to take sexual advantage of a girl from a nearby farm. Predictably, the predatory Matthew grows enraged. Who knows what might have happened if Patience's husband, the jolly, ursine Gideon Danks, had not happened along just in time? It is time, Gideon tells Matthew, for him to reap what he has sown.

Gideon soon has the upper hand. "Not a word was spoken. Matthew's gasps and sobbing swallows of his own blood were the only sound." But the foolish young man, "an animal gone ugly," will not give in, forcing Gideon to dole out still more punishment, even though "there was no more fight to it. Matthew was as stubborn as a mad bull but Gideon's fists were battering rams that beat him back over ground until he could neither see nor sense direction, and a final swing knocked him to earth like a poled ox. He lay there without motion, beaten to a soggy, bloody coma." Like the "poled steer" Joe Denter, the "poled ox" Matthew Crabtree has met with a better man – and the better man is always the stronger man too. In this comforting world, to quote the lovely June from *Here Stays Good Yorkshire*, "Right always wins ... if we'll only believe it."[207]

We can instantly identify people in the right because they exude wholesome vitality. Lancelot and Jonathan of *Here Stays Good Yorkshire* "were both over six feet in height, blond and blue-eyed ... with soft golden beards."[208] John Hildreth, the kindly hero of "Out of the Past," was "a giant of a man, with a fair skin burned by wind and sun, and his expression was that of a patient ox."[209] Honesty Bartley of *To Love and to Cherish* "had firm, even features, a dimple in her cheek and a set to her chin that promised good-natured tolerance in most things."[210] Good people are easy on the eyes. They are pictures of health. They are faithful, pleasant, and normal – qualities that seem to have shaped their physiognomies. Many women in Bird's novels bear the names of virtues – *Honesty* Bartley, *Unity* Lemming, and *Patience* Crabtree – names to which they always live up.

Good people are uncomplicated, dutiful and contented. Even as adults, there is something childlike about many of them. Asa Crabtree, the simpleton who is father to the principal characters of *Here Stays Good Yorkshire*, is a sort of woodcarver-savant whose family recognizes that he has grown "childish" in his middle age. Back in Yorkshire, as his shrewish, scheming, unfaithful wife lies on her deathbed, still issuing commands to her grown children, "Asa wetted his lips with his tongue, rubbed his head. He did not like the odours of the room and he wished his wife would not say such harsh things." This man is an innocent. He has neither ambition, nor sexuality, nor a capacity for reflection. He simply is. He tries to be good and to enjoy simple pleasures. Bird has an uncommon empathy for such people. They are, one might say, the truest citizens of Birdland. Asa, indeed, is perhaps the most admirable character in this novel. Throughout the story, he quietly busies himself with projects that have no discernible usefulness but which end up being the most important things that anyone does. Because he so loves to feel the soil of Yorkshire in his hands, he brings a sack of it with him to Nova Scotia when his children take him there. Thereby, unbeknownst to him, he assures the spiritual continuity of the Yorkshiremen on both sides of the Atlantic. Once his family has settled in

Chignecto, he placidly sets about carving, in the stump of a lightning-struck tree, the words "Here Stays Good Yorkshire," an apparently useless preoccupation that draws only puzzlement and condescension from the more pushy and ambitious characters. They do not realize that Asa has foreseen his death and the stump will serve as his gravestone. More than that, in the final scene of the novel, we learn that the apparently dead stump is still alive and growing. His daughter-in-law Unity observes, "It's a sign of perpetuity or t' like."[211]

Asa stands in contrast to his "sons" (who, as we have seen, are not really his progeny), Matthew and Tristram, who do only what seems most profitable but thereby miss out on all the important things in life. Talking about Tristram, who had wanted to marry her back in England, Unity "pointed at a goldfinch hovering over a ripened dandelion, its plumage bright in the sun. 'T' man I marry will see that. Tristram never had time.'"[212] Asa's blissful ignorance, dreaminess, and simplicity make him lovable. Tristram's obsessive forethought, industry, and ambition – qualities unsettlingly implicated in his aggressive personality – stop him from being human, let alone endearing.

Bird seldom goes in for all-embracing statements about the human condition, but his differential handling of different sorts of characters nevertheless conveys a clear message. Priscilla Murolo usefully suggests that "all novels, whatever the aims of their writers, suggest answers to questions concerning human agency: How can people affect the world around them? What can they expect to achieve? Why do they succeed or fail?"[213] For Bird, the quiescent, the innocent, and the wholesome will always triumph because they will always have overwhelming strength and providential serendipity on their side. As such, the childlike enjoy good prospects. What need would they have for long-range planning, painstaking analysis, or attempts to change the world? The world is good. Those who protest its iniquity must be grouchy; those who fail to prosper in it must be bad; those who want to change it must be evil.

Childhood stands as a reproach to adulthood. Adulthood is not a stage of life to which one should aspire, but a temptation that one must resist. It is not that Bird excoriates all results of growing up. As we have seen, he glories in bodily maturity in his loving descriptions of the champion physical specimens populating his novels. Rather, he distrusts the forms of consciousness commonly associated with adulthood: sexuality, intoxication, and politics, for example. They have no place in the sort of life conducive to human flourishing. One does better to remain entirely innocent of them.

Lovers of whom Bird approves have studiously preserved their sexual naivety. Their concerns overwhelmingly revolve around being good and resisting the temptation to be bad. The romantic leads of *To Love and to Cherish*, Heber Marrack and Honesty Bartley, meet in eighteenth-century New York where their Loyalist families are taking refuge from the marauding American revolutionaries (of whom more anon). Heber has had his eye on Honesty for a little while. They have sat together several times in the pretty garden between their respective homes. The time comes when Heber decides they should get serious. "Would you go for a walk with me?" he asks. She would. His elation at hearing her say yes comes accompanied by uneasiness, though, because "she was so vibrant with life that I wondered how she would behave." To reassure himself that his beloved will keep her worrisome vibrancy in check, he requests that the habitually barelegged Honesty wear stockings for the occasion. Even for Honesty, who takes good behaviour seriously, this is a bit rich. "La, but you are modest," she teases him. "Don't you like my legs?" Heber allows that he has never heard a girl speak of her legs before. This is just the right answer. Honesty, now "sobering," levels with her beau that, of course, nice girls never mention their legs. Heber has proven to her that "your mother has made you a proper young man, and I like proper young men." The trio of Honesty, Heber, and Heber's mother having conspired to assure the continuance of propriety, the walk can proceed free from uneasiness over the unpredictable workings of vibrancy.[214]

Different sorts of women will cross Heber's path as the novel progresses, ones in whom vibrant life cannot be restrained even by the application of stockings. He is ready for them, however. While he is living in his adoptive home of Shelburne, Nova Scotia, whence he has fled the revolution in the Thirteen Colonies, the pretty widow Sabina Dallow tries to seduce him. On an occasion when the two are left dangerously alone, Heber "saw her warm lips moving toward mine. They touched my cheek, and waited. It was all there, mine for the taking. Sabina was soft and vibrant with life, ardent for love, filled with the thousand lures Nature has given her favoured sex." To her frustration, he resists. Propriety in this case seems to have afforded Heber certain compensations for his forbearance. He has experienced her vibrancy, ardour, and warmth. Yet he has conceded nothing, has not betrayed to Sabina that he has so much as noticed her, has not contracted any ongoing commitment to her now that the experience is past. He could have had her, but he was better than that. Better than her, in point of fact, and he can return home to confidently tell his mother that she had no reason at all to worry because the wiles of a woman like Sabina could never ensnare the likes of him.[215]

Janet, too, overflows with vibrant life. When she marries the widower Amos, Heber has his doubts about the wisdom of their union. He explains, "She was a big woman, not fleshy, but nicely moulded and big. It surprised me that she was so young and of such size, and it didn't seem possible that she could be Amos' wife, not after what he had told me about his first bride, her slenderness and beauty." While Janet too has beauty, it strikes him as of a vaguely indecent kind, for "she was blonde and had nice skin and a pile of lovely hair, and full breasts and strong thighs … it was easy to see she was almost smoldering with emotion, or passion." She radiates sexual excitement in the form of "a faint bodily sweetness such as an animal would have."[216] Predestined to be a sexpot, she soon proves herself unfaithful to poor Amos and runs off to New York. Amos learns the cost of physical attraction.

Janet, too, will learn the error of her ways in short order. After her New York sojourn ends badly, the chastened adulteress returns to Shelburne. She has no one to whom she can turn. Honesty decides to reconcile Janet with her estranged husband. She insists, "seemingly naïve as a child," that Heber should raise the matter with the local legislative representative, Wilkins, who has influence with Amos. Heber "check[s] an impulse to say" what he thinks and then goes on what he considers a fool's errand to Wilkins. When the assemblyman agrees with Honesty, Heber is flabbergasted, and "again I checked myself, for he seemed as artless as Honesty." Sure enough, though, Amos does take back Janet, who now seems most contrite and much less charged with the sort of vibrant life Amos had found it so difficult to control. Heber is astounded. As his pious friend Tim Roly observes, "Wonders never cease."[217] Not for the last time, naivety proves wiser than experience.

◆

Heber's private doubts about naive sincerity register a disquieting trend in the hitherto dependable character's mentality – an emerging taste for analysis. By this point, Shelburne has fallen into such terminal decline that Heber makes his living by tearing down abandoned houses to sell the timber. His faith is sorely tested as the town goes to wrack and ruin. He admits, "Something of the fear that was spreading pricked at me as I pried boards from rafters and hammered nails free of them. I was taking down houses that had not been up three full years … It didn't make sense." At first, he retains his equanimity, for "no drab thoughts could stay with me long." He confides his doubts openly to good old Tim Roly, who promptly upbraids his wavering friend: "Don't be a Job or a Jonah … Just tell yourself that we're down near as low as we can get, and the next swing is up. If you can make yourself believe that without a mug of rum to help you'll do."[218] Reinforced by Roly's injunction to cheerfulness, temperance, and faith in Shelburne, Heber survives another close brush with realism.

Clearly, however, Heber is slipping. Soon he can hold out no longer. Without warning, Honesty's long-lost husband, Ned Clay (whose very existence had been a secret from Heber), appears in Shelburne, demanding his conjugal rights. This "heaving, hacking wreckage" had entrapped Honesty in marriage under false pretences and then abandoned her later on.[219] Nevertheless, Honesty insists she must abide by her vows, protest though Heber might. Heber falls into brooding. It seems so unfair. All social ties, all pledges of loyalty, begin to strike him as arbitrary and unnatural. Clearly, Heber has lost a great deal of his innocence and he is perforce in grave danger.

For disaster truly to strike, however, Heber will require more than discontent. He will need rum. Normally, he never touches the stuff. Earlier in the novel, he learned all about the drinker's downfall from the sad case of his mother's cousin Melinda. But old verities are dissipating all around him. Soon he has gotten roaring drunk in the streets of Shelburne in the middle of the night. In his altered state, it comes to him that the tie of loyalty to the Crown that brought him to Shelburne looks suspiciously similar to the patently iniquitous tie of marriage that binds his beloved Honesty to the execrable Ned. The sodden Heber accosts the hapless parson, forcing him to perform a farcical marriage ceremony between himself and a tree in the town square. "This tree's 'Shelburne,'" he rants. "Marry me to it. Tell me the words about to love and to cherish. Marry me to Shelburne." Heber wakes up in jail. He has more than enough time there to reflect upon the recent error of his ways, repenting of it at length in a letter to Honesty. He writes, "All I want now is a chance to show you that I can be a decent man and a good husband. I had the best mother ever a man can have and now I'll be waiting for when you come back to me … and I'll love and cherish you while life is in me."[220] He has regained his innocence. Now he can go back into the world, having realized that in a child's trusting faith the truest wisdom in the universe reposes.

What undid Heber was his undue analytical preoccupation with social arrangements. Had he carried on regardless, he would have made out fine. There are no meaningful politics in Birdland. To care about them implies that one is deluded (like Heber) or after something else. Heber's family, for instance, were assailed by rebel Americans who forced them off their Connecticut farm. These men were not just taking a civil war a little bit too far; they were brigands, led by the repulsive lout Joe Denter. Heber tells one of these freebooters, authoritatively, "You and this pig-eyed slack-gut are nothing but cattle thieves anyhow, pretending it has to do with the war."[221] Readers of this novel can be forgiven if they come away from it believing that the American War of Independence was an expedient by which the shiftless stole from the diligent.

Anything that might initially seem like a matter of political economy quickly reduces to a matter of individual moral continence. Heber, for example, wishes to avoid wage labour in Shelburne. He just refuses to do it. Local moneybags George Ross wants very much to hire Heber, but Heber consistently rebuffs his advances until the Scots merchant asks bluntly, "Is there something you have against me, man?" Heber truthfully says he bears no grudge against Ross ("I wish there were more like you in Shelburne"), but the fact is "I like to be independent. I'd sooner work for myself than anyone else." Ross recognizes a kindred spirit and they part on good terms. Waged work, it appears, is a refuge for weak-kneed people who cannot stand on their own two feet. No man of good character would sink into such an abject condition of helpless dependence. Heber is a self-employed small businessman because that is his character.[222]

Different people have different characters, leading them to have different roles in the economy. Amos "King" Seaman of Minudie, for example, became a local magnate because of his quasi-magical powers: "[E]verything he touched seemed to turn into money."[223] Meanwhile, in *The Misadventures of Rufus Burdy,* the eponymous Burdy lives in rural poverty because he likes it. Living as he does along the "lazy curves" of the gravel Old Road, "instead of moving to more fertile acres abutting the macadam," he has thereby opted for membership in an "easy-going fraternity" who would rather have unemployment, deprivation, and isolation than jobs, prosperity, and progress. But "live and let live."[224] The Burdys have made their choice. Who are we to gainsay them?

The same thing applies on a social structural level (if we can speak of one in Birdland) as on an individual level. Visiting a textile mill in Riverport, whose male owner takes him on a tour, Bird immediately sees why his women employees have chosen to work there. The windows afford them a view of "amazing seascapes." And then there is the absence of trade unions and strikes, which allows a "family spirit" to guide productive relations in this "friendly" factory. The garment workers have clearly opted for benign patriarchy over a bargaining unit, because they prize family values. He visits an abandoned shipyard in Pugwash soon thereafter, a paradisiacal workplace that had flourished for years until troublemakers began to demand the right to drink liquor on the job. As Bird explains ruefully, "so buckets of the refreshment [were] served and soon the old story had been repeated. Rum had ruined the industry. Its cost had been too high. Workers had lost their usefulness."[225]

Bird insinuates that the order of the world, from the character of people to the distribution of property in the community, is unalterable short of divine intercession. Positive thinkers cheerfully adapt to the inevitabilities of character and circumstance. They do not question or analyse, for farther down those quixotic lines of inquiry the perils of negativity and despair await. A positive historian will realize these truths. Like Bird shielding little Mickey from the acerbic Professor by telling him tales about coaches of crystal and gold, the true historian realizes that his job is to entertain and divert, not to analyse and explain. In fact, Bird's imagined Nova Scotia does not really have a history. There are only events, one after another. Over their course, the order of the world confirms and reconfirms its imperviousness to all alteration.

4

Down the Twisting Path of Destiny:
The Impossible Liberalism of Thomas Raddall

Bird's particular construal of Nova Scotia, which we call Birdland, has deliquesced into the ambient Innocence of tourism/history. The works of Bird's contemporary Thomas Raddall, on the other hand, have retained and perhaps even improved their standing.[1] Conferences, dissertations, and awards keep his name alive.[2] Raddallian Nova Scotia is still on the map in a way that Birdland no longer is. Bird's image over time has become that of the tourism promoter, but Raddall retains his good reputation as a significant historian and serious novelist, one of the most influential cultural figures in twentieth-century Nova Scotia. Bird himself would have admitted that his books fell several notches below those of his friend Raddall.[3] Bird wrote blatantly boosterish histories, fodder for the tourist mill; Raddall wrote *Halifax, Warden of the North*, an award-winning volume that even today is often the one book people have read about the city. Bird wrote melodramas, while Raddall wrote works of literature, some of which still find a place in the CanLit canon. Raddall would clearly take precedence over Bird as a respected figure in high culture, towering over his middlebrow contemporary. Yet, as we will argue in this chapter, such a differential treatment seems suspect. In fact, both Bird and Raddall worked within the same networks, jointly argued for the same linkage of history to tourism, and shared similar perceptions of Nova Scotian identity. Although they thought of history in different ways, they reached by divergent routes a common destination: the Province of History.

The history of the province would nonetheless look importantly different in Raddall's hands. Bird's work presents us with a rather uniform, homogeneous regime of time. Events and happenings are manifold, but the timeless principles of character always hold true no matter what. Raddall gives us a much clearer sense of historical progression, with strongly delineated epochs and eras that succeed each other. Like Bird, he consistently points to abiding essences (of race, of gender, and of the individual, for example), but these are articulated in different ways depending on the period under discussion – whether the eighteenth century or the twentieth, for example, or the time before European settlement or the time after. The manner in which these essences express themselves in each era is also (much as in Bird) not primarily a product of historical events themselves, though again as in Bird's case there are thrilling occurrences aplenty. Rather, the cosmic forces of evolution and degeneration determine the historical dynamic of each Raddallian era – whose proliferous events simply confirm the underlying evolutionary tendencies that relate essences to their circumstances and to historical time. Raddall's novels and histories present us with the metaphysical workings of evolution in the recorded history of Nova Scotia. There was a slow up-building of bioethical excellence in the seventeenth and eighteenth centuries (where excellence equates to the Victorian liberal individual); evolution triumphantly fulfils itself in the nineteenth-century Golden Age of Sail (which Raddall curiously chooses not to represent directly); finally, the Golden Age withers away in the twentieth century as evolution reverses itself, leaving us with an unsettling sense that time is out of joint. At the chronological extremity of Raddall's work, we see that liberalism has become impossible – impossible either to enact in twentieth-century Nova Scotia or to leave behind as a normative standard.

◆

By any reckoning, Thomas Head Raddall (1903–1994) stands among the foremost intellectuals who shaped the interpretation of Nova Scotia's history. He played a founding role in historical societies and in the Historic Sites Advisory Council, figured as an influential promoter of historically based tourism, and addressed scores of audiences on historical themes. His books achieved even greater renown. At the end of 1972, he estimated his total sales at 2,434,710 and counting.[4]

Born in Hythe, England, Raddall was the son of an instructor for the British Army School of Musketry. His family came to "small and depressing" Halifax in 1913, leading Raddall to reflect in later years that they were "in all probability the last of a long procession of imperial soldiers and their families who had settled in Halifax all the way back to 1749 [when Cornwallis had founded the city]."⁵ Raddall survived the 1917 Halifax Explosion, lost his father in the Great War in 1918, and trained with the Canadian School of Telegraphy, which qualified him to take up positions with Marconi in New Brunswick, aboard merchant ships, and on Sable Island. Resigning from this work in 1922, he settled in Potanoc, Queens County, where in May 1923 he became an accountant with the MacLeod Pulp and Paper Company of Liverpool. He wrote in his spare time.

In 1928, *Maclean's* published his first short story, "Three Wise Men," and he began contributing to pulp magazines such as *Sea Stories* and *Adventure*. He decided to become a full-time professional writer in 1935, which meant quitting a secure job in the middle of the Depression, a terrible risk for a man with a family to support. It was, though, something he felt he had to do. Keeping the books for a pulp mill hardly ranked as his ambition in life. As he later said, "[T]o do the thing you want in life is a success in itself ... All the rest is emptiness." In keeping with this tenet, he refused to write what he thought would be most saleable, instead concentrating entirely upon the quotidian milieu of rural Nova Scotia or on tales from regional history. He made this decision out of deep patriotic and aesthetic commitments, later explaining that "while every man must consider himself a citizen of the world, it seems to me that if he is not to dissipate his energies he must find some corner of it that he loves, whose people he understands, whose past and present he knows, whose future is his concern, and spend himself there in the best way he knows."⁶ Though he still sold to the pulps as he eked out a living, he soon graduated to higher-toned outlets like *Blackwood's Magazine* in Britain (the beloved "Maga") and that American standby, the *Saturday Evening Post*. By the 1940s, he was a novelist too.

Raddall produced twenty-two major books. He published seven short-story collections – *The Pied Piper of Dipper Creek and Other Tales* (1939), *The Wedding Gift and Other Stories* (1947), *Tambour, and Other Stories* (1945), *A Muster of Arms & Other Stories* (1954), *At the Tide's Turn, and Other Stories* (1959), *Footsteps on Old Floors: True Tales of Mystery* (1968), and *The Dreamers* (1986). His five historical novels – *His Majesty's Yankees* (1942), *Roger Sudden* (1944), *Pride's Fancy* (1946), *The Governor's Lady* (1960), and *Hangman's Beach* (1966) – all work to recreate Nova Scotia's history over a "long eighteenth century," 1713 to 1820, the years when the French Acadie became British Nova Scotia. He also wrote three romantic novels focused on twentieth-century Nova Scotia – *The Nymph and the Lamp* (1950), *Tidefall* (1953), and *The Wings of Night* (1956). As far as nonfiction is concerned, there are four commissioned histories – *The Saga of the 'Rover'* (1932; brought out in revised form as *The Rover: The Story of a Canadian Privateer* in 1958), *West Novas: A History of the West Nova Scotia Reg-*

iment (1948), *Ogomkegea: The Story of Liverpool, Nova Scotia* (1951), and, with Charles Hugh Le Pailleur Jones, *The Markland Sagas: With a Discussion of Their Relation to Nova Scotia* (1934); much more widely read and influential, his two more substantial historical works, *Halifax, Warden of the North* (1948) and *The Path of Destiny: Canada from the British Conquest to Home Rule, 1763–1850* (1957); and finally his autobiography, *In My Time* (1976), widely hailed as a gripping account of one Nova Scotian's rise to literary fame and fortune. In addition, he prepared promotional works for the Nova Scotia government (such as *This Is Nova Scotia, Canada's Ocean Playground*, in 1970). Three of his books (*The Pied Piper of Dipper Creek; Halifax, Warden of the North;* and *The Path of Destiny*) won the Governor-General's Award – indeed, award founder and bestselling author John Buchan, Lord Tweedsmuir, approved of Raddall unreservedly[7] – and some of his books were translated into other languages.[8]

By the 1950s, McClelland and Stewart could acclaim Raddall "Canada's outstanding author."[9] One wonders what Gabrielle Roy or Morley Callaghan might have said to that,[10] but at home in Nova Scotia no one had much doubt. We can get some sense of his Halifax reputation from Phyllis Blakeley, Raddall's colleague in the Canadian Authors Association. Blakeley told her aunt and uncle about a literary club meeting attended by Raddall. The hostess, the folklorist Helen Creighton, was in a "fever of anxiety" before the arrival of "her lion, Dr. Thomas Raddall." Once he appeared, she announced that Raddall had a secret admirer – one of her own tenants – who had asked to know when "Tom" was approaching "so she could look out the window to see him." Helen had said to her, "'I wish there was some way you could meet him.' 'Oh, don't bother, Helen. It'll be enough to know we're both under the same roof!' Great shouts of laughter at this." Raddall, we learn, had worn a grey flannel suit, wine-coloured shirt, and blue tie to the meeting: "His hair is white now and beginning to get thin on top, but he is tanned and fit and his blue eyes sparkle."[11] To many eyes, he was the brightest star in the Nova Scotia cultural firmament. The provincial government even offered to make him lieutenant-governor (ever the maverick, he refused).

With the possible exception of the aforementioned Helen Creighton, no one could rival Raddall when it came to explaining Nova Scotians to themselves in the pursuit of what Archibald MacMechan had once called the "Nova Scotia-ness of Nova Scotia."[12] Raddall enjoyed such authority in large part because he claimed to base even his novels upon sound archival research. As he wrote his fellow historical novelist Thomas Costain, people like them had a heavy responsibility to the truth. Everyone knew that "many people get their notion of history in this palatable form; and I have a great contempt for those too-numerous costume pieces which display the writers' ignorance of history and often the very costumes they fling on their characters."[13] From the late

1930s onward, Thomas Raddall haunted the Public Archives of Nova Scotia (PANS), although it had initially struck him as an uninviting "tomb of documents."[14] It helped reconcile Raddall to archival work when the assistant archivist, Jim Martell, finagled the novelist a private office where he could smoke and use his typewriter (blatantly contravening official policy). Further, Martell and his colleague Margaret Ells answered his historical queries and edited his drafts.[15] Raddall's status as the novelist of the archives, so to speak, gave him considerable prestige.

Raddall spent long months in the archives or visiting the sites where he set his historical fiction. He constantly reminded his readers of how this research had informed his creative process. "Ellen Dewar and Michel Cascamond are creatures of the author's fancy," Raddall remarks in his preface to *Hangman's Beach*, "but I venture to say their adventures might well have happened in this place and at this time, for their background is the result of long and diligent research and of personal observation on the ground and the sea."[16] Raddall wanted to tell his readers "what really happened" – to recreate the past as it actually had been, had felt like, had looked like.[17] His experiences while examining historic sites afforded him special access to what the people of the past must have been thinking and doing. Preparing to write *Roger Sudden*, whose climactic final scenes take place at the fortress of Louisburg during the Seven Years' War, Raddall spent weeks in that "grim and lonely place" exploring the bogs and underbrush in quest of the trenches dug into the bare rock by the besieging British army. He told Kenneth White, the editor of *Adventure* (which was serializing the novel), "I like to think that all this going over the scene produces secondary effects in the writing – a sixth sense if you like – which an author can acquire no other way." His diligence was rewarded: "It was in these lonely walks on the ramparts, with the sea fog drifting mysteriously over the ruins and the gulls crying, that I saw Roger Sudden and his fellow characters in my mind like a film." Assuring White that he was no "romantic" (a term of opprobrium in the Raddallian lexicon), he explained, "If you soak yourself first in the documents, and then in the actual environment, sooner or later the characters suggest themselves, and talk and move, and all you have to do is write them down."[18] Immersion in the facts opened the way to a hidden universe of meaning.

Looking back on his intense involvement with historical fiction in the 1940s, Raddall said his "main discovery" was that "I could plunge myself into the eighteenth century and swim about freely under its surface, entirely at home with its inhabitants because I had learned to talk and think as they did and because I knew life in the forest and on the sea from experience, not just from reading about it." His inner self having been pervaded by this embodied knowledge of the past, he could "dream deliberately" to make his historical characters real.[19] Raddall's modus operandi involved accessing the spiritual essence of history through the inspired workings of his own imagination as he communed with the voices of the past.

This play of imagination and historical research put Raddall in a unique, and in some respects very odd, position. "With the exception of actual historical personages," ran the customary introductory caveat to *The Governor's Lady*, "the characters are entirely the product of the author's imagination and have no relation to any person in real life."[20] But the real/imagined polarity suggested by this conventional disclaimer is actually hard to sustain in Raddall's texts. For example, Frances and John Wentworth, the leading characters of the novel *The Governor's Lady*, undoubtedly did once exist as Nova Scotia's vice-regal couple in colonial times, in which capacity they feature prominently in the history *Halifax, Warden of the North*. Yet, exercising poetic licence, and in both his fictional and factual modes, Raddall supplies us with their thoughts and emotions. In *The Governor's Lady*, Lady Frances is a calculating seductress given to manipulative micromanagement: "She tapped a foot. She had always been able to twist him round her finger, and she wondered which approach was best now. An angry storm? Or tears and outraged innocence? Or just her coaxing mood, teasing him into laughter with some pert bit of wit at the right moment?"[21] Is this a dialogue proceeding in her mind? In the mind of the omniscient narrator? Although she seems a one-dimensional representation of the archetypal feminine schemer, at least one male reviewer found the novel "a masterful re-creation of the personality and character of Fannie Wentworth."[22] How did he know? In *Halifax, Warden of the North*, the external attributes of "Mrs Wentworth" ("slender, vivacious, adept and experienced in the arts of the drawing room and the bedchamber") are much the same, but Raddall-as-historian, though able to tell that she was "clever and ambitious," confesses his inability to make a realistic assessment of her capacity for "womanly calculation."[23] Do we, in fact, know she was calculating? Can we be sure she was "womanly"? Or that "woman" is essentially calculating? The reader who accepts Raddall's version of Lady Wentworth has been invited into a haunted twilight to see in the ghostly personalities of the past a re-enactment of the heterosexual gender ideals of the 1920s–1950s.

Momentarily adopting an unworkably ultra-empiricist definition of history, Raddall would deny that *Halifax, Warden of the North* was a history at all, for "a history must record every incident, every date, and copious statistics, all documented with care."[24] A history that recorded every incident in the life of Halifax would run to thousands of volumes merely to recount what happened to each resident in a single day (and, even then, only if it could impose some limit on the potentially infinite number of such occurrences). In fact, despite authorial disclaimers, readers of *Halifax* conventionally approach the book as a nonfictional account of happenings in the past and trust it as a well-researched, reasonably balanced assessment of the facts – that is, as a history. Rather than starkly opposing *historical fiction* to the *historical facts*, Raddall subtly develops an intermediate historical space where he combines his intuitions with his researches to dazzling effect. The Lady Wentworth he presents both in history and in historical fiction is the product of his professedly profound grasp of woman's true nature as well as the outcome of his feats of research in the archives.

Subtle shadings and different rhetorical emphases, but no profound epistemological divide, separate the factual from the fictional Mrs Wentworth. The very categories would lose much of their clarity, as the Province of History was increasingly called upon to turn the profits of tourism. Entering this Province of History means entering a vast historical novel made up not only of books, but also of monuments, restored mansions, and commemorative rituals. The uncertain boundaries between fact and fiction (exacerbated by the absence of footnotes) make it difficult to separate the voice of Raddall from the voices of the past. When he gives us the inner thoughts and casual conversations of a real or imagined character, we do not know if any textual evidence supports his representation. Voice-of-Raddall narration omnisciently gazes beyond what any person in the past could have experienced – a commonplace of historical fiction that becomes downright ahistorical in nonfictional history and commemoration. In "Raddallia," natural attractions are beautiful, aboriginal peoples alternately shabby and alarming, whole neighbourhoods disgusting – but to whom? The omniscient narrator, presumably; but then, how does he know?

Raddall's narrative voice rules out the exculpatory expedient of countering criticisms of the harsh bias evident in so many of his novels simply by saying, in effect, *such were the narrow views of a distant age*. Raddall himself often reads these views back into the past. It is not only that Raddall filters past words and deeds through his own interpretive grid, as must happen in every attempt to describe historical events, but rather that he reconstructs virtually every speech and deed with only loose reference to documentation. When we encounter the "scum" of Halifax or the "sluts" of its Upper Streets, we might imagine that we are encountering the dialect of the past. Yet all such words emanate from Raddall. Whether eighteenth-century Haligonians actually used these words as frequently, or with the same sense, remains uncertain. The intrusive authorial voice tells us what we should think and how we should see. In place of any explicitly acknowledged theory, Raddall relies upon characterization to keep his narrative flowing. Intuition and commonsensical values would guide him when he came to paint vivid portraits of the individuals who performed in this vast historical pageant. Here, for all their differences, lies a close connection between Bird and Raddall.

Like Bird, Raddall was a Victorian liberal adrift in a twentieth-century world that discomfited many of his assumptions. History offered an inviting avenue for revitalizing them. In his writings, it appears as though history itself communicates these positions and Raddall simply records them. As with Bird, Raddall did not simply read back his own opinions, but powerfully strengthened them and rendered them more plausible by associating them with a mass of historical details.

◆

In the Province of History, man and woman continually re-enact the timeless scripts of romance. No less than in Birdland, women enter the Raddallian narrative to follow, amuse, and seduce their men. The burden of making history falls onto the sturdy shoulders of rugged male individuals. Writing of colonial America on the eve of the American Revolution, Raddall notes that – contrary to the British policy of not settling west of the Appalachians – "the Americans were eager to burst across the mountains and spread into the West. Their frontiersmen already had crossed the barrier, and wherever they went their women were eager to follow."[25] The frontier-defying Americans in this passage are exclusively men, as are the Haligonians in *Halifax, Warden of the North*: "The sober middle-class Haligonian made his way to church or counting-house in the midst of all this brawling and brotheldom, and kept his womenfolk off the streets after dark."[26] Raddall portrays women through externals, as shadowy presences within the action and drama of historical men.

The names change, but natures stay the same. The fundamental determinant of gender roles lies in invariant biological dispositions. Late in *The Governor's Lady*, John Wentworth reflects that his wife "couldn't help being what she was, made as she was. You had to get along with her and with the serpent somehow, even in the wilderness." The "serpent" here refers, through its metonymic association with Eve, to female sexuality – which in this novel, as generally throughout the Raddallian world, poses the risk of overthrowing reason itself. Indeed, Raddall repeatedly associates women with creatures of lesser intelligence. "The guns leaped and spat flame," in the opening pages of this novel, and "there was a sound of great planks clapped together by a giant, followed at once by a squealing of silly females and a scuttle of startled dogs."[27] There is something intrinsically "silly" about "females." Raddall himself remembers a soirée in Halifax, attended by "two dozen people, mostly ladies of a certain age, with papers at the ready." One after another, "earnest ladies" (a particular bête noir of his) "read their rhymes aloud, to solemn applause by the others. During a long lecture on Keats, read from a book, comic relief was supplied by a little old man whose specialty was writing hymns. He simply went to sleep and snored."[28] This comes as a startlingly savage critique of the Halifax circle of Raddall enthusiasts who did so much to organize the rapturous reception of his works.

Not all women are such write-offs. Isabel Jardine in *The Nymph and the Lamp* and Frances Wentworth in *The Governor's Lady* attain an unusual degree of self-sufficiency and intelligence. Isabel works in a Halifax office. When this "new woman" travels to Sable Island to commence her love affair with Matthew Carney, she even finds herself drawn to working with the telegraph instruments. When she puts on the headphones, she experiences the liberating thrill of a "flight into another existence." Lest we worry about her essential femininity, however, Raddall quickly adds that "her feminine mind was not hampered by ... male self-discipline."[29] Her lack of an inner discipline becomes all the more evident when she takes up with the hard-hearted Skane, leaving the decent but inexperienced Matthew in the dust – a move that retrospectively seems even more ethically suspect given Matthew's growing blindness (which somehow or other she has failed to register).

Frances Wentworth, the femme fatale of Raddallian Halifax, was "Becky Sharpe and a Ninon de Lenclos rolled up in one artful bundle of petticoats."[30] Whether in a fictional or nonfictional mode, John Wentworth's "clever and expensive wife" brazenly uses her husband to accomplish her own selfish objectives.[31] One should believe nothing she says. As she welcomes John home, a clued-in male character watches her effusion of emotion "with the pursed smile of a man who has had too much to do with women ever to believe this little scene." Nor does she have a capacity for real human attachments. Her husband, set to return to Halifax as governor, is shocked at the expression on Frances's "taut ivory face" as he looks into her "smoldering eyes": "Johnnie was startled. A woman's eyes should only look like that when one is making love ... She was past the age for love at last, and what glowed in her eyes made her face look older still. It was hate."[32] Vanity, malice and libido pretty well sum her up; she has no inner life.

Raddall often has us experience the essence of womankind by having us smell his women, fictional and nonfictional. Passage after passage conveys molecular evidence of woman's radical otherness. Describing the aftermath of an eighteenth-century party, *The Governor's Lady* (fictional) recreates "the empty rooms swimming in an invisible mist of bohea tea and warm and scented femininity." Upon entering a room, Fannie – a habitué of this social jungle – can instantly pick up "the scent of women" within the "faint mingled scent of elegant people."[33] Meanwhile, *Halifax* (factual) remembers packed governor's balls, crowded with "gorgeous women" complete with decaying teeth, pimples, and offensive body odour. They "*smelled* in the heat of the dance despite liberal dashes of scent," a bodily indignity apparently not suffered by their male dance-partners.[34]

Even more than smells, Raddall loved describing costumes, often from an imagined female perspective. He has a minor woman character supply this description of Fannie's portrait: "[S]he posed in a silk gown that would have thrown old Justice Atkinson into a fit. Bodice down to here, and the stays laced tight below. She daresn't take a good breath the whole time she was sitting, lest she pop her pretty dumplings. She told me that herself."[35] Raddall often trains our gaze upon women whose bodies – particularly their bosoms – strain against the confines of their garments. Men do not come in for such scrutiny. Male bodies, in Raddall's typology, tend to be hard and unyielding; those of women are soft and pliant, amenable to being moulded by their raiment. Such vignettes are inscribed within a normative discourse about naturalness and authenticity. The heroine of *Tidefall* is Rena Caraday, a young woman from the Fundy shore whose new husband is the cruel Sax Nolan. The single-minded shipping entrepreneur Sax drags Rena with him to Europe on an ostensible honeymoon that is really a business trip. Disconnected and alone, she has nothing to do but buy fashionable clothes that do not really become her. It comes as a relief to return home and feel the clean salt air wash over her. Alone on the coast, "she filled her lungs with it now as if driving out the last cloying reek of that other atmosphere; and beneath the dress her breasts strained at the impudent Paris brassiere as if eager to be free of that too, and of everything that had to do with the world into which she had been carried."[36] She understands now what she has done in marrying this unnatural man, hearkening to the message nature itself imparts to her through the agency of her body. Soon she has escaped to a remote and rocky island where she can breathe freely.

Stylish outfits represent all the coercive forces that modern society brings to bear upon nature as incarnated by the female form. *The Wings of Night* supplies a scene in which the hero Neil comes upon Tally Pendergrass, a young schoolteacher, swimming with her rural family. These "half-wild" people have "an easy independent look" that comes of living off the land.[37] They are utterly unself-conscious before Neil – save for Tally herself, who remains underwater so that the visitor from town will not see her. She alone of her family wears a store-bought swimsuit, purchased two years before, which has grown rather too tight. When she finally emerges from the water, Neil sees that "true enough the wet suit clung to her plump young breasts, to the long waist and round hips." She feels mortally embarrassed, to his mirth. He is "tickled" to think of "this healthy young creature from the backwoods with … her notion that she'd got beyond everything that savored of the Old Back Road; and that fresh picture of her at the lake, swimming with the simple pleasure of a deer in hot weather, a pure Back Road creation that the cheap mail-order bathing suit couldn't hide in any way at all."[38] There is more than one way in which Tally's suit does not fit her. Her efforts to look more sophisticated than her origins have made her look silly instead.

Paradoxically, this passage asserts that Tally's beauty lies in the unadorned naturalness of her form, but Neil is also "tickled" to think of how her "plump breasts" look in the tight swimsuit that supposedly mars her appearance. Like the imagined Lady Wentworth before her, Tally's contrived vanity actually makes her more attractive. Furthermore, while true feminine beauty purportedly lies outside the influence of self-regard and pride of appearance, it is also true that a powerful tendency to vanity in Raddall's "woman" prevents his female characters from actually realizing it is so. Neil – not Tally – understands the truth about her that is given to him by the sight of her body. They are not thinkers, these women. It is in their nature to become preoccupied with artificial frippery to an extent that they neither apprehend nor comprehend the beauties of nature, which they nonetheless embody. Pretty things drive Raddallian women to distraction. When eighteenth-century ladies visited the governor in Halifax, their eyes darted "with bright feminine curiosity" across the room to admire his "silver-mounted brushes, combs, and powder box; a wardrobe whose open door gave a glimpse of elegant London clothes; the rich carpet in which their painted wooden heels sank as if in snow; the huge mahogany bed with its tester and valances and looped curtains."[39] Is it women or Raddall who tries to understand the world by obsessive attention to mere appearances?

On the subject of women's deaths in nineteenth-century Halifax, for example, Raddall the historian observes that it "was fashionable for young ladies to be pallid; and so they were, poor things, what with a studied avoidance of sunshine, no exercise, stuffy rooms, tight stays, monotonous diet, and a constant huddling over fires and stoves. And they suffered a fashionable disease in consequence – consumption – which carried them off right and left."[40] These silly women were more the authors of their own deaths than they were the victims of patriarchal power relations or inadequate public sanitation. Their fate – death by vanity – typifies a world where (as in Birdland) explanation seldom extends farther than characterization.

Social class does exist in this world of characters – but only as a judgment upon one's intrinsic qualities, not as an overarching socio-economic reality. Raddall typically disregards relations of production and their associated social preconditions, to focus instead on the picturesque extremities: debauched soldiery, effete aristocracy, shiftless paupers. When he does depict working people, he confines himself to describing the bodily and psychological consequences of their working lives. Labour itself and its place within a larger world never become visible. In his autobiography, he tells us of his outrage at the treatment of the pulp workers in his area, but trains his anger upon "the comfortable owners whose schemes and practices had brought about these conditions" – that is, upon particular individuals, not upon an economic relationship. Indeed, systematic thinking about social structure and its relation to the labour process and capital accumulation is viewed with overt hostility. When, for example, Marx rears his head in Raddall's world, he is quickly ushered off the page in a blaze of liberal indignation. When one of Isabel Jardine's acquaintances in *The Nymph and the Lamp* indicts an employer as a "specimen of his type," Isabel steps out of character to deliver a sharp Raddallian rebuke: "Brock, you're a specimen of your own type. The man who got hurt in the war and feels he owes the world a grudge. I met your type once before; only he didn't go about preaching a backwoods version of Marx; he went off to sulk on a desert island. There seem to be a good many others – all this talk about a 'lost generation'! And you're all alike, the lot of you. All you've lost is your sense of decency. Sooner or later you hurt other people."[41] People attracted to social theory should take a time-out on a desert island until they are ready to be sociable again.

Raddall often describes the working class in biological terms implying a less-evolved and subhuman nature, rather than portraying it as a requisite component of a mode of production dependent upon access to large numbers of people compelled to sell their labour in order to secure the necessaries of life. As governor of New Hampshire, the fictional John Wentworth is besieged by the "scum of Portsmouth."[42] Such defectives also proliferate in Raddall's factual description of Halifax. The city's original settlers (a "rabble of cockneys") were a truly "shiftless lot, full of complaints, many in rags, others sick or feigning sickness to avoid the labor of clearing the townsite." The city was "little better than a transatlantic almshouse for the London poor." The outbreak of typhus among the early settlers – "[u]nclean, undisciplined, clutched together for warmth" – was, implicitly, their own fault.[43]

"It seems brutal to suggest that all this was for the best," Raddall says, struggling for balance as he describes their deaths, but he goes on anyway: "It is the truth." Typhus sought out dirty, drunken, improvident people (society's "dregs"), leaving Halifax "purged of its worst human element." Better yet, "the loss was neatly offset by an influx of New Englanders, tough, resourceful scions of the Pilgrims and Puritans, accustomed to making a living in a stony land." If we skip ahead to the 1810s, we find a city that has benefited from Mother Nature's evolutionary tough love. Natural selection has allowed the best to flourish by making the worst to wither away. Hence, "in place of the rabble of doubtful cockneys there was now a population of more than eleven thousand, the majority Nova Scotia born, busily employed, some of them rich, and all convinced of the town's eternal prosperity."[44] Nature intervened with a resolution worthy of Herbert Spencer to remove such degenerates from history, saving the city for those more rugged men of the north whom biology had predestined to predominate in Nova Scotia.

The above reference to how working "stony land" induces moral virtue brings us to a theme much beloved of Raddall. Like a twentieth-century Montesquieu, he insistently connects environmental conditions with moral development. Some climates and landscapes induce torpor, others vigour. Raddall upholds the windswept, rock-bound, frostbitten climate of Nova Scotia as an ideal locale for fostering real liberal individuals. The fictional Rev. George MacLeish gives voice to this conviction in "A Muster of Arms": "It took a bold man to venture here and a steadfast woman to follow him. No attraction for the rich, no field for the merely clever, no ease for the sluggish, no security for the craven or weak." Only the "bold" could succeed. The very hardship and difficulty of life sufficed to weed out the unfit to leave only healthy, resourceful stock to populate the province. As the minister impresses upon us, "[T]hey had to fight with savages for a foothold and with the climate for existence … Struggle, struggle, that was the story, all down through the years."[45] With a concluding evolutionary flourish, Raddall's mouthpiece MacLeish establishes rural Nova Scotia as the natural habitat of the self-reliant and the strong.

"A Muster of Arms," intended to summon up all the sterling qualities that Canadian soldiers could bring to the fight against Hitlerism, fairly radiates the flush of wartime patriotic fervour. Elsewhere, Raddall did not wax so sanguine about the bioethical health of twentieth-century Nova Scotians. Defective individuals seemed to have appeared in their midst. This came as an unstoppable consequence of a historical process that had stalled as the capitalist development of Nova Scotia petered out. In *The Wings of Night,* Jim, an old-timer from Oak Falls, explains the state of the region to his young friend Neil, who has just returned after a decade's absence. He offers up a folksy metaphor: "You ever notice a l'il whirlpool in a brook, in the lee of a big boulder, say, in December when the first real cold weather comes? The brook don't freeze over if the water runs fast enough, but there in the lee o' the boulder is a disc of ice, perfec' circle, slowly goin' round and round but never gettin' any place. That's Oak Falls." On Jim's advice, Neil turns to history for answers. The verdict is clear; as Neil reads, he sees "one cold fact standing out more and more, that usually it was the ambitious and energetic who went away, leaving the village and the breed to what was left."[46] It had taken the forces of nature centuries to carefully winnow out the unfit, but now that work is being undone before their eyes.

Neil gets vivid confirmation of this gloomy Spencerian *aperçu* on a visit to the local pulp mill. Peering into "the moist gloom of the mill's interior," he espies "a hundred pallid men, the separate tribe of Oak Fallers known as the 'pulp crowd,' and the name was apt, for they looked like [the mill's] product: their faces had the same tallowy tint, and it seemed to me that if you put any of them under the big hydraulic press where the bales were made it would wring water, not blood, out of him."[47] Oak Falls, no longer the stronghold of vigorous homesteaders, hosts a vitiated strain of enervated mill hands. Their way of life throws them into an abject dependence upon the mill owner, whose generosity and savoir-faire alone furnish them with wages and work. No elemental struggle tests their evolutionary mettle, so natural selection has halted – even reversed.

In a Raddallian cosmos, only direct confrontation with an unmediated and implacable natural world can instil the powerful instincts of self-mastery and self-sufficiency that furnish the necessary supports to individuality. Once acquired, these characteristics entail to one's descendants with Lamarckian fatalism. Thus, a rugged and hardy race grows up. Wage labour, though, has no such fundamental purpose. With brutal irony, industrialism emerges thanks to the hardihood and enterprise proverbially characteristic of Anglo-Saxons only to undercut the very conditions that had instilled such qualities to begin with. Whole communities were degenerating. Under the influence of the distorted conditions they lived amidst, the biological fabric of these unfortunate people rotted away until they became something less than human.

Raddall traces these decrescent evolutionary patterns through physical descriptions of degenerates or richly suggestive reflections upon the course of history. Yet he neither theorizes nor even names them. In this, he was a man of his time. Degeneration did not enter intellectual history as a positive hypothesis susceptible to verification. Instead of a clearly understood biopsychological phenomenon, degeneration appeared as the uncanny complement to a liberalism that prized progress above all else. This imprecision did little to hinder its expressive power. Left untheorized, degeneration almost magically became immanent – a malign presence whose workings were observable in the material world, but which resisted direct representation. It appears in Raddall's books (as in those of authors to whom he has often been compared, such as Jack London and Joseph Conrad) as "a process which could usurp all boundaries of discernible identity, threatening the very overthrow of civilisation and progress."[48] Degeneration encapsulated a potential that lurked within the central components of liberalism. It could not be banished to the antipodes of inferior races, the working class, and economically stagnant regions – much as intellectuals would try.

The novel *Tidefall* presents us with a telling example of this truth. It promises the story of a rugged individualist: "Here is a strong, masculine story told by a strong, masculine talent. The world of Sax Nolan is a violent place where men of action pit their resources against society and the elements and each other: and only a Conrad or Kipling or Jack London has written of that world with the drive and familiarity of Thomas Raddall." Saxby Nolan works his way up from humble beginnings to become, by the early 1930s, a local magnate with a mansion on the hill. As such, he represents something of a throwback to an earlier type of hard-working, hard-headed, hard-bargaining Bluenose, one who has usually passed from the scene by the time Raddall reaches the twentieth century. The local member of Parliament (MP), Hilliard Cuff, gives a little speech when Sax launches a ship, "recalling the days of Nova Scotia's glory, when the great windjammers sailed in every sea. The days of wooden ships and iron men … Good old Nova Scotia still had ships and men like that." Cuff upholds Sax as an indomitable "iron man" who sums up the liberal individual's legendary capacity to stand above mere circumstances. Let others rationalize their personal failures with appeals to the inscrutable ups and downs of the economy; Saxby Nolan made his own luck: "The talk of hard times he heard with contempt, the babble of weaklings. Prosperity wasn't 'just around the corner' either, as some of the optimists said. Prosperity, Sax said with his little grin, was something you dug up for yourself."[49] There is only one problem. Sax Nolan is a simian.

Nolan is nasty, brutish, and short. His hirsute body has the terrible strength of a wild animal. He is subject to fits of unreasoning anger provoked by the atavistic impulses coursing through him. When he was a boy, the little girls called him "Monkey Eyes." After such humiliating episodes, Sax would return to the family shack, "sitting in one of his moody fits beside the shore and promising himself that someday, somehow, he would master one of those tittering creatures and satisfy the hatred and longing that he had for them."[50] From this suddenly sharp appraisal of the transposition of class antagonism onto sexual politics, Raddall (here resembling Jack London in his striking description of the *Sea Wolf*) proceeds to construct an evolutionary parable.

Sax must amass money and power so that someday he will gain possession of a well-bred young woman with a refined sensibility. Although he comes by money with relative ease (thanks to his unflagging energy and steely determination), he is simply not made of the right stuff. Early in the novel, he charms Ellen, the beautiful daughter of a Bostonian lawyer. Ellen loves how it feels to control "an original male" who seems "all chained and locked up by some whim of his own will. That she had the key to the lock and chain occurred to her sometimes in a puzzling and lightly amusing way, as if she had found a means of unlocking a cage in a zoo and did not know quite what to do about the tenant." When Sax finally realizes that she regards him as a pet, his true nature conclusively breaks through the thin veneer of civilization. Beyond reason now, "he threw an arm about her waist and clutched at her breast with the other, dragging her towards him and thrusting his lips on her mouth." The horrified Ellen slaps him and slips his grasp, accusing him, "You — yo*u* ape!"[51] She is not far wrong.

An insurmountable barrier keeps Sax from the likes of Ellen. Pamela, his eventual mother-in-law, correctly surmises that he desperately craves the respect of fully realized human beings for just the same reason that he can never get it. He is subhuman. She taunts him, "[S]omething about you ... repelled everyone. And nothing you could do about it. That's the pitiful thing about you, Saxby. You can't help being what you are. You have the power to do many things but not that." Her daughter Rena finds this out the hard way, by marrying Sax, not realizing the truth until it is too late. Rena imagines a conversation with her mother: "Sax Nolan isn't any ordinary man. He isn't really a man at all. He's an animal. Oh, a very clever animal, very pleasant when he wants to be, full of energy and courage in his own way, but still an animal." While she spares nothing in her criticism of Sax, she does try to be fair-minded. She knows that "he can't help any of this" because he resembles "an ape that had wandered out of the jungle and learned some rather clever tricks inside a cage."[52]

Sax's baseness does not interfere with his attainment of agency. He is clever, energetic, and courageous. He knows what he wants, abetted in his pursuit of his desires by something in his character, "something cruel. Something without conscience." The relentless self-discipline with which he furthers his designs seems inhuman. Rena insists that "there's even something animal about the way he shies away from alcohol and tobacco — as if he had to keep his sense of taste and smell for catching prey." What is he? A primate of a lower order, spawned in the genetic cesspool of the shacks around Herring Point? Or a man among men, a hell-bent-for-leather fire-eater of the old school (as Cuff suggests) who is also a rational calculator of risk and reward, a man who makes a fortune by his own efforts — in short, "the kind of fellow who made the heroes in books look pale and soft"?[53] Really, he is both at the same time — and for the same reasons. He represents a point of contact between the liberal individual and his negation. His humble beginnings mean that he is both a self-made man and a lower order of primate. His pursuit of self-interest gives him agency in the wider world, but also enslaves him to his own impulses. His defiance of circumstance gives him the strength to accomplish what other men would never do out of faint-heartedness and moralizing qualms, even as it further attenuates his connection to the rest of humanity. Perhaps with the character of Saxby Nolan, Raddall wanted to explore the fate of the individual during a conjuncture when history itself seemed to have stagnated and the predominance of much-prized British biological and moral characteristics no longer seemed assured.

———————◆———————

Unlike Bird, who had no social vocabulary, Raddall had an implicit evolutionary theory. However, like Bird – but on evolutionary rather than strictly characterological grounds – Raddall felt unswervingly convinced as to the superiority of Anglo-Celtic civilization and the inferiority of all other racial, ethnic, and national groups, whose irrationality, collectivism, and weakness handicapped them in the struggle of the fittest to survive. Raddall's archetypal Nova Scotians, Barry Moody observes, were the New Englanders who settled parts of the province in the 1760s (and whose loyal status as "His Majesty's Yankees" immunized them against the radicalism of their kindred): "[I]t becomes increasingly clear that, for Raddall, these New England settlers and their descendants, and a select few of the other English immigrants and Loyalists, really *are* Nova Scotia, or at least constitute the parts that count."[54] As for aboriginal peoples, African-Americans, Acadians, and Europeans of non-British descent, social evolution has condemned them to racial inferiority.[55]

Aboriginal peoples fascinated Raddall. One of his first stories, "Tit for Tat," tells of an "old Indian" with a penchant for stealing wood. Raddall went on to acquire a reputation as an expert on the Mi'kmaq, having acquired a smattering of their language. Yet, in his published writings, First Nations people appear as "savage folk." They supply the rude foil for the Euroamerican colonizers. That they preceded Europeans in North America suggests not that they should enjoy the privileges often associated with first-comers, but rather how much the continent has benefited from its subsequent deliverance of their savage grasp. John Wentworth in *The Governor's Lady* admires the good prospects of fishing and hunting, riding and rambling "in a forest where only yesterday the savages lurked with tomahawk and scalping knife."[56] In *Halifax,* the Mi'kmaq are first depicted as credulously believing in a "queer whimsical mythology," then as bloodthirsty scalpers under the influence of a "famous and ferocious savage who for a decade filled [Haligonians'] ancestors' days and nights with horror," not to speak (but of course!) of the "half-mad priest Le Loutre."[57] In *The Path of Destiny*, pre-contact North America features as "an unknown wilderness ... haunted by ferocious savages." By the 1780s, native peoples had devolved into a "shabby puzzle," having lost their old fighting power, though they seemingly staged a remarkable comeback in time for the War of 1812.[58]

Indeed, Raddall's "Indians" typically figure as pawns in the struggle between the British and Americans in the late eighteenth century. In one of the many struggles that convulsed Lake Champlain, Raddall introduces "a greasy swarm of Indians with war paint daubed over the grime of a winter's fires" who added to the "travelling circus" atmosphere that enveloped the campaign. (Once more, we wonder who is watching the procession and deciding it looks carnivalesque?) When native peoples figure as historical agents, tawdry considerations motivated them. The Mi'kmaq and Malecite, trying to play the English off against the Americans, were merely "greedy for gifts." Assuming the voice of Lord Dorchester (but ventriloquizing him, not quoting), Raddall asks, "The Indians, those brown creatures of the forest on both sides of the lakes, what could a British gentleman make of them? There had been promises (and a gentleman lived up to promises), so he had done his best to honor old pledges to these crapulous and unclean creatures upon whose whim the western trade depended."[59] No voices of these supposedly "crapulous and unclean creatures" counterbalance this little vignette by suggesting that differently placed actors in North America might have had reason to characterize nineteenth-century Euroamericans as something other than endlessly patient, put-upon, pledge-honouring gentlemen.

The African-Americans who came to Nova Scotia after the early days of European colonization fare little better. "Happy-go-lucky Negroes" pop up in *The Governor's Lady*,[60] and in *The Nymph and the Lamp*, Matthew Carney worries about the fate of Sable Island ponies at the hands of "darkies from Preston";[61] but most of Raddall's comments on people of colour come in his nonfiction. Even there, they factor as a problem, not a people. When a party of black settlers left for Sierra Leone in the 1790s, "it seemed for a time that the Negro problem in Nova Scotia had been solved." Yet both free blacks and even slaves remained, so "the problem" persisted.[62] This problem worsened in 1796 with the arrival of five or six hundred "wild black men, women and children" from Jamaica – the Maroons, who made the "nocturnal forest about Preston" ring with "voodoo chants and orgiastic laughter ... There were whispers also of something else."[63] (That the Maroons also laboured mightily in the creation of Halifax's military infrastructure is a fact Raddall passes over – and certainly does not celebrate – in a few sentences.) When the Maroons ("untamed, unhappy, pinched by the bitter winters and hungry land" – we notice they were never oppressed, exploited, or marginalized) are summarily dispatched to Sierra Leone, Raddall's race-conscious readers might breathe a sigh of relief. They would relax too soon. During the War of 1812, the fleets "brought something else back to Halifax – the Negro problem." Characteristically, he pays attention to them mainly because they wore captured American uniforms: "The memory of these Africans cavorting about the streets in the blue and buff of the United States Army and the green and scarlet of the York Rangers was long cherished in the town."[64]

We next glimpse the "Negro Problem" in the mid–twentieth-century relocation of Africville, depicted not as a longstanding community but as a perplexing anomaly, a "squalid shack town." The "Negro community" may have misguidedly cherished the hope that it would remain intact, but as a city report advised them "firmly," it was "not right that any segment of the community should continue to exist in isolation."[65] Africville, and by implication Afro–Nova Scotian history more generally, was a "sad problem." The face of Nova Scotia was essentially British, and people of colour were discolorations – to echo the very figure Raddall uses to describe the "rash of Chinese restaurants" that "broke over the city's face" during the Great War.[66] Raddall might have explained that he was trying to inhabit and incarnate bygone worldviews and mindsets. He nevertheless makes it tricky to separate his own views from those of his characters. Indeed, it sometimes seems as though he avails himself of the historical-accuracy defence in order to say things he could not otherwise get away with uttering in polite public discourse.

Nowhere, perhaps, is this issue more troublesome than with the seemingly gratuitous proliferation of the word "nigger" throughout his historical novels. This word's deployment follows a number of rules. It does not appear in modern-dress stories, only in costume ones. Furthermore, only a certain sort of character ever says it. Raddall's women never utter anything so unseemly. Nor do his heroes, just as they never speak in dialect. The man who says "nigger" in the Raddallian cosmos is a man who is even tougher than the hero is – one who is unsentimental and hard, walking tall in proud possession of a take-no-guff masculinity. Thus, in *His Majesty's Yankees*, Raddall reserves the word for the hero Davy's older brother Mark, who is taller, thicker of limb, and unburdened by Davy's romanticism. He says "nigger" where sensitive Davy opts for "negro."[67] Mark represents a type of character who is neither the hero nor the villain but the man who pushes history along. If such men appear inconsiderate or rough-edged on occasion, it hardly signifies – they are the doers who, as such, command respect. Rough-hewn, plain-spoken, and hard-nosed, they have a practical knowledge of the historical process. They are on its side. If they sometimes say things that seem insensitive, that is because they have no bleeding-heart sympathy for history's victims. They know where evolution is heading and have few tears to shed for those whom it shoulders out of its way.

Amos Pride, of *Pride's Fancy*, is such an agent of evolution. Pride, an old merchant prince, remembers regretfully a time when he forwent the chance to become a Caribbean sugar planter. In the West Indies, he saw "nothing … but parched earth and mountains and the long road home. Blind! – for there was

Africa full of idle niggers, very easy to be had by the Middle Passage, and those rich plains ... wanting nothing but the brush cleared off and a few canals dug."[68] Amos Pride is one of any number of characters Raddall used to explore a particularly stark formulation of Western manhood in the age of liberal capitalism. Pride makes history and speaks on its behalf. He serves as a mouthpiece for the way capitalism sees the world, as an assemblage of materials awaiting commodification. Insofar as Pride conceives of Africans as passively awaiting operations that would commodify their persons and their labour (i.e., insofar as a capitalist mode of production has yet to incorporate them), and insofar as he has grasped the *realpolitik* of his situation, he is simply being accurate when he refers to them by means of a dehumanizing slur.

In Raddall's Nova Scotia, the Amos Prides of the world had long since gotten the job done, but dehumanization still had certain useful applications. Working in the context of a vogue for folklore identified with Helen Creighton and a host of other enthusiasts, Raddall offers his own suitably hyper-masculine take on what in other hands was an exercise in gentle historical sentimentality: the pursuit of fine, old, simple traditions, traditions that defined who really belonged to the community. In "Blind MacNair," Raddall recreates a nineteenth-century singing contest between Singing Johnny Hanigan, the eponymous MacNair, and "a big, handsome negro man with a voice like the sound of great bells." This nameless black sailor leads the contest in its early going, excelling at chanties and frivolous novelties. Then the contest turns serious. Now the singers must show their mastery of ballads, the genre that represents the highest emotions and the noblest sentiments. Balladeers perform the most precious cultural heritage of Nova Scotia. The black sailor has no aptitude for this form. Hanigan crows, "I never saw a nigger yet could sing ballads!" The remark, characteristic of Johnny the showboating braggart, cements our affection for MacNair the quiet dreamer. At the same time, in the terms of the story, Johnny is right: "So the negro man dropped out of the game."[69] The soulful MacNair wins the singing contest, but he is a doomed man trapped in the past; fittingly, he is a ghost by the time the story has ended. The future really belongs to the aggressive Hanigans. What about the nameless black man with the voice like bells? He just disappears. Black people can take no important place within the sublime folk community of Nova Scotia. Like Bird, but following a different path, Raddall reduces people of colour to mere local colour, with no hand in shaping the province's identity.

French Canadians fare somewhat better, depending on how completely they have bought into the overarching project of British liberal order. If their history reflected badly upon the extension of British civilization, Raddall would not touch it. Although a man who prided himself on his willingness to face the plain facts, he resolutely declined to countenance the "French fact" in

North America. His editor, Thomas Costain, urged him to no avail that, since *Roger Sudden* took place during the 1750s, Raddall would absolutely have to reckon with the Expulsion of the Acadians – if only to satisfy the pragmatic financial considerations of marketing the novel to Americans enamoured of *Evangeline*. "You don't visualize or dramatize it," he upbraided Raddall. "This is throwing away a grand opportunity." Knowing of Raddall's British partisanship, Costain suggested an even-handed approach rather than a one-sided lament of atrocities (which he knew Raddall would never accept). Why not write a lead-up to the events of 1755, telling the reader all about Acadian "refusal to cooperate, their obstinacy, and their willingness to play the game of the Indians"? Having done that, Raddall could then recreate the scene of the deportation "and so give the other side of the picture, the misery and the agony and the heartbreaks."[70]

Raddall prized creative freedom, priding himself on his refusal to take direction.[71] Yet he respected Costain, a successful historical novelist in his own right.[72] He often adopted Costain's suggestions, which explains why we know more about Roger Sudden's love life than Raddall had originally planned. Yet this time Raddall resisted tooth and nail. As a Canadian himself, Costain surely knew, Raddall remarked, that the whole episode of the Expulsion had been "written to death" long ago. And cutting, one suspects, to the chase, what did Costain mean by the implied even-handedness of giving "the other side of the picture"? For, in fact, the British had had no choice in what they did: "the Acadians themselves brought it on their heads." He would have none of the woolly-headed, soft-hearted romanticism he discerned in Longfellow and his ilk. Such sentimentalists had allowed their sympathies to interfere with their appraisal of factual accuracy and historical significance. He dearly wished that reviewers of *Roger Sudden* might say of him, "Here at last is an author who can write of eighteenth century Nova Scotia without lingering sentimentally over the Acadians."[73] Indeed, no fair-minded reader of the finished novel could hesitate to pronounce this verdict. Raddall in *Roger Sudden* gives us vivid descriptions of the Acadians' slovenly farms and personal ugliness (small, lean, and sharp-featured). They were no great loss.[74]

During a Halifax radio interview, Raddall advised the archivist Jim Martell that he hoped *Roger Sudden* would recall history with an unflinching willingness to face facts. After all, "the history of Nova Scotia has been romanticized to death. In this book I have tried to show things and people as they really were."[75] Martell had read earlier drafts of the novel – before Costain had advised Raddall to up the Acadian quotient – and the harshness with which Raddall treated them in the published work startled him. In a personal letter, the archivist expressed his reservations. Raddall's friend and collaborator sheepishly explained, "You may be thinking that we [Martell and his co-worker

Margaret Ells] don't want to see anything reflecting on the French because of the situation today … but our main concern is that you keep your reputation for historical objectivity."[76] The novelist responded by asking Martell to take the scales from his eyes so that he might see the Acadians for what they were rather than as "maudlin and untrue literature" showed them. Martell would have only to drive from Digby to Yarmouth to see the houses "without beauty," the ugly women ("the only pretty Acadian girls I've seen were in Moncton"), and the "small and dour" men. Then he should continue driving down the road to Port Maitland, where he could compare the prosperity of its anglophone inhabitants with the squalor of the French Shore. Anyone would have to conclude that "there is the same soil and the same sea, and the same forest beyond – the same resources on which the Acadians live so meagrely … It is in the marrow of their bones: they don't know how to live, *and never did*. And they don't care." There was no point to indulging in sympathetic Acadian history now that the deed was done: "The world moves."[77] Martell backed down. He had no particular interest in Acadian welfare. He pointed out, defensively, that though his name sounded French, his ancestors were in fact Huguenots who had settled as Foreign Protestants near Lunenburg, and so he naturally felt solicitous towards the British.

Throughout this exchange, both sides underlined their objectivity. Martell's first letter to Raddall had asked his friend to remain objective. Raddall responded by appealing to the objective facts of socio-economic development. It is hard not to suspect a mechanism of displacement at work here, a de-centring of the discussion from the Acadians, their present marginalization, their historic grievances, and the threat these represented to a historical narrative that recounted the spread of British civilization. By their very presence, Acadians called into question the notion of Nova Scotia as the cradle of British civilization and the concomitant priority of the British as a founding people. Instead of facing such worrisome matters head-on, Martell and Raddall recast the debate so that it seemed to hinge on empiricism, best practices, and clear-headedness. The results were wonderful. The historians appeared to be nobly renouncing something cherished, namely romance (which they had stored elsewhere, in stories of British heroism); they made themselves appear very modern; and they effectively placed their cultural outlook beyond reasonable reproach, since opposition to it was equivalent to silliness or fanaticism. For these two Nova Scotian intellectuals, the manifest content of their discussion (all about being undeceived and objective) displaces its emotional heart (the legitimacy of anglophone ascendancy) onto something relatively minor (historical methodology). The disguised underlying wish (that they deserve their high social status) is bound up in too much anxiety to be admitted.

Raddall felt convinced that the real tragedy of the French in North America lay not in their subordination to British imperialism, but rather in their tragic inclination to unwise liaisons with native peoples and their subsequent retention of primitive traits. Englishmen, by contrast, had abjured such ill-advised couplings, and they owed their great success to this doughty perseverance in racial continence. Here one thinks of Roger Sudden's epiphany as he ponders whether he should sleep with Wapke, a Mi'kmaw woman to whom he has been given as a captured slave. One moonlit night, as the two of them camp out, she sheds her habitual garb in an attempt to seduce him. Roger "had come to accept Wapke as a shapeless caribou-hide smock with a black repulsive mask at one end and a pair of muscular legs at the other," but now "the bronze pixie before him was young and slender as to waist, with rounded hips and plump thighs and a pair of breasts neither large nor small, pink-nippled and erect." Roger, who brings to this encounter a long résumé of seductions in Europe, nevertheless felt "profoundly disturbed" at this sight. "He shivered, for she was tempting," Raddall writes. "Look at me, Bosoley," cries Wapke, using the name she has selected for Roger. "I am strong and alive. I am like a young maple by the water."

"Am I not well made, Bosoley?"

"As the moon," he answered. She was turning herself again, displaying all her perfections with the pride of a naked child, but at his words she broke her pose and dropped upon her knees before him, saying softly:

"Then let us make love together, Bosoley."

How many women had said that to him in other lands and other tongues! And how easy it had been to take what they offered and pass on, without the shadow of a thought! Yet it was just that, the shadow of a thought, that hung between him and the splendid animal at his feet – the notion of a plunge into darkness from which there was no return. Gautier's voice came back to him: "When you have spent a year ... you will not wish to leave ... hundreds like you mated to savage women in the woods ..." All his impressions of this enormous loneliness confirmed the Acadian's words, and all his instincts rebelled. To mate with this wild thing, to produce hybrid things, half beast and half himself, and to live year in year out among these mockeries, like a man shut up in a room hung with distorted mirrors ... ugh! Darkness! Darkness!

"No!" he said violently.[78]

Raddall, versed in evolutionary theory, knows that a lot hangs on Roger's decision. When, at the end of the book, Roger faces a French firing squad at the fortress of Louisbourg, his last thoughts turn to the inevitable triumph of the English. Unlike the French, they did not wall themselves up in fortresses, but saw "fields in the unbroken forest," envisioning "new earth to tread, new rivers to cross, new mountains to behold." Unlike the French, they were never distracted by native women: "Only a handful of *coureurs de bois* and priests had ever penetrated the continent – and the *coureurs* had mated with savage women and spilled their seed in the wilderness ... They had not left a mark." Conversely, the English – with a better grasp of what colonization entailed – "took their women with them everywhere, resolved not merely to penetrate the wilderness but to people it!" Uplifted by these patriotic thoughts, Roger "faced the muskets with a proud, unflinching gaze."[79] He meets his death thinking, as always, of his one true love: the emergent liberal order.

In some ways, then, passages that seem to be about sex are really about property. If, after their somewhat rocky start, Roger had managed to settle down with Wapke, he might well have gone native in other respects. If the *coureurs de bois* had "spilled their seed," a Biblical image equating interracial sex to masturbation or *coitus interruptus,* they had consequently failed in their duty to the white race.[80] They mixed up its bloodlines so that their progeny, nightmarish "hybrid things," would inevitably lack the connatural European capacity for enlightenment, civilization, and industry.

Yet these reflections capture only some of the energies that drive these remarkable passages from *Roger Sudden*, passages that fuse sexuality and colonialism with a candour unusual in Canadian letters. Peter Stallybrass and Allon White remark that "disgust always bears the imprint of desire. These low domains, which have apparently been expelled as 'Other,' return as the objects of nostalgia, longing and fascination. The forest, the fair, the theatre, the slum, the circus, the seaside-resort, the 'savage': all these, placed at the outer limit of civil life, become symbolic contents of bourgeois desire."[81] In Raddall's colonialist fantasy, multiple transgressors underlie this primal scene of Roger and Wapke: the sexually aggressive woman-master, the humiliatingly dependent man-slave, the empowered natives, the natural people far removed from the city, and above all the European, aroused by the sight of a native woman. Folded within "scientific" accounts of race, Robert J.C. Young reminds us, was "a central assumption and paranoid fantasy" seldom articulated but compulsively repeated as a leitmotif: "the uncontrollable sexual drive of the non-white races and their limitless fertility" that invariably feature in Western accounts of essential racial difference. Furthermore, "this extraordinary vision of an unbounded 'delicious fecundity' ... only took on significance through its voyeuristic tableau of frenzied, interminable copulation, of couplings, fusing, coalescence, *between races.*" Such Western accounts feverishly represented in art and literature the very acts of misalliance they sought to forestall in reality.[82]

Wapke and Roger thus restage in backwoods Nova Scotia a long and arduous debate over hybridity. What might seem inexplicable in Raddall's text –

how, for instance, could Wapke have miraculously transformed into the object of Roger's desire instead of disgust, and why would she have fantasized about him (her slave) as a suitable father for her many sons? – becomes much clearer when one remembers the undertow of European racial theory. In many respects, Raddall re-enacts of the tragic narrative of Count Gobineau, the very authority on race, esteemed by many fascists, who figured in chapter 2 as an admirer of Evangeline. Gobineau believed that white men feel a magnetic sexual attraction to non-white women as they act out a self-destructive civilizing instinct that leads them to seek to spread whiteness everywhere. Yet for Gobineau (as for Raddall), the prospect of a generalized human hybridity fills him with a horror that, as Young remarks, "recalls Frankenstein contemplating the possibility of the results of a female companion for his monster deserting her own species for the 'superior beauty of man': 'No limits, except the horror excited by the possibility of infinite intermixture, can be assigned to the number of these hybrid and chequered races that make up the whole of mankind.'"[83]

Young's observation returns us to Raddall's crucial theme of English superiority to the French as colonizers of America. Roger, by contemplating the horrid hybrids ("half beast and half himself") that might issue from any union with Wapke, withstands her sexual attractiveness. He realizes, in fact – and Raddall prepares us for this with his rapt description of her uncanny physical transformation – that she is not exactly human, which is why their imagined children would be "half beast." The English can see, as the French cannot, that the aboriginal peoples of North America lay outside the pale of humanity. Roger's refusal to make love to Wapke condenses a whole theory of hybridity, colonialism and race. Herein resides much of Raddall's thinly disguised impatience with the French Canadians. Their ancestors had succumbed to the temptation of betraying the white race in the North American wilderness. Raddall once considered writing a book about the La Tour family, closely associated with the earliest days of French colonization, but found disturbingly complicated the evidence suggesting Charles La Tour had fathered children by "Indian women, some of whom bore his name."[84] For him, a spectre of racial miscegenation haunts the French colonial enterprise.

Raddall skilfully transfers his critique of miscegenation from the eighteenth century to the twentieth in "Reunion at Grand Pre," a short story that distils all his contempt for the Evangeline Phenomenon. Raddall writes from the perspective of George Fortin, a fifty-two-year-old professor holidaying at an old farmhouse near Grand Pré. Fortin, who hopes to become a major authority on the Mi'kmaq, spends most vacations roaming about the province "conversing with Indians, learning their ancient tongue and a good deal about the ancient customs and legends." His idyll is agreeably punctuated by the visit of four sightseeing American women, "spinsters of deliberate choice," who regularly motor about North America. The physique of one of them, Miss Eva Trusdell, a math teacher, is appraised with Raddall's trademark attention to detail – she has the "trim figure of a young girl with legs carved out of alabaster." Ms Trusdell has a secret. Her full name is "Evangeline Trusdell," and she has established, through genealogical research in the American South, her Acadian descent. She quotes Longfellow endlessly and pushes her somewhat reluctant companions to extend their visit to Grand Pré so that she can thoroughly study the place. "Eva" is also a mystic who believes in the transmigration of souls. She confesses to George, "I'd read *Evangeline* of course, but now I read it again – and again, and suddenly it seemed to me that I'd known those people a long time. There were certain things – certain passages you understand? – that gave me the queerest feeling, as if I'd lived twice, and all this belonged to my earlier existence."[85] Persuaded that the spirit of Evangeline moves within her, she becomes convinced that the famous statue of Evangeline at Grand Pré Park is trying to communicate to her the whereabouts of her lover Gabriel, presumably likewise transmigrated into a twentieth-century body.

The story comes to a climax in a terrific thunderstorm, amid pelting rain and vapour rising from the marshes, as Eva has a mystic vision of the Acadians of two centuries before, on the very day of their exile. She runs over the field crying, "Gabriel!" but her voice seems to make the vision evaporate into the mists of the marsh. Later she recounts, "I fell, and found myself on my knees in the road, alone, and the rain coming down in sheets. It poured. It was awful. I shrieked 'Gabriel!' again and again, hopelessly." With a start, she then saw an old man walking towards Blomidon: "He was like an ape, so bent at the knees and shoulders, and his arms so long, with big gnarled hands. He had a dark wrinkled face, and strings of grey hair hanging down his neck from under an old felt hat. He had a grey shirt and trousers of some thick stuff, cut very short, with a lot of grey wool sock showing, and on his feet were a pair of very dirty tennis shoes, much too big for him. He'd begged the shoes somewhere, I suppose. He was an Indian – I knew because he had a dozen baskets tied together and slung on his back, the kind you see Indians selling from door to door." Eva asks him if he has seen the Acadians, and – with eyes "dark and small, and old and very wise, with a little gleam of malice in them" – he tells her that his ancestors remembered the day that their settlement burned to the ground, and many of their young men vanished into the woods.[86]

Suddenly the situation becomes plain to George. "The woman was a psychopathic case," he muses. "He could see it all now; the years of mathematics, the growing restlessness of the forties manifest in these furious summer journeys, and now at the turn of life the pixie fancies creeping in. Into her sterile existence she had conjured a dream-lover with a name out of a poem, and the dream had brought her to hysteria." First, he disabuses her of romantic illusions about Evangeline's statue. There are a few possible explanations for the statue's distinctive pose, but one stands out as most "probable": "she's seeking in despair for her lover, one of the runaways, up there in the woods with the Indians." Then he presents her with a very different story of the Acadians:

> "You see," he went on deliberately, "your Indian spoke the truth. A lot of the young Acadian men got away and joined the Micmacs. Eventually most of 'em took Indian wives. Nearly all present-day Micmacs have a drop of Acadian blood. And most Micmac family names today are simply a garbled version of the Christian names of Acadian men. The Micmacs couldn't pronounce an R to save his soul; he substituted L, just like a Chinaman. In the same way he gave the French C a guttural sound, like G. And the French J was sounded as an S. So the Acadian squaw-man Jean became *San* and Pierre became *Peyal*. Martin became *Maltee*, Claude became *Glode* and so on."

Getting to the point, he reveals that he knows a thing or two about the old Indian whom Eva saw carrying the baskets. For one thing, he is quite real. Eva asks his name. "George Fortin waited a moment. He felt like a murderer, but he steeled himself with the notion that it was for her own good. After all, it was the truth. 'Gabliel,' he said harshly."[87]

Underneath the romance of Evangeline lay, according to Raddall's proxy, the sordid secret of the Acadians: intermarriage with the Mi'kmaq, now epitomized by "Gabliel" – its inevitably degenerate, even apelike, outcome. Now it seems easier to understand what prompted Raddall's apoplectic screeds against the Acadians, which so took Martell and Costain aback and seemed such disproportionate reactions to their judiciously phrased suggestions. Their advocacy of even-handedness implied an essential equality in the dignity of both peoples, an equality – Raddall believed – that evolution had emphatically ruled out after the French had squandered their substance in misalliance. In the deepest biological bedrock of the race, the English were better than the French. Claims to the contrary went against nature.

True, Raddall rather liked the French-Canadian *habitants*, who "clung to their small farms by the St. Lawrence, peaceful, happy-go-lucky, content with a rude subsistence and no more." He bore them no grudge so long as they remembered their place. As their nationalism cohered, gaining influence over the course of Canadian history, however, Raddall's historical survey of Canada increasingly disparaged their credulity, parochialism, and demagogic political leadership. Concurrently, as French colonialism extended beyond the St Lawrence Valley, becoming even more dangerously embroiled in relations with less-evolved "savages," Raddall's descriptions become even more charged. "In the wry phrase of the plains the *métis* were half French, half Indian, and half devil," Raddall remarks. "Although they lived like savages they were always conscious of their white blood. Most of them had sprung from the loins of Nor'west *engagés* and they inherited the Nor'west hatred of everyone and everything that came to the plains by way of Hudson Bay." They were not in any sense central to the history of the West. Even the Métis heartland in Manitoba is defined by Raddall as "a small clan of half-wild Scots almost lost in the growing swarm of *métis*" – a formulation that recalls his eviction of all women from the ranks of the "Americans" and the "Haligonians."[88]

◆

Roger Sudden's moment of decision suggests how, in marked contrast to Bird, Raddall displays an avid interest in sex. In his autobiography, Raddall wistfully contrasts the postwar freedom of the young with the inhibited sexual secrecy he experienced in the 1930s and 1940s. "During the long depression," he writes, "the most intimate and exquisite part of conjugal life had to be carefully insulated, like a dangerous electric current."[89] In his earlier work, Raddall, worried about censorious editors and readers, handled sexual issues cautiously – even earning retrospectively ironic plaudits from earnest clergymen.[90] His caution was warranted. In this early period in his career, Raddall's British editor and early champion George Blackwood objected that his work incorporated "too much 'sex.'"[91] As he grew more successful, however, Raddall took more and more literary forays into the sexual. At a Royal Society seminar on censorship, a Queen's University professor who took contemporary authors to task for contributing to the "present flood of fiction devoted to violence and sex" noted that the front cover of *The Nymph and the Lamp* "shows a good deal of the Nymph but not very much of the Lamp."[92] In his context, Raddall broke new ground in trying to bring discussions of sexuality into serious literature.

Raddall interpreted his willingness to write about sex as evidence of his superiority to the common run of closed-minded, mealy-mouthed puritans. When he heard that "a group of organized prudes in Manitoba" had banned Hugh MacLennan's novel *Barometer Rising,* he used the occasion to write MacLennan a letter reminiscing about how "a middle-aged schoolma'am in the American mid-west" had removed *The Nymph and the Lamp* from her school library. The woman had had the temerity to write Raddall a letter accusing him of producing "highly indecent and immoral" books, further noting how "she was amazed that a married man with children could write a book so obsessed by sex. Believe it or not, she closed by saying that she would pray for me." If she had hoped to shame him into moral rectitude, she had miscalculated entirely. Criticism like hers actually emboldened Raddall, because

227

it endued him with an exhilarating sense of himself as a progressive thinker well in advance of blinkered public opinion. He gleefully composed a response. First, he tallied up all the passages in the offending book that alluded to "sexual congress" – which, by his reckoning, amounted to scarcely eight or nine pages out of 376. In triumph, he wrote his critic a letter, thanking her for her interest before encouraging her to "go on and read the other pages, which obviously she must have skipped. I closed by saying that I, too, would pray – not for her, but for the children in her school."[93] Now he had a funny story he could retail to his colleagues, about how he had utterly humiliated a silly woman who had hypocritically condemned him for writing the sexy passages that, in truth, had absorbed her entire interest.

Not everyone was as convinced that *The Nymph and the Lamp* really captured sexuality in a way so lifelike that it verged on indecency. A letter from Isabel LeBourdais proved much thornier for him to deal with than the letter from the benighted Midwestern teacher. LeBourdais knew Raddall as a fellow member of the Canadian Authors Association and paid him great professional courtesy in the matter of his first modern novel: "I found myself saying aloud to no one – My God, Tom knows how to write!" She particularly admired his deft characterization of the heroine Isabel, a portrait so true to life that "she gave me several shocks." She had to say, though, that she found Isabel's paramour Matthew unsatisfactory. His whole persona as a middle-aged man experiencing a sexual awakening seemed impossibly far-fetched in a novel otherwise distinguished by its unsparing realism. To wit: "I find it difficult to believe that a man of 46 who had lived an entirely sexless life by choice and inclination, could suddenly turn into an expert and entirely adequate lover without inhibition, hesitancy, or even the blunderings of the inexperienced!"[94] Raddall hardly knew what to say. He confessed that he was "a little surprised" by her objections. Then he promptly turned to another subject.[95] If he provoked censorship, embarrassment and shock, it reinforced his self-conception as a maverick – a man who would rather be right than be popular, with no time for the Sunday school notions of propriety that shielded more demure souls from those aspects of human experience that they could not handle. LeBourdais confronted him with something else, the possibility that he did not have any special insight into sex just because he wrote about it.

Indeed, while Raddall often wrote about sex, his goal in doing so seldom seems to have been realism or even eroticism. He often used sex as a means of talking about other things, such as the evolutionary credentials of the people with whom he populated his novels. Sexuality supplies a symbolic terrain upon which to test one's character and fitness. Characteristically, Raddall often portrays sexuality as seen through the lens of people far removed from the liberal ideal of a propertied self-possession. Raddall lavished his attention on women sex-trade workers. They fascinated as well as disgusted him. In *The Governor's Lady*, Frances Wentworth condemns the women of Halifax as a "little huddle of prudes in a crowd of common sluts."[96] A scene in *Hangman's Beach* depicts one reputable woman protagonist inadvertently sharing a boat with May, Kay, and Sal, all *habituées* of "dolly-shops," whose "wretched stockings and scrubby shoes, and … dirty and torn petticoats" are brought to our attention.[97] Raddall speculates that the American invaders of Quebec in 1775 wearied of their quest to conquer the St Lawrence Valley because, although "the pillaged wine, the rude fare of the farms, [and] the occasional embraces of a fuddled hag in St. Roch were all very well," they could not make up for the comforts of home.[98] (He left unspecified how he had documented the existence of the "hag" or ascertained her state of befuddlement.)

Halifax, Warden of the North cannot afford even one paragraph enumerating the city's industries. Yet it lavishes dozens of passages on its "unwashed sluts," "daughters of joy," "strumpets," "harlots," "kept women," "naughty women," "courtesans," "eager prostitutes," "harridans," "streetwalkers," "nymphs," "trollops," and "queer denizens of the Hill." Raddall's attention seems glued with something like misogynistic intensity to the figure of the sex-trade worker, simultaneously appalled and fascinated, nauseated and intrigued. We see Barrack (now Brunswick) Street as "an evil slum of grog sellers, pimps, and prostitutes who battened on the dissolute soldiery." The long wars from the 1780s to the 1810s transformed the city into "a sink of depravity notorious in every cantonment and dockyard of the empire." In the descriptions of both world wars, the sex trades ("the old evils") loom large, with Raddall even providing a rough guide to their migration to the suburbs. The 1945 riots at the conclusion of the Second World War offered a moment of truth when Halifax could "see all at once the evil face of its own criminal element, grinning and triumphant, in the broad light of day." The whole situation is incarnated in the figure of a "filthy harridan" proceeding drunkenly along Barrington Street, clutching armfuls of stolen goods and "shriek[ing] again and again, 'Never had so much fun in my life!' There spoke the voice of Chaos, which lurks in every modern city waiting patiently for the sailors to break the windows."[99]

This last remark suggests the problem with the sex trades. It was not that they improperly commercialized the personal, but that they compromised the autonomy, integrity, and rationality of the free-standing male individual. Like Matthew Carney in *The Nymph and the Lamp*, Raddall perceives women generally – and transgressive women particularly – as agents of disorder who threaten to make fools out of men who go too far with them. (Carney, as LeBourdais remarked, holds this conviction with such tenacity that he remarkably preserves his virginity into his forties.)[100] Like John Wentworth in *The Governor's Lady*, whose inner voice tells him he must not let Frances make him a fool and a villain, Raddall's texts construct women as temptresses who lure men into treacherous waters: "Johnnie was lost in a sea storm of his own, with waves that swelled and lifted him up to the sky and dropped him into warm deeps, with the sound of wild surf in his ears, with nothing to save him but a slim pine log, peeled and white, that he clasped urgently in the storm. There were times when he fainted and drowned in a fatal plunge. And then, after a death whose length he could not measure, he was alive and alone with the white log again on the mysterious sea, and with new waves rising."[101] In this description, the elemental storm of sexual intercourse is one that threatens the boundaries of the individual. Only the strong can weather it. Those who succumb to sexuality risk losing their reason.[102] "Chaos" will consume them. Even the small details of daily life – the combined smells of men and women in a boarding house, "mingled in vulgar intimacy from morn to night" – signal sexual danger on the molecular level.[103]

Raddall felt uneasily aware of other transgressors even further out on the margins of his imagined world. One character in *The Governor's Lady* wonders if John Wentworth is "lacking" something, inviting the quick rebuke: "Stuff! Johnnie's all man in spite of those dancing-master ways he picked up in England." If the reader feels momentarily reassured, his or her doubts immediately reawaken at the description of Charles-Mary Wentworth, son of John and Frances, whose very name intimates a certain degree of gender flexibility. "Her son was not quite what she had expected," Raddall says of Frances Wentworth as she visits her son in England. "Charles-Mary seemed not quite so much Charles as Mary. An exquisite creature of course. Such beautiful speech and manners." John puts it plainly: he "could not even picture Charles-Mary taking a wife and siring boys to carry on his name."[104]

Miss Benson in *The Nymph and the Lamp* likewise pushes against the frontiers of normality. She toys with the young men ("healthy animals following natural instincts") who are attracted to her like "wasps to jam." They then discover – after many dinners, flowers, chocolates, stockings, scarves, and jewels – that no sexual conquest will follow. Our hero considers her a "heartless fraud." Isabel's landlady, drawn according to specifications familiar to readers of Daphne du Maurier, presents an even more disquieting figure. Entering Isabel's room after a drunken male fellow tenant has accosted Isabel, the Mrs Danvers-like landlady observes Isabel with a certain unnerving intensity: "the sight of the trembling young woman excited her. The silken wisp drawn so tightly about Miss Jardine betrayed a figure slender but well filled at the breast and hips, and it revealed to the landlady's gaze a pair of comely legs. She had not suspected the typist of such properties." Her gaze assaults Isabel's heterosexual boundaries in a way that dwarfs the physical assault she has just endured: "She felt defiled ... by something evil in [the landlady's] hard black eyes that searched her flesh as if the scrap of silk did not exist. She made a picture of despair, and for a moment the woman in the doorway was almost mollified."[105] In his attention to sex, Raddall remained fundamentally constrained by the classic liberal paradigm within which he categorizes and understands all of social reality. This theme serves him only as another instantiation of how his characters did or did not measure up to the protocols of self-possessed individualism.

◆

In 1972, as Raddall's career was winding down, W.H. New (professor of English at the University of British Columbia) considered the history of English Canadian fiction. He decided upon "realism" as the key concept whose changing fortunes would serve as his principle for periodization:

> A history of modern English-language Canadian fiction traces a journey into "realism" and out of it again. Whereas earlier nonfiction had been deceptively realistic, nineteenth-century fiction largely relied on the stock figures and the elevated style of romantic adventures. Twentieth century writers, for about five decades, tried to make their landscapes more specific, to lock them, for example, in southern Saskatchewan, Halifax, Montreal or Manitoba. They tried also to ensure that their characters were fully motivated and behaved credibly in such locales. The commitment to psychological motivation, however, led a number of writers by the 1960s to explore the nature of the mind itself ... Symbolic and mythic landscapes overlapped regional geographies.[106]

Raddall cuts across all of the categories New offers in his graceful and economical analysis.

Raddall holds himself to a high standard of realism – especially in the way of historical accuracy – but it is a somewhat deceptive realism wholly compatible with stock figures like hard-bitten old salts and savage "Indian" braves, conveyed in the most elevated prose style employed by any writer this side of Francis Parkman. At the same time, he makes his landscapes as specific as possible. Has any writer rendered the South Shore with such attention to fine detail? His characters are not only *in* this landscape, but also *of* it: they behave credibly according to the geographical origins Raddall assigns them. (He generates most of his stock characters this way.) Most important, finally, all of his landscapes are mythic ones that brood over the fates of his characters. Psychology is present throughout his oeuvre, but in a curiously externalized form revealed through physical description.

Raddall's nationalist preoccupations led him to generate a form of his own, the romance of Nova Scotia. He represents Nova Scotia as what Anthony Smith calls a "historic land," a realm whose people and territory "belong to each other" after generations of reciprocal influence.[107] The spiritual connection of Nova Scotians – particularly the descendants of Yankees and Gaels – to Nova Scotia appears as a crucial theme in any number of Raddall's novels. The sea, wind, rocks, and wild woods nourish and feed all of Raddall's Nova Scotian characters, in a way no other milieu ever could. Saxby Nolan, the antihero of *Tidefall*, feels utterly alienated from the West Indies when he cruises there. To his Fundy shore eyes, "the lush West Indian landscapes were like a scatter of picture post cards seen in the wavering air." He found these foreign landscapes "too lofty and too rich a green to be quite credible."[108] Nolan cannot fully inhabit the Caribbean. He may sail on it, for more than a decade as it happens, but it will never live for him. Small wonder that he finds himself drawn back to his hometown far to the north, for reasons he can neither fathom nor resist. Nolan is but one of many characters who sense almost at the cellular level where they belong, responding instinctively to blood and soil.

The interplay between alien lands and historic lands has particular importance for the 1946 novel *Pride's Fancy*. Its story takes place in Nova Scotia and the West Indies during the Haitian Revolution of the 1790s, giving our hero Nathan Cain ample opportunity to compare the two locales. Nova Scotia is crisp and clear in an environmental sense that quickly takes on a moral dimension as well. Nathan rejoices to return there after a nightmarish voyage to Hispaniola. The island was "a savage and threatening wilderness. The beautiful villas … had seemed to me besieged the whole year round – by the mountains, the forest, the damp and choking heat … and by something else I could not name, a sense of doom perhaps." The Caribbean is simply not a natural place for Nathan to live. Nova Scotia is, for Nathan descends from the blood of Yankees. Conversely, Nova Scotia is not for everyone. Victor Brule, a French colonist who has fled the slave uprising in Haiti, finds himself passing a tedious exile in Nathan's town of Gosport. He languishes in a country where the sky is "gray always, and that sea always cold, and that land … nothing but melancholy trees and stones," and where the people "have a lean and starved look all the time, and rush about doing this and that."[109] Everything about Gosport – its natural setting and its inhabitants – alienates Brule; both nature and history have rendered him completely unsuited to any of it.

Brule is not the only French West Indian exile trapped in Gosport. On his voyage home, Nathan brought along the sugar planter Dolainde and his daughter Lia, forced to flee the slave revolts sweeping the French colony of Saint Domingue (present-day Haiti) on the island of Hispaniola. If Nathan cannot live in Hispaniola, Lia cannot live away from it. Matters come to a head when Nathan and his stern foster-father Amos Pride catch Lia in the furnace room engaged in a lewd and diabolical dance with their black servants. She defies them and says she only feels at home there and in such company: "Ah, you cold people! ... I come here because it is like home to me, it is like the old days at the *manoir* when I was small and went to see the black people of my father, and they danced for me and made music and sang, and we were happy." Lia pinpoints the difference between Nova Scotia and Saint Domingue: the former is a land of whiteness, the latter a land of blackness. Hence, Lia may long for her home, but as a white woman, she must remain separated from it forever. While she feels uneasy in the land of whiteness, return to the land of blackness is impossible. Her father – an embittered wretch – has come to realize this, but too late, recalling how he had worried about "the blacks, always the blacks, the savages from Africa, like a pot of boiling tar that gleams, that bubbles, that stinks, that someday will boil over ... My poor Luz [his slain wife] had no fear of them. Our little Lia loved them. But I – I knew, down in my heart I knew." The French presence in the colony affronted the natural order, and the colonists could only maintain their ascendancy by "a cruelty beyond a northern imagination."[110]

The insolvent Dolainde entices his biggest creditor, the titular Pride, to bankroll a fanciful expedition back to his abandoned plantation where he says he has left a buried treasure. Nathan commands the doomed adventure. Homesick, Lia stows away on the ship. After many hair-raising adventures, they discover there is no treasure. The lying Dolainde had only wanted to return to the island so that he could die there and spend the hereafter buried next to his wife. The Nova Scotians must go home empty-handed, thankful just to be alive. Lia begs Nathan to leave her behind in what she still considers her homeland. He insists he cannot. The whole place is oppressive and unfit for white people, including the sunshine that she craves. He reminds her that even in the old days only the "slave folk" had dared walk abroad, while their fearful masters "shut the sunshine out," so that the apparently sunny island was really enveloped in "darkness": "not just the shadow cast by the sun or moon, but something more that seemed to come out of the earth itself." Metaphysical blackness shrouds this island "where every man or woman with a drop of white blood must creep and stay and gasp for breath till nightfall. Prisoners – prisoners always – prisoners of the sun and prisoners of that black multitude about them."[111]

According to the social order, of course, the slaves who chopped cane on the plantations of Saint Domingue had been prisoners of their white masters.

They had been spirited across the ocean, then worked unto death under the lash, with incorrigible runaways lawfully punished by the slicing of a hamstring.[112] According to Raddall's natural order, however, the opposite situation obtained. White men were "prisoners of the sun" – their very presence an affront to the order of things, their history consisting entirely of borrowed time. Nathan must convince Lia of this in order to save her from death or worse. He entreats her: "Lia, where we are going the sun is a lover, not an enemy. It is a pleasure to be outdoors, to walk about in the full shine of it, to feel it on the skin. Even the earth is greedy for our sun – there is no monstrous mass of green to shut it out, the trees stand tall and clean, and there is a pleasant smell under the branches. Do you remember the smell of the pines? And there is the rocky shore and the cool smell of the sea, and the brown sails of the fishing boats, and the sound of the calkers making music in the shipyards." She resists. What about violent storms and long northern nights? Nathan ingeniously replies, "Storms and nights! There must be a time to shut out the world and turn to each other, Lia. There must be a time to love." Nova Scotia's very climate will coincide with the biorhythms of their white bodies. It is their homeland, even for Lia who was not born there. She sees he is right, so their tale ends happily.[113]

Even after reflecting upon it for decades, Nathan finds the emergent black state of Haiti (which arose from the ashes of the razed French plantations) incommensurable, incompatible, and, ultimately, incomprehensible. The novel begins with an aged Nathan remembering with a shudder "the houses burning and the dark savage faces swarming through the streets athirst for blood." As his ship sails away from that netherworld, "where Satan has a face as black as night, and howls a mixture of French and Fulani, and shows a glitter of polished teeth and staring bloodshot eyes in the lights of the fires," he thinks he hears a voice on the wind that commands, "Never come back again ... never ... never." Overcome by the horror of it all, the men go mad. Even resilient Nathan cannot stand this ordeal. They are in hell: "Hades – or Haiti if you like, Hispaniola, Saint Domingo, it has many names."[114] We must resort to supernatural metaphors and demonology because to face the reality would pose grave risk to the integrity of the subject.

Haiti represented the first complete reversal of a successful European imperialist project, the only known example of a slave society dismantled by the slaves themselves. As such, it stood as a lasting challenge to racial hierarchies, notions of economic development, and liberal verities about historical agency. This challenge has been so potent that down to the 1990s most Western intellectuals chose not to face it. The Haitian Revolution amounted to an unthinkable history, something processed as a world historical event (rather than a simple slave revolt, or a spasm of unreasoning violence, or an

annex to the French Revolution) only at the risk of upsetting all the carefully maintained exclusions that comprise the framework of Western
culture.[115] Sibylle Fischer argues that a mechanism of disavowal has served to
regulate this danger, casting the decolonization of Saint Domingue outside
history and into a twilight world of horror, fantasy, and monstrosity.[116] *Pride's
Fancy* presents the revolution as an upwelling of baleful energies that seize the
human participants – particularly the black ones – stripping them of their
humanity to leave only the will to violence, revenge, and destruction. The
uprising has neither causes nor effects. It is not a historical event because it is
the wholesale eradication of history itself. Raddall gives us Haiti as the negation of Nova Scotia, for one is white and the other black, one healthful and
the other diseased, the one is a successful colony and the other is the undoing of colonialism as such.

◆

The intense concern for colonialism reflected in *Pride's Fancy* suggests the
inadequacy of associating Raddall with a sort of regionalism of the type familiar
today, one that begins with the assumed cultural and historical distinctiveness
of Nova Scotians or Maritimers and works outward to theorize a fixed and
firm identity extending back in time and ahead into the future. We can call
Raddall a regionalist only on the understanding that he had an overriding
attachment to the civilizing mission of the British Empire, the imagined community to which he belonged before all others. Its triumphant worldwide
extension gave Canadian history (and by the same token the history of Nova
Scotia) its shape and meaning. He thus sacralized those moments in Nova
Scotia history that he could readily incorporate within an English Canadian
imperial/nationalist narrative. In his telling, the province's resistance to the
American Revolution and subsequent involvement in privateering from 1812
to 1814 counted as moments within a larger process of Canadian nation-
building. Long before Confederation, "the future of Canada hung upon what
happened in Nova Scotia between 1775 and 1783." Nova Scotia mattered
primarily for the great developments that it precipitated, but that ultimately
unfolded largely outside its borders, such as the "cheerful comradeship [of] the
two races, British and French," who together "discovered the great Canadian
land and ... stamped the Canadian character with their own simple faith in the
country and their ability to do things and do them quietly."[117]

Within this British imperial framework, Raddall worked to construct a
coherent saga of Nova Scotia history. J.M. Bumsted has justly observed that
Raddall's hallmark was "always in forceful narrative and accurate setting,
rather than in characterization."[118] The sum of Raddall's "forceful" narratives

is a compelling and consistent emplotment of a wide swath of history in the "accurate setting" of Nova Scotia. This chronology overarches, determines, and situates all of the various literary characters who populate his stories. Raddallian history would begin in the time immemorial before European settlement, an undifferentiated and unbounded duration without historical events, properly speaking. From thence we would move onwards – after the briefest tip of the hat to the Norsemen – to the great age of European settlement, which begins with the foundation of Port Royal in 1605 and continues through the colonial wars that so interested Raddall. After the struggles between the British, Americans, French, and Mi'kmaq have subsided (the War of 1812 could provide a convenient endpoint, given its prominence in *The Path of Destiny*), the romance of history reaches its climax with the Golden Age of Sail. This era of Victorian equipoise, when Nova Scotia becomes a successful realm of liberal capitalism, redeems all the hardship, strife, and dissension of previous history. The brilliant but brief Golden Age tarnishes as the nineteenth century turns into the twentieth. Raddall sets his modern novels in this later, post–Golden Age period. In addition, a propulsive, totalizing modernity is developing at the same time, but it emerges mostly in other places (Toronto, New York, Europe), and there are grave doubts about its compatibility with Nova Scotia. Having established the bare contours of this chronology, we will flesh it out in the balance of this section.

Raddall's history begins with the inscription of European norms and forms onto American terrain. He knew in his bones just how long a prospect this was. The short story that tackles the seventeenth-century foundation of Port Royal is accordingly entitled "The Dreamers." In its pages, the French boy Biencourt talks to his "Indian" friend the Pigeon about a ship from France said to arrive "soon." The Pigeon exclaims, "Soon! Always you say soon … You are dreamers, you Normanni. You dream and tell us your dreams." The French are a visionary people in this story, while their Mi'kmaw neighbours have no capacity to understand the unfolding of historical time, whose movements baffle them. When the ship comes, "the savage camp broke into outcry, and a swarm of Indian men, women and children and dogs came running." They react to history, but the "Normanni" make it out of their dreams. Raddall brings this point home with the figure of the "map-maker" (unmistakably Samuel de Champlain) who, recounting the historical importance of the Port Royal settlement, "looked as if he saw exactly what he had described, a new French empire stretching on towards the China Sea."[119] Before it could be made, history needed to be envisioned. Then these visions could be imposed on a natural setting to make it a historical one.

Dreaming does not imply idleness. Sweat, toil, and the prudent husbanding of scarce resources define the first great age of Euroamerican history. Nathan observes in *Pride's Fancy*, "It's no land of milk and honey, our [eighteenth-century] Nova Scotia." The common run of men will not prove equal to its rigours. Rather, a self-possessed rational calculator such as Nathan's adoptive father, Amos Pride, must follow his shrewd, hard insights into what the doctrines of development demand if a place like the South Shore settlement of Gosport is to thrive. Nathan explains, "My foster father was a merchant and a stirring one, with a hound's nose for an opportunity and the courage to reach out and seize it, often at a risk that frightened lesser moneybags." Amos is not a likeable man, but "a harsh and calculating god who ruled the house as he ruled the town, and would like to have ruled the world."[120] That, however, is beside the historical point.

A certain authoritarian masculinity fascinated Raddall. He was simultaneously repulsed by its coldness and attracted by its association with historical agency. For him, the eighteenth century represented the era *par excellence* of the unalloyed classic liberal individual whose pursuit of enlightened selfishness ensured the advance of civilization across the world. The individual is a civilizational product himself – made, not born. Amos handles his family relationships with all the care he gives his business ones to ensure he inculcates the right mental and moral habits in his children. He sees to it that his adopted son Nathan grows up self-sufficient and tough by having the youth serve for years as an ordinary seaman on his ships before he tells him that he will be his sole heir. Sloth would have ruined Nathan: "I've seen too many sons 'o rich men spoiled ... Well, I've bided my time ... No fear of turning your head – a man grown – brought up seaman fashion – discipline – a taut hand and frugal mind."[121] In the terms of the story, Amos appears narrow and inflexible, but fundamentally correct, the evidence being that Nathan's strength of character saves his crew in a climactic naval battle.

A stark struggle to win a living on one's own account, with no expectation of ease or luxury, distinguishes this era from its successor. David Strang, narrator of *His Majesty's Yankees*, set in Nova Scotia during the American War of Independence, remembers growing up in a little seaport "with little time and less money for social graces; even the merchants lived simply ... Our town was a good place to live in, then. All that came after, while it gave some ease to the hard life, and some gaiety and polish, brought first and foremost bloodshed and suffering and bitterness."[122] Nova Scotians bought prosperity dearly, securing it only by a series of wars over the course of which they lost certain homely virtues for good. In this way, the Golden Age, when it came, was already somewhat tarnished. The classic liberal utopia really existed before its own triumph.

Raddall never shows us the Golden Age of Sail. It is always *about to happen* or *already over*. While the action in "Blind MacNair" may take place during the nineteenth-century halcyon days of wooden shipbuilding, the story comes to the reader only through the mediation of a narrator who meditates on the sad decline of Shardstown in the 1940s. Raddall's whole oeuvre takes place on either side (as Barry Moody has noted) of a magnificent event that never actually occurs.[123] His celebration of Nova Scotia's heroic rise to a Golden Age during the eighteenth century does not have as its sequel a description of that Golden Age – instead, it gives way to a lament for its melancholy dissolution during the twentieth century. The Golden Age is always already absent, just over the horizon or vanishing into the distance, a spectre that announces the destiny of the past or indicts the limitations of the present – but never comes to life itself. Despite its ineffability, it would haunt the Raddallian twentieth century.

As he sheepishly admitted, Raddall tended to write his historical fiction in the mode of romance. The same does not hold true of his modern-dress stories. An atmosphere of decadence, decay, and degeneration pervades the stories set during his lifetime. "The Miracle," for example, takes the reader on a journey through the outskirts of Tropesville in the 1940s. Nature is reclaiming this terrain from the vanished timber industry that can no longer produce anything but poignant reminders of what once was: "There was a mound of sawdust, gray with winter and frozen hard. Bits of rotten edgings and slabs stuck out of it like bones. Beside it tottered the ruin of a sawmill." We see it all through the eyes of RCMP constable Cawfield as he leads a rescue party through the woods on a desperate search for a missing boy whom the landscape seems to have swallowed up. Seeking to orient himself, Cawfield consults his map but to no avail. The map is but "a soiled sheet badly worn at the folds, a relic of bygone logging operations on Black River," its cartography consisting of "jumbled squares and rectangles in faded red ink marking the boundaries of timber lots cut and forgotten years ago." Contrary to what the map decrees, the uplands "were veined with faint paths kept open by moose and deer, all that was left of the old logging roads."[124] Cawfield finds himself caught in a terrain that the map, an obsolescent artifact of an era of capitalist development now passing out of existence, can scarcely describe anymore. In a way, the story amounts to a study in regional underdevelopment.

Raddall set his modern tales in the twilight of a liberal capitalism whose failure his protagonists can neither accept nor ignore. Herein lies their affective charge. The prosperity, progress, and optimism of the Golden Age return to the present in spectral form to torment the living. Set during the 1950s, *The Wings of Night* recounts Neil Jamieson's postwar return to his birthplace of Oak Falls. Its lumber business in irreversible decline, it seems to him "a village under an evil spell in some old tale." The glory days now exist only in sepia-tinted photographs of Victorian dandies, pictures that had once enthralled the youthful Neil, since they seemed "full of romance, the romance of another and better time, before the village fell under its evil enchantment." The photographs unsettle him now as he reflects on how some of the people in the photos have died, others have moved on, and the rest remain as "human relics of that pleasant time of the big timber and the easy prosperity ... moving about like shabby phantoms amongst the solid furniture."[125] The photos seem to portray a history moving in reverse. The dynamic progress that the future ought to hold actually exists only as a memory, while the static, undifferentiated time without events – the time *before* progress – actually exists *after* progress. The future of Oak Falls belongs to its past, in a disturbance of the liberal order that Neil processes as a malefic enchantment. The townspeople appear strangely unreal, as though they were their own ghosts, haunting themselves.

Raddall wrote at a time when liberalism had become impossible. It could, impossibly, neither be relied upon as an adequate guide to the condition of the present nor be consigned to the dustbin of ideas. Liberalism tells a compelling story about where human beings have come from and where they are going. Francis Fukuyama won great fame after the Cold War by recapitulating the old idea that liberalism offers itself as "a universal history" positing the unstoppable advance of humankind towards "the realization of freedom in the here and now," where freedom means the conjunction of free men and free markets calculated to produce free, self-possessed liberal individuals.[126] It was no small part of Raddall's appeal that he could articulate such a "universal history" in the terms of Nova Scotia history and life. Writing near the end of the novelist's life, John Bell hailed him for "his rare ability to uncover universal truths within the distinctiveness of his own community."[127] Mediating universal truths (pre-eminently the tenets of liberal individualism) through local conditions, in his modern novels Raddall produced moving reflections on the feeling of melancholy decline that comes when progress cannot sustain itself and when the Moloch of modernity has outrun the capacity of classic liberalism to define the terms of social life. The universal truth he discovered in twentieth-century Nova Scotia was perhaps that faith in liberalism comes easily when free men and free markets seem already to exist in Fukuyama's "here and now," but is harder to sustain when they seem a ways off – in this case, already receding into the distant past.

Raddall describes a historical process utterly beyond conscious manipulation. History has become a fate to be borne, whose dynamics derive from natural or occult forces metaphysically inaccessible to mere mortals. *Tidefall* contains a scene in which our heroine Rena Caraday must decide whether she will accept a proposal of marriage from Saxby Nolan, whom she does not love but whose suit has the strong backing of her controlling mother – in part because he seems like the only hope to save their declining family firm.

Walking to the shore so she may think, Rena fixes her eyes on the sea and sees the tide "at full ebb out of [the Bay of] Fundy now and streaming through the islands." She remembers what the fishermen said about the tidal race: "If you got caught in the ebb or flow it was useless to fight the tide. You had to go with it and hope for the best, putting all your trust in a stout heart and the boat."[128] Raddall hardly need tell us in so many words that Rena's sublime reflection signifies her capitulation to her mother and her suitor.

The marriage, predictably, is disastrous. Rena's efforts to escape it come to naught. Only the mysterious powers of time and tide can free her from her demonic husband. Sax Nolan is a brutal man of monstrous strength. Alone of the characters, he continues to believe he can defy fate by relying on nothing but his own powers and audacity. Here is an unreconstructed individualist. Sax feels sure he can take over Port Barron's struggling shipping firm and make it thrive by sheer force of will. He is wrong. Supra-individual forces hem him in, and inevitably the business fails. He is driven mad with frustration at the locals who mock him as a fool for "planning to take up a life that didn't exist any more! ... What had deceived him was Port Barron, the poor community isolated on the cape, where the tradition of the old time remained untouched, with nothing new for contrast."[129] He could not discern destiny as it crept up on him because he had gotten lost in a land out of time, a fragment of Victorian liberal assumptions adrift in a Fordist tide of the impersonal and hierarchical concentration of capital.

In a last desperate bid to stave off the inevitable, Sax decides to wreck his biggest ship for the insurance money, just when the terrifying tide race would make such an event seem normal to his underwriters. He must run the ship into the rocks, thereby to destroy it, but avoid actually sinking it, which would mean death to all hands. It all goes wrong. He ends up off-course in a lashing storm. Indomitable to the end, he inwardly insists, "You've been through worse than this and come out grinning, Sax. You'll beat 'em all yet ... Beat 'em all. All!"[130] The ship goes down anyway. His hyperbolic invocation of his own individuality is pathetically impotent. The tide, having driven Rena into Sax's power, sweeps him away again.

Raddall's obsession with destiny and fate, which provoked much of his best writing, helped make sense of the era in which he found himself. The course of history seemed to have slipped the grasp of human beings, an aberration that called out for an explanation. But liberals of Raddall's generation never had much of a vocabulary for the historical context that impinges upon the individual, because, although increasingly well equipped with general evolutionary concepts à la Herbert Spencer, they lacked more specific ways of describing social relations as real constraints upon people. In order to talk about that context at all, they had recourse only to metaphors, metaphysics, and mythology. The tide stands in allegorically for the sweeping forces that govern the terms of the human relationships portrayed in *Tidefall*, but that defy all scrutiny. Such reflections always have a tragic or elegiac cast. By their very nature, they rule out the possibility of meaningful agency. Raddall's later oeuvre records his dismay at the historical annihilation of the individual. The early novels prepare us for a triumph of liberalism and progress that the later novels demonstrate never took place.

Nova Scotia's relative underdevelopment made it an obvious novelistic setting for such reflections upon the strange death of classic liberalism. The perceived backwardness of the place admitted of multiple readings, as Raddall shows us. The very fact that liberal capitalism had stalled in Nova Scotia meant that its operations would never bring forth here the era destined to succeed it elsewhere. Centralized state capitalism, which characterized the more successful world economies from the Great Depression through the early 1970s, did not take root in this proverbially undercapitalized locale. As a result, some of the dehumanizing effects associated with that particular social formation seemed not to intrude so obviously upon Nova Scotia as they did in, say, Raddall's Toronto.

Neil, hero of *The Wings of Night,* must travel to Toronto for a meeting with business tycoon Luther Kinnoul. He begins to feel uneasy when he sees the Kinnoul Investment Corporation housed in "a granite structure like a hornet's nest designed by a cubist and stood on the ground wrong end up." Inside, where he "found the hornets busy in their cells and corridors," he heard a terrible sound, "not the bumbling of fat and stupid bees that you hear in a hive but the more sinister buzz of smart slim-waisted creatures whose business it is to be alert."[131] Kinnoul's insectival employees are so many instruments of the "hive," their very humanity evacuated from them in the interests of serving the corporation. Neil recoils. Refusing a job offer, he returns to Nova Scotia, where he will do his best to make it on his own in the moribund pulp woods.

Yet, as they say, you can never go home again. Neil's soul-crushing experience as a soldier in the Second World War has irreparably disrupted his connection to his boyhood home. He came back in the first place so that he could recover. Memories of Oak Falls had comforted him: "I had thought of the Jamieson place [his ancestral home] many times in Italy, in the drilled routine of an infantryman's life between battles, and I had fetched up the memory of it almost without tears sometimes in the humdrum hell of Stalag VIII B."[132] Stalag VIII B, the German prison camp where Neil spent two years, often occupies his thoughts. We never learn what happened to him there. There is a strong intimation that whatever it was has so traumatized him that he cannot engage anymore with the high modern world that had created such a place as Toronto. Flight to Oak Falls, which amounts to a flight back in time, is all he can think to do.

Neil, however, cannot extricate his personality from the army, the corporation, and the camps: "Queer how my mind kept going back to all that. The machine. All the big and little wheels, and the cogs and cams and shafts and spindles, and everything jerking and turning and bobbing and coming back to the same point again." Even after he has escaped from the mechanized social form that enlisted him as a component, Neil carries the impress of the mechanism upon his own mind as an ever-present threat to his individuality. His attempt to climb back into an earlier era is not only quixotic, but is doomed to be disastrous – as it indeed becomes when he kills his estranged friend Steve in a hunting accident that seems preordained by some dark fate. After the deadly mishap, he guards Steve's body all night in the woods. At daybreak, he paddles the corpse back to town. The police immediately take a statement. At a crucial point during the subsequent trial, an argument ensues over whether Neil's statement should be admissible as evidence, given that his grief, exposure, and exhaustion may well have prevented him from thinking clearly. A conference in the judge's chambers reveals that in his debilitated condition, Neil had not even signed his name to his statement. Instead, he had written "Stalag VIII B."[133] This not only attests to Neil's confusion at a particular time, but in a larger sense shows how his encounter with modernity has irreparably compromised (indeed, almost annihilated) the content of his personality.

When the court exonerates Neil, the verdict comes as an anticlimax. It has become clear by now that he has failed. His hometown holds nothing but ghosts and he is still haunted by the horrifying historical future in which he was immured during his personal past. Deciding he has to leave, he hurries to the Jamieson Place to collect his things. He tells us, "I was ready to go. There was nothing to stay for now. Yet something troubled me. Something that remained to be done ... The notion was so strong that I had an uncanny prickling in my hair, as if all the old shadows of the house were whispering together and whispering one thing."[134] Burn down the house. He must raze it to lay to rest the ghosts of his ancestors, thereby liberating himself from an earlier stage of history that continues to have claims on him. Its outdated *habitus* keeps Neil from living in the outside world, because he can only react to its social forms with unreasoning horror, insofar as they systematically violate the canons of individualism. Perhaps, Raddall suggests, it is best to simply scorch the earth and start over again. How difficult must it have been for such a historically attuned writer as Raddall to face such a conclusion!

◆

Though a tireless advocate of heritage preservation, Raddall was no sentimental antiquarian. He set forth his views in a 1943 brief to the provincial Commission on Post-war Development and Rehabilitation that he wrote on behalf of the town of Liverpool. His brief argued that the provincial tourist trade went disproportionately to the Annapolis Valley for one reason: Longfellow, by writing *Evangeline,* had unwittingly marketed its history to millions of Americans. Yet the South Shore also had historic towns that the commission could induce tourists to visit if only it could muster a "sense of showmanship." And it was pre-eminently history that should be shown off: "The tourist is willing to be diverted with bathing, sailing, fishing and golfing, but as the primary object of his trips he wants to 'see something historic' … And since he demands to be 'shown' we must provide him with things to see." Why not reconstruct Liverpool's privateer redoubt of Fort Morris? American wayfarers would thrill to stories about the exploits of privateersmen in three wars, Liverpool's role in the American Revolution, and the romance of the square-riggers sailing the seven seas. They would flock to Liverpool's Simeon Perkins House, which should become a museum exhibiting relics of aboriginal peoples, pioneer Yankees, and Loyalists. Raddall insisted, "By good planning and a cooperative effort on the part of our citizens, Liverpool could in ten years become one of the show places of the continent."[135] Raddall was already showing them the way. After the Queens County Historical Society had purchased Perkins House in 1936 for $2,500, he had become the key figure in the repair and restoration of the house, acting as an unofficial architectural conservator.[136]

Two years after submitting the brief, Raddall gave similar counsel to the Halifax Commercial Club. What did any tourist expect to find in Nova Scotia? Why, "a country different from his own, with a story of its own, and someone who can tell him all about it." Haligonians ought to do more with the "fascinating and historic scene" surrounding them.[137] It was advice one influential attendee relayed directly to the premier.[138]

Given its prominence in public life today, it is hard to remember how far down the political agenda heritage preservation had been when Raddall began promoting it. He accused his fellow Nova Scotians of having turned their backs on the history that expressed their authentic essence. "Blind MacNair" dramatizes his conviction, lamenting how twentieth-century Nova Scotia no longer understood that the Golden Age had even been golden. "In Shardstown they sing ballads no more," the story opens. "It is a village enchanted." Under a spell of torpor, Shardstown's wharves rot out, its songs disappear, and its residents do not care: "[N]owadays men say the wind ships were hell ships and well lost; and they say the chanteys had no music and the ballads no poetry. Blind they are, more blind than Blind MacNair."[139] Over the course of the tale, Raddall's narrator restores the lustre of the Golden Age by

dramatizing a long-ago singing contest that pitted Blind MacNair of Shardstown against Singing Johnny Hanigan of Revesport – a Herculean mnemonic
combat that hinged on who could remember the greatest number of verses
to ancient ballads. If you listen closely, they say, you can still hear the ghost of
the victorious MacNair singing *Mo Run Geal Dileas* on windy nights. The
moral of the story: Nova Scotians were allowing a priceless array of heritage
objects to waste away – a particularly shameful circumstance, since these cultural treasures were not inert but sang with the life of ages past.

"Blind MacNair" exemplifies Raddall's determination to further popular
historical education, not only by edifying readers but also by inducing patriotism. It worked. Nova Scotians, dispersed across North America, who had
never known him except through his published stories, thanked him profusely
for rendering their cultural identity so effectively. An anonymous reader from
California, inspired by "Blind MacNair," wrote him a warm remembrance of
his Nova Scotian childhood: "Many a time my father sang 'The Braes of
Balquidder' ... The tears ran down my face before I had finished the story."[140]
Raddall meant his stories to serve as sites for the cementing of Nova Scotian
cultural associations into a cohesive ethnicity. His readers understood this in-
tuitively and instantly. He had allayed a deep longing they had hardly known
they harboured, but that all of a sudden overwhelmed them. As a displaced
Maritimer wrote from Kansas City, "The 'Blue-nose' may never return to
his old haunts, but memories even though silent are lasting, and your ROGER
SUDDEN awakens them, so we are grateful."[141]

C.L. "Ben" Bennet of Halifax was even more emphatic in a letter he wrote
to Raddall praising *Tambour:* "Once again, you have put Nova Scotia into a
book ... You say about Nova Scotia the things that I feel and can't express."
Not only did Raddall have a rare gift for finding the words to express collective feelings of identity, he also had the still rarer gift of making them
comprehensible to outsiders. Only he could show to "foreigners" the "character and value" of this "neck of the woods." Bennet presented Raddall with
the mantle of a culture hero, "a spokesman for us all – seeing more than the
rest of us, and saying for us what we dimly see but cannot say ourselves."[142]
Here was a vindication of all that Raddall had ever done, whether abandoning
his secure job for full-time writing, or remaining stubbornly devoted to his
home province, or blending historical research with romantic themes. Speaking on behalf of all Nova Scotian writers, the poet and journalist Andy Merkel
told him, "You certainly sit at the head of the table and I feel we are all very
much in your debt."[143]

Raddall's English birth and imperial attachment presented no bar to his
acceptance by either the Halifax cultural elite or his South Shore neighbours.
Phyllis Blakeley admiringly described his total integration into his local com-

munity: "[H]e is an ordinary man, he is close to the people who think he earns his living in an extraordinary way – in a small town he knows the men and women and children – in easy reach of the sea and woods and factories and townspeople."[144] Raddall's autobiography ends with a long endorsement from the proprietor of a small fishery business in Moose Harbour, Queens County, where Raddall owned a cottage: "Tom, I'm not much of a hand for talking and I don't rightly know how to say this, but I am proud of you and proud to know you, because you write about our own people and our own country, and you live here and you're one of us."[145] It was a compliment that the English emigrant obviously treasured as a sign that he had truly passed the test of regional authenticity.

Raddall had effectively naturalized himself as the most Nova Scotian of Nova Scotians. It was a triumph, though perhaps of a strange kind. Consider one of his most successful stories, "Bald Eagle," almost a *roman à clef* about Archie Belaney (alias Grey Owl), the Englishman who so successfully impersonated an Indian that he became the much-heralded spokesman for all aboriginal peoples everywhere. Raddall's crypto Grey Owl, the Cockney lad Selby Higgins, arrives in Halifax as a naive, awkward teenager but goes on to find great fame in the guise of the wise, dignified Mi'kmaw "Chief Bald Eagle." Bald Eagle publishes poems through an agent in New York, tours the world as a speaker, and lives an ostentatiously authentic lifestyle in a secluded South Mountain shack.

Natives knew Higgins for a "charlatan," but "fortunately they did not write to newspapers." White people, however, accepted him "at his face value, which was considerable. Nobody asked why he did not call himself Joe Something-or-other like the rest of the Micmacs. And nobody questioned the 'chief' – for Micmac 'chiefs' are as common in the Maritime provinces as colonels in Kentucky." Higgins gets away with so much for so long because his white confreres cherish a profound ignorance about aboriginal life. As the narrator remarks, "the Micmac remains as aloof and mysterious as ever. He slips along the busy street, as quiet, as anonymous as a shadow, and then he is swallowed up in the woodland." Bald Eagle's readership knew no better, nor did they wish to. He "fooled white people without effort, because they wanted to be fooled, because in his person he dramatized for them the Indian of the story-book."[146] Bald Eagle fits into their cultural universe and that is enough for them. As Daniel Francis observes, popular culture has consistently preferred the "imaginary Indian" to the real thing, eschewing portrayals of "life on the reserve or on the other side of the tracks" for ritualized depictions of feathered warriors in fringed buckskin or Pocahontas-like princesses in beaded doeskin.[147] "Bald Eagle" performs an implicit cultural criticism to expose and indict such attitudes.

Bald Eagle becomes a sad figure because of the way his intense desire to connect with an aboriginal reality outside the bounds of his own culture ends up connecting him only to hackneyed English ideas about the Wild West. His insincerity is painfully sincere. Although his career brings him wealth, "with him the role was everything, the money less than the dust. He ... ceased to be a white man in Indian dress; he *was* an Indian, he was Bald Eagle! But because his shack was now a shrine for literary tourists, the very simplicity of his life had a theatrical touch about it." Because he has set out to become more Indian than the Indians – which, in the symbolic economy of the story (and Western culture), amounts to becoming more natural than nature – he actually arrives at the *ne plus ultra* of artificiality. Everything about him becomes an affectation embraced as an expedient in his quest to counterfeit authenticity. This includes his famed poetry, which meant no more to him "than the eagle feather or the romantic cabin on the hillside."[148] He tried so hard to write like an Indian that he turned out a mass of clichés.

Comparing the imaginary career of Bald Eagle to the actual career of Thomas Raddall is irresistible. Raddall, though he came to Nova Scotia from England (albeit when young), made a career of epitomizing a certain widespread image of the Maritimes in ways that the native-born seemed unable to do, both in his writings and in his person. Although he retained a literary agent in New York, he resisted all entreaties to go there, preferring to live in the out-of-the-way port town that represented the privileged site of the Bluenose persona he celebrated.[149] Rather like the ideal-typical "Red Indian," the ideal-typical Bluenose was a creature widely believed (not least by Raddall)[150] to be fading into the mists of history as the heroic time of legend was eclipsed by the sordid intrusion of deracinating modernity. These parallels are inexact. Aside from the fact that Bald Eagle is a fictional character and Raddall his author, Raddall did not purposefully come from England to impersonate a New World archetype. His performance as a real Bluenose did not involve hoodwinking a credulous public. (Nor would it have had to, since Raddall had the right bloodlines.) Most importantly, he captivated the insiders as well as the outsiders, in a way that he assures us Bald Eagle never could. People born and bred in Halifax, Windsor, and Sydney readily accepted Raddall as one of their own.[151] Raddall was involved in something more akin to self-essentialization than to the ethnic masquerade of Bald Eagle. As the author put it in the introductory note to the volume of stories that collected "Bald Eagle," "if the tales in this book have a strong flavor of Nova Scotia it is because I have lived and played and worked almost my whole life as a Bluenose among Bluenoses. I *am* a Bluenose."[152] All of these things separate Raddall from Bald Eagle.

The most telling point of comparison between Bald Eagle and Raddall is their art, which in each case serves as a vehicle to promote and proclaim a certain cultural essence – in Bald Eagle's case the noble savage version of First Nations people, in Raddall's the "jewel of true Nova Scotiana." For Raddall as for Bald Eagle, such a project seemed especially urgent, since unstoppable forces of change were fast sullying the precious essence in question beyond all recognition. (That, indeed, helps make it precious.) In the 1950s, Raddall regretted that "it is no longer possible to put forth one's hand, so to speak, and touch the remote past as I was able to touch it in those days of the 1920's."[153] Either works of art would summon up the pure essence or it would cease to exist at all. We might ask any number of questions at this point. Did he faithfully recreate a bygone way of life? Or did he create its simulacrum, a genuine copy of an original that had never existed before? Why did he believe that he had to find and defend such a timeless essence? What purpose would that serve?

Clearly, one purpose it might serve was to make money – for Raddall personally, for other cultural producers, and for the provincial government. His first efforts at historical writing were commercial ventures designed to boost the sales of a paper company.[154] From the 1930s on, he worked with the tourism bureaucracy writing copy on such spectacles as the tuna fishing competitions off the South Shore and contributing to the province's general tourism brochure (not always a happy position for a man who prized his artistic integrity and personal freedom).[155] Raddall took pride in his sales figures and consciously pitched his histories and novels to a large, relatively untapped market for "intelligent entertainment."[156] The success of a historical product in the age of mass consumption hinged less on verisimilitude than sensual appeal. The ideal consumer of a Raddallian history is someone hungry for colour, excitement, romance – and costumes (an enthusiastic publisher boosted his stories in just these terms, as "brilliant costume pieces").[157]

As he strove for the most effective manner of conveying colour, excitement, and romance, Raddall became an absolute master of creating long and evocative lists of exotic items whose very names sing out the romance of days gone by. The actual Frances Wentworth's shopping excursions in London may have been tedious or humdrum affairs (we cannot know), but in Raddall's fiction, they become moments of enchantment: "She set off with Mrs. Barradale the very next day, in the phaeton with its spanking gray four and her coachman in a livery to match, and there followed a whirl of shops and milliners and mantuamakers beyond anything she had dreamed. For a week she lived in a haze of velvets and tiffanies and Cantons and Florentines, of moreens and crepes and satins and lutestrings, of buttons and ribbons and silver lace and gauze, of silken shoes and morocco shoes, of clocked silk stockings, of hats and bonnets and caps and plumes and bows and fichus and bandeaux."[158]

Through an omniscient voice-of-God narrator, Raddall summons up sublimely satisfying (if in actuality impossible) sweeping vistas and grand panoramas. History is, one might say, *simply breathtaking*. Here is Raddall, in *Halifax, Warden of the North*, picturing the busy streets of the city as it experiences "the clang, the jostle and the prosperity of large-scale war":

> Now the streets were thronged with Boscawen's merry seamen in their short petticoat trousers, their red or checkered flannel shirts, their Barcelona handkerchiefs and tight little thrice-cocked hats. Lawrence's redcoats woke the dust of the narrow streets as they marched from barracks to forts, to church parade at St. Paul's, and to Grand Parade for inspections or the changing of the guard. The air was pierced with their drums and fifes and shaken by the boom of signal guns. Gaunt pig-tailed rangers, padding soft-footed in their moccasins about the town, set the taverns ringing with their songs and whoops.[159]

For all Raddall's proud insistence on his hard-boiled, hard-earned realism, his factual history often has the structure of a screenplay. Come to the past, he beckons, to savour the enchantment and colour of a bygone age! The drama! The excitement! The triumph! The tragedy! At the Battle of Queenston Heights, where General Isaac Brock met his patriotic end during the War of 1812, we behold the whole tableau laid out before us:

> It was a splendid little scene; the "dark October day" of the song, the wet grass of the slope, the trees in autumn color, the Niagara surging below: the American regulars on the crest in their blue jackets, white trousers, and black fire-bucket shakos; the British regulars in their sun-faded scarlet jackets, gray trousers, white shoulder belts and tall black stovepipe shakos, each with its leather sun visor and colored tuft, its glittering brass regimental badge and chain strap: the Canadian and American militiamen alike in the plain dress of the woods and farms, buckskin or gray homespun or a mixture of both, and rough boots of beefhide sewn like moccasins.[160]

The "splendid little scene" could only have been seen as such by God Himself looking down on his Creation, much as Raddall surveys his historical re-enactment. Raddall produces a reality effect through the steady accumulation of seemingly exact detail, so that in his most successful historical dramas he paints a vivid portrait of an imagined past. His knack for "eloquent preciseness" enabled his "lyrical" literary style, as John Gray observed.[161] His panoramic *trompe l'oeil* has such immense persuasiveness because it seems composed of an infinite number of concrete details, each known with complete precision by the author. Such bravura passages mean to convince us that he could go on elaborating them forever, if he so chose. He knows all because he smells, hears, touches, tastes, and (especially) sees it all.

The author's foreword to *Pride's Fancy* tells us that "the pistol of one privateersman lies at my elbow as I write."[162] His total knowledge of such heritage objects guarantees utter fidelity to the spirit and the specifics of the long ago. Not just a quaint old period survival, an old gun preserves the life of the people who made it, ever ready to impart its message across the mists of time. Rev. Mac, stroking a flintlock in "A Muster of Arms" – set during the Second World War – holds forth on its spiritual properties: "All the stored-up thrust of the past, the pressure of all the old bold spirits thronging out of the darkness, all the courage and faith that went into the making of the New World, and the living instinct to defend a thing hard-won – that's what's behind us in this war, my friend." We can access all that through the flintlock, this history's "badge and totem."[163] The exactitude of its stage properties lets the splendid theatre of the past re-enact for an audience of readers a lost world of pure values for which they long, but that seems to have faded into indistinct haziness. Here we have the "eloquence" that Gray identifies in Raddall's "preciseness."

Yet for all its magnificent costumes, breathtaking set-pieces, crafty *femmes fatales*, fierce natives, salty New Englanders, and vast army of strumpets, we leave Raddall's theatre none the wiser about why any of these historical characters made a difference. Part of Raddall remained unsure whether they had. He concedes, *à propos* of the merchants of Halifax, that they could not fight the "law of economics," which fated them to lose their fight to make their city a metropolis.[164] More generally, the hand of destiny worked behind the backs of historical actors, as fate overmastered all of their ambitions so as to hold the vanity of human wishes up to derision yet again.

"Those who can find no pleasure in the past must look with a single eye to the future, and in the end they are the conquerors," writes Raddall with respect to the founders of Halifax.[165] Yet the opposite would also seem to hold. The sweeping tableaux of character and circumstance are in detail exotic, yet in substance familiar and unthreatening. They tell us only what we already know. Even the evolutionary theory implied in the modern novels does not function as the logico-historical scaffolding of a general framework, but rather as a way to evoke the atmosphere of a land caught in a degenerative spiral. It introduces no new possibilities. History in this reading is a diversion (and a profitable one). It never raises the prospect that things could be otherwise than the competitive, individualistic cosmos a good liberal knows is the only possibility for humankind. It raises no warnings. It teaches no lessons. Destiny, especially in a land where liberalism has failed, lies out of reach. Its invisible hand moves of its own accord. Raddall's history discloses the timeless pattern of individuals competing with each other only to recapitulate their own essential natures against the sublime and unfathomable backdrop of time, nature, and destiny.

◆

Bird and Raddall were the cultural cartographers who mapped the Province of History – or, perhaps, the songwriters who most fully developed many hits beloved within tourism/history. We conclude by considering their different roles, which might be summed up under the rubrics of the "Songs of Innocence" and "Songs of Experience."

Bird, one might say, sings a song of innocence. His service in the trenches confronted him with shattering experiences incommensurable with the moral categories acquired in a small-town Methodist childhood. In common with many soldiers of the Great War, he became convinced that spirits from the afterworld influence our lives. His turn to the spiritual entailed a rejection of the analytical. He came to fear the dangers that realist analysis pose for optimistic faith in the future or happy contentment in the present. Denying much of the society around him – especially any conceptual grasp of its hierarchies – became a signal feature of his stance towards the world. War left its mark on Bird, but in a paradoxical way. Rather than pushing him towards modernism, it convinced him that he must insist all the more implacably on the simple homilies of his childhood. When he became the principal architect of the provincial propaganda campaigns of the 1930s–1950s, he transfigured this defensive formulation of innocence into a doctrine of Innocence applicable to the entire province. His brand of positive thinking required a child's faith in the truth of appearances, in the simple-hearted goodness of Nova Scotians (certain ethnically marginal persons excluded), and in each individual's ability to re-experience history directly, as a set of happenings unmediated by any categorical framework.

Positive thinking meant writing and acting with folksy immediacy and childlike spontaneity, unburdened by (indeed resistant to) any analytic categories. Bird's Nova Scotians repeat, over and over again, certain immutable character traits over which individuals exert relatively little influence and that explain everything that ever befalls them. One cannot study Bird's corpus without thinking that he had internalized a powerfully compelling story about the goodness and inevitability of a predominantly Protestant, male-dominated, white Nova Scotia, but neither can one imagine him ever mounting a coherent defence of this master narrative. As a professional *faux-naïf*, he could hardly be expected to think past his next tall tale, heritage sound-bite, or entertaining after-dinner speech. Thus, calling Bird a classic liberal can only work in the special sense that Horatio Alger was liberal: that is, in the sense that Alger's turn-of-the-century, rags-to-riches stories showed how go-getters could better themselves, how good people triumph over bad ones, and how, above and beyond the boundaries of one's own particular career, one simply ought to mind one's own business. Bird's most enduring descriptions of character can all be explained with reference to the underlying grid of Protestant, middle-class, small-town assumptions he had acquired in childhood, endlessly rehashed as an adult, yet which he never brought into any explicit form.

Raddall would seem the exact opposite of Bird. He sings the song of hard-won experience. Having entered the world of men at the age of fifteen, he never quite dispensed with the expedient of performing the role of the tough guy who has seen it all, the maverick who can take anything life throws at him, the aloof backwoodsman who disdains the tinsel and tawdriness of the big city for the manly world of the hunting lodge and fishing shack. Raddall brings this tone of hard-bitten experience to his characterization of human relationships, to his expositions of Nova Scotia history, and to his portrayal of various ethnicities and races, all of which he weighs on finely calibrated scales, evaluating them according to their respective divergences from the liberal norm.

Even when confronted with challenges clearly beyond his conceptual grasp (such as patterns of socio-economic development or cultural variation), Raddall retains his pose of tough-minded realism by pretending that otherness equals fantasy, inferiority, irrationality, or nonsense. Thus, calling Raddall a liberal can only work in the special sense that, say, Herbert Spencer was a liberal. One could simultaneously hold that there are social evolutionary patterns that place Britons at the apex of human development, yet at the same time warn that any divergence from the rule of self-possessed male individuals might place social evolution at risk or even (as in the case of Oak Falls) reverse its course. An evolutionary principle, a driving force of selection that casts entire peoples into the shade, governs Raddallian Nova Scotia.

Whereas a typical Bird story gives one a sense of having revisited a world of children, each of whom instantiates the lessons of a schoolmarm, a typical Raddall story gives one a sense of having passed through a world of undeceived adults who see through such cant as they cannily pursue their self-interest. These two renditions of reality are two sides of the same coin. Both the song of innocence and the song of experience praise the autonomous individual, this white Anglo male who strides masterfully through history, his shoulders back, chest out, eyes clear. Neither song can develop a theme extending much beyond that individual. If the one disavows realism where the other affirms it, in a deeper sense both stances leave history deeply inexplicable. In Bird's case, this is by design, and in Raddall's, it results from his dependence on a reductionist telos of social evolution and degeneracy. Hence, although there is an infantile clinging to eternally recurring essences in Bird and an impressive appearance of dialectical change in Raddall, in fact both authors effectively take an anti-historical tack. Neither can see history as anything other than a pageant. It can never be for them, say, a series of politico-ethical problems contextualized by social transformations and mediated by human experience.[166]

Neither innocence nor experience, as an aesthetic or political mode, necessarily has reactionary implications. Innocence, as for example in the case of the "estrangement" cultivated within Russian formalism, can mean the radical refusal of the conventional definitions that frame experience – as when a child, describing in simple terms a ritual adults take very seriously, inadvertently exposes its emptiness and artificiality.[167] Indeed, Bird's *And We Go On* comes close to this, as he turns his innocent gaze upon the capricious and irrational hierarchy of the army. On the other side of the equation, experience, as for example in the case of Niccolò Machiavelli's political realism, can mean the reconstruction of traditional categories, adequate to interpreting the world in new and striking ways.[168] And, in *The Nymph and the Lamp*, Raddall does undertake a realistic and imaginative reconstruction of the interwoven political and personal realities of the people who work and live on Sable Island.

Nonetheless, the Province of History, as a compound of Birdland and Raddallia, was in truth a deeply reactionary construct. Via Bird, it entailed seeing all history and society with the gaze of a child, as an entertaining spectacle, a massive diversion from reality – a series of isolated moments, events, and sites unconnected by any underlying process – in essence, an anti-historical history. Via Raddall, it entailed the ruthless application to history of purportedly realist criteria that reserved historical significance for those moments, events, and sites that he could connect to the British victors and their Canadian successors – the elite in whom social evolution had vested power and prestige.

One might plausibly trace a distinction between their two forms of liberalism. Bird's liberalism corresponds to the mid-nineteenth-century classical individualism of the mythical frontiersman, in which character types are relatively immutable, a function of hereditary processes that themselves do not seem to evolve. Raddall's corresponds to the late-nineteenth-century evolutionary individualism of the social imperialists, in which individuals and societies transmit characteristics developed through external environmental stimuli. It follows that, whereas Bird steadfastly resists any form of historical explanation, Raddall feels comfortable with a crude (untheorized but potent) form of determinism. Yet the two of them arrive, by somewhat divergent routes, at a common destination – the Province of History. Here the categories and practices shaping social life escape critical scrutiny, firstly because no such scrutiny is possible and secondly because it is constrained at the outset by an unquestioned teleology.

5

Marketing Race:
Angus L. Macdonald, Tartanism, and the
Cultural Politics of Whiteness

In 1952, Harold Connolly, the plain-spoken Halifax cabinet minister of Irish descent closely identified with the development of the tourist industry, wrote a letter to Nova Scotia's Liberal premier Angus L. Macdonald. For years, Connolly had been hearing from his party leader about things Gaelic and events Scottish. As minister of industry and publicity in the 1940s, Connolly had done his bit to make Nova Scotia into the "Scotland of the New World." Once, in 1946, he had wondered why a man bearing the impeccably Irish name of Patrick Meagher should have written to the Nova Scotia government requesting information on the newly established Scots Gaelic College. In his response at that time, Macdonald had half-jokingly assured Connolly that the apparently "strange" question had a "very simple" answer. Mr Meagher's interest in the college was only natural, since "[i]t is well known to students of such matters that since the doctrine of the Master Race has come to the fore, many persons endeavour to hold themselves out as Scotsmen."[1] Now, six years later, Connolly could not refrain from poking fun at the alacrity with which the province was pursuing a Scottish image. He reminded Macdonald of a paper he had once written (suggestively titled "Let's Cash In on Antiquity") about Nova Scotia's potential for tourism, advising the province to exploit the "English, Irish, German and even Scotch origin of our peoples" to the hilt. Yet, somehow, the last had become first: the Scots had come out on top in the province's self-representation. At the New Brunswick border, a Scottish bagpiper even piped summer visitors into the province. Connolly imagined what a more ecumenical representation of ethnicity might look like: "Visualize if you can at the [border] alternating groups of Irish harpists – English trumpeters – French Fiddlers and German Bands of the well known variety referred to in that great ballad, Macnamara's Band."[2]

Ethnic jokes made in passing can say as much about cultural politics as the more elaborate and pious declarations of the politicians. An easy sense of camaraderie and entitlement suffused Macdonald and Connolly's quips. In a province exerting itself as never before to project a tartanized quasi-Scots image, Connolly still found it possible in 1952 to joke about the piper at the border and slyly undercut the notion that the province was essentially Scottish. Just a year after the defeat of Hitler, Premier Macdonald felt comfortable joking about the "Master Race." Both men assumed that racial and ethnic representations were not to be taken too seriously, while – paradoxically and simultaneously – they invested substantial amounts of time, energy, and public money into making sure that they were.

As we noted in the Prologue, in 1936 the province officially recognized it as historical fact that five white races had founded Nova Scotia. The Provincial Co-ordinating Committee for the 1959 royal tour of Canada would reassert this truism. In Nova Scotia, the committee announced, one found a province "settled by five races, the French, the English, the Irish, the Hanoverians and the Scottish. These different races have preserved many of their characteristics down the centuries, retaining their languages and customs to an extent that makes the old province seem a 'different' part of America."[3]

Our consideration of Bird's and Raddall's works makes it plain that the concept of bioethical fitness implicitly underwrote their visions of the Province of History, such that racial and ethnic hierarchies explained the trajectory of events. They reached a wide and appreciative audience. Yet without a *third* intellectual, one much more centrally associated with the provincial government, the Province of History might have remained the enthusiasm of a small coterie of bourgeois Haligonians. Tourism/history would never have become such an incontrovertible aspect of daily life throughout civil society had the state not massively promoted it. Even though a whole bureaucracy got behind the effort, we can reasonably identify the process of state promotion with a third and in some respects paramount "organic intellectual" of tourism/history: Premier Angus L. Macdonald.

The public history that Macdonald championed was, in large part, an exercise in ethno-racial re-description. Tartanism[4] – a matrix of ideas about and images of nature, history, and race, all testifying to the Scottishness of Nova Scotia – stands out as the most visible and obvious element of a more general antimodern dispensation in which history became a function of racial and ethnic identity. It had five primary effects. As Connolly would have been the first to point out, the new dispensation represented an attempt to accelerate the commodification of the past. In David Lowenthal's terms, it turned the artifacts of history into marketable items of heritage. This does not mean that heritage construction aimed only to promote tourism – quite the contrary. Within Nova Scotia, tartanism subsumed rational protest against the fiscal imbalances and injustices suffered by the province within Confederation into a politically aimless exercise in recreational nationalism. It is nonetheless incontestably true that tartanism offered the expanding tourist industry a way of branding the province, burnishing its therapeutic lustre as a haven of antimodern authenticity. Brand-name clarity demanded a single primary essence, preferably suggestive of romance and adventure. Not only could one come to Nova Scotia to appreciate its older-and-better folkways and enjoy tales of its blood-soaked battlefields; one could also commune with the oldest white races on the continent and savour the melancholy splendour of the "last stand" of the Gael in North America. In developing these images, the provincial government was precocious in the Canadian context, but it was also contributing to international tourism patterns of reconstructed ethnicity (well described by Dean MacCannell)[5] by anticipating the demands of the "armies of semioticians" (analysed by Jonathan Culler) that modern tourism loosed upon the world.[6]

Second, the new dispensation reasserted Britishness – both the province's eternal destiny within the Empire as well as (if perhaps contradictorily) its elevated status within Canadian Confederation. Official ethnic doctrines gave Nova Scotians a way to conceive their identity at a time when definitions of self and nation in imperial terms no longer sufficed and the emergent framework of "Canadianism" excluded or marginalized them. In defining the truest Nova Scotians as the Scots, tartanism gave Nova Scotians a new subject position from which, equipped with a new past and an intensified sense of belonging to an ancient and holistic community, they could develop rhetorical explanations of their distinctive features. Citing their Scottishness, Nova Scotians too could claim a distinct – perhaps even paramount – place among the founders of Canada. A deeply conservative nationalism emerged from tartanism, one that was romantically individualistic in its social vision, backward-looking in its political economy, and mystificatory in its insistence upon an organic national community underlying all other ascriptions of class and region. Reaching beyond (and before) the emergent symbols of pan-Canadian nationalism, the Nova Scotia government officially adopted symbols that spoke plainly of the kilted regiments of the Great War, the ties of blood that linked Nova Scotia to Scotland, and even those aspects of Nova Scotia's natural environment that rendered it inherently Scottish.

Third, the new dispensation cleansed Nova Scotia history of controversy and awkwardness. Articulated in the antimodern language of belonging, the past raised no difficult issues. Hence the treatment of the province's substantial ethnic German population as Hanoverians – a designation that, while wildly inaccurate, preserved them from any association with the maligned Huns by linking them to the British royal family. Tartanism in particular responded to the Evangeline Phenomenon and Acadian counter-readings of the Nova Scotia past (discussed in chapter 2). These had long raised perplexing questions for certain Nova Scotians about the legitimacy of their claims to ascendancy within the province. While mimicking many of the Evangelinizers' tactics, the leading tartanizers tried to rebut their message. The Land of Evangeline was progressively displaced by the Highland Heart of Nova Scotia.

Fourth, tartanism suggested a form of multiculturalism that could harmonize particular identities within a hierarchy (provided no one took the exercise so seriously as to alter it). Tartanism implied not only a ranking of white races, with Scots on top – as suggested by the photomontage that opened this book – but also that the primary mode of racial expression lay in folkloric display – expressions of identity sufficiently quaint as to preclude the generation of unseemly political divisions. In equal measure, tartanism would ward off the miscegenation against which Raddall had warned so eloquently. It instead celebrated the persistence in Nova Scotia of a racial hierarchy, each element of which maintained its separate and unequal identity across the ages.

Fifth, finally, and perhaps most obviously, this new network of representations was a determinate application of a general politics of whiteness – a symbolic statement that peoples of colour (and sometimes recent immigrants too) could never count as true Nova Scotians in any foundational sense. In fact, Nova Scotia remained a racially divided society. Race riots had recurred since the 1780s. The province featured racially segregated schools, churches, and cinemas.[7] As we hear echoed in the works of Raddall, racist epithets punctuated everyday life within larger modalities of disparagement. In Macdonald's Nova Scotia, people of colour – Chinese, blacks, and Mi'kmaq particularly – had been and still were the targets of jokes, segregation, and even violence. The elevation of the "white" necessarily entailed the abasement of the "coloured," symbolically as well as practically. Judging from official statements and publications, no natives, blacks, or Asians were *really* settlers of Nova Scotia. Nor, for that matter, were the province's numerous Eastern Europeans, Jews, or Lebanese. While seeming to speak historically, the state and its promoters actually developed a form of racialized heritage that obscured the facts of that history and ruled out alternative interpretations of its meaning.

We call this new form of public heritage "tartanism" because its most visible manifestation was the proclamation of Nova Scotia's culture and identity as essentially Scottish. Yet we do so on the understanding that tartanism belongs to a complex whole that contains a diversity of heritage resources that have implications not only for the minority of Nova Scotians of Scottish descent, but for everyone in the province as well. We will also associate this new form with Angus L. Macdonald, who presided over Liberal governments in the province from 1933 until 1940 and again from 1945 to 1954. He was hardly its sole author, but without him, the new ethnic doctrines would not have attained such enduring power. If many voices called out for the comprehensive redefinition of Nova Scotia as a Province of History from the 1920s to the 1950s, Angus L.'s was perhaps the loudest and most influential.

Before we can explore tartanism further, we must first address some commonsensical objections to even questioning it. Skeptics might say something to the effect of, "But, as a matter of fact, the province simply *is* Scottish. Given the name itself ("Nova Scotia" = "New Scotland"), the use of the Gaelic language, and the vast Scottish population, describing Nova Scotia as Scottish merely acknowledges reality." That these facts seem obvious pays eloquent tribute to the triumph of heritage over history, ideology over experience, and tartanism over previous representations of the province.

◆

The commonplace notion of provincial Scottishness, attested by the provincial flag, coat of arms, and official tartan, insists that Nova Scotia is New Scotland in more than name. Summer visitors to the province are still piped in by a bagpiper stationed at the border, and greeted by a Gaelic motto (*Ciad Mile Failte* [A Hundred Thousand Welcomes]). The Gaelic College at St Ann's and St Francis Xavier University at Antigonish both offer instruction in the ancient language of Scotland. Ceilidhs and clan gatherings orient sociability around the province's Scottish identity. Most contemporary residents and visitors may find it hard to understand what Harold Connolly had found odd or amusing about the new emphasis on things Scottish, unaware that Nova Scotia has never had a Scottish majority and that by most estimates Scots have never constituted more than a third of the populace.

Seventeenth-century New Scotland, comprising the modern Maritime provinces and Gaspé Peninsula, represented just one of three major European claimants on the region. (The others were represented by the patent of the Council of New England on all lands between the 40th and 48th parallels, and the grant of the Compagnie de la Nouvelle-France, which extended from Florida to the Arctic Circle). Nor do Scots loom very large in early regional history, compared to the English or French. Furthermore, the vast majority of the seventeenth-century population within the present borders of Nova Scotia was aboriginal. To suggest that the contested claim of the Scottish king over lands populated by aboriginals made the peninsula Scottish would confuse Stuart ambitions with North American realities and discriminate against the equally worthy (or unworthy) claims of other Europeans.[8]

In short, we cannot confidently say the Scots founded Nova Scotia. Those who insist that they did typically point to King James VI of Scotland (who ruled in his native land from 1567 to 1625 and who, as James I, reigned as the first king of both England and Scotland beginning in 1603). James decided that the only way he could match the colonizing exploits of the French and English kings was to found "a new Scotland comparable to New France and New England." Accordingly, he prevailed upon the Council of New England to cede him all their lands north of the Sainte-Croix. He then instructed the Scottish Privy Council to issue a grant of this territory for his favourite, Sir William Alexander, a document that in September 1621 made Sir William the lord proprietor of "New Scotland or Nova Scotia."[9]

Sir William's poems *An Elegie on the Death of Prince Henrie* and *Doomes-Day, or, the Great Day of the Lords Judgement* had made him a well-known literary figure. Although his poetry often underlined the futility of all human ambition, as a member of the Scottish Privy Council he met enthusiasts of English colonization who inspired him to dream of making a name for himself as a colonizer – in which capacity he was energetic, imaginative, and almost completely unsuccessful. His principal colonial legacy is a description of New Scotland, *An encouragement to colonies* (1624), in which he sprinkled Scottish names generously if unrealistically over the North Atlantic coastline of the continent. He also drew royal attention to the recent plantation in Ulster, founded by the creation of knights-baronetcies. Soon thereafter, James informed the Privy Council of Scotland that he had decided "to confer the dignity of knight-baronet upon any worthy Scot who would undertake to furnish a number of settlers in return for a portion of New Scotland and instructed the council to prepare a proclamation to that effect." The Crown instituted this order of knights-baronets in 1624. In a small section of Edinburgh Castle symbolically designated "Nova Scotia," some of the baronets took sasine (or possession) of their lands.

The experiment failed. James conferred very few knights-baronetcies, and none of the baronets followed up their claims to their lands by taking physical possession of them. In 1626, James's successor, Charles I, empowered a committee of the council to ensure "that the petitioners for the dignity of knight-baronet had satisfied Alexander and that he was prepared to surrender the lands specified, and to award the dignity forthwith." As part of this commission, the king awarded the armorial bearings from which Nova Scotia derives its present flag and coat of arms. If, until 1627, the principal obstacles to Sir William's dream had been inadequate finances and Scottish reluctance to emigrate, after that date he had also to contend with both the powerful

Compagnie des Cent-Associés, organized by Cardinal Richelieu to control
New France, and the Brothers Kirke, adventurers who menaced French colonization but whose schemes also challenged Sir William's primacy. Under a
commission issued to Sir William Alexander the Younger, the Kirkes seized
Quebec and Sir William planted a short-lived colony at Baleine on Cape
Breton Island and (along with Claude de la Tour) a colony at Port Royal. The
Cape Breton settlement lasted only a very short time, and the second just until
1632, when the Treaty of Saint-Germain-en-Laye surrendered it to France,
although without any renunciation of Scottish claims.

The dreams of the Alexanders came to grief because, as D.C. Harvey tells
us, the cash-strapped Charles I agreed to give up New Scotland if the French
paid him the half of his wife's dowry that they still owed him. His decision
"sounded the death knell of Sir William's colonizing efforts … and his hope
of solvency, for by the end of 1632 the colony had been withdrawn and the
king's warrant for £10,000 in compensation for his losses had been dishon-
oured." By the end of his life, Sir William had fallen so deeply into debt that
"his creditors surrounded his death-bed in London, and denied him a peaceful burial in the church of Stirling."[10] As a colonial venture, Alexander's
scheme, like so many others of the period, left behind little except a name, coat
of arms, and flag. Nevertheless, the name "Nova Scotia" regained official
standing when France ceded Acadia (not including Île Royale, the present-day
Cape Breton) to Britain in 1713.[11]

To make this tangled history into a claim for Nova Scotia's Scottish origin
entails at least four hazardous procedures. First, it means projecting back into
the distant past our own contemporary sense of nationhood, attributing to
early-modern colonizers national identities they may not have shared. We
would need to discount the awkward fact, noted by John Reid, that Scotland's
colonists on Cape Breton appear to have been chiefly English.[12] Then we
would need to reckon with the complicated identity of James I, sovereign of
Scotland, England, and Ireland (indeed, according to official foreign policy, of
France too). Second, an insistence on Scottish origins would seem to claim
that short-lived New Scotland somehow had more contemporary significance
than Acadia did – not to mention the more remunerative pursuits of the Portuguese, Basques, and others.[13] Third, it means trying to argue that, contrary
to most evidence, there was a substantial continuity to Scottish interest in the
region; in fact, it would take almost two centuries for large numbers of
Scottish colonizers to arrive. Fourth, and most fundamentally, it means arguing that only Europeans could be the originators – slighting the Mi'kmaw
peoples permanently resident in the area for thousands of years.

Only long after the early misadventures of the Scots in the New World,
and even after the British conquest of Acadia in 1710–13, did a steady stream

of Scots immigrate to Nova Scotia. We need much more data on Scottish settlement before generalizing about many topics with any authority.[14] Faithful
to the Highland bias of Macdonald's Scottish Myth, commentators more often
assume than document Highland predominance, and the role of Lowlanders
awaits extensive research. Detailed investigation of Scottish immigration to
those areas of the province that industrialized after the 1820s, involving hundreds of miners from southern Scottish coalfields, remains to be carried out.
The impact of the breakdown of the Scottish clan system needs thorough evaluation; the typicality of group settlements has not been established; and even
the number of Scottish immigrants is hazy.[15] Here, in brief summary, is what
one might say about the Scottish presence in Nova Scotia – whose historical
significance is not at issue. They were enticed by opportunities in the New
World and, especially after 1815, pushed out by their clan chiefs-turned-
landlords. Many, though by no means all, of the Scots who came to Nova Scotia between 1770 and 1840 were Highlanders.[16] Many settled in the province's
northern counties, particularly in mainland Pictou and Antigonish Counties
and on Cape Breton Island (a separate colony between 1784 and 1820).[17]

Some have argued that Highlanders recreated the communities they had
left in Scotland, which made their departure less exile than transplantation.
Such group migrations populated at least some rural Cape Breton districts.
Protestant and Catholic Scots gravitated to co-religionists.[18] Some of them
brought their Gaelic language, which they would preserve in many parts of
the northern counties, particularly rural Cape Breton. In the 1931 census,
24,303 Nova Scotians listed Gaelic as their mother tongue, making it the third
most widely spoken language in the province, well behind English and French
to be sure, but ahead of German and Mi'kmaq.[19] Sermons were preached,
books and periodicals published, and daily business transacted in Gaelic.[20]
Throughout much of northern Nova Scotia, recently arrived Scots recreated
some of the atmosphere of Scotland. One could point to the passions aroused
by doctrinal questions among Scottish Presbyterians in Pictou County, the
appeals that educational reformers made to Scottish precedents in struggles for
nondenominational universities, or the calls-to-arms of such Scotland-born
trade union leaders as Robert Drummond and J.B. McLachlan. Scottish
national societies also formed during the nineteenth century to "foster a taste
for the literature ... and develop the noble characteristics of the Scottish people," as the "loyal Scotch of River John" put it in 1871.[21] Perhaps the most
important of these was the Highland Society founded at Antigonish in 1862.[22]
The Society's Highland Games, first held in 1863, have long featured prominently in the province's summer calendar.

None of these historical phenomena substantiate the claim that Nova
Scotia was in a primordial sense the Scotland of the New World. According to

the 1921 census, 148,000 Nova Scotians of "Scottish origin" represented just over 28 per cent of the provincial population of 523,837. The 202,106 Nova Scotians of "English origin," representing about 39 per cent of the population, easily outnumbered them. The remaining 83,731 Nova Scotians were assigned a wide range of "principal origins," including Irish, French, German, black, native, and others. Nor did Nova Scotia's Scots make the province conspicuously more Scottish than other areas of Canada. Prince Edward Island, which developed a much less pronounced concept of itself as a New World Scotland, was actually far more Scottish in this demographic sense (38 per cent of Islanders told the 1921 census that they considered their "origins" to be Scottish). As for the raw numbers, far more Ontarians (fully 465,400) than Nova Scotians claimed Scottish origins.[23] Beyond these statistical and historical considerations, however, before the 1920s, Nova Scotians – even Scottish Nova Scotians – did not imagine themselves in the ways implied by tartanism.

◆

In fact, before the 1930s, no single ethno-cultural vocabulary of "Nova Scotianness" predominated. No official and influential notion of an essence underlying (and somehow explaining) how Nova Scotians in general thought and behaved had won out. Everyone would have known the Latin meaning of "Nova Scotia," but that Nova Scotia *was Scottish* in some much more profound way was a far different proposition. It would never have occurred to most writers before the 1920s. We can divide earlier writings on the "Scottish fact in Nova Scotia" into two subcategories. Some looked at the Scots, especially those who had arrived quite recently, as backward castoffs of civilization, off-scourings of the British Isles, deficient in appearance, industry, and culture. Others looked at the Scots as improvers who brought with them enlightened ideas about education and business. Both of these mutually opposed readings actually participate in the same larger discourse of progress.

A surprising number of prominent nineteenth-century texts deride the Scots. Since the areas of Scottish settlement often bore little resemblance to the green and pleasant landscapes of the Home Counties esteemed throughout the Empire, sharply critical assessments of such unprepossessing locales rubbed off on those unintelligent enough to settle them.[24] "The settlers here [Cape Breton] were a peculiar set of people, almost all Highland Scotch and Roman Catholics, speaking Gallic in addition to English, some even not knowing the latter language," remarked Richard Dashwood in 1872. "These people were most kind and hospitable, but some of them very ignorant, and rather lawless. As an instance of their ignorance, we were actually asked by a well-to-do settler, if it was true the Duke of Wellington was dead, and if he was not a great general!"[25] Other travellers felt aghast, not at the insularity of the Scots, but conversely at their dreadful immersion in transatlantic religious debates. William Moorsom memorably described the Scots in Nova Scotia as a set of raving religious fanatics. He put down "all the feuds of all the Macs from A to Z, throughout the Scottish alphabet" to imported zealotry combined with the jealous "self-importance of individual nothingness." They should get on with workaday matters more suited to their particular gifts. "Pity it is, that with a little population which has plenty of fish to pickle outside of its harbour's mouth, and plenty of forest to clear, and of land to cultivate within its township, should distract its brain with political arguments upon abstract questions of privilege, and party squabbling for sectarian aggrandizement," huffed Moorsom.[26]

The American traveller Frederick Cozzens agreed. Remarking upon the absence of bagpipes, pistols, sporrans, or philabegs, he called the Nova Scotia Scots a "canting, covenanting, oat-eating, money-griping, tribe of second-hand Scotch Presbyterians: a transplanted, degenerate, barren patch of high cheekbones and red hair, with nothing cleaving to them of the original stock, except covetousness and that peculiar cutaneous eruption for which the mother country is celebrated."[27]

Nor did come-from-aways alone arrive at such bleak assessments. Thomas Chandler Haliburton, the province's most renowned man of letters, regretted that most Cape Bretoners were "indigent and ignorant Scotch islanders," of whom the province could count on receiving one or two thousand more each year, "equally poor and illiterate, and almost all of the Roman Catholic persuasion."[28] No less than Joseph Howe, though sympathetic to victims of the Clearances, agreed in substance with the critics of "dirty-phiz'd radicals and red-headed Highlanders" when he condemned the "degrading and paltry bickerings" of the Scots – as evidenced in the recondite sectarian squabbling between Kirkmen and Antiburghers.[29] Here we see the Scots weighed, and often found wanting, on universal scales of progress and civilization. They often violated unspoken but generally understood norms of physical beauty, political economy, and civility. One searches high and low for a representation of the Scot as the archetypal Nova Scotian.

The Scot was often a figure of fun. The key text here is Charles Dudley Warner's *Baddeck, and That Sort of Thing* (1874), whose primitive Scots can be safely indulged and patronized. Among the first to establish Nova Scotia as a North American travel destination (particularly by launching Baddeck as a noteworthy holiday resort), Warner angered Cape Bretoners by portraying them as good-natured savages far removed from the modern age.[30] A Victorian like him found Scots quaint, pathetic, and ignorant. He emphasized Cape Breton's supposed isolation, but in a mockingly ironic way. He delighted, for example, in meeting a Scot who had never heard of Robert Burns, and wrote of one isolated farm near Middle River, "I could conceive of no news coming to these Highlanders later than the defeat of the Pretender."[31]

Warner established a way of seeing that influenced many tourists. Even some early twentieth-century publications celebrating industrial progress sought to reassure visitors that Warner's diverting peasant communities remained open for viewing. The Intercolonial Railway's 1908 guide, *Forest, Stream and Seashore,* for example, after long descriptions of coalfields and steel mills, noted that the simple Gaelic primitives who had so "amused" earlier visitors still abided along the Mira: "Quaint, indeed, are the ways of many of them, amusing their maxims, and droll their wit."[32] "The primitive simplicity which amused Charles Dudley Warner and other humorous writers is still to be found in many districts," advised another pamphlet, "but it is no longer a troublesome journey to reach even the mysterious Baddeck."[33]

The isolated rural Scots of Victorian and Edwardian accounts, although in some respects similar to their later tartanist kindred, differed in crucial ways. While this era too had its racial politics, no special conception of whiteness regulated the appraisal of Scots. Some readers of imperialist bard Rudyard Kipling's *Captains Courageous* hoped they would find in Cape Breton large numbers of black Gaels, influenced by the novel's image of the cook, a "coal-black Celt" from "the innards of Cape Breton" who spoke a "home-made Scotch."[34] Moreover, within this framework of the picturesque, Gaelic simplicity and highland isolation did not come in for idealization, but for either censure or condescension. In no way did Scots count as the truest Nova Scotians who bore the provincial essence. Indeed, no single ethnic group stood out as "typically Nova Scotian,"[35] and all were weighed and assessed on the scales of progress and civility according to measurements familiar to readers of Adam Smith or John Stuart Mill. In general, the conspicuously clannish Scots did not pass this test with flying colours.

Early twentieth-century accounts tend to overpower ethnographic description with economic data. We still find a "typical Highlander" in Beckles Willson's 1911 *Nova Scotia* ("Tall and spare, with florid skin and high cheekbones, and hair and beard which a decade ago or so must have been violently red, the beard jutting out in true Highland aggressiveness"), but now he lives in a society wondrously transformed by coal and steel.[36] C.W. Vernon plays even more sharply against our expectations. His "cosmopolitan" Cape Breton welcomes all comers; one finds, especially in polyglot Cape Breton County, "Americans, English, Italians, Austrians, Swedes, Germans, and negroes from the United States, who are employed about the blast furnaces at Sydney." As for the Highland customs that a Victorian would have either condemned or patronized, Vernon writes, with specific reference to massive open-air religious services, that their passing might be a "pity," but "the remorseless march of modern ideas" and "the busier lives that men live to-day" made it inevitable. More than inevitable, salutary: while Britain, after two millennia of "gradual and successful development," stands "possibly at the very zenith of her commercial and maritime supremacy," Cape Breton, which "has not yet seen two hundred years of Anglo-Saxon energy and skill," "but sees in dim outline the imperial destiny that nature and Providence have in reserve for her."[37] "Anglo-Saxon" progress, not the quaint Celtic custom of the country, was the needful thing. Vernon's Cape Breton photographs lavish attention on the mansions of industrialists, the bankheads of coal mines, and the triumphantly belching chimneys of the steel mills, with no piper or kilt in sight. Even more remarkably, the province's own 1930 official tourist brochure proffers a briskly factual description of the province's Scottish settlers, with nary a tartan, tam, or caber toss.[38]

Yet how did Scottish Nova Scotians understand their ethnicity? While none can say with certitude, available sources yield much to discredit tartanism. While some of the usual Scottish suspects come up for memorialization – Sir Walter Scott and Robbie Burns, chief among them – they do not always appear in their latter-day antimodern guise. Labour leader J.B. McLachlan, for instance, nominated Burns as the "poet laureate" of the coming socialist revolution.[39] Nova Scotia Scots often insisted they were a progressive people. Consider how Antigonish, a town rightly identified as a citadel of Scottishness, presented itself to the world in 1916. The Board of Trade and Town Council, no doubt egged on by the Ladies' Civic Improvement League and the Forward Movement, placed their town in the vanguard of progress:

> Where once the Indian wigwam stood and where the bears a pathway trod, a town of large proportions and every new convenience stands. Where once the savage lived in sloth and superstitious fear, a group of buildings have been raised to hold aloft rich learning's torch, to those who dwell within their walls. It is the centre of a noble shrine, a symbol of the faith which conquers by the words of hope and love, while stretching outward all around lie smiling farms, wrought from the formless forests of the past, and from which the golden threads of time and change have woven a panoramic nature scene as rare as any which the eye could care to see.

What did the Board of Trade highlight about Antigonish? Its splendid cathedral, women's college, and St Francis Xavier University – equipped with the most up-to-date scientific apparatus and European-trained professors. Nor should one omit the town's fine water supply, telephone system, recently macadamized Main Street, and, the *pièce de résistance,* the Eastern Automobile

Company's four-storey palace, complete with "a modern two and a half ton elevator," the headquarters for Ford cars. Only the most alert reader would have picked up the faintest trace of the Highlander, buried in a discussion of the progressive town's religious life.[40]

Early twentieth-century literature fairly brims with this sense of a province transformed. Gaelic poems celebrated railways and progress, or cursed the iniquity down in the mine. People experiencing massive industrialization used Gaelic as a living language, so it reflected their experience.[41] Labour and capital fought in a Scottish idiom – an appropriate strategy, David Frank has noted, when Gaelic could be heard in the wash-house and on the street corner. *Mosgladh,* the organ of the conservative Scottish Catholic Society (which had formed in 1919 to defend Gaels from the "materialism of the age"), received support from the advertising of the mammoth British Empire Steel Corporation. The opposite side in the labour wars, put forward by the *Maritime Labour Herald,* included numerous rhetorical flourishes citing nationalist touchstones such as the Clearances, Culloden, and Bannockburn.[42]

Ever since historian Hugh Trevor-Roper documented the invention of the modern kilt by an Englishman after the Union of 1707, it has been commonplace to point out how Scottish forms have been particularly prone to reinvention and appropriation by romantic consumerism.[43] Trevor-Roper's famous essay on "the invention of tradition" was anticipated in Canada in 1964 by the novelist Hugh MacLennan. He recorded it as a "plain fact that the kilt was never worn in Cape Breton until the tourists came."[44] Now, this fact is not so plain as he implies. If he meant that until the advent of mass tourism in the 1920s no Cape Bretoner ever wore a kilt, he was plainly wrong.[45] Yet his comment exaggerated a valid point. Until the advent of tourism/history, kilts – along with the bagpipes, heather, Gaelic, and so on – were hardly signs of Nova Scotia (not necessarily even of Scottish Nova Scotia) identity. As we have already had occasion to mention, startling evidence of this comes from *Nova Scotia, The Ocean Playground*, brought out as the province's key tourism pamphlet in 1930. Its section on "History," while dutifully recounting the details of Annapolis Royal and Louisbourg, omits King James, Sir William Alexander, and the knights-baronets of Nova Scotia. When it comes to describe "The People," it merely mentions "fifty thousand Scots who emigrated after the eighteenth century troubles in the Highlands," with nothing on the famous *Hector* or any suggestion that these immigrants had more importance than the others. It never once intimates that the province is essentially Scottish. No tartan-weaver, Gaelic proverb, or Highland dancer graces its pages – not even in Cape Breton.[46]

Even as late as 1930, then, even the men responsible for promoting the province had not yet seen its deep Scottishness. This was a fact that they, and others, had to learn in decades to come. While Scottish elements pervaded the life of some people in the province, before the 1930s few would have suggested that, singly or cumulatively, these elements meant anything about Nova Scotia in itself. That transition required not so much the *invention* of these forms as their *re-articulation* in a new framework – a symbolic infrastructure ultimately constructed and maintained by the state.

◆

This transition, though still largely invisible in 1930, goes back to the Great War. Across the country, smouldering ethnic and racial antagonisms flared up. The struggles over conscription that divided francophone from anglophone added a new intensity to postwar celebrations of Evangeline, who more than ever before became a figure celebrated by French-Canadian nationalists – a contentious identification that would prompt some local anglophone opposition down to the 1950s. In this sectarian atmosphere, some groped for a non-French alternative to the Evangeline Phenomenon. The Halifax *Daily Star* drew a parallel between Scottish pilgrimages to Bannockburn (site of the legendary 1314 victory of Scots, led by Robert the Bruce, over the invading English) and the *Le Devoir*–sponsored pilgrimages to Grand Pré. In the 1950s, proposals for a Highland village historic site would point to the case of the Acadian memorial as precedent.[47] The localized and specific Evangeline promotion, in this sense, served as the prototype of the much more all-encompassing rise of tartanism in the 1940s and 1950s.

The 1920s abounded in signs that, at least retrospectively, seem to foreshadow the tartan shift. Archibald MacMechan, a leading figure in the Nova Scotia Historical Society, would verge on an argument for Scottish essentialism in 1924. He gave the Scots of Cape Breton more attention than any other ethnicity, even if he stopped significantly short of making them the bearers of "Nova Scotia-ness."[48] Of all the provinces, he noted, only Nova Scotia had a provincial flag that was

not English, not French, in origin, but all its own. It is a white flag with the blue St. Andrew's cross (saltire) dividing the "field" in four. In the centre is the double-tressured lion of Scotland, the ruddy lion ramping in gold. You recognise, of course, the arms of Sir William Alexander, first grantee of the province, still borne in part by the Baronets of Nova Scotia, that order of nobility ... Sir William was a Scot, a poet, and a favorite of that kindly Scot, King James, First of England, but Sixth of Scotland ... The King himself, as became the pupil of Buchanan,[49] may well have stood sponsor for the Latin name. This was to be a new Scotland, to match new England, new France, new Spain.

Though an incipient essentialist who claimed priority for the Scots, MacMechan qualified his flag-waving. He admitted that this banner had long drawn scorn as the "flag of a trading company." It commemorated a history made by "Indian, Frenchman, Acadian, Gael, Scot, Englishman, German, Catholic Huguenot, explorer, fur-trader, privateer, fisherman, pirate, loyalist, land-grabber, settler, farmer, miner, sailor" – not necessarily just by Scottish lords.[50] Nevertheless, something was afoot.

The three-hundredth anniversary of Sir William Alexander's 1621 charter prompted a wave of interest in claiming him as the father of Nova Scotia. An August 1921 ceremony featured the unveiling of three plaques – one marking the tercentenary of "New Scotland," another the bicentenary of the establishment of English Common Law in the province, and the third the centenary of Thomas Chandler Haliburton – all three symbolizing, said the Halifax *Chronicle*, "in a remarkable manner the dowry of race, law and literature which Nova Scotia gave to Canada." The trio of tablets also made an implicit argument, at the very site of Port Royal, for Scottish primacy. The Saint Andrew's Society of Glasgow presented the "flags of New Scotland" to cover the tablet erected by the province and formally "presented to the Nation" by Premier George Murray.[51]

In a long Halifax *Chronicle* article in 1921, Rev. W. Bruce Muir of Sherbrooke described the "Scottish Foundation of Nova Scotia," taking special note of "Sir William Alexander, the Poet, Courtier, and Statesmen." In this article (which immortalized an earlier address to the Nova Scotia Historical Society), Muir paddled upstream against the evidence to make the best of Alexander as the father of his people. True, critics found Alexander's verse rather a mixed bag (even Muir thought he rose at best to the status of a "minor poet"). True, Sir William, having received a vast grant of land in Nova Scotia, settled no enduring community there. True, the colonists who eventually did come out under the leadership of his son failed miserably, but – and here Muir resorted to a classic essentialist ploy – by their very failure, they revealed that "they could not have been of the *same hardy, persevering type as those of my fellow countrymen who settled the County of Pictou.*" True, Sir William himself became acutely unpopular with his fellow countrymen ("an unpopularity which seems to have followed him to his dying day"), but his "outstanding ability" was somehow affirmed by the very office conferred upon him by the Scottish king. In essence, William Alexander needed to become the Anglo-Celtic answer to Samuel de Champlain – despite the slight problem that he had never in fact set foot in the province. Yet the province could not dispense with his services as the fountainhead of the provincial essence: "I cannot help but feel, that Scottish characteristics have been a mighty factor in making Nova Scotia what it is today ... it is the character of a people that can alone determine national greatness." Muir went even further. Taking inspiration from the Statue of Liberty in New York, he thought Halifax might consider adorning its harbour with a statue of Sir William Alexander that would "stand for ever as a lasting memorial to the man who was a pioneer of colonization of these lands by a healthy, virile, British stock." Canadians must not forget "the rock out of which we have been hewn" – namely Britain. "As we cast our eyes to those little islands set like diamonds in the northern seas; why! they look mere specks upon the ocean wave" – but appearances can be deceiving, for the steadfast islanders had spread their genius across the world to form the greatest empire the world had ever known. This fact was of the highest importance as Canadians became "ever more determined to uphold the glory honor and renown of the flag 'That has braved a thousand years / The battle and the breeze.'"[52]

Muir concocted a precocious statement of the Scottish Myth that within fifteen years would become something of an official ideology. No matter that King James had truculently argued for the divine right of kings, or that his grant to Alexander and the scheme of knights-baronetcies mirrored similar plantation policies in Northern Ireland, or that Alexander failed miserably as a colonizer, besides being a sarcastic, vilified, and bankrupt poetaster. In Muir's inspired rereading of history, Alexander remained worthy of an imposing statue and the Stuarts remained the province's romantic founders. One almost wishes Muir had known of King James's predilection for trysts with male courtiers, if only to savour more of the reverend's deft spinning of the historical record.[53]

Muir gave voice to an idea whose time had come. Jackson Lears has discerned in crisis-ridden *fin-de-siècle* American culture a vogue for a simplified medievalism, shorn of its scholastic philosophers and arcane political theology. In crisis-ridden interwar Nova Scotia, one might discern a parallel vogue for dimly perceived figures of Highland warriors and royal Scots. In the terms of this simplified perception, theology, political economy, and philosophy (not to speak of sexual versatility) simply disappear. One would neither celebrate the byzantine intricacies of the feudalized Scottish clans nor critically assess James VI's notions of God-given sovereignty, but rather treasure warm memories of gallant lairds, colourful tartans, and stout-hearted crofters.[54]

It was helpful, especially at first, that (as the Alexander tercentenary suggests) antimodernism and British imperialism harmonized. Many Nova Scotians delighted in imperial pomp and circumstance. Their reading of Scottish identity always placed it within an imperialist context where happy Scottish attachment to the Empire confirmed its historical inevitability and civilizing beneficence.

This was a heroically selective reading, given that, after the rout of the Jacobites at Culloden in 1746, the regnant Hanoverians had forbidden the playing of bagpipes and the wearing of tartan (both of which were considered material supports to violent insurrection, not folkloric curiosities). But the Hanoverians did allow an exemption for men in military service. The kilted regiment symbolized the reconciliation of Highlanders and Hanoverians, especially after the Great War, in which Canada raised several such regiments (recall that Will Bird served in one, the Black Watch). From "The 85th Feather," the first song in the *Song-book of the 85th Battalion* (the Nova Scotia Highlanders), we find this celebration of Scottish martial prowess:

Now we wear the feather, the 85th feather,
We wear it with pride and joy,
That fake Advertiser, Old Billy the Kaiser [Kaiser Wilhelm II of Germany],
Shall hear from each Bluenose boy,
Where trouble is brewing, our bit we'll be doing,
To hammer down Briton's foes,
With the bagpipes a-humming, the 85th's coming,
From the land where the maple leaf grows.

alongside this celebration of the British Empire:

Britain's flag has always stood for Justice,
Britain's hope has always been for Peace;
Britain's foes have known that they could trust us
To do our best to make the cannons cease.
Britain's blood will never stand for insult,
Britain's sons will rally at her call,
Britain's pride will never let her exult,
But we'll never let the old flag fall.[55]

The Great War offered fertile ground indeed for reinvented Scottish traditions. The image of the rugged Cape Breton Highlander, fearless in battle, magnificent in physique, and gruffly taciturn in manner, informed Thomas Fraser's 1919 sketch of "The Spirit of the Maritimes." Fraser imagined two returning soldiers of the prized Scottish stock ("There could not be any finer men in the world physically than the Highlanders of Cape Breton"). He visualized them "climbing the hills together, perhaps thinking about some of the companions who had gone away with them but who did not come back, and keeping the thoughts to themselves." When the time came for them to go their separate ways, they would do so "without any elaborate ceremony of leave taking." As for their long-awaited homecoming, "I question if either got any more effusive greeting, from the head of the house, at least, than an: 'Aye, Sandy, you're back!'"[56] Perhaps – but in 1919 Sydney saw the first of many effusive "Gatherings of the Clans" welcoming returned servicemen back home.[57] The kilted regiments interwove the romantic garb of the Highlanders with the red thread of patriotism and wartime sacrifice.[58] The kilt no longer signified Scottish resistance to unjust English occupation, but the valour of soldiers fighting for king and country. Moreover, the interwar emergence of tartanism coincided with a nationwide resurgence of imperialism, exemplified by royal visits and even the forlorn Depression-era attempt to resuscitate the British honours system in Canada. None other than Governor-General Lord Tweedsmuir (famous as the novelist John Buchan – remember his backing of Raddall) thought of Canada as a "Scotland-writ-large."[59]

No part of Canada would pursue Tweedsmuir's dictum with more alacrity than Nova Scotia. In 1923, Nova Scotians set a major benchmark with the *Hector* celebrations that foreshadowed, in almost uncanny detail, the subsequent articulation of the provincial Scottish Myth (our name for the insistence that Nova Scotia has a Scottish essence).[60] Attempts to present this vessel (which arrived in Pictou on 15 September 1773 carrying 189 Scottish passengers) as the Nova Scotia equivalent of the *Mayflower* date back to 1871. These first celebrations amounted to formulaic filiopietistic declarations of admiration for stalwart ancestors, enlivened by Celtic music and baseball games but not by mythic claims about the supposed Scottish essence of the province.[61] The Pictou Academy centenary observation in 1916 occasioned more ambitious claims of provincial Scottishness and a "virtuous past" for students to emulate, but kept itself to a local scope.[62] In contrast to these earlier Scottish commemorations, the 1923 *Hector* event included an official attempt at marketing Scottishness to the travelling public.

The *Hector* anniversary came at a pivotal moment in the relationship between Nova Scotia's government and its history. Just months before, the foundation of the Tourist Association of Nova Scotia had marked the first province-wide attempt to create a viable state presence in tourism. Henceforth, the state would always employ bureaucrats charged with monitoring and improving the "tourism plant."[63] Economic chaos engulfing the heavy industry upon which northern Nova Scotia depended, a rising tide of class conflict, and a dramatic out-migration of Nova Scotians to more prosperous locales, all lent new urgency to attempts at developing tourism as an industry – even a way of luring wayward sons and daughters home. Michael Boudreau has shown how policy-makers closely watched the 1923 *Hector* celebration as a measure of how well summer campaigns to bring émigrés back as tourists would work (well enough that the "Old Home Summer" campaign of 1923 would be restaged repeatedly). An unremarkable "honour-the-pioneers" moment, fostered as usual by local enthusiasts, suddenly took on startling new dimensions. The newly empowered tourism planners, especially Tourist Association secretary A.J. Campbell, believed that "upon the work accomplished in 1923 will depend the future of the Tourist Traffic in Nova Scotia."[64]

The grandiose *Hector* commemoration marked a decisive step in the development of tourism/history. First, it revealed the Nova Scotia government's willingness to play with historical facts in the interests of developing tourism/history. While the good ship *Hector* had landed on September 15th, 1773, the state-sponsored spectacle occurred in June; mid-September came "rather late in the season for an appropriate national celebration."[65] At this founding moment and forevermore, in any conflict between factual accuracy and commercial profitability, the odds favoured the latter.[66] The new dispensation that the *Hector* event betokened also placed a novel emphasis on Highlanders. When the *Hector* landed in Nova Scotia, many Scots already lived there. Predominantly Lowlanders had settled in Halifax, Colchester, and Pictou, and even after the *Hector*'s landing, many Scottish immigrants would hail from the country's southern coalfields. The Highland motif marginalized them all. Not only that, but its relentless focus on martial masculinity and pious spirituality virtually expunged the entire history of the Scottish Enlightenment – David Hume, Adam Smith, and James McPherson, among others, who perhaps constituted a contingent too plainly secular and civil for inclusion in the antimodernist dispensation.[67] History, the painstaking reconstruction of past complexities in the light of logic and evidence, was already being transformed, essentialized, and commodified into tourism/history.

The *Hector* event brought these new interests to the fore. Although the government monies involved did not amount to much by twenty-first-century standards (a general provincial grant of $10,000 to the Tourist Association, a $5,000 provincial grant to the *Hector* commemoration, $15,000 from the federal government, $2,500 from Pictonian ratepayers), they augured a momentous shift in governmental priorities. Such funding raised eyebrows. The local Tories worried with good reason that henceforth every county in the province would come begging for commemoration money. At the federal level, Edward J. Garland, MP for Bow River, Alberta, memorably (but ineffectually) remarked, "I, like all Irishmen, love Scotchmen, but I do not love Scotchmen dearly enough to vote them money like this at a time like this."[68] Such voices cried out against an emergent mnemonic politics according to which history was an industry too, as deserving of subsidy as any other because it promised economic development.

Goosing the local economy depended upon a novel use of publicity. A.E. MacKinnon, a Pictonian adman resident in New York, orchestrated press coverage for the *Hector* commemoration, direct mail-outs to recent emigrants, and the systematic inflation of the event's actual historic significance. Its stock accordingly rose from only middling importance – the *Hector* was neither the first boatload of Scots to the province, nor very remarkable among the host of such ships, nor even all that renowned among Scottish Canadians – to become a milestone in the history of the entire Dominion. Like the *Mayflower* in the United States, the *Hector* became the bearer of true national virtues. Tourists unmoved by the prospect of visiting Nova Scotia as a "premier vacationland" might come for a world-historical event. Parades, balls, picnics, re-enactments, and speeches from dignitaries like the governor-general and premier, all bespoke the *Hector*'s capital importance – to Nova Scotians and to all Canadians, who were also advised of the Dominion's Scottish roots.

The *Hector* commemoration demonstrated that a pseudo-event (which would not otherwise have occurred had the state not backed it) could draw a crowd. The population of Pictou rose overnight from three thousand to twenty-five thousand – a captive audience for "half a ton" of promotional literature brought in under the auspices of the Nova Scotia Tourist Association. A tent city sprouted. Catered meals fed those without accommodation. Merchants plied tourists with their wares, including cameras for those yearning to "keep the story of this epoch-making week" forever fresh.[69]

"Epoch-making" – the notion that the Scots stood first among the races of the Dominion suffused every moment, designedly so. According to this early version of the myth, Scottish pioneers had been the true go-getters of the province and the Dominion. Their offspring, dubbed the "Pictou Product," grew up as natural leaders endowed with that "particular quality of mind and energy which had much to do with the up-building of the great Dominion." Modest nineteenth-century claims that the *Hector* had provided Pictou County with a number of Scottish settlers, some of whom became significant local figures, metastasized into claims of moral (indeed, racial) superiority. Michael Boudreau draws attention to the speech given by the mayor of Pictou, who claimed that the *Hector* pioneers had "blazed [a] trail for thousands of loyal sons of the Motherland whose influence has been potent in molding the destinies of Canada and in giving her that place in our Empire of which, as Canadians, we are proud." The *Hector* monument (whose unveiling provided the centre-piece of the commemoration) celebrated Scottish manliness and fighting spirit by depicting a young kilted Highlander holding a rifle in one hand and an axe over his shoulder. It stood as a metonymic depiction of a master race specially favoured by God, a proposition clinched by its inscription dedicated to the "vanguard of that army of Scottish Immigrants whose intellectual ideals, moral worth and material achievement have contributed greatly to the good Government and upbuilding of Canada. 'God of our Fathers be the God of their succeeding race.'"[70] The last line referenced "O God of Bethel, By Whose Hand," a 1736 hymn all true Scots learn at their mother's knee.[71] The Scots are tops, one infers, because God wills it.

In his keynote address to the assembled masses, the ultra-conservative Sir Andrew Macphail of McGill University combined God's racial preferences with the more terrestrial imperatives of building the white man's dominion. He warned his audience of the declining morality and work ethic of Canadians. What diabolical force menaced these worthy qualities? Immigration, of course: "I see no evidence that the immigrant of today is bringing that quality with him. We must supply this vital principle from ourselves or we shall perish."[72] Such themes would become staples of Robbie Burns Nights and other elite gatherings, which called together affluent middle-aged men to bear witness to their individual and collective prowess with copious amounts of alcohol and haggis.[73] They would also flourish within another demonstration of the mass appeal of images and ideas drawn from the Scots tradition, the Ku Klux Klan, which made quite considerable inroads during the interwar period, particularly in the Canadian West.[74] In Nova Scotia, with its segregated schools and theatres, the Scottish Myth played into a prevailing politics of whiteness. The Scottish Myth also played an essential role in regional politics. According to mainstream liberal political economy, Nova Scotians could blame only themselves for their faltering economy. They were failed individuals living in a failed region. Tartanism let them identify with the world's most successful imperial power and the country's most successful pioneers.

Yet if the *Hector* commemoration counts among the first moments of the new tourism/history matrix in Nova Scotia, in other ways it remained a relic of an earlier time. Notwithstanding the strenuous attempts to make this particular vessel the carrier of virtues applicable to the entire country, many speakers kept coming back to specific local memories. A succession of Presbyterian divines laboured to underline the appropriate denominational character of the occasion, in a manner out of keeping with a later era of the Scottish Myth dominated by a Catholic premier. Moreover, as the tourist promoters looked back over the event, some felt unsure about its success. Tourism czar A.J. Campbell declared flatly that he considered the *Hector* celebration a failure. Designed in part to attract Nova Scotians back to their province, it may have had the opposite effect. Some young Pictonians, having heard from their visitors about American prosperity, had likely been lured away. As for the pageant itself, the image of the master race foundered on some practical difficulties. Having drawn thousands of people thousands of miles to see the *Hector* glide triumphantly into Pictou Harbour, the organizers reckoned without the tides. The vessel had to dock an hour early, bitterly disappointing many in the crowd (some of whom, it was said, burst into tears). Later, when it came time to unveil the

Contemporary *Hectoriana* from the town of Pictou, which as the "Birthplace of New Scotland" now boasts a *Hector* replica, a *Hector* festival, and a *Hector* heritage quay, from Nova Scotia, Department of Tourism, Culture and Heritage, *Doers' & Dreamers' 2007 Guide* (Halifax, 2007).

statue hailing the God-given racial superiority of the Scots, it transpired that this superiority did not encompass knowledge of mechanical contraptions. The governor-general pulled the ceremonial cord. It proved tangled and useless. The cloth covering the gallant Highlander would not budge. Nothing went quite according to plan in the Pictou commemoration – perhaps the only way it resembled the actual history to which it supposedly bore witness.

◆

If by the early 1930s all the elements of the Scottish Myth were present and accounted for, they had not cohered. As a one-off commemoration, the *Hector* event did not launch a more general program. Various Highland games and clan gatherings remained merely local happenings. There was a significant difference between an episodic, historically specific, and local development of Scottish themes and the sustained, mythic, and province-wide intensity of official tartanism after 1933. Here we must factor in Angus L. Macdonald. Raddall and Bird could write dozens of books on Nova Scotia without recourse to the improbable notion that the province was essentially Scottish. Yet by the end of the 1950s, an official tartan, a piper welcoming visitors to the border, a newly renamed region called the "Cape Breton Highlands," a host of Scottish-themed historic sites, and a Gaelic college all testified that the province clearly had become so. It would have been unthinkable without Angus L.

Angus L. Macdonald (1890–1954) was Liberal premier of Nova Scotia from 1933 to 1940 and again from 1945 to 1954. No twentieth-century political figure in the province enjoys anything even approaching his posthumous prestige.[75] Here is George Farquhar, the editor of the Halifax *Chronicle* (and himself no mean advocate of the Scottish Myth), recalling the Macdonald touch: "The son of a Gaelic-speaking father and a French mother, Macdonald grew up in a home where Gaelic, French and English were as familiar as the morning sun." Macdonald enjoyed a sterling education, but more than that, his "native eloquence" really "gripped an audience, and the result was a wide personal following not seen in this province since the days of [Joseph] Howe. At times, his words were winged with an almost mystic quality, in striking contrast to the cold, matter-of-fact Anglo-Saxon."[76] Macdonald's federal ambitions foundered after he opposed Prime Minister William Lyon Mackenzie King in the conscription crisis during the Second World War, but at home no one could touch him. After he died in office, an estimated hundred thousand people turned out for his funeral in Halifax, where the *Mail-Star* eulogized him as the "most beloved Nova Scotia statesman and scholar since Joseph Howe."[77] Macdonald was accorded a lying-in-state in Province House, the first since Charles Tupper in the nineteenth century. Phyllis Blakeley eloquently described the scene in a letter. For nearly five days he lay in the Red Room of Province House, while an honour guard watched over him: "Angus was laid out in kilts and looked calm and dignified. The room was half filled with flowers. There was one 8 foot cross made of calla lillies from the government of Nova Scotia, and another 8 foot cross of white carnations and red roses from the members of the assembly. Zaidee Harris went down Sunday night about 9.30 with Percy Scott and Dot Smith. They stood in line 40 minutes before getting into the Red Room – had to line up on Hollis Street and go in the main door and up the marble staircase."[78]

The sophisticated, brilliant premier taught at Dalhousie Law School from 1924 to 1930, became leader of the Nova Scotia Liberals at their first modern American-style convention in June 1932, and then led his party to victory in 1933. In power, he spearheaded the groundbreaking Provincial Economic Inquiry (popularly known as the Jones Commission), whose mandate was to investigate the province's interwar-era collapse – vividly symbolized by the absolute fall of its population from 523,827 to 512,846 during the 1920s. Drawing on research by Norman McLeod Rogers, a Nova Scotian who taught at Queen's University, the commission documented the fiscal imbalances that had grievously affected the province and tracked deindustrialization in steel and coal. Many of its recommendations dealt with enhancing the state's administrative capacity – in research and development, assistance to coopera-tives, and electrification.[79] Of particular significance for tourism, the commis-sion called for a new national park in the province, improved hotel facilities, and road-building – all of which Macdonald would vigorously pursue. In many ways "Angus L." seemed like Nova Scotia's answer to "FDR," whom he greatly admired. His government initiated old age pensions and brought in legislation (influenced by the New Deal's Wagner Act) to guarantee collective bargaining rights for Nova Scotian workers. In an age of virulent reaction across Canada, he stood virtually alone in reaching a historic compromise with the labour movement. Workers won only a partial victory, but this should not conceal the significance of Macdonald's acknowledgment that organized labour had legitimate interests within the polity. He led a broadly centre-left government generally considered a friend to the little guy – which, in addi-tion to his reputation for incorruptibility, explains why the crowds lined up to pay their respects to him in 1954.

Yet this complicated and deeply introspective man was embroiled in a crisis that would test the liberalism that held his political allegiance. Macdonald's individualism went beyond a simple tenet to encompass a whole style of governance. Though he ran a government, his intense personal distrust of the state led him to operate as a nineteenth-century politician who insisted upon day-to-day involvement with each major portfolio. Since he saw balancing the budget as government's chief responsibility, he eccentrically kept provincial finances in his own hands rather than managing them through a ministry.[80] Key cabinet minister Henry Hicks rankled at what he considered an ill-judged retention of an obsolescent model of leadership. He noted that the Nova Scotia budget amounted to only seven million dollars when Macdonald first became premier, reflecting a small government amenable to personal control, but Macdonald never quite adjusted to changed circumstances after he resumed the office: "Angus L. tried desperately when he came back from Ottawa in '45 to regain that kind of relationship with the control of Government business in Nova Scotia and, of course, could never succeed in doing it."[81] Harold Connolly put it bluntly: "Angus was completely unable to delegate authority. He had a terrible deep-rooted suspicion of anybody's efforts except his own, that was true even with people in whom he had complete trust."[82]

No mere foible, Macdonald's compulsive micromanagement reflected the programmatic individualism of a convinced liberal. Unlike his fellow liberals Bird and Raddall, Macdonald worked publicly to articulate his political philosophy. "If a statement of fundamental aims is soundly conceived and faithfully followed by leaders and followers alike," he reasoned, then "the particular problems that arise from time to time will be solved wisely under the guidance of these general basic principles." Accordingly, Macdonald's liberalism sought "to gain and hold a true understanding of the proper relation between the state and the individual." Drawing upon the work of historian Arthur Lower, who had undertaken to define "The Essence of Liberalism," Macdonald argued that "liberalism is best defined as that way of life which emphasizes the absolute value and dignity of human personality. That is the pith and substance of the definitions reached by the great liberal writers of England and America." Liberals who stressed "the importance of human personality and the inalienability of certain individual rights" could brook "no compromise" with those who believed that "the state is supreme and that the individual must in all things subordinate himself to the state and to its agents."[83]

In making such a declaration in 1948, he had a good sense of occasion. For a consistent liberal, the level of direct state involvement in the economy of the 1940s worryingly signalled that wartime *dirigisme* might become the counter-individualist model of the future. Macdonald tasked liberalism "to set the [Liberal] Party's feet firmly on the old and well-proved paths, to align itself definitely against any encroachment, no matter how speciously attractive may be its garb on those fundamental human rights that liberal effort and liberal sacrifice have won throughout the long years of the past." He particularly abjured any truck or trade with socialists. "Those who say lightly that political liberty has little meaning for those who lack economic security, those who suggest that economic security must be provided at no matter what sacrifice of other securities, may one day find themselves without either political liberty or economic security," he warned. "Furthermore, I think it would be highly unwise to combine complete economic power and complete political power in one agency, even if that agency be government."[84]

The Halifax *Chronicle* spelled out the contemporary application of Macdonald's liberal theory in an editorial prompted by his speech. "Statism is an insidious doctrine," it announced. "Because of the pressure of immediate needs it often seems to offer the easy way out of difficulties. It appears to provide a specious short-cut to efficiency, and it invariably promises the cheap achievement of every man's material desires." Yet "statism" offered but a slippery slope to totalitarianism. There could be no compromise, because "once a people becomes committed even to relatively small adventures in state ownership state ownership must be pursued from salient to salient until the whole terrain is occupied. There is no half-way house on the road to socialistic statism, and Liberalism must recognize this potent fact before it is too late." This analysis betrays the influence of *The Road to Serfdom*, F.A. Hayek's influential right-wing tract of the 1940s, clearly repudiating the accommodation of state intervention in British liberal thought under the aegis of men such as Sir William Beveridge, T.H. Marshall, and John Maynard Keynes. In effect, the editorialist was firing an early salvo in the looming Cold War.[85]

Thus, while Macdonald might have become the prudent architect of a modest provincial welfare state, he remained the most classic of liberals who instinctively suspected any collectivizing impulse. One could easily construe even his state-building activities in the 1930s, such as his massive road-improvement program, as conventional pro-business measures designed to further private capitalist accumulation (as Macdonald rightly liked to remind people, liberal governments had served business interests for decades). The development of a tourism/history complex fit comfortably into such an agenda. Many besides Macdonald came to identify it as the industry of last resort, a have-not province's one remaining hope for economic development. A liberal premier could build roads, fund craft programs, and orchestrate pseudo-events without experiencing any cognitive dissonance because such measures seemed perfectly consonant with an underlying goal of shoring up the propertied individual – in this case, the entrepreneur turning a profit in the tourism sector.

Not only did Macdonald lay down the infrastructure of tourism, but he also helped to formulate the distinctive cultural content that would set Nova Scotia apart from other possible destinations. In September of 1934, following in the footsteps of Archibald MacMechan, Premier Macdonald addressed the Nova Scotia Tourist Advisory Council on the subject of "Nova-Scotianness." His speech advocated the promotion of "the distinctive habits and customs that characterize the various races represented in our population," whether Highlander, French, or Hanoverian,[86] as the "genuine tourist resources" that more than anything else "will help attract more visitors to our shores." The Halifax *Herald* approved of his idea, affirming that tourists "desire to see not so much what they can find in their own lands, but something authentically Nova Scotian – something with the atmosphere of Nova Scotia and the lure of bygone days in its presentation."[87] The 1930s and 1940s saw the articulation of this marketable "something." As Macdonald had suggested, representations of the various (white) "races" would propel this effort. And, under Macdonald, Scots would stand front and centre among the "five white races" to become first among equals.

On its face, a doctrine that the state should promote the Scottish race does not seem inherently liberal. Indeed, in some respects the Scottish Myth was in fascinating contradiction with others of Macdonald's liberal tenets, while in other respects it achieved remarkable symbiosis. As the "Laird of Winwick" (his elegant South End Halifax home), Macdonald savoured the romance of the Gael, which he elaborated into the commercialized Scottish Myth, in essence the ethnic face of Innocence. For all the self-assurance of his liberal convictions (securely hegemonic in Canada), Macdonald, like so many other interwar, middle-class, urban cultural producers, reached for something outside of and better than the changeful, anxious world he inhabited. Tartanism triumphed because Macdonald, a believer in the Scottish tradition and in the redemptive role of tourism, used the government to fuse these two truths into one commanding commonsense. He built on tartanism's modest local beginnings in the 1920s to construct something like an official Scottish Myth. He thereby naturalized tartanism, making it seem like a self-evident summation of the province's cultural identity – the expression of an essence that visitors (to say nothing of many Nova Scotians) believe in to this day. The triumph of tartanism illustrates the cultural impact that tourism could have when powerfully focused through the active twentieth-century state.

Where did Macdonald's commitment to the Scottish Myth actually come from? As for the province, as for Will R. Bird, so for Macdonald: the Great War seems to have been a great turning point for him. Macdonald's pursuit of the romantic Scottish past was quite literally escapist, a diversion from the grim realities of combat. Macdonald spent three weeks' leave in the Scottish Highlands, touring Inverness and Moidart, birthplace of his grandfather in 1811. He returned to the battlefield heavily burdened with heather from the Moidart hills, stone from Castle Tirrim (for many years the seat of the chiefs of the Clanranald), souvenirs of Culloden, and two heavy volumes: *History of the Highlands and Gaelic Scotland* and *A History of the Macdonalds and Lords of the Isles*.[88] He liked to remind audiences that an ancestor of his had drawn the first sword that flashed in Scotland for Bonnie Prince Charlie, the lad born to be king as scion of the exiled House of Stuart.[89]

As Murray Beck has pointed out, notwithstanding his Scottish name, Angus L. was only about as Scottish as Nova Scotia itself – approximately 25 per cent. He could have, with equal lineal warrant, established himself as a true Acadian (from his mother) or a genuine Irishman (from his half-Irish father).[90] Nevertheless, he became enthralled with the Scottish Myth. Perhaps the compromised (from a bloodlines standpoint) nature of his Scottishness abetted an abiding ecumenicity in extending its rubric to others with even more tenuous claims. Raddall recalled how one day the premier had stopped him in the street, having noticed the novelist sporting a tartan tie. "So you're a Scot too?" he enquired. Raddall confessed not. Upon hearing of Raddall's Cornish ancestry, though, Macdonald interjected, "Wait a minute! If your father was a Cornishman, your blood is half Celtic. That makes you a half-brother to a Scot."[91] Scottishness mattered so much to Macdonald because, beyond a common history, it implied a substratum of shared affective and spiritual characteristics transmitted over generations. Hugh MacLennan remembers the first time he met the premier: "With a suddenness that would have been startling to anyone but another clansman, Mr. Macdonald turned to me in a company of people and from the depths of a mutual empathy he said: 'To be a Celt is never to be far from tears.'"[92] The spiritual progression from Nova Scotian to Scot to Celt and back again in Macdonald's representations of ethnicity suggests a move towards an even more mystical and primordial racial realm. Macdonald's fascination for the Scottish tradition only heightened because he felt out of sorts in a modern world that so little reflected his idealized racial characteristics – a modern world whose exigencies he had mastered in his professional life, whose particular logic he would abet and extend in his public life, but which perhaps for just this reason made him profoundly uneasy in his mind.

It is entirely typical of Angus L. that the pan-Celticism he embraced in large part because of his misgivings about modernity would enable him to enjoy a successful career in business. Indeed, when he spoke of using race as a way of promoting tourism he expressed no ethical misgivings. He does not seem to have believed that tourism raised the problems Dorothy Duncan likened to "prostitution" in her travel book *Bluenose*.[93] He felt so few qualms about commercialization that he urged one correspondent who asked his opinion on the proper representation of Highland dress to "follow pretty generally the famous Macdonald Tobacco ad which appears on a card that I am sending herewith."[94] The clearest expression of his thoughts about invented tradition comes out in his reminiscence of Flora Macdonald College in Red Springs, North Carolina, which he visited in 1937. In 1896, the school's founders had called it the "Southern Seminary for Young Ladies,"[95] but a "very enthusiastic Scot" successfully intervened to recommend the substitution of "Flora Macdonald College." Macdonald drew this moral from the story: "They at once passed from being just another school to a school with a distinctive and appealing flavour, and they received gifts from Scotsmen in every part of the world." A cynic might draw from this episode a jaded impression of a money-hungry institution manipulating cultural tradition. (Flora Macdonald College's Scottish credentials amounted to little more than its name and the possession of a brooch, alleged to contain two locks of hair from Flora Macdonald and Prince Charlie.)[96] Macdonald took away precisely the opposite impression, urging that Nova Scotia's St Francis Xavier University should follow the North Carolinian example by stressing "the Scottish side of things."[97] To him, the very profitability of the Scottish tradition demonstrated its underlying value. In developing Scottishness as the brand name of Nova Scotia, he honoured his own ancestry by developing an attractive tourism package.

Macdonald was also following the example of his neighbours in South End Halifax, a comfortable cultural elite who influenced the Canadian Authors Association, the Nova Scotia Historical Society, and Dalhousie University. Like them, he did not intend to abandon the comforts of Winwick on the North West Arm in favour of the rural life for which he expressed such nostalgic affection. Yet, unlike most of them, he could use the full resources of the state to express his romantic fantasies. Macdonald inscribed the Scottish Myth on the enduring public text of the province itself: parks, mods, gatherings of clans, bronze plaques, highway maps, and the very landscape. A vast network of words and things told Nova Scotians that their society was in some profound sense Scottish. It was one thing to play at being a member of a primitive clan society one Robbie Burns Night a year, escaping into a therapeutic but temporary otherness. It was another thing entirely to do it wholly, to write a fictional sense of belonging to a clan into the province's icons, historic sites, and public memory.

Even without Macdonald, antimodernism would still probably have become the new vocabulary of tourism. It was an international trend. Even without Macdonald, the Scottish theme would likely have developed as an analogue of tourism, perhaps as a minor motif applied particularly to Cape Breton Island and the northern mainland, where it had a semblance of demographic plausibility. Then Nova Scotians might (like their more Scottish fellow Canadians, the Prince Edward Islanders) have shifted the ethnic emphasis of their tourism promotion from one year to the next. But with Macdonald, a general tendency to antimodernism and the general international popularity of things Scottish crystallized in a more powerful way, permanently naturalizing Scottishness as a persuasive commonsense.

Such a project led Macdonald into uncharted territory. Under the ostensibly anti-statist Macdonald, the state's role in tourism expanded enormously. As premier, he encouraged investment of public monies in tourist accommodation through generous grants to private entrepreneurs and the establishment of the publicly owned Keltic Lodge at Ingonish. Along with A.S. MacMillan (a fellow Cape Breton Liberal), he planned a massive paving program, including the construction of Cape Breton's Cabot Trail – a road whose expensive construction was justified on the grounds of projected tourism revenues. The state's role in tourism promotion massively expanded through a new department bearing the vaguely Orwellian name of "The Department of Industry and Publicity."

Although an orthodox liberal, Macdonald also used his position in the state to make his romantic Scottish attachments into official policies. He presided over a program of state involvement in economic and cultural life far more extensive than most Victorian liberals had publicly contemplated. Macdonald sometimes spoke as though he wished for a nineteenth-century "nightwatchman state," and the ideology promoted by his expanding state apparatus remained individualist. So how could he, in good faith, actually expand the state? The answer would probably be that statism in Nova Scotia expanded rather than circumscribed the sphere of market relations. The entire tourist administrative machine worked to bring hitherto uncommodified activities (most obviously the production of cultural goods) into capitalist exchange relations. This required a massive reshaping of the provincial culture.

No one could mistake the new influences at work in the mid-1930s. The 1935 *Nova Scotia, Canada's Ocean Playground* (*chef-d'oeuvre* of promotional literature) represented a new stage in the marketing of ethnicity. Admittedly, it portrayed the Acadians in all "the pleasing simplicity that marked the lives of their ancestors," recycling humdrum nineteenth-century notions of Evangeline – "They still speak the French of their forefathers and, in their cottages, many century-old customs remain, even to spinning wheels and kirtles" – but now they had to make way for the Scots, depicted in traditional Highland dress.[98] D. Leo Dolan, a New Brunswicker who had risen to become director of the Canadian Travel Bureau, hailed the new promotional vocabulary in an address to the Nova Scotia Motor League. "Keep this province distinctively Nova Scotian, Canadian, and British," he advised. In order to garner a share of the five billion dollars that Americans spent yearly on travel, Nova Scotians needed to play up their supposed cultural essence. Americans "were being educated to the fact that they might 'be foreign' – go abroad – merely by crossing a borderline without necessity for an ocean voyage." He picked up *Nova Scotia, Canada's Ocean Playground*, which he praised for reflecting "the Nova Scotian atmosphere." That atmosphere was Scottish. Nova Scotia could be a popular destination if people believed that "here was to be found a larger percentage of Scottish population than in any other country outside the old land itself. There was no need to compete with the French atmosphere of Quebec or with the mountains of Alberta and British Columbia."[99]

Dolan would sound this theme repeatedly. After the Gaelic College opened in 1939, he wrote Macdonald a glowing letter suggesting how closely they agreed on the benefits of marketing race. Dolan expressed the pious hope that, after he had launched a suitable promotional campaign, "Sons of Scotland" would throng to the new temple of all things Celtic. He confided to Macdonald that "like yourself, I sometimes think I am a bit of an idealist, but I visualize the day when this Gaelic College may become a new Scottish Shrine for Cape Breton, if not North America."[100] Macdonald warmed to the prospect, agreeing that "the most attractive feature of Nova Scotia is her interesting people."[101] "You and I both have the same idea with respect to these matters," Dolan replied, "and it has always been a mystery to me why the people of Nova Scotia generally have not grasped the importance from a tourist standpoint of the character of the people who reside within that province."[102] Dolan was clearly preaching to the converted. So was I.H. Macdonald of the Canadian Daily Newspaper Association, who informed the premier that "our considered opinion is that Nova Scotia, with the development of the celtic motif, holds out a travel lure that is hard to beat."[103] Yet, if the "celtic motif" had really been no more than a "travel lure," it would not have moved so many people. Macdonald's unqualified success in naturalizing the Scottish Myth and branding the province stemmed from his sincere belief that in stepping up the promotion of Scottishness for tourists he was presenting the province's innermost nature. As one self-identified Cumberland County "Scot" remarked, Macdonald seemed to appreciate the work of the Scottish societies, not only from a tourism perspective, but also "from a pride of race standpoint."[104]

This "race standpoint" marks the extent to which a tartanist "celtic motif" exceeded previous representations of Scots. In the 1930s, following Macdonald's lead, writings about northern Nova Scotia (especially Cape Breton) took a turn towards racialized depictions. An area once portrayed as a progressive industrial hive of coal mines and Ford dealerships now reappeared as the haven of simple folk. Neil MacNeil, a college friend of Macdonald's, won renown in 1948 with *The Highland Heart in Nova Scotia*. Paralleling in many respects the quasi-Darwinian social thought of Thomas Raddall, MacNeil painted a heartwarming portrait of the MacNeils of Barra, who exemplified the "survival of the fittest, for only the strong, the brave and the intelligent could survive the rigors of their climate and the hardships of their life." Life in Washabuckt "was simple and innocent and its tempo was sluggish." The Highlanders "felt sufficient unto themselves and did not court the frills and artifices, the luxuries and mechanics, of modern civilization." No, these dour folk "looked with contempt upon such effete influences ... They were content with little, and thus they had the deepest secret of life." Houses were left unlocked, crime and illness unknown. Living "a wholesome but primitive life close to the soil," the Highlanders' needs were elementary. These folk were also rather stupid, though that was part of the charm. While, occasionally, new ideas or inventions did disrupt the Highlander's "complacency," they never did so "with enough force to cause him to delve more deeply into the problems of life, government and the hereafter." Happily, though, his kind did find a lot of time for "pride of name and pride of race."[105]

"Pride of race" required a novel reading of Cape Breton geography. Progressive-era writings had emphasized industrialized Cape Breton County, sidelining rural areas. The new dispensation reversed this hierarchy. Attention refocused on the unspoiled interior and north. In the new tourism vernacular, these areas of the island became "the Highlands." Nova Scotia had known other "Highlands" before. Pre-1914 visitors to southern Nova Scotia had learned, for example, that they were just a hop, skip, and a jump from Nova Scotia's "Highlands," where they might discover in Yarmouth County "the scenic beauties of 'Bonnie Scotland,' with a road winding around mist-capped hills and a silver chain of lakes which have a true Gaelic quality of their own."[106] The foundation of Cape Breton Highlands National Park in 1937 voided such competing Highland claims. Gordon Brinley's *Away to Cape Breton* illustrates a new cultural geography, conjuring a purely preindustrial island brimming with stout-hearted fisherfolk and quaint Scots, cleansed of coal mines and steel mills – a feat he accomplished by the simple expedient of steering clear of those urban areas where most Cape Bretoners lived.[107]

The Scottish Myth required a methodical strategy of selection when it came to placing the island's racial essence in an appropriate antimodern light. Dorothy Duncan found a daringly essentialist solution (in *Bluenose: A Portrait of Nova Scotia*) to the problem of making this *Gesellschaft* out to be a *Volksgemeinschaft*. Throughout *Bluenose,* Nova Scotians live and die as social evolution decrees. We get long descriptions of their bodies, which Duncan construes as documents proving that history moves according to the dictates of heredity. In this anatomical tourism, Duncan's readers pleasurably view bodies with a distanced and objectifying gaze. The rural "Highlanders" of Cape Breton are "broad-shouldered creatures with pale-blue opaque eyes, high complexions, gnarled hands, and features so inelegant as to seem handsome. The girls are pretty, and the mature women are fair to look upon at any age. All of them, including their polite children, speak with a lilt in their voices that clings to one's memory like the odor of lavender or the sound of the sea."

The Highlanders owe their happiness to their bloodlines. This is emphatically the case for one MacGregor, who once dug the trench for a cesspit behind Duncan's house. Looking into his eyes, she can discern a deep folk wisdom, "knowledge that he had no needs which he could not fulfill, no questions about what he must do next, and no doubts about the sense in what he had done so far. Here was one of the rarest persons left alive – a strong man who was gentle, a wise man who was simple, a thoughtful man who was contented." Alas, MacGregor's breed was dwindling. Duncan must regrettably inform us of the adulteration of the racial stock, debased by mining and diluted by crossbreeding:

> The Highlanders who first went down into the mines two or three generations ago have produced children smaller in size, duller of the eye, and slower of wit. Their stubbornness has grown into combativeness, their dignity can often seem nothing but sullenness, and their imagination has required strong drink in order to be still. So they work until they are bone-tired, and enough of them fight after they have become roaring drunk on Saturday night to give Glace Bay the reputation of being one of the toughest towns in Canada. Intermarriage with the Poles and Bohemians who have joined them for work underground has produced a further mutation of character, but every once in a while the real Highlander will show through a coal-begrimed face.[108]

The Scottish Myth here becomes something frankly racist. It encompasses not only the notion that the Scottish race exists biologically, but that mongrelization can pollute it. Like almost everything in the ambit of tourism/history, Duncan's bioethical melodrama is tellingly impervious to empirical disconfirmation. Duncan can admit ethno-cultural diversity on the one hand, yet deny it any validity on the other. She posits an essential Highland nature even if she also concedes that it rarely appears in a world tainted by proletarianization and misalliance. Some Scots count as pure Celts who proudly uphold their lineage. Others lose their way, developing (as Wilfred Campbell had explained in 1911) the "modern vulgar mind of a mongrel people, which has lost its race individuality."[109] And since the miners are not real 100 per cent Highlanders, nothing they do – strikes, radical politics, wage labour – can challenge those "deep insights" that Duncan has acquired (largely via her husband, the romantic novelist and professional Highlander Hugh MacLennan) into their true "racial" nature.[110]

Angus L. Macdonald expressed his blood-and-soil romances more gently than Duncan. Given his own maximum 25 per cent Scottish composition, he would not have seconded her condemnation of "mutation." As a good Liberal premier, he would not have disparaged the miners whose votes he assiduously courted and whose industry generated the coal royalties that kept the province solvent. Nonetheless, he too emphasized the Scottish tradition as somehow truer, more essential, and in effect superior to those of other peoples. His position, too, implicitly subordinated other races.

Macdonald voiced his views on the Scottish essence most clearly in nineteen major addresses he delivered to Scottish societies from 1924 to 1944. They ring with antimodern paeans to the past. Macdonald treasured Scottish history as the "lamp of memory" that burned in Scottish breasts, that flickered to life at the sound of those stirring airs and ancient melodies that had been sung "by Scotsmen around their hearth-fires" and had "soothed the Scot in his sorrows, emboldened him in his wooing and cheered him on many a battlefield."[111] "We spring from the same soil, you and I," he told Prince Edward Islanders at a memorial to commemorate the late Bishop MacEachern, "we honour the same heroes, we venerate the same names ... The call of the blood is strong and our hearts are still Highland."[112] These carefully crafted speeches have, like his liberalism, a nineteenth-century feel. One hears echoes (and at times the actual rhetorical flourishes) of Thomas D'Arcy McGee, the Irish-born father of Confederation and exponent of the Celtic genius.[113]

Unlike the blazingly optimistic McGee, however, Macdonald the speechmaker conjured up an antimodern and preservationist sense of a heritage besieged – perhaps even doomed to extinction. Even when opening a new athletic facility in Antigonish, home of the Highland Games, he talked, not of a bright shimmering future for the high-jumper and pole-vaulter, but of the melancholy grandeur of this "last great stronghold of the Gael in America," echoing "the beautiful accents of the ancient tongue of the North." He exhorted his university audience to keep faith with their Scottish forebears by preserving the Gaelic language and folkways, and, more than that, "the spiritual and moral virtues of the pioneers. Let us not forget the rock from which we are hewn."[114] Even at the Scottish stronghold St F.X., not everybody could straightforwardly claim to have been "hewn" from that "rock" (certainly not the premier, himself an alumnus). That did not really matter. Macdonald rhetorically gave the "we" a homogeneous ethnic identification. Nova Scotia had a mission in the world, Macdonald argued, to preserve Scottish heritage. "I come from a part of Canada which, in its name, in its racial character, in its traditions and even in its language, is the greatest outpost of Celtic Scotland in the whole world," he told the St Andrew's Society of Philadelphia in 1948.[115] Nova Scotia still had something that others had lost.

Macdonald reinterpreted history in an emotionally powerful way. For progressives, history ran forward triumphantly into the present. For Macdonald –

at least when operating in his romantically pessimistic Celtic mode – an immense gulf separated the past from the present. The new heritage of the 1920s–1960s commemorated a lost Golden Age. It did so by eliding past and present, by introducing into the present rarefied traces of the golden past that connoisseurs could savour with a fond melancholy pleasure. Macdonald tangibly focused this generalized essentialism in speeches and gestures invoking ancient traditions. This reading of the Scottish legacy operated, like other elements of Innocence, through the reduction of complexity to essence. It remembered only those events closely linked to the romantic episodes in Scottish history. In a sense, Macdonald was, like Bird, a "stranger to himself" who viewed the history of his own province from a distanced vantage. Also like Bird, Macdonald imagined history as a series of static and colourful moments. Since it did not change over time, this history presented no contradictions or complications. It perfectly suited a burgeoning tourism program that likewise profited from the dissemination of decontextualized artifacts and isolated historical nuggets.

Perhaps the most important single moment in the Scottish Myth of Nova Scotia had occurred in Scotland itself. As we noted above, in the seventeenth century at Edinburgh Castle, James VI had set aside a spot where the knights-baronets of Nova Scotia took sasine of their New World estates. Macdonald fixated on this patch of earth. He pursued international negotiations from 1948 to 1952, which culminated in an October 1953 ceremony that saw him sprinkle Nova Scotian earth on the castle grounds. "Nova Scotia more than 300 years ago was annexed to Scotland by a fiction," Macdonald said. "Let me complete the task today by depositing … a handful of Nova Scotia earth. Thus the fiction becomes a reality and Nova Scotia and Scotland are united in soil."[116] He was re-enacting the supposed deposit of a quantity of earth from seventeenth-century New Scotland, allegedly covered up by the pavement of the castle's esplanade. Even the Halifax *Herald* admitted that the whole story was probably apocryphal, but the re-enactment nonetheless brought blood-and-soil romantic nationalism to a new level of concretion.[117]

The heroes and heroines of the Scottish Myth also came in for felicitously partial presentations that made them into suitable figures of romance with compelling connections to the Province of History. Flora Macdonald, as Angus L. told a perhaps somewhat receptive Flora Macdonald College audience, called out for the spotlight. Her name summoned up "high courage," "unswerving loyalty," "the aura of romance," "chivalrous gallantry," and "unselfish devotion," not only for Scots but for "all to whom such qualities have any appeal." Macdonald hoped the example of this woman, who had sheltered Bonnie Prince Charlie during his escape from the redcoats, would guide "a world that is now sorely distressed."[118] In 1950, the provincial Historic Sites Advisory Council approved a plaque commemorating the hitherto obscure fact that in 1779 Flora had wintered in Windsor, Nova Scotia, en route from North Carolina to her native Skye.[119] The previous obscurity of the episode accurately reflected its negligible historical significance. From the perspective of the Scottish Myth, though, it was irresistible. Flora Macdonald became an honorary and suitably be-plaqued Nova Scotia heroine, notwithstanding her detestation of the province where she had suffered near-starvation, cold, and confinement sufficient to make her desperate to escape it, "tho' in a tender state."[120]

Rev. Norman McLeod posed some thornier issues. In 1851, having decided that his Presbyterian followers in St Ann's, Cape Breton, would fare better elsewhere, he led several hundred of them on a remarkable voyage to New Zealand. In different hands, the story might have spoken of poverty, out-migration, and unbridled patriarchal authority in the nineteenth century. Furthermore, it did not easily cohere with the new tartanism because it inherently raised the issue of religious zealotry. In the romantic framework, one might refer vaguely and generally to ancestral piety; one very rarely brought up the relish with which Scots had disputed with (and even slaughtered) each other over doctrinal matters. John Knox, the Great Disruption, and the violent riots pitting Burgher against anti-Burgher (which had their Pictou County analogues) made for an inappropriately divisive history, especially in a province with a Catholic plurality. Macdonald judiciously conceded that McLeod had been "in some respects a peculiar man." Yet ethnic essentialism could transmute the emigration from Nova Scotia of several hundred people with an almost cultish collective obedience to a charismatic preacher into one more episode of romantic Scottish legend and lore. Here one did not find a story of collective poverty and suffering, culminating in out-migration, but rather the tale of a rugged individual, undaunted by adversity, whose voyage from Cape Breton to New Zealand "will stand as one of the great sagas of the New World."[121]

Describing a re-enactment of the McLeod emigration in 1947, the Halifax *Mail* noted in passing that, at a time when Cape Breton workers were emigrating in large numbers "to the greener economic fields of Upper Canada, their friends and relatives paused during the Gaelic Mod to honour the memory of other migrants."[122] In 1952, when Waipu, New Zealand, celebrated the landing of Reverend McLeod and his flock, Nova Scotia sent them a provincial flag and noted its official pride in "a voyage of courage and enterprise, an adventure worthy of the true Scottish spirit of accomplishment."[123] It was yet another proof of plucky Scottish individualism – and a determined liberal could look past the collective pressures and traditions (and the bleak record of colonial poverty and backwardness) that had made such a remarkable voyage possible.

These retellings of old tales depended upon a carefully monitored cultural environment. Outsiders could easily misunderstand Nova Scotia's Scottish Myth. Scottish Nationalists might have hoped that it portended support for their cause. D.H. McNeill, the honorary secretary of the Scottish National Party, sought Macdonald's endorsement of the party's objective of forming a separate government for Scotland. Macdonald's reply was distinctly cool.[124] He did not intend to dismantle British dominion but to celebrate it. Moreover, his fascination with the primordial Scottish race precluded interest in contemporary Scottish politics – which gave his reading of Scottish history an entirely different valence. A Scottish nationalist might have expected that Macdonald's sympathy for Flora Macdonald and the Jacobite rebels of 1745 would spur him to denounce the illegitimate royal family who had vilely usurped the true Stuart kings, for whose rights the gallant Jacobites had given their lives. In fact, though, the Scottish Myth treasured only the generic romance of the '45, not its purpose. When he unveiled a plaque to Flora Macdonald, just weeks before a visit by Princess Elizabeth, Angus L. carefully distanced himself from any neo-Jacobitism. Nothing about honouring Flora Macdonald, he argued, implied reservations about the House of Windsor, whose forebears she had implacably opposed.[125]

Nor did Jacobites represent only an isolated case of Macdonald's squeamishness. The Scottish Myth also determinedly omitted any sustained attention to the socio-economic processes through which Scots had arrived en masse in North America. The capitalist transformation of the Highlands from 1745 to 1840 could stand, in a different analysis, as the central issue of Scottish history in Nova Scotia. Yet Macdonald's approach to history – which, like Bird's, was simultaneously heroic individualist and racially determinist – lacked any vocabulary for grasping social and economic change. Macdonald's framework could not accommodate capitalist transformation in general or the Clearances more specifically. Although once a touchstone of the Scottish experience, the Clearances became the property of increasingly marginalized left-wingers. Official public history deftly wrote them out.[126]

If the premier seldom concerned himself with the historical politics of Scotland, he often intervened decisively in matters of regalia, heraldry, and costume. In 1936, he wrote a long confidential letter to Ian Mackenzie, the minister of defence, asking him to consider forming a "Macdonald Regiment." ("Here and there, as with nearly every clan, there may be found an instance of selfishness and treachery," he wrote somewhat apologetically about the Macdonalds' rather controversial record in Scotland, "but, on the whole, the clan stood firm in all the struggles for Scottish independence.")[127] He stood ever ready to intervene on behalf of Scottish aficionados everywhere. In 1946, the Antigonish Highland Society faced the grim prospect of celebrating its centenary during an acute postwar shortage of kilts and plaids in the Black Watch tartan. On hearing of their plight, Macdonald urgently cabled the deputy minister of national defence to see if he might rush in Scottish supplies.[128] Three years later, Macdonald wrote a long confidential letter to J.A. MacKinnon, whose Ministry of Mines and Resources administered the national park in Cape Breton. Macdonald raised three pressing issues:

1   Would it not be an excellent idea to have the foresters wear the kilt? For visitors to the Park this would appear as a very spectacular garb and very distinctive. As you know, when the King goes to Scotland he dons the kilt, and I see no reason why, in this Scottish area, the kilt should not be worn. It might be, at first, a little more expensive but in the long run I think it would prove cheaper because it is practically everlasting in its wearing qualities. Furthermore, it is a very becoming costume to a man who has any figure whatever.

2   There is some question as to the color of the bonnet. The traditional Scottish bonnet is blue. It is true that green is a forester's color, but I think perhaps some attention should be given to maintaining the tradition of the Scottish blue. Of course, blue is in every respect a Scottish color, it being the background of the St. Andrew's Cross, and the "bonnets of blue," the "buff and the blue," are all well known phrases in Scottish poetry.

3   As to a tartan to be worn under the badge, this would be quite correct. The question is, of course, as you put it, which tartan to select. There is something to be said for several tartans. The name Macdonald is the most common Scottish name here, as it is in Scotland … I should, of course, be very pleased to see the tartan worn more generally. On the other hand, I suppose the Stuart tartan would be acceptable to all clans, it being a Royal tartan … There is something, of course, to be said for your own tartan, and something also for the MacIntosh tartan, inasmuch as it was a bequest of the late D.S. MacIntosh that, in a certain sense, started us off on the idea of a Park in the beginning …

   If the kilt should be considered unsuitable for use by Park officials, possibly the use of tartan breeches might be considered. Doubtless you are familiar with the appearance of these and you have probably seen some officers of Highland Regiments wearing the breeches with leather leggings. They make a very attractive garb. The coat could be, I think, of almost any color, and a bonnet could well be worn with such a costume.[129]

Such matters occupy file after file (often solemnly designated "Scottish Affairs") of the chief of the Clan Ranald and the first grand noble chief of the Scottish Clans of Nova Scotia – also known as the premier of Nova Scotia.[130]

The 1949 Macdonald-MacKinnon exchange provides only a foretaste of how tartanism – the visual representation of the Scottish Myth – would take hold. Two years later, the brawny piper Wally Roy made his debut at the border to "pipe" tourists into Nova Scotia. "This move," wrote W.C. Wilson, the president of the St Andrew's Society of Amherst, was a "splendid advertising medium for 'New Scotland.'" Tourists took to Roy immediately. He cut "a colorful figure due to his size, and his willingness to oblige those who wished to hear him and photograph him … made a great hit with the tourists." Perhaps the department might consider adding a second, suitably clad, piper who could alternate shifts with him? "The reason for suggesting this is the fact that tourists were continually asking for Wally and I must say he came out to play for them at all hours."[131] The government had a hit on its hands: the travelling public greeted Roy with deafening applause. Amherst tourism authorities related the following testimonials in 1955: "What pleases the heart of every Scotch person is to be greeted by a piper dressed in Nova Scotia tartan and the sound of the pipes," "the burly Scotsman in full dress playing bagpipes gave us a warm reception," and "The serenading of the bagpiper was most impressive on our entry into the province."[132]

No less a personage than Neil MacNeil, author of the *Highland Heart,* "revelled in the beauty of the scene" at the border (though he did wonder why the Information Centre had neglected to display his book).[133] Piper Roy offered a flesh-and-blood spectacle of a piece with contemporary Highland box-office hits such as *Whisky Galore!* (1949), *Rob Roy* (1953), and *Brigadoon* (1954) that "brought the mythic kilted Highlander living in a land of milk and heather to the attention of the whole spellbound world."[134] How wonderful to think there was a real province, headed by a real kilted Highlander named Angus, where one could hear the real sounds of the Gaelic language. Macdonald had himself photographed repeatedly at the annual Gaelic Mod at St Ann's, and the public could also see him sitting at a loom in a display of Highland handicrafts in Scotland itself.[135]

Tartanism called out for the transformation of Nova Scotia's very nature. The land itself must testify to the province's Celtic essence. A significant difficulty presented itself. Most of Nova Scotia does not look like the Scotland of song and story. Much of Cape Breton, while appropriately hilly, is distressingly forested. It lacks an appropriate sense of Highland desolation. Worse, it lacks heather. Although nineteenth-century travel writing does occasionally refer to a patch here or there, nobody rhapsodizes over the inspiring purple-clad glens of Nova Scotia.[136] Skeptics wondered why they should consider *Calluna vulgaris* Scottish in the first place, since it flourishes around the globe.[137] The Scottish Myth, though, would confront skeptics with the non-falsifiable claim that heather was the botanical analogue of the Scottish race. Heather, one writer argued in 1929, eloquently bespoke the province's "Scottish character," since "the wiry, brave, patriotic nature of the Scot has in it much of gentleness, sensitiveness, and deep emotion. Does not the heather typify these national qualities?"[138] A provincial heather deficiency would insinuate a concomitant deficiency in the truest qualities of the race. Scandalously, one rarely encountered heather even in Cape Breton Highlands National Park (the "only true Highlands in America"). Could one have a Highlands without heather? Macdonald, inspired by some promotional literature from New Hampshire, suggested planting it in Cape Breton Highlands National Park – "If we could get some hillside covered with heather," he wrote to Thomas Courtney, the director of information, "the growth would make a tremendous appeal to tourists."[139] Soon, all three levels of government had set about increasing provincial heather stocks. They even contemplated an emergency airlift of heather from Scotland, in exchange for maple trees.[140]

Meanwhile, the premier had turned his rapt attention to another vexing absence in the Nova Scotia landscape, this time at publicly owned Keltic Lodge. Each hole of the hotel's golf course already carried a Scottish name – "Cuddy's Lugs," "Dowie Den," "Muckle Mouth Meg," and the 18th, "Hame noo."[141] However, the links offered scope for even more Scottishness. The newspaperman I.H. Macdonald perceptively remarked that a "celtic motif" could give Nova Scotia an answer to the dog carts and bread ovens of Quebec. Keltic Lodge needed redecoration in recognition of the fact that "[p]ipers, tartans, shieling, are all individual parts of a montage that makes up the whole highland scene." Given that "no one part of that montage is more colourful than highland cattle with their magnificent heads and shaggy hides," why not, "if for no other reason than a publicity stunt," set two or three Highland steers wandering the grounds in full view of the lodge's dining room? Why shouldn't the waitresses in the dining room, already attired in a distinctive clan tartan, carry a small card identifying the clan for the convenience of diners who might want to purchase tartan gifts after their meal? When diners turned their eyes to the hills, visual cues could thus remind them that beneath the surface reality of everyday events lay the true racial essence of the province. Macdonald loved it.[142]

Redesigning hills, golf courses, and border crossings – and, in thousands of pieces of propaganda, educating the tourist gaze about what it should expect to encounter in the province – had an immediate impact. Albert Deane of

Kilted Cape Breton Scots set within their very own North American "miniature Scotland," from Nova Scotia, Department of Highways, *Nova Scotia, Canada's Ocean Playground* (Halifax, n.d. [1936]), 33.

"Keltic Lodge, Cape Breton," from Department of Industry and Publicity, *Sea-Conditioned Nova Scotia* (n.p. [Halifax], n.d. [1949]), 27. "Keltic Lodge, operated by the Provincial Government and opened in 1940, offers high-class accommodation. Fishing, boating, bathing, hiking, golf, tennis and motoring can be enjoyed to the full," the pamphlet advises. The lodge was also the site of some of the most ambitious attempts to tartanize the landscape and the experiences of tourists.

New Rochelle found the leitmotif so completely convincing he titled his article on Nova Scotia "How to See Scotland without Crossing the Atlantic." He explained that he had visited Nova Scotia with a party including a woman of Scottish extraction who had pined for the sight of her notional homeland, but (bowing to practical considerations) had settled for Nova Scotia. It did not disappoint. The topography confirmed its essence: "Its rocky coast *was* Scotland; its rugged hills *were* Scotland; its clear, tumbling streams sang of Scotland." Nor did ethnically appropriate folk fail to grace this tartan landscape. A visit to the Gaelic College at St Ann's afforded a glimpse of "Scots tots learning the Highland fling to the skirl of the bagpipes played by kilted Scots, while all around was the savour and the sight of heather, one swiftly knew that one *could* really be in Scotland without crossing the ocean."[143] Nor would one have visited just any old Scotland – not, for instance, the enlightened Edinburgh of Adam Smith or the Red Clydeside of John MacLean – but "the old, the original" Scotland, purged of such excrescences.

If plants and animals could both bespeak the Scottish essence to which the Nova Scotia landscape perversely refused to conform, so might the built environment. Only a few of Nova Scotia's houses could be mistaken for Hebridean dwellings. Many of them resembled the Cape Cod homes of New England. Yet an efficient administration could fix this problem too. It all started with the MacIntosh bequest. In 1934, Professor Donald S. MacIntosh, who for years held the chair of geology at Dalhousie University, died in Halifax. MacIntosh was a native of Pleasant Bay, Inverness County, a past president of the North British Society of Halifax, and a proud Scot. Although he had not been a man of wealth, his will had an enormous posthumous effect by leaving to His Majesty a hundred acres at Pleasant Bay. "It is my wish," the will read, "that the government of the Province will maintain a small park at the Intervale and will build there a small Cabin which will be constructed in the same design or plan as the lone shieling on the Island of Skye, Scotland." His generosity truly moved Angus L. Macdonald. Dalhousie students, he said, had thought the professor a quiet man interested in his home, books, and work. They had missed his racial essence, the "rich vein of sentiment which is never absent from the Celtic soul," dramatized by this "appealing and magnificent gesture, expressive of deep affection for the two Scotlands, the Old and the New."[144]

MacIntosh's bequest referenced "The Canadian Boat-Song," which a generation of Nova Scotian schoolchildren knew by heart. Published anonymously in the September 1829 issue of *Blackwood's*, this affecting poem with a diffusely Gaelic tone expresses a Highlander's longing for the land of his forefathers, as remembered in Canadian exile. (Alas, a Lowlander resident in London probably wrote it and probably did *not* translate it "from the Gaelic.")[145]

From the lone shieling of the misty island –
  Mountains divide us, and the waste of seas –
Yet still the blood is strong, the heart is Highland,
  And we in dreams behold the Hebrides.

Once the province accepted the gift under the conditions attached, the campaign to establish a national park in Cape Breton gained immeasurably in strength. T.A. Crerar, the minister of the interior and enthusiastic supporter of things Scottish, was reported to have been deeply impressed. In 1947, after long and intricate negotiations, Flora MacLeod of MacLeod unveiled the tablet at the newly constructed Lone Shieling, while a piper played "Over the Sea to Skye."[146] This was perhaps the crowning moment of the Scottish Myth. It represented the full naturalization of the new truth of the province's inherently Scottish nature. The shieling quickly became a prominent – if, to some uninformed visitors, rather mysterious – part of the province's tourism repertoire.[147]

Only one verse of the poem appeared upon the plaque placed on the reconstructed Lone Shieling. Subsequent verses did not make the cut:

We ne'er shall tread the fancy-haunted valley
  Where 'tween the dark hills creeps the small clear stream,
In arms around the patriarch banner rally,
  Nor see the moon on royal tombstones gleam.
When the bold kindred, in the time long-vanished,
  Conquer'd the soil and fortified the keep –
No seer foretold the children would be banish'd,
  That a degenerate lord might boast his sheep ...

"That a degenerate lord might boast his sheep": such a line would never fit within the Scottish Myth. It suggested an actual history of social disruption whose recounting might, more to the point, insult the various "degenerate" aristocrats who would adorn the clan gatherings and mods that ritually erased such unhappy memories.

◆

In the idiom of the picturesque, Julian Stallabrass observes, interpretation becomes a simple matter of examining signs inscribed on the surface, with a view to generating a description obsessed with colour and ornament.[148] Tartanism belonged to a wide range of twentieth-century practices that used description to render otherness safe by regulating it through representation.

As elsewhere, the use of primitive otherness in tourism and in politics had nothing to do with preserving alternative traditions in a cultural world increasingly homogenized by mass consumption and mass communications. In a bitter irony, while Nova Scotia appeared more Gaelic every year, Gaelic – whose survival in Nova Scotia supposedly distinguished the province from other locales – was fast disappearing. The official acceptance of Gaelic in the province's overarching tourism motto "*Ciad Mille Failte*," a greeting repeated frequently since Macdonald wrote it into the touristic program, coincided with official neglect of the needs of Gaelic speakers. Tartanism exploited Gaelic as a raw material, but it was a non-renewable resource.

Macdonald's roots in the Gaelic tongue were a great selling point for the premier and, in a sense, the litmus test of his Scottishness. Yet, like many Nova Scotians of Scottish descent, he had an ambiguous relationship to the language. He spoke it only haltingly.[149] He nevertheless let himself be put forward as a true Gaelic speaker, a veritable Celtic sage most comfortable in the ancient language of his mystic forefathers. The Halifax *Chronicle* and many other newspapers retailed a story about British prime minister Ramsay MacDonald's visit to the province in 1933. As befit a province still closely tied to the British Empire, the local press interpreted his visit as the publicity coup of the year (although, in the most widely distributed photographs, the British politician looks utterly haggard and stricken – as though he had already encountered his posthumous reputation as a man who would betray all the causes he had championed in his youth). Angus L. reportedly greeted his fellow Macdonald with a flowery Gaelic speech. A perplexed Ramsay MacDonald understood not a word.[150]

The story said, in effect, that the language of the race still flourished over the distant seas in romantic Nova Scotia. Like the Child Ballads that folklorist Helen Creighton "discovered" and publicized, Macdonald's Gaelic "proved" the cultural (indeed racial) purity of Nova Scotia, cast as the innocent counterpart to metropolitan decadence. Yet, in fact, a journalist had made up the whole thing. "Some newspaper man conceived the idea that the thing would make a good story," the premier said in a private letter, "which it did, having been referred to in papers as far away as South Africa and Australia."[151] He made no effort to correct the false impression in the public record.

Although he sometimes signed "Aonghas MacDhomhnuill, Priomh Mhinistir, Albainn Nuadh," Macdonald needed expert assistance even to draft a short note in *Gaìdhlig* – let alone the text of a Gaelic tablet marking a historic site.[152] As he explained to the secretary and organizer of the Highland Association, Glasgow, in connection with his forthcoming visit to the Gaelic Mod in Oban, Scotland, "I must … apologize for not replying to your letter in the ancient language. To do this would require more time than the writing of an

English letter, and I am now in the midst of a Parliamentary Session."[153] "Like many others in this country," he told one correspondent, "I can speak Gaelic and read it, but I cannot write it sufficiently well to attempt a reply to your letter."[154]

Lack of fluency did not really matter in the grand scheme of things. Macdonald thought of Gaelic as more a racial than a linguistic entity. Gaelic represented the "real link between the new lands over the seas and the old country."[155] Gaelic nourished the Highlander; without it, he was like a plant "that has been plucked from rich and well watered soil and placed in poor and arid ground."[156] Gaelic tied the Gaels to their immemorial past. As such, it was not the language of a people but of a *race* whose heroism and glory it alone could convey. "No Highlander can fully understand the great history of his race, unless he can understand the language of that race," Macdonald told an audience of the converted at the founding meeting of the Gaelic Foundation of Cape Breton in 1939: "It is in Gaelic, in Gaelic song, in Gaelic story, in Gaelic music that the long tale of Highland glory, Highland joy and sorrow, is told. It is in Gaelic that the Highland nature expresses itself. Therefore, the Highlander who cannot understand the language of his race is likely to be cut off from the past. He may be a good man, a great man, but it is hard for him to be as good a Highlander as he would be if he had Gaelic ... I believe that every Highlander who is proud of his blood should be interested in the survival of Gaelic and in all steps that are taken for the purpose."[157]

The paradox of Macdonald's cultural legacy lies in this mystic racialization of Gaelic. He loved it as the storied tongue of a distant time, but as both a liberal and an antimodern romantic, he felt indisposed to do much to help it survive. The *Gàidhealtachd* had sustained itself as a major Nova Scotia language community when Macdonald came to power in 1933. His inaction left its future far more uncertain at the time of his death in 1954. The problem with Macdonald's relationship with Gaelic went beyond his awkwardness in the language. He cherished it as he did history, as a changeless treasure handed down from the romantic Scottish past. He cared much less about it as a living language expressive of the modern world, whose speakers would need words for "telephone" and "electricity" as well as "sporran" and "sword." In three areas – the training of primary school teachers, broadcasting, and adult education – Macdonald's practical measures for the defence of Gaelic proved almost entirely ineffectual.

Throughout the first half of the twentieth century, supporters of Gaelic considered the education of children their paramount issue.[158] One of the most prominent advocates in the 1930s was James MacNeil, the Gaelic editor of the Sydney *Post-Record,* who implored Macdonald to give Gaelic more security in the province's education system. Macdonald perhaps suspected that Mac-Neil, who noted his forty-five years of service to the Liberal Party, sought a government job.[159] In his *pro forma* responses to MacNeil, Macdonald phlegmatically reminded him that if a school board wished to have Gaelic in the curriculum, it could by all means engage someone with a Nova Scotia teacher's licence to teach it.[160] MacNeil persisted. If the government could not waive the teacher's certificate requirement in the case of Gaelic, then the Normal School must hire a Gaelic instructor who could enable prospective teachers to learn the language.[161] Aghast at government apathy, he warned, "The sacred right of having Gaelic taught to our children in the schools is a live issue."[162] Macdonald thought it better to place Gaelic in the curriculum of the summer school, where some teachers went to improve their pedagogical standards. Their instruction would have amounted to one hour per day for six weeks, hardly enough time to acquire the written language.[163] When James MacNeil died in 1939, his obituary noted that two of his central goals had been the restoration of Gaelic to the school curriculum and the preparation of suitable textbooks.[164] Macdonald, self-proclaimed myrmidon of Gaelic, had done virtually nothing to help him.

MacNeil's obituary also noted that another great purpose in his life had been the defence of Gaelic broadcasting. The issue of broadcasting was a proxy for upholding Gaelic as an acceptable language of public discourse in Canada, a matter very much in doubt. A major controversy erupted on 30 November 1940, when the Western Union office in Sydney refused to accept a message of greeting written in Gaelic from the secretary of the Scottish Catholic Society to a group of Scots who had assembled at Baddeck to celebrate St Andrew's Night. The wartime censor banned Gaelic as an alien language like German or Italian. A wave of indignation swept Cape Breton. The Municipal Council of Victoria County, in a move seconded by many other communities, passed a unanimous resolution protesting the ban on Gaelic and pointing out its British character. Gaelic, activists argued, deserved the same respect as English or French.[165] Macdonald supported the protest, but quietly. He implored Senator Donald MacLennan, the only Gaelic-speaking Cape Bretoner in Parliament (out of Cape Breton's three MPs and two senators), to offer his "help to the Gaels." Macdonald seemed more fatalistic than activist, however, openly wondering if perhaps the CBC, tired of the fierce political debates that had attended its Gaelic program *Cotter's Saturday Night,* was simply trying to "be rid of the whole business."[166]

A few years later, in 1949, Macdonald finally did something concrete to help embattled Gaelic speakers when he appointed Major Calum Iain MacLeod, of Ross-shire, as the head of a special Gaelic section in the Adult Division of the Department of Education. Proponents of the Gaelic revival warmly congratulated him.[167] Macdonald got great mileage out of this appointment when he addressed the National Mod in Oban, Scotland. He thanked God that the evil time "when some people were ashamed to acknowledge that they had Gaelic" was "gone forever," dispelled by a resurgence of "the ancient language" and "all that goes with it." He extended the credit for this happy circumstance to "one of your own," Dr MacLeod (and thus, indirectly, to himself), "whose work in the schools and communities of Nova Scotia has already begun to bear rich fruit."[168] In the mists of this Gaelic romanticism, one could lose track of the fact that Macdonald had not recruited MacLeod from Scotland. His arrival in Nova Scotia undoubtedly helped the cause of Gaelic there, but that had little to do with the premier. Moreover, one appointment hardly represented an adequate response to the massive erosion of the language community.

Gaelic benefited little from Macdonald's twenty-one years in active politics, sixteen as premier.[169] Macdonald reproached St Francis Xavier University for waiting so long to specialize in Gaelic language, literature, and music, but could he really boast a much more inspiring record himself?[170] True, he bragged that Scotland, with five million people but only ninety thousand Gaelic speakers, ran second to Nova Scotia, where one out of every twenty-five people could "use the ancient language of Scotland." He felt convinced that "the last stand of Gaelic outside of Scotland, itself, and perhaps not excepting Scotland, will be in Eastern Nova Scotia."[171] However, the very way he thought about the issue – an "ancient language" making its "last stand" – conveyed melancholy fatalism, not a practical strategy for language maintenance. Macdonald had nothing to fall back on except a vague romanticism when critics of the Gaelic revival such as Rev. Alexander D. Murray, a Presbyterian minister in Sydney, argued that "to revive the Gaelic language will be about as successful as to revive a dead horse." Murray saw no hope when the young took no interest in the language. In short, "it is only a matter of a very few years when it will die out with the old people."[172] Murray understood that liberal voluntarism, if applied to Gaelic, meant quietly letting it die.

Rather than a politics of language, Macdonald elaborated a quasi-historical reverie of language, played out as much for the benefit of American tourists as for that of Nova Scotians. The epicentre of this tartan fantasia was the Gaelic College at St Ann's. St Ann's was founded in 1938 as the brainchild of Angus William Rugg MacKenzie. Born in Portree, Skye, Scotland, in 1891, MacKenzie moved to the United States in 1913 and graduated from Montreal's Presbyterian College in 1929. He came to Baddeck in 1935 as the minister of Knox Presbyterian Church, going on to serve various Presbyterian churches between Baddeck and Ingonish.[173] MacKenzie brought excellent qualities to the role of Gaelic activist. He had such a talent for persuasion that in 1939 he talked the Victoria County Council's Property Committee into giving him one hundred acres of land to commemorate the memory of the Scottish pioneers in general and of Rev. Norman McLeod in particular. MacKenzie inspired locals to donate their labour, to cut and peel logs, and to erect a large log cabin – the main building of the college. He was single-minded and selfless. "I have not known any man with such an ardent and enthusiastic desire to benefit our country people," said an admirer. He soldiered on "without any direct monetary advantage to himself, in fact I think all his own money has gone into this work without any return."[174] Handicrafts organizer Mary Black pronounced A.W.R. MacKenzie a "visionary," "very kind + interested in helping the people all he can."[175] In short, MacKenzie had many of the things that one would want in a crusader for Gaelic – persuasiveness, determination, industry, selflessness. There was, however, a catch. He could not speak Gaelic.[176]

As with Macdonald, Gaelic existed for MacKenzie as a racial ideal rather than a living language. Although he called it the "Gaelic College," his institution did little to teach it. By 1946, after three years of exposure to the place as a teacher of weaving, even erstwhile admirer Black, in her capacity of state advisor on such issues, told the government bluntly that it should discontinue the Gaelic College as an educational centre. It had a future only as a weaving, not a language, facility.[177]

A.W.R. MacKenzie commanded the Gaelic language only in his heated imagination, but he could create a veritable whirlwind of Gaelic-sounding activities – to the chagrin of numerous local opponents. Some of this opposition may have had roots in long-standing Catholic-Protestant tensions in Cape Breton, but by no means all. Simon MacKenzie, councillor of District 4, South Bar, blanched at the thought of the provincial government entrusting thousands of dollars to Reverend MacKenzie. As he wrote the premier, "while we are not opposed to any work along Craft Center lines … I trust that any money granted by your Government, to the 'Gaelic Foundation' will be spent in some project of benefit to the whole community."[178] John A. Smith of North River Bridge added his impression that "Rev. MacKenzie is a domineering Man, Who is not popular in the district of St. Ann's, or surrounding districts."[179] The aforementioned Rev. Murray of Sydney warned both Macdonald and Harold Connolly against funding Rev. MacKenzie: "You might as well put the money into a sack with no holes."[180] "The Man is honest enough," concurred another correspondent, "but is the Kind that Can't Handle Money."[181]

MacKenzie's chief success lay in persuading people that the Gaelic College merited the name as an educational institution of recognized standing. He may have sincerely believed this. When he protested against the war censor's attack on Gaelic, he claimed that St Ann's placed "High Scottish Gaelic" in a "high ranking position with the other two main languages of Canada; namely English and French."[182] In a second imaginative leap, MacKenzie painted a picture of the college as the busy hub of a Great Gaelic Revival. He accomplished this feat with a swirl of letterheads. When he wrote to Macdonald in August of 1947 to thank the premier for his participation in the recent mod, the letterhead was almost as long as the letter itself. It proclaimed:

The Canadian-American Gael (Illustrated) Vol. II.
Published by the Gaelic College, St. Ann's, Cape Breton, Nova Scotia.
Devoted to the Preservation of all Things Cultural, Traditional and Spiritual Pertaining to the Scottish Heritage. Articles on all Phases of Celtic Culture in Canada and the United States. Featuring: The Romantic Nova Scotia Highlands, Eilean Cheap Breatann. The Cradle of Celtic Culture in North America.[183]

The first issue of this *Canadian-American Gael* carried the motto *"Clanna Nan Gaidheal Ri Guaillibh A Cheile"* ("Children of the Gael Shoulder to Shoulder"). An unsuspecting reader of this publication might come away with the impression of a revitalized Gaelic community coming into its own. It first listed the ten existing "wings" of the imposing Gaelic College –

1. The Annual Highland Gathering (1938). 2. The Gaelic College Summer School (1939). 3. The Gaelic College Library (1939). 4. The Highland Folk Museum (1939). 5. The Annual Gaelic Mod (1939). 6. The Annual Registration of Clans (1940). 7. The Gaelic College Scholarships (1940). 8. The Gaelic College Extension Department (1941). 9. The Handcrafts (weaving) Summer School (1943). 10. The Canadian-American Gael (1943)

– with eleven more sub-institutions, departments, and programs in the works:

11. The Cape Breton Ceilidh [a radio broadcast]. 12. The Gaelic Weavers Home Industry. 13. The Gaelic College Primary and Home Department. 14. A Folk-Art Summer School. 15. A Celtic Music Summer School. 16. An Annual Folk-Art and Handcrafts Exhibition. 17. Annual Highland Games. 18. An Annual "Ceist" Day. 19. A Gaelic School of the Air. 20. A Canadian National Gaelic Mod. 21. An International Gaelic Mod.[184]

An impressive list, but many of its items existed only in the realm of publicity. Indeed, after he had alienated the cohort of long-standing activists who had rallied to his project in the late 1940s, most of these institutional names were simply so many synonyms for "MacKenzie."[185]

The firebrand MacKenzie put Macdonald in a delicate position. The premier could not take his customary passive stance on this issue, because the expansionist college looked to the state for fresh resources. On the other hand, many Liberals opposed MacKenzie. Their ranks included Harold Connolly, the no-nonsense minister of industry and publicity, whose department would have to foot the bill. He thought the college misconceived and said the Gaelic Foundation should raise its own money.[186] Yet how could Macdonald say no? In a moment of enthusiasm, he had once promised MacKenzie funding for a new college building – at least MacKenzie thought so.[187] MacKenzie ingratiatingly flattered Macdonald, bestowing such titles upon him at the annual Gaelic Mod as "Chief of the Clanranald" and "Grand Noble Chief" of all the "Clans of Nova Scotia." If the Gaelic College disappeared, so would these newly minted sobriquets. Macdonald came up with $12,000 for the Gaelic College in 1947, enough to build a new handcrafts building for the college, though not quite enough if that building were to have water and electricity. Soon even Macdonald must have doubted the wisdom of his decision. The irascible MacKenzie quarrelled violently with the contractor and also with Connolly, who finally exclaimed, "I wash my hands of the whole business. Your constant interference has forced me to conclude that I will not have anything more to do with the water installation."[188] Connolly, nobody's fool, refused to have any future dealings with MacKenzie. "They consider that you are the fairy godmother," Connolly wrote acidly to Macdonald.[189] If the premier wanted to give MacKenzie any more money, he would have to find it himself. Macdonald scrounged a further $2,500 to hook up MacKenzie's utilities.

Macdonald felt beholden to the college because it appealed to his romantic conception of Gaeldom. Moreover, it cohered in his classically liberal respect for the small businessman and independent craftsman. "I think it is true to say that there is some possibility of establishing a small industry in Cape Breton in the weaving of tartan scarves, ties, rugs and other like articles," he argued in response to Reverend Murray's criticisms. While handcrafts would never become an economic mainstay, they deserved some public support, since "[m]uch of the work can be done in homes in spare time and a few extra dollars brought into the household exchequer in this way." Why not invest money in a permanent building, "where the product of the workers could be shown to tourists and other visitors"?[190]

Nonetheless, Macdonald had to face down serious arguments against the rationale of a Gaelic college. Was weaving at St Ann's a realistic activity, when only three persons – all non-residents – attended the lessons in 1946? Reverend MacKenzie's slogan was "More sheep on every hill and a loom in every home." To the contrary, Reverend Murray insisted, "[t]here are less sheep on the hills than ever, and as for a loom in every home, where are the young people who are going to weave as did their grandmothers?"[191] Farmers were not breeding sheep. MacKenzie's dream of importing from Scotland a flock with a genuine Highland shepherd to look after them was just that – a dream.

Grasping the strangeness of MacKenzie's dreams, Murray concluded, "The whole thing is in the air and will never materialize."[192]

In the Nova Scotia of the 1940s and 1950s, however, such things *did* materialize. One could re-describe a province, making people see it as a romantic manifestation of a culture foreign to two-thirds of its actual residents. One could change the perceptions of (and, over time, the actual appearance of) the landscape. Airy fantasies could become material realities. One merely needed to believe. Also, one needed to spend and to publicize. The press loved the idea of a Gaelic college ("the only Gaelic college in North America") and lapped up every detail about the annual Gaelic Mod. *Time* magazine covered the Clan MacLeod festivities in 1947. Wildly inaccurate accounts of "misty glens" in the American press prompted Helen Champion, herself a writer of romantic travel books, to exclaim, "How we like to fool ourselves … and all for a bit of sentiment or romance."[193] "You cannot realize what an attraction you had in the Gaelic Mod or you would have had news of the 1948 meeting mailed in quantity all over the continent," a Montreal travel promoter told Macdonald.[194] President Alexander Kerr of Dalhousie University heartily agreed. In his 1951 address to the mod, he contrasted the wholesome image presented by the Gaelic festivities with the movie *Johnny Belinda* – a "pathetic story" of a "backward and benighted" community that Hollywood publicity had, through some gross error, attached to Cape Breton.[195]

The annual Gaelic Mod conduced perfectly to tourism promotion. It serendipitously occurred in the middle of the newspapers' silly season. It featured a different clan theme each year, ensuring a steady parade of Scottish potentates who deigned to pay their nostalgic courtesies to the people whose lands many of their ancestors had opportunistically seized and whose actual clans they had unsentimentally demolished. Now, united within the Celtic race, all such tensions could ease. In a masterstroke, the mod would showcase the "election" of prominent would-be Gaels to semi-fictional clan positions. Even normally hard-nosed politicians (but not Connolly) succumbed to the romantic charm of St Ann's. Charlotte Whitton, a right-wing expert on social welfare not usually associated with tender-hearted romanticism, wrote especially to Macdonald in 1947 to make sure Agnes MacLeod – a personal friend and "holder of the largest nursing job in Canada" – got an invitation to the 1947 mod, at which the MacLeod of MacLeod (her clan chieftain) was the guest of honour.[196] Every year, A.W.R. MacKenzie told Macdonald, "It will be our duty to invite one of the hereditory [sic] Chieftains of Scotland to Cape Breton which will be a great source of inspiration to Cape Breton Gaels."[197] He did not need to add that it also gave the premier a chance to distribute honours, win some free publicity, and hobnob with the Celtic notability.

Thus, the same premier who could not find the money to support a struggling language community often found money and time for the tartanism of St Ann's. True, he did grumble about MacKenzie's tendency to add "speech upon speech and dance upon dance," which sated even his appetite for things Scottish. "I must say," he said with some feeling, "that having seen five girls, say under twelve years of age, on the sword dance, and then four or five between twelve and sixteen do the same dance, and then a similar number over sixteen, I am a little weary of sword dancing."[198] He might acknowledge to his correspondents that the "College" did not deserve the name and "may never amount to a college in the real sense of the term."[199] In the end, though, the Gaelic College perfectly embodied his conception of Scottishness. It provided a living example of that hierarchy and loyalty that Macdonald thought characterized the "traditional clan system," with the premier at the top. The annual visits of Scottish luminaries bearing the names of high romance (the MacLeod of MacLeod!) perfectly suited the romantic temperament of someone like Macdonald. The clan lived on. The Highlanders still hearkened to the language of their race.

The college survived Macdonald's death; it even managed (barely) to survive MacKenzie. Its connection to the Gaelic language became increasingly fictive, as its role as craft centre and gift shop grew ever larger. Already in 1952, it had been renamed "The Gaelic College of Celtic Folk Arts & Highland Home Crafts."[200] The mods became less and less Gaelic. The link to Gaelic stretched to the breaking-point when, perhaps in the name of a misguided notion of pan-Celtic unity, the college invited leading Boston Irish personalities to a "Massachusetts Day." (It snared only the president of the Ancient Order of Hibernians, "as Irish as Paddy Murphy.")[201] Perhaps the mods reached their nadir in 1958, when the "official bard and historian of the worldwide clan MacMillan," one Rev. Somerled MacMillan of Paisley, Scotland, introduced into this strange world the fatal word "farce." In a heated quarrel with MacKenzie, fiery as ever, the visitor insulted his host in Gaelic. The head of the Gaelic College seemed suspiciously unresponsive. He plainly did not have the language. "The St. Ann's affair is a travesty on a genuine mod," jeered the vengeful MacMillan, "the biggest farce I ever attended … a phoney from top to bottom." Just where was the "Cradle of Celtic Civilization in America," which MacMillan had been promised? "This island, I was told was the stronghold of Gaelic in North America. I received a shock when I found out how little Gaelic was spoken in Cape Breton. All I could find who could speak the language were a few older people."[202]

MacKenzie, like Macdonald, died on the job. His successor as head of the college was one Leonard Jones, who brought to the position no previous history of interest in Gaelic. He had much clearer credentials in tourism, having for many years run a hotel and the local garage. In 1979, a major controversy

"Highland dancing at Antigonish," from Department of Industry and Publicity, *Sea-Conditioned Nova Scotia* (n.p. [Halifax], n.d. [1949]), 26. Visitors to Nova Scotia were "thrilled by fiddlers who play jigs, reels and pipe marches, the old-time square dances and sets of Scotch-eights," the pamplet remarks. From the 1930s to the 1950s Angus L. Macdonald's Liberal government made the branding of Nova Scotia as a Scottish province a top tourism priority.

erupted that (depending on one's perspective) was either about a Halifax coup and the rights of local people to decide the college's direction or about whether a Conservative should control the lucrative gift shop.[203] These controversies simmered on, the legacy of an immensely tangled institutional inheritance and a broader failure "to make language the basis of its [the college's] existence, having concentrated instead on the easier identification of the Gael with the tartans, the popular Highland dancing, and the military pipe and drum tradition."[204] The Gaelic Mod continued its success as a tourist attraction. It won the high honour of being one of only two Canadian events listed by the American Bus Association. Children from outside the area attended the college's summer school. By their teacher's own admission, they learned very little Gaelic. On the other hand, they received a fine education in the new memories of Innocence:

> "How we danced," she [the teacher] remembers, looking into that shining, innocent past. "There was also step dancing and the Lancers at all the frolics. And we sang like larks, we were that happy ..."
>
> In those unbelievable days of fresh-churned butter and home-baked bread; on Sunday walks after kirk down pine-shaded paths to the sea, the language of the countryside was Gaelic.[205]

It was a memory, not of the college, nor of any actual Cape Breton, but of the timeless realm of romanticized Innocence that Macdonald had so durably superimposed on twentieth-century Nova Scotia.

◆

Macdonald, rivalled perhaps only by his fellow Liberal, Prime Minister William Lyon Mackenzie King, mastered the art of winning consent. But unlike King, he made men and women of very different backgrounds love him and identify wholeheartedly with his program. (As one admirer exclaimed, "You represent more than any other man the character and the traditions which everyone of Highland blood holds dear.")[206] The most obvious example of Macdonald's nonpareil extension of hegemony was the historic compromise he achieved with the labour movement. The more important example, perhaps, was tartanism itself – the enchantment of the drab realities of underdevelopment and economic crisis through the magic of language and heraldry. Baldly stated as a political sermon to working people in times of crisis, Macdonald's brand of liberalism would hardly have made hearts beat faster. Paving roads and luring tourists did not form the stuff of legend, especially not when many people desperately needed solutions to urgent economic and social problems. Repositioned as part of a great and noble tradition, the true clan legacy of every real Nova Scotian, threadbare liberal nostrums suddenly seemed far more attractive.

One begins to understand how so conventional a politician could exert so powerful a moral and intellectual leadership when one attends seriously to Macdonald's speeches. Macdonald found in Scottish essentialism a vast reservoir of individualist ideas. Furthermore, and by the same token, the Scottish idiom made liberal ideas much more persuasive. Scottishness furnished the unquestionable bedrock of public virtue. "In a day when there are great questionings and vast stirrings in men's minds," he proclaimed in 1937, "when we hear doubts as to the validity of much that once was regarded as almost sacred – doubts, economic, social, political and religious," we should give due respect to "the inquiring mind" but nonetheless remember that "there are some things about which there should be no questions asked and no doubts raised."[207] Invoking the essential traits of the race, wherein resided all that was right and holy, Macdonald could make statements with powerful political implications without actually having to take anything that looked like a political (i.e., contestable) position.

Thus, in the Depression of the 1930s, facing down the forces of dread statism, Macdonald summoned up the "chief characteristics of the Scot," viz.:

his strong religious sense, amounting sometimes to mysticism; his love of education; his high sense of loyalty; his pride, and his self-reliance. These, it seems to me, are the very foundation stones of Scottish character. Scotland is a rugged country, and something of the strength and endurance of the Scottish hills seems to have impressed itself on the nature of the Scottish people. The ruggedness of their character and its sturdiness, the strengths and yet the humility of it, the reverence with the independence – in one word, the greatness of that character, constitutes the magic of Scotland.[208]

There you had it. Topography predestined Scots to be rugged individualists with a weakness for the romantic. Red Clydesiders and their ilk, then, could not really be Scots – appearances, ancestry, and accents notwithstanding. True Scots could never be socialists, for Scots were essentially true individuals for whom "paternalism" (Macdonald's code word for socialism) held no attractions.

There actually turned out to be a good many "things about which there should be no questions asked." "The great homely Scottish virtues of thrift, of honesty, of reverence, of independence, of self-reliance, of honest pride" all lay somewhere "beyond the scope of reckoning or argument." Why did they? "If we lose those, it seems to me that we shall have lost much of the salt and savour of life." Macdonald sounded the alarm: these virtues were beleaguered. While he promised not to talk politics, he could not help but mention that "I see in some countries, happily not in yours or mine, every lamp of freedom extinguished, and every web of liberty torn into tatters." The culprit was devilish paternalism. Paternalism "must rob manhood of much of its character, and life of the joy of individual achievement." He knew that "the vigorous manhood of Scotland's sons" would fight for freedom, but insidious dangers were moving through the world – notably the siren of collectivist politics. The times demanded that manly Scottishness "also assert itself against all forms of action which will tend to produce, it may be slowly, unsuspectingly, but nevertheless surely, a generation whose pride has vanished, and whose sense of independence has been lost."[209]

There could be no arguing with him. That a few Scots worried over the Celtic Revival's unsettling resemblance to fascism and thousands more had found socialism attractive could not stand as counter-evidence. The very fact of their political choices voided their Scots credentials. Indeed, even those who espoused a mild Keynesianism risked their identity. After noting the "thrift and frugality" instilled in the Scots by their tough environment, Macdonald in 1936 loosed his wrath on "a large and increasingly vocal school" of economists who told people "that the sense of thrifty independence which centuries of struggle with such conditions bred into the Scot, no longer has a place in this new and kindlier American dispensation."[210] Macdonald offered no real argument that a "sense of thrifty independence" sufficed as a regulative principle for a complex industrial society in the depths of the Great Depression, but he had no need: his logic proceeded from ascribed identities, not political economy.

The same Scottish essence that spoke so eloquently against collectivism during the 1930s began to recommend the democratic principle during the Second World War. Rather than rooting this in the Scottish Reformation or Scottish Enlightenment, Macdonald rested his case for the "democratic principle" on a romantic confection of the "Clan System," which he touted as "the finest illustration of democracy." The clan system counted as democratic because the humblest clansman might be a blood relative to the chief himself. Consequently, Macdonald argued, "there was no caste system. All were equal members of one great family. Hence it is that the Scots, wherever they have gone, have carried with them, as a sacred fire, the true spirit of democracy."[211] Thus democratized, the Highland tradition threw itself into the struggle against fascism, with the Gael doing his bit against Hitler.[212] Macdonald argued that Scottish independence was so firmly ingrained that Nova Scotia could never succumb to Nazism: "[I]f the worst should come and if our shores stood in danger of feeling the oppressive tread, our people here would chain themselves to the rock on our coasts and fight the invader unto death."[213]

Many ideologies drew upon Scottish traditions, but usually they showed up in support of classic liberal argumentation.[214] Thrifty, independent, self-reliant; pious, mystical, spiritual; proud, brave, self-sacrificing; democratic, sage, cultured: in brief, the true Scot was an idealized nineteenth-century liberal individual – someone, in fact, who shared the ideals of Angus L. Macdonald. Given the essential status of liberalism in this true Scottishness, was Macdonald's resistance to the postwar welfare state so surprising? How could he reconcile the welfare state with the rock from which he believed himself hewn? And how much more powerfully could he voice his resistance to labour organization and social democracy when he could claim that there was something intrinsically *alien* in collectivism that all true Nova Scotians must oppose? It is commonplace to contrast the young, idealistic Macdonald of the 1930s with the older-but-wiser Macdonald of his second administration. The contrast is indeed striking. Yet one suspects that the conservatism of the second Macdonald followed directly from the ethnic essentialism of the first.

Macdonald often perceptively discerned the ways that postwar centralization could work against Nova Scotia. His *aperçus* did not issue in any coherent regional politics, however. Macdonald took a general Nova Scotian sense of regional grievance, merged it with a doctrine of the Scottish essence, and thereby helped transform regional protest from something historian Ernest

Forbes has persuasively connected to urban progressivism before the war into something that after the war was more like the conservatism other scholars have diagnosed (albeit sometimes in a misleadingly essentialist and eternalized manner).²¹⁵ Consider how appeals to Scottish identity could handle out-migration, always a key regionalist issue. Out-migration might look like an indictment of a system that does not allow Nova Scotians to live in their own province, but the Scottish Myth repositions out-migration as the expression of an ethnic essence. If the true Scot was footloose, perhaps out-migration could be glossed – as we have seen that it was in the case of Reverend McLeod – as an adventure, one more chapter in the romantic Scottish conquest of the world. "Scotsmen in the past have gone into every corner of the earth, exploring, colonizing, settling; establishing schools, churches and universities; contributing greatly to civilization in its every form, and enriching mankind by the splendour and the stability of their achievement" was how Macdonald put it.²¹⁶ Did it really matter if they did so in Nova Scotia, Alberta, or Boston? Others who believed in the Scottish Myth argued that the crisis of the regional economy itself followed from the Scottish essence (and consequently not of economic exploitation or mismanagement): an older generation of Scots had simply been *too* thrifty and had discouraged their young.²¹⁷ Increasingly, the Scottish Myth could simply function as part of an antimodernist culture of consolation. Fiddle music and Gaelic on the CBC were the equivalent of W.R. MacAskill's fervently nostalgic photographs: they consoled the sadness of the guest worker. "The Cape Bretoner has not yet been born," Macdonald wrote to a lonely correspondent, "who does not long for the feel of Cape Breton soil beneath his feet and the sound of the Cape Breton accent in his ears."²¹⁸ The remedy for such homesickness and anomie would remain a strictly individual one.

Yet, while it had an individualist moment, the Scottish Myth was not necessarily as individualist as Macdonald often liked to suggest. The Scottish Myth implied ethnic and racial hierarchies. Most of the time, these hierarchies supported racism subtly, not overtly. Neither MacKenzie nor Macdonald would have justified racial discrimination. For his time and place, Macdonald commendably refrained from racial epithets and slurs in his correspondence. MacKenzie's *Canadian-American Gael* clearly tried to distance itself from any suggestion of racism, proclaiming itself without "Religious, Political, Racial or National Prejudice, Believing in the human right of every race to liberty and a place in the sun." "Let no one harbor the idea that The Gaelic College or … The Canadian-American Gael, are established for purposes of racial aggrandizement," MacKenzie announced. He worked for a common pan-racial good, so "as to ensure the perpetual supply of these superb Highland-Lowland qualities of spirit and character, carrying their influence for good intact, to the common melting-pot of races."²¹⁹ Macdonald explained to a (possibly somewhat doubtful) South Carolina audience that history had favoured "mixed races," "despite the talk of racial supremacy and the desirability of preserving a pure and unmixed strain." The "mingling of bloods" – as American history showed – made a country strong and "the result will be, as in Scotland, a sturdier and braver people and a healthier nation," so long as each race maintained healthy respect for the others.[220]

Macdonald's comments are certainly not racist insofar as he was not strictly allocating human beings to races, "which accurately described and identified discrete groupings of the human species," or arguing that one's race "conferred unalterable characteristics and qualities that, precisely because of their biological provenance, were not prone to melioration."[221] Racism, at least according to one rigorous treatment of the subject, requires not only the apprehension that races exist but also the conviction that some are better than others and that the preservation of this distinction requires that they be kept as separate as possible. It is difficult to discern this position in any of Macdonald's musings on race. Rather, his comments might be more accurately read as "racializing." They transpose a concept of race onto a diversity of cultural phenomena, in a manner that takes for granted that race refers to a real essence, an actual generative mechanism that accounts for visible differences.

Howard Winant argues that "racialization signifies the extension of racial meaning to a previously racially unclassified relationship, social practice, or group."[222] Today scholars generally agree that "classifying human populations into races was a theoretical exercise that only corresponded to superficial differences between human beings."[223] In the 1930s and 1940s, on the other hand, the concept "race" ruled over an immense conceptual terrain. This was an era that saw a pervasive racialization whereby strategically located social actors (like Macdonald, Bird, and Raddall) imposed the idea of race on a wide diversity of social relationships and practices. In arguing as he did that the Scots constituted a race, and invoking the term "racial" to describe what we would today more readily call a "cultural" phenomenon, Macdonald implied that beneath the surface of events one could discern a long-term racial pattern peculiar to this group. He, then, racialized the social world around him. He was not, as was the case with the more ostensibly Darwinistic interpreters, overtly insisting that races were subspecies with "different capacities and inherent antagonisms toward each other."[224] Nor, at least most of the time in the public record, were most of his fellow Scottish Myth–makers.

At the same time, the Scottish Myth did imply – and sometimes stated outright – a stable hierarchy of races. The myth exalted the Scots, implying – by spinning deterministic metaphors of blood and soil – that they deserved social and cultural leadership positions. As one theorist remarks, race in such discourses "not only tends to subsume other sets of social relations, namely, gender and class, but it blurs and disguises, suppresses and negates its own complex interplay with the very social relations it envelops." Race has this magical discursive power because, on the one hand, it presents itself as natural and appropriate – beyond reasonable contestation – while, on the other hand, it is "strategically necessary for the functioning of power in countless institutional and ideological forms, both explicit and subtle."[225]

Constantly hailing the white races of Nova Scotia in tourism literature, for example, does not overtly call for the subordination of people of colour. Nevertheless, such a practice applied the concept of race to a host of phenomena, from heather to folksongs, which it then assorted into a hierarchy of significance. As the Scots became the most celebrated of the white races in the fast-expanding tourism industry, that industry privileged things that were Scottish over things that were not. Scots deserved special treatment. As this notion of the true "white" essence of the province became a commonplace, it was easy for many – Angus L. Macdonald's government most prominently – to largely ignore the oppressive conditions suffered by racial and ethnic minorities.[226]

In MacKenzie's case, the very issue of the *Canadian-American Gael* that carried the strident disclaimer of "racial aggrandizement" also promotes a discriminatory immigration policy aimed at strengthening the Scottish character of rural Cape Breton. The college, worried about the number of abandoned farms around it and the rural depopulation they betokened, proposed to resettle them with either "Native Sons" or, more interestingly, "Highland Scottish immigrants who are suited to the soil, sea and forest way of life."[227]

In 1949, Angus L. Macdonald would receive a revealing letter from James A. MacKinnon, the federal minister of mines and resources. He wondered if Macdonald could recommend "a young Canadian, Scottish background, with suitable qualifications" for a public-relations job in Cape Breton Highlands National Park.[228] Was this Scottish proviso racializing? One could object that it was not, since a Scottish Canadian would be most appropriate for employment in a park named after "the Highlands." Yet this, of course, would merely beg the question of how the park got to be "the Highlands" in an area far from being homogeneously Scottish.[229]

On a strictly symbolic level of provincial iconography, the Scottish Myth implied a hierarchy of races. The rediscovery and reinstitution of the province's seventeenth-century Scottish emblems in the 1920s – the coat of arms and the provincial flag – show vividly how Scottishness could help naturalize the idea of white dominance. This coat of arms derives from the Earl of Stirling's arms of the period 1633–35, in which the dexter supporter of the arms is an "Indian savaidge," attired (rather improbably) in a short kilt of feathers. The motto reads *"Munit haec et altera vincit,"* which translates either as "This one protects and the other one conquers" or as "One defends and the other conquers."

Like all good mottos, its meaning is not altogether clear. Perhaps the gist of it is that the king of the Scots will defend those who engage in conquering New Scotland.[230] The restoration of the coat of arms paved the way for the issuance of a royal warrant for the Nova Scotia flag, based on the arms, in 1929.

The flag is richly symbolic. David Lowenthal remarks that claims of historical priority may rest on prestige and title, proximity to God, legacies of unbroken stability, or importance to furthering the progress of civilization.[231] (We shall revisit his sage observation in the following chapter.) This flag put all four elements in play. It suggested the prestige and title of the Scots as the first among the Nova Scotians. The Cross of St Andrew upheld the role of divine providence in securing this noble enterprise. The armorial shield suggested Nova Scotia's age-old stability as a community from the most unfathomably feudal past. The flag's widespread full-colour reproduction on a range of products pleasingly suggested that from this feudal past a technically efficient and well-regulated civilization had emerged. Thus, through its constant reiteration and transposition into a vast diversity of contexts − from government stationery to tourist kitsch − the flag, in becoming naturalized as an obvious traditional symbol, secured a particularly Scottish version of official history.

Macdonald did not orchestrate the reinvention of the coat of arms and other symbols, but he does deserve credit for their contemporary ubiquity. He made the province's emblems a top priority, patiently lobbying the Lord Lyon to allow the widespread flying of the flag.[232] (For a time, Nova Scotia was the only political jurisdiction in Canada − including even Quebec − with its own official standard.) By about 1935, the ever-adaptable Will R. Bird, in a publication that hailed Nova Scotia as the first colony of Great Britain to fly its own flag, remarked that "New Scotland sprang, as it were, direct from the loins of Old Scotland."[233]

Through an arbitrary association of the Earl of Stirling with the founding of Nova Scotia, the quite contestable concept of Scottish priority thus became part of everyday life. In consequence, a highly debatable description of the "savage" (who in modern renditions has lost his peculiar kilt of feathers in exchange for something that looks more like leather) became an intrinsic part of that network of words and things that have attached themselves to the Province of History. The symbols would naturalize, through constant repetition, a proposition soon taken as self-evident: not only was the province Scottish, but its existence implied the subordination of its First Nations, symbolically attired in a way that suited the colonizer. Covering buildings and stationery with images of white triumphs over native peoples (or perhaps happy native cooperation in the processes through which Europeans settled in Nova Scotia) is not politically neutral. These reinvented traditions naturalize a

HISTORIC
NOVA SCOTIA

·ΜVΝΙϚ·ℏÆϹ·ЄϚ·ᎯꝈϘЄℜᎯ·ᏉΙꝈϹΙϚ·

Armorial Achievement of Nova Scotia
Granted by King Charles 1,
in 1625.

PUBLISHED BY AUTHORITY OF
HON. PERCY C. BLACK
MINISTER OF HIGHWAYS

The provincial coat of arms, as high-lighted in Department of Highways, *Historic Nova Scotia. A Land for Pilgrimage for all Time, Beloved for its Natural Beauty and the Romance of its History* (Halifax, n.d. [c. 1930]), cover. "The ancient Arms of Nova Scotia, in the changes following the union of the Provinces in 1867, were officially supplanted for a time by a commonplace design of a salmon and thistles, but they are now offi-cially restored to their proper place, and this unique and ancient armor-ial achievement of the romantic days of the Stuart Kings is after three centuries of colorful history the official badge of Nova Scotia and the basis of her famous Flag" (6). The Latin motto was sometimes rendered: "With this (the naked hand) he labours and with the other (the armed hand) he protects."

certain ethnic essentialism that clinches the rightness of conquest. They are, in essence, about the triumph of the white races.

How completely have the symbols naturalized these truths? A romanticized Scottishness interwove with other strands of antimodernism to powerful effect. Wallace R. MacAskill, the great romantic photographer, lived in a house called "Brigadoon," was reputed to drink only Drambuie and the finest Scotch, and "every New Year's Eve ... asked his dinner guests to rise, put one foot up on a bench, and drink a toast to Bonnie Prince Charlie."[234] Large numbers of Nova Scotians tried to live out the Scottish Myth, to one extent or another. People of mixed background might choose, like half-Acadian Angus L. himself, to highlight their Scottishness. A long tradition of intermarriage among ethnic groups in Nova Scotia meant that many Nova Scotians could claim Scottishness, if only through one distant branch of their family or even through marriage. The television journalist and writer Robert MacNeil suggests just this possibility in *Wordstruck,* his reminiscence of childhood in Nova Scotia. Although his mother was an Oxner of Lunenburg and on her mother's side came from a family that had been Virginians and Tennesseans since the American Revolution, she embraced tartanism passionately after she married

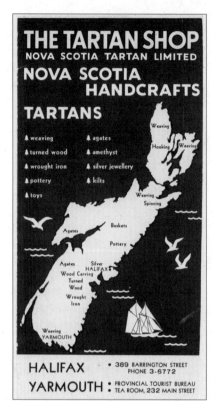

Historical tartanism. The history of the Nova Scotia tartan is proudly distilled in a 1950s advertising brochure from the "Tartan Shop, Nova Scotia Tartan Limited." That the Nova Scotia tartan was the recent invention of an English emigrant is not apparent.

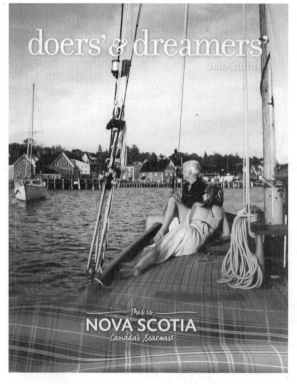

Twenty-first-century tartanism, from Nova Scotia, Department of Tourism, Culture and Heritage, *Doers' & Dreamers' 2007 Guide* (Halifax, 2007), front cover. In contemporary tourism/history, even the sea itself, the ultimate signifier of "Maritimicity," bears tartaned witness to the province's supposedly essential Scottishness. This boomer couple are drinking in the sights of historic Lunenburg.

MacNeil's father in the 1930s. Indeed, she became far more enthusiastic about Scottishness than her husband ever was.[235] For Nova Scotians like her, Scottishness became something to teach the children, a new mythical vocabulary of the self.

Since Macdonald's day, tartanism has attained a stature far beyond his ambitions. He died before the "Nova Scotia Tartan" became part of official heraldry. This new sign of Scottishness (invented by an English immigrant from Crewe) meant a rethinking and extension of the very concept of tartan. A tartan, the Lord Lyon informed Macdonald, who of course enthusiastically supported such an official sign of the province's true essence, designated one particular clan (exceptions had sometimes been made for military regiments). Extending such a traditional symbol to a political jurisdiction was audacious. Nonetheless, the tartan would gain official status and from the 1960s went on to grace bookmarks, ashtrays, and coffee mugs the world over.[236]

Macdonald's piper at the border still pipes away, at least during the tourism season, in the vanguard of a vast tartan army. As one writer noted in the 1980s, with a curiously chilling phrase, visitors would find their stay "inescapably enhanced" by Scottish dances, Scottish games, Scottish tartans, Scottish memorials, and Scottish advertisements.[237] Yet, could he observe his province from beyond the grave, Macdonald might note something strange about today's hyperbolically tartanized Scottish Myth. His antimodern Scottish Myth–making owed its ultimate allegiance to a romantic ideal of the clan. It always meant to say something deep, offering glimpses of origins, responding to calls of the blood, honouring the rocks from which "we" were hewn. On his bedrock of identity, his truths beyond question, Macdonald planted his liberal church. Would something in him rebel against a definition of the Scottish essence that includes "good parties"?[238] Or would he find one more way to trump any such purism with the higher card of capitalist accumulation?

What message does the officially sanctioned Scottish Myth, this vast tartan patchwork quilt, actually convey?[239] Have we not shifted, in ways difficult to analyse, from a substantial if controversial official legendry to a vapid tartanism driven solely by profit? Macdonald's weird identity politics can at least be confronted with the factual record. But under the aegis of neo–liberalism, such debate seems entirely futile. It would wrongly presuppose that, under such conditions, identities as Macdonald had imagined them could even exist. All that is left now is a series of discontinuous and vaguely Scottish sensations, a vast ocean of kitsch and a harrowing sense of inner emptiness. Macdonald wanted tartanism to represent a meaningful world of human community. We have irretrievably lost that world, in large measure through the very forces of commodification that Macdonald helped set in motion.

◆

In the last days of 1953, Macdonald received yet another breathless note from MacKenzie. In a romantic moment, Macdonald had mused that, at the opening of the new Canso Causeway between Cape Breton Island and the mainland scheduled for 1955, it might be nice to have "One Hundred Pipers" play "Road to the Isles." While he knew the premier was speaking figuratively, MacKenzie seized the opportunity to involve the Gaelic College in a crash course for training pipers, whom MacKenzie – perhaps in line with the overall tendency within Innocence towards the simplistic and infantile – thought should be "child pipers." "To produce this Pipe Band is a major task in our program in promoting Celtic Culture in Nova Scotia," MacKenzie advised Macdonald.[240] It was another partnership of tartanism and commerce. The pipers would march Cape Breton into the brave new world of spectacular tourism.

Macdonald died in his sleep on 13 April 1954, a year before the Causeway, Cape Breton's modernized link to a motorized North American tourism industry, was officially opened on 13 August 1955 in a ceremony that bore the unmistakable imprint of his romantic notion of Scottish history. An estimated forty thousand people flocked to a ceremony scheduled to fit into an increasingly busy summer season of recently contrived festivals and happenings. C.D. Howe, the federal Liberals' renowned "Minister of Everything," sang the praises of Cape Breton's "heather-clad hills," not to mention the "gathering of the clans" and the "magic sounds of the ancient and honorable tongue." An appropriately Scottish tartan ribbon was cut with an equally fitting instrument, a ceremonial claymore.[241] Soon tourists would arrive en masse. In his mournful eulogy to Macdonald, Harold Connolly fondly remembered how, in his droll fashion, Macdonald had enjoyed twitting him about his Irish forebears, "only to reassure me before the evening ended – thinking perhaps I might have been hurt – that the Highland Scot and the Irish were really one and the same people." Connolly concluded with dolour, "He will not lead the hundred pipers across the Canso Strait ..."[242]

But, in truth, he already had.

6

Of Runic Stones and Lockean Dreams: The Triumvirate and Its Treasures, 1935–1964

It weighs about 420 pounds, was reputedly discovered in 1812 by retired army surgeon Dr Richard Fletcher, and from the 1880s to the 1940s conveyed an almost magical message to its many enthusiasts – first on location in Yarmouth, Nova Scotia, and then across the continent. On 5 February 1880, the Numismatic and Antiquarian Society of Philadelphia dispatched its corresponding secretary Henry Phillips Jr to investigate this massive relic of an ancient time, the Yarmouth "runic stone." Phillips reported that he had found the markings on its surface inscrutable at first, but "like a kaleidoscope, word after word appeared in disjointed forms, and each was in turn rejected until at last an intelligible word came forth, followed by another and another, until a real sentence with a meaning stood forth to my astonished gaze: – 'HARKUSSEN MEN VARU' – 'HARKO'S SON ADDRESSED THE MEN.'"[1] It seemed that the medieval Vikings had once settled in Nova Scotia, as had long been rumoured. The runic stone provided hard evidence that Nova Scotia equated to the Markland of the Norse sagas.

Or did it? Skeptics stepped forward almost immediately. Upon seeing the stone on special exhibit in Oslo during the Great War,[2] the renowned Norwegian philologist and runologist Professor Magnus Olsen commented that its marks might be a "freak of nature" but were definitely not runes (to which they indeed bore very little resemblance).[3] Sir Daniel Wilson – president of the University of Toronto and perhaps the greatest Canadian ethnographer of his day – had evinced similar skepticism in an 1890 article on "The Vinland

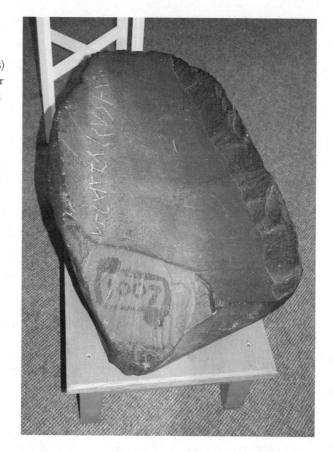

The famous (or infamous) runic stone – the Fletcher Stone – as it now appears in the Yarmouth County Museum and Archives (photograph courtesy Robert Vanderheyden, 2007). On earlier illustrations of the stone, the markings are less clearly visible and the official-looking if decidedly non-Viking "1007" had not been added as an extra "authentic" detail.

of the Northmen" for the Royal Society of Canada.[4] Among local historical authorities, Moses H. Nickerson, Harry Piers, and K.G.T. Webster all expressed equally substantial doubts about the stone's Norse credentials.[5] At the same time, the discovery in Yarmouth around 1896 of a second "runic stone" with a very similar inscription undermined the earlier dismissal of the marks upon the first as a freak of nature. If this one proved genuine, it would confound the skeptics.

Naysayers had romance against them. The Yarmouth runic stone delivered an excitingly enigmatic signal from the distant past: an ancient mystery, a tantalizing clue, a hidden message awaiting intrepid decipherers. From the mists of time came this strange sentence that would soon serve as the nucleus for hundreds of texts, pictures, and events – each struggling to fix its flow of meanings. Could these runes, if runes they were, be stabilized as a text within the master narrative of European colonization? Could they tell us how the white race had mastered the continent? Could the stone take up its seemingly predestined role as yet another unit of exchange within the common political economy of tourism?

By 1905, the runic stone was already attracting hundreds of tourists each summer, according to one account.[6] North Americans had lapped up tales of the Vikings since the mid-nineteenth century. The stone placed Yarmouth in the select if eccentric company of sites such as Taunton River, Massachusetts, and Kensington, Minnesota (in this second case, a quite elaborate and apparently Norse relict commemorated the truly mind-boggling exploits of Vikings who had somehow found themselves deep in the Midwest). Patriotic expatriate Scandinavians championed such local artifacts with an almost religious zeal. Others took a more prosaic interest in them. Yarmouth businessmen gazing upon the stone discerned the unmistakable signs of big money in its arcane inscription. One of them, George R. Hoskins, wrote in 1923, on the letterhead of the Yarmouth Inn ("Where the Norsemen First Landed"), to ask if he could borrow the stone from the trustees of the Yarmouth Public Library, which had obtained custody of it sometime in the 1880s. He reassured them, "The historic rock will be kept from harm, as I am using the Norseman as a tremendous advertising feature for Yarmouth [;] you can readily see what a value it will have in creating interest in Yarmouth to have my guests *see* the rock and write home about it, thus arousing the curiosity of others in an endless chain."[7] However enigmatic the inscription on the stone, its message blazed forth for contemporaries – *this* historic property could generate vast tourism returns.

Voices near and far hailed Yarmouth's stone. The county aggressively promoted its Norse legacy. The second stone – the "Bay View Stone," now revealed as a crude hoax associated with a local resort – disappeared into a rock wall,[8] but the first artifact, the "Fletcher Stone," became Yarmouth's most famous sight and one of the great attractions of the interwar period.[9] Beyond potential profitability, the Fletcher Stone also had potent racial significance. It could authorize the province to claim the *oldest* and *first* white settlers in North America. Some even implied that factoring in the Norse made many troubling anomalies of Nova Scotia history simply evaporate. White people could now, C.H.L. Jones and Thomas Raddall argued in *The Markland Sagas*, think of themselves as virtually first peoples, since, they argued, the Mi'kmaq had probably arrived *after* the Vikings: "Is it nothing that a Scottish man and woman from the Hebrides set foot in New Scotland six hundred years before the men of Sir William Alexander? Or that the first white child in North America was born in Nova Scotia five hundred years before Columbus crossed the sea? ... We live in what we believe to be the very land visited by our blood kinsmen of long ago."

The authors puzzled over why such Norsemen-cum-Scotsmen had not prevailed, given their bioethical brio. "It may seem strange that the courageous Norsemen, conquerors of half the known world, should thus retreat before an ill-armed mob of savages," remarked Jones and Raddall. "We incline to agree with the virago Freydis:[10] 'Why do you fine men run away before these inferior people, whom you could butcher like cattle?'" Jones and Raddall determined that the description of Markland's "savage people," "swarthy and ugly men, with unkempt hair, large eyes and broad cheeks,'" might well fit "either MicMac or Eskimo." It seemed incontrovertible to them that "the stout warrior strain, equipped with a belief in triumphant and picturesque deities, inevitably must have gained sway over the imaginative Indians of the continent, its domination sealed with a knowledge of the use of metals." They ascribed their inexplicable failure to do so to an accident of history, namely Erik the Red's premature death after falling from his horse. The prospect of what might have been intoxicated the historians. If things had only gone a little differently, the stout-hearted Vikings would have pre-empted the perplexing French as the first white race to claim the province. On their arrival centuries later, the French might have encountered "a vigorous Norse or Indo-Norse race, spreading along the Atlantic seaboard and penetrating into the interior by the great rivers." Alas, this "Nordic Empire of the West" never came to pass – foiled by neither the Little Ice Age nor inadequate transatlantic communications, but by the fate of accident-prone Erik. Still, the Norse had bestowed an invaluable legacy (the runic stone most obviously) upon the province. They had also left behind somewhat more tractable "savages": "During these three centuries and a half the Norsemen must have left some impression upon the savage inhabitants of Markland, for we have seen that they traded peacefully upon occasion."[11] Ancient relics, however enigmatic, could thus give rise to powerful white fantasies about the foundational civilizing mission of their race. From the nineteenth century on, speculative histories have suggestively fantasized about a Nova Scotia where, from virtually its earliest days, white races held sway.[12] The runic stone played beautifully into the local romance of the white race, because it gave an imagined Scottish-Norse Nova Scotia a central place in that race's great worldwide victories.

With regard to the runic stone's actual inscription, the word "Haku" that some discerned in it might refer to the Scottish slave "Haki" identified in the sagas. If it did, then the blood coursing through the Highland heart of Nova Scotia had a venerable pedigree indeed, for it had also run through the veins of the province's true founders – the white men who arrived from the East, not the red men who arrived from the West. In fact, the inscription was about to become even more prestigious. In 1934, Olaf Strandwold, a pugnacious runologist of Prosser, Washington, retranslated the stone to read "LAEIFR ERUKI RISR" or "Leif to Erick Raises [this monument]," an electrifying phrase for seekers after white origins, for it tied Nova Scotia directly to heroes from Norse lore.[13] Strandwold put skeptics on notice: "By the time I get thru these people will have the surprise of their lives." With the fervid authority of a true believer, he proclaimed, "I have now identified enough of the runes to know the words on the stone and even the year in which it was written or inscribed. The date is very plain, so there is no guesswork about that; but there are four runes whose identity I have to judge from the context." In some ways, though, a cryptic rune counted for more than a clear one: "The fact that the inscription is so difficult to decipher should add to the proof of its authenticity." How could anyone still object to the stone "when it can be shown so plainly that any schoolboy can understand it that these runes spell words and dates and that these have absolute historical background?" Strandwold predicted that with the publication of his slim volume (price: 25 cents) his interpretation would cause a sensation: "I am starting to work through Leif Erikson clubs in this country, which seems to me to be the best way to disseminate the wonderful message on the rock."[14]

Knute Haddeland, the Manitoba-based president of the League of Norsemen in Canada, took note. Since runology had "established beyond doubt that the Norsemen were the first discoverers of what is now Canada," he urged the establishment, post-haste, of a Leif Erikson museum in Yarmouth, where it "would draw tourists from all parts of North America and would focus the eyes of the entire world upon Nova Scotia." If Yarmouth devoted the summer of 1937 to "Leif Erikson Year," the town would become "the stage for a grand pageant portraying this great event in Canada's historic past." Looking ahead, he also anticipated a full-scale reconstruction of the first Norse settlement.[15]

Premier Macdonald also sympathized with the Strandwold argument, though he remained cautiously aware that scholarly research might undercut any provincial claim to such a Norse pedigree. Soliciting the support of the provincial archivist D.C. Harvey, he explained that "if Nova Scotia was the first part of the mainland of North America which Erikson touched, we should prove that fact beyond dispute and erect some sort of monument to commemorate the event ... We wish to claim all our rights, but, on the other hand, we do not wish to make claims that cannot be substantiated and accepted by scholars of the world."[16] "Our rights" effectively meant property rights – a claim to a monument, to public commemoration, and to the abundant publicity and profits that might flow from both. This was of no small moment to the Depression-era government. Nevertheless, Harvey proved discouraging, even dismissive. His files contained decades-old correspondence deprecating the Fletcher Stone as a prank.[17] He blandly summed up his position on the authenticity of the stone: "I doubt whether it can ever be decided satisfactorily." He pointed out that the Historic Sites and Monuments Board of Canada (HSMBC) on which he sat, having wrestled with a long memorandum on the subject, had resolved that, "as the question of the Norse landing in any part of eastern North America is so obscure and as so little evidence of value has been presented in support of this proposal, the Board is not prepared to take any action in the matter." Harvey even failed to see how Leif could meaningfully contribute to Nova Scotia's history, "to our discovery, life or settlement." Surely the province should prioritize commemorations of "those who actually did something to settle and develop this province. That is why I have during the past five years tried to avoid the controversial romantic elements of our history and to become familiar with the work of those who have contributed to the continuity of our life and achievements."[18] Even in the face of these scholarly and patriotic objections, Premier Macdonald persisted. Sensing what a coup for tourism an authentic Viking relic would represent, he entreated the Nova Scotia Historical Society to investigate the matter: "While Leif Erikson did not institute a permanent settlement here, there is no doubt in my mind that it would be worth a good deal to us to establish that he was here and that the stone at Yarmouth is authentic."[19]

Some local historians in the Yarmouth area already considered the authenticity of the stone beyond question. In the "Leif Erikson Memorial Issue" of *Norge Canada* (distributed by the League of Norsemen of Canada), H. Leander d'Entremont of the De La Tour Museum in Centre East Pubnico drew a map of the Tusket area showing the site of Leif Erikson's settlement and outlining a "Canadian National Park" commemorating the Vikings.[20] The *Yarmouth Light* proclaimed, "We believe that the first white settlement in America was made at Tusket, and was later extended to Raynardton." The architectural remains aligned with the Viking record; the topographical descriptions in the sagas matched up "exactly" with local geography; but the stone itself clinched the county's Norse origins: "We have the Fletcher Rock, which according to the only successful translation which has been made, bears the name of a man whom we know to have been a member of one of the Norse expeditions to America [i.e., Leif Erikson]."[21] By 1937, J.L. Johnston of the Yarmouth County Historical Society could begin his appeal for a national park by saying, "[T]he fact [h]as generally been conceded that Leif Eriksson visited the shores of Nova Scotia, and tradition very generally names Yarmouth County as one of the places where he landed."

In 1938, Rev. Gordon T. Lewis (president of both the Yarmouth Historical Society and the Yarmouth Leif Erikson Memorial Society) published *The Cruise of the Knorr: An Account of Early Norse Exploration in America*. Lewis mainly compiled the work of other writers, but he took care to state unambiguously, "Leif Erikson and members of his family visited Yarmouth, left the Yarmouth Stone with his name on it, built a village at Tusket and explored the neighborhood for 12 years and we know not how much longer."[22] More than anyone else, as another heritage promoter later remembered, Lewis really "took hold of the yarn – talked it morning noon and night – got experts here – and really developed it."[23]

According to a plausible if not fully substantiated report, Lewis believed in the stone so passionately that he took the bold step of "improving" it. The recalcitrant markings were allegedly "clarified" under his ministrations with hammer and chisel, transforming the faint tracings described in the nineteenth century into the much more emphatic text of the twentieth.[24] (Herein lies one possible explanation for the striking difference between pre- and post-1930s images of the artifact.) Just as Evangelinizers improved the Annapolis Valley with the legacies of fictional characters and tartanizers improved Cape Breton's landscape by adducing its Scottishness, so now (if we can credit this account) an ardent Vikingizer improved the runic stone by revealing its true and inspiring message.

Yarmouth soon buzzed with plans for rebuilding Leif's capital, reconstructing Leif's vessel, and celebrating an annual Leif Erikson day. Leif Erikson National Park would encompass fifty square miles surrounding the supposed Norse campsite on the Tusket River. The park would house its administration building in a replica of the chieftains' hall of Leif Erikson, built in "the old Norse Fashion." If the province would get behind the Erikson commemoration, Knutte Haddeland remarked, it would make front-page news for years to come.[25] More than mere profit was involved. There was also the discovery of the "essential" Canadians, the Norse. The Norse deserved priority, for "these early settlers were almost a true prototype of our Canadian citizen of today ... this is not a race issue of interest only to the Norsemen but a National issue to establish a historic fact, now fully admitted by students of history, and which will add over five hundred years to the age of Canada."[26] Since, in the later words of *Historic Nova Scotia*, "the Norse discoveries are the first recorded contacts of *our race* with this continent," such a discovery ought to interest "the race" worldwide.[27] This definition of the prototypical Canadian, "our race," neatly excised the aboriginal peoples – no more native to this Norse Canada than they had been to Will Bird's and Thomas Raddall's historical novels.

The discursive explosion around the runic stone so unequivocally established its authenticity that by 1943 the provincial guidebook *Historic Nova Scotia* treated it with the utmost respect as the genuine article. Then the bubble burst. Professor A.D. Fraser, an expatriate Nova Scotian now with the Division of Archaeology, School of Ancient Languages, at the University of Virginia, apparently advanced the fatal criticism. He noted that the stone showed the plain marks of saws, probably emery saws, suggesting an inauspicious provenance as a discarded quarry block:

The cutter of the letters was quite obviously not the man who shaped the block. He worked, as far as I could discover with the aid of a magnifying glass, with a single tool, the stone-cutter's punch, or pointed chisel. His method of cutting the letters was that of driving in the punch so as to form holes a few mm. apart, and then breaking away the stone between hole and hole. It is an interesting point that I have noted in connection with the famous Dighton Rock cuttings and other New England inscriptions discovered in the 18th and 19th centuries that the same technique of cutting has been found on, I think, all of them.

I cannot see that the characters on the stone resemble runes in any way apart from the fact that in a series of simple letters some of them inevitably bear a likeness to the forms of a regular alphabet, but I cannot see anything here that is more runic than Roman or Cypriote or of any other system that one might name. The Norsemen, on the other hand, cut their letters with great definiteness and precision in all the specimens I have seen from Norway, Iceland and Greenland. There is a strong probability, I think, that the thing is the work of an Indian of perhaps a century back who found a discarded ballast block and utilized it for his own purposes.

(Revealingly, the stone's currency within tourism/history would instantly fall to almost nil were it merely "Indian.") Fraser dealt just as harshly with the ruins upon which so many "capitals of Norse America" had arisen in so many imaginations. He discounted accounts of cellars attributed to the Norse: "I found that there is a shrewd local suspicion that they were dug by a local rumseller (or moonshiner, as I suspect he was) whom tradition associates with the spot. At least I was so told by more than one of the inhabitants of the village, and such traditions are, as you know, likely to be true in the main." Fraser thought it unlikely that the Norse would have used such cellars – why locate such a community so far from shore? – nor did he uncover any telltale trace of pottery.[28]

With a reluctance evidenced by the lapse of time between Fraser's critique and the stone's excision from *Historic Nova Scotia*, the provincial heritage bureaucracy finally decommissioned the runic stone as a site of official memory. With a refusal to explain that calls to mind the strategy followed by the editors of the *Great Soviet Encyclopedia* who retrospectively airbrushed Leon Trotsky out of heroic representations of the revolution, the officials in charge of Nova Scotia's mnemonic apparatus quietly disappeared the stone. "[T]he photograph was hastily removed from [*Historic Nova Scotia*] and the print destroyed," as Bird put it.[29] In Bird, the stone had encountered a powerful enemy. He characteristically noted that so many stones in so many places in Nova Scotia bore so many odd markings "that making such markings was a sort of amusement for the teenagers of other years."[30] To the writer Evelyn

Richardson, he suggested that the "Runic Stone" was probably the work of a hoaxer – there was even some speculation as to his identity.[31] In his correspondence, Bird pointedly quoted a skeptical author from the daily press who hoped "that no ridiculous move for tourist publicity will be foisted on the public."[32]

Most runologists shared his skepticism. Olaf Strandwold, whose expertise on antiquities had overawed various Yarmouthians, turned out to possess no runological credentials. A humble school superintendent, he spoke modern Norwegian but not Old Norse – his slippage from the former to the latter amounts to claiming insight into eighth-century Anglo-Saxon on the basis of speaking twentieth-first-century English. "Strandwold," confided one authority decades later, "arrived at his interpretations via a well-developed imagination combined with a highly creative use of a modern Iceland[ic]-English dictionary."[33] Moreover, Strandwold actually based his transcription on photographs of the artifact. He had never laid eyes on the runic stone.[34]

Despite the bad news of the 1940s, some Yarmouthians – including mayors and heritage activists – kept hoping for a runic resurgence. Bloodied but unbowed, the museum steadfastly ordered a hundred more copies of Strandwold's pamphlet in 1947.[35] Robert Blauveldt (who had publicized "Norse Yarmouth" across Canada in *Maclean's*) protested eloquently that the county's Viking heritage might lack definitive proof, but "men have been hanged on less evidence."[36] He would never change his mind. In 1959 he declared, "[T]he Sagas, the Vatican records, the terrain, and certain inscribed stones, cellars and other relics, otherwise unexplained and inexplicable, build up a strong chain of evidence that Leif Ericson's 'great house' and the seat of the Norse colony of Vinland was at the head of tide on the Tusket River." Visiting experts on things Norse who had carefully examined the stone and allied Viking paraphernalia certified them "beyond any question, Norse relics, and of the period of Leif Ericson."[37] Yarmouth mayor Willard F. Allen started a campaign in 1954, appealing for support to the provincial Historic Sites Advisory Council and the federal Historical Sites and Monuments Board.[38] Notwithstanding truly discouraging reports from runologists – "it is hopeless, there is not a single true rune in this inscription" – the trustees of the Yarmouth Public Library appointed a committee in the 1950s to reissue the 1934 pamphlet that had celebrated the stone.[39] "Advice to our Committee was to continue the research, and to think further about the pamphlet," Grace S. Lewis wrote to Laura Salverson (who described herself as "a descendant of the Vikings" and hence a true believer in the equally contested Kensington Stone of Minnesota). Lewis founded her claims for the stone's provenance on the proposition "As Nova Scotia is a tourist haunt, much local thought turns towards things in which our visitors will find interest."[40] As a member of the Runic Stone Committee – which some locals nicknamed the "Norse-of-Course Coterie" – she insisted in 1958 that the town should present Strandwold's *The Runic Stone* as an official town gift to Her Royal Highness, Princess Margaret, on the occasion of her visit to Nova Scotia. "Of all the places in Canada which she will visit," Lewis remarked, "none can have a similar souvenir to present."[41] Of this, at least, there could be no doubt.

For Lewis, as for many Yarmouthians, the stone was the "one thing that we have, that no-one else can take away from us."[42] The committee still imagined a future in which the stone might stimulate inspiring historical sites and grand happenings. As late as 1974, *Yarmouth, Nova Scotia, Canada*, a guide to the town, placed the runic stone on its cover, encouraged tourists to take the "Leif Erikson Drive," and offered advice on how best to encounter, in "favourable lighting," a mysterious vessel "[t]hought to be a skeleton of an unidentified ship, possibly French or Norse."[43] Yet the stone no longer had a shred of credibility by the 1990s.[44] In 1993, even the *Yarmouth Vanguard* vehemently editorialized against its inclusion as part of "Yarmouth's heritage": "Bury it, use it for a gigantic doorstop, do anything but brag about it, before even more people see merit in the claim that history is indeed bunk."[45] It had faded into a kind of liminal heritage space, that twilight zone of Masonic conspiracies, ghostly ships, transatlantic Irish monks, and an amazing array of treasure-concealing pirates, that makes up such a profitable region of the Province of History.[46]

Against all odds, the Stone still commands a certain spectacular value in this shadowy realm. Unburdened of Norseness, the mysterious text can work its signifying magic in any number of contexts. Even in the nineteenth century, its apparently ancient Japanese inscription had been authoritatively deciphered (in the Royal Society of Canada, no less) to read: "Kuturade, the eminent warrior has died," or perhaps, "Kuturadem, the eminent warrior, has died in peace," a pronouncement rather more grammatical than the Viking alternatives.[47] The stone's Mycenaean translation imparted an even more eloquent, if also more obscure, message: "The pure Lions of the royal household sent into the sunset to protect, to seize, and to make a hole in the mighty waters at the summit have been sacrificed – the whole corporate body."[48] For their part, the stone's Basque inscribers went for a much blunter declaration of sovereignty: "Basque people have subdued this land and dwell here."[49] Passing with regrettable haste over the Carthaginian,[50] Hungarian,[51] and Welsh[52] readings – all with impassioned advocates – one feels compelled to make special mention of the stone's Mayan interpreters, who broke new semiotic ground as they treated the marks not as putative letters, but rather as possible signs of numbers. Intricate calculations could show that these supposed digits corresponded to the Calendar Stone in Mexico City, not to speak of Mayan artifacts found in other surprisingly far-flung locations.[53]

As the stone rolled from one interpretive context to another, it lost the capacity to speak authoritatively within any of them. In its second life, the stone left behind history as such as it catapulted into the virtual world of legendry and apocrypha that increasingly enraptured visitors to the Province of History. Liberated from the straitening limitations of Vinland, the stone could inspire New Age archaeologists across the planet. Indeed, why stop at the planet? In 1993, the *Yarmouth Vanguard* ran an editorial headlined, "The 'runic stone' – why don't we just say it was left by aliens?"[54] Given that one of the most interesting new twenty-first-century sites of memory in the province commemorates the supposed sighting of a UFO at Shag Harbour in 1967 (now duly commemorated with a gift shop, commemorative book, and museum, complete with a plastic little green man), this idea might merit serious consideration.[55]

◆

The Runic Stone Affair reconfirms that *cashing in on antiquity*, to remember the phrase of Minister Harold Connolly and Premier A.S. MacMillan, often entailed racializing claims.[56] For an artifact to have profound historical significance, it had to provide access to the *first* things of the *white* races. Any object doing so could expect both the touring public and the increasingly elaborate tourism/history network to lavish it with attention and honour. From the perspective of tourism/history itself, these heritage objects functioned not as elements within a *whole* made up of qualitatively different parts (like, for instance, a human body) but rather as aspects of a *totality* comprised of moments that were, at bottom, qualitatively identical – expressive of the same essence. Had its advocates managed to authenticate the stone as a unit within this totality, it would have functioned, interchangeably, with elements of the Scottish Myth. Indeed, in Jones and Raddall's treatment, one can already discern an attempted convergence of the "Norse" into the "Scots." Tartans or runic stones, sheilings or imaginary Norse capitals, each and all function as units in a mythic complex. Tourism/history works much the same way as commodity exchange in general (with each commodity having a particular concrete *use value* but also a common, abstract *exchange value*). Commodity exchange construes incommensurable objects as having an abstract essence that differs in magnitude but never in kind. The logic of commodification, which we can see all the more clearly in the case of the runic stone because its application did not ultimately succeed, thus worked to restructure the objects that it incorporated – to make them units of exchange within a common myth of white colonization and a common political economy of tourism.

As one Yarmouth newspaper had significantly explained of the runic stone, the artifact constituted an untapped resource, especially because of the fact "that Yarmouth has so little of historic importance to exploit prior to its founding."[57] Under conditions of capitalist modernity, history too can function as a generative mechanism for the production of commodities. Remembering the premier's advocacy of the runic stone ("we wish to claim our rights"), we can think of these commodities as a kind of historic property. If we follow C.B. Macpherson to define property as "an enforceable claim to some use or benefit of something,"[58] a "historic property" is an enforceable claim to the benefits – both symbolic and economic – of something generated by historical research or preservation.[59] As in the work of Marx, the form of property at issue here is not so much a thing as a set of relationships that establish entitlement.[60] These relations can obtain between humanity and the rest of the natural world, among different human societies, within the ruling blocs of the "neo-Europes" that from 1750 to 1900 transformed much of the world, and, in this case, between different generations of state and private entrepreneurs.[61] What counts as property depends very much upon the social relations that structure objects, rather than just upon the intrinsic excellences of objects themselves. In early modern France, under the Old Regime that flourished before the revolution of 1789, many kinds of social status and public office were lawfully heritable and monetized forms of property in a way they are not for us – a plum Parisian magistracy would reputedly fetch about fifty thousand *livres*, as of 1750.[62] Magistracies – and their attendant honorific status – are not inevitably property, but under a certain social regime they can be so. In like manner, the social relations of twentieth-century Nova Scotia were drawing history and commemoration into market relations as they never had been before.

This does not involve the straightforward debunking claim that everything within the tourism/history complex actually reduces to its economic dimension. The construction of a modern mnemonic apparatus might, and usually did, have non-economic justifications – as, in so many cases, the elaboration of a nationalist myth-symbol complex celebrating whiteness and empire. Nor does it mean, as the runic stone episode shows so well, that the mere existence of a formula for the homogenization and commodification of "historic properties" guaranteed the success of heritage entrepreneurship in every case. A minimal correspondence with the evidence left by an empirically verifiable past was requisite. Nor, then, can it mean that the flawless calculations of heritage elites produced everything within this system of exchange. Sometimes their plans went awry in the socio-political world, as in this case of an unsuccessful bid to transform the discovery of an artifact into a unit of exchange. Nor does it mean that we can discern just one regime of property relations. As the imagined "Viking National Park" and the actual Cape Breton Highlands National Park both demonstrate, public as well as private investment had its place in the network of heritage objects and sites. Nor, finally, does it mean that people on the ground looked on helplessly as commodification proceeded around them, since commemorative demands coming from local communities strongly influenced the new mnemonic practices. Rather, it means we can discern from the 1920s onward an overwhelming tendency to treat history as a resource mined for marketable properties. More and more, one looked upon the *ancien régime* of history and dreamt of a brave new world of profitability.

In classic liberal fashion, all three figures we have considered in depth championed the rights of property and made it into a measure of all value. As we have seen, Bird evaluated communities in terms of the orderly appearance of their properties. Recall his critique of European townspeople who perversely resisted "anything orderly or clean"[63] and his fierce denunciation of the fictional Purple Rocks, with its dreadful "jumble" of shacks, each with "mean little windows," interspersed with winding paths and infested by free-ranging dogs.[64] In such places, what ought to be clear rules governing property, cleanliness, and order have given way before disobedience, disorder, and dogs. For Raddall, faithfully echoing in this respect the work of John Locke in his *Second Treatise of Government*,[65] both the Mi'kmaq and the Acadians – having failed to grasp the rudiments of enclosing and improving property, so evident in Halifax in the 1750s – were content to stagnate. If the native encampments were disorderly and chaotic, the Acadians had done little better: "It was a typical Acadian farm [muses Roger Sudden in 1755]: a small clearing at the edge of the upland, a few staked fields in the wild meadows, a miserable cabin of logs (overflowing with children, dogs, fowls, and lean pigs), a crazy barn, and one or two outhouses. The people were small and lean and sharp of feature, living in a sort of dour content with themselves and at odds with the rest of the world. The women were shapeless in homespun, none too clean, and the men wore a mixture of homespun and buckskin."[66]

Locke himself actually might have taken the view that the historical Acadians had "mixed their labour" with their enclosed farms so as to earn titles of rightful ownership to them, but Raddall is obviously having none of it. In his treatment of them, the Acadians possess only a "few staked fields," the meadows are wild, the cabins miserable. Accordingly, their deportation, rather than a crime against property as well as humanity, was the cruelly necessary precondition of the full development of progress. Property here means enclosure, order, and sanity. "What the deuce was Canada?" asks Peter McNab in *Hangman's Beach*, set in the Halifax of the 1790s. He answers his own question: "A jabber of Frenchmen between Québec and Montréal; a few stump farmers grumbling in English by the shore of Lake Ontario; west of that nothing but a wilderness haunted by wild Indians and a scattering of frost-bitten ragamuffins in the fur trade!"[67] "A wilderness haunted by wild Indians," for both

Locke and Raddall, was the antithesis of that settled and orderly process of enclosure upon which one founded legitimate claims to property. Finally, Angus L. Macdonald too considered property rights paramount. In 1936, he hailed Adam Smith as "the Scotsman whose ideas were to do so much toward releasing the economic energies of mankind from the shackles of authoritarian government."[68] And as we have seen, his manifesto against the seductions of socialism was pitched in terms of the rights "inherent in individuals as human beings," among which freedom of enterprise was emphatically a central one.[69]

In a province where liberalism had exercised hegemony since the 1840s, those who wanted to cash in on antiquity simply transferred long-standing conventions with respect to property ownership to the realm of history. Ownership of the properties generated by the past came to be regarded as an absolute right (as in Macdonald's concern that the province should claim the rights coming to it from the runic stone). Yet the commodification of history did not pass without incident. Because individuals and organizations could unconditionally own historic properties as marketable commodities in a cash economy, debates over them sometimes reached the dramatic intensity of struggles over the control of natural resources. Premodern relationships to the past based on other norms – honour, mourning, patriotism – would be marginalized by the new commodifying dispensation, which regarded the past not as something to revere but as something to sell. This represents a transition from an *embedded* liberalism that operated within a past/present relationship that respected many social and cultural limits to a *facilitative* liberalism that, privileging "the will of the owner over other interests," sought the "maximum exposure" of history to the marketplace.[70] Tourism/history partook of a facilitative liberalism as it aimed to liberate the traces of the past from their traditional contexts in order to transform them into freely exchangeable items in the capitalist marketplace.

The older forms of history might help one to recall an ancestor, venerate a sacred site, find inspiration in a heroic exemplar, establish social status, or even make a political point. The point of the new tourism/history was perforce to display and sell commodities. The historic site was ipso facto a tourist site. Whether one actually carted home souvenirs or merely acquired memories, heritage was a commodity marketed to tourists. Community-based, often patriotic and religious, sites of memory would persist, but they no longer held pride of place. After the 1930s, historic mansions,[71] restored fortresses, historic pageants and other pseudo-events, and even decontextualized but intriguing factoids became much more prominent in a mnemonic apparatus increasingly under the aegis of the state.

"It is my hope that you and your cabinet will appreciate the fact that I am doing more than getting our historical assets on array in the shop window for our visitors," Will R. Bird wrote to Premier Robert Stanfield in 1960.[72] A thorough study of all the "historic assets" placed on display in the twentieth century, from the massive reconstruction of Fortress Louisbourg to the elaborate staging of each Gathering of the Clans, could occupy many volumes. In this chapter, we focus closely on those historical assets proximately connected to Macdonald, Bird, and Raddall. Drawing upon the records of the Historic Sites Advisory Council, which involved all three, we will look first at the geographical and social patterns that help explain which things the council deemed historical. We will also look at the historical assets themselves to discern the logic behind the success of some and the failure of others. Finally, we will draw out the activities of Bird, Raddall, and Macdonald as builders of this council before venturing an assessment of the council's activities during its most active years, from 1948 to 1964.

◆

Angus L. Macdonald's Liberal government established the Historic Sites Advisory Council in October 1947. The new council fulfilled a key recommendation of R.M. Dawson's *Report of the Royal Commission on Provincial Development and Rehabilitation* of 1944. Dawson had noted that Nova Scotia tried hard to attract tourists, but "she has not exerted herself enough to ensure that when the tourist arrives he will find what he really wants, and therefore make a lengthy stay and perhaps return the following year." He went on to consider the Department of Industry and Publicity's suggested "initiation of a number of restoration projects designed to interest the tourists." The report recommended rebuilding part of Fortress Louisburg, as well as the stockade and fort of La Tour, to capture the touristic imagination. It also approved of a scheme "to build a few Acadian cottages at Grand Pré," for the cost "would not be great, and there is every reason to believe that the tourists would go there by the thousands." The province would need a coordinating body to preside over so many historical ventures involving so much public money. Dawson also intended to link the Public Archives of Nova Scotia with the envisaged Historic Sites Advisory Council, but in such a manner as to shield the archives from direct involvement in tourism promotion – which might jeopardize the "austere detachment so essential to conscientious historical scholarship."[73]

The provincial archivist, D.C. Harvey, thought hard about how to implement Dawson's scheme. He cautioned Premier Macdonald that, after fifteen years on the federal Historic Sites and Monuments Board, he knew that even "getting one tablet prepared and erected" consumed a lot of time and energy.[74] However, since the premier had already made up his mind, the archivist recommended that the provincial government set up the Historic Sites Advisory Council under Order-in-Council rather than by statute. Further, he urged that appointments to the council "should be for a limited period subject to renewal at the end of that period."[75] The resulting Order-in-Council noted that despite "increasing interest in the long and eventful history of Nova Scotia," even Nova Scotians themselves – to say nothing of visitors – knew little enough about it. The province might rectify this sad state of affairs "by marking the sites of historical events, commemorating the names and activities of prominent men and women, and preserving some of the more typical residences or structures associated with personages or events." Since "the Historic Sites and Monuments Board of Canada commemorates only what it deems of national importance and therefore of necessity neglects many other subjects of great interest to each Province," the new Historic Sites Advisory Council of Nova Scotia would devote itself to marking such places after investigation and also to maintaining historic buildings. Members earned no salary but could claim their expenses for matters such as travel and secretarial assistance. Their terms would last three years, with reappointment a distinct possibility. The council would meet annually before the legislative session began in Halifax and throughout the year as circumstances warranted. Between meetings, work would carry on by correspondence with the chairman.[76]

By appointing Bird and Raddall to the council, with Bird in the strategic chairman's position, the Macdonald government held true to its pattern of placing tourism interests first. Bird really controlled the council, with Raddall as his trusted advisor. Macdonald provided the necessary political backup. (Harvey, meanwhile, was the acerbic and occasionally resented professional amongst the council's plurality of amateurs.) While the council reached most decisions by consensus, it usually accorded with Bird's own views. On occasion, he would single-handedly reverse a ruling he found ill-advised.[77]

All three members of the triumvirate certainly count among the key players in the marketing of Nova Scotia's antiquity. All three had close connections to Halifax, specifically to its South End cultural elite. Bird and Macdonald lived there. Raddall, as we have seen, would become the city's most famous twentieth-century historian. Raddall greatly admired Macdonald, Bird patterned himself on Raddall, and Macdonald was friendly to both. More importantly, we can discern thematic unities in their historical imagination. They believed in mining the history of Nova Scotia to yield up marketable resources; all three had spoken (Bird hundreds of times) on this theme to service clubs, historical societies, and cultural associations. Paying attention to history paid off because it let Nova Scotians make money. It followed that all who loved the province had a duty to turn the past into something profitable. Bird did the most to make this happen, but he had the unflagging support of Macdonald and Raddall. Close research into all three men has located no fundamental criticism of the commodification of history.

When it came to the content of this new tourism/history, all three committed themselves to establishing the province as deeply, primarily British. British ascendancy in Nova Scotia was inevitable, unquestionable, and good. Bird celebrated the small group of Yorkshire pioneers in Cumberland; Raddall remembered the daring adventures and commercial acumen of New England settlers; and under Macdonald, as we have seen, Scottishness became an official cult. Each of these approaches ended up suggesting the beneficence of British rule, a proper reverence for which befitted true Nova Scotians. Whatever the rest of the Empire may have been doing in a postwar era of decolonization, the triumvirate stayed by Britain's side. Reverence for empire would persist in tourism/history well after all three had passed from the scene.

Imperialism involved an implicit politics of race that privileged white settlers. Each author put a slightly different spin on whiteness. Macdonald located the Scots – most noteworthy of the white races of Nova Scotia – in the golden past and ritually evoked them in the present to bolster individualism, encourage loyalty to the Empire, and instil an appreciation for cultural achievements. The motif could tactically be extended to include all Celts who shared something of the Scots' genius, but at bottom it extolled Scottish superiority. Bird imagined the past in a slightly different way. In his Nova Scotia, individuals lived and died according to bioethical natures that they could not really change. The fair and fit flourished, the dark and unfit suffered, as decreed by the inheritance of their acquired characteristics. Hence, in contrast to Macdonald's Scots, Bird's Yorkshire settlers contained some bad characters as well as many good ones (with the good inevitably forcing out the bad). White characters, often fair-haired and attractive, did better in this world than dark ones, and the logic of this postulate lay in age-old character patterns transmitted from one individual to the next over generations. Raddall worked with a yet more evolutionary conception of history. He acclaimed his Yankees as racially superior because they embodied the march of progress. In contrast to stagnantly unhistorical peoples, such as aboriginal peoples and Acadians, the New Englanders – aided by certain enterprising Britons – had insurmountable advantages in the competition of the fittest to survive. Alone of the three authors, Raddall also worked to understand the province's twentieth-century decline in racial terms, through figures of evolutionary degeneration.

Finally, all three figures eschewed any explanatory sociology when they tried to understand the world. They remained doctrinaire classical liberals unmoved by the "new liberalism" of the twentieth century, with its implicit acknowledgment of an irreducible social dimension to human affairs. This is not to say they were blinkered. The notion that the past might seem very different if glimpsed from the standpoint of a worker, a woman, or a member of an ethnic minority would not have startled them. Raddall in *Roger Sudden* makes an effort to reproduce the childlike and primitive mentality of the about-to-be-expelled Acadians of 1755, for example. Nevertheless, none of the three would have seen any particular reason to give such views analytical or moral weight. They remained self-assuredly convinced that they were enunciating the univocal truth about their province, not merely describing Nova Scotia as it appeared from their own perspective. None felt any need to answer to divergent or dissonant conceptions of reality. This remained true when they were called upon to make decisions on behalf of the whole community, as with their work on the Historic Sites Advisory Council. Although the underfunded council that these three men so influenced never became all-powerful, its records offer a window onto the transformed world of Nova Scotia heritage in the twentieth century. Macdonald, Bird, and Raddall took active part in the process of commemoration in postwar Nova Scotia, corresponded with each other about matters of historical significance, and made decisions about what was historically significant. The council's papers demonstrate just how pervasive the concept of historic property had become by the 1950s and 1960s.

In June of 1961, for example, Will R. Bird sounded like a man besieged. He had never been busier since becoming chairman of the Advisory Council in 1949. Every day brought more phone calls, letters, and meetings. Parrsboro wanted a plaque honouring it as the site of the first airmail flight (Bird suggested reconstructing a nearby blockhouse instead). In Joggins, he conferred with "leading citizens" about honouring "King" Seaman, a legendary nineteenth-century merchant. In Amherst, he promised the Tourist Committee of the Board of Trade that they would get their plaques in the next year. Requests rolled in from Yarmouth and Shelburne, Baddeck and Milton, Sherbrooke and Port Wallis, Marble Mountain and the Ovens. Bird found it overwhelming. "It is little more than six weeks since our Annual Meeting," he exclaimed in a letter to Premier Stanfield, "and already I have half an agenda for May 1962. I have spoken at ten widely different meetings this spring and all want the same topic – historic Nova Scotia. History has become almost a mania in some communities, who feel they can attract tourists if their history is made known."[78] Three years earlier, Bird had struck the same note: "Nova Scotians," Bird remarked to Stanfield in 1958, "are becoming the most history-conscious people in Canada."[79] He intensified that statement two years later: "Nova Scotia is almost feverish with desire to win attention to matters historical."[80]

"We have first raised a dust and then complain we cannot see" – in a manner recalling Bishop Berkeley, Bird drove historical societies, service clubs, and local businessmen wild with "feverish desire," then complained about all the excitement. In a 1953 letter to Premier Macdonald, he said that in the previous year he had addressed sixty-eight public meetings on council business. Many of his listeners got a fiscal reality check: "In the beginning all had the idea that they could dream up a project for their district and present it to our Council as a definite task. No group thought of doing any work thereafter." The clueless locals had expected the council to handle all their commemorative needs. He swiftly put them right: "Now, after two years of preaching self-support, I have been able to make them understand that if they want things they must do them, and not confine their efforts to begging for handouts."[81] Like a good classical liberal (such as his character Heber Marrack), Bird distinguished the undeserving from the deserving applicants, as failure to do so might unleash a flood of mnemonic relief applications, history running wild with desire and bankrupting the penny-pinching state. The state he served sought to maximize opportunities for profitable activities without itself directing them, and Bird extended that modus operandi to history. Describing his work to one correspondent, he noted his many visits to "Historical Societies, Boards of Trade, etc., that are working to mark or restore some particular place of historic interest," before bluntly adding that "[t]he job is to get such work done without offering too much aid from the government."[82]

The material prospects that history offered had entranced Nova Scotians. Some made it a central focus of their lives. Andrew Merkel – a leading figure in regional journalism, poetry, and historical reconstruction – bought a twenty-five-acre lot near the Port Royal Habitation, where he intended to erect a radio station, install a swimming pool, and provide other tourist attractions. Merkel claimed that his land marked the site of the Scottish fort that had first flown the Nova Scotia flag. No such fort had stood on his land, nor had the Scots even contemplated a Nova Scotia flag during their stay in the neighbourhood.[83] Nonetheless, when the time came to sell the property, he would advertise its "unparalleled advantages as a tourist centre, located as it was next to the most impressive memorial in America."[84]

In the same spirit, the sellers of an old Bedford coaching inn touted its authenticity as shown in "true homespun decor incorporating local Nova Scotia color," which "would definitely strike a chord in glamour weary patrons." The interior of the old inn "gives you a quaint and cozy feeling upon which to build a beautiful atmosphere of old fashioned charm and hospitality reproducing the old English Inn. With copper kettles, wood-burning fireplaces and ladder backed chairs one could make this place outstanding in the Jet age." It was a good long-term investment for the "profit minded innkeeper of the 1960s," since "the Colonial simplicity never goes out of style and it belongs to the realm of the classic." Potential buyers unsure about the market value of quaintness might find reassurance in the inn's fortuitous highway location and the excellent prospects for installing outdoor neon lighting.[85]

The mania Bird described in 1962 came merely as the intensification of a phenomenon already visible in the 1930s. Nova Scotians hoped to receive economic benefits from living in an old province. The aspirants ranged from the humble – for example, the members of the Canadian Corps of Commissionaires, who received about five dollars a day as guides to the Halifax Citadel in 1939 – to the rather less humble – such as interior decorators from New York who marketed rare prints to the provincial premier and supplied American antique furniture to "authentic" Nova Scotia historic mansions.[86] They included contractors in Cape Breton who attempted to stick the province with a preposterous bill of $414.50 for putting up one post, then attaching a plaque to it with four screws.[87]

Some of the history enthusiasts became local public intellectuals. William Coates Borrett, the managing director of radio station CHNS, attained minor celebrity status in Halifax after he began presenting talks on Halifax history on his radio show "Tales Told under the Old Town Clock." His folksy book of the same name, based on his show, enjoyed a wide readership. Phyllis Blakeley of the Public Archives of Nova Scotia was just one of many who contributed material to his show. ("He murdered my best phrases by stumbling over them, but the publicity is a good thing, I suppose," she complained in 1952.)[88] Private museums were common. The Pioneers' Museum at Green Hill, Pictou County, won accolades for its early farming implements and the very big shoe of notable giantess Anna Swan.[89] Many such ventures depended for their success on the small-town notability, such as the members of service clubs, small businessmen, and middle-class club women. Such volunteers in the heritage crusade could succeed only if they had sufficient respectability to mobilize local sentiment and money – and, most importantly, to interest the state.

Many municipalities applied for "history" as if it were a government program to which they had a right. Promoters of tourism in Parrsboro, for example, demanded recognition of the forced landing of a Handley-Page bomber in 1921. The town pleaded for "something" because "it feels out of the regular tourist path." Indeed, explained a weary Will Bird, communities from Springvale to Marble Mountain believed "the erection of something historical or the arranging of some yearly celebration will bring the visitors to their door."[90] Mrs K.G.T. Webster, trying to persuade the council that the Ross-Thomson House in Shelburne deserved preservation, wrote that the "house would make a wonderful setting," and then asked, in the spirit of the new history, "Is it an unopened mine?"[91] The idealistic Margaret Pugsley, who championed the restoration of Amos "King" Seaman's home at Minudie, Cumberland County, believed so fervently in the power of heritage that she predicted the sight of the restored mansion would inspire local farmers to paint their houses and clean up their barnyards.[92]

As Pugsley's case suggests, reducing the demand for a new kind of history to the selfish pursuit of profit would give us at best a partial picture. Heritage activists often selflessly pursued community salvation, at least in their own terms – fresh paint, pleasant streetscapes, local pride, rising property values all around. (The population of preservationists has yet to receive quantitative study, but one feels safe in underlining the importance of the middle class.)[93] These activists were also struggling to re-endow the drab and alienating world of capitalist modernity with at least the memory of something more authentic and more human. Historical artifacts – in and of themselves, whether contextualized or not – could almost magically transport one to an earlier time. Mrs Webster caught such a moment of enchantment within the walls of Ross-Thomson house, which she opened as an unofficial museum in 1949. She described boys captured by the aura of the "authentic" historical object: "As they turned the old treasures over, gently turning cranks and trying the works, they taught me how much history is learned by what you handle; and how vivid the past becomes as you finger the things people used. Perhaps that's all there is to it – an enriching sense of the past."[94] Especially when it came to local voluntarism, the invisible spiritual dimension of heritage preservation counted for just as much as its showier economic dimension did.

From the 1950s on, the provincial government faced an increasingly history-conscious middle class that had embraced antimodernist romanticism as its creed. These heritage activists felt particular dismay over the visible decline of prominent historic buildings that seemed to stand for a Golden Age of elegance and refinement, and they repeatedly drew the problem to government attention. James D. How of Annapolis Royal contemplated with horror the destruction of a house that the writer Thomas Chandler Haliburton had once called home, to make way for a car dealership. "The town of Annapolis Royal – historic Annapolis Royal – former cultural centre – and capital of Nova Scotia – birthplace of Canada – is in my opinion no longer historic," he lamented. To tell the truth, little distinguished it from other small Annapolis Valley towns. Yet it had the potential to become "a second Williamsburg Va." Who wanted to see a little plaque eulogizing something that had disappeared? Tourists wanted to visit the sites of memory themselves. Tugging at Bird's heartstrings, How exclaimed, "I appeal to you – give it your consideration because if and when it 'gets the axe' – perhaps in after years, a brass tablet marks its grave, I can say – 'I tried to save you!'"[95]

Miss Laura Lawson of Yarmouth struggled even more tenaciously to persuade the government it should buy "a beautiful home in our town built in the early years of the days of wooden ships," which had belonged to a Miss Clara

Caie. With the house and its contents destined for the auction block in March 1956, Miss Lawson's campaign persuaded even the premier and attorney general to examine the house. Using a characteristic metaphor of the preservationists, she urged them to look upon it as "a treasure trove": "Full of beautiful furniture, rugs, china, silver, etc. Much of it brought from Europe ... There is a crystal chandelier and a lovely white marble mantel. Too many things to enumerate." Such valuable estates had abounded for over two hundred years in Nova Scotia, but suddenly it had become urgent to avert their loss. "Very soon," Lawson warned, "there will be little left to show coming generations how people lived graciously in their homes, not in hotels and box-like apartments."[96]

Lawson's brand of conservation had more to do with preserving beautiful things that vaguely recalled an older and better time than with commemorating or understanding specific events. From this perspective, based on elegance alone, a house without any obvious claim to historical significance could merit serious consideration for restoration. To take but one example, Yarmouth's Rock Cottage – an American millionaire's nineteenth-century hideaway – had played no apparent role in the political or social history of the province as conventionally narrated. Still, it boasted extraordinary home furnishings and marble busts from Italy. Bird's inventory alone would have aroused feverish desire in many enthusiasts of antiquing: "A cabinet in the dining room reaches from floor to ceiling and is filled with the very best cut glass and china."[97] Lawson had clearly caught the zeitgeist.

Preservationists like Lawson worked most effectively in historical societies. Even the redoubtable Halifax Citadel, intermittently a federal restoration project (the largest in the region during the 1950s), only eluded the clutches of developers partly through the efforts of a "Committee on Citadel Restoration of the Halifax Civic Improvement League," which included two provincial cabinet ministers.[98] At the provincial level, since the turn of the century the Nova Scotia Historical Society had agitated for the restoration of decrepit sites (such as Prince's Lodge), fought what its members perceived as attempts by the Dominion Archives to spirit away prized provincial antiquities, and participated in the commemorative events orchestrated by the federal Historic Sites and Monuments Board (as well as initiating some thirty-five of its own plaques by 1948).[99] The most energetic local historical society – Bird called it the "one active Society in Nova Scotia" – was the Yarmouth County Historical Society, established in 1935, revived in 1956, and incorporated in 1958.[100] This society marked the landing place of the first settlers, commemorated Sir James Pearl (a Yarmouthian who won renown in Newfoundland), and erected memorials to Yarmouth seamen and shipbuilders. The society tried to disseminate local history through signage on main streets and even quizzed Yarmouthians on their grasp of their local history ("Where, in the County, is the grave of the famous 'Petrified Woman'?" asked the Quiz in 1959).[101] Outside of Cape Breton (whose society mounted a strong campaign on behalf of John Cabot as a local hero – more about which in a moment), most of the successful societies formed between Digby and Liverpool, on the province's southwest coast.[102]

Over and above the local heritage movements, the provincial government was taking a much more energetic role in tourism/history. In 1948, the Ministry of Industry and Publicity issued a revised and much-enlarged edition of *Historic Nova Scotia* that superseded earlier, rather rudimentary publications in the field of provincial history. Bird had "prepared" the text, after (at times unwelcome) consultation with D.C. Harvey. William E. DeGarthe's accompanying illustrations constitute a veritable Raddallian costume-drama interpretation of some of the leading personalities. There is, predictably, no visual representation of the Expulsion, but there is a large inspirational image of the Planters (who, as one expects of Anglo-Saxon heroes, had evidently clambered ashore in their Sunday best). If pre-1930s tourism/history products had almost entirely overlooked the Scots, the new Macdonald-era *Historic Nova Scotia* had a full-colour provincial flag on the cover, along with the announcement: "The Flag of Nova Scotia traces its origin to the Charter of New Scotland granted in 1621 to Sir William Alexander (afterwards the Earl of Stirling) by King James VI of Scotland and I of England." None could doubt the founding moment of the province of Nova Scotia.

As for Bird's text, it offered a mild and muddled version of his interpretation of Nova Scotia history. Bird set out confidently from origins, but then went, so to speak, "off trail in Nova Scotia" as he followed each picturesque byway. The Norse question he treated gingerly, forbearing mention of the disgraced runic stone. Both the First Nations and Acadians received their customary short shrift. The treatment of the former, though entirely reliant on outsiders' opinions and perpetuating simplistic and sensationalistic views of Mi'kmaw culture – "The women were natural singers and the tribe changed with harmony but their dancing was a crude mixture of jumping, contorting, and grimacing" – nonetheless steers clear (likely thanks to Harvey) of the racist excesses in Bird's fiction. At least he allowed them some historical agency in their raids upon helpless Europeans in the 1750s: "War parties would emerge from the leafy forest, shoot, knife, tomahawk and burn, then vanish into the woods as silently as beasts of prey. In one week, 1758, a settler wrote that three of his neighbors, two women, two children and two soldiers were victims of the savages."

As one would expect, the real history of "Nova Scotia, Land of Romance," begins with French colonization and ends, more or less, with the coming of the Loyalists. Le Loutre makes his customary bow as the chief troublemaker,

In their Sunday best and looking remarkably fresh from their sea
voyage, the New England Planters arrive in 1760. Illustration in
Will R. Bird, *Historic Nova Scotia* (Halifax: Government of Nova
Scotia, 1948), 50.

with a "complete domination of the savages, the Acadians and his fellow
priests." As for the Expulsion of the Acadians, it was really their own fault.
They constituted "in fact ... an enemy encamped in the heart of the province."
The French bore much more blame for what the British had done than the
British themselves did: "The records ... show how, with a heartless perfidy and
a reckless disregard of [Acadian] welfare and safety, the French government and
its agents labored to keep them hostile to the Crown of which it had acknowledged them to be subjects." The villainous meddling of France left the
Acadians prey to "a state of restless disaffection," in which they refused to pro-
vision the British ("except at most exorbitant rates"), blithely continued
trading with Louisbourg, spied for the French, "and sometimes, disguised as
Indians, robbed and murdered English settlers." Unsurprisingly, Bird broaches
no discussion of the British or New Englanders as instigators of conflict or
perpetrators of "perfidy." Most glaringly, and against reams of evidence, all
violence is inflicted on the British. The Expulsion itself is described in neutral

terms: we learn that "[a]ltogether a little over six thousands inhabitants were thus forcibly removed," without really learning who specifically did the removing or how they accomplished it.[103] Even if the account carries Harvey's imprimatur, its tone veers pronouncedly to Bird – to such an extent that the province's official history reproduced the emphases and the silences of Bird's fictional works.

Under the Macdonald administration, the vision of Nova Scotia that Bird and Raddall had developed in their novels became something like the province's official narrative. With *Historic Nova Scotia,* the state now took up their concepts, categories, and values in a book distributed in much higher numbers and to a much broader public than any work of academic history. Note as well Harvey's cautious, but very real, involvement. Not only did the state publish the book, but its various institutions – the Public Archives of Canada, the Historic Sites and Monuments Board of Canada, and, more crucially, the Public Archives of Nova Scotia – worked both to produce and then to accredit it. Mustn't it be the simple truth, if it had the apparent approval of the archives?

A state mnemonic complex attained coherence and consistency in the 1930s and 1940s. Long-standing but isolated and episodic commemorative acts differed quantitatively and qualitatively from the new sustained mnemonic program geared specifically to tourism. Even the Evangeline Phenomenon, though it far exceeded individual voluntarism, had remained confined to one theme and (generally speaking) one area. After 1935, though, a consistent policy of developing historical resources in the interests of promoting tourism would tie together previously ad hoc localized commemorations. Haphazard generalizations about the true racial essence of the province gave way to a consistent ideological program that celebrated five canonical white races (but of course the Scots most of all). A jumble of private, semi-private, and public sites of memory cohered into a system of parks and heritage sites concurrently administered from Halifax and Ottawa. A vigorous Ministry of Highways, with the interests of tourists in mind, renovated a transportation system that had left large areas of the province inaccessible to motor vehicles. Soon entire "trails" provided them with scenery and historic sites.[104]

Emblematic of this new state presence was the Macdonald government's re-establishment of Samuel de Champlain's seventeenth-century "L'Ordre du bon temps," under the somewhat unidiomatic English name "Order of the Good Time."[105] Here was a pseudo-group for the era of the pseudo-event. Visitors who spent at least ten days in Nova Scotia automatically qualified to join an order avowedly designed to encourage "the maintenance of good fellowship amongst our summer visitors."[106] In return for filling out a registration card, a tourist received a handsome certificate and wallet-sized membership card. These had a practical purpose. If stopped by the police, the motoring tourist could avoid paying a fine by flourishing such proof of his special status.[107] The main point of the exercise was to give tourists something attractively historical as a gesture of goodwill and as a reward for staying ten days (thus boosting the tourism economy). "The new members definitely do not look upon this as a 'gag,'" we read in the 1949 *Tourism Report*. "They appear to be appreciative of the opportunity to be associated with the oldest social club in America, and the certificates they carry home and display provide a good form of advertising for Nova Scotia."[108] Close to two hundred thousand members of an order that never convened spanned all the world's continents by 1956.[109] The revived order tied in neatly with the restored Port Royal Habitation. The first significant historical simulacrum created by the Canadian state, its life-size reproduction was based on Champlain's plans and some American archaeological work (although, C.J. Taylor dryly observes, subsequent investigations "failed to confirm that the [restored] habitation was in fact on the original site").[110]

"Order of the Good Time, Nova Scotia," from Nova Scotia, Department of Highways, *Nova Scotia, Canada's Ocean Playground* (Halifax, n.d. [1936]), inside front cover. A casual reader of this description of the Order of the Good Time might reasonably assume that, by joining the "oldest social club in America," he or she was actually taking part in a tradition established by Champlain in 1606. Almost exactly the same wording was used down to the 1960s.

No matter its dubious historical status, the Order of the Good Time had a secure place in a tourism/history nexus. As a glossy government publication proclaimed, "The Spirit of the Order of the Good Time is everywhere in this province. Here the vacationist finds escape from the tension and tedium of his work-a-day world." The back cover displayed a sepia-tinted photograph of

Imagining the good old days at the Port Royal habitation, from Will R. Bird, *Historic Nova Scotia* (Halifax: Government of Nova Scotia, 1948), 10.

jolly French explorers clad in hose and leather jerkins, carrying heaped platters of food, and sporting luxuriant (if not wholly convincing) beards.[111] The canny A.J. Campbell at the Bureau of Information and Publicity even concocted a spectacle to re-establish the revamped order, attracting thousands to Fort Anne – including the governor-general, Lord Tweedsmuir – to witness "the colourful proceedings."[112] The reconstructed habitation could take its place on the fold-out map of the tourist province alongside the bagpiper at the New Brunswick border and Cabot's landfall at Cape North.

The crowds who flocked to Campbell's "colourful proceedings" took in a florid display of imperial grandeur. Bird's "provincial shop window" metaphor became straightforwardly literal, since for days before the ceremony itself Haligonians and tourists alike had gawked at the "special ceremonial cake" displayed in the Barrington Street shop window of Moirs, Ltd. Attention fastened itself even more intently further down the street at Henry Birk & Sons, Ltd, where all marvelled at the official Collar of Office – twenty inches in diameter, composed of "massive links, heavily gold plated in the conventionalized form of the fleur-de-lis, thistle, rose, shamrock and mayflower" – that Tweedsmuir would sport as the head of the order. For the ceremony itself,

Francis J. Hiltz had fashioned a special Cloak of Office for Tweedsmuir, a flowing blue velvet number that would offer "a striking background for the beauty and form of the Collar of Office."[113] Who could buy such good press?

All this splendour had a clear political purpose. The Collar of Office symbolically united French, Scottish, English, Irish, and Nova Scotian in the figure of Tweedsmuir, the emissary of the Empire by way of Ottawa. One might well ask what the ceremony commemorated – Champlain or the status quo of interwar Nova Scotia? His Excellency, leaving no doubt that this celebration honoured triumphant Britishness above all else, recited Robbie Burns at the ceremony. It concluded with "God Save the King." In the meantime, Tweedsmuir "smoked the pipe of peace" with Mi'kmaw Grand Chief Gabriel Silliboy and received avatars of the inevitable white races of Nova Scotia.[114] Marjorie Ayer of the Halifax *Chronicle* found it especially moving to see ethnic representatives of the Indians and the French "offering an homage" to "an English nobleman" on behalf of their ancestors (who had not always been so quick to bend the knee).[115] The re-enactment gave Ayer and her compatriots a chance to view Nova Scotia history as they knew it should have been like: not the interminable, tortuous vicissitudes of early modern alliance politics, but the blessedly concrete pledging of fealty to the invariant Crown by grateful envoys from the eternally subject peoples.

Of course, as the ballyhooed shop window displays would indicate, the revivified Order of the Good Time was just the latest of the provincial government's ingenious self-promotions. History would yield an excellent "return upon the investment," argued Ella K. Cork on behalf of the Canadian Tourism Association in 1950. "The tourist industry offers history its greatest market and its greatest opportunity … If the tourist can be encouraged to tarry, he will spend money for goods and services which will penetrate to every economic level in the community."[116] By the 1950s, she was preaching to the long-since converted.

◆

One might think that the middle-class heritage advocates would have considered the new dispensation a dream come true, but often they did not. Problems remained. If history could and should be converted into property (i.e., the "enforceable claim to some use or benefit of something"), on what grounds could one individual protest the property rights of another? For example, why should Americans not buy up as many such commodities as they wanted? Was free enterprise not a human right, as Angus L. Macdonald himself had argued? Should sentimentalists not abandon their old-fashioned arguments about the place of history in the community, in the tough-love environment of the new heritage economy? Visitors who called on L.B. Firth's private marine museum (chock full of ships blocks, a brass sundial, cavalry swords, muskets, pepper-box pistols, muzzle-loading Colts, greased cartridges from the 1857 Indian Rebellion, a spoon horn from Iceland, an Italian hair iron, a boarding pike, sea shells, a high-wheeled bicycle, among other things) had told him, "[Y]ou have a small fortune here." Why, in the name of property, should the government not then allow him to realize a fair return on it?[117]

Yet preservationists greatly feared the consequences of too many Nova Scotians trying to do just that. As early as 1921, W.C. Milner of the Dominion Archives had sounded the alarm about the curios, documents, and relics gathered from the descendants of Nova Scotia Loyalists. He feared "that nine tenths of the early records bearing on local history have entirely disappeared."[118] Similarly, a collection of rare maritime artifacts in Lockeport – which Will Bird guessed "may possibly be the finest collection of old ships blocks in existence" – seemed equally imperilled, if not by storms sweeping away the ramshackle old building sitting on posts over the water, then by tides of American tourists making off with treasures in exchange for a few dollars.[119] In the 1950s, Miss Laura Lawson of Yarmouth feared that the antiquities of Rock Cottage would be lost to the clutches of time or perhaps to "the hands that are seeking to grasp [them] for other purposes."[120] Property and propriety seemed rather in conflict.

The alarmist image of tourists swooping down upon the innocent locals overlooked the extent to which many locals themselves jumped at the chance to "cash in," however they could, on their "antiquities." Tourists acted as the vanguard of market relations. They spread the word to those possessing "things historic" that the market for such commodities had never been better. This could cause the council problems. When the Green Hill Museum in Pictou County went out of business, causing widespread alarm expressed in "a deluge of phone calls and protests,"[121] its proprietors had persuaded themselves that the collection was worth $10,000. Rather contradicting his own gushing treatment of their museum's treasures in *Historic Nova Scotia*, Bird privately appraised the value of the mere thirty items (out of four hundred) with *any* historical value at a paltry $1,500.[122] In another case, Bird found it difficult to negotiate a price for antiquities belonging to the Quinlans of Lunenburg County because they were "afraid to state a sum lest they might learn later that they might have had more."[123]

Yet what right did Bird have to censure the Quinlans, especially since he made a good living out of "things historical" himself? Tourism/history had always promised to turn the romance of the past into the profits of tomorrow. Public and private investment in reconstructions and restorations was supposed to pay off in increased numbers of visitors. Those visitors were supposed to buy things. In an unintended consequence of this relationship to the past, a key measure of how much visitors liked the historical assets on display was found in their willingness to cart them back home. In tourism/history, acquisition was the sincerest form of admiration.

Even as American interlopers were making off with the family silver, they were also developing at home (and in some cases bringing with them as tourists to Nova Scotia) more ambitious models of how to package and sell history. As early as 1908, J.S. McLennan, the historian of Fortress Louisburg, had looked to the American example of Fort Ticonderoga when he proposed "that the site of the ruins be acquired by the Canadian government and restored as a national monument."[124] Similarly, Professor K.G.T. Webster resolved to save Ross-Thomson House after the Yarmouth native saw how much it resembled the various New England houses he had tried to restore while teaching at Harvard.[125] American soldiers visiting Halifax's Citadel Hill in 1951 asked a local newspaper reporter, "Why doesn't somebody get a franchise to use this place? ... This is a gold mine ... Don't you value old things in Canada? ... Children should know those things ... Gosh, we'd sure like to have this in my home town. Would we ever fix it up fast."[126] Those who envisaged a renovated provincial museum took their cues from the Mariners' Museum at Newport News, Virginia, which had single-handedly created "a new tourist locality."[127] Elsewhere in the same state, Nova Scotians found John D. Rockefeller Jr's Colonial Williamsburg – the "exquisite little eighteenth-century town, clean, tidy, and tasteful" that commemorated Virginia's Planter elite – especially inspiring.[128] When Mrs K.L. Dawson appealed to the council on behalf of her old Halifax dwelling, Acacia Cottage, she referred to Williamsburg. Margaret Pugsley, who wanted to save the Seaman Mansion, lamented, "[I]f only a Rockefeller could become interested in it and restore it to its past glories, as Williamsburg in Virginia was restored."[129] (And not only Minudie but also Annapolis Royal could become another Williamsburg, as we have already learnt from James How.)[130] Katharine McLennan, a prominent Louisburg preservationist, pointed out the implausibility of the Williamsburg comparison (Nova Scotia lacked the requisite Rockefellers, sunny days, and nearby big cities), but few heritage enthusiasts heeded her skepticism.[131] There were also precedents closer to home than Chesapeake. When C.H. Wright asked Bird about marking the sites of three blockhouses ("I *know* tourists are interested. The city should be a Mecca for such"), he enclosed a note on "What Massachusetts Has Done For History." With its 116 Historical Societies, restored vessels, the Bourne Whaling Museum in New Bedford, and Old Sturbridge Village, Massachusetts earned $250 million annually from tourists. The Bay State was doing rather more for (or perhaps to) the past than Nova Scotians had dreamt of.[132]

Besides the paradoxical influence of Americans on the expression of Nova Scotia's timeless essence, another oddity of the new dispensation was that the property value of any given heritage object was determined by its status as a "priority item" – that is, by whether or not it was a "first" of some description. David Lowenthal has shown how thoroughly "claims of priority suffuse every realm of heritage. Everyone eagerly insists their lineages, languages, fossils, even rocks are previous to those of others."[133] This was not an altogether new fixation in Nova Scotia; early in the century, for example, the Halifax Memorial Tower had commemorated the first representative government in British North America (as discussed in chapter 1). Yet after the 1930s, as tourism/history predominated, the link between property and priority became ever tighter.

Firsts (which some aficionados called "primary occurrences") commanded top dollar in the marketplace of significance. "Nova Scotia has been first in many things which it is a duty to recall, and a pleasure to read," we learn from the Dominion Atlantic Railway's *High Lights of Nova Scotia History*. Who had milled North America's first wheat? Who had grown its first apples, their orchards "still sending their golden fruitage down the years"? Who had started the first "fraternal society"? Or built the first church? Planted the first public gardens? Erected the first wireless installation? Inaugurated the first parliament "in any British dominion"? Nova Scotians had. Let no one forget it.[134]

In 1936, J.W. Regan (under the penname "John Quinpool") dramatically extended this list in *First Things in Acadia: "The Birthplace of a Continent."* Regan's book, published by First Things Publishers Limited and dedicated ("by permission") to Governor-General Lord Tweedsmuir, established a jaw-droppingly long list of "primary occurrences" associated with "Acadia" (defined broadly to include Nova Scotia, New Brunswick, Prince Edward Island, parts of Maine, Quebec, and Newfoundland). Judging from the preface, Regan's motivation for making priority claims had everything to do with progress. He urged his readers not to think of his book as only "instrumental in defeating Father Time's ancient tendency to consign poor mortals to the limbo of the lower orders and forgotten things," though it certainly was that. More importantly, though, he had written a "constructive as well as preservative" history that offered a "dynamic reminder that nothing is final and that a constant stream of fresh enterprise is necessary to take up the slack and keep the wheels of progress harmoniously humming." His paean to progress paid a "polite tribute to pioneers at large, who help ever so little to push back the interior limits of the big unknown universe, that surrounds the world's small clearing."[135]

As we proceed through the 100 chapters and upwards of 250 "primary occurrences" of Regan's book, we encounter striking evidence of the "modes of priority" noted by Lowenthal. As we saw in chapter 5, staking a priority claim will usually entail suggesting that the phenomenon in question (a) suggests divine Providence; (b) cements the prestige and title of the established social order; (c) connects the present to a legacy of unbroken stability in antiquity; or (d) indicates how well and how swiftly society has evolved since the heyday of the antiquity in question.[136] Regan invoked religious priority frequently. John Cabot got credit for having planted the first cross on the mainland of the Western Hemisphere, at a point near Cape North ("one of the world's oldest headlands"). Regan acclaimed Cape North "the genuine American 'Hill of the Cross' where the translation of Christianity to the west was definitely commenced." The cross, majestically surveying "the immemorial ocean" from atop "the most ancient geological system," presided over "one of the oldest neighborhoods of time," where terrain is more venerable than geography of Egypt or the Holy Land."

Prestige and title also underwrote many firsts. By adroitly assimilating the early French history of Port Royal, then casting ahistorical definitions back onto a very different society, Nova Scotians could lay claim to the first surgeon, first stocking of pools with game fish, first portable dwellings, first regulated workweek, first distillation of tar and turpentine, first baker's bread, first daily wine allowance for workmen, first theatrical performances, first graded highway in Canada, first Canadian poet and lawyer, first literary visitor especially to write up America, first titled lady in America, first white woman resident in Canada, and so on and so forth.

Above all, though, Regan chronicled the many "primary occurrences" that spoke of progress: "First aviation and Supreme Court in the British Empire, commercial telephones, organized temperance, first distillery in Canada, rail operation, Bible Society, Sunday School, Responsible Government, orders of the Daughters of the Empire, libraries, shipbuilding, orcharding, Masonry, Oddfellows, Indian baptism, ice-skating, hockey, school inspection of teeth, iron bridge-building." Combining progress and religion, Nova Scotia could even claim the honour of having the first Mass celebrated in the air – because the dirigible *Hindenburg* had been passing over the "Sable Island Zone" when its passengers celebrated the Mass. Nova Scotia could also claim the first government lottery in Canada, the first American missionary (Leif Erikson, naturally), the first Portuguese colonies on the mainland of the Western Hemisphere, quite possibly the very first North American Swedenborgians, and the first nine-hundred-pound tuna in the world caught by rod and line, off Liverpool, Nova Scotia, on 17 August 1934 – and so on, for 304 engrossing pages.[137]

Throughout the mnemonic apparatus, the quest for primary occurrences ate up countless hours. Professional archivists privately cursed this tourism-driven obsession. In Ottawa, the Dominion Archivist W. Kaye Lamb bemoaned requests for rulings on firsts as the "bane of an archivist's existence" because they invariably involved anachronistic definitions.[138] Harvey concurred. Scholars could not rein in the new mnemonics, however. Bird considered establishing firsts as a fundamental part of the council's operation, fully justifying vast amounts of archival labour.[139] Many saw in such claims to first things a validation of the province's precocious modernity. As J.C. Webster argued to Harvey in making the case for a tablet to mark the first birth under anaesthesia, "This indicates the progressiveness of N.S."[140] As Bird knew only too well, tourists loved firsts because they somehow ratified their decision to make the trip to Nova Scotia; and locals loved firsts because they showed that their community had been on the *qui vive* since time immemorial. The theme of firstness pervaded postwar tourism. At Annapolis Royal, the road sign welcoming tourists even read, "Annapolis Royal welcomes you to a town of First Things."[141]

Not everyone can come first. The new dispensation held out the promise of tourist dollars to all, and hence implicitly promised that every community could prosper equally if only it found the appropriate historical assets, but in fact tourism/history largely intensified pre-existing patterns of winners and losers. Winning communities had middle classes, service clubs, historical societies, and political connections. Losing communities were working class, often underdeveloped, often with numerous visible minorities, and featured rudimentary volunteer sectors and isolated or eccentric advocates. This held true even if they held sites with strong claims to historical significance by any other standard. Despite the best efforts of Margaret Pugsley, the government passed over the Seaman Mansion near Minudie, a magnificent structure built by Amos "King" Seaman, perhaps the richest man in mid-nineteenth-century British North America and a visionary with a fascinatingly Unitarian approach to religious tolerance. It would fall victim to vandals in the 1960s.

Minudie was not the only community that lost out. Mining towns such as Springhill, Sydney Mines, and Joggins made few claims for public recognition, perhaps because they lacked historically conscious middle classes and also because they were thought to lack tourism potential. Canso, far removed from the tourist trails of the day, had nonetheless seen some of the earliest and most influential episodes in eighteenth-century European and New England colonization, as well as fascinating if troubling moments in eighteenth-century Mi'kmaw/newcomer relations. (Through many of these early years, it was the largest, albeit seasonal, community on the Atlantic coast of Nova Scotia.) It too lacked clout in the world of tourism/history. Communities without a sufficiently large class of small businessmen and professionals to sustain a functioning historical society or service club would labour at a disadvantage, thanks to the state's continuing emphasis on helping volunteers and communities to help themselves. In fact, Bird's council would explicitly cite the absence of a local historical society when turning down appeals for commemoration.[142]

As with Macdonald's stance on Gaelic, the provincial government contented itself with a more or less passive response to demands from localities, which meant that those already favoured by tourists and equipped with prosperous heritage elites did well, but many others went by the boards. This new framework paid no more attention to distributive justice when it came to the fruits of tourism/history than did the other elements of Macdonald's liberalism. Because of this imbalance, many irreplaceably *sui generis* artifacts from Nova Scotia history crumbled, while many that were rather similar to each other – one perhaps uncharitably thinks of the umpteenth Victorian bigwig's mansion restocked with imported antiques – crowded the provincial roster of historically significant sites. In perhaps the ultimate irony, although the Province by the Sea buzzed with much talk about the Golden Age of Sail, the winning communities and sites tended rather more to be within sight and sound of the emergent highway system, whereas the losers were often found in coastal, archetypically maritime locations well off the tourist trails. Most tourists were motorists, not sailors.

Bird's succinct description of his role – "getting our historical assets on array in the shop window for our visitors"[143] – reminds us that the astute shop owner places in the window only those items that please the customers. The window display should coincide with the expectations and values of the middle-class travelling public at whom these historical attractions aimed. Sites (or sights) became meaningful as they attracted the tourist gaze – which had to do with not just what tourists actually looked at, but what a hypothetical average tourist *might* look at. Just as he researched his travel books by pretending to be a tourist, Bird often assessed historical projects with what he fancied to be a tourist's eye.

The council's first decision, in fact, was to urge all municipal governments to put up large signs at their borders advertising "any historical details of its founding, the identity of the first settlers, data regarding any interesting feature of the locality, its recreational facilities, and leading industries." With any luck, visitors would take photographs of such signs, which would be taken home "and shown far and wide," affording the province a decisive "advantage in publicity advertising."[144] Eleven years later, trying to come up with something that could give suburban Bedford a sliver of historical significance, Bird hit upon the idea of restoring the town's toll bridge. He proposed to the premier that "[i]t might be that if old-looking gates were erected near the bridge at Bedford with appropriate signs, headed by such lettering as 'FREE ENTRY,' it might rouse the curiosity of tourists and cause many pictures to be taken."[145]

If only Port Mouton would put up a sign explaining that its name derived from the sheep that had jumped off Pierre Dugua, Sieur de Monts's ship, then "[t]hink of the numbers who would stop to take a picture," said a visitor whose comments Bird reported. He boldly predicted, "Port Mouton would be talked about and written about in hundreds of American books."[146] Bird's advice typified the new mnemonics according to which people sought not contexts, inspirations, narratives, or explanations, but sensations; this imagined past increasingly resembled a vast attic of fascinating oddities or a massive *Ripley's Believe It or Not* museum.

Tourism/history emerged within this empire of the gaze, where Bird the bureaucrat put the panoramic sensibility of his books to work in his tourism planning. He gave serious consideration, for example, to making the Digby Gap more scenic. "You can see," he wrote to Premier Stanfield, "that if the two block houses were restored and the cannon put back in place, what a thrill the scene would give all visitors entering Nova Scotia on board the Princess Helene."[147] Various communities that requested markers commemorating the Planters met strong opposition from Bird, whose grounds were that "it will make the tourist confused to see two or three [plaques] telling the same story."[148] Cairns, Bird and many of his correspondents agreed, should not stand on the sites they commemorated if this meant placing them where tourists might not see them. A marker seen only by local residents was hardly worth putting up.[149] Monuments that visitors would not easily understand – such as the "French Cross" at Morden, an old monument, heavily damaged by frost and souvenir hunters, identified only by its name and the date "1755" – drew sharp rebukes from Bird: "This means absolutely nothing to a visitor. Three cars from the U.S. drove in while I was there. They had no idea what the cross meant."[150] Bird rarely sounded outraged in his correspondence, but this enigmatic (and for many subtly moving) Acadian cross had clearly struck a nerve.

Sites that lacked direct commercial impact fared poorly. The travelling public was once urged to visit cemeteries – those of Yarmouth, for instance, provided a particularly lovely picturesque vista.[151] The more pragmatic paradigm of the 1950s, however, found cemeteries a headache. They could hardly "pay for themselves." Bird informed Stanfield that the council, taking into account the probable cost of maintaining a very large number of cemeteries, "does not feel justified in recommending that the Government of Nova Scotia undertake their restoration and perpetual care."[152] Bird reported over fifty requests to restore graveyards in an eleven-year period. Restoring just one would open the proverbial floodgates for scores of other demands, not to mention exciting denominational rivalry.[153] Expatriates disturbed by weeds on ancestral graves made heartfelt appeals to no avail. Though many Nova Scotians still considered cemeteries especially important sites of memory that deserved public support, the council disagreed.[154] This was not its sort of history.

On similar grounds, the council avoided bicentenaries. Beginning with the 1955 bicentenary of the Acadian Expulsion, the province found itself swept up in bicentennial celebrations for many communities. "All are plaguing me for some sort of assistance, and I cannot agree," Bird complained. He again discerned the thin edge of the wedge: "There will be no end if government funds were extended for such celebrations as from now on there will [be], every year, some place celebrating a 200th birthday."[155] This was perhaps a somewhat inconsistent position for someone whose operetta in honour of Halifax's "200th birthday" ("in rather weak Gilbert and Sullivan style," Phyllis Blakeley thought) had featured prominently in the state-funded 1949 Halifax bicentennial celebrations.[156] Perhaps the difference was that many of the 1950s commemorations concerned Acadians, always awkwardly located in Birdland. In any case, the council ruled that it would assist no community in staging such anniversary celebrations.[157]

◆

So diffuse a sentiment as preservationism needed leaders. It required a mnemonic vanguard capable of distilling the clear elements of a liberal policy from so many competing claims. Here the triumvirate of Macdonald, Bird, and Raddall played a decisive role.

Although as the very busy premier he had many other things to attend to, Macdonald closely monitored provincial ventures into tourism/history. His correspondence suggests both his passionate drive to make Nova Scotia a tourism Mecca and also his penchant for micromanagement. Let us begin with a single example from 1945. On November 15th, Raddall addressed the Commercial Club of Halifax on the subject of "Halifax and the Tourist Trade." His forceful speech urged the city to upgrade its image in the interests of tourism. "Get to know this fine old city of yours, and when a stranger stops you in the street with a question, tell him what you know," Raddall counselled the businessmen. "You are busy men I know, but surely there is room for ten minutes' courtesy in business. For this is business. The success or failure of the tourist trade in Halifax depends on every citizen. Every tourist who goes away from Halifax impressed with its color and romance will send three to see what he has found."[158] He impressed Harold Ball of the *Chronicle-Herald*, at any rate. Ball wrote Macdonald to reiterate Raddall's message that tourists travelled to Halifax "not for our scenery, our Public Gardens, our hotels, our food, because they can get as good and better at home, but to see a country different from their own and to learn its story." Unfortunately, Ball continued, Raddall had been equally correct to maintain "that Halifax and Nova Scotia as a whole has done a very poor job to date in telling the story of the city's and the province's romantic past." Ball wanted the province to "check up on our points of historic interest in Halifax." Small repairs would make "a world of difference – and make the visitor think that we care about our place in history." For instance, why not do something about St Paul's Burying Ground, which "looks pretty much like a scene of decay"? And what about the terrible coffee tourists encountered in Nova Scotia?[159]

Macdonald responded in detail. He would see to the refurbishing of the two guns at Province House. As for the ruined historic cemeteries in Halifax, it would be a fine thing for them to look more presentable – but, alas, their upkeep lay firmly within municipal jurisdiction. He confided that he had witnessed a similarly derelict cemetery in Annapolis Royal, "older even than St. Paul's," terribly neglected despite its central location. Fortunately, when he had pointed out the sad state of affairs to the locals, "they appeared to be quite willing to undertake the job." Finally, Macdonald turned his attention to the quality of provincial coffee: "For some reason or other our people do not seem to be able to make it as well as Americans. There is no reason in the world for this, as I assume we get the same sort of material as they have there." Numerous such letters testify not only to Macdonald's obsession with detail, extending from property to percolation, but also to his willingness to act as tourism's advocate-general, reminding all of the imperative need to improve the tourism product.[160]

Macdonald appointed Bird head of the Historic Sites Advisory Council in 1948, empowering the novelist to make important decisions about heritage. The appointment also freed Bird to write a slew of historical novels and travel accounts (as Bird said himself, without such state employment he could never have freed himself from the weary round of hackwork). Right away, Macdonald gave Bird a detailed list of the historical places that the council should consider:

1 Uniacke House, Mount Uniacke, Hants County.
2 Sir Robert Borden's Home, Grand Pre, Kings County.
  (There are, I understand, two houses here of some significance – one the house in which he was born, and the other the house in which he grew up.)
3 The first house in Wolfville.
  (This matter is now being looked after by the Wolfville Historical Society.)
4 Certain spots near Annapolis, such as the site of the first grist mill in North America, the first road, and so on.

5 A memorial to Longfellow at Grand Pre.
6 Something on the French Shore to mark the return of the Acadians after their trek from Massachusetts Bay.
7 Shelburne – First House.
 (I think that already a certain Mrs. Webster or daughter of Mrs. Webster has offered the Shelburne Historical Society an old house.)
8 Simeon Perkins House, Liverpool, N.S.
9 The French Settlement at LaHave.
10 Lunenburg – Something to commemorate the arrival of the Hanoverians.
11 Cape Breton – Louisburg, of course, takes care of much of the history of the Island, but there are some spots that I will give you later.

Would it not be a good thing to have any town which has any historical significance marked by a large sign, as one sometimes sees in the United States at the entrance to the town. That is, at Annapolis Royal you could have a square sign of some three or four feet on each side, with something like this on it:

"Annapolis Royal, formerly Port Royal, site of the first permanent white settlement in America north of St. Augustine [Florida], founded in 1605 by the French, captured by the British in 1710, and so on."

Guysboro could be marked as having been established by Loyalists. There are very few of our towns that have not some claim on our historic sense.[161]

The memo suggests that, although plainly committed to the Scottish Myth, Macdonald wanted to extend tourism/history to the entire province. Even a county like Guysborough, which despite the ancient settlement of Canso almost invariably fell outside the canon of tourism/history, could take the Loyalists (although not, significantly, the hell-raising New England fishermen or their Mi'kmaw opposition) as their entrée into historical significance.

The Historic Sites Advisory Council probably would not have succeeded without Macdonald. Harold Connolly technically oversaw it as the minister of industry and publicity, but found it an irritating distraction. He demanded to know who in fact sat on the board, if it had done any useful work, and under what authority it would operate. "If we could have ten minutes at an early moment," he remarked, "we could straighten out the matter and set a course."[162] Macdonald replied that Bird would be chairman, while the members would include, in addition to Raddall, Professor W.J. Belliveau, Collège Saint-Anne; C. Bruce Fergusson, MA, assistant archivist; Professor R.S. Longley,

PhD, Acadia University; Miss Katharine McLennan, honorary curator, Louis-burg Museum; and, as ex-officio member, Professor D.C. Harvey, MA, LLD, FRSC, archivist of Nova Scotia and member of the Historic Sites and Monu-ments Board of Canada.[163] Harvey, who often worried that tourism/history would undermine the academic seriousness of historical research, was there not only as Macdonald's personal friend, but as a widely respected historian whose scrupulous scholarship would save the board from embarrassment.

Routinely confused in the public mind with the much more powerful HSMBC, the little council lacked much of a profile. During the first three years of its existence, Chairman Bird had little time for it.[164] Without appropriations in the government's estimates, it clung to a precarious existence within the Department of Industry and Publicity.[165] Furthermore, this department sent the council mixed signals about how to evaluate proposals for commemora-tion. On one occasion, it mandated that the council should consider costs when it made its recommendations, while on another, it insisted the council make recommendations on "purely historical grounds."[166] By 1954, the coun-cil had grown so unhappy with this cloudy arrangement that it passed a motion demanding some clarification of its place in the bureaucracy and of what the government expected it to do.[167] During a period that stretched from Macdonald's death in 1954 until January of 1955, Bird found himself "quite adrift," with "no one to whom I could refer matters for advice."[168] When the council's three-year term lapsed in 1955, Bird had to appeal directly to the new premier for an Order-in-Council granting another one.[169]

Under parsimonious Premier Robert Stanfield, the council cut costs by supplying only the plaque, leaving the community to supply the cairn or platform on which to mount it and then to handle the actual installation. Even then, the council could issue only three plaques per year – which, Bird remarked to Stanfield, "pretty well uses up the money."[170] (A Halifax firm could make the all-weather bronze plaques in three weeks, at a price per plaque ranging from $130 to $220 in 1960, depending on its size and number of words.)[171] If one sought a major commitment to a significant heritage project, the council was the wrong place to look. Its activities captured only one small dimension of the triumvirate's effective work.

Yet, despite these limitations, the council mattered. Nova Scotians anxiously sought its plaques and hotly debated its decisions. Its judgments taught peo-ple which things were historically significant and which were inaccurate or inconsequential. Of 152 requests for commemoration between 1948 and 1964, only 38 succeeded (i.e., met with a favourable decision from the council), 77 failed outright, 21 were referred to another body (frequently the federal HSMBC), and in sixteen additional cases we do not know the outcome. The difference between the successful cases and the general pattern tells us something about the bias and impact of this particular council. Half (86) of the demands sent to the council were for plaques and monuments, a further 45 favoured restoring various historic structures. The remaining 21 asked for help in preserving private collections, financial aid for existing historical facilities, and a combination of plaques and restoration. These data have their limitations – Bird did not record all of his decisions, only the most important. Nonetheless, the numbers do give us some clues about how the council presented the past, about public demand for the new history, and about how the master narrative associated with Bird and Raddall shaped the process of commemoration.

Demands for historical recognition came from across the province, but particularly from areas with heavy tourist traffic: Cumberland (18 cases), Annapolis (14), the Halifax-Dartmouth metropolitan area (13), Hants (13), Lunenburg (12), Yarmouth (11), and Digby (10). We find slightly less demand for public history from Cape Breton County (9), Pictou (8), Kings (8), Shelburne (7), Halifax County (5), Colchester (7), and then dramatically less from Antigonish (2), Inverness (3), Victoria (6), Guysborough (3), Queens (2), and Richmond (1). As for success rates, we find no fewer than 25 (66 per cent) of the successful cases in the counties of the Annapolis Valley and South Shore. Yarmouth led all other counties with 6 successes. Only Cumberland (5) and Victoria (3) approached the totals of the southern counties.

Before a case reached the council, it usually had already won support from small businessmen and professionals. Of the 135 requests about whose instigator we know something, private individuals living in the same county as the site they wanted commemorated raised the largest number (61). Individuals who indicated their links to historical societies and women's institutes brought forward a further 13 cases. Historical societies acting corporately initiated no fewer than 15 cases. Business groups – often local boards of trade, sometimes with their own "tourist committees" – generated a further 9 cases. The remainder came from many different quarters: municipal governments, service clubs, provincial politicians, and the council itself.

What kinds of historical events did the council consider? No fewer than 103 (68 per cent) cases represented attempts to commemorate pre-Confederation history, surely a tribute to the tenacious hold of the "Golden Age." Only 20 (13 per cent) represented post-Confederation history, with the remainder not fitting into either category (historic houses, for example, typically spanned them both). Looking more specifically at century, we find that 4 cases referred to events predating 1600, 17 to seventeenth-century events, 44 to eighteenth-century events, 58 to nineteenth-century events, and only 9 to events in the twentieth century (a further 22 are unclassifiable in this way). Perhaps a more illuminating standard would correlate cases with well-known historical epochs. We can plausibly classify a total of 123 cases in this way. Only 4 cases referred

to the period before the foundation of Port Royal in 1605. Twenty-two referred
to the French colonial epoch of Acadia (1604–1755). No fewer than 76 cases
(62 per cent of the 123 classifiable in this way) refer to the triumphant British
colonial period after the Expulsion and before Confederation. Breaking this
figure down further, we find 12 from the Expulsion to the American Revolution, 24 for the period 1783–1800, 29 for 1801–48, and 11 for 1849–66. Only
14 cases pertained to 1867–1924. Only 7 pertained to 1925–64. The council
clearly preferred events that fell between 1783 and 1866 (55 per cent of the
successful cases, as opposed to 42 per cent of all cases), whereas it tended to
filter out cases from the period 1604–1755 (only 11 per cent of the successes
compared to 18 of all requests).[172] Looking at the cases topically, immigration – usually of Planters or Loyalists – topped the list at 20 cases; Acadian
cases followed at 19; "economic growth," much of it concerning sailing ships,
at 18; "social institutions" – schools, churches, and universities, primarily – at
12; pre-1900 politics at 8; "French/English hostilities" at 7; "labour" at 3;
nineteenth-century economic growth at 3; twentieth-century politics at 1; and
Mi'kmaw history at 1.[173]

At first glance, the council seems to have capriciously refused commemoration here but granted it there, invoking in one case a rule blithely overlooked
in another. Take the case of Shelburne's Ross-Thomson House. Bird found it
in a "dreadful state of disrepair and decay." Worse, it lacked a strong claim to
historical significance. "If it were simply old houses we needed," he wrote to
its advocate Mrs Webster, "we would have six or seven on our hands at
Annapolis Royal and three at Granville Ferry." These other old houses, moreover, were "in first-class condition ... lived in, with old beams and ironware
and ovens and fireplaces in excellent condition. But there must be more than
simple age for recommendation when funds for restoration are so limited." At
its second meeting, the council unequivocally ruled that "the Thomson House,
Shelburne, is not a typical house of the Loyalist period and has no recorded
history to recommend it." Then, out of the blue, Bird overturned the verdict.
It seems that the house had subsequently been certified as a viable restoration
project. Suddenly he recalled its historical importance as an early post office
and school.[174]

Behind the council's apparent caprice, however, logic did govern its decisions – a two-tiered system of triage meant to eliminate unworthy events, persons, and buildings from the running. All cases first had to pass a means test.
History had to pay its way. It had value insofar as it could generate historical
commodities to set in the shop window of the province. Local traditionalists
had all kinds of sentimental fixations, but the pragmatic council would always
inquire as to the economic potential of any relic. The much-vaunted quality
of *firstness* bolstered the rule of political economy. The council dismissed many

a beloved historical landmark because, being neither *the first* nor *the only*, it had no scarcity value in the significance sweepstakes. Ten Mile House, near Halifax, was one of seven or eight old stagecoach inns still extant. The council objected that if it recognized this stagecoach inn, then it would have to recognize the others too. Similarly, they denigrated Earltown's claim to have the first gristmill and thus a site of history. Nova Scotia boasted dozens of first gristmill sites, complete with their original millstones.[175] What was so special about that one? The council, ever inattentive to the social, the structural, or the causal, had its eyes on the individual and the unusual – preferably the unique.

Under these conditions, claimants sometimes resorted to truly desperate arguments on behalf of their cases. The owner of Acacia Cottage in Halifax initially claimed that it had been the first house in Halifax to have a Christmas tree. This expedient having failed, she relied on the backup argument that, in the past month, the house had also "made history" as Halifax's first house moved by trailer.[176] Bird apparently spent much of his time combating such claims to significance: "I have this summer dealt effectively with no fewer than fourteen requests that had no foundation in fact," he advised Premier Stanfield in 1962, with something like a charity visitor's grim satisfaction at exposing cheats and malingerers.[177]

As we might remember from his harsh descriptions of the slovenly Belgians and untidy Mi'kmaq, looks mattered profoundly to Bird. Property should exemplify propriety. History should not look too old. Romantics had long loved ruins for the wistful melancholy and gentle mysticism that lingered as a gracious and forgiving mist upon their quaint and lovely stones. They would not have done well on this council. Tourism/history did not favour structures that looked their age or hinted plaintively at the vicissitudes of time. Chapman House in Cumberland County, a giant eighteenth-century dwelling built of marsh brick, had special significance for Bird – author of *Here Stays Good Yorkshire* – since it was the last original home remaining from the Yorkshire settlers who came to the Chignecto area in the 1700s. Having fallen into the wrong hands, however, the house no longer merited a plaque. It had degenerated into "a pig sty" during the tenancy of a widower and his adult son who kept "a large flock of geese which foul the ground. I have told the people repeatedly that until this situation changes we will not recommend a plaque."[178] Bird found it intolerable to see history in the hands of a "dirty-lazy widower … who sleeps on an iron cot in the kitchen to save climbing the stairs."[179] One would not give a plaque to Jigger Loney of *So Much to Record,* and this squalid widower clearly reminded Bird of such a character.

The rule of attractiveness also applied to people chosen for commemoration. Over the winter of 1958–59, controversy raged in Halifax over plans of St Mary's University to demolish Gorsebrook, a mansion once belonging to Enos

Collins, one of British North America's most important merchant capitalists. Estimating it would cost $65,000 to repair the building, the university preferred simply to raze it. Bird strongly endorsed their position, as did other members of the council, their principal argument being the personal unattractiveness of Collins. Raddall contended, "Collins made a huge fortune but never contributed anything to the city or province, historically or in any other way, [he] was a cold, hard, grasping man." Bird concurred: "He never raised a hand to help anyone or any cause. His sole claim to notice is that he was one of Nova Scotia's first millionaires."[180] He was too reminiscent, perhaps, of Saxby Nolan from Raddall's *Tidefall*. Despite his undoubted significance to the history of Canadian capitalism, Collins was not plaque material. The demolition of Gorsebrook, later averted on other grounds, had the council's blessing.

Certain kinds of people seem to have merited commemoration more than others did. The male hero dominated the world of public commemoration as thoroughly as he did the swashbuckling novels of Bird and Raddall. Of our 38 successful cases, no fewer than 17 (45 per cent) commemorated individual men as compared with 44 (29 per cent) of all cases submitted to the council. Only one woman, Flora Macdonald, invaded this old boys' club of historical significance; she only did so because her case enjoyed Angus L. Macdonald's personal support (and she, of course, attracted Macdonald's notice primarily because of her association with the male hero Bonnie Prince Charlie). Gallant fighting men, on the other hand, even those without much connection to the province (like two brothers who had won Congressional Medals of Honour during the Spanish-American War) inevitably made it into the pantheon of historically significant Nova Scotians.

As the premier's successful advocacy of Flora Macdonald's few days in Nova Scotia might indicate, the council deferred to powerful men, especially when it seemed politically expedient. Sidney E. Smith served Prime Minister John Diefenbaker at External Affairs. Virtually no one remembers him today, and he had long resided outside Nova Scotia, yet he won commemoration shortly after his death in 1961.[181] The hero need not even have died yet to earn eulogies. Bird drafted the wording of a plaque for Yarmouth's C. Sydney Frost while he was still alive, hailing him as a "NATIVE SON WHO THROUGH DILIGENCE AND ABILITY BECAME PRESIDENT OF THE BANK OF NOVA SCOTIA, AND WAS RESPONSIBLE FOR THE CREATION OF AN OUTSTANDING BANK BUILDING IN HIS HOME TOWN."[182]

While rich white men amassed dozens of plaques, Afro–Nova Scotians could not claim historical significance. As we have seen, they played little role in either Raddall's or Bird's imagined Nova Scotia. To place Nova Scotia's

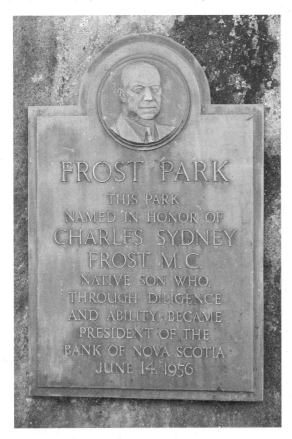

Frost Monument, Yarmouth. Will R. Bird wrote the text, which in its original form also hailed Frost for his role in the creation of an "outstanding bank building in his home town" (photograph courtesy Robert Vanderheyden, August 2007).

society and economy in an Atlantic world where transatlantic slave migrations and staples trades reliant on plantations were vital parts of the Empire, of significance wherever rum, sugar, and fish were traded, was simply not in the minds of men who so often blithely spoke of "our" race. Blacks were "historical" to the extent that slaves provided a certain *Gone with the Wind* ambience to some of the province's newly restored stately homes. True, William Hall, who had won the Victoria Cross in the nineteenth century, had received an official commemoration before the council even formed. Apart from him, however, blacks could secure no claim to remembrance in their own right. When Bird informed Premier Stanfield that Birchtown – a black settlement near Shelburne dating back to the eighteenth century – had asked for recognition of its history, he lumped it in with the other communities "with very little in the way of historic importance" that wanted things done for them. "There is simply no foundation to their stories," he remarked to Stanfield, "but I am being as tactful as possible with them."[183]

Bird felt less compunction when considering whether labour might deserve commemoration. Apart from a small mining museum in Stellarton (which company officials controlled), labour's part in developing Nova Scotia had yet to receive public recognition.[184] Even trade unions that could make a claim to be first were unhistorical by definition. J.M. Murphy of the Truro Board of Trade asked the council to recognize the little-known fact that on 22 August 1882 the first railroad labour organization in Nova Scotia – "Granite Rock" Division No. 149, Brotherhood of Locomotive Engineers – had formed in Truro. Bird found the very idea of recognizing such an event rather funny. He wrote sardonically to Stanfield about Murphy's request "that the Council provide plaques to go up inside the railway station at Truro and tell the world that the first Brotherhood of Locomotive Engineers was formed there in 1822 [sic]" and reported the council's belief that "railway unions should provide their own plaques as the formation of a union was not an outstanding event." In rejecting this outré request, Bird allowed himself a rare degree of candour when dealing with a client. He bluntly told Murphy that the council had refused the request because it "felt there were many items of greater historic significance needing attention."[185] He dealt more gently but no less firmly with cooperatives. No matter how venerable or internationally famous, they had no history worth commemorating.[186]

French colonization and Acadian life posed a more difficult problem for the council. Bird and Raddall shared a pronounced distaste for Acadians, but one could hardly expunge them from the Land of Evangeline. Bird knew perfectly well that 1955 marked the bicentenary of the Expulsion, and Acadians brimmed with a newfound pride. Furthermore, as J.W. Regan could have reminded him, erasing the French would also inadvertently excise a phenomenal number of firsts. The federal Historic Sites and Monuments Board had covered a smattering of Acadian history, but a good many cases awaited commemoration. Nonetheless, the council weeded out a disproportionate number of them. They represent only 8 per cent of the successful cases, as opposed to the overall success rate of 18 per cent. On three occasions, the council even allowed local anglophone communities to convert plaques initially awarded for Acadian themes into plaques commemorating British themes. Bible Hill switched the commemoration of a "Holy Well" attributed to the Acadians to a commemoration of the landing of the first English-speaking settlers. At Mira, commemoration of a monastery connected with Louisbourg changed to commemoration of Mira's "pre-Loyalist, Loyalist and Scottish pioneers."[187] Perhaps most egregiously, in Grand Pré itself – site of some of the deportation's most wrenching scenes – the plaque honouring this history gave way to one that celebrated the arrival of the Planters who seized their farms.[188]

Perhaps even more than Acadian claims, those of the native peoples gave the council headaches. On the one hand, a strong economic case favoured commemorating aboriginal themes. Tourists always flocked to "prehistoric" relics.[189] As late as 1949, a note for tourists visiting Shubenacadie (unsigned, but most likely written by Bird) recommended that they bring a shovel – a "little digging" would turn up "crumbled pieces of pottery, barely discernible as remains of cooking utensils," the crude remains of a people who "did not do much with clay beyond biscuit firing."[190] Whatever else one might say of it, such an approach to aboriginal artifacts had little to do with the preservationism that regulated the treatment of the historical record left by other ethnicities. In 1961, Arthur Merry complained to Bird that tourists visiting his property near Kejimkujik Park defaced petroglyphs by carving their names over them. The thoughtless holidaymakers also imperilled a native cemetery.[191] Today's cultural politics would have treasured such artifacts as components of a world heritage of quite possibly far greater importance than the aggregated stately homes of the province. It was not so in 1961. The blasé Bird advised Merry that the council had a fixed policy against restoring cemeteries. As for the petroglyphs, the council decided that it "would not recommend any action to preserve the rock markings."[192]

The council *did* commemorate the site of a large native encampment at Shubenacadie. The Mi'kmaq may have slipped through the backdoor in this case, because this site marked the "largest Micmac encampment when Le Loutre arrived in Nova Scotia."[193] Since both Bird and Raddall had made the eighteenth-century Abbé Le Loutre carry such a heavy explanatory burden as the chief villain in their histories and historical fiction, helping them make their polemical case against the perfidious French and the deceptive Acadians, they were understandably keen to mark the site. Thus, this one major exception to the rule of whiteness actually underlines its pervasive influence. The keynote speakers at the official marking of the site included the local Indian agent and another well-known authority on the Mi'kmaq, indeed the man whom Bird considered the "best qualified person in the province." He meant, of course, Thomas H. Raddall. Aboriginal voices would not be entirely absent, for choirboys from the nearby residential school would sing a song or two, thus providing a little "something to add to the occasion."[194]

The most significant moments of the Nova Scotia narrative happened, unsurprisingly, where and when the novels of Bird and Raddall had located them. Insofar as the council could set a stamp upon Nova Scotia, it was theirs. As such, the council systematically *liberalized* the past, paying close attention to exceptional individuals (especially businessmen) and usually overlooking any subalterns who had the temerity to request commemoration. To this extent, it was also a *racializing* council that worked (perhaps unconsciously) to perpetuate the image of a Nova Scotia founded by and rightly centred on the white races.

◆

We can illustrate the typical modus operandi of the new mnemonic apparatus and its politics of commemoration with reference to the vexed question of John Cabot (alias Zuan, alias Giovanni, Caboto), the Genoese navigator who in 1497 made landfall somewhere in eastern Canada on behalf of his employer King Henry VII of England. Cabot became a sort of Columbus for the British Empire.[195] In the New World, however, two different colonies, Nova Scotia and Newfoundland, would hotly contest the honour of claiming Cabot's landfall for their own.[196] As early as 1930, Nova Scotia sought to make Cabot a Nova Scotia hero by attaching his name to the Cabot Trail, a new scenic highway in Cape Breton.[197] The province effectively declared that Cabot had made landfall on Cape Breton Island.[198] According to Peter Pope, documentary evidence for this position – in particular a map of 1544 – had become widely known in North America in the last quarter of the nineteenth century. For many Canadians, Cabot's Cape Breton landing had become "conventional wisdom."[199]

In 1935, A.S. MacMillan, the minister of highways, wrote D.C. Harvey to check whether the province really had firm grounds for claiming Cabot. Harvey noted that despite "prolonged and widespread" controversy, knowledge about Cabot's landfall remained "inconclusive owing to the fragmentary nature of the materials which historians have had to use and the vagueness of geographical knowledge at the time of Cabot's first voyage in 1497." He nonetheless felt, after "considerable research and reflection," that the province could confidently claim that Cabot had landed on Cape Breton Island, at or near Cape Breton (the island's easternmost extremity) on 24 June 1497.[200] He reiterated this opinion five years later when Angus L. Macdonald asked him whether the province could attach the name "Cabot" to a new golf course. Harvey replied that, with the support of three scientific geographers, he no longer feared "that we might be criticized legitimately for using the name of Cabot to give us a greater sense of antiquity."[201]

Harvey's confidence aside, Newfoundland had a serious rival claim to Cabot that it pressed with increasing vigour after entering Confederation in 1949. The Newfoundland Historical Society informed Macdonald and Harvey that, unless they found some new evidence, Nova Scotia had no case. The crucial map on which Nova Scotia founded its claim lacked meridians and parallels. Newfoundland historians, moreover, found Cabot an emotional as well as a scholarly priority. "We of the Historical Society of Newfoundland cling to these records: maps, documents, unbroken tradition, etc. as to a life-line and will not let go," Memorial University's S.P. Whiteway warned Harvey.[202] G.R.F. Prowse, son of Newfoundland's greatest historian, contested the Nova Scotia claim with a demonstration of rigorous scholarly reasoning and cartographical evidence that the renowned University of Toronto economic historian Harold Innis, for one, found persuasive. "The mass of materials I have collected since 1904," Prowse wrote definitively, "points unmistakably to a landfall at Bonavista and to the practical and demonstrable impossibility of the one at Cape Breton."[203] Prowse also wrote vividly of the depth of feeling this issue aroused in Newfoundland: "There has been a continuous Bonavista tradition; IT IS IN OUR BLOOD. There is nothing in Cape Breton with this."[204] Innis would remark in 1941, "The bias of nationalism in the study of exploration would make an interesting study ... The vested interests of nationalism are concerned with territorial rights, and perhaps more recently with the tourist trade. The mayor of St John's, Newfoundland, once assured the writer that 'John Cabot landed right out here in this bloody harbour.'"[205] This rather histrionic challenge to the Cape Breton claim made Harvey uneasy. He equivocated. "I have always felt that no one could speak with absolute confidence on this matter in view of the uncertain nature of the evidence available," he explained to Macdonald. "We should be very careful of the wording of any tablet that may be erected."[206] Bird suspected that Harvey, as a native Prince Edward Islander who by implication lacked a vested personal interest in the matter, had settled upon indecision as the path of least resistance.[207]

Harvey merely exercised a scholar's caution. To this day, no one has irrefutable evidence that would settle the quarrel.[208] It might go on indefinitely, incidentally generating (one might hope) new evidence, theories, and grounds for reflection. Yet the new tourism/history rejected the cautiousness, inconclusiveness, and incremental progression of many historiographical developments. The demands of the tourism economy dictated that Cabot land in Cape Breton. In 1935, after the City of Sydney officially recognized Cape Breton as the landfall of Cabot, its Publicity Committee started to promote him as a tourist attraction. In 1940, prominent Cape Bretoners had proposed that a cross be erected: here would be a "great drawing card for tourists, especially in view of the current vogue to visit the scene of 'first things' in America."[209] Pressure to commemorate Cabot mounted steadily in the 1950s but encountered newly confederated Newfoundland's articulate presence on the federal HSMBC. The feds withheld recognition from Nova Scotia. On 24 June 1952, the Cape Breton Historical Society – whose letterhead defiantly carried a picture of the

Mathew, Cabot's ship, with the date 24 June, 1497, referring to his landfall[210] – held its first "Cabot Day" at Cape North, with a large crowd and the past lieutenant-governor, Hon. J.A.D. McCurdy, in attendance.[211]

Mrs Maie Munro, president of the society, had made the recognition of Cabot her personal crusade. She considered truth cumulative. The recognition of Cabot at Cabot Day in 1952 and a landowner's gift of a site at Cape North for the Cabot Memorial both argued in favour of Nova Scotia's claim to Cabot. So, she would later add, did the naming of the Cabot Trail and the public recognition of Cape Breton's claim by the seafarer's home port of Bristol.[212] According to Munro, the collective weight of these actions meant "that the claim of Cape Breton is on sound ground and *Cannot be disproved*." How could the provincial government, she asked Bird, unaccountably delay official acknowledgment of Cabot's historical significance?[213] Bird simply replied that "no proof of Cabot's landing has been discovered. In 1894 and in 1897 the greatest experts in maps and history gave a considerable period to research on the subject – and came to a dead end." The HSMBC was considering the matter, at Newfoundland's insistence. Any attempt on Nova Scotia's part to commemorate Cabot in opposition to a finding by the federal board would make the province look ridiculous. Bird added, however, that he had repeatedly written in to press Cape Breton's claim to Cabot "because I have felt our claims were as well founded as those of Newfoundland, and also because I hoped such statements would produce arguments and new data that might help settle the problem."[214]

Cabot partisans in Cape Breton pressed on. A 1953 open letter from Emily E. Brown, the secretary of the Cape Breton Historical Society, written to show the HSMBC the depth of provincial commitment to Cabot, established a new precedent for the overt politicization of public history. "IT IS IN THE INTEREST OF THIS PROVINCE THAT SUCH RECOGNITION BE GIVEN," the letter proclaimed. "TO YOU, AS A NOVA SCOTIAN, and a representative of the people, it is the purpose of this letter to solicit your support for this Cabot Memorial Project. A project which will gain for Nova Scotia *official Federal recognition* of being the province on which Cabot made his landing in 1497." The society urged Nova Scotians to petition the board, for "the decision will rest more secure in our favor by 'out-voicing' competing claims from another province."[215] In the new kind of history, which seemed to echo mass-market advertising, claims became ever more true as ever-increasing numbers of their proponents restated them ever more stridently.

Yet the federal board remained noncommittal. So did the Historic Sites Advisory Council, which in 1953 and again in 1955 demurred that the decision was up to Ottawa. "This is a neat way of avoiding the issue," Bird confided to Premier Henry Hicks.[216] But the issue would not go away. MLAS, MPS, the

Municipal Council of Victoria County, all supported Cape Breton's claim to Cabot. As a letter from Victoria County pointed out, the truth of Cape Breton's claim became more evident annually as "celebrations of the Landing of Cabot have been held three years and attended by members of the provincial government and the lieutenant-governor. The presence of so many at such celebrations, and of officials of high rank, would indicate that the celebrations are considered in order."[217] Finally, in April of 1958, after Bird had received another weighty missive from the Cape Breton Historical Society – their fourth request for official recognition of Cabot – the chairman reached his limit. He informed his council that "[s]omething must be done about providing a suitable memorial to Cabot's Landing on this side of the Atlantic ... I urge that you give the matter much thought during the next two weeks and come with some concrete proposals for action."[218] At the council's meeting of 9 May 1958, the truth of Cape Breton's claim to Cabot – as established by petitions, political activism, and adroit marketing – received official recognition.[219]

Or did it? The text of the plaque that the council supplied provides an apt illustration of the negotiated language in which tourism/history couched itself:

CABOT'S LANDFALL.
On 24th June, 1497, in the "Mathew" out of Bristol, England, with a crew of eighteen men, John Cabot discovered the continent of North America. His landfall, "First land seen," was in this vicinity, and it is believed to have been the lofty headland of North Cape Breton. It is to commemorate this important event that this monument has been erected by the Cape Breton Historical Society.

"This inscription places all credit for the memorial to the Cape Breton Historical Society, which pleases them very much," Bird candidly explained to Premier Stanfield. It thereby also "places on that Society whatever criticism is made."[220] Bird also kept his distance from arrangements to dedicate a bust to immortalize "the intelligent, athletic features of John Cabot,"[221] an undertaking so poorly managed that the ceremony scheduled for 1960 dissolved – the Boston gallery making the bust was late, Mrs Munro had "wild ideas" about perhaps substituting another one, and the society was finally compelled to postpone the great event.[222] Meanwhile, certain Cape Bretoners had gotten sick of the whole thing. The prospect of yet another official Cabot Day in Victoria County proved too much for newspaperman Frank Keating, who vented his exasperation with the pointed question, "Except as a periodic reviver of regional cock-a-doodle-do, what does any of it matter?"[223]

The monument to Cabot aimed to bring a knowable order out of the unknowable infinitude of the past. It created the reassuring illusion of solid foundations where there were, in fact, no such foundations. This new kind of history, so tightly bound together with tourism, soothes doubt with a politically contrived certainty. It counteracts a dangerously destabilizing historical process with the comforting solidity of the tangible. It addresses a profound sense of deracination with engineered identities. And it presents the past as a vast profusion of commodities – statues, plaques, restored houses, memorabilia, all the bric-à-brac of commodification. It thus renders history harmless, for it has become just a collection of more things, more exchangeable commodities, more properties – more convertible units within capitalism. Tourism/history made everyone a prospective permanent resident of the Province of History. Its raison d'être was to produce just one more set of reasons to feel at home in the world.

The tale of the alleged Yarmouth runic stone suggested that public history in Nova Scotia could not ultimately succeed in passing for truth a delicate filigree of circumstantial evidence, suggestive hearsay, and flamboyant theorization. Historical re-description had its political and social limits. The runic stone lay well beyond them. It engendered skepticism in runologists and local historians almost from its inception, with an accredited American professor delivering the *coup de grâce* in 1938. The case of Cabot, however, suggests that within these limits tourism/history could develop its own truths in its own manner by a cumulative process of political and social acceptance abetted by special pleading in the name of revenue. Cabot's memorial still stands at Cape North, even though the province's own archivist, assigned the task of sifting the evidence, thought that the explorer had probably landed elsewhere.[224]

The stark materiality of the monument conceals the radical ambiguity of an irremediably unrecoverable past. We do not, in fact, know where Cabot landed.[225] Moreover, this logistical detail only leads us to our deeper ignorance. We do not really know why Cabot came here. Or why Tudor claims to an already populated continent should count as a momentous discovery at all. Or why the fifteenth-century peregrinations of a navigator for hire, possibly Italian or perhaps more likely Catalan, in the pay of an English king, ought to look like the founding gesture of Nova Scotia – and, indeed, Canada (and, controversially, Newfoundland). Yet we do know that vast amounts of time and emotion went into deciding such questions in the mid-twentieth century. Does this mnemonic efflorescence not call out for a commemorative monument of its own?

Conclusion: Is the Romance Ended?

Surely not. For the young couple captured by the well-known Canadian painter Franklin Arbuckle in a promotion for the Dominion Atlantic Railway, the romance seems to have only just begun (see page 370). They are surely in love, caught up in the transfiguring glow of restrained but palpable pleasure. We see them seated in the dining car on the DAR, amid white linen, glistening salt and pepper shakers, a glowing pitcher of water, gleaming silverware. He sits with his back to us, so we cannot see his face – but we sense by the positioning of his shoulders and neck how thoroughly he is drinking in the sights before him. His attractive partner (reminiscent perhaps of a younger and more innocent Joan Crawford), adorned with a pearl necklace and dressed in a smart suit, joins him in gazing upon the beautiful Nova Scotia seascape. Although these two are post-Edwardians, they still communicate that era's pleasant ambience of refinement and decorum. At least they have the means and the manners to dress properly for dinner. As they look on, the Province of History works its trademark magic – a tranquil fishing cove, as though untouched since the nineteenth century; a picturesque lighthouse; quaint saltbox houses; and beautiful hills, receding into an eternal distance – all of it bathed in the luminescence of a radiant sky. Nova Scotia is for lovers. Its historic sites, glimpsed from the train and in the tourist brochure, offer so many props for their individual journeys into the promised land of eternal love, middlemost comfort, and perpetual consumption. This is a happy couple in Longfellow's "home of the happy." Their white faces are all aglow with light, as though beaming, not

Promotional painting by Franklin Arbuckle, for the Dominion Atlantic Railway, c. 1950, with the permission of the Musée acadien, Université de Moncton.

so much at the thought of the delicious meal to come, but at the tableau that Nova Scotia has unfolded before them. Here is romance.

On their table, we find a menu from the Land of Evangeline, with the little Grand Pré church and Hébert's statue just discernible – a frame within a frame within a frame. Does this historical reference retain anything factual? Evangeline now stands at eight considerable degrees of separation removed from any hypothesized woman who may have suffered from the cruel violence of 1755 (see chapter 2). Like Evangeline and Gabriel, this young couple has found love in Nova Scotia. They have also brought with them a propertied propriety. They can just sit back, absorbing at their leisure the panoply of sights and sounds which the province serves up to them, much as their *maître d'* will shortly arrive with their dinner. The faint reminders of historical events are safely miniaturized and enticingly consumable. Everything is in its proper place. Evangeline, fine food, the crisp linens, the (implied) European service, and – above all – the panoramic view. Indirectly or directly, everything has now become an article of exchange. ("Dreamlike traveling on the railroad," commented Ralph Waldo Emerson in his journal in 1843. "The towns which I pass between Philadelphia and New York make no distinct impression. They are like pictures on a wall.")[1]

As our young couple peers into the shop window of the province to glimpse the historical and cultural assets on display – to recall Will Bird's deft formulation of his life's work – we in turn gaze at the window of the advertisement, where the young couple themselves are objects of our desire. Which desire, you ask? Take your pick: for young love, for the elegance and leisure of the glamorous days of railway travel, for the Old World, for the home of the happy, for Evangeline – unburdened of historical significance until her name triggers associations of apple blossoms. The distance our romantic couple can rightly feel from the sights framed by their picture window – for it is just an evanescent picture that has resulted from the mechanization of perception made possible by the railway's annihilation of space by time[2] – is also the distance we in turn feel from them, for they are just props in a railway promotion. A virtual reality has caught them up and us too. History is now a passive vista, easily held at a distance, or safely contained as an illustration upon a menu card. As one charming tableau succeeds another, indiscriminately, none of the sights within the choreographed landscape requires study.[3] In this historic Nova Scotia, the tourist gaze has magically miniaturized all histories, reduced them (as with Evangeline on the menu card) to the faintest whispers from a now safely remote romantic past.

Let us concede the vividness of the dream – love, beauty, fine food, security, ease. This couple lives in quiet equipoise and Nova Scotia is helping them do so, with its quaint lighthouse, hearty sailormen, and picturesque hills. History holds no terrors any more. After a stormy adolescence of exposing the transiency and contingency of every social and economic system, or of invoking concepts of collective guilt or innocence, history has settled down cosily with all the amenities of modern middlemost life. We have domesticated history. Tourism has helped us do it.

The tourist gaze requires the *tourist frame,* the careful boundaries within which we know that the rules of reality are suspended and those of virtuality apply. We sense this as soon as we enter the artificial world of museums, Victorian bed-and-breakfasts, heritage districts and heritage moments, or the loosely historical advertisements for Alexander Keith's beer – all holo-decks upon which we can safely play at history. Tourism/history poses no questions, issues no challenges, demands no recognitions, and presents no contradictions. It presents no difficult-to-grasp underlying logics. It entertains us with a parade of beautiful objects, but relieves our couple – and, by extension, us all – of any responsibility to know how these beautiful objects came into existence and why they are dancing before our eyes. To demand that this couple reflect on the long and winding road that led from the actual ethnic cleansing of 1755 to the elegant Evangeline menu card on their tablecloth would be gauche. Here the Land of Evangeline is not really about Acadians or their deportation at all. It is merely about itself. History is no longer a root, an inspiration, a curse, or a blessing. It is merely a curiosity – a diversion from real life. History is just something that happens every summer.

This book has wanted to probe beneath the genteel surface of tourism/history, revealing it as a form of knowledge that is contradictory, hence problematical. It has wanted to ask how, from the 1860s in the case of Evangeline and from the 1920s and 1930s more generally, Nova Scotia became the Province of History – the childlike romantic history one might expect in a perpetual playground. In field after field – from Evangeline to runic stones to tartanism – we have discerned a similar logic that can reframe this lighthouse, that "first thing," or a thousandth image of Evangeline as classy merchandise in the shop window of Nova Scotia. Everything here is reified. Nothing (not even history) is historicized. Even abstract discursive entities – the Land of Evangeline, the roistering Raddallian eighteenth century, the mystical Macdonaldian Highlanders – are themselves processes that generate consumable things. All of the ahistorical essentialist talk echoing through twentieth-century Nova Scotia appeared to recount a history that it actually occluded. Worse, it placed the present condition of Nova Scotia beyond all possible critique. The only history one could reference was already the uncanny double of that very hegemonic constellation of ideology (and the social relations for which that ideology covered). The historical narrative was not, as it purported to be, an alternative to the twentieth-century liberal consensus. Instead, history presented one more form of that consensus's ideological self-justification, as a myth-symbol complex that could mediate between personal experience and the conclusions one draws from that experience.[4]

Let us look beyond the veil of ideology for a moment to see the history obscured by this imaginary couple and the relationship between the past and present that they incarnate. They can gaze out upon the Playground with a History so serenely because they have accepted an implicit philosophy of history that shelters them from its storms and allows them the comfortable illusion that history happens to other people. They themselves can relax and enjoy its by-products, secure in the unspoken belief that history can be tamed, consumed at a distance, or referenced indirectly to create an impression of local colour.

Yet history is, all at once, a process, a form of disciplined knowledge about that process, and the integration of that knowledge into a strategic awareness of the structures and possibilities of the present moment. We cannot keep it at bay – safely framed in a picture window, contained in little boxes, appropriated as a fashion accessory. Against Arbuckle's understated but palpable sense of an easily itemized and contained spectacle, the real world, in all its volatility, violence, and complexity, demands stark political and ethical choices. Confronted with this burden of history, the Playground with a History seems a profoundly dissatisfying response. And yet – here is its uncanny power – it also seems beguiling and beckoning, at the same time and for the same reasons.

Herein lies the ultimate problem with the Province of History, the commodity-generating network of words and things that business and the state brought forth in twentieth-century Nova Scotia. This consumable past offers nothing that can help one live one's life or reflect upon one's situation. It offers nothing except ever-increasing consumption itself. Its products, arranged in the shop window of the province or here in the window of the dining car, promise some magic moments of enchantment and escape in an aestheticized mode of retail therapy. Once those products are manufactured, sold, and circulating, they constitute a veritable currency of acceptable attitudes and appropriate beliefs, even though they refer to a vaguely apprehended and hazily conceived reality. We all become Birdians committed to his radical form of infantine innocence. Or, tiring of that, we could become Raddallians, social Darwinist liberals identifying ourselves with the Anglo winners of our heroic narrative. Or, more likely today, we could become Macdonaldians who reorganize our perceptions according to primordial imagined identities. The individual is still free to choose in the affective marketplace between all the many dialects of the lingua franca of Innocence.

No dialect of this language can speak of history itself. Innocence almost systematically precludes sequential thought, making it seem impossible, hubristic, and tiresome to think about oneself or the world as historical processes. Its soothing coo lulls us into the illusion that if we passively withdraw from history, leaving it safely ensconced in its picture window, it will somehow stop happening. History becomes the tale of kings and queens we recite in a strife-torn world, to keep sadness and mortality at bay. Just as Will R. Bird shielded little Mickey from the acerbic Professor by telling the innocent man–child fairy tales about coaches of crystal and gold, true historians realize that their job is to entertain, to laud, and above all to reassure.

Innocence – the notion that the conflicts of the twentieth century somehow did not implicate Nova Scotia – became a way in which both locals and tourists framed the events of their past. The new kind of history serialized in the 1920s to 1960s entailed commemorating a lost golden age – in Arbuckle's painting, a golden age of bucolic tranquility just within sight of one's railway car. Past and present effortlessly elide. As we have argued, Innocence might have, in some contexts, a radical edge – as when, by assuming the eyes of a child, one declares a powerful emperor to have no clothes. Such would rarely have been the case in Nova Scotia. Here, Innocence meant insisting with faithful credulity that the emperor did indeed have clothes (and such clothes!). Innocence characteristically meant engaging with past and present as if one were a little child watching a parade go by, a series of isolated moments, events, and sites unconnected by any underlying process and orchestrated by someone else – in essence, an *anti-historical history*. History is attractive. History is safe. Above all, history is over – we are not part of history ourselves, but merely consume it. This vacationing couple has learnt to savour reality indirectly, with the same rapture as their modern counterparts today might immerse themselves in virtual realities on their HDTV. Everything has become a tableau. Nothing is a problem.

This happy couple should not ponder the landscape as it drifts lazily by their window, nor wonder about the deeper reasons for the statue of Evangeline. Should they do so they might stumble into a mode of critical engagement that would dispel the Romance of History – this being the meta-commodity Nova Scotia was offering, in a variety of guises, to its own populace and to the travelling public. That it did so very early, and continues to do so with a totalizing will curiously at variance with an otherwise conventional liberal state, is a pattern traceable to its peculiar status as Britain's colony and New England's (and later central Canada's) therapeutic outpost – simultaneously integrated into and distanced from the cultural requirements of people undergoing accelerated capitalist development.

Many locals were neither passive recipients of, nor helpless hostages to, this process. They actively promoted it. Communities imagined that historical significance would yield prosperity, as spokespeople of the new kind of history advocated the exploitation of the "mines," "treasures," "properties," and "resources" of the newly constructed Old World of Nova Scotia. As though Lockean liberals approaching North America for the first time, they dreamt of enclosing as much history as they could in order to establish legitimate property rights over its most lucrative areas. The tourism/history thus generated was classically liberal in a twofold sense. Thematically, it characteristically sang the praises of the liberal order. Less obviously, in the very structures it generated – from the Land of Evangeline to tartanism – it replicated possessive individualist logics of appropriation and consumption, alienation and exchange. The point of the various golden ages developed within the Province of History was to yield *gold* – state revenues, business profits, and (eventually, one hoped) community prosperity. If other uses of history conflicted with tourism/history, they were swiftly sidelined.

Business *and* government threw their weight behind tourism/history. It had at its disposal some formidable weapons to make its form of historical truth persuasive. Jobs, respectability, and plausibility could all depend upon a willingness to believe what, at some level, one must have also realized could not actually be the case. The most alert and persistent promoters of tourism/history – and here we have focused on Bird, Raddall, and Macdonald – believed that they were enunciating the univocal truth about their province, not describing the province as it appeared from their perspective, not attempting to balance competing or complementary perspectives from a variety of angles. Since they worked within a stable (indeed, hegemonic) liberal framework, their historical thinking rarely included moments of self-reflection or doubt. Each developed a particular past based on liberal principles, and none felt the need to answer to divergent or dissonant conceptions of reality. Rather than praise their acumen at managing dissonance, we fault them for imprisoning history in such a way as to deny its potentially useful and critical insights to generations wrestling with the implications of modernity.

Within the force field that tourism/history generated, an unstoppable logic simplifies, isolates, freezes, and reifies the historical events and patterns from which it draws its motifs, blurring them into swirling, all-encompassing, promethean processes of accumulation and exchange. Within such processes, it is certainly possible to grasp threads – the Evangeline Phenomenon, tartanism, Parkmanesque fife-and-drum commemorations in the period covered in these pages, or the *Titanic* commemorations, the Parade of Sail, the Gathering of the Clans of later years – and follow them. Yet in the context of a mature tourism/history plant, this procedure can also be somewhat misleading. For all such threads and strains – and the products they generated – functioned not as elements within a *whole* composed of qualitatively different parts, but rather as aspects of a *totality* made up of moments that we can construe as qualitatively identical insofar as they express exactly the same essence. The vertiginous proliferation of heritage objects, with their relentlessly particularistic details and fetishized material characteristics, belies the fact that they actually express the same thing. Their outward particularities (colour, model, brand name, style) are endlessly dwelt upon because they are interchangeably equivalent as bearers of value whose entire social function (as opposed to their concrete use, which is personal rather than social) is to mediate human contacts by their production, sale, and distribution.

The tendency to universality and totalization inherent in the commodity form had an important consequence for the heritage program that dallied with advanced capitalism. Forces of abstraction went to work on the content of the heritage itself. Remember, if you will, Thomas Raddall's joke about how his plaid necktie fooled Angus L. Macdonald into thinking he must also be a Scot – how the gracious premier, nonplussed at discovering Raddall was really English, triumphantly found a way to include the novelist under the purview

375

of pan-Celticism by citing his distant Cornish ancestry. The joke is sweetly funny in the way it shows the premier's endearing solicitude to his friends. But it is also funny because it subtly shows the vacuity into which the self-serious Scottish Myth always threatened to collapse at any moment. It supposedly expresses the innermost selfhood of the ancient race of Gaels, connecting each of them to the most deeply buried recesses of their blood history, but anyone can buy in for the price of a suitably tartaned accessory – even if this purchase expresses no subjective intention at all – in such a way that even the ultimate Gael (the Grand Noble Chief of the Clans of Nova Scotia, as it happens) cannot tell the difference. In jest, quipped Freud, we may even tell the truth.

Macdonald, a past master of essentialist effusion, did not skip a beat. He simply reframed the terms of the discussion in order to make Raddall an honorary Gael too. His deft reformulation makes the joke funnier. In making Gaeldom more capacious, he also makes it more abstract – less determinate, less tied to any particular locus of identification, more casually applicable to all comers. In other words, much more like the deracinated modernity to which the Scottish Myth supposedly offered an alternative way of being in the world. Was it, potentially, a snazzy synonym for citizenship? Raddall can be a Gael – if we call him a Cornishman and extrapolate like mad. Minister of Industry Harold Connolly, as he remembered in his eulogy to Angus L., could be one too – if we remember how the Irishman is the brother to a Scotsman. Gaelic College mastermind A.W.R. MacKenzie can be a Gael – if we remember that Gaelic is a racial essence of which linguistic fluency is purely optional. This Scottish Myth made no sense at all to many of those who had devoted their lives to safeguarding Gaelic lore, whether at home (James MacNeil) or abroad (Somerled MacMillan). But it made perfect sense in this new Province of History. In fact, if we carefully examine those definitively barred from notional Gaeldom – be it because of who they were (Mi'kmaq) or what they thought (Communists) – we notice that the exclusions correspond neatly to the insiders and outsiders that liberal capitalism created on its own. The crucial difference, of course, is that liberal capitalism is an avowed politico-economic strategy susceptible to interrogation, whereas the Scottish Myth is metaphysically inaccessible to such scrutiny.

It is inadequate to present tourism/history as an inert set of sights, sounds, things, and experiences for tourists – phenomena whose production and distribution have no implications for the producers themselves, who can manipulate them at will. The magical thinking that tourism/history recommends will endow its beneficiaries with only a false sense of security, by imparting a delusive impression that social disruption represents only a passing, surface phenomenon in a world that still fundamentally operates according to the deeper working of ineffable essences, which have always been there and always will be. A more substantial antimodernism – one that advances a serious conservative critique of modernity's social and cultural implications – might facilitate a more critical and creative politics. In this highly commercialized form, however, much of antimodernism's potential critical charge dissipates in retail therapy. In this form, antimodernism is not so much the antithesis of modernity as it is one of its tools – a branding strategy that might beckon romantic couples to the Land of Evangeline.

Tourism/history has an ideological function too. It collapses the boundaries between fact and fantasy. Some may feign to deem such a manoeuvre liberating or playful, but – especially when systematically propagated by a state apparatus allied with big business – we view such irrationalism as irresponsible, both epistemologically and ethically. Some stories are qualitatively different from others. It matters which ones we tell each other and how we relate them to the surrounding world. As tourism/history takes hold, it becomes harder and harder to distinguish one story from another. The past, ironically enough, becomes more and more inaccessible as anything other than a series of radically decontextualized but (or hence) marketable stimuli.

The foregoing explanation is a bit too conspiratorial. It is to speak as though well-placed Nova Scotians all went to a meeting around 1920 and decided deliberately to leverage their marginal position within a continental economic system into a profitable business model by offering tourists a marketable haven from the wheelhouse of capitalism. In reality, even Nova Scotia's elite did not fully grasp the implications their choices would have. Although plainly influenced by antimodernism and clearly exercising hegemonic powers of cultural selection, even the key players were not entirely consistent in, or fully conscious of, their own activities. They may not have clearly understood why large-scale social change was occurring, even if they certainly knew it required a response. There was a great deal of eclecticism and *bricolage* in the making of the public past of Nova Scotia – a blurring between history and landscape, past and present, not to speak of fact and fiction, that makes a general attribution of an antimodern *strategy* somewhat flattering. The representation of the Province of History was never as ideologically antimodernist as it was market-driven.

Had tourists arrived in their thousands yearning to see the Halifax equivalent of the Statue of Liberty, the Bureau of Industry and Publicity would have accommodated them with a handsome monument to progress, pronto. Indeed, it would have been as though Rev. W. Bruce Muir had gotten his wish (see chapter 5) and Nova Scotia really had erected a proud statue of Sir William Alexander overlooking Halifax Harbour to "stand for ever as a lasting memorial to the man who was a pioneer of colonization of these lands by a healthy, virile, British stock." At least when Muir spoke in 1921, such a statue actually would have quite unsurprisingly represented the extension of the earlier narrative about Nova Scotians as world-beating Britons overseas, the most progressive people who ever lived. It would have been as though the province had never used the semiotic alchemy of antimodernism to convert its position within the Empire into misty pseudo-Gaelic nostalgia. But as Nova Scotia came more and more to be defined as a therapeutic space, the playground wherein stressed-out urbanites regained their vital energies, these older senses of history as progressive were sidelined.

One theme that this new therapeutic reading of history took over from the progressive reading, and radically reconceived, was whiteness. The construction of the Province of History was, in large measure, about the construction of the white races of Nova Scotia. As we have seen, whiteness performed many functions on a symbolic level. It offered a way to construct a romantic teleological narrative out of the liminal and nonlinear materials presented by much of Nova Scotia history. Whiteness was not a monolithic theme. It could be grasped partially and statically, as in Macdonald's case: the elaboration of a Golden Age of the Scot, located outside time and history, a vivid fiction about the ostensible age of manly independence and fervent chivalric fealty. It could be expressed magically, as in Bird's case: the fair and fit flourish, and the dark and unfit decline, just as they do in so many storybook tales. Or it could be given a social-evolutionary, quasi-scientific treatment, as with Raddall, for whom the racial superiority of the Yankees both contributes to and is reflected by their superior material progress. In all three cases, one is looking for the properly historic peoples whose deeds moved history forward, in implicit contrast to the non-historic, primitive peoples (Acadians, Mi'kmaq, blacks) who are condemned to a perpetuity of pointless repetition.

Whiteness was always racializing – always according an ontological and epistemological reality to race. Sometimes, though, it became more stridently racist – encompassing notions that the superior races must guard against pollution by their bioethical inferiors. In a very real sense, buying into the conventional narrative constructed by tourism/history meant having a disregard for the province's actually existing race problem – its segregated theatres, brutally impoverished communities of colour, its unresolved questions over native land claims. Beyond mere disregard, however, whiteness often meant the active articulation of an exclusionary concept of the Nova Scotian that worked to stigmatize any critic of racial hierarchy as "not one of us." To believe in tourism/history was to incapacitate oneself as an informed participant in reshaping a racially divided colony into a democratic post-colonial polity. To the considerable extent that Nova Scotia's tourism/history was an exercise in essentialist ethno-racial re-description, attributing to one group an essential worthiness implicitly denied to others, it could only work to ratify the rule of the powerful and disqualify the challenges of their critics. Racial and ethnic essentialism, pervasive in historical consciousness since Haliburton wrote in the 1820s, would prove a very stable and powerful form of cultural politics – especially when conjoined with Innocence during the twentieth century.

The cultural politics of Innocence made extraordinary claims upon the innermost recesses of the self: Nova Scotians must demonstrate to themselves and to others that they share in the timeless essence of Nova Scotianness and express it without adulteration or change. As the self-selected ethnic Nova Scotian Stan Rogers put it in a devout hymn to Innocence, "I used to be so different, now I know I'll always stay the same."[5]

An old humanist idea – which still has its attractions – holds that some day we can live history directly, without mediation, in lives of active historicity.[6] We hope so. We doubt it will be easy, though. Robert Graves, in his moving memoir *Good-bye to All That,* remembered his adolescent rambles in Wales. The Anglo-Irish Graves siblings found there "a place with a history too old for local legends; while walking there we made up our own. We decided who lay under the Standing Stone and who had lived in the ruined round-hut encampment, and in the caves of the valley where the big rowans grew."[7] They could never have experienced their native land this way. Freed from the burden of his lordly heritage, spared the irresistible imperative of subordinating his every experience to the exigencies of some essentialist national identity, Graves grasped total historical freedom. The whole overburden of assumptions that bear down upon every landscape we glimpse suddenly dissipated for him. This was an adolescent sort of liberation, however. It did not really free him from the duties and burdens he had of identifying with the British ruling class. (Indeed his membership in that ruling class had facilitated such vacationing and crucially informed his sense of entitlement to mentally reorder the landscape of a conquered nation.) Soon he would be in the trenches, commanding troops in a First World War he found barbaric yet felt an adamantine, unyielding duty to fight insofar as he knew himself to be British and of a certain class. We cannot wish these things away.

What we hope to offer, less grandly but more honestly, is a preliminary to reflection on the possibility of opening up the politics of tourism/history to the challenge of a dialogue with both the tourist and the toured-upon. If the conversations around present-day tourism/history are today limited to a few planners and investors, there is a cast of extras waiting to crash the gates. And for many of them, the romance *is* over. It was never, in truth, much of a romance to begin with. They might refashion tourism/history in profoundly different ways, ones that reflect a much more sophisticated and challenging sense of the ties of responsibility and tradition that properly commit us collectively to a more respectful and rigorous concept of history. Tourism/history can, in principle at least, be opened up, analysed, and reconstructed. And it should be. We hope the romance can be ended. There must come a time when the train pulls into the station, we unfix our eyes from the window, and walk onto the platform, back into the onward rush of real life.

Notes

ABBREVIATIONS

DUA   Dalhousie University Archives
HSACP   Historic Sites Advisory Council Papers
JHA   *Journals of the House of Assembly, Nova Scotia*
PANS   Public Archives of Nova Scotia

ACKNOWLEDGMENTS

1 "Tartanism Triumphant: The Construction and Uses of Scottishness in Nova Scotia, 1934–1954," *Acadiensis* 22, no. 1 (Autumn 1992): 5–47; "History and the Tourist Gaze: The Politics of Commemoration in Nova Scotia, 1935–1964," *Acadiensis* 22, no. 2 (Spring 1993): 102–38.

PROLOGUE

1 Ian McKay, *The Quest of the Folk: Antimodernism and Cultural Selection in Twentieth-Century Nova Scotia* (Montreal and Kingston: McGill-Queen's University Press, 1994), xiii. The present volume comes as partial fulfilment of a promise made to readers of *Quest* to provide a "related" volume examining a broader range of the forms that emerged in interwar Nova Scotia, accompanying those of the "Folk" and working alongside them to construct an imagined Nova Scotia. However, there will remain at least one more "road to innocence" to explore before this saga is ended.

2 McKay, *Quest of the Folk*, 30.

3 Throughout this book, "race" denotes not a biological but a social fact. Historical actors will repeatedly advance race as a *bioethical reality* structuring human capacities and dispositions. We, however, consistently take the position that race is a *conceptual reality* structuring the analytic categories that enable people to interpret their world.

4 This spelling will be retained in the citation of original documents; Mi'kmaq will be used in the main text, with Mi'kmaw as the adjectival form.

5 Nova Scotia, *Nova Scotia, Canada's Ocean Playground* (Halifax: Nova Scotia Department of Highways, n.d. [1936]), unpaginated insert.

6 Drawing upon the *Encarta World English Dictionary* (Microsoft Corp., 1999).

7 Susan Smith, "Whitewashing Womanhood: The Politics of Race in Writing Women's History," *Canadian Review of Comparative Literature,* March 1995, 96.

8 See Michael Banton, "Historical and Contemporary Modes of Racialization," in Karim Murji and John Solomos, eds, *Racialization: Studies in Theory and Practice* (Oxford: Oxford University Press, 2005), citations at 51, 52, 53, 54, 56–7.

9 Bob Carter, *Realism and Racism: Concepts of Race in Sociological Research* (London: Routledge and Kegan Paul, 1985), 24.

10 This phrase occurs in the tourism literature of the time: see Nova Scotia Tourist Association, *Halifax, Nova Scotia: The Garrison City by the Sea* (Halifax: Nova Scotia Tourist Association, n.d. [1903]), 4.

11 Carter, *Realism and Racism,* 9.

12 The publication, interestingly, places the Irish among the "five distinct white races" in the montage but omits them altogether in the earlier discussion of "The races that settled the Province … the English, Scotch, Acadians and Hanoverians." As we shall see in chapter 6, the Irish were ambiguously positioned as a "founding race."

13 David Lowenthal, *The Heritage Crusade and the Spoils of History* (London: Viking, 1996), 121.

14 Henri-Dominique Paratte, *Acadians* (Halifax: Nimbus, 1998), 10.

15 Winthrop Pickard Bell, *The 'Foreign Protestants' and the Settlement of Nova Scotia: The History of a Piece of Arrested British Colonial Policy in the Eighteenth Century* (Toronto: University of Toronto Press, 1961), 304–5. The Foreign Protestants only became Hanoverian during the Great War of 1914–1918, when conflict with Germany made it advisable to pre-empt attacks on their own Teutonic character by rhetorically associating it with the home principality of the British royals.

16 This conception draws on Antonio Gramsci's influential notion of "organic intellectuals," for which see David Forgacs, *The Antonio Gramsci Reader: Selected Writings, 1916–1935* (New York: New York University Press, 2000), chap. 10.

17 As in a Nova Scotia tourism advertisement, "[s]ome places have incredible museums. Some places *are* incredible museums" (emphasis in original), Advertisement, *Harper's Magazine* 314, no. 1883 (April 2007): 69. Or, as the province's *Doers' and Dreamers' 2007 Guide* (Halifax: Nova Scotia Tourism, Culture and Heritage, 2007) advises: "We're not stuck in the past. We're blissfully embracing it" (17).

CHAPTER ONE

1 Lowenthal, *Heritage Crusade,* citations at 121, xi, 119, 121, 122, 128, 132 (see Prologue, n. 13).

2 For an illuminating discussion, see Jonathan Joseph, *Hegemony: A Realist Analysis* (London and New York: Routledge, 2002), 33.

3 Historians have known all too well for a few decades now that they do not innocently transcribe the facts (which then speak for themselves), but – even despite themselves – they emplot these facts according to metahistorical poetic modes such as tragedy, comedy, and irony. While this revelation rules out dustbowl empiricism, it does not rule out engagement with reality altogether. David Carr suggests that narrative forms "reveal themselves to be not distortions of, denials of, or escapes from reality, but extensions and

configurations of its primary features." To engage reality is not to reproduce it, of course. This is emphatically true of engagement with the past, which we can only conjecture by examining its faint traces. To follow Keith Jenkins, the people of today and the people of the past are separated by a yawning "ontological gap" that no amount of "epistemological effort" can ever close. We do not bridge this gap by gesturing proudly to the facts. Facts, as Thomas Haskell advises us, are themselves "low-level interpretive entities" that emerge from a process of "imaginative construction" (although never out of whole cloth). Themselves abstractions of a modest sort, facts are generated and acquire their meanings within shared conceptual frameworks. Constantin Fasolt cautions that the historian's insistence on total objectivity when examining unqualified facts discloses an uneasy worry that we may be unable to separate facts from the politically saturated contexts that have generated them: "Like an ugly frog, that fear sits right in the middle of the well from which historians draw water. Nothing has shaped the destiny of history more deeply. Nothing has been a sharper spur to history than the desire to defeat that fear with knowledge. What was the point of Ranke's ringing call for history 'wie es eigentlich gewesen,' if not precisely to proclaim the danger that history was all too likely *not* to report what actually happened?" Historians might find it tempting to evade this prophecy simply by adopting a commonsensical tone and marshalling footnotes. But appeals to common sense about the facts undermine the scholarly imperative to suspend or bracket the common sense of our own time in the interests of historical understanding. History inevitably involves frameworks of analysis, if only because factual evidence must be addressed within them if it is to be meaningful. Mere chronological sequence will not satisfy the disciplinary requirements of history. This gives rise, as Hayden White has often noted, to a tricky problem for historians: "It is the fact that they [events] can be recorded otherwise, in an order of narrative, that makes them, at one and the same time, questionable as to their authenticity and susceptible to being considered as tokens of reality ... The authority of the historical narrative is the authority of reality itself; the historical account endows this reality with form and thereby makes it desirable by the imposition upon its processes of the formal coherency that only stories possess." However much it might make us anxious, we cannot engage evidence outside such a framework (without which there would be no way to make the facts commensurable with human experiences and concepts). Interpretive problems arise, however, because these frameworks are never simply vehicles for factual content, but bring along a content of their own that arises from the eras and actors who birthed them. These historical narratives contain the seeds of present-minded concerns with the socio-political world and thus present the facts in a certain light – indeed, formulate the facts themselves in a particular way. The frameworks themselves thus become historical facts in their own right, facts of great interest to the historian. Bill Sewell explains it like this: "Significant and enduring changes in semiotic practices – that is to say, in social life – can only be explained by tracing out the temporally extended effects of semiotic innovations in the material world, by showing how they lead to the construction of facts on the ground whose presence and perpetuation reinforces (but may also inflect) the initial semiotic innovations." The framework that we have called Innocence arose in a particular economic and social context. Any framework that might replace it will do so as well. Such frameworks, by virtue of shaping facts and endowing them with meaning, redound upon their context in ways that preclude objectivity *stricto sensu,* but do fairly cry out for critical scrutiny. David Carr, *Time, Narrative, and History* (Bloomington: Indiana University Press, 1991), 16; Keith Jenkins, *Rethinking History*, 3rd ed. (London: Routledge, 2003); *On 'What is History?' From Carr and Elton to Rorty and White* (London: Routledge, 1995); Thomas L. Haskell, *Objectivity Is Not Neutrality: Explanatory Schemes in History* (Baltimore: Johns Hopkins University Press, 1998), 157; Constantin Fasolt, *The Limits of History* (Chicago: University of Chicago Press, 2003), xix; Hayden V. White, *The Content of the Form: Narrative Discourse and Historical Representation* (Baltimore: Johns Hopkins University Press, 1987), 20; William H. Sewell, Jr, *Logics of History: Social Theory and Social Transformation* (Chicago: University of Chicago Press, 2005), 362.

4 J.E. Tunbridge and G.J. Ashworth, *Dissonant Heritage: The Management of the Past as a Resource in Conflict* (Chichester: John Wiley & Sons, 1996), citations at 20, 21, 29–30.

5 There is a significant difference between the two regions, notwithstanding their close links. New Englanders could trade on a myth-symbol complex that proceeded from a notion that when Americans came to Salem or Plymouth, they were revisiting the birthplace of a nation that, from its seventeenth-century beginnings, had continuously pushed a frontier of settlement across a great continent. In contrast, the demographics of Canadian settlement – in an archipelago of distinct patches, settled at distinct times by distinct peoples – militated against the propagation of a myth of origins in such a "continuous national history." When a central Canadian comes to Halifax or Yarmouth, he or she is not presented with the same myth. For a discussion, see Cole Harris, "Regionalism and the Canadian Archipelago," in L.D. McCann and A. McGunn, eds, *Heartland and Hinterland* (Scarborough: Prentice-Hall, 1998).

6 Harold Connolly to Angus L. Macdonald, 4 September 1946, Angus L. Macdonald Papers [hereafter Macdonald Papers], vol. 904, file 28 f/2, Public Archives of Nova Scotia [hereafter PANS].

7 Ella K. Cork, Memorandum to the Members of the Historical Committee of the Canadian Tourism Association, 21 June 1950, Historic Sites Advisory Council Papers, MG 20, vol. 933, PANS.

8 See Malcolm Chase and Christopher Shaw, eds, *The Imagined Past: History and Nostalgia* (Manchester and New York: Manchester University Press, 1989); John Davis, "The Social Relations of the Production of History," in Elizabeth Tonkin et al., eds, *History and Ethnicity* (London: Routledge, 1989); David Gross, *The Past in Ruins: Tradition and the Critique of Modernity* (Amherst: University of Massachusetts Press, 1992); Robert Hewison, *The Heritage Industry: Britain in a Climate of Decline* (London: Methuen, 1987); Eric Hobsbawm and Terence Ranger, eds, *The Invention of Tradition* (New York and Cambridge: Cambridge University Press, 1983); D. Horne, *The Great Museum: The Representation of History* (London: Pluto Press, 1984); Michael Kammen, *Mystic Chords of Memory: The Transformation of Tradition in American Culture* (New York: Alfred A. Knopf, 1991); Michael Kammen, *In the Past Lane: Historical Perspectives on American Culture* (New York: Oxford University Press, 1997); Lowenthal, *Heritage Crusade*; Martha Norkunas, *The Politics of Public Memory: Tourism, History, and Ethnicity in Monterey, California* (Albany: SUNY Press, 1993); Richard Terdiman, *Present Past: Modernity and the Memory Crisis* (Ithaca and London: Cornell University Press, 1993); Susan Porter Benson et al., eds, *Pre-*

senting the Past: Essays on History and the Public (Philadelphia: Temple University Press, 1986); Patrick Wright, *On Living in an Old Country: The National Past in Contemporary Britain* (London: Verso, 1985), among many other titles.

9   See G.J. Ashworth and B. Goodall, eds, *Marketing Tourism Places* (London: Routledge, 1990); Louis Turner and John Ash, *The Golden Hordes: International Tourism and the Pleasure Periphery* (New York: St Martin's Press, 1976).

10 Shelley Baranowski and Ellen Furlough, introduction to Shelley Baranowski and Ellen Furlough, eds, *Being Elsewhere: Tourism, Consumer Culture, and Identity in Modern Europe and North America* (Ann Arbor: University of Michigan Press, 2001), 10. For a most impressive recent collection, see David M. Wrobel and Patrick T. Long, eds, *Seeing & Being Seen: Tourism in the American West* (Lawrence, Kans.: University Press of Kansas, 2001).

11 See Alisa Apostle, "Canada, Vacations Unlimited: The Canadian Government Tourism Industry, 1934–1959" (PhD thesis, Queen's University, 2003); Michael Dawson, *Selling British Columbia: Tourism and Consumer Culture, 1890–1970* (Vancouver and Toronto: University of British Columbia Press, 2004); Karen Dubinsky, *The Second Greatest Disappointment: Honeymooning and Tourism at Niagara Falls* (Toronto: Between the Lines Press, 1999); Patricia Jasen, *Wild Things: Nature, Culture, and Tourism in Ontario, 1790–1914* (Toronto: University of Toronto Press, 1995); Tina Loo, *States of Nature: Conserving Canada's Wildlife in the Twentieth Century* (Vancouver and Toronto: University of British Columbia Press, 2006).

12 For some of the major titles, see Beverly Boutilier and Alison Prentice, eds, *Creating Historical Memory: English-Canadian Women and the Work of History* (Vancouver: University of British Columbia Press, 1997); Caroline-Isabelle Caron, *Se créer des ancêtres: Un parcours généalogique nord-américain, XIXe et XXe siècles* (Sillery: Éditions du Septentrion, 2007); Colin M. Coates and Cecilia Morgan, *Heroines and History: Representations of Madeleine de Verchères and Laura Secord* (Toronto: University of Toronto Press, 2002); Alan Gordon, *Making Public Pasts: The Contested Terrain of Montréal's Public Memories, 1891–1930* (Montreal and Kingston: McGill-Queen's University Press, 2001); Alan Gordon, *The Hero and the Historians: Historiography and the Uses of Jacques Cartier* (Vancouver and Toronto: University of British Columbia Press, 2010); Patrice Groulx, *Pièges de la mémoire: Dollard des Ormeaux, les Amérindiens et nous* (Hull: Éditions Vents d'Ouest, 1998); José E. Igartua, *The Other Quiet Revolution: National Identities in English Canada, 1945–71* (Vancouver and Toronto: University of British Columbia Press, 2006); Viv Nelles, *The Art of Nation Building: Pageantry and Spectacle at Quebec's Tercentenary* (Toronto: University of Toronto Press, 1999); Gerald Pocius, *A Place to Belong: Community Order and Everyday Space in Calvert, Newfoundland* (Montreal and Kingston: McGill-Queen's University Press, 1991); Jennifer Reid, *Louis Riel and the Creation of Modern Canada: Mythic Discourse and the Postcolonial State* (Albuquerque: University of New Mexico Press, 2008); Ronald Rudin, *Founding Fathers: The Celebration of Champlain and Laval in the Streets of Quebec, 1878–1908* (Toronto: University of Toronto Press, 2003); Ronald Rudin, *Remembering and Forgetting in* Acadie: *A Historian's Journey through Public Memory* (Toronto: University of Toronto Press, 2009); Gerald Sider and Gavin Smith, eds, *Between History and Histories: The Making of Silences and Commemorations* (Toronto: University of Toronto Press, 1997); C.J. Taylor, *Negotiating the Past: The Making of Canada's National Historic Parks and Sites* (Montreal and Kingston: McGill-Queen's University Press, 1990); Jonathan

Vance, *Death So Noble: Memory, Meaning, and the First World War* (Vancouver: University of British Columbia Press, 1997). For introductions to academic history-writing in English Canada, see Carl Berger, *The Writing of Canadian History: Aspects of English-Canadian Historical Writing since 1900,* 2nd ed. (Toronto: University of Toronto Press, 1986); Marlene Shore, ed., *The Contested Past: Reading Canada's History* (Toronto: University of Toronto Press, 2002); Donald Wright, *The Professionalization of History in English Canada* (Toronto: University of Toronto Press, 2005).

13 She defines the contact zone as the "space of colonial encounters, the space in which peoples geographically and historically separated come into contact with each other and establish ongoing relations, usually involving conditions of coercion, radical inequality, and intractable conflict." Mary Louise Pratt, *Imperial Eyes: Travel Writing and Transculturation* (London and New York: Routledge, 1992), 6.

14 Over the course of history, the words "Nova Scotia" have named several very different territories and societies. When we use the name without qualification, we mean the area *now* encompassed by the Province of Nova Scotia – that is, all that territory within the confederation over which the Nova Scotia government is regarded to be the provincial government.

15 John Bartlet Brebner, *The Neutral Yankees of Nova Scotia: A Marginal Colony during the Revolutionary Years* (Toronto: McClelland & Stewart, 1969), 309–10.

16 Drawing principally upon Stephen A. Davis, "Early Societies: Sequences of Change," in Phillip A. Buckner and John G. Reid, eds, *The Atlantic Region to Confederation: A History* (Toronto: University of Toronto Press; Fredericton: Acadiensis Press, 1994), 3–21, citation at 20.

17 Drawing principally upon Ralph Pastore, "The Sixteenth Century: Aboriginal Peoples and European Contact," in Buckner and Reid, eds, *Atlantic Region to Confederation,* 22–39, citations at 37, 39; John G. Reid, "*Pax Britannica* or *Pax Indigena*? Planter Nova Scotia (1760–1782) and Competing Strategies of Pacification," *Canadian Historical Review* 85, no. 4 (December 2004): 669–92; Geoffrey Plank, *An Unsettled Conquest: The British Campaign against the Peoples of Acadia* (Philadelphia: University of Pennsylvania Press, 2001), 26; William Wicken, *Mi'kmaq Treaties on Trial: History, Land, and Donald Marshall Junior* (Toronto: University of Toronto Press, 2002), 57.

18 They could draw upon the emergent work of early-modern political theory, exemplified by John Locke (himself, perhaps not coincidentally, a shareholder in the colonizing Virginia Company), to argue that unenclosed, uncultivated land was free for the taking. Edmund Morgan summarizes their view: "land could rightly be taken, even in Utopia, from those who did not work it. Work came first, property rights second." Edmund S. Morgan, *American Slavery, American Freedom: The Ordeal of Colonial Virginia* (New York: W.W. Norton & Company, 1975), 24.

19 Elizabeth Mancke and John G. Reid, "Elites, States, and the Imperial Contest for Acadia," in John G. Reid et al., *The 'Conquest' of Acadia, 1710: Imperial, Colonial, and Aboriginal Constructions* (Toronto: University of Toronto Press, 2004), 25–47, citation at 29.

20 John Bartlet Brebner, *New England's Outpost: Acadia before the Conquest of Canada* (Hamden, Conn.: Archon Books, 1965 [first published 1927]), 21.

21 The Treaties of Saint-Germain-en-Laye (1632), Breda (1667), and Ryswick (1697) punctuated this process.

22 Drawing principally upon Elizabeth Mancke and John G. Reid, "Elites, States, and the Imperial Contest for Acadia," in Reid et al., *'Conquest' of Acadia, 1710,* 25–47, citation at 37–8; and from Naomi Griffiths, *The Contexts of Acadian History 1686–1784* (Montreal and Kingston: McGill-Queen's University Press, 1992).

23 A perception echoed in the U.S. name for the disturbances of the period: "The French and Indian Wars."

24 Drawing upon Maurice Basque, "The Third Acadia: Political Adaptation and Societal Change," in Reid et al., *'Conquest' of Acadia, 1710,* 155–78, citations at 169; he in turn draws upon Donald Desserud, "Nova Scotia and the American Revolution: A Study of Neutrality and Moderation in the Eighteenth Century," in Margaret Conrad, ed., *Making Adjustments: Change and Continuity in Planter Nova Scotia 1759–1800* (Fredericton: Acadiensis Press, 1991), 89–112. Naomi Griffiths, *From Migrant to Acadian: A North American Border People 1604–1755* (Montreal and Kingston: McGill-Queen's University Press, 2005), is a 633-page magisterial narrative that brings new depth and complexity to Acadian history.

25 Other moments of abortive Scottish imperialism in the seventeenth century included ventures in New Jersey (1683), Carolina (1684), and Darien (Panama) in 1695, the latter an enormously expensive failure.

26 George A. Rawlyk, *Nova Scotia's Massachusetts: A Study of Massachusetts–Nova Scotia Relations 1630 to 1784* (Montreal and London: McGill-Queen's University Press, 1973), xiii.

27 Geoffrey Plank, *An Unsettled Conquest: The British Campaign against the Peoples of Acadia* (Philadelphia: University of Pennsylvania Press, 2001), citations at 11, 15.

28 Barry Moody, "Making a British Nova Scotia," in Reid et al., *'Conquest' of Acadia, 1710,* 127–54, citation at 139.

29 On Louisbourg, note especially Christopher Moore, *Louisbourg Portraits* (Toronto: Macmillan of Canada, 1982).

30 Wicken, *Mi'kmaq Treaties,* 82–3.

31 For an overview, see John Grenier, *The First Way of War: American War Making on the Frontier, 1607–1814* (Cambridge, Mass.: Cambridge University Press, 2005). As he remarks, "[E]arly Americans understood war to involve disrupting enemy troop, supply, and support networks; gathering intelligence through scouting and the taking of prisoners; ambushing and destroying enemy detachments; serving as patrol and flanking parties for friendly forces; operating as advance and rear guards for regular forces; and, most important, destroying enemy villages and fields and killing and intimidating enemy noncombatant populations" (1).

32 Plank, *Unsettled Conquest,* 78.

33 Wicken, *Mi'kmaq Treaties,* citations at 219. Also see Plank, *Unsettled Conquest,* 86.

34 For an interesting discussion, see A.J.B. Johnston, "Borderland Worries: Loyalty Oaths in *Acadie*/Nova Scotia, 1654–1755," *French Colonial History* 4 (2003): 31–48.

35 Given the high levels of Mi'kmaw/Acadian intermarriage suggested by William Wicken, this would have been a matter of no small concern. Wicken, *Mi'kmaq Treaties,* 47.

36 For a sterling account, see James Pritchard, *Anatomy of a Naval Disaster: The 1746 French Expedition to North America* (Montreal and Kingston: McGill-Queen's University Press, 1995).

37 Drawing upon Stephen E. Patterson, "1744–1763: Colonial Wars and Aboriginal Peoples," in Buckner and Reid, eds, *Atlantic Region to Confederation*, 125–55, citation at 129.

38 The French kept French Guiana, Saint-Domingue (present-day Haiti), and Saint Pierre et Miquelon; Guadeloupe and Martinique were returned to them.

39 Reid, "*Pax*," 673. This essay can also be found in John G. Reid, *Essays on Northeastern North America, Seventeenth and Eighteenth Centuries* (Toronto: University of Toronto Press, 2008), citation at 174.

40 The historians of the 1970s and 1980s often explored Nova Scotia history outside the geo-historical parameters suggested by the Brebners of an earlier generation. We might cite the micro-histories of crime, propriety, and reform of Judith Fingard; or the recreation of the elite of Halifax, in essence seen as a failed metropolis, by David Sutherland; or the explorations of labour history by David Frank, to name but three central figures.

41 For a useful summary of the evidence, see Dean Jobb, *The Acadians: A People's Story of Exile and Triumph* (Mississauga: John Wiley & Sons, 2005): "Artifacts unearthed at Acadian sites over the years include shards of English and Chinese porcelain, French pottery and New England earthenware, evidence of prosperity and proof of the extent of trade between Acadie and the outside world. Archeologists have found English clay pipes, French wine bottles, and fancy buckles, along with oversized iron keys that show a few folks locked their doors. And Acadie's economy was not completely moneyless – eighteenth-century British, French, and even Spanish coins have been found. The basement of the harbormaster's house that stood at Port-la-Joye, near present-day Charlottetown, Prince Edward Island, until the 1740s yielded four weathered coins, including a gold piece the size of a quarter" (49).

42 These considerations must remain fragmentary and unspecific, since we lack a major monograph that would allow us to relate this period of Nova Scotia's history to the rise of merchant capitalism in the world economy.

43 M. Brook Taylor, *Promoters, Patriots, and Partisans: Historiography in Nineteenth-Century Canada* (Toronto: University of Toronto Press, 1989), 55.

44 Ibid., 259. Taylor is citing in the second instance W.J. Eccles, "The History of New France according to Francis Parkman," *William and Mary Quarterly*, ser. 3, vol. 18 (1961): 163. For the phenomenal hold of Parkman over writers of school textbooks in Canada down to the 1960s, as evidenced by George Brown's *The Story of Canada*, see José E. Igartua, *The Other Quiet Revolution: National Identities in English Canada, 1945–71* (Vancouver and Toronto: University of British Columbia Press, 2006), 64–5.

45 Francis Parkman, *A Half-Century of Conflict* (New York and London: Collier, 1962 [first published 1892]), 144.

46 Parkman revealingly pays no attention to the costs in lost labour and time incurred by Acadians at Minas pursuing a case in Annapolis Royal. Nor does his account attend to the de facto subsidization of the institution of private property that state-run law enforcement invariably provides in any liberal society, nineteenth-century Boston included.

47 The key text here is D.C. Harvey, "The Intellectual Awakening of Nova Scotia," *Dalhousie Review* 13, no. 1 (April 1933): 1–22.

48 "The golden age of Nova Scotia," Harvey's disciple J.S. Martell lamented during the Depression, "is to-day almost a forgotten age." J.S. Martell, "The Progress of Nova Scotia after 1815," *Journal of Education* 7, no. 6 (December 1936): 1021–3, citation at 1023.

49 Brebner, *New England's Outpost*, 33, 225, 232, 231, 38, 40. W.S. MacNutt erred when he said, of Brebner's *New England's Outpost*, that "[b]eneath the clear exposition of what really did happen, considerations of morality and of man's inhumanity to man, beloved by dialecticians and controversialists who labour out of context, disappeared." Such considerations in fact subtly permeate Brebner's account. See W.S. MacNutt, introduction to J.B. Brebner, *Neutral*, xi. MacNutt compounded his error when he went on to argue that "Governor Charles Lawrence, the victim of a hundred years of biased and sentimentalist writing, emerged as a more than usually competent and relatively decent officer who did what he had to do in the line of duty" (xi). His description utterly falsifies Brebner's portrait of a man who, although "no human ogre," lacked "the imagination or moral courage to draw back" from a fateful step, a misplaced martinet who "found escape from the dictates of humanity, in the manner of soldiers, by regarding as enemies the people who would not bend to his will" (*New England's Outpost*, 233).

50 Brebner, *Neutral Yankees*, 13. For a similar appraisal of Nova Scotia's economic history from 1740 to 1815, see Julian Gwyn, *Excessive Expectations: Maritime Commerce & the Economic Development of Nova Scotia, 1740–1870* (Montreal and Kingston: McGill-Queen's University Press, 1998), 226: "In the early economic history to 1815, which was dominated by wars and their aftermath, public enterprise, in the form of British governmental spending, was crucial to the still painfully underpopulated colony. In that long, early phase, private capital appears mainly to have been derived from the public trough."

51 Brebner, *New England's Outpost*, 233.

52 Brebner, *Neutral Yankees*, xix.

53 Ibid., 309–10.

54 Brebner, *New England's Outpost*, 222

55 J.S. Martell, review of *The Neutral Yankees of Nova Scotia*, *Journal of Education* 8, no. 7 (December 1937): 1055–8.

56 Moody, "Making a British Nova Scotia," 128.

57 Rawlyk, *Nova Scotia's Massachusetts*.

58 Gordon Stewart and George Rawlyk, *A People Highly Favoured of God: The Nova Scotia Yankees and the American Revolution* (Toronto: Macmillan of Canada, 1972).

59 See Margaret Conrad, ed., *They Planted Well: New England Planters in Maritime Canada* (Fredericton: Acadiensis Press, 1988), citation at 9; also Conrad, ed., *Making Adjustments*.

60 This is so even though Brebner was, with gross injustice, impugned as a "continentalist" – read: U.S. annexationist – by certain of his central Canadian colleagues who felt he accorded too little importance to the St Lawrence–bound trajectory of national history as he became more insistent about contextualizing historical events within an integrated Atlantic world wherein eighteenth-century New England bulked rather larger than the thinly settled contemporary Canadian Shield. Sadly, this author of *The North Atlantic Triangle* did not live long enough to see transatlanticism become modish within

academe. See Rohit Aggarwala, "'Non-resident Me': John Bartlet Brebner and the Canadian Historical Association," *Journal of the Canadian Historical Association* 10 (1999): 237–77.

61 See George Rawlyk, "J.B. Brebner and Some Recent Trends in Eighteenth-Century Maritime Historiography," in Conrad, ed., *They Planted Well*, 97–119, citation at 103, 99.

62 Brebner, *New England's Outpost*, 28.

63 Reid, "*Pax*," 669–92.

64 See Brebner, *Neutral Yankees*, 40. For newer work, see J. Sherman Bleakney, *Sods, Soil, and Spades: The Acadians at Grand Pré and Their Dykeland Legacy* (Montreal and Kingston: McGill-Queen's University Press, 2004).

65 Robert Sauvageau, *Acadie: La guerre de cents ans des Français d'Amérique aux Maritimes et en Louisiane, 1670–1769* (Paris: Berger-Levrault, 1987); for this description, one of many, of the entirely peaceful Acadians, see Bleakney, *Sods*, 3; Jean Daigle, "Acadia from 1604 to 1763: An Historical Synthesis," in Jean Daigle, ed., *Acadia of the Maritimes: Thematic Studies from the Beginning to the Present* (Moncton: Chaire d'études acadiennes, 1995), 1–43; Brebner, *New England's Outpost*, 45; Maurice Basque, "The Third Acadia: Political Adaptation and Societal Change," in Reid et al., eds, '*Conquest' of Acadia*, 155–77, citation at 159.

66 See especially D.G. Bell, *Early Loyalist Saint John: The Origin of New Brunswick Politics, 1783–1786* (Fredericton: New Ireland Press, 1983).

67 On early divisions of opinion among the New Englanders, see George Rawlyk, *Yankees at Louisbourg* (Oronto: University of Maine Press, 1967), which points out that some New England merchants were glad to see Louisbourg returned to the French in 1748; on the blacks, see James W. St G. Walker's classic study *The Black Loyalists: The Search for a Promised Land in Nova Scotia and Sierra Leone 1783–1870* (New York: Africana Publishing and Dalhousie University Press, 1976); on the Loyalists, see especially Neil MacKinnon, *This Unfriendly Soil: The Loyalist Experience in Nova Scotia 1783–1791* (Montreal and Kingston: McGill-Queen's University Press, 1986); and also Marion Robertson, *King's Bounty: A History of Early Shelburne, Nova Scotia* (Halifax: Nova Scotia Museum, 1983); on the Scots, see J.M. Bumsted, *The People's Clearance: Highland Emigration to British North America, 1770–1815* (Edinburgh: Edinburgh University Press; Winnipeg: University of Manitoba Press, 1982).

68 Sewell, *Logics of History*, 101.

69 Taylor, *Promoters, Patriots, and Partisans*, citations at 267, 268, 268–9, 269, 270–1.

70 Joseph Howe, *Western and Eastern Rambles: Travel Sketches of Nova Scotia* (Toronto, 1973 [Halifax, 1821]), 92–3. For a stimulating recent study of British travellers' impressions of Halifax, see Jeffrey L. McNairn, "'Everything was new, yet familiar': British Travellers, Halifax and the Ambiguities of Empire," *Acadiensis* 36, no. 2 (Spring 2007): 28–54, which notes there were only "a few half-hearted attempts to identify the most 'romantic spot' of Halifax harbour or to invest it with patriotic grandeur by associating it with the sinking of the French fleet in the Bedford Basin in 1758" (32).

71 Andrew Learmont Spedon, *Rambles among the Blue-Noses; or, Reminiscences of a Tour Through New Brunswick and Nova Scotia, During the Summer of 1862* (Montreal: John Lovell, 1863), 9.

72 Herbert Crosskill, *Nova Scotia: Its Climate, Resources and Advantages. Being a General Description of the Province, for the Information of Intending Emigrants* (Halifax, 1872), 1.

73 R.R. McLeod, *Markland or Nova Scotia. Its History, Natural Resources and Native Beauties* (Halifax, 1903), 247 (emphasis added).

74 Richard Lewes Dashwood, *Chiploquorgan; Or, Life by the Camp Fire in Dominion of Canada and Newfoundland* (London, 1872), 199. For an insightful analysis that reveals how such writers of travel accounts saw hunting as "fraught with economic and moral lessons," see Jeffrey L. McNairn, "Meaning and Markets: Hunting, Economic Development and British Imperialism in Maritime Travel Narratives to 1870," *Acadiensis* 34, no. 2 (Spring 2005): 3–25 (citation at 23).

75 Crosskill, *Nova Scotia*, 2–3.

76 Copy of *Chiploquorgan* at the Nova Scotia Archives and Records Management, PANS.

77 *Herald* (Halifax), 21 March 1913. The Liberal premier's endorsement of Willson did little to temper the Tory newspaper's outrage at a book that was, despite its title, a generally admiring portrait of a progressive province.

78 For a more general discussion of progressivism in the province, see Ian McKay, "The 1910s: The Stillborn Triumph of Progressive Reform," in E.R. Forbes and D.A. Muise, eds, *The Atlantic Provinces in Confederation* (Toronto: University of Toronto Press; Fredericton: Acadiensis Press, 1993): 192–229.

79 Paul B. Williams, "A Vision of Progress and Nostalgia: The Halifax Memorial Tower," *International Journal of Heritage Studies* 9, no. 3 (2003): 243–65, citations at 252–4, 254, 255, 256, 258, 261, 262, 264–5. See also Paul Williams, "Erecting 'an instructive object': The Case of the Halifax Memorial Tower," *Acadiensis* 36, no. 2 (Summer 2007): 91–112.

80 Williams, "Vision."

81 G.F. Parker, *A Tripod Trip along the South Shore of Nova Scotia* (Yarmouth, 1899), 21, 24.

82 Lady Aberdeen, *My Canadian Journal 1872–8* (Don Mills: Longmans Canada, 1969 [first published London, 1891]), 103. Even the renowned Canadian poet Charles G.D. Roberts (whom we shall meet again as a master of romantic Victorian travel writing) advised all visitors to experience first-hand the "great grim pile of Mount Hope Lunatic Asylum." Charles G.D. Roberts, *The Land of Evangeline and the Gateways Thither* (Kentville: Dominion Atlantic Railway, n.d. [1895]), 51. The same building greatly impressed the French race theorist Joseph Arthur de Gobineau: "[O]n high ground covered with woods and in the middle of an English-style park laid out with unusual care and good taste, stands a huge structure, so elegantly built that one first imagines it to be the residence of some rich or powerful dignitary. This is a cardinal error. There the colony has erected at great expense an asylum for its insane." Joseph Arthur de Gobineau, *A Gentleman in the Outports: Gobineau and Newfoundland*, ed. and trans. Michael Wilkshire (translation of *Voyage à Terre-Neuve Suivi de la Chasse au Caribou* [Paris, 1861]) (Ottawa: Carleton University Press, 1993), 72.

83 Herald (Halifax), *Nova Scotia, the Atlantic Pier of America*, special ed. (n.p. [Halifax], n.d. [1931]).

84 Halifax & South Western Railway, *The Ocean Shore* (n.p. [Halifax], n.d. [c. 1908]), 7; *The Evangeline Land: made famous by the expulsion of the Acadian farmers by the British government on account of their fidelity to their French King, and afterwards immortalized by Longfellow*

(Kentville: A.L. Hardy, n.d. [c. 1902]); *Yarmouth, Town and County, Nova Scotia, Canada: 'Western Gateway of Nova Scotia'* (Yarmouth, 1918; repr. Yarmouth County Historical Society, 1995), which includes a lovely photo spread of the "Noted Hawthorn Hedges" of Yarmouth (10).

85 Robert Everest, *A Journey Through the United States and Part of Canada* (London: John Chapman, 1855), 4–5.

86 Frederic S. Cozzens, *Acadia; or, A Month with the Blue Noses* (New York: Derby & Jackson, 1859), citations at 20, 22, 23.

87 Ian Radforth, *Royal Spectacle: The 1860 Visit of the Prince of Wales to Canada and the United States* (Toronto: University of Toronto Press, 2004), citations at 254–5, 255–7.

88 A[lexander] Heatherington, *A Practical Guide for Tourists, Miners, and Investors And All Persons Interested in the Development of the Gold Fields of Nova Scotia* (Montreal: John Lovell, 1868), citation at 12.

89 Beckles Willson, *Nova Scotia: The Province That Has Been Passed By* (London: Constable and Co., 1912), 40.

90 Margaret Warner Morley, *Down North and Up Along* (New York, 1912), 134.

91 Canada, Minister of the Interior, *Nova Scotia Canada: The Country and Its People and the Opportunity It Offers to Other People* (Ottawa, 1907), 13–14.

92 Canada, Minister of the Interior, *Nova Scotia Canada: Fertile, Productive Lands, Free School System, Contented and Law-Abiding People* (Ottawa, 1914), 33.

93 Crosskill, *Nova Scotia,* 74–5.

94 Nova Scotia Tourist Association, Report, *Journals of the House of Assembly* [hereafter JHA], 1923, 21.

95 For a superb study of this phenomenon on the West Coast, see Dawson, *Selling British Columbia.*

96 One reason for changing the "Nova Scotia Tourist Association" to the "Nova Scotia Publicity Bureau" in 1923 was to avoid the unfortunate connotations of the very word "tourist," which the association feared would evoke distaste among "the most desirable class of summer visitors," for whom the term suggested "an organization for the exploitation rather than the assistance of the stranger." Nova Scotia Tourist Association, Report, 1923, JHA (1924): 15. For the genealogy of the term "tourist," see Stephen Prickett, "Circles and Straight Lines: Romantic Versions of Tourism," in Harmut Berghoff, Barbara Korte, Ralf Schneider, and Christopher Harvie, eds, *The Making of Modern Tourism: The Cultural History of the British Experience, 1600–2000* (Basingstoke and New York: Palgrave, 2002), 69–84. As Prickett remarks (70), "The word 'tourist' was in fact a very recent addition to the English language. One of the first recorded uses in the OED is in 1800, when Samuel Pegge, in his *Anecdotes of the English Language* notes that 'A traveller nowadays is called a tour-*ist.*' The model for this, of course, was the so-called 'Grand Tour' of Europe, which was almost an obligatory rite of passage for the young eighteenth-century English aristocrat."

97 Note James H. Morrison, "American Tourism in Nova Scotia, 1871–1940," *Nova Scotia Historical Review* 2, no. 2 (1982): 40–51.

98 Dashwood, *Chiploquorgan,* 77. As Jeffrey McNairn points out, "In the hands of British officers, antimodernism denigrated the middle-class 'tourists' who later sustained it" ("Meaning and Markets," 18).

99　Nova Scotia, Tourism Reports, JHA, 1922–39. In 1899, the 411,588 citizens of New Hampshire welcomed 174,000 summer visitors. Brown, *Inventing New England*, 155.

100　Brown, *Inventing New England*, 201.

101　The broader North American historiography of tourism might pursue the more general theme of the northward march of a "therapeutic frontier," pushing up from New York and southern New England first into coastal New Brunswick, Quebec, and Nova Scotia, then into the "provincial north," and finally – in the 1990s – extending all the way to chilly Ellesmere Island.

102　*Chronicle* (Halifax), 14 June 1938.

103　Local tourist historians have yet figure out how to assess the proportions of Canadian-versus-American tourists. Until the late 1950s, the inclusion of all auto traffic coming across the New Brunswick/Nova Scotia border inflated the Canadian totals, since much of this traffic would have consisted not of tourists in any meaningful sense, but rather of commuters.

104　See Halifax Herald, *Nova Scotia, the Atlantic Pier of America*.

105　See E.R. Forbes, *Challenging the Regional Stereotype: Essays on the 20th Century Maritimes* (Fredericton: Acadiensis Press, 1989).

106　Brown, epilogue in *Inventing New England*. The parallels between the touristic discovery of post-fishery Cape Cod and that of Nova Scotia's South Shore are uncanny.

107　See Michael Berkowitz, "A 'New Deal' for Leisure: Making Mass Tourism during the Great Depression," in Baranowski and Furlough, eds, *Being Elsewhere,* 185–212.

108　See Ian McKay, "Among the Fisherfolk: J.F.B. Livesay and the Invention of Peggy's Cove," *Journal of Canadian Studies* 23, nos 1/2 (Spring/Summer 1988): 23–45.

109　See McKay, *Quest of the Folk* (see Prologue, n. 1).

110　For an indispensable guide to these developments, see Alisa Apostle, "Canada, Vacations Unlimited: The Canadian Government Tourism Industry, 1934–1959" (PhD thesis, Queen's University, 2003).

111　For example, in the 1923 festivities surrounding the anniversary of the landing of the *Hector* (the province's first large publicly funded historical extravaganza), this vessel carrying Scots to Nova Scotia was represented as a proud moment not just in Nova Scotia history but also in Canadian history; the governor-general himself was on hand to commemorate this Scottish-Canadian equivalent of the *Mayflower*. See Michael Boudreau, "A 'Rare and Unusual Treat of Historical Significance': The 1923 Hector Celebration and the Political Economy of the Past," *Journal of Canadian Studies* 28, no. 4 (Winter 1993–94): 28–48. For an important new statement on the theme of antimodernism and Canadian nationalism, see Benedict Anderson, "Staging Antimodernism in the Age of High Capitalist Nationalism," in Lynda Jessup, ed., *Antimodernism and Artistic Experience: Policing the Boundaries of Modernity* (Toronto: University of Toronto Press, 2001), 97–103.

112　Stan Rogers, "Bluenose," on the posthumous *Home in Halifax* CD (1994).

113　Archibald MacMechan, *Storied Halifax, the Warden of the Honour of the North,* 3rd ed. (n.p. [Ottawa]: Canadian Government Railways, 1913), 8–9.

114　*Sketches of Halifax: presented by the Halifax Hotel Halifax Canada* (n.p., n.d. [Halifax, c. 1916]).

115　Nova Scotia, *Nova Scotia by the Sea* (n.p. [Halifax], n.d. [c. 1928], 5.

116　Emma-Lindsay Squier, *On Autumn Trails and Adventures in Captivity* (London, 1925), 9.

117 *Sydney Post-Record*, 1 July 1936.

118 Betty D. Thornley, *Acadia* (n.p. [Kentville]: Dominion Atlantic Railway, n.d. [1920s]).

119 Thomas H. Raddall, "The Literary Tradition," *Canadian Author and Bookman* 25, no. 3 (Autumn 1949): 3–7, citation at 7.

120 T. Stephen Henderson, *Angus L. Macdonald: A Provincial Liberal* (Toronto: University of Toronto Press, 2007), 212.

CHAPTER TWO

1 Henry Wadsworth Longfellow, *Evangeline: A Tale of Acadie* (Halifax: Nimbus, 1985). This was the seventeenth local printing of the poem.

2 Drawing upon the account in M. Brook Taylor, "The Poetry and Prose of History: Evangeline and the Historians of Nova Scotia," *Journal of Canadian Studies* 23, nos 1 and 2 (Spring/Summer 1988): 50; Naomi Griffiths, "Longfellow's *Evangeline*: The Birth and Acceptance of a Legend," in P.A. Buckner and David Frank, eds, *Atlantic Canada after Confederation: The Acadiensis Reader*, vol. 2 (Fredericton: Acadiensis Press, 1985).

3 Christopher Irmscher, *Longfellow Redux* (Urbana and Chicago: University of Illinois Press, 2006), 3, 60, 70, 179.

4 Paul Friedland glosses the state of nature as an ur-past without events in his *Political Actors: Representative Bodies and Theatricality in the Age of the French Revolution* (Ithaca: Cornell University Press, 2002), 115.

5 Griffiths, "Longfellow's *Evangeline*." Also see T.C. Haliburton, *An historical and statistical account of Nova-Scotia: illustrated by a map of the province, and several engravings*, 2 vols. (Halifax: Joseph Howe, 1829).

6 The whole point of the ingenious *aboiteaux* was to desalinate the coastlands of the Fundy shore by allowing saltwater marshes to drain into the Minas Basin through an opening in the dykes at low tide yet preventing the ingress of additional seawater at high tide. Longfellow, then, got it exactly backwards.

7 See John Frederic Herbin, *History of Grand Pré*, 5th ed. (Kentville: Kentville Publishing Co., 1969 [first published Toronto: W. Briggs, 1898]), 158–61. As he points out, even the priest who figures in the poem had already been apprehended by the British and was, consequently, unavailable for the purposes Longfellow assigned him. See also Robert Viau, in *Grand-Pré: Lieu de mémoire, lieu d'appartenance* (Longueuil: Publications MNH, 2005), who adds that the single-child, single-father Lajeunesse and Bellefontaine families described by Longfellow were highly atypical of Acadia.

8 Naomi E.S. Griffiths, *The Contexts of Acadian History 1686–1784* (Montreal and Kingston: McGill-Queen's University Press, 1992), 63–4.

9 Thomas Garden Barnes, "'The Dayly Cry for Justice': The Juridical Failure of the Annapolis Royal Regime, 1713–1749," in Philip Girard and Jim Phillips, eds, *Essays in the History of Canadian Law* (Toronto: University of Toronto Press, 1990), 10–41 (examples from 29).

10 In 1961, even the provincial archivist would still describe "[t]hese people" as a "close-knit, homogeneous and almost self-sufficient colony. On the whole they were happy, healthy and virtuous, attached to their religion and their traditions, influenced by their environment, and almost independent of the outside world." C. Bruce Fergusson, introduction to Longfellow, *Evangeline*, 17.

11 Reid et al., *'Conquest' of Acadia, 1710,* xiii (see chap. 1, n. 19).
12 Griffiths, "Longfellow's *Evangeline,*" 66–7.
13 Cited in Taylor, "Poetry and Prose," 51.
14 For a discussion, see Emanuele Saccarelli, *Gramsci and Trotsky in the Shadow of Stalinism: The Political Theory and Practice of Opposition* (New York and London: Routledge, 2008), 98–9; David Harvey, *The Condition of Postmodernity* (Oxford: Blackwell, 1989); and, most particularly, Michael Löwy, *The Politics of Combined and Uneven Development: The Theory of Permanent Revolution* (London: Verso, 1981).
15 For an extended discussion of this theme in the regional context, see McKay, *Quest of the Folk* (see Prologue, n. 1).
16 Karl Marx and Frederick Engels, "The Manifesto of the Communist Party," in Karl Marx and Frederick Engels, *Collected Works* (Moscow: Progress Publishers, 1976), vol. 6, especially 507–14, for their critique of "Reactionary Socialism" and "Conservative, or Bourgeois Socialism."
17 It seems heartless, but necessary, to point out that contemporary historical evidence suggests not only the existence of locks in pre-1755 Acadia, but even the presence of at least one actual locksmith. See Jobb, *Acadians,* 49 (see chap. 1, n. 41).
18 Marx and Engels, "Manifesto of the Communist Party," 516.
19 Cozzens, *Acadia,* 60 (see chap. 1, n. 86).
20 A.J.B. Johnston, "'Imagining Paradise': The Visual Depiction of Pre-deportation Acadia, 1850–2000," *Journal of Canadian Studies* 38, no. 2 (2004): 105–29.
21 Cozzens, *Acadia,* 38–9.
22 Barbara Le Blanc, *Postcards from Acadie: Grand-Pré, Evangeline & the Acadian Identity* (Kentville: Gaspereau Press, 2003), 51.
23 Mde Morel de la Durantaye, *A Visit to the Home of Evangeline. Historical Romance of the Acadians* (Detroit: Wilton-Smith Co., 1892), 9–10.
24 Cited in Johnston, "Imagining Paradise," 112.
25 Charles G.D. Roberts, *A Sister to Evangeline: Being the Story of Yvonne de Lamourie, and how she went into exile with the villagers of Grand Pré* (Boston, 1898), 7–8.
26 Johnston, "Imagining Paradise."
27 Cozzens, *Acadia,* 56.
28 L'Abbé H.R. Casgrain, *Un Pèlerinage au Pays d'Évangéline* (Quebec: J.L. Demers, 1887), 84. "Quant à leur moralité, elle n'a pas besoin d'autres preuves que l'étonnante fécondité des familles, qui n'a été égalée que par celle des pasteurs boers du Transvaal."
29 T.J. Jackson Lears, *No Place of Grace: Antimodernism and the Transformation of American Culture, 1880–1920* (New York: Pantheon Books, 1981). As he remarks, "Embracing premodern symbols as alternatives to the vagueness of liberal Protestantism or the sterility of nineteenth-century positivism, antimodern seekers nevertheless adapted those symbols for modern ends. Craftsmanship became less a path to satisfying communal work than a therapy for tired businessmen. The martial ideal ennobled not a quest for the Grail but a quest for foreign markets. Even Catholic mysticism, art, and ritual were adjusted to secular purposes" (xv).
30 For an interesting discussion, see Jean Daigle, *The Acadians of the Maritimes* (Moncton: Centre d'études acadiennes, 1982), especially chap. 1.
31 Bernard Pothier, "Sigogne, Jean-Mandé," in Frances G. Halpenny, ed., *Dictionary of*

Canadian Biography, vol. 7: *1836 to 1850* (Toronto: University of Toronto Press, 1988), 800–6, citations at 802, 803.

32 Gobineau, *Gentleman in the Outports*, 64 (see chap. 1, n. 82).

33 Casgrain, *Pèlerinage*, citations at 85–6, 386, 389. "La population de Grand-Pré était répandue par essaims dans le village, ou apparaissait aux fenêtres ouvertes et devant les portes des maisons. Çà et là s'élevaient des cris joyeux d'enfants attroupés sous les arbres des vergers chargés de fruits, ou des voix de femmes qui chantaient pour endormir leurs nouveau-nés. Quelques vieillards, assis sur les clôtures, fumaient tranquillement leurs pipes en devisant du lendemain. Des groupes de garçons et de jeunes filles, vêtus de leurs habits du dimanche, passaient, en causant, aux abords de l'église; les jeunes gens habillés d'étoffe tissée à la maison; les jeunes filles portant jupon et *mantelet*, coiffées de chapeaux de paille tissée de leurs mains. Bien des couples qui, en ce moment, se faisaient des aveux et formaient des projets d'union, étaient loin de se douter qu'ils étaient à la veille d'être séparés pour ne plus jamais se revoir." "Comment! leur dit-il, n'avez-vous pas honte? Vous, des Acadiennes? Vous rougissez de votre nationalité! Je vous connais au reste; vous êtes loin de valoir ces deux braves femmes dont vous vous moquez. Je les connais elles aussi, ce sont d'excellentes mères de famille, l'exemple de leur paroisse; et vous!" "Toutes les races, toutes les sectes de l'Amérique du Nord s'accordent à regarder les Acadiens comme un peuple honnête, paisible, soumis aux lois. Voilà l'école où leurs générations ont été formées."

34 Jean-Paul Hautecoeur, *L'Acadie du Discours: Pour une sociologie de la culture acadienne* (Québec: Les Presses de l'Université Laval, 1975). For other insightful analyses of the "providential" interpretation of Acadian history, see Viau, *Grand-Pré*, 79, 113, and especially 155, where this framework is nicely summarized as follows: "Les Acadiens sont revenus au pays malgré de nombreuses vicissitudes. Après la traversée d'une longe période obscure, ils connaissent une résurrection, mettent en place des institutions sociales, construisent des églises et des écoles, et peuvent maintenant poursuivre leur mission rédemptrice. Les Acadiens forment un peuple élu au destin providentiel et dans les romans qui se déroulent à Grand-Pré, dans les sermons des prélats, dans les discours des dignitaires, on les enjoint de poursuive leur tâche et de se conformer à leur mission apostolique afin de hâter l'avènement du royaume éternel des justes. Par leur courage, leur travail et leur foi, ils participent à l'avènement du royaume de Dieu sur terre." See also Caroline-Isabelle Caron, "Se souvenir de l'Acadia d'antan: Representations du passé historique dans le cadre de celebrations commemoratives locales en Nouvelle-Écosse au milieu du 20e siècle," *Acadiensis* 36, no. 1 (printemps 2007), 65–6, for a fascinating look at providentialism in local historical commemorations.

35 A.I. Silver, *The French-Canadian Idea of Confederation, 1864–1900* (Toronto: University of Toronto Press, 1982), 220, 223.

36 Griffiths, "Longfellow's *Evangeline*," 66.

37 Irmscher, *Longfellow Redux,* 247.

38 This estimate is a bit dicey. The concluding section, although not literally set in Nova Scotia, urges the reader to reflect on it.

39 As he neglects to tell them, but Longfellow the well-informed abolitionist probably knew, one key to their future profits will come from owning African slaves, as most of the Acadian households in Louisiana would eventually do, but such was the price of

progress. Carl A. Brasseaux, "A New Acadia: The Acadian Migrants to South Louisiana, 1764–1803," *Acadiensis* 15, no. 1 (Autumn 1985): 123–32; *The Founding of New Acadia: The Beginnings of Acadian Life in Louisiana, 1765–1803* (Baton Rouge: Louisiana State University Press, 1987), chap. 11.

40 See Pamphile Lemay, *Essais poétiques* (Quebec: G.E. Desbarats, 1865). It is available on microfilm in the CIHM/ICMH Microfiche series, no. 45240. For an excellent discussion, see Irmscher, *Longfellow Redux*, 245–50. Throughout this discussion, we follow the National Library's version of his name.

41 Casgrain, *Pèlerinage*, 85–6, 141.

42 Rumilly cited in Griffiths, "Longfellow's *Evangeline*," 72–3. "Évangéline devient l'héroïne nationale et non seulement la plus touchante, mais la plus vivantes des filles de sa race." On Bourassa, see Viau, *Grand-Pré,* 124.

43 Mrs [Catherine R.] Williams, *The Neutral French; or, The Exiles of Nova Scotia* (Providence: the author, 1841), citations at 1, 12, 13, 23.

44 Cozzens, *Acadia*, 298.

45 Irmscher, *Longfellow Redux*, 67.

46 For an interesting recent discussion, see John Mack Faragher, *A Great and Noble Scheme: The Tragic Story of the Expulsion of the French Acadians from Their American Homeland* (New York and London: W.W. Norton, 2005). Contemporary evidence of Louisianan designs on Evangeline abounds. The Wikipedia page for the town of St Martinville, Louisiana, proudly proclaims: "The Evangeline Oak, made famous in Henry Wadsworth Longfellow's poem, 'Evangeline,' stands on the bank of the Bayou Teche." (http://en.wikipedia.org/wiki/St._Martinville,_Louisiana, accessed 29 January 2009). For a fascinating discussion of this Louisiana tradition, see Carl A. Brasseaux, *In Search of Evangeline: Birth and Evolution of the Evangeline Myth* (Thibodaux, La.: Blue Heron Press, 1988).

47 Hezekiah Butterworth, *Zigzag Journeys in Acadia and New France. A Summer's Journey of the Zigzag Club through the historic fields of the early French settlements of America* (Boston: Estes and Lavriat, 1885), 188.

48 Anonymous review of *Evangeline*, cited in Taylor, "Poetry and Prose," 51.

49 See Ronald Rudin, "The Champlain–De Monts Tercentenary: Voices from Nova Scotia, New Brunswick and Maine, June 1904," *Acadiensis* 33, no. 2 (Spring 2004): 3–26; Greg Marquis, "Celebrating Champlain in the Loyalist City: Saint John, 1904–10," *Acadiensis* 33, no. 2 (Spring 2004): 27–43; H.V. Nelles, *The Art of Nation-Building: Pageantry and Spectacle at Quebec's Tercentenary* (Toronto: University of Toronto Press, 1999).

50 Benedict Anderson, *Imagined Communities: Reflections on the Origin and Spread of Nationalism* (London and New York: Verso, 1983). The federal Canadian state, sworn both to uphold the honour and dignity of the Crown (hence in some sense to stand by the results of 1755) and yet also to maintain the rights and privileges of religious and ethnic minorities, has little choice but this option when it comes to the contemporary commemoration of the expulsion.

51 Le Blanc, *Postcards,* 111.

52 This book, which skirts any realistic description of the callous implementation of the Expulsion, skips optimistically ahead to proclaim how "[t]he present British Commonwealth of Nations, and in it the bi-lingual dominions of Canada, South Africa, New Zealand, and Ireland, afford ample evidence that it is easier to hold an empire

together by concessions to national and racial particularism than by attempting to impose on it a rigid imperial constitution to which all sections must conform." Brebner, *New England's Outpost*, 274.

53 Le Blanc, *Postcards* 127.

54 Williams, *Neutral French*, 11.

55 It is not even clear that Evangeline still speaks French at the end of the poem. It is difficult to imagine that a Sister of Mercy operating in a Philadelphian institution would have been able to do so. Longfellow, for his part, shows no interest in such issues of Acadian cultural heritage or survival. He even declined invitations extended by prominent people to visit the "Land of Evangeline" in 1877. See P.B.Waite, "A Brief Footnote to Naomi Griffiths on Longfellow's *Evangeline*," *Acadiensis*, 12, no.1 (Autumn 1982): 186.

56 It is suggestive that recent American developments of the Acadian story have increasingly focused on the figure of Joseph Broussard *dit* Beausoleil. The main hall of the Acadian memorial in Louisiana is dominated by a large mural depicting forty-five Acadians arriving in Louisiana, smiling with relieved joy upon their arrival to the Promised Land. Broussard stands front and centre. See Jobb, *Acadians*, 253, 208. Broussard has such appeal, especially to Americans, because he actually resisted the British and can thus be represented as a freedom-fighter. The cover of Warren A. Perrin, *Acadian Redemption: From Beausoleil Broussard to the Queen's Royal Proclamation* (Opelousas, La: Andrepont Publishing, 2005), depicts Broussard, whose actual appearance is unknown, very much in the manner of the well-known iconic revolutionary image of Che Guevara (and not by accident, since the book's author requested that the illustrator approach his hero in this Che-like manner when he painted the portrait). Although Broussard's political views are unknown, Perrin develops a case for him as an American revolutionary, in part based on the fact that he fathered an illegitimate child: "*Beausoleil* was a man of action, one who thought of freedom as mankind's natural tendency, one who loathed oppression. In this respect, he could be compared with other contemporary figures in North American history, such as Thomas Jefferson, who may also have fathered a child out of wedlock, and who, tired of British oppression, led the American Colonies into a revolution against that government with a poorly trained and poorly equipped army. Both men shared the qualities of being passionate, somewhat elusive men of tantalizing inner complexity, whose aggressive actions drew formal rebukes from British authorities. Both men are revolutionaries who became cultural icons" (16). For another account emphasizing Acadian resistance, see Claude Le Bouthillier, *Le Feu du Mauvais Temps* (1989; repr. Montreal: XYZ éditeur, 2004). Increasingly resistance-focused accounts of Acadian history are well described in Rudin, *Remembering and Forgetting*, chap. 6.

57 Drawing upon Le Blanc, *Postcards*, 64 and *passim*.

58 For an interesting discussion, see James C. Scott, *Domination and the Arts of Resistance: Hidden Transcripts* (New Haven and London: Yale University Press, 1990).

59 This last point is well made by Caron, "Se Souvenir," 68. Caron adds that in the relatively recent folklore developed around Gabriel and Evangeline, they even became something like the "Adam and Eve" of Acadia.

60 Pothier, "Sigogne," 804.

61 Here is J.B. Brebner: "Phillips was instructed to give 'all possible encouragement to

intermarriages' and endow each white man or woman who complied with £10 sterling and fifty acres of land free of quit-rent for twenty years." Brebner, *New England's Outpost*, 74.

62 Dashwood, *Chiploquorgan*.

63 D.E.H. [D.E. Hatt], *Digby Chickens: Caught and Cured in Digby, Nova Scotia* (n.p. [Digby], n.d. [1920?]). See, for example, "Feeshin" (Acadian-French dialect):

> T'ree summer touris' feller,
> Dunno nam' de House dey stay,
> Ax me I will tak' dem feeshin'
> In ma motor boat nex' day.

Such attempts at "local colour" were typical of the day, as suggested by the dialect verse of William Henry Drummond.

64 Brebner, *New England's Outpost*, 42, 86. The uneasiness liberals like Brebner felt about the liquidation of the property rights of a minority, defined not as individuals but as members of a community, comes out in their rhetorical efforts to somehow come up with a Lockean position that showed – appearances notwithstanding – how Acadians had not really "mixed their labour" sufficiently with their farms, nor enclosed their properties from the "chaos" of native collectivism, to allow them to count as free-standing, property-holding individuals (forgetting that, as Patricia Seed would remind us, agricultural improvement connoted rightful ownership for the English in a way it has never done for the French. See Seed's *Ceremonies of Possession in Europe's Conquest of the New World, 1492–1640* [Cambridge, U.K.: Cambridge University Press, 1995], 38–48).

65 They were said to harbour (in the words of Dr Lucien Belliveau, the president of the nationalistic Société nationale l'Assomption [SNA], founded in 1881) *too great* a love for France. Cited in Le Blanc, *Postcards*, 111 (emphasis added).

66 Le Blanc explains that Evangeline sparked a sense of pride and belonging in "being part of the first European group to establish roots in North America." *Postcards*, 167. Of course, many other European applicants – Basque, Portuguese, Spanish, Scottish, Dutch, etc. – could make a similar claim. As Rudin explores very imaginatively, Pierre Dugua de Monts was a problematic ancestor because as a Huguenot he would hardly fit as the father of a Catholic people; yet he was plainly a more far more important figure in the founding expedition than the more easily accommodated Catholic Champlain. See Rudin, "Champlain–De Monts Tercentenary," 5; Rudin, *Remembering and Forgetting*, chap. 1.

67 See Paulette Chiasson, "As Others See Us: Nova Scotia Travel Literature from the 1770s to the 1860s," *Nova Scotia Historical Quarterly* 2, no. 2 (1982): 9–25.

68 See, for instance, Arthur de Gobineau, *The Inequality of Human Races*, trans. Adrian Collians (London: Willian Weinemann, 1915).

69 Gobineau, *Gentleman in the Outports*, 177–8.

70 On the question of Acadian/Mi'kmaw relationships, see Griffiths, *From Migrant to Acadian*, 36–7, 131–2, 172 (see chap. 1, n. 24). This theme is also addressed in some fictional treatments: see Margaret Marshall Saunders, *Rose of Acadia* (Halifax: Formac Publishing, 2002; first published 1898), 210.

71 Audre Lorde, *Sister Outsider: Essays and Speeches* (New York: Ten Speed, 2000), 100. For a fascinating analysis of the ways in which the figure of Evangeline came to serve as an icon of all of Acadia's pre-deportation history and was then put to work in local historical representations emphasizing the Acadians as modern, savvy, and tenacious, see Caron, "Se Souvenir," 67.

72 Note, for instance, H. Beaudé, *La deportation des acadiens* (Montreal: Bibliothèque de l'Action française, 1918).

73 Jeannette A. Grant, *Through Evangeline's Country* (Boston, 1894), 32.

74 See Taylor, "Poetry and Prose," 46–67.

75 For a discussion, see B.C. Cuthbertson, "Thomas Beamish Akins: British North America's Pioneer Archivist," *Acadiensis* 7, no. 1 (Autumn 1977), 86–102; for a contemporary commentary, see Cozzens, *Acadia*, 280–2n., which summarizes the *Sun* (Halifax), 9 December 1857.

76 Ibid., 93–4.

77 Ibid., 94.

78 Francis Parkman, *Montcalm and Wolfe*, vol. 1 (Part 7 of *France and England in North America* (Boston: Little, Brown, and Company, 1885), 284.

79 Cuthbertson, "Akins," 96–7.

80 Only the intervention of Chezzetcook's priest induced the two Acadian women, niece and aunt, to visit the unfamiliar daguerreotype gallery in Halifax. The "shy creatures," terrified by the thought of climbing the stairs to the gallery, only did so on the prompting of the operator's wife. Cozzens, *Acadia*, iv–v.

81 Ibid., 36, 38–9.

82 Ibid., 299.

83 Butterworth, *Zigzag Journeys*, citations at 16, 176, 179, 181–3, 187, 188.

84 Viau, *Grand-Pré*, 70; Charles G.D. Roberts, *The Land of Evangeline and the Gateways Thither* (Kentville: Dominion Atlantic Railway, n.d. [1895]), 1.

85 The details in the previous two paragraphs are all drawn from Margaret Woodworth, *History of the Dominion Atlantic Railway* (n.p. [Kentville], n.d. [1936]), 108–21, citation at 119.

86 Dominion Atlantic Railway, *High Lights of Nova Scotia History* (n.p. [Kentville], n.d. [1936]). Whatever its merits as tourist fodder, this guide's merits as history are rather dubious. While it ecumenically allowed a profile to New Englander Samuel Argall, perhaps on account of his colourful privateering past, it drew the line at Lawrence, even though he orchestrated the Expulsion.

87 Dominion Atlantic Railway, *Illustrated Guide, Land of Evangeline Route* (n.p. [Kentville], n.d. [1928]), 1. "Cuyp-like" refers to the seventeenth-century Dutch painter Albert Cuyp, who favoured idyllic rusticity.

88 Dominion Atlantic Railway, *The Land of Evangeline, Nova Scotia: Historical and Descriptive Annotated Guide* (n.p. [Kentville], 1947), n.p.

89 See Alan MacEachern, *Natural Selections: National Parks in Atlantic Canada, 1935–1970* (Montreal and Kingston: McGill-Queen's University Press, 2001), for an excellent discussion of how federal parks planners wrestled with the dilemma that most eastern landscapes were not considered striking enough to be "park-worthy."

90 *Canadian Magazine* 15, no. 1 (May 1900), special issue on "Canada and the Tourist": 67.

91 Boston and Yarmouth Steamship Co., *The Playground with a History: Vacation Days in Nova Scotia: The Land of Evangeline Route* (New York: Boston and Yarmouth Steamship Co., n.d. [1929]). The citation admittedly comes from a later period, but it is entirely consistent with the corporate promotion of the theme from the 1880s to the 1940s.

92 Elizabeth B. Chase, *Over the Border. Acadia. The Home of 'Evangeline'* (Boston: James R. Osgood and Company, 1884), 24.

93 Frank Bolles, *From Blomidon to Smoky and Other Papers* (Boston and New York, 1894), 14, 70.

94 As will be discussed in chapter 6, historical claims based on "primacy" are apt to be question-begging and trivializing, and we are not suggesting that Nova Scotia was the birthplace of contemporary tourism/history. Perhaps the most interesting parallel case, likewise inspired by poetry, would be the Lake District in England. William Wordsworth, whose poetry had inspired thousands to visit his beloved landscape, wrote a poem as early as 1800 bemoaning the tourist hordes descending upon it. Thus the Lake District was "among the first places ... reorganized for the emerging tourist market in response to popular demand." See Tobias Döring, "Travelling in Transcience: The Semiotics of Necro-Tourism," in Harmut Berghoff, Barbara Korte, Ralf Schneider, and Christopher Harvie, eds, *The Making of Modern Tourism: The Cultural History of the British Experience, 1600–2000* (Basingstoke and New York: Palgrave, 2002), 249–66, citation at 250; see also N. Nicolson, *The Lakers: The Adventures of the First Tourists* (London: Robert Hale, 1955). However, if Lake District tourism was largely about visiting the beautiful sublimity evoked by Wordsworth and was equally dependent on the advent of railway travel, it seems to us that the Land of Evangeline Phenomenon, in investing so much energy in shaping the perceptions of tourists, went several steps further down the theme-park path by getting them to re-experience a fictionalized history. Nova Scotia is often a curiously precocious forerunner of developments later generalized throughout world tourism, even as its initiatives always partake of transnational trends that attend capitalist culture in a global fashion. This transnational dimension, indeed, explains how Nova Scotia's tourism/history could find a ready audience outside the confines of the province to begin with: other people instantly knew how a Province of History could satisfy their affective needs.

95 Later North American literary landscapes developed within tourism/history include Monterey, California ("Steinbeck-land"), and Hannibal, Missouri ("Twain-land"). Even here, though, one might argue that they are less ambitious in that they at least memorialize places that had a documented connection with the commemorated authors. For a discussion, see Norkunas, *Politics of Public Memory*, chap. 3 (see chap. 1, n. 8). We suspect a detailed comparison with Scotland – or "Scott-land," as those ironically disposed to its romanticization termed it – would yield rich results and probably undermine any ambitious case for Nova Scotia's primacy. Still, David McCrone, Angela Morris, and Richard Kiely's *Scotland – the Brand* (Edinburgh: Edinburgh University Press, 1995), although discussing "theme park Scotland" in a provocative fashion, does not introduce much evidence from the mid-nineteenth century suggestive of a systematic coordination of sights and sites with a coherent tourist gaze on a par with Nova Scotia. Nor do most of the U.S. examples cited in the literature.

96 One thinks here of Charles G.D. Roberts, Bliss Carman, and Margaret Marshall Saunders. Among the leading titles are Charles G.D. Roberts, *The Raid from Beauséjour* (1894) and *A Sister to Evangeline* (1898); Carrie Jenkins Harris, *A Modern Evangeline* (1896); and J.F. Herbin, *The Heir to Grand-Pré* (1907) and *Jen of The Marshes* (1921). We draw these titles from Gwendolyn Davies, introduction to Saunders, *Rose of Acadia*, n.p.

97 D.M.R. Bentley, "Charles G.D. Roberts and William Wilfred Campbell as Canadian Tour Guides," *Journal of Canadian Studies* 32, no. 2 (Summer 1997): 79–100.

98 *Canadian Magazine* 15, no.1 (May 1900), special issue on "Canada and the Tourist": 66–7.

99 Canada, Minister of the Interior, Nova Scotia Canada, *The Country and Its People and the Opportunity It Offers to Other People* (Ottawa, 1907), 17.

100 Willson, *Nova Scotia*, 70 (see chap. 1, n. 89).

101 See Parker, *Tripod Trip*, 6 (see chap. 1, no. 81). He no doubt remembered "Evangeline's beautiful heifer, / Proud of her snow-white hide, and the ribbon that waved from her collar." It would be only a slight exaggeration to describe some of these highly emotional moments of the *Evangeline*-hunters as analogues of the ecstatic responses, at times harmful to their mental stability, of contemporary tourists in Britain and Italy (the so-called Stendhal syndrome, named for the self-dramatizing and serially pseudonymous French novelist). Note the interesting discussion of "Suddenly Unhinged Tourist Syndrome" in Wrobel and Long, introduction to *Seeing & Being Seen*, 12 (see chap. 1, n. 10). Could some American tourists have been as overwhelmed by their proximity to the site of a poem they had so deeply internalized?

102 See John Urry, *The Tourist Gaze: The New Edition* (London: Sage, 2001). For a fascinating discussion, see Adrian Franklin, "The Tourist Gaze and Beyond," *Tourist Studies* 1, no. 2 (2001): 115–31.

103 Chase, *Over the Border*, 22.

104 Thornley, *Acadia*, n.p. (see chap. 1, n. 120).

105 G.H. Gerrard, *A Four Weeks' Trip in Nova Scotia: Hunting and Fishing on the Clyde River and Its Tributaries* (n.p., n.d. [c. 1903]).

106 Arthur P. Silver, *Farm-Cottage, Camp and Canoe in Maritime Canada, or The Call of Nova Scotia to the Emigrant and Sportsman* (Toronto and London, n.d. [c. 1908]), 22.

107 As one publication remarks, à propos of the rock-bound coast, "[H]istory knew what she was about. She experimented here, to provide the enduring quality of her sons. Then she loosed the tides into their predestined channels, and reserved the early testing-places to be the playground of a more genial epoch, furnished with examples of her own half-formed, tireless, magnificent powers." Halifax & South Western Railway, *The Ocean Shore of Nova Scotia* (n.p. [Halifax], n.d. [c. 1905]), 6.

108 Charles G.D. Roberts, *The Canadian guide-book: complete in one volume: a guide to Eastern Canada and Newfoundland, with full descriptions of routes, cities, points of interest, summer resorts, information for sportsmen, etc.* (Toronto: G.N. Morang, 1899), 254.

109 *Canadian Magazine* 15, no.1 (May 1900), special issue on "Canada and the Tourist": 67.

110 Roberts, *Land of Evangeline and the Gateways Thither*, 1.

111 Grand Rapids: James Bayne Co., n.d. [c. 1902].

112 Graeme Wynn, "'Images of the Acadian Valley': The Photographs of Amos Lawson Hardy," *Acadiensis* 15, no. 1 (Autumn 1985): 59–83, citation at 83.

113 For instance, when the members of the British Association for the Advancement of Science visited Montreal in the 1880s, they were told that the Acadians' "unchangeable conservatism is a phenomenon in the western world," and that, therefore, Longfellow's description of the Acadians still applied. The province as a whole was represented, however, as a field of scientific and progressive endeavour. See S.E. Dawson, *Hand-Book for the Dominion of Canada* (Montreal, 1888) (prepared for the Montreal meeting of the British Association for the Advancement of Science). And some, rather than being lured with historical romance, were also drawn by the prospect of nabbing the Acadians' supposed buried treasures. See, for instance, Carrie J. Harris's novel *A Modern Evangeline* (Wolfville, 1896). As demonstrated in the next chapter, Will R. Bird also developed this theme of hidden gold in the 1920s.

114 Hardy, *The Evangeline Land*, unpaginated.

115 See Le Blanc, *Postcards*, 63.

116 See Caron, "Se Souvenir," 70. Caron subtly brings out how such a borrowed costume might nonetheless represent a declaration of identity: "Ce costume est un symbole. Il est immédiatement reconnaissable et représente à la fois l'histoire acadienne et le peuple acadien tout entier. En revêtant le costume, les Acadiens et, surtout, les Acadiennes s'investissent de ce passé et déclarent leur 'acadianité.' Dans une parade, la simple apparition du costume établit instantanément un rapport au passé collectif des Acadiens et à leur communauté. Plus encore, le costume symbolise la présence du passé acadien dans le présent. C'est là que se situe le véritable paradoxe. Les Acadiens, et particulièrement les Acadiennes, ne s'habillaient pas de cette façon ni avant, ni après la Déportation. Ils et elles ne s'habillaient pas ordinairement comme cela non plus au milieu du 20e siècle. Nous sommes en présence d'un faux vieux costume, d'une invention historique" (70).

117 Rising interest in Montreal in things Acadian correlated with mounting tensions over conscription. On 30 May 1917, at the Monument national, la Société Saint-Jean-Baptiste organised a "Soirée de Grand-Pré," which was addressed by such orators as Abbé Lionel Groulx, to become the leading clerico-nationalist historian, and Henri Bourassa, the editor of *Le Devoir*. See Viau, *Grand-Pré*, 94.

118 Herbin, *History of Grand Pré*, 5th ed., frontispiece.

119 Le Blanc, *Postcards,* 117.

120 John F. Herbin, *The Land of Evangeline: The Authentic Story of Her Country and Her People* (Toronto: Musson Book Co., 1921), 8.

121 Le Blanc, *Postcards,* 117–19.

122 Leo Dolan in 1936, quoted in Le Blanc, *Postcards,* 98.

123 The Protestant Herbin would erect such a cross in 1909. The nearby "Deportation Cross" at Horton Landing, erected by the emphatically non-Protestant pilgrims of *Le Devoir*, followed in 1924.

124 In 1950, for example, a giant three-day reunion of Le Blancs – reputedly North America's largest family – would bring together many generations of Acadians from across the continent. Le Blanc, *Postcards,* chap. 7.

125 Viau, *Grand-Pré*, 99–100.

126 Napoléon Bourassa, *Jacques et Marie: Souvenir d'un peuple dispersé* (Montreal: E. Senécal, 1866).

127 Brasseaux, *In Search of Evangeline*, 36–46; Viau, *Grand-Pré,* citation at 131.

128 Cited in Le Blanc, *Postcards*, 124.

129 M.S. Spigelman, 'The Acadian Renaissance and the Development of Acadien-Canadien Relations, 1864–1912, 'des frères trop longtemps séparés'" (PhD thesis, Dalhousie University, 1975), 13. We were drawn to this citation by Le Blanc's work.

130 Will R. Bird, *Done at Grand Pré* (Toronto: Ryerson Press, 1955). In 1930 there was a concerted effort to erect a plaque to commemorate the site of this "Battle of Grand-Pré," recognized as a site of historical significance by the Historic Sites and Monuments Board of Canada in 1924; only in 1938 was such a plaque erected, near but not on the grounds of Grand-Pré. See Rudin, *Remembering and Forgetting*, 192, 316n; Roger Marsters, "'The Battle of Grand-Pré': The Historic Sites and Monuments Board of Canada and the Commemoration of Acadian History," *Acadiensis* 36 (2006): 29–50.

131 Phyllis Blakeley to Aunt Annie, Cousin Louise and Family, 10 August 1955. Some authorities have placed the number of participants at about 10,000, but this figure is convincingly contested by Ronald Rudin in *Remembering and Forgetting* (195); Rudin thinks the contemporary Canadian Press figure of 5,000 is nearer the mark. Bicentennial commemorations took place across the francophone Maritimes in 1955, and some of the local celebrations, such as the 20,000-strong fête at Caraquet, overshadowed in size and perhaps in lasting significance the more official celebrations at Grand Pré. See Rudin, *Remembering and Forgetting,* 196–200; Caron, "Se Souvenir," 57–8.

132 Le Blanc, *Postcards,* 140–3.

133 Nova Scotia, *Nova Scotia, Canada's Ocean Playground* (n.p. [Halifax], n.d. [1950]).

134 Irmscher, *Longfellow Redux*, 19, 52, 17.

135 Cozzens, *Acadia*, 38–9, 39, 299, 312–13. Cozzens, unlike Longfellow and unlike other American travellers, thought the tragedy of 1755 reflected poorly on the United States. He urged Americans not to boast about it: "Let us take a fresh start in history and brag of nothing that antedates Bunker Hill [in 1775]. But for the age that preceded it, the least said about it the better!"

136 Bernard Pothier, *Battle for the Chignecto Forts, 1755*, Canadian War Museum Battles series, no. 1 (Toronto: Balmuir Books, 1995); A.J.B. Johnston, "Borderland Worries: Loyalty Oaths in *Acadie*/Nova Scotia, 1654–1755," *French Colonial History* 4 (2003): 48n3. John Mack Faragher has recently reiterated that Americans share in the responsibility and, furthermore, that the revelation of their complicity played a major role in the relegation of the Expulsion to the margins of historical interest in the United States. See his *A Great and Noble Scheme*: "The expulsion of the Acadians, which Longfellow claimed as an American story, remained a part of the historical canon only so long as it told a tale of British perfidy. Once New Englanders were implicated in the chain of responsibility the story was relegated to a dimly remembered chapter in the history of Canada, about which Americans are notoriously ignorant. But *le grande dérangement* was an Acadian, French, British, Canadian, *and* American story" (479).

137 Hautecoeur, *L'Acadie du discours*. A violently hostile introduction to the book suggests some of the risks run by questioning so powerfully instituted a myth-symbol complex.

138 See Antonine Maillet, *La Sagouine: Pièce pour une femme seule* (Montreal: Lémeac, 1990). See as well Maillet's other works: *Evangéline Deusse* (Montreal: Leméac, 1975); *Par-derrière chez mon père* (Montreal: Leméac, 1987); and *Pélagie-la-Charrette* (Paris: B. Grasset, 1979). As Viau, *Grand-Pré*, notes, Maillet and others argued that *Evangeline* was the cre-

ation of an American author, had as its subject an idealized woman thought up by a man, and was devoted in large part to a description of the grandeur of the United States and the assimilation of Acadian refugees in Louisiana (166).

139 See, for example, Jacques Paul Couturier, "La République de Madawaska et l'Acadie: La construction identitaire d'une région néo-brunswickoise au XXe siècle," *Revue d'histoire de l'Amérique française* 56, no. 2 (automne 2002): 153–84. Couturier charts the gradual supersession in the twentieth century of an official pan-Acadian nationalism in the Madawaska region of northeastern New Brunswick.

140 For a discussion of the marginalization of the Atlantic region within mainstream Canadian history, see Margaret Conrad, "My Canada Includes the Atlantic Provinces," *Histoire Sociale/Social History* 34, no. 68 (2001): 392–402. Rudin, *Remembering and Forgetting,* chap. 6, masterfully reconstructs the tangled threads of official and unofficial Acadian commemorations in the twenty-first century.

141 Mark Blanchard, "Separate Acadian History Branch Needed – Comeau," *Chronicle-Herald* (Halifax), 10 August 1987.

142 John Reid, "The 1750s: Decade of Expulsion," in John Reid, *Six Crucial Decades: Times of Change in the History of the Maritimes* (Halifax: Nimbus Publishing, 1987), 49.

143 See, for example, Clive Doucet, *Notes from Exile: On Being Acadian* (Toronto: McClelland & Stewart, 1999); Rudin, *Remembering and Forgetting,* 134–5, and chap. 4.

144 Saunders, *Rose of Acadia.*

145 Le Blanc, *Postcards,* 53, 107.

146 For a fascinating discussion, see Le Blanc, *Postcards,* 135.

147 Ibid., 164.

148 See Libby Hughes and Marian R. Carlson, *American Genius: Henry Wadsworth Longfellow* (New York: iUniverse, 2006).

149 Griffiths, "Longfellow's *Evangeline,*" 66.

CHAPTER THREE

1 He fictionalized many of his formative experiences – moving to Amherst from a rural area as a child, harvesting grain on the Prairies, fighting in France – in his novel *The Shy Yorkshireman,* where they befall the stalwart Robin Crabtree. Bird readily avowed that "there is very much of myself in the story." See Will R. Bird, *The Shy Yorkshireman* (Toronto: Ryerson Press, 1955); Will R. Bird to Mrs Nora L. Balders, 12 September 1966, Dal MS-2-367, Correspondence File [hereafter Corres.] 1, Dalhousie University Archives (hereafter DUA).

2 Will R. Bird, "My First Book," *Canadian Author and Bookman* 19, no. 1 (Spring 1953): 5; W.R. Bird to Miss May Martyn, 2 April 1969, Bird Scrapbooks, DUA.

3 Bird, "My First Book," 5.

4 Phyllis Blakeley to Uncle Welton and Aunt Annie, 27 November 1953 [enclosing letter of 19 December 1953], Phyllis R. Blakeley Papers, MG 1, vol. 3045, no. 18, PANS.

5 W.R. Bird to M. Caroline Prince, 2 June 1966, Bird Scrapbooks, DUA. There are fourteen Ryerson titles counting *The Misadventures of Rufus Burdy,* brought out by McGraw-Hill Ryerson in 1975. In the 1960s, after Lorne Pierce's resignation, Bird had turned to Macmillan and Clark, Irwin. W.R. Bird to Ruth Fraser, 4 February 1972, Bird Scrapbooks, DUA.

6 W.R. Bird to T.J. Courtney, 16 November 1950, Historic Sites Advisory Council Papers [hereafter HSACP], MG 20, vol. 933, PANS.

7 We should reiterate that this is no way to void Bird's status as an intellectual. The most learned among us can consciously choose to eschew rationality in the name of a higher morality and such choices involve their makers in schemas strongly reminiscent of Birdian Innocence. Harold Mah records a fine example in a recent article on "the predicament of experience." A large portion of his article examines the art historian Frank Ankersmit, an erudite exegete if ever there was one, who has grown suspicious of all attempts at contextualization or theorization. Ankersmit ultimately "opts for what he calls … a strategy of 'reinfantilization' – of the intentional return on the part of an adult of advanced years to experiencing the world as a child, which Ankersmit claims is to see the world afresh." Mah, unimpressed, counters that "[w]hat it actually means is to force oneself to be naive." Ankersmit's move to naivety does not actually make the world new or reinstate pure interpretive innocence, but it certainly does serve to privilege unsubstantiated cliché as somehow aesthetically – even morally – unquestionable. His attempts to free himself of context do not actually eliminate it, but rather elevate the refusal to see it as the hallmark of good aesthetic judgment. He also places his judgments beyond all scrutiny; such scrutiny by definition succumbs to the illicit temptation of context as soon as it reaches for any evidence or explanation in order to make itself convincing. Ankersmit could have been the dean of a college in Bird's imagined Nova Scotia. Harold Mah, "The Predicament of Experience," *Modern Intellectual History* 5, no. 1 (2008): 97–119, citation at 110.

8 When we call Bird an intellectual, we mean he acted as one. While he did not dwell in an ivory tower or self-consciously opt to live the life of the mind, he found his calling as a writer who articulated a particular way of being in the world – no one else had ever formulated it so aptly, cohesively, or ubiquitously. In this sense, he was indeed an intellectual. With respect to the elaboration of tourism/history, he worked as an intrinsic (or organic) element in a new structure linking the state to civil society, through which elements of the past were manipulated, symbolically and physically, to produce profitable historic properties. Thus we also call him an "organic intellectual" of the new tourism economy of twentieth-century Nova Scotia.

9 Will R. Bird, *And We Go On: A Story of the War by a Private in the Canadian Black Watch; a Story without Filth or Favor* (Toronto: Hunter-Rose, 1930), 11.

10 This outline is substantially indebted to "William Richard Bird, 1891–1984," postscript to Will R. Bird, *Private Timothy Fergus Clancy: A Novel of the Great War* (Ottawa: Graphic Publishers, 1930; repr. Ottawa: CEF Books, 2005), 194–6.

11 Norm Christie, introduction to Bird, *Private Timothy Fergus Clancy*, n.p.

12 He would later lose his own son, Stephen, his brother's namesake, in 1944 during the Second World War.

13 Norm Christie, preface to Will R. Bird, *Thirteen Years After: A Great War Veteran Revisits the Old Battlefields* (Ottawa: CEF Books, 2001 [first published Toronto: Maclean Publishing, 1932]), n.p.

14 Will R. Bird, *Ghosts Have Warm Hands* (Toronto and Vancouver: Clarke, Irwin & Co., 1968), 250.

15 Bird, *And We Go On*, 5. He reserved particular ire for Erich Maria Remarque's *All*

Quiet on the Western Front, the "poorest" of the new additions to the fast-growing "veteran's library" of the early 1930s. Will R. Bird, *The Communication Trench* (Amherst, N.S.: the author, 1933), 85.

16 Jonathan Vance, *Death So Noble: Memory, Meaning and the First World War* (Vancouver: University of British Columbia Press, 1997), 263, 29, 267, 136, 261.

17 As Vance notes, in a 1926 session of Parliament, Macphail disputed the claim that the sacrifice of Canada's war dead had been for high and noble motives. To the over-matched G.B. Nicholson of East Algoma she posed the pointed question, "Will the honourable member admit … that the prime cause of the war was an economic one, and that the protection of women and children was not part of it?" (262). "There may well have been some truth to what she said," Vance remarks, "but there was no room for her truth in Canada's myth" (263). One can only surmise that Macphail's constituents in Grey Southeast (later Grey-Bruce), a socially conservative rural Ontario riding, who returned her to the House repeatedly after her declaration of resistance to Canada's myth, must have been mysteriously oblivious to it themselves. For a stimulating and detailed exploration of Canadian attitudes towards peace and war, see Victor Huard, "Armageddon Reconsidered: Shifting Attitudes towards Peace in English Canada, 1936–1953" (PhD thesis, Queen's University, 1995).

18 Vance, *Death So Noble*, 48, 195, 196. Vance does not engage any of Bird's other war books.

19 Jay Winter, *Sites of Memory, Sites of Mourning: The Great War in European Cultural History* (Cambridge: Cambridge University Press, 1995), 9–10, 225, 5.

20 Vance, *Death So Noble*, 261.

21 Bird, foreword to *Communication Trench*, 131–2.

22 Bird, *And We Go On*, 13–14, 10–11, 66.

23 Bird, *Ghosts*, 5.

24 Vance, *Death So Noble*, 34 (emphasis added).

25 Bird, *Thirteen Years*, 246.

26 Bird, *Ghosts*, 245.

27 Bird, *And We Go On*, 66.

28 Bird, *Ghosts*, 95.

29 Bird, *And We Go On*, 159–60.

30 Ibid., 143. This chapter uses his spelling "Passchendale" rather than the conventional "Passchendaele."

31 Bird, *Thirteen Years*, 161.

32 Bird, *And We Go On*, 189–90.

33 Bird, *Ghosts*, 200.

34 Bird, *And We Go On*, 15–16, 33.

35 Ibid., 20, 65, 336.

36 Ibid., 192–3, 337.

37 Ibid., 4, 100.

38 Ibid., 137.

39 Vance, *Death So Noble*, 196.

40 Nor is the passage singular. See also this account of the death of a little girl at Noultes Mitnes: "The Hun shelled [the town] the next day and killed a few of the civilians,

one a little girl from the house where we were staying. I helped the mother pick her from the street. Her eyes were open, looking up, her hair thrown back from frightened, pinched features, a frail little elf, who had smiled at me and shyly called me 'Canada.'" Bird, *And We Go On*, 154.

41 Ibid., 25.
42 Bird, *Communication Trench*, 332.
43 Bird, *And We Go On*, 133–4, 139, 147, 326.
44 Bird, *Thirteen Years*, 225.
45 Bird, *And We Go On*, 148, 140, 339.
46 Ibid., 4, 107.
47 Ibid., 108, 108–10.
48 Ibid., 342.
49 Bird, *Ghosts*, 96.
50 Bird, *And We Go On*, 105, 100.
51 Bird, *Thirteen Years*, 126, 188.
52 Bird, *And We Go On*, 12. Bird refers to a Bible story about the extremely close friend-ship (perhaps even verging on romance) between David, the slayer of Goliath, and Jonathan, the son of King Saul of Israel, as described in the Old Testament Book of Samuel.
53 Bird, *Ghosts*, preface.
54 Bird, *And We Go On*, 342.
55 Ibid., 41, 202–3.
56 Bird, *Ghosts*, 132.
57 Bird, *Private Timothy Fergus Clancy*, 23, 27. Ultimately, Clancy himself will – to evade the Germans and to fool his own compatriots – cross-dress and even play the part of a seductress: "He tore loose his big skirt, and stood in a pink frilled petticoat, the skirt loosely piled above his boots and puttees. His waist was loose over the top of the pet-ticoat, and he pulled his bonnet down so as to hide the most of his Irish countenance." All, indeed, is fair in love and war. Bird, *Private Timothy Fergus Clancy*, 191.
58 Ibid., 24.
59 Bird, *Communication Trench*, 327.
60 Bird, *And We Go On*, 91–2.
61 Bird, *Ghosts*, 122.
62 Bird, *Communication Trench*, 80. This occurs in a doggerel verse.
63 See the "coon song" in *Thirteen Years*, 105.
64 Bird, *And We Go On*, 44, 51, 103.
65 Ibid., 107, 4.
66 Ibid., 4, 148. The statement would translate as "God with us."
67 Winter, *Sites of Memory*, 76.
68 Bird, *And We Go On*, 4, 6.
69 Bird, *Ghosts*, 171.
70 Bird, *And We Go On*, 17–18, 146.
71 Ibid., 111–12.
72 Bird, *Thirteen Years*, 40.
73 Ibid., 76.

NOTES TO PAGES 153–61

74 Ibid., 219–20, 213, 143, 220, 56.

75 Ibid., 231, 76.

76 Ibid., 200, 93.

77 H. Napier Moore to W.R. Bird, 18 February 1930, Bird Scrapbooks, DUA. Admittedly, the comment occurs in a letter in which Moore accepts, as an exception to his own rule, a war story submitted by Bird.

78 R.V. Gery to W.R. Bird, 2 April 1932, Bird Scrapbooks, DUA.

79 Marshall Berman, *All That Is Solid Melts into Air: The Experience of Modernity* (New York: Simon and Schuster, 1982).

80 Paul Fussell, *Abroad: British Literary Traveling between the Wars* (New York and Oxford: Oxford University Press, 1980), 210.

81 Bird to Angus L. Macdonald, 11 February 1953, HSACP, MG 20, vol. 933, PANS.

82 W.R. Bird to R.L. Stanfield, 22 April 1960, HSACP, MG 20, vol. 934, PANS. To the incensed ratepayers of the province, Bird did point out in his own defence that he had not claimed one day of sick leave in all his years with the government.

83 For instance, the moving of the Fort Cumberland whipping-post in *Judgment Glen* (Toronto: Ryerson Press, 1947), 8, is recorded in the Orderly Book of Fort Cumberland, 1759–1760 – as documented extensively in Bird's own *A Century at Chignecto: The Key to Old Acadia* (Toronto: Ryerson Press, 1928), chap. 15.

84 Bird, *And We Go On*, 38.

85 Will R. Bird, *This Is Nova Scotia* (Toronto: Ryerson Press, 1950).

86 *Star-Phoenix* (Saskatoon), 29 July 1950.

87 *Daily Standard-Freeholder* (Cornwall), 13 May 1950.

88 *Winnipeg Tribune,* 10 June 1950.

89 Will R. Bird, *Off-Trail in Nova Scotia* (Toronto: Ryerson Press, 1956), 100. One American tourist bewails the fact his wife will oppose his plan of moving to the Digby Neck because "[s]he likes noise. She wants people elbowing her. She wants to ride elevators, to eat in a restaurant, to be in a rat race" (157). In typically backhanded fashion, Bird has just told us that Nova Scotia is peaceful, its people are considerate, its lifestyle is gracious, and that anyone with any sense would live there if possible. All the better, he has offloaded the entire burden of proof onto a nameless foreigner who did not really say exactly that and who may not even have existed.

90 In a half-hearted admission that he may have overstated the friendliness of which even a Nova Scotian might be capable, Bird cautions in the foreword to *Off-Trail in Nova Scotia,* "I must ask my readers to remember one thing. Every person you meet will not have an unusual story to tell, though the way this book reads would make it appear so" (vii). In effect, he has sold a compelling image of the province while retaining plausible deniability in the fine print.

91 Bird, *This Is Nova Scotia,* 256–8.

92 Will R. Bird, *So Much to Record* (Toronto: Ryerson Press, 1951), 202.

93 Bird, *This Is Nova Scotia,* 71–2.

94 Bird, *Off-Trail,* 24. He soon meets other happy Americans in Noel and Summerville (43, 49).

95 Ibid., 100.

96 Will R. Bird, *These Are the Maritimes* (Toronto: Ryerson Press, 1959), 330.

97 Ibid., 126–7.

98 Ibid., 176.

99 Bird, *Off-Trail*, 19–20.

100 David Lowenthal, "Nostalgia Tells It Like It Wasn't," in Christopher Shaw and Malcolm Chase, eds, *The Imagined Past: History and Nostalgia* (Manchester, U.K.: Manchester University Press, 1989), 18–32, citation at 29.

101 Bird, *These Are the Maritimes*, book jacket.

102 Ibid., 323, 313.

103 W.R. Bird to Angus L. Macdonald, 11 February 1953, HSACP, MG 20, vol. 933, PANS.

104 Percy C. Black and L.W. Fraser, foreword to Will R. Bird, *Historic Nova Scotia* (Halifax, n.d. [1935]).

105 Bird, *Historic Nova Scotia*. That all such claims were predicated on undisclosed narratives of race and that many of them (even when applied strictly to white Europeans) were factually suspect would have been a critique appropriate only to growling grouches.

106 Bird, *Century at Chignecto*, 151.

107 Ibid., 174–5, 198, 239.

108 Even the grandiloquent Francis Parkman, who could wring romance from a stone, only found this to say of the Missiquash: "When the tide was out, this river was but an ugly trench of reddish mud gashed across the face of the marsh, with a thread of slime lazily crawling along the bottom; but at high tide it was filled to the brim with an opaque torrent that would have overflowed, but for the dikes thrown up to confine it." Parkman, *Montcalm and Wolfe*, vol. 1 (Part 7 of *France and England in North America. A Series of Historical Narratives*) (Boston: Little, Brown, and Company, 1885), 118.

109 Bird, *Century at Chignecto*, 198–9.

110 Bird, "Canada's Newest National Park: Fort Cumberland, on the Borders of New Brunswick and Nova Scotia," *New Outlook,* August 1928, 6, 19.

111 Bird, *Century at Chignecto*, ix. It is actually rather difficult to imagine schoolchildren thrilling to the book's undigested primary documents and long lists of names.

112 Ibid., 235.

113 Note "Stories and Legends are Big Tourist Attraction," an undated clipping in the Bird Scrapbooks, DUA; Bird, *This Is Nova Scotia,* 269–70.

114 Robin Brass to W.R. Bird, 17 January 1972; W.R. Bird to Robin Brass, 20 January 1972, Bird Scrapbooks, DUA.

115 Bird, *This Is Nova Scotia,* 8th ed. (Toronto: McGraw-Hill Ryerson, 1972), back cover.

116 W.R. Bird to E.A. Batchelor, 20 October 1948, HSACP, MG 20, vol. 933, PANS.

117 W.R. Bird to Stanfield, 25 April 1957, HSACP, MG 20, vol. 933, PANS.

118 Bird made $3,876 and got a raise to $4,884 from Macdonald in 1953. W.R. Bird to Macdonald, 11 February 1953, HSACP, MG 20, vol. 933, PANS.

119 W.R. Bird to Ruth Fraser, 4 February 1972, Bird Scrapbooks, DUA.

120 W.R. Bird, untitled note, Bird Scrapbooks, DUA.

121 Dr Will R. Bird, "Keep Your Powder Dry," *Telephone Lines,* January 1953.

122 *Telephone Lines,* March 1953.

123 *Telephone Lines,* May 1953.

124 See W.R. Bird to Robert Coates, 4 September 1977, Bird Scrapbooks, DUA.

125 Both cited in Will R. Bird to Betty Miller, 21 January 1972, Bird Scrapbooks, DUA.

126 Will R. Bird, *Here Stays Good Yorkshire* (Toronto: Ryerson Press, 1945), dust jacket.

127 Ibid., viii–ix, vii.

128 Ibid., v. He dedicated it, "To my mother, a courageous daughter of Cumberland settlers, and to all descendants of our Yorkshire pioneers."

129 Ibid., dust jacket.

130 Ibid., 2, 27.

131 Ibid., 47.

132 Ibid., 288.

133 Ibid., 146, 150.

134 Ibid., 124.

135 Ibid., 324, 325, 329.

136 W.R. Bird to Vida Mann Keyworth, 4 December 1959, Dal MS-2-367, DUA.

137 For a useful commentary on "types" within racial thought, see Robert J.C. Young, *Colonial Desire: Hybridity in Theory, Culture and Race* (London and New York: Routledge, 1995), 79–80.

138 Bird, *Shy Yorkshireman*, dust jacket, 23.

139 Ibid., 38.

140 Ibid., 90.

141 Ibid., 249, 250.

142 Bird, *Good Yorkshire*, 95.

143 Bird, *Off-Trail*, 285–6, 76, 72, 218.

144 Bird, *Century at Chignecto*, 32–3, 39, 170.

145 Will R. Bird, *Despite the Distance* (Toronto: Ryerson Press, 1961), 128, 187–8.

146 Bird, *Century at Chignecto*, 115, 119. Bird was citing Parkman, *Montcalm and Wolfe*, i, 113.

147 Parkman, *Half-Century of Conflict*, citations at 367, 366 (see chap. 1, n. 45).

148 Brebner, *New England's Outpost*, 120 (see chap. 1, n. 30).

149 J.C. Webster, *The Career of the Abbe Le Loutre in Nova Scotia, with a Translation of His Autobiography* (Shediac: privately printed, 1933), 4. Webster dissented from the view that Le Loutre initiated most of the troubles of the 1740s.

150 Norman McLeod Rogers, "The Abbé Le Loutre," *Canadian Historical Review* 20 (1930): 105–28.

151 Grenier, "Father Le Loutre's War," in *First Way of War*, 77–86 (see chap. 1, n. 31).

152 Micheline D. Johnson, "Étienne Bâtard," in Frances G. Halpenny, ed., *Dictionary of Canadian Biography*, vol. 3 (Toronto: University of Toronto Press, 1974), 34–5.

153 Bird, *Century at Chignecto*, 87. Here Bird exceeds even Parkman, who conceded that the charge against Le Loutre with regard to the murder of How "has not been proved." Parkman, *Half-Century of Conflict*, 367.

154 Bird, *Century at Chignecto*, 67–8, 71, 167.

155 For an introduction to the labile ethnic and national ascriptions of the eighteenth-century Maritimes, see Geoffrey Plank, "The Two Majors Cope: The Boundaries of Nationality in Mid-eighteenth Century Nova Scotia," *Acadiensis* 25, no. 2 (Spring 1996): 18–40.

156 Bird, *This Is Nova Scotia*, 57.

157 Bird, *Done at Grand Pré*, vii (see chap. 2, n. 125). Note that no one had ever extended

the Acadians citizenship, British or otherwise, in any but the most second-class fashion. As late as 1958, the Historic Sites and Monuments Board considered a plaque to the events of 1755 that discreetly implied that the Acadians came to accept the "rights and duties of citizenship" only after returning to the province. The offending phrase was later replaced. See Viau, *Grand-Pré,* 185.

158 Ibid., 170. Here Bird oversimplifies a passage in Brebner, *New England's Outpost:* "If one is tempted to seek a single and therefore incomplete explanation of why the Acadians suffered as they did, it is far more likely to be found in the expanding energies of New England than in the character of Charles Lawrence, although the latter seems conclusively to have been the agent of the removal" (233). This is far from a clear assignation of blame. In fact, the whole tenor of the statement casts doubt upon the usefulness of assigning the blame to any one party.

159 See Taylor, *Promoters, Patriots and Partisans: Historiography in Nineteenth-Century English Canada* (Toronto, 1989), 188–208. See also W.C. Milner, "Chief Justice Belcher and the Acadian Expulsion," *Herald* (Halifax), 2 July 1915. We discussed the nineteenth-century views of Akins, Murdoch, et al. in chapter 2.

160 Bird, *Done at Grand Pré,* 2, 172.

161 Bird, *Century at Chignecto,* 241.

162 Bird, *Despite the Distance,* 5, 64–5.

163 Will R. Bird, *An Earl Must Have a Wife* (Toronto and Vancouver: Clarke, Irwin & Co., 1969), 173–4. Bird would seem to be borrowing directly here from Thomas Raddall's description in *Halifax, Warden of the North,* 2nd ed. (Toronto: McClelland & Stewart, 1971 [1948]), 121–2. For an interesting analysis of British travellers' impressions of Halifax blacks in the early nineteenth century, see Jeffrey L. McNairn, "'Everything was new, yet familiar': British Travellers, Halifax and the Ambiguities of Empire," *Acadiensis* 36, no. 2 (Spring 2007), 28–54, which demonstrates how often such travellers interpreted the blacks' poverty as an indication that the abolition of slavery had failed to make them "industrious, self-sufficient economic agents" (44).

164 Bird, *Judgment Glen,* 298.

165 Will R. Bird, *The Passionate Pilgrim* (Toronto: Ryerson Press, 1949), 135, 137, 141.

166 Will R. Bird, "The Original Nova Scotians," *Sunday Leader* (Halifax), 19 July 1925, 26 July 1925.

167 Rosemary Bauchman, *Scotia Story Tellers: Personal Glimpses of 21 Nova Scotia Writers* (Hantsport, N.S.: Lancelot Press, 1983), 40–1.

168 We do not mean to imply that Bird manifested an unheard-of bias by insisting so implacably on Native viciousness. In fact, most Anglo-Canadians of his generation likely believed as much. One correspondent of D.C. Harvey, the Nova Scotia representative on the Historic Sites and Monuments Board, having learned of a proposal to bestow a Native name on Cape Breton's new national park, exclaimed, "It is a profanation … We must not immortalize the tomahawk and scalping knife." M.H. Nickerson to D.C. Harvey, 10 August 1936, PANS, Harvey Papers, MG 1, box 1798, file 10.19. For an impressive new study of hegemonic representations of Native peoples as dying races, see Patrick Brantlinger, *Dark Vanishings: Discourse on the Extinction of Primitive Races, 1800–1930* (Ithaca and London: Cornell University Press, 2003). Daniel Coleman, *White Civility,* notes that within the project of "white civility" – his term

for "the central organizing problematic of English Canadian whiteness," whereby it is able "to organize a diverse population around the standardizing ideals of whiteness, masculinity, and Britishness" (9–10) – the settler was obliged to construct, "by a double process of speedy indigenization and accelerated self-civilization, his priority and superiority to latecomers: that is, by representing himself as already indigenous, the settler claims priority over newer immigrants and, by representing himself as already civilized, he claims superiority to Aboriginals and other non-Whites" (16) – hence, perhaps, Bird's anomalous combination of hostility to the Natives with eagerness to adopt certain of their customs. As Coleman suggests, "Civility dynamites *and* memorializes the spectres of the past; it grieves *and* reproduces the ever-vanishing 'Indian'" (34).

169 Bird, *Century at Chignecto,* ix–x, 3, 25.
170 Ibid., 171, 174, 29.
171 Bird, *Judgment Glen,* 56, 278–80, 283.
172 Bird, *Despite the Distance,* 264, 279.
173 Will R. Bird, "The Original Nova Scotians," *Sunday Leader* (Halifax), 19 July 1925, 19, 26.
174 Bird, *Passionate Pilgrim,* 5, 205.
175 W.R. Bird to Joseph A. Hamelin, 27 November 1956, HSACP, MG 20, vol. 933, PANS. He notes that the Maine men "were not much better."
176 Bird, *Passionate Pilgrim,* 161, 190, 300, 221, 138, 245.
177 Ibid., 310.
178 Bird, *Judgment Glen,* 117–18, 15, 42, 248.
179 Bird, *Despite the Distance,* 106–7.
180 Bird, *Passionate Pilgrim,* 95.
181 Bird, *So Much to Record,* 23, 36, 130, 141.
182 Ibid., 134, 136, 137.
183 Bird, *This Is Nova Scotia,* 273.
184 Bird, *Passionate Pilgrim,* 294–5, 34.
185 Ibid., 202, 208.
186 Bird, *An Earl Must Have a Wife,* 29, 156.
187 Bird, *Passionate Pilgrim,* 99–100, 45, 120–5.
188 Ibid., 100, 200.
189 Ibid., 282.
190 Bird, *So Much to Record,* 129.
191 Bird, *Passionate Pilgrim,* 37.
192 Bird, *Despite the Distance,* 148.
193 Bird, *So Much to Record,* 44–5.
194 Bird, *Ghosts,* 56.
195 Bird, *Passionate Pilgrim,* 84.
196 Bird, *Judgment Glen,* 57.
197 Bird, *Despite the Distance,* 141, 221, 225. This scene is almost certainly borrowed from Thomas Raddall. See Thomas H. Raddall, *Halifax, Warden of the North,* 2nd ed. (Toronto: McClelland & Stewart, 1971), 107.
198 Bird, *Passionate Pilgrim,* 91.
199 Bird, *So Much to Record,* 111.

200 Bird, *Passionate Pilgrim*, 238, 255.

201 Bird, *An Earl Must Have a Wife*, 178, 235.

202 Bird, *Despite the Distance*, 6, 10, 22, 102.

203 Bird, *Passionate Pilgrim*, 46–7, 201.

204 Bird, *So Much to Record*, 77–8.

205 M.W.S. Eagles, "Will R. Bird," *Canadian Literature*, 1958, Dal MS-2-367, DUA.

206 Will R. Bird, *To Love and to Cherish* (Toronto: Ryerson Press, 1953), 28.

207 Bird, *Good Yorkshire*, 253–63.

208 Ibid., 5.

209 Bird, "Out of the Past," in *Sunrise for Peter and Other Stories* (Toronto: Ryerson Press, 1946), 106–21, citation at 107.

210 Bird, *To Love*, 46.

211 Bird, *Good Yorkshire*, 18, 331.

212 Ibid., 163.

213 Priscilla Murolo, "History in the Fast Lane: Howard Fast and the Historical Novel," in Susan Porter Benson, Stephen Brier, and Roy Rosenzweig, eds, *Presenting the Past: Essays on History and the Public* (Philadelphia: Temple University Press, 1986), 53–64, citation on 63.

214 Bird, *To Love*, 55.

215 Ibid., 179.

216 Ibid., 210–12.

217 Ibid., 259–63.

218 Ibid., 269.

219 Ibid., 291.

220 Ibid., 302, 307.

221 Ibid., 15.

222 Ibid., 255.

223 Bird, *Off-Trail*, 5.

224 Will R. Bird, *The Misadventures of Rufus Burdy* (Toronto: McGraw-Hill Ryerson, 1975), 1.

225 Bird, *Off-Trail*, 148, 306.

CHAPTER FOUR

1 The British Studies Workshop at the University of Chicago hosted a discussion of this chapter in February 2007. The authors would like to thank all the participants, particularly Ted Cook and John Acevedo for making the arrangements and Arvind Elangovan for his insightful response paper.

2 A few examples: each year the Writers' Federation of Nova Scotia honours a fiction writer from the Atlantic provinces with the Thomas Head Raddall Atlantic Fiction Prize (past winners include Wayne Johnston, David Adams Richards, and Alistair MacLeod); near Port Joli Harbour in Nova Scotia, Thomas Raddall Provincial Park conserves about 650 hectares of the South Shore coastline so dear to Raddall's heart; and in his adopted home town of Liverpool, Nova Scotia, the Queens County Historical Society (which he helped to found) maintains the Thomas H. Raddall Research Centre as the chief local archives repository – nothing, one imagines, would have pleased him more.

3 Note Thomas Raddall to W.R. Bird, 28 November 1950; W.R. Bird to Martha Miner, 25 April 1950, both in HSACP, MG 20, vol. 933, PANS.

4 Thomas Raddall Papers, Dal MS 2-202, Corres. "Raddall," DUA. These figures include 686,036 copies of *The Nymph and the Lamp*, 471,858 copies of *The Governor's Lady*, 348,286 copies of *Roger Sudden*, 323,612 copies of *Tidefall*, 188,189 copies of *The Wings of Night*, and 114,169 copies of *His Majesty's Yankees*. Although his nonfictional historical works were not as widely sold or read, both *The Path of Destiny* (88,075 copies) and *Halifax, Warden of the North* (21,583 copies) achieved great success by Canadian standards.

5 Thomas H. Raddall, *Halifax, Warden of the North*, 2nd ed. (Toronto: McClelland & Stewart, 1971), 22, vii.

6 Thomas Raddall to Paul J. Gelinas, 21 August 1944, Dal MS 2-202 S 508–509, Corres. P.V. Gelinas, DUA.

7 Raddall told Charles Clay that winning the Governor General's Award meant all the more to him because of Buchan's association with it. He "was one of the first to see virtue in my work. He could always find time to write an encouraging little note when he read something of mine that pleased him, and the first of those notes came at a time when my prospects were deep indigo." Thomas Raddall to Charles Clay, 14 August 1944, Dal MS-202 S-113-125, Corres. C.A.A., DUA.

8 For translations of his work into German, for instance, see *Die Nymphe unterm Leuchtturm: Roman* (Hamburg; Wien: P. Zsolnay Verlag, 1957) and *Schwingen der Nacht: Roman* (Hamburg: P. Zsolnay Verlag, 1959).

9 Thomas H. Raddall, *A Muster of Arms and Other Stories* (Toronto: McClelland & Stewart, 1954), dust jacket.

10 Lorne Campbell of Thorold, Ontario, specifically boosted Raddall over Callaghan. Soon, said Campbell in 1940, "you will be known as THE Canadian Author and the much tooted Morley Callahan [*sic*] will be – as he should have long ago been – buried beneath his insipid drivel." Lorne Campbell to Thomas Raddall, 1 November 1940, Dal MS-2-202 S-112, Corres. L. Campbell, DUA.

11 Phyllis Blakeley to Uncle Welton and Aunt Annie, 27 November 1953, Blakeley Papers, MG 1, vol. 3045, no. 18, PANS.

12 See Archibald MacMechan, *The Book of Ultima Thule* (Toronto: McClelland & Stewart, 1927), 15.

13 Thomas Raddall to Thomas Costain, 18 September 1944, Dal MS 2-202 S357-462, Corres. Doubleday Doran, DUA.

14 Thomas H. Raddall, *In My Time: A Memoir* (Toronto: McClelland & Stewart, 1976), 197. By 1944, he was defending the archives to the illustrator Harve Stein, a collaborator on the serialization of *Roger Sudden:* "I may say that the Archives isn't the gloomy hole one is apt to imagine." Thomas Raddall to Harve Stein, 18 December 1944, Dal MS 2-202, Corres. Adventure, DUA.

15 To a correspondent, he said, "Research from time to time carried me to the Public Archives in Halifax, where Dr. [D.C.] Harvey gave me every facility; and Jim Martell and Margaret Ells were a joy, full of ideas and sound knowledge and both very keen to see an honest novel." Thomas Raddall to Mrs Allan F. Dill, 8 May 1944, Dal MS 2-202 S350-351, Corres. A.F. Dill, DUA.

16 Thomas H. Raddall, *Hangman's Beach* (Halifax: Nimbus, 1992), vi.

17 Raddall, *In My Time*, 197.

18 Thomas Raddall to Kenneth S. White, 18 July 1944, Dal MS 2-202, Corres. Adventure, DUA.

19 Raddall, *In My Time* 198.

20 Thomas H. Raddall, *The Governor's Lady* (Garden City, N.Y.: Doubleday & Co., 1960), opening note.

21 Ibid., 215–16.

22 Robert Cockburn, "Raddall, Thomas," in William Toye, ed., *The Oxford Companion to Canadian Literature* (Toronto: Oxford University Press, 1983), 692.

23 Raddall, *Halifax*, 103.

24 Ibid., ix.

25 Thomas Raddall, *The Path of Destiny: Canada from the British Conquest to Home Rule: 1763–1850* (Toronto: Doubleday Canada, 1957), 6.

26 Raddall, *Halifax*, 137.

27 Raddall, *Governor's Lady,* 436, 20.

28 Raddall, *In My Time,* 226.

29 Thomas H. Raddall, *The Nymph and the Lamp* (1963; Toronto: McClelland & Stewart, 1982), 193.

30 Raddall, *In My Time*, 327. Becky Sharpe appears in William Makepeace Thackeray's novel *Vanity Fair,* while Ninon de Lenclos was a courtesan and authoress in seventeenth-century France.

31 Raddall, *Halifax*, 138–9.

32 Raddall, *Governor's Lady,* 295, 460–1.

33 Ibid., 25, 227.

34 Raddall, *Halifax*, 82–3 (emphasis in original).

35 Raddall, *Governor's Lady*, 46.

36 Thomas H. Raddall, *Tidefall* (Boston: Little, Brown and Company, 1953), 114–15.

37 Thomas H. Raddall, *The Wings of Night* (Garden City, N.Y.: Doubleday, 1956), 128.

38 Ibid., 133, 136.

39 Raddall, *Governor's Lady*, 39.

40 Raddall, *Halifax*, 83. He does go on to call attention to puerperal fever, which struck "wives rich and poor" (83).

41 Raddall, *In My Time,* 143; Raddall, *Nymph,* 275.

42 Raddall, *Governor's Lady*, 187.

43 Raddall, *Halifax,* 20, 26, 33.

44 Ibid., 34, 158.

45 Thomas H. Raddall, "A Muster of Arms," in *A Muster of Arms and Other Stories* (Toronto: McClelland & Stewart, 1954), 218–36, citation at 235. For a wide-ranging analysis of such environmental determinism in the writing of Canadian history more generally, see Jennifer Reid, *Louis Riel and the Creation of Modern Canada: Mythic Discourse and the Postcolonial State* (Albuquerque: University of New Mexico Press, 2008), 57–8; a classic exploration of the theme can be found in Carl Berger, "The True North Strong and Free," in Peter Russell, ed., *Nationalism in Canada* (Toronto: McGraw-Hill,

1966), 3–26. No less à figure than Vincent Massey credited climate with endowing Canadians with "our special character," especially "a sober temperament." Vincent Massey, *On Being Canadian* (London and Toronto: J.M. Dent, 1948), 29–30.

46 Raddall, *Wings of Night*, 40, 71.

47 Ibid., 83–4.

48 Daniel Pick, *Faces of Degeneration: A European Disorder, c. 1848–c. 1918* (Cambridge: Cambridge University Press, 1989), 9.

49 Raddall, *Tidefall*, dust jacket, 70, 65.

50 Ibid., 9, 20.

51 Ibid., 46–7, 51.

52 Ibid., 206, 132–3.

53 Ibid., 133, 88.

54 Barry Moody, "The Novelist as Historian: The Nova Scotia Identity in the Novels of Thomas H. Raddall," in Alan R. Young, ed., *Time and Place: The Life and Works of Thomas H. Raddall* (Fredericton: Acadiensis Press, 1991), 140.

55 See David Creelman, "Conservative Solutions: The Early Historical Fiction of Thomas Raddall," *Studies in Canadian Fiction* 20, no. 1 (1995): 127–49. As Creelman astutely notes, with specific reference to *Roger Sudden*, Raddall's conviction of Mi'kmaw inferiority emerges with particular force through his tendency, when describing them, to use particular animal imagery and metaphors that implicitly critique their "swarming" homogeneity rather than their distinctive individuality – a turn that we (unlike Creelman, who is convinced of Raddall's "conservatism") would relate to the novelist's more profoundly *liberal* formation.

56 Raddall, *Governor's Lady*, 47.

57 Raddall, *Halifax*, 3, 48, 61.

58 Raddall, *Path of Destiny*, 2, 13.

59 Ibid., 60–1, 75, 117.

60 Raddall, *Governor's Lady*, 35.

61 Raddall, *Nymph*, 159.

62 Raddall, *Halifax*, 121.

63 Ibid., 122. We suspect that the intriguing mention of "something else" may allude to ritual murder. Margaret Ells sent Raddall, as per his request, information about Jamaican obi, which the archivist assured him involved black sorcerers "poisoning their victims in the name of magic." This alarming piece of intelligence may amount to garbled reportage of slave efforts at resistance in the Caribbean, which sometimes included strategic poisoning to stop the especially cruel projects of some slave-masters. Margaret Ells to Thomas Raddall, 18 May 1944, Dal MS 2-202, Corres. M. Ells, DUA. A discussion of poisoning as a technique of slave resistance can be found in C.L.R. James, *The Black Jacobins: Toussaint L'Ouverture and the San Domingo Revolution*, 2nd ed. (New York: Vintage Books, 1989), 15–17.

64 Raddall, *Halifax*, 123, 153.

65 Ibid., 328–9. Taken literally, of course, this suggestion would have caused many long faces in the South End of Halifax.

66 Ibid., 249.

67 Thomas H. Raddall, *His Majesty's Yankees*, ed. Malcolm Ross and James Gray (Toronto: McClelland & Stewart, 1977), 221, 227. Jeffrey McNairn, "Halifax," 46, 54, cites elite nineteenth-century British travellers making use of the word. For a general assessment of racial attitudes among local white intellectuals, see Greg Marquis, "Haliburton, Maritime Intellectuals and 'The Problem of Freedom,'" in *The Haliburton Bi-Centenary Chaplet: Papers presented at the 1996 Thomas Raddall Symposium*, ed. Richard A. Davies (Wolfville, N.S.: Gaspereau Press, 1997), 195–235.

68 Thomas H. Raddall, *Pride's Fancy* (Garden City, N.Y.: Doubleday & Company, 1946), 24–5.

69 Thomas H. Raddall, "Blind MacNair," in *Tambour and Other Stories* (Toronto: McClelland & Stewart, 1945), 371–88, citations at 377, 380.

70 Thomas Costain to Thomas Raddall, 5 April 1944, Dal MS 2-202 S357-462, Corres. Doubleday Doran, DUA.

71 He called George Blackwood "my idea of the perfect editor" because "not once did he tell me how to write." Thomas Raddall to Edith Rogers, Dal MS 2-202 S279, Corres. E. Rogers, DUA.

72 A native of Brantford, Ontario, Costain enjoyed a long Canadian career as an editor for *Maclean's* and the *Saturday Evening Post* before relocating to New York in the late 1930s, where he worked as an editor for Twentieth-Century Fox and then Doubleday. His first historical novel, *For My Great Folly,* appeared to great success in 1942 when he was fifty-seven. During the period of this correspondence with Raddall, he was at work on *The Black Rose,* destined to be a publishing blockbuster in 1945 and, in 1950, a feature film starring Tyrone Power and Orson Welles. Its success (over two million copies sold) would allow him to retire from Doubleday the following year to write full-time, winning a reputation as "Canada's Sir Walter Scott." It is perhaps no accident that Raddall's string of classic historical novels ended with *Pride's Fancy* in 1946, just when Costain left Doubleday. See Mel James, "Thomas B. Costain, 1885–1965," Library and Archives of Canada Digital Collection online, http://epe.lac-bac.gc.ca/100/205/301/ic/cdc/heirloom_series/volume6/74-75.htm (accessed 10 July 2009).

73 Thomas Raddall to Thomas Costain, 10 April 1944, Dal MS 2-202 S357-462, Corres. Doubleday Doran, DUA.

74 See also Creelman, "Conservative Solutions," which catalogues no fewer than seventeen pejorative adjectives on a single page of *Roger Sudden* to characterize the Acadians – "indolent," "extremely ignorant," "half savage," etc.

75 Thomas Raddall, Interview with J.S. Martell, CJCH Radio, 19 November 1944, MS-2-202, box 50, folder 8, Thomas Raddall Interviews, DUA.

76 J.S. Martell to Thomas Raddall, 7 January 1945, MS-2 202 44.8, DUA.

77 Thomas Raddall to J.S. Martell, 16 January 1945, MS-2 202 44.8, DUA. Raddall rehearses two liberal bromides. The first is that the sufferings of subaltern groups can be justified as the price of progress, in this case the peopling of the province by New Englanders who knew "how to live." The second is that suffering is essentially the fault of the sufferer, for individuals shape their own destiny. If Acadians were poor, it was evidence that

they could not husband the resources of the "soil" and the "sea." It was not evidence that an anglophone and anglophile elite jealously guarded its privileges – the sort of notion that classic liberals dislike because it seems to give priority and agency to groups and institutions rather than to individuals.

78 Thomas H. Raddall, *Roger Sudden* (Toronto: McClelland & Stewart, 1972 [1944]), 164–6. "Bosoley" is a corruption of the French "Beau Soleil" (Beautiful Sun) as filtered through negligent aboriginal pronunciation. As Creelman observes in "Conservative Solutions," this is a more highly detailed description of a woman than is generally found in Raddall's early fiction.

79 Ibid., 357–8.

80 The spilling of seed, or semen, occurs in Genesis 38.7–10 where God smites Onan for the transgression. The passage clearly refers to *coitus interruptus,* which Onan employs to get around the obligations of Leverite marriage, but since the eighteenth century the Western tradition has appropriated the story of Onan to condemn masturbation (or "onanism," as Dr Tissot dubbed it), making these verses into an all-purpose interdiction of non-generative sex acts. *The New Oxford Annotated Bible,* New Revised Standard Version (NRSV), 3rd ed., ed. Michael D. Coogan (Oxford: Oxford University Press, 2001), 64n. For the modern hyperbolic interpretation of spilling seed, see Thomas W. Laqueur, *Solitary Sex: A Cultural History of Masturbation* (New York: Zone Books, 2003).

81 Peter Stallybrass and Allon White, *The Politics and Poetics of Transgression* (London: Methuen, 1986), 5, 191, as cited in Robert J.C. Young, *Colonial Desire: Hybridity in Theory, Culture and Race* (London and New York: Routledge, 1995), 115.

82 Young, *Colonial Desire,* 181.

83 Ibid., 113.

84 Raddall, *In My Time,* 343–4.

85 Thomas Raddall, "Reunion at Grand Pre," in *Tambour and Other Stories,* 103, 106, 105, 104, 112.

86 Ibid., 115–16.

87 Ibid., 116–17.

88 Raddall, *The Path of Destiny,* 11–12, 340, 456.

89 Raddall, *In My Time,* 180–1.

90 A Baptist minister in Springhill commended Raddall for "producing 'clean' novels that do not stoop to that present-day literary emphasis upon profanity and sexual vulgarity," and a United Church minister from Campbellton, New Brunswick, wrote Raddall an appreciative note on *His Majesty's Yankees* to say, "A man can give it to his son without wishing some of the pages out, and that is something these days." Rev. James D. Davison to Thomas Raddall, 21 March 1945, Dal MS 2-202 S337-339, Corres. J.D. Davison; Rev. Chester N. Brown to Thomas Raddall, 2 December 1942, Dal MS 2-202 S1-S12, Corres. C.N. Brown, DUA.

91 George W. Blackwood to Thomas Raddall, 15 March 1939, Dal MS 2-202 Corres. Blackwoods, DUA.

92 Raddall, *In My Time,* 303.

93 Thomas Raddall to Hugh MacLennan, 12 December 1960, Dal MS 2-202 S773, Corres.

H. MacLennan, DUA. Raddall was disingenuously restrictive in counting only those passages that refer specifically to "sexual congress." Many other passages in the book have obviously sexual overtones.

94 Isabel LeBourdais to Thomas Raddall, 3 August 1953, Dal MS 2-202 S632-633, Corres. I. LeBourdais, DUA.

95 Thomas Raddall to Isabel LeBourdais, 12 August 1953, Dal MS 2-202 S632-633, Corres. I. LeBourdais, DUA.

96 Raddall, *Governor's Lady*, 360.

97 Raddall, *Hangman's Beach*, 62–3.

98 Raddall, *Path of Destiny*, 35.

99 Raddall, *Halifax*, 42, 172, 305.

100 Raddall, *Nymph*, 25.

101 Raddall, *Governor's Lady*, 77–8.

102 Raddall's contemporary Simone de Beauvoir wrote about this notion of sex as a test in which a man tries to preserve his boundaries. Woman "makes her lover in truth her prey. Only a body can touch another body; the male masters the flesh he longs for only in becoming flesh himself; Eve is given to Adam so that through her he may accomplish his transcendence, and she draws him into the night of immanence." The magic often ascribed to women – sirens, Circe, the succubus – has this play of immanence and transcendence as its source: "The man captured by her charms no longer has will-power, enterprise, future; he is no longer a citizen, but mere flesh enslaved to its desires, cut off from the community, bound to the moment, tossed passively back and forth between torture and pleasure. The perverse sorceress arrays passion against duty, the present moment against all time to come; she detains the traveler far from home, she pours him the drink of forgetfulness. Seeking to appropriate the Other, man must remain himself; but in the frustration of impossible possession he tries to become that other with whom he fails to be united; then he is alienated, he is lost, he drinks the philter that makes him a stranger to himself, *he plunges into the depths of fleeting and deadly waters.*" Simone de Beauvoir, *The Second Sex,* trans. and ed. H.M. Parshley (New York: Vintage Books, 1989 [1949; trans. 1952]), 163–5 (emphasis added).

103 Raddall, *Nymph*, 40.

104 Raddall, *Governor's Lady*, 42, 443.

105 Raddall, *Nymph*, 46, 65, 67.

106 W.H. New, "Modern Fiction," in Robert Fulford, David Godfrey, and Abraham Rotstein, eds, *Read Canadian: A Book about Canadian Books* (Toronto: James Lewis & Samuel, 1972), 219–27, citation at 219.

107 Anthony D. Smith, *National Identity* (Reno: University of Nevada Press, 1991), 9.

108 Raddall, *Tidefall*, 27.

109 Raddall, *Pride's Fancy*, 45, 290. Raddall has transparently modelled Gosport on his adoptive home of Liverpool, Nova Scotia.

110 Ibid., 69, 113, 245.

111 Ibid., 307.

112 See Laurent Dubois, *Avengers of the New World: The Story of the Haitian Revolution* (Cambridge, Mass.: Belknap Press of Harvard University Press, 2004), 36–59.

113 Raddall, *Pride's Fancy*, 307–8.

114 Ibid., 1–2.

115 See Michel-Rolph Trouillot, *Silencing the Past: Power and the Production of History* (Boston: Beacon Press, 1995), 70–107.

116 Fischer explains that disavowal "is productive in that it brings forth further stories, screens, and fantasies that hide from view what must not be seen." *Pride's Fancy* easily qualifies as among these "further stories, screens, and fantasies." Sibylle Fischer, *Modernity Disavowed: Haiti and the Cultures of Slavery in the Age of Revolution* (Durham, N.C.: Duke University Press, 2004), 38.

117 Raddall, *Path of Destiny*, 75, 143.

118 J.M. Bumsted, "Historical Writing in English," in Toye, ed., *Oxford Companion to Canadian Literature*, 350–6, citation at 354.

119 Thomas H. Raddall, "The Dreamers," in *The Dreamers* (Porters Lake, N.S.: Pottersfield Press, 1986), 8–17, citations at 9, 13, 16. This story originally appeared in the magazine *Weekend* on 30 July 1955. Biencourt was, of course, the real-life son of the French governor Poutrincourt.

120 Raddall, *Pride's Fancy*, 16, 62. Raddall modelled Amos Pride after the historical Enos Collins.

121 Ibid., 76–7.

122 Raddall, *His Majesty's Yankees*, 15. In this novel Raddall again stages the genesis of fully-fledged liberalism among the eighteenth-century merchant class of Liverpool.

123 Moody, "Novelist as Historian," 150–3.

124 Thomas H. Raddall, "The Miracle," in *The Dreamers* (Porters Lake, N.S.: Pottersfield Press, 1986), 128–41, citations at 130–1. This story first appeared in the *Saturday Evening Post*, 9 January 1943. The mention of Black River and uplands suggests that this story may take place on South Mountain.

125 Raddall, *Wings of Night*, 11, 14.

126 Francis Fukuyama, "On the Possibility of Writing a Universal History," in Arthur M. Melzer, Jerry Weinderger, and M. Richard Zinman, eds, *History and the Idea of Progress* (Ithaca, N.Y.: Cornell University Press, 1995), 13–29, citation at 13.

127 John Bell, foreword to Raddall, *Dreamers,* 5–7, citation at 7.

128 Raddall, *Tidefall*, 107.

129 Ibid., 155–6.

130 Ibid., 221.

131 Raddall, *Wings of Night*, 154.

132 Ibid., 16.

133 Ibid., 304, 271. Raddall may have cadged this trope of the prisoner who conflates his identity with his prison from the Victorian literary colossus Charles Dickens. In his runaway bestseller of 1859, *A Tale of Two Cities,* the English novelist gives us the tormented Dr Manette. By 1775, after eighteen years of solitary confinement in the notorious Bastille, Manette has lost all connection to his former life. On deliverance from his internment, the poor deluded physician gives his name as "One Hundred and Five, North Tower." As with Neil, Manette's imprisonment haunts him throughout the novel and to some extent cuts him off from normal relationships with his family and friends (to which he nonetheless returns). In addition, Manette also suffers from traumatic memory loss associated with his ordeal – which prevents him, at one point, from

giving unfavourable testimony in court that would have convicted the noble Charles Darnay on false charges of treason. At crucial moments in the novel, Manette, under crushing psychic pressure, will – like Neil – suffer a compulsive, unwilling return to the dehumanized automatism associated with his immurement. It continues to lurk within the psyche like a fifth column of the soul. Charles Dickens, *A Tale of Two Cities,* ed. Huber Gray Buehler and Lawrence Mason (New York: Macmillan, 1922), 44.

134 Raddall, *Wings of Night*, 315.

135 Brief submitted to the Royal Commission on Post-war Development and Rehabilitation, on behalf of the Town of Liverpool, N.S., 27 July 1943, Thomas Raddall Papers, Dal MS 2-202, file "Addresses," DUA.

136 Allen Penney, "Thomas R. Raddall in the Role of Conservator of Historic Buildings," in Young, ed., *Time and Place*, 98–108.

137 An Address by Thomas Raddall to the Commercial Club, Halifax, N.S., on the subject "Halifax and the Tourist Trade," 15 November 1945, Thomas Raddall Papers, DUA.

138 Harold Ball to Angus L. Macdonald, 24 November 1945, Macdonald Papers, MG 2, vol. 907, file 37B/8, PANS.

139 Raddall, "Blind MacNair," 371, 373.

140 Anonymous letter to Thomas Raddall, 7 August 1940, Dal MS 2-202 S20, Corres. Anonymous, DUA.

141 D.G. Burrill to Thomas Raddall, 21 March 1945, Dal MS 2-202 S106, Corres. D.G. Burrill, DUA.

142 C.L. Bennet to Thomas Raddall, 9 January 1948, Dal MS 2-202 S33, Corres. C.L. Bennet, DUA.

143 A.D. Merkel to Thomas Raddall, 10 November 1944, Dal MS 2-202 S818-845, DUA.

144 Phyllis Blakeley to Uncle Welton and Aunt Annie, 27 November 1953, Blakeley Papers, MG 1, vol. 3045, no. 18, PANS.

145 Raddall, *In My Time,* 365.

146 Thomas H. Raddall, "Bald Eagle," in *Tambour and Other Stories,* 25–47, citations on 45–6, 35, 31, 32. The third-person narrator lacks any distinguishing marks that could establish whether the voice is Raddall's or not, Nova Scotian or not, white or not.

147 Daniel Francis, "Marketing the Imaginary Indian," in Ken S. Coates and Robin Fisher, eds, *Out of the Background: Readings on Canadian Native History*, 2nd ed. (Toronto: Copp Clark, 1996), 310–19, citation at 311.

148 Raddall, "Bald Eagle," 37, 46.

149 Literary contacts in New York and Toronto often tried to coax Raddall to visit them. These included Ken White, editor of *Adventure* ("Do you ever come to New York?"), Raddall's magazine agent Jacques Chambrun ("Do you ever come down to our part of the continent?"), and Raddall's editor at Doubleday Doran, Thomas Costain ("I'd love to meet you"). Raddall inevitably demurred. Kenneth S. White to Thomas Raddall, 12 July 1944, Dal MS 2-202, Corres. Adventure; Jacques Chambrun to Thomas Raddall, 8 May 1940, Dal MS 2-202 S145-291, Corres. J. Chambrun; Thomas B. Costain to Thomas Raddall, 14 May 1944, Dal MS 2-202 S357-362, Corres. Doubleday Doran, DUA.

150 Raddall told Edith Rogers of Acadia University that, as a young man, "I was keenly aware that I was seeing things and people and a way of life that were passing rapidly …

I saw the last real log-drives brought down the Mersey River, and saw the closing, one by one, of old water-driven saw-mills. Although I was only in my 'teens and early twenties when these things were passing I felt a pang, for they seemed to me full of the romance of another time." Thomas Raddall to Edith Rogers, 21 March 1954, Dal MS 2-202 S279, Corres. E. Rogers, DUA.

151 The aspiring author Frank Robertson of New Waterford, having read "Blind Mac-Nair" and "Bald Eagle," wrote to Raddall: "Primarily, I was interested because they were written in Nova Scotia, about Nova Scotia, by a Nova Scotian – if you don't mind being called a Nova Scotian – I gather you are really English." Frank F. Robertson to Thomas Raddall, 20 August 1940, Dal MS 2-202 S921, Corres. F.F. Robertson, DUA.

152 Thomas H. Raddall, "Author's Note," in *Tambour and Other Stories*, unpaginated front matter.

153 Thomas Raddall to Edith Rogers, 5 June 1954, Dal MS 2-202 S279, Corres. E. Rogers, DUA.

154 In a letter to the bookseller Charles P. Burchell (of Halifax's venerable Book Room), Raddall explained that pulp-and-paper entrepreneur Colonel C.H.L. Jones had commissioned the *Saga of the Rover* and *The Markland Sagas* from his bookkeeper Raddall, with illustrations by his marine engineer Tom Hayhurst. Jones wanted to publicize his mill's position on an ice-free harbour, making it the only mill in Eastern Canada to operate year-round. In 1931, the enterprising colonel shipped the initial 250 copies of the *Rover* to prospective clients in Australia, New Zealand, the West Indies, the United States, and the United Kingdom to drum up business and – as Raddall remembered admiringly – "[b]efore long, Mersey mill was shipping paper to all these places." Thomas Raddall to Charles P. Burchell, 30 April 1968, Dal MS 2-202, Corres. The Book Room, DUA.

155 In 1944, a furious Raddall wrote Director A.J. Campbell of the Nova Scotia Bureau of Information to protest what he considered the misappropriation of his image. Campbell, a born wheeler-dealer, had paid Raddall to sketch White Point for a provincial bulletin on "Hospitality." Campbell leveraged the value of this sketch by attaching Raddall's name and photo to it. The flustered writer complained, "Thus I have been placed in the position of giving a personal endorsement to the White Point Beach Company, its management and all its works – a position which I absolutely abjure." Thomas Raddall to A.J. Campbell, 12 June 1944, Dal MS 2-202 S-108-110, Corres. A.J. Campbell, DUA.

156 Raddall, *In My Time*, viii.

157 Thomas H. Raddall, *The Wedding Gift and Other Stories* (Toronto: McClelland & Stewart, 1947), dust jacket.

158 Raddall, *Governor's Lady*, 230.

159 Raddall, *Halifax*, 46–7.

160 Raddall, *Path of Destiny*, 205–6.

161 John Gray, introduction to Raddall, *His Majesty's Yankees*, xi–xviii, citation at xiv.

162 Raddall, *Pride's Fancy*, v.

163 Raddall, "Muster," 235.

164 Raddall, *Halifax*, 213.

165 Ibid., 39.

166 Dominick LaCapra gestures towards casting experience as a bridging category between

human feeling and social structure in *History in Transit: Experience, Identity, Critical Theory* (Ithaca, N.Y.: Cornell University Press, 2004). Of course "price fluctuations," "demographic movements" and "the long-term process of commodification" structure material conditions of human life and as such "have experiential effects." However, despite generating experiential effects, they "are not directly objects of experience. Hence one may experience the effects of commodification as fetish, but there is an important sense in which one does not experience the long-term structural process of commodification" (48).

167 Carlo Ginzburg recommends such a technique of "estrangement" in "Making Things Strange: The Prehistory of a Literary Device," *Representations* 56 (Fall 1996): 8–28, as "a good antidote to a risk we all face: that of taking the world, and ourselves, for granted" (22).

168 In Sheldon Wolin's percipient account, Machiavelli's practical advice to princes – the bitter fruit of his own failed political career – expresses the Florentine's melancholy intuition that the demands of rulership were radically incompatible with the tenets of personal ethics. He cast aside medieval political theology to formulate a theory of political power as such. In his work, "there was a marked shift away from questions of legitimate authority, with their connotations of a stable political world, to questions of power, or the ability to exert mastery by controlling an unstable complex of moving forces. Similarly, the old values of *pax, ordo,* and *concordia,* were treated by the new science not as ends, but as ironies: the nature of the political condition was such that good often issued in evil, order in disorder, culture in anarchy." Sheldon Wolin, *Politics and Vision: Continuity and Innovation in Western Political Thought,* expanded ed. (Princeton, N.J.: Princeton University Press, 2004), 192.

CHAPTER FIVE

1 Harold Connolly to Angus L. Macdonald, 4 September 1946, and Angus L. Macdonald to Harold Connolly, 11 September 1946 (copy), Macdonald Papers, MG 2, vol. 904, file 28F/2, PANS.

2 Harold Connolly to Angus L. Macdonald, 25 August 1952, Macdonald Papers, MG 2, vol. 972, file 40-1/12, PANS.

3 Nova Scotia, Provincial Information Co-ordinating Committee, Royal Tour of Canada, 1959, *Public Information Handbook and Amended Arrangements, Nova Scotia* (Halifax, 1959), 2.

4 Tom Nairn, *The Break-up of Britain: Crisis and Neo-Nationalism* (London: New Left Books, 1977), speaks of "tartanry" (286) and the "vast tartan monster" (285). The word "tartanism" connotes a less pejorative image, simply conveying the notion that this network of Scottish words, images, and things had the internal coherence to communicate real political ideas for those who developed and received it. For a serious, if polemically nationalist, critique of Nairn's concept, see Craig Beveridge and Ronald Turnbull, *The Eclipse of Scottish Culture* (Edinburgh: Polygon, 1989). For suggestive recent work on the international spread of "Scottishness," see Paul Basu, *Highland Homecomings: Genealogy and Heritage-Tourism in the Scottish Diaspora* (London: Taylor & Francis, 2007).

5 Dean MacCannell, "Reconstructed Ethnicity: Tourism and Cultural Identity in Third

World Communities," *Annals of Tourism Research* 11, no. 3 (1984): 377. MacCannell notes, "The institutions of modern mass tourism are producing new and more highly deterministic ethnic forms than those produced during the colonial phase. The focus is on a type of tourism in which exotic cultures figure as key attractions: where the tourists go to see folk costumes in daily use, shop for folk handicrafts in authentic bazaars, stay on the alert for a typical form of nose, lips, breast, etc., learn some local norms for comportment, and perhaps learn some of the language."

6 Jonathan Culler, "Semiotics of Tourism," *American Journal of Semiotics* 1, nos 1/2 (1981): 127–8: "The tourist is interested in everything as a sign of itself, an instance of a cultural practice: a Frenchman is an example of a Frenchman, a restaurant on the Left Bank is an example of a Left-Bank-Restaurant: it signifies 'Left-Bank-Restaurantness.' All over the world the unsung armies of semioticians, the tourists, are fanning out in search of the signs of Frenchness, typical Italian behavior, exemplary Oriental scenes, typical American thruways, traditional English pubs." Nova Scotia was a world leader in the timing of its turn to branding, as suggested by its original request for its own tartan, evidently a first for a political jurisdiction.

7 For one interesting reminiscence, see Doris Evans and Gertrude Evans, *Telling the Truth: Reflections, Segregated Schools in Nova Scotia* (Hantsport: Lancelot Press, 1995).

8 See John Reid, *Acadia, Maine, and New Scotland: Marginal Colonies in the Seventeenth Century* (Toronto: University of Toronto Press, 1981), 80.

9 D.C. Harvey, "Alexander, William, Earl of Stirling," in George Brown, ed., *Dictionary of Canadian Biography*, vol. 1: *1000 to 1700* (Toronto: University of Toronto Press, 1967), 50–4.

10 Ibid.

11 See Reid, *Acadia*, chap. 1, for a detailed discussion of New Scotland.

12 See ibid., 31.

13 In many respects, the fleeting Scottish contribution rather resembled that of the generally forgotten Dutch, who from 1665 to 1678 played a key role in the complex imperial rivalries that periodically brought wars to the region. They staked claims to sovereignty, established short-lived forts, and even occupied Port Royal before swiftly fading from the scene.

14 For example, many scholars have been content to repeat nineteenth-century condemnations of the Highland Catholic as a farmer; for an exploratory reassessment of these negative impressions, see Alan MacNeil, "Cultural Stereotypes and Highland Farming in Eastern Nova Scotia, 1827–1861," *Social History/Histoire Sociale* 29, no. 37 (May 1986): 39–56.

15 For some estimates, see J.M. Bumsted, *The Scots in Canada* (Ottawa: Canadian Historical Association, 1982), 10.

16 "Highlander" is a term commonly applied to Scots living on the Western Islands or on the mainland of Scotland north of the "Highland Line," which runs from Dumbarton on the Firth of Clyde east to Stonehaven on the North Sea.

17 See J.M. Bumsted, *The People's Clearance, 1770–1815* (Edinburgh: Edinburgh University Press; Winnipeg: University of Manitoba Press, 1982), which should be read in conjunction with Rosemary Ommer's important critical review in *Labour/Le Travail* 14 (Fall 1984): 291–6; James Hunter, *The Making of the Crofting Community* (Edinburgh:

John Donald, 1976); and D. Campbell and R.A. MacLean, *Beyond the Atlantic Roar: A Study of the Nova Scotia Scots* (Toronto: McClelland & Stewart, 1974).

18 Gilbert Foster, *Language and Poverty: The Persistence of Scottish Gaelic in Eastern Canada* (St John's: Institute of Social and Economic Research, Memorial University, 1988), 4–8.

19 *Census of Canada,* 1931, vol. 4, Table 61. The census probably underestimated the number of Gaelic speakers in later years.

20 D. MacLean Sinclair, "Gaelic in Nova Scotia," *Dalhousie Review* 30 (October 1950): 252–60.

21 *Colonial Standard* (Pictou), 26 September 1871. The Antigonish Highland Society was founded in 1861. Angus L. Macdonald was president of the North British Society of Halifax in 1930; this, the oldest of the Scottish societies, began in 1768.

22 It was initially founded as the Highland Society of the County of Sydney, but its name was changed in 1864 to the Antigonish Highland Society to reflect the change in the boundaries and name of the area in which it was situated. Alice Taylor Cheska, "The Antigonish Highland Games: A Community's Involvement in the Scottish Festival of Eastern Canada," *Nova Scotia Historical Review* 3, no. 1 (1983): 51–63; Patrick F. Walsh, *The History of Antigonish* (Antigonish: Scotia Design Productions, 1989); Pat Lotz, "Scots in Groups: The Origin and History of Scottish Societies with Particular Reference to Those Established in Nova Scotia" (MA thesis, St Francis Xavier University, 1975).

23 *Census of Canada,* 1921, vol. 1, Table 23.

24 See Mary Sparling with Scott Robinson, *Great Expectations: The European Vision in Nova Scotia 1749–1848* (Halifax: Art Gallery, Mount St Vincent University, 1980), for an exemplary treatment of this theme as it pertains to landscape.

25 Richard Lewes Dashwood, *Chiploquorgan; or, Life by the Camp Fire in Dominion of Canada and Newfoundland* (London: Simpkin, Marshall & Co., 1872), 75. Dashwood, here as elsewhere, is in some respects the limit case of imperial condescension. In this instance, one has to wonder if he had bridged the language divide between himself and these Gaels in order to make himself understood.

26 W. Moorsom, *Letters from Nova Scotia; comprising sketches of a young country* (London: H. Colborn and R. Bentley, 1830), 353; William Scarth Moorsom, *Letters from Nova Scotia,* ed. Marjory Whitelaw (Toronto: Oberon, 1986), citation at 129–30.

27 Frederick S. Cozzens, *Acadia; or, a month with the Blue Noses* (New York: Derby & Jackson, 1859), 150.

28 Cited in Brian Tennyson, ed., *Impressions of Cape Breton* (Sydney: University College of Cape Breton Press, 1986), 101. One wonders if Haliburton would have appreciated being included on Wilfred Campbell's exceedingly catholic list of the "Scots Who Founded Canada." Wilfred Campbell, *The Scotsman in Canada,* vol. 1 (Toronto: Musson Book Co., 1911), 114.

29 Joseph Howe, *Western and Eastern Rambles: Travel Sketches of Nova Scotia,* ed. M.G. Parks (Toronto: University of Toronto Press, 1973), 152, 149.

30 C.W. Vernon, *Cape Breton, Canada, at the Beginning of the Twentieth Century* (Toronto: Nation Publishing, 1903), documents the resentment of Warner felt by citizens of Baddeck (302). D.J. Rankin, in his vigorously right-wing *Our Ain Folk and Others* (Toronto: Macmillan Co. of Canada, 1930), remarks, "We have still some old copies of *Baddeck and That Sort of Thing* written by Charles Dudley Warner whose account of his stay among

our people was very offensive to them. It is true, the work is written in a humorous vein, but even those of us who are fond of humour can hardly see the reason for a traveller who has enjoyed the hospitality and friendship of a people, exposing to the gaze of future generations skeletons that would have been better off untouched" (162).

31 Charles Dudley Warner, *Baddeck, and that Sort of Thing* (Boston: James R. Good and Company, 1874), 149. He refers, of course, to the Young Pretender, Bonnie Prince Charlie, whose infamous rout at Culloden in 1746 ended all real hope of restoring the Stuart kings to their throne.

32 Intercolonial Railway of Canada, *Forest, Stream and Seashore* (n.p. [Ottawa]: Intercolonial Railway and Prince Edward Island Railway of Canada, n.d. [1908]), 176.

33 Intercolonial Railway of Canada, *A Ramble and a Rest. Pure Air, Sea Bathing, Picturesque Scenery on the Intercolonial Railway of Canada, Summer of 1895* (Ottawa: Government Printing Bureau, 1895).

34 Rudyard Kipling, *'Captains Courageous': A Story of the Grand Banks* (London: Macmillan and Co., 1897), 42, 121, 244.

35 A point made well by Paulette M. Chiasson, "Travellers in Nova Scotia, 1770–1860" (MA thesis, Queen's University, 1981).

36 Willson, *Nova Scotia,* 222, 53, 228 (see chap. 1, n. 89).

37 Vernon, *Cape Breton, Canada,* 14, 61, 237.

38 Nova Scotia, *Nova Scotia, The Ocean Playground* (n.p. [Halifax]: Nova Scotia Department of Highways, n.d. [1930]).

39 James B. McLachlan, "Where Would Robert Burns Stand Today in Labor Problems," *Herald* (Halifax), 24 January 1908.

40 *Antigonish Town and Country* (Antigonish: Town Council and Board of Trade, 1916), 5 and *passim*.

41 C.W. Dunn, *Highland Settler: A Portrait of the Scottish Gael in Nova Scotia* (Toronto: University of Toronto Press, 1968 [c. 1953]), 158–9.

42 David Frank, "The Cape Breton Coal Miners, 1917–1926" (PhD thesis, Dalhousie University, 1979), 81–99.

43 Hugh Trevor-Roper, "The Invention of Tradition: The Highland Tradition of Scotland," in Eric Hobsbawm and Terence Ranger, eds, *The Invention of Tradition* (Cambridge: Cambridge University Press, 1983), 15–41. For a restatement and extension of his theme, see Trevor-Roper, *The Invention of Scotland: Myth and History* (New Haven: Yale University Press, 2008). The concept of "invented tradition" has a place, provided we keep in mind that all traditions are historically constructed, not merely those held dear by non-academics and marginalized nationalities. Trevor-Roper's influential essay relies on a naive historical realism (which allows him to debunk Highland traditions rather than ask why these traditions came to mean so much to so many) and on an unsubstantiated concept of the real, authentic, uninvented traditions. The essay provides a safe adventure in relativism, problematizing only certain traditions and not others. As with other of Trevor-Roper's writings, there is an implicit prejudice that, if applied to groups other than Scots (whose traditions are, for some reason, treated as inherently hilarious), would become immediately obvious. As Daniel Coleman, *White Civility: The Literary Project of English Canada* (Toronto: University of Toronto Press, 2006), remarks, "Although Trevor-Roper takes clear delight in exposing the chicanery involved in the

elaboration of these elements of the Highland myth, he notes that this invented tradition remains a lasting triumph in that it elevated Scottish culture from the Celtic periphery to a world-renowned cultural myth celebrated in story, song, and popular history ... Indeed, an equally valid reading of the power of tartanism would attend to the desperation of people who had suffered genocide, treachery, and displacement to construct for themselves the signs of a coherent, continuous identity that would be transportable and adaptable to the farthest reaches of empire" (100).

44 Hugh MacLennan, "The Scottish Touch: Cape Breton," *Holiday*, April 1964, reprinted in Elspeth Cameron, ed., *The Other Side of Hugh MacLennan* (Toronto: Macmillan of Canada, 1978).

45 George Patterson, in his classic *History of the County of Pictou, Nova Scotia* (Montreal: Dawson Brothers, 1877), has the young men on board the *Hector* wearing "kilts, with *skein dhu,* and some with broadswords" (82). Patterson may have been succumbing to High Victorian romanticism, but he was unlikely to have selected this particular detail if he thought it would be contradicted by the still relatively fresh stories of the *Hector.* In any case, Scottish paraphernalia had a long-term presence in the province. Even in 1919, even in progressive Antigonish, one could find the Macdonald Music Store, specializing in "Celtic Music and Literature," whose catalogue included "Highland bagpipes and costumes, 'Brian Boru' Irish warpipes, bagpipe and Celtic music, novelties, such as clan post cards, tartan playing cards, maps of Scotland and of Ireland, and Celtic literature in one or more of the Gaelic, Irish or English languages, including dictionaries, grammars, readers, books of folk-lore, fiction, travel, biography, history, heraldry, dancing and poetry." *Antigonish Town and Country,* 38–9.

46 Nova Scotia, *Nova Scotia, The Ocean Playground* (Halifax, n.d. [1930]), citation at 3.

47 Le Blanc, *Postcards,* chap. 6, 126–7, 135 (see chap. 2, n. 22).

48 Archibald MacMechan, *The Nova Scotia-ness of Nova Scotia,* Nova Scotia Chap-Books no. 2. (Halifax: published for the author by T.C. Allen, 1924).

49 "Buchanan" refers to the consummate Scottish humanist George Buchanan (1506–1582) who served as tutor to King James VI – then no more than a boy – between 1570 and 1578. As implied by MacMechan, his Latinity had virtually no peer.

50 Archibald MacMechan, "Singularity of the Province," in *The Book of Ultima Thule* (Toronto: McClelland & Stewart, 1927), 17.

51 *Chronicle* (Halifax), 30 August 1921.

52 *Morning Chronicle* (Halifax), 13 August 1921. Rev. Muir quotes a snatch from the Scottish poet Thomas Campbell's fervently patriotic "Ye Mariners of England" (1800).

53 Michael B. Young, *King James and the History of Homosexuality* (New York: New York University Press, 2000).

54 Jackson Lears, *No Place of Grace: Antimodernism and the Transformation of American Culture, 1880–1920* (New York: Pantheon Books, 1981), 142.

55 *Songs of the 85th Overseas Battalion, Canadian Expeditionary Forces, 'Nova Scotia Highlanders'* (n.p. [Halifax], n.d. [c. 1921]), vertical file 75, no. 11 and no. 1, PANS. The Nova Scotians in the 185th Cape Breton Highlanders wore kilts in the Argyle and Sutherland tartan, in recognition of its status as the authorized tartan of the 92nd Cape Breton Military regiment; the kilts were worn at all times, except in cold weather and in

the front of support lines. See Frank Parker Day to Charles Bruce, 26 November 1947, Charles Bruce Papers, MS 2 297, DUA.

56 Thomas Fraser, "The Spirit of the Maritimes," *Busy East,* July 1919.

57 Norman Macdonald, "Anglo-Canadian Disengagement in the 1930s and the Growth of the Scottish Simulacrum in Nova Scotia," unpublished paper.

58 Even men without Scottish connections find a place within the romantic myth-symbol complex of the kilt. Consider the Black Watch Memorial Window of the Church of St Andrew and St Paul in Montreal, the regimental church of the Black Watch of Canada. Alongside St Andrew bearing the Cross of Scotland, an armoured crusader, a private of the Royal Highlanders of Canada in battle array, and the Black Watch regimental badge, one can also espy the six-pointed Star of David, included to honour fallen Jewish soldiers of the Highland Regiment.

59 "Lord Tweedsmuir's Address at St Andrew Day Dinner, Winnipeg," 1936, Macdonald Papers, MG 2, vol. 1507, file 436, PANS.

60 Most of the details in these paragraphs on the *Hector* celebrations are drawn from Michael Boudreau, "A 'Rare and Unusual Treat of Historical Significance': The 1923 Hector Celebration and the Political Economy of the Past," *Journal of Canadian Studies* 28, no. 4 (Winter 1993/94): 28–48.

61 *Acadian Recorder* (Halifax), 16 September 1873, 17 September 1874; *Eastern Chronicle* (New Glasgow), 21 September 1876.

62 See Anne Wood, "Constructing Nova Scotia's 'Scottishness': The Centenary Celebrations of Pictou Academy in 1916" (paper presented to the annual meeting of the Canadian Association for Foundations in Education, Charlottetown, P.E.I., 6 June 1992).

63 See Order-in-Council, Certified Copy, vol. 667, file 8, E.H. Armstrong Papers, MG 2, PANS; *Herald* (Halifax), 8 December 1923.

64 Cited in Boudreau, "Rare and Unusual Treat," 31.

65 Cited in ibid., 30.

66 Here the *Hector* commemoration was anticipated by the Port Royal tercentenary celebrations of 1904, which, as Ron Rudin points out, made little sense, given the establishment of Port Royal in 1605. Ronald Rudin, "The Champlain–De Monts Tercentenary: Voices from Nova Scotia, New Brunswick and Maine, June 1904," *Acadiensis* 33, no. 2 (Spring 2004): 5; see also Rudin, *Remembering and Forgetting in* Acadie: *A Historian's Journey through Public Memory* (Toronto: University of Toronto Press, 2009), chap. 1.

67 In this the Nova Scotians followed the lead of "ben and glen" nationalists in Scotland who routinely derided the Scottish Enlightenment as inherently un-Scottish and rootlessly "cosmopolitan," as Tom Nairn notes in *The Break-up of Britain.*

68 Cited in Boudreau, "Rare and Unusual Treat," 33.

69 Ibid., 38.

70 Ibid., 36, 39, 40.

71 Of course, true Scots would want this sentiment expressed in their true tongue:

. Dhe Bhetel le d'làimh thoirbhear taic
'S tu beathaich t'Israel fèin

'S a threòraich feadh an turuis sgìth
Ar sinnseara gu leir.

Ar bòid 's ar n-urnuigh nis a tà
Aig làthair do chathair gràis
Bidh leinn o Dhia ar n-aithriche
'S na diobair sinn gu bràth

72 Cited in Boudreau, "Rare and Unusual Treat," 41.

73 Under conditions of postwar consumerism, the "piping in" of the haggis (canned) became part of the ritual of St Andrew's Day dinners (see *Chronicle-Herald* [Halifax], 28 April 1958). Those who liked it liked it a lot. The Wartime Prices and Trade Board, by ruling that Tuesdays should be meatless in deference to the exigencies of wartime food supply, endangered the supply of haggis on St Andrew's Day in 1943, when the dinner fell on a Tuesday. According to at least one newspaper report, the board then yielded to pressure to make an exception for haggis. *Whig-Standard* (Kingston), 26 November 1943.

74 Warren Kinsella, *Web of Hate: Inside Canada's Far Right Network* (Toronto: Harper-Collins, 1994).

75 The surest way to grasp his appeal is to peruse Angus L. Macdonald, *Speeches of Angus L. Macdonald* (Toronto: Longmans, 1960). For a recent political biography, see T. Stephen Henderson, *Angus L. Macdonald: A Provincial Liberal* (Toronto: University of Toronto Press, 2007).

76 Transcript of Interview Regarding Angus L. Macdonald with George Farquhar, C.B. Fergusson Papers, MG 1, vol. 1857, file 1/5, PANS.

77 *Mail-Star* (Halifax), 13 April 1954.

78 Phyllis Blakeley to unidentified correspondent, 21 April 1954, MG 1, vol. 3046, PANS.

79 See Danny Samson, "Learning to Plan: State, Class and Intellectuals in the Nova Scotia Economic Inquiry, 1933–1937" (unpublished paper, Queen's University, 1990).

80 Transcript of Interview Regarding Angus L. Macdonald with George Farquhar, C.B. Fergusson Papers, MG 1, vol. 1857, file 1/5, PANS.

81 Transcript of Interview with Henry Hicks Regarding Angus L. Macdonald, C.B. Fergusson Papers, MG 1, vol. 1857, file 2/3, PANS.

82 Transcript of Interview with Harold Connolly Regarding Angus L. Macdonald, C.B. Fergusson Papers, MG 1, vol. 1857, file 2/2, PANS.

83 Angus L. Macdonald, *The Task of Liberalism* (Winnipeg: Winnipeg Free Press, n.d. [c. 1948]).

84 Ibid.

85 *Chronicle* (Halifax), 14 July 1948. This editorial, "A Man with a Message," was also included in reprints of the Winnipeg speech.

86 Of course, as we noted in the Prologue and chapter 1, this "Hanoverian" business provides another example of the re-description of ethnicity. Most of the Foreign Protestants who settled in Lunenburg in the eighteenth century did not originate in Hanover; they came from a wide range of German states, Swiss cantons, and Protestant communities in France. They became Hanoverian because of a mistaken inference from the place-name "Lunenburg" and because it was much easier during the Great War to be Hanoverian (with implied connections to English royalty) than German. See Winthrop

Pickard Bell, *The 'Foreign Protestants' and the Settlement of Nova Scotia: The History of a Piece of Arrested British Colonial Policy in the Eighteenth Century* (Toronto: University of Toronto Press, 1961).

87 *Herald* (Halifax), 29 September 1934.

88 Speeches to Scottish Societies, 1924 to 1944; Speech to the St Andrew's Society, New Glasgow, 1924, Macdonald Papers, MG 2, vol. 1507, file 436, PANS. Macdonald provides a general description of these volumes, which were probably Dugald Mitchell, MD, *A Popular History of the Highlands and Gaelic Scotland From the Earliest Times Till The Close of the 'Forty-five* (Paisley: Alexander Gardner, 1900), which weighed in at 707 pages; and Alexander MacKenzie, *History of the Macdonalds and Lords of the Isles; with Genealogies of the Principal Families of the Name* (Inverness: A. & W. Mackenzie, 1881), which was a slightly less impressive 534 pages long. Ian McKay thanks Professor Elizabeth Ewan of the University of Guelph for pointing these volumes out.

89 Speech at Flora Macdonald College, 7 May 1946, Macdonald Papers, MG 2, vol. 904, file 28–file 1/16.

90 J.M. Beck, *Politics of Nova Scotia,* vol. 2: *Murray-Buchanan, 1896–1988* (Tantallon, N.S.: Four East Publications, 1988).

91 Raddall, *In My Time,* 179.

92 Hugh MacLennan, *Scotchman's Return and Other Essays* (Toronto, 1960), 10.

93 Dorothy Duncan, *Bluenose: A Portrait of Nova Scotia* (Toronto: Collins, 1946 [1942]), 249.

94 Angus L. Macdonald to T.J. Courtney, 2 February 1953, Macdonald Papers, MG 2, vol. 979, file 40-2/5.

95 Macdonald was not being quite accurate here. According to the *Souvenir Program, Semi-centennial Celebration, Flora Macdonald College* (n.p., 1946), the college was founded by the Fayetteville Presbytery in 1896 under the name of the Red Springs Seminary and became the Southern Presbyterian College and Conservatory of Music in 1903. It was renamed at Dr J.A. Macdonald's suggestion in 1914.

96 See Frank Baird to Angus L. Macdonald, 14 May 1946, Macdonald Papers, MG 2, vol. 904, file 28 and file 1. Baird, clerk of the Synod of the Maritime Provinces, Presbyterian Church of Canada, informed Macdonald that the college's name had been changed "mainly for FINANCIAL reasons – so as to appeal to Scots outside not from real interest in Flora." The college was rumoured to contain other sacred relics as well – the bodily remains of two of Flora Macdonald's children – but this view was dealt a severe blow by Dorothy MacKay Quynn, "Flora Macdonald in History," *North Carolina Historical Review,* July 1941.

97 Angus L. Macdonald to Charles J. MacGillivray, 3 May 1944, Macdonald Papers, MG 2, vol. 1518, file 746/27.

98 Nova Scotia, *Nova Scotia, Canada's Ocean Playground* (n.p. [Halifax], n.d. [1935]).

99 *Herald* (Halifax), 26 April 1935.

100 D. Leo Dolan to Angus L. Macdonald, 1 August 1939, Macdonald Papers, MG 2, vol. 1505, file 409/14.

101 Angus L. Macdonald to D. Leo Dolan, 4 August 1939, Macdonald Papers, MG 2, vol. 1505, file 409/15.

102 D. Leo Dolan to Angus L. Macdonald, 16 August 1939, Macdonald Papers, MG 2, vol. 1505, file 409/16.

103 I.H. Macdonald to Angus L. Macdonald, 3 September 1952, Macdonald Papers, MG 2, vol. 972, file 40-2/12.

104 W.C. Wilson to Angus L. Macdonald, 22 April 1953, Macdonald Papers, MG 2, vol. 979, file 40-2/9.

105 Neil MacNeil, *The Highland Heart in Nova Scotia* (New York: C. Scribner's Sons, 1948); reprinted – amazingly enough – in 1997 (Wreck Cove, N.S.: Breton Books), citations at 6, 21, 23, 33, 34, 51, 58, 90–1. As is typical of such descriptions of rural simplicity, the narrator does not include *himself* or *his family* among the "extremely simple." His Washabuckt grandfather subscribed to three newspapers and read extensively in Gaelic and English. Somehow, too, the author reconciles the image of the crime-free community with an account of a local murder. The *Highland Heart* formed the basis of a radio play by Nova Scotia playwright Don Wetmore, and a stage play, in Canada's Centennial Year. See Jim Lotz, "Straight from the (highland) heart," *Atlantic Insight,* June 1983, Special edition for the Gathering of the Clans, 'Ciad Mile Failte.'"

106 Halifax & South Western Railway, *Summer Resorts along the Road by the Sea* (n.p., n.d.), unpaginated.

107 Gordon Brinley, *Away to Cape Breton* (New York: Dodd, Mead & Co., 1936).

108 Duncan, *Bluenose,* citations at 232–3, 236, 247. Her crucial historical claim that coal mines had operated in Cape Breton for just a couple of generations, ending a previous era of rural idyll among Cape Breton Scots, is egregiously wide of the mark. See Daniel Samson, *The Spirit of Industry and Improvement: Liberal Government and Rural-Industrial Society, Nova Scotia, 1790–1862* (Montreal and Kingston: McGill-Queen's University Press, 2008); and, on images of Cape Breton, Don Macgillivray, "Glace Bay: Images and Impressions," in Benjamin H.D. Buchloh and Robert Wilkie, eds, *Mining Photographs and Other Pictures 1948–1968: A Selection from the Negative Archives of Shedden Studio, Glace Bay, Cape Breton* (Halifax and Sydney: Press of the Nova Scotia College of Art and Design and the University College of Cape Breton Press, 1983), 171–91.

109 Campbell, *The Scotsman in Canada,* vol. 1, 29. Campbell's credibility on questions of race was rather diminished by his suggestion that the Scots were descendants of the Lost Tribes of Israel, a claim lightheartedly adapted by Neil MacNeil in *The Highland Heart.*

110 In terms of period sources, Dunn, *Highland Settler: A Portrait of the Scottish Gael in Nova Scotia,* while certainly romantic in places, nonetheless generally avoids the essentialism of other contemporary descriptions.

111 Speech of Angus L. Macdonald at New Glasgow, 1924, Macdonald Papers, MG 2, vol. 1507, file 436.

112 Memorial to the Late Bishop MacEachern of Prince Edward Island, 1929, Macdonald Papers, MG 2, vol. 1507, file 436.

113 His repeated likening of himself to a debtor acknowledging his accounts to his creditors (a rhetorical opening he used in 1953 when he addressed the National Mod in Scotland) came directly from McGee. Macdonald noted in one of his addresses on Robert Burns that he had consulted a symposium of tributes paid to Burns over the past 150 years (Speech of Angus L. Macdonald on Burns' Night, St John's, Newfoundland, Macdonald Papers, MG 2, vol. 1507, file 436).

114 Address to the Antigonish Highland Society, 1937, Macdonald Papers, MG 2, vol. 1507, file 436.

115 Address to St Andrew's Society of Philadelphia, 30 November 1948, Macdonald Papers, MG 2, vol. 1507, file 437.

116 *Daily News* (Truro), 21 October 1953. For the Edinburgh Castle negotiations, see numerous letters in Macdonald Papers, MG 2, vol. 933, file 24 and vol. 972, file 40, PANS.

117 *Herald* (Halifax), undated clipping in the Macdonald Papers, MG 2, vol. 979, file 40-4/10, PANS.

118 Speech at Flora Macdonald College, 7 May 1946, Macdonald Papers, MG 2, vol. 904, file 28, file 1/161, PANS.

119 Minutes of the Seventh Meeting, Historic Sites Advisory Council, 27 October 1950 PANS.

120 James A. Roy, *The Scot and Canada* (Toronto: McClelland & Stewart, 1947), 80.

121 Draft of a Speech by Angus L. Macdonald to the Gaelic Mod, n.d. [1940], Macdonald Papers, MG 2, vol. 1507, file 437/2.

122 *Mail* (Halifax), 6 August 1947.

123 Statement "To the People of Northland, New Zealand," 15 December 1952, Macdonald Papers, MG 2, vol. 980, file 41, PANS.

124 D.H. McNeill to Angus L. Macdonald, 23 July 1935; Macdonald to McNeill, 6 August 1935, Macdonald Papers, MG 2, vol. 1518, file 747, PANS.

125 Speech of Angus L. Macdonald at the Unveiling of a Plaque for Flora Macdonald at Windsor, 13 September 1951, Macdonald Papers, MG 2, vol. 966, file 40/6. Perhaps he mollified the shade of Flora Macdonald by noting that the non-Stuart queen was at least a "noble Scottish lady."

126 For an example of an attempt to mobilize a popular memory of the Clearances by a left-wing cultural figure, see Kenneth Leslie, "In Halfway Cove," *Commonweal* 25 (26 February 1937): 490. Leslie was a brilliant poet and noted proponent of Gaelic, which, unlike many of its professed champions, he spoke fluently. In the late 1930s, he organized Gaelic Broadcasts for the Canadian Broadcasting Corporation (CBC); he believed that his programs were "just *ahead* of the people and educative to the glory of the Gael." He blamed the cancellation of his program on the opposition of the conservative Gaelic revival interests associated with the Cape Breton *Post*. Interestingly, Angus L. Macdonald was on very friendly terms with Leslie and rather tended to see the controversy from his point of view, not because he was politically sympathetic to him, but because he liked him personally. See Kenneth Leslie to Angus L. Macdonald, 26 March 1938; Gladstone Murray to Kenneth Leslie, 7 March 1938 (copy), Macdonald Papers, MG 2, vol. 1504, file 403, PANS. For Leslie's radical career, see Burris Devanney, "Shouting His Wares: The Politics and Poetry of Kenneth Leslie," *New Maritimes* 4, no. 10 (June 1986): 4–11. Rev. Frank Baird, in a sermon delivered to the Cape Breton Island Gaelic Foundation at St Ann's on 25 August 1940 (*Eastern Chronicle* [New Glasgow], 24 September 1940), did draw a parallel between the Clearances and the German occupations of Norway, Denmark, Holland and Belgium – a somewhat doubtful strategy if one were attempting to develop the argument that the British were intrinsically better than the Germans.

127 Angus L. Macdonald to Ian Mackenzie (Personal and Confidential), 20 October 1936, Macdonald Papers, MG 2, vol. 1535, file 1384/51, PANS. He forbears mention of the fact that enmity for Clan Campbell dictated the political and military stance of Clan Mac-

donald far more consistently than did any putative clan position on national sovereignty, "firm" or otherwise.

128 Angus L. Macdonald to A. Ross, 23 May 1946, Macdonald Papers, MG 2, vol. 904, file 28/2, PANS.

129 Angus L. Macdonald to James A. MacKinnon, 17 February 1949, Macdonald Papers, MG 2, vol. 951, file 19-8A/1, PANS. MacKinnon first raised the matter by asking which tartan should be represented on the patch fixed on the green bonnet worn by Park officials. He considered this letter so sensitive that he called for Macdonald's "personal, wholly confidential reaction," reassuring him, "I am not keeping a copy of this letter and I will keep wholly confidential, of course, your view." James A. MacKinnon to Angus L. Macdonald, 12 February 1949, Macdonald Papers, MG 2, vol. 951, file 19-8A/2, PANS.

130 Both positions were twentieth-century inventions, as was the very idea of the Nova Scotia "clan" as a distinct and organized entity.

131 Angus L. Macdonald to Harold G. Sutherland, 17 April 1952, Macdonald Papers, MG 2, vol. 972, file 40/2, PANS.

132 Nova Scotia, *Journals of the House of Assembly*, Department of Industry and Publicity, 1955, 14; ibid., 10; 1956, 21.

133 Neil MacNeil to Angus L. Macdonald, 17 August 1952 (copy of extract); Angus L. Macdonald to Harold Connolly (copy), 22 August 1952, Macdonald Papers, MG 2, vol. 972, file 40-1/13, PANS.

134 Malcolm MacLean and Christopher Carrell, eds, *As an Fhearann: = From the Land: A Century of Images of the Scottish Highlands* (Edinburgh, Stornoway, Glasgow: Mainstream Publishing/Lanntair/Third Eye Centre, 1986), 99.

135 *Post* (Sydney), 16 November 1953 (reporting on the *Scotsman's* coverage of Macdonald's tour of Scotland).

136 For an early heather reference, see Cozzens, *Acadia*, 151 (see chap. 1, n. 86).

137 *Morning Chronicle* (Halifax), 5, 13, and 15 August 1878. For more on this debate, see Suzanne Zeller, "George Lawson: Victorian Botany, the Origin of Species and the Case of Nova Scotian Heather," in Paul A. Bogaard, ed., *Profiles of Science and Society in the Maritimes prior to 1914* (Fredericton: Acadiensis Press, 1990), 51–62.

138 *Dalhousie Review* 8 (1928–29): 54–5.

139 Angus L. Macdonald to Thomas Courtney, 19 September 1949, Macdonald Papers, MG 2, vol. 956, file 40-5/14, PANS.

140 On importing heather from Scotland for New Glasgow, see H. Garside to Arthur Hambleton, 13 April 1949, MICRO: Biography: Hambleton, Arthur: Papers no. 18, PANS; *Post-Record* (Sydney), 18 May 1949. For provincial plans, see N.V. Jankov to T.J. Courtney, 31 October 1949 (copy), Macdonald Papers, MG 2, vol. 956, file 40-5/12, PANS; and numerous other letters in the same file. For a contemporary discussion, see Alison Day, "Highland Heather: Digging for Its Folklore Roots," *Atlantic Insight*, April 1987, 57–8.

141 Albert Deane, "How to See Scotland without Crossing the Atlantic – Impressions Gained While Roaming the Province of Leisurely Loveliness – Nova Scotia," unidentified clipping [1950], Macdonald Papers, MG 2, vol. 972, file 40-2, PANS.

142 I.H. Macdonald to Angus L. Macdonald, 18 August 1952; Angus L. Macdonald to I.H. Macdonald, 28 August 1952, Macdonald Papers, MG 2, vol. 972, file 40-2/11, PANS.

143 Deane, "How to See Scotland."

144 *Chronicle* (Halifax), 25 July 1934. Macdonald wrote to the secretary of state for Scotland to obtain "designs or drawings or pictures" of a shieling – evidently local memories of shielings had dimmed. Angus L. Macdonald to Lt Col. D.J. Colville, M.P., 10 July 1939, Macdonald Papers, MG 2, vol. 1505, file 409, PANS. A "truly authentic" ancient shieling – a rude thatched hut on a mountainside – should ideally have been made of tough heather stems, twined with wisps of straw, and plastered with peat mud. This, however, would have severely strained the province's limited heather supply.

145 See Roy, *The Scot and Canada*, 73, which cites G.H. Needler, *The Lone Shieling* (1941), and Edward MacCurdy, *A Literary Enigma* (1935).

146 For negotiations with the National Parks Bureau, see Angus L. Macdonald to J. Smart, 24 February 1947, Macdonald Papers, MG 2, vol. 921, file 31/9J, PANS; for the ceremony itself, see Flora MacLeod of MacLeod to Angus L. Macdonald, 6 November 1947, Macdonald Papers, MG 2, vol. 921, file 31-9j/40, PANS. Again, the official celebrations ransacked the symbolic repertoire of Jacobitism for its affective charge in a way that systematically falsified its content. The lines of "Over the Sea to Skye" seem to unambiguously uphold Stuart claims to the very throne to whose incumbents – mortal enemies of the Stuarts – Macdonald had sworn loyalty as premier of Nova Scotia: "Speed, bonnie boat, like a bird on a wing, / Onward! the sailors cry, / Carry the lad that's born to be king / over the sea to Skye." The song records the incognito flight of Bonnie Prince Charlie – whose claims to sovereignty appear to be straightforwardly ratified in the verses – from the Scottish mainland to the Isle of Skye, accompanied by Flora Macdonald (the premier's heroine) after the defeat of his effort to reclaim his realm. One wonders whether the last verse was sung: "Burned are our homes, exile and death / Scatter the loyal men / Yet, e'er the sword cool in its sheath, / Charlie will come again." This might have presented Premier Macdonald with an awkward dilemma had the whole song not been already pre-emptively tartanized, its lyrics by Sir Henry Boulton constituting a late nineteenth-century English-language pastiche of diffuse Jacobite mythography that only retrospectively (and bizarrely) gained popular standing as an authentic cry of rebellion translated out of the Gaelic.

147 Some visitors thought that a shieling was a rock formation peculiar to Scotland. See Bird, *This Is Nova Scotia*, 233 (see chap. 3, n. 85).

148 Julian Stallabrass, "The Idea of the Primitive: British Art and Anthropology 1918–1930," *New Left Review* 183 (September/October 1990), 110.

149 As Macdonald noted himself in his address to the National Mod in Scotland in 1953, English was the language of his childhood. Although Gaelic was the mother tongue of his father, Macdonald's own mother did not speak it. *Weekly Scotsman*, 1 October 1953.

150 *Chronicle* (Halifax), 20 May 1947.

151 Angus L. Macdonald to W.F. Chisholm, 21 August 1934, Macdonald Papers, MG 2, vol. 1535, file 1369/54, PANS.

152 Angus L. Macdonald to K.A. Greene, 6 June 1947, Macdonald Papers, MG 2, vol. 921, file 31/9H, PANS.

153 Angus L. Macdonald to Neil Shaw, 19 March 1953, Macdonald Papers, MG 2, vol. 978, file 30/A, PANS.

154 Angus L. Macdonald to Judge Caldair, 9 September 1935, Macdonald Papers, MG 2, vol.

1535, file 1384/7, PANS. It was thought that of approximately thirty thousand Gaelic speakers in Nova Scotia during the 1940s, only about 15 per cent could read or write in the language. (However, all the statistics pertaining to Gaelic in Nova Scotia seem like educated guesses at best.) *Chronicle* (Halifax), 15 May 1947.

155 Report of Angus L. Macdonald's speech to the National Mod in Scotland, 1953, in *Daily News* (Truro), 21 October 1953, PANS.

156 *Weekly Scotsman* (Edinburgh), 1 October 1953, clipping in Macdonald Papers, MG 2, vol. 978, file 30/A, PANS.

157 Untitled address by Angus L. Macdonald, n.d. [1939], at the founding of the Gaelic Foundation, Macdonald Papers, MG 2, vol. 1505, file 409/48, PANS.

158 The Keltic Society met in Halifax as early as 1903 to discuss the fate of the language; it heard A.H. MacKay, superintendent of education, argue against the idea of bilingual education. *Morning Chronicle,* 11 December 1903.

159 James MacNeil to Angus L. Macdonald, n.d. [c. 1935], Macdonald Papers, MG 2, vol. 1535, file 1384/64, PANS; 14 November 1935, vol. 1535, file 1384/66, PANS.

160 Angus L. Macdonald to James MacNeil, 4 March 1936, Macdonald Papers, MG 2, vol. 1535, file 1384/65, PANS. James G. MacKinnon, a towering figure in Gaelic circles who had once edited *Mac-Talla,* advised Macdonald that a certificate from clergymen and others fluent in the language be accepted as a supplementary license to teach the subject. The shortage of teachers and teaching materials presented a basic problem. J.G. MacKinnon to Angus L. Macdonald, 20 March 1939, Macdonald Papers, MG 2, vol. 1505, file 409/33, PANS.

161 James MacNeil to Angus L. Macdonald, 25 February 1938, Macdonald Papers, MG 2, vol. 1504, file 403/3, PANS.

162 James MacNeil to Angus L. Macdonald, 22 July 1938, Macdonald Papers, MG 2, vol. 1504, file 403/4, PANS.

163 Angus L. Macdonald to James MacNeil, 15 March 1939, Macdonald Papers, MG 2, vol. 1505, file 409/35, PANS. The premier restated this position in a public address later in the year. Untitled address by Angus L. Macdonald, n.d. [1939], at the founding of the Gaelic Foundation, Macdonald Papers, MG 2, vol. 1505, file 409/48, PANS.

164 *Post-Record* (Sydney), 23 November 1939; *Cape Breton Highlander* (Sydney), 24 November, 8 December 1971.

165 A.W.R. MacKenzie and C.W.K. McCurdy to W.L.M. King, 2 May 1940 (copy), Macdonald Papers, MG 2, vol. 1506, file 419/16, PANS.

166 Angus L. Macdonald to Senator Donald MacLennan, 10 May 1940, Macdonald Papers, MG 2, vol. 1506, file 419/19, PANS.

167 A.W.R. MacKenzie to Angus L. Macdonald, 7 February 1950, Macdonald Papers, MG 2, vol. 953, file 32/1, PANS.

168 *Weekly Scotsman* (Edinburgh), 1 October 1953, clipping in Macdonald Papers, MG 2, vol. 978, file 30/A, PANS.

169 See D. Maclean Sinclair, "Gaelic in Nova Scotia," *Dalhousie Review* 30 (October 1950): 252–60; and Foster, *Language and Poverty,* chaps 4 and 5.

170 Angus L. Macdonald to Senator Donald MacLennan, 10 May 1940, Macdonald Papers, MG 2, vol. 1506, file 419/19, PANS.

171 Angus L. Macdonald to Roy Fraser, 11 December 1953, Macdonald Papers, MG 2, vol. 1507, file 443/33, PANS.

172 Rev. Alexander D. Murray to Angus L. Macdonald, 2 April 1947, Macdonald Papers, MG 2, vol. 921, file 31-9h/81, PANS.

173 See *Chronicle-Herald* (Halifax), 22 May 1967, for his obituary; we thank Norman Macdonald for correcting the biographical data at certain points.

174 Charles W.K. McCurdy to Angus L. Macdonald, 15 March 1947, Macdonald Papers, MG 2, vol. 921, file 31-9L/63, PANS.

175 Mary Black Diary Notes, 27 July 1943, Mary Black Papers, PANS.

176 Foster, *Language and Poverty*, 91.

177 Mary Black to Harold Connolly, 29 October 1946, Macdonald Papers, MG 2, vol. 904, file 28–f2/25, PANS.

178 Simon J. MacKenzie to Angus L. Macdonald, 16 December 1946, Macdonald Papers, MG 2, vol. 921, file 31/9H, PANS.

179 John A. Smith to Angus L. Macdonald, 17 April 1947, Macdonald Papers, MG 2, vol. 921, file 31/9H, PANS.

180 Rev. Alexander D. Murray to Angus L. Macdonald, 2 April 1947, Macdonald Papers, MG 2, vol. 921, file 31-9h/81, PANS.

181 Angus Morris to Angus L. Macdonald, 11 January 1946, Macdonald Papers, MG 2, vol. 921, file 31/9H, PANS.

182 A.W.R. MacKenzie and C.W.K. McCurdy to W.L.M. King, 2 May 1940 (copy), Macdonald Papers, MG 2, vol. 1506, file 419/16, PANS.

183 A.W.R. MacKenzie to Angus L. Macdonald, 23 August 1947, Macdonald Papers, MG 2, vol. 921, file 31/9H, PANS.

184 *Canadian-American Gael* 1 (1943–44): 2.

185 Foster, *Language and Poverty*, 86–90, suggests that in its first decade the Gaelic College enjoyed substantial support and attained a high cultural level, particularly given its scant resources, but that MacKenzie was unable to hold the allegiance of Gaelic scholars. Foster seems radically to underestimate the structuring role of the tourism industry, right from the beginning (98).

186 Connolly to A.W.R. MacKenzie (copy), 22 March 1947, Macdonald Papers, MG 2, vol. 921, file 31-9h/75, PANS.

187 A.W.R. MacKenzie to Angus L. Macdonald, 26 March 1947, Macdonald Papers, vol. 921, file 31-9h/76, PANS.

188 Cited in A.W.R. MacKenzie to Angus L. Macdonald, 30 June 1948, Macdonald Papers, MG 2, vol. 933, file 31/29, PANS.

189 Harold Connolly to Angus L. Macdonald, 21 October 1947, Macdonald Papers, MG 2, vol. 921, file 31-9h/88, PANS.

190 Angus L. Macdonald to Rev. Alexander D. Murray, 8 April 1947, Macdonald Papers, MG 2, vol. 921, file 31-9h/80, PANS.

191 Rev. Alexander D. Murray to Angus L. Macdonald, 2 April 1947, Macdonald Papers, MG 2, vol. 921, file 31-9h/81, PANS.

192 Rev. Alexander D. Murray to Harold Connolly, 11 April 1947, Macdonald Papers, MG 2, vol. 921, file 31-9h/82, PANS.

193 *Herald* (Halifax), 13 August 1947; see also *Eastern Chronicle* (New Glasgow), 21 August 1947.

194 S.R. Gordon to Angus L. Macdonald, 22 September 1948, Macdonald Papers, MG 2, vol. 933, file 31/46, PANS.

195 *Chronicle-Herald* (Halifax), 11 August 1951. *Johnny Belinda* had been well received on its release in 1948, even garnering an Academy Award for its leading actress, Jane Wyman. However, this does not mean that Cape Bretoners welcomed the attention it paid them. The film depicted rural poverty, intolerant provincialism, and sexual violence with a relative frankness very unusual for the period. Such themes had absolutely no place in the Cape Breton of the Scottish Myth. Particularly irksome for someone like Kerr, the plot had its basis in events that had occurred on Prince Edward Island – not Cape Breton Island – but the filmmakers had cavalierly transported the story to Nova Scotia at just the time when the province was in the midst of tartanizing itself.

196 Charlotte Whitton to Angus L. Macdonald, 25 March 1947, Macdonald Papers, MG 2, vol. 921, file 31/9H, PANS.

197 A.W.R. MacKenzie to Angus L. MacDonald, 14 February 1947, Macdonald Papers, MG 2, vol. 921, file 31/9H, PANS.

198 Angus L. Macdonald to A.W.R. MacKenzie, 11 June 1948, Macdonald Papers, MG 2, vol. 933, file 31, PANS.

199 Angus L. Macdonald to D. Leo Dolan, 4 August 1939, Macdonald Papers, MG 2, vol. 1505, file 409/13, PANS.

200 A.W.R. MacKenzie to Angus L. Macdonald, 30 December 1953, Macdonald Papers, MG 2, vol. 978, file 30/1, PANS.

201 *Chronicle-Herald* (Halifax), 9 August 1957.

202 Ibid., 7 August 1958.

203 Heather Laskey, "A Big Gaelic Squabble in the Land of the Giant MacAskill," *Atlantic Insight,* June 1986, 8–9.

204 Ellison Robertson, "The Hidden Cape Breton," *ArtsAtlantic,* Summer/Fall 1987, 46–9.

205 *Cape Breton Post,* June 1970.

206 Roy Fraser to Angus L. Macdonald, 5 December 1953, Macdonald Papers, MG 2, vol. 1507, file 443/34, PANS.

207 A.L. Macdonald, *Scotland Forever! Being an Address by Angus L. McDonald [sic], Premier of Nova Scotia to the St. Andrew's Society of Charleston, S.C.* (n.p., n.d. [1937]).

208 Ibid., n.p.

209 Ibid.

210 Angus L. Macdonald, "The Day We Celebrate," Response to the toast by Col. Robert S. Henry at the two hundred and seventh anniversary dinner of the St Andrew's Society of Charleston, November 30th 1936, Macdonald Papers, MG 2, vol. 904, file 28/file 1/46, PANS.

211 Angus L. Macdonald, speech at Gaelic Mod, n.d. [1940], Macdonald Papers, vol. 1505, file 409/16, PANS.

212 Lord Sempill, who was not only a peer, but a "Baronet" of Nova Scotia, called upon the "Gaelic Race" in Nova Scotia in 1944 to carry on the romantic history of their race, whose latest chapter was "Gaelic Triumphs in Aeronautics." *Chronicle* (Halifax), 7 March 1944.

213 Angus L. Macdonald, speech at Gaelic Mod, n.d. [1940], Macdonald Papers, MG 2, vol. 1505, file 409/16, PANS.

214 As the Second World War turned into the Cold War, Scottish history continued to be plundered for examples that purportedly shed light on contemporary questions. A.R.M. Lower, for example, told the eighty-third annual banquet of the St Andrew's Society in Winnipeg that Scottish history illuminated the Gouzenko Affair by showing how a small nation might resist a larger one. As well, the history of a once bicultural Scotland possibly suggested that "before Canada can truly become a united nation, one of its languages, like Gaelic, will have to go" (*Winnipeg Free Press*, 1 December 1953). Meanwhile, the Toronto *Globe and Mail* denounced local Communists for holding a "gala Burns Night," when everyone knew that Burns was "mightily opposed to snivelling sneaks and double-dealers, and, consequently, would not have been pleasant company for those who now try to use his name as sucker-bait." "Commies," the newspaper intoned, "should leave him alone" (clipping in the Macdonald Papers, n.d. [January 1952]).

215 See Ernest Forbes, "The Origins of the Maritime Rights Movement," in *Challenging the Regional Stereotype: Essays on the 20th Century Maritimes* (Fredericton: Acadiensis Press, 1989), 100–13; Forbes, *The Maritime Rights Movement, 1919–1927: A Study in Canadian Regionalism* (Montreal and Kingston: McGill-Queen's University Press, 1979); R.A. Young, "Teaching and Research in Maritime Politics: Old Stereotypes and New Directions," in P.A. Buckner, ed., *Teaching Maritime Studies* (Fredericton: Acadiensis Press, 1986), 153–73.

216 Macdonald, *Scotland Forever!*

217 Hugh MacLennan, "The Miracle That's Changing Nova Scotia," *Mayfair*, July 1953, 60.

218 Angus L. Macdonald to Judge Caldair, 9 September 1935, Macdonald Papers, MG 2, vol. 1535, file 1384/7, PANS.

219 *Canadian-American Gael* 1 (1943–44): 1–2.

220 Macdonald, *Scotland Forever!*

221 See Bob Carter, *Realism and Racism: Concepts of Race in Sociological Research* (London and New York: Routledge, 2000), 2.

222 Karim Murji and John Solomos, introduction to Murji and Solomos, eds, *Racialization: Studies in Theory and Practice* (Oxford: Oxford University Press, 2005), 22.

223 Carter, *Realism and Racism*, 2–3; see also Elizar Barkan, *The Retreat of Scientific Racism: Changing Concepts of Race in Britain and the United States between the World Wars* (Cambridge: Cambridge University Press, 1991).

224 Michael Banton, "Historical and Contemporary Modes of Racialization," in Murji and Solomos, *Racialization*, 53.

225 Evelyn Brooks Higginbotham, "African-American Women's History and the Meta-language of Race," in Joan Scott, ed., *Feminism and History* (London: Oxford University Press, 1996), 185–6.

226 The Nova Scotia in which the Scottish Myth emerged was a place where people of colour suffered systematic discrimination. If the Great War apotheosized the Highland regiments, it also saw military authorities forcibly marginalize black men. Recruiting officers initially refused to admit them and later relegated them to a construction unit under white command. The exclusion of people of colour from the Highland regiments was no accident. In Pictou County, where the legacy of the *Hector* so warmed

Scottish hearts, Afro–Nova Scotians were segregated in the movie houses – a policy that, when challenged by one courageous black woman, the courts upheld. In general, blacks and whites went to different schools. Almost no blacks made it to university. Most trade unions quietly excluded them. Calvin W. Buck, *Canada's Black Battalion: No.2 Construction 1916–1920* (Halifax: Society for the Protection and Preservation of Black Culture in Nova Scotia, 1986); Constance Backhouse, "'Bitterly Disappointed' at the Spread of 'Colour-Bar Tactics': Viola Desmond's Challenge to Racial Segregation, Nova Scotia, 1946," in *Colour-Coded: A Legal History of Racism in Canada, 1900–1950* (Toronto: Osgoode Society for Canadian Legal History and University of Toronto Press, 1999).

227 *Canadian-American Gael* 1 (1943–44): 2. The paradox is patent: if Highland Scottish immigrants were intrinsically suited to "the soil, sea and forest way of life," why had so many of their descendants apparently failed at it, thus necessitating MacKenzie's immigration scheme?

228 James A. MacKinnon to Angus L. Macdonald, 2 March 1949, Macdonald Papers, MG 2, vol. 951, file 19-8A/7, PANS.

229 In this instance, the idea of "Scottish essence" read into the name of the area clearly slighted the numerous Acadians at Chéticamp, who had lived in the area long before anyone thought of establishing a park there.

230 Charles I granted the original Scottish coat of arms in 1629. Between 1805 and 1810, the arms of Nova Scotia were re-entered in the Register of His Majesty's Lyon Office in Edinburgh. (The Lyon Office or Court of the Lord Lyon King of Arms is the department of the British government that determines and places upon record the arms used in Scotland and the arms of a Scottish connection used abroad.) However, committing – in the shocked words of John Stewart, the armorial historian – "a blunder worse than a crime," the *original, Scottish,* and indeed *royal* coat of arms was simply forgotten in 1868, as a new coat of arms ("a rather commonplace design of a salmon and thistles") was issued. Only in the 1920s was the "true" coat of arms restored to the province. John A. Stewart, *Notes on the Arms of Nova Scotia* (Glasgow: privately published, 1928), 26–7.

231 Lowenthal, *Heritage Crusade*, 146 (see Prologue, n. 13).

232 Angus L. Macdonald to Rev. Andrew MacDonnell, 18 April 1939, Macdonald Papers, MG 2, vol. 1505, file 409/26, PANS.

233 Bird, *Historic Nova Scotia*, 9.

234 Harry Bruce, introduction to *Wallace MacAskill: Seascapes and Sailing Ships* (Halifax: Nimbus 1987), 14.

235 Robert MacNeil, *Wordstruck: A Memoir* (Markham, Ont.: Penguin Canada, 1989), 70.

236 See Marjorie Major, "History of the Nova Scotia Tartan," *Nova Scotia Historical Quarterly* 2, no. 2 (March 1972), 191–214. Here is Nova Scotia's own distinctive contribution to what Tom Nairn called the "boundless realm of short-cake tins, plaid socks, kilted statuettes and whisky-labels that stretches from Tannochbrae to Tokyo." Nairn, *Break-up of Britain,* 168.

237 Glen Hancock, "The Clans Are Gathering Again," *Atlantic Advocate*, June 1987, 27–32.

238 Ibid., 32.

239 To paraphrase George Moncrieff's discussion of the Victorian appropriation of Scottish history in Roy, *The Scot and Canada,* 313.

240 A.W.R. MacKenzie to Angus L. Macdonald, 30 December 1953, Macdonald Papers, MG 2, vol. 978, file 30/1, PANS.

241 For a fine study of the causeway and an analysis of the opening ceremony, see Meaghan Beaton and Del Muise, "The Canso Causeway: Tartan Tourism, Industrial Development and the Promise of Progress for Cape Breton," *Acadiensis* 37, no. 2 (Summer/Autumn 2008), 36–69.

242 *Mail-Star* (Halifax), 19 April 1954.

CHAPTER SIX

1 J. Murray Lawson, *Description of the Runic Stones Found Near Yarmouth, Nova Scotia* (Yarmouth: *Yarmouth Herald*, 1898), 2–3; Harry Piers, "Remarks on the Fletcher and Related Stones of Yarmouth," *Collections of the Nova Scotia Historical Society* 17 (1913): 53–6.

2 It was evidently sent to Norway in 1913 or early 1914, with some involvement by Beckles Willson, who wrote on the "Runic Mystery" in *Nova Scotia: The Province That Has Been Passed By*, 101–6 (see chap. 1, n. 89). See G.S.L. [Grace S. Lewis] to Irving Pink, 2 February 1966, Yarmouth County Museum and Archives, Runic Stone Fonds [hereafter RSF]. It was stored in London for much of the war, under the auspices of the Canadian Pacific Railway.

3 Moses H. Nickerson, "A Short History on the Yarmouth 'Runic Stone,'" *Collections of the Nova Scotia Historical Society* 17 (1913): 51–2. Such remains the predominant view of almost every runologist who has considered the stone. There is "virtually no similarity between its markings and those of runic inscriptions," reaffirmed Birgitta Wallace Ferguson, staff archaeologist of the Atlantic Region of Parks Canada in 1992. See Birgitta Wallace Ferguson to Eric Ruff, 25 August 1992, RSF.

4 Sir Daniel Wilson, "The Vinland of the Northmen," *Transactions of the Royal Society of Canada*, sec. 2 (1890): 109–25 (read 27 May 1890); ser. 2, vol. 2 (read 20 May 1896): 49–51.

5 See Piers, "Remarks on the Fletcher and Related Stones."

6 Henry G. Farish [?] to R.R. McLeod, 26 September 1905, Harvey Papers, MG 1, vol. 1793, file 10/1, PANS.

7 Correspondence 1923–1935, George R. Hoskins to the Trustees of the Yarmouth Public Library, 19 June 1923, RSF.

8 Robert Blauveldt later remarked, "The Bay View stone was a fake for gullible tourists. I know where it is – but we'll let it stay there, and forget it." No name [Robert Blauveldt] to Robert R. Brown, 12 December 1949; see also Grace S. Lewis to L.S. Loomer, 28 November 1963, RSF.

9 Yet, given the pervasiveness of the themes of progress and Britishness in the years before the 1930s, even as late as 1918 the town's official guide placed far more emphasis on factories (lovingly illustrated and documented with scores of impressive-sounding statistics), stately public buildings (including both the Yarmouth South Fire Station and the Yarmouth North Fire Station), and the "noted hawthorn hedges of Yarmouth" than it did on the runic stone, which was briefly described and displayed along with these other attractions. See *Yarmouth, Town and County, Nova Scotia, Canada: 'Western Gateway of Nova Scotia'* (Yarmouth, 1918; repr. Yarmouth County Historical Society, 1995), 7, 18, 14.

10 The wilful Freydis Eriksdottir, daughter of Erik the Red and sister (or perhaps half-sister) of Leif Erikson, appears in both of the medieval Vinland sagas.

11 See C.H.L. Jones and Thomas H. Raddall, *The Markland Sagas: With a Discussion of Their Relation to Nova Scotia* (Montreal: Gazette Printing Company, 1934), 7–8, 111, 109, 115–16. See also Thomas Raddall to "Librarian, Yarmouth," 18 May 1933, RSF, for his early interest in the runic stone.

12 For example, Frederick J. Pohl elaborated a whole chronicle of pre-Columbian Nova Scotia from the Zeno Narrative published in sixteenth-century Venice, which recounted the adventures of two of the ancestors of the author, Niccolò Zeno. According to Pohl, the narrative clearly established that Prince Henry Sinclair of Scotland had visited Nova Scotia in 1398. He insisted that the Zeno Narrative's land of Drogio must be Nova Scotia because the smoking hills and flowing pitch of Drogio corresponded remarkably to the landscape of Pictou County, with its combustible coal seams. Moreover, a translation of "Sinclair" into the Mi'kmaw language would derive, through a rather complicated process, something a bit like the word "Glooscap," the central figure in Mi'kmaw religion. A bevy of such circumstantial evidence established that "Henry Sinclair was 'the first to place a really civilized foot' on North America, the continent Columbus never saw." Pohl had also spent twenty years studying Viking voyages to North America, attempting to pinpoint Vinland as Cape Cod. Arthur Godfrey, "Archeologist Sees Glooscap as Pre-Columbian Discovery," *Pictou Advocate*, 30 June 1955.

13 Olaf Strandwold, *The Yarmouth Stone* (Washington: Prosser Printing Co., n.d. [1934]).

14 Olaf Strandwold to George Perrin, 12 March and 2 October 1934, RSF.

15 *Chronicle* (Halifax), 11 December 1935.

16 Macdonald to Harvey, 6 June 1936, MG 1, vol. 1793, file 10/3, PANS.

17 Some identified the prankster as Richard Huntington of Yarmouth. Henry G. Farish wrote with respect to Huntington: "In his younger days he was always up to pranks & clever ones too. My father Dr. Farish & my two elder brothers Dr. Joseph & James all practicing in Yarmouth were very much interested in the Norse Stone or Runic Stone so called. It was discovered on Dr. Fletcher's premises – and they always thought that the inscription on it had its origin in Dick Huntington's fertile brain. He lived most of his youthful days with his grandmother Fletcher." Farish to R.R. McLeod, 26 September 1905, in Harvey Papers, MG 1, vol. 1793, file 10/1, PANS. Another popular theory, supported by some of his own descendants, has Fletcher himself as the prankster. See *Yarmouth Vanguard*, 13 August 1976; Eric Ruff to Dr. Herbert Brown, 25 February 1992, RSF.

18 Harvey to Macdonald, 9 June 1936, MG 1, vol. 1793, file 10/4, PANS.

19 Macdonald to Harvey, 3 August 1936, D.C. Harvey Papers, MG 1, vol. 1793, file 10/10, PANS.

20 *Norge Canada: A Magazine for Norsemen in Canada.* "Leif Erikson Memorial Issue," 1936. D.C. Harvey Papers, MG 1, vol. 1793, file 10/19, PANS.

21 *Yarmouth Light,* February 1936.

22 Gordon T. Lewis, *The Cruise of the Knorr: An Account of Early Norse Exploration in America* (Yarmouth: the author, 1938), unpaginated. Lewis documents none of these claims; nor could anyone very well do so.

23 No name [Robert Blauveldt] to Robert R. Brown, 12 December 1949, RSF.

24 See Laura Bradley to William Schröder, 17 August 1996, RSF: "One thing that you should be aware of is that many years ago a well meaning but unthinking Curator of the Museum had the inscription re-chiseled because he felt that the markings were faded. Unfortunately, this has meant that carbon dating tests will not be accurate, therefore we have not had any done. Also, because of this, the stone has lost some of its integrity." The underlying authority for this account of the stone's twentieth-century transformation was William Lent, the curator of the museum from 1969 to 1974. See RSF, file YMS 13, file-2, "Pamphlets, Books, Essays"; Eric Ruff to Birgitta Wallace Ferguson, 7 November 1992. No one has produced direct evidence.

25 Lewis, *Cruise of the Knorr;* Knute Haddeland to H. Leander d'Entremont, 13 January 1935 (copy for A.S. MacMillan), Harvey Papers, MG 1, vol. 1793, PANS.

26 Knute Haddeland, Starbuck, Manitoba, to H. Leander d'Entremont, Curator, De La Tour Museum, Centre East Pubnico, Nova Scotia (copy for A.S. MacMillan), n.d., MG 1 vol. 1793, file 12/9, PANS.

27 Will R. Bird, *Historic Nova Scotia* (Halifax: Government of Nova Scotia, 1948), 4 (emphasis added).

28 A.D. Fraser, of the School of Ancient Languages, Division of Archeology, University of Virginia, Va., to D.C. Harvey, 7 September 1938, MG 1 vol. 1793, file 12/21, PANS.

29 Bird to A.L. Kelsall, 24 November 1950, HSACP, MG 20, vol. 933, PANS.

30 W.R. Bird to Miss Mae Chisholm, 22 November 1954, HSACP, MG 20, vol. 933, PANS.

31 W.R. Bird to Evelyn Richardson, 11 February 1954, HSACP, MG 20, vol. 933, PANS.

32 W.R. Bird to Grace S. Lewis, 5 January 1954, HSACP, MG 20, vol. 933, PANS.

33 Birgitta Wallace Ferguson of Parks Canada to Eric Ruff, 25 August 1992, RSF. Skepticism about Strandwold's accreditation also surfaced in the local press; see Charles Spencer Goldring, letter to the *Yarmouth Vanguard,* 27 August 1975. He quotes a Scandinavian runologist who remarked that Strandwold "was able to find runes in any crevice or groove in any stone and decipher them."

34 See Olaf Strandwold to Miss C.A. Caie, 18 August 1947, RSF: "I have made three trips to New England, but the nearest I came to Yarmouth was Port Clyde and Thomaston, Maine."

35 Miss C.A. Caie to Mr Olaf Strandwold, 25 September 1947, RSF.

36 No name [Robert Blauveldt] to Robert R. Brown, 12 December 1949, RSF.

37 Robert Blauveldt, "Tusket: Capital of Vinland," *Yarmouth Herald,* 21 October 1959.

38 Allen would later lose faith in the stone after none of the experts on runes he consulted would confirm that the Yarmouth stone was authentic, with the Smithsonian Institution being particularly categorical. See W.F. Allen, Letter to the Editor, *Yarmouth Vanguard,* 14 December 1967 [repr. 17 August 1993].

39 Hjalmar Holand to Miss [Grace] Lewis, 11 July 1954 (copy), RSF; W.R. Bird to the Historic Sites Advisory Council, 15 January 1954, HSACP, MG 20, vol. 933, PANS.

40 Laura S. Salverson to Grace Lewis, 15 June 1954; Grace S. Lewis to Laura Salverson, n.d. [1954], RSF.

41 Grace S. Lewis to G. Harold Hopkins, President, Yarmouth Public Library, 14 July 1958, RSF.

42 Grace S. Lewis, citing Dr H.D. MacLeod, to *Yarmouth Herald*, 2 February 1966. MacLeod's statement was carried in the same *Herald* issue.

43 John C. Kernick, *Yarmouth, Nova Scotia, Canada* (Yarmouth, 1974).

44 In the blunt words of Stephen A. Davis in his "Early Societies: Sequences of Change," in Buckner and Reid, eds, *The Atlantic Region to Confederation* (see chap. 1, n. 16): "The search for the Norse settlements of Vinland, so prominent in the sagas, has generated a large volume of literature. With few exceptions the evidence presented is highly speculative or based upon shoddy fakes. It seems reasonable to suggest that Vinland may have been somewhere in eastern Canada, but until substantial physical evidence is discovered, its location will remain uncertain" (14–15).

45 *Yarmouth Vanguard*, 17 August 1993.

46 On pirate treasure, see especially William S. Crooker, *Oak Island Gold* (Halifax: Nimbus, 1993). It is indicative of the enormous appetite for such histories that by 2004 this volume was into its eighth printing.

47 John Campbell, "The Ancient Literature of Nova America," *Transactions of the Royal Society of Canada,* ser. 2, 1896, 49–51 (read 20 May 1896). For a discussion, see Willson, *Nova Scotia*, 103–4. As Willson noted, Campbell advanced the opinion that the script on the stone was "identical" with that found in Siberia, Mongolia, and Japan. This apparently far-fetched correspondence came as no surprise to the linguist, who had earlier established that many native languages – Choctaw and Cree, for instance – were "simply Japanese dialects" (103).

48 Elbert S. Esmiol, of Arvada, Colorado, advanced this translation. See Esmiol to Eric Ruff, 4 July 1974, RSF.

49 Barry Fell to Eric Ruff, 12 April 1976, RSF.

50 See Robert Silva of Baltimore to Eric Ruff, 26 July 1982, RSF. Libyan explorers were also thought to have carved rocks in Gaspésie, a claim treated with skepticism in Jean-Marie M. Dubois, "Même des pierres écrivent l'histoire du Québec et de l'Amérique," GEOS 12, no. 2 (1983).

51 Zoltán Andrew Simon to Eric Ruff, 29 October 1983, RSF.

52 According to Dr William Evans of Anglesey, North Wales, the stone was in fact an inscription by Meredydd (Meredith) registering that Welshmen had settled in Nova Scotia in AD 950. See Thomas Dunbabin, "Canada's First 1000 Years," *Chronicle-Herald* (Halifax), 31 August 1961.

53 See John T. Reid, Mining Engineer, Lovelock, Nevada, 1 May 1935, to Miss E.F. Raymund, Yarmouth Public Library, RSF. Reid requested extensive on-the-spot research from the Yarmouth librarians: "I [have] seen enough in the photographs that you sent me to know now that this is an important stone related to Mayan Mathematics, but I cannot get all the information I want from the stone without the measurements, for these people spoke, literally, in mathematics. Now, the place where this was found, that is the exact spot, by longitude and latitude, is the next matter I must learn something about. If you could give me this, which perhaps some engineer there could tell you that would aid me greatly." Weeks later, he made even more detailed and insistent research requests: "I note that you feel it would be impossible to give me the measurements that I require and as mentioned in mine of the 1st instant. As to anyone who would be willing to do that for you, I imagine that you have someone familiar with the use of

calipers in your vicinity, almost any carpenter, and a ship-carpenter especially could, if he would, do this for you. If he was unable to get a very fine measurement, then to the closest tenth of an inch would suffice for what I have in mind ... As to the thickness, the measurements take one inch from the outside of the stone at four places on the stone where it is widest and narrowest, would be desirable." Reid to E. F. Raymond, Yarmouth Public Library, 22 May 1935. September found Reid regretting that the library had not yet given him a satisfactory reply. Nonetheless, even in the absence of his requested measurements, he argued that there could be no doubt that the runic stone was Mayan. Furthermore, it had links to the Kensington Stone: "[T]he Stones in each case are Mayan Stones and each are very important ones, being of the nature of philosophers stones, in which there are incorporated mathematics used for instruction purpose." The connection of both stones with a central point in his home state of Nevada would, he hoped, be the subject of a projected volume on the "philosophers stones" used by Mayan mathematicians. See John T. Reid to Yarmouth Public Library, 2 September 1935, RSF.

54 *Yarmouth Vanguard*, 17 August 1993.

55 See Don Ledger and Chris Styles, *Dark Object: The World's Only Government-Documented UFO Crash* (New York: Random House, 2001). The book is available for purchase at the Shag Harbour Incident Society Museum, which opened in June 2007. Those interested in exploring Nova Scotia's UFO heritage may consult the museum's webpage – http://cuun.i2ce.com/misc/shagHarbourMuseum/ (accessed December 2007) – or they can write to the Shag Harbour Incident Society Museum, P.O. Box 53, Shag Harbour, N.S., B0W 3B0.

56 Harold Connolly first used this phrase in the 1930s. He reports on it in Harold Connolly to Angus L. Macdonald, 4 September 1946, Macdonald Papers, MG 2, vol. 904, file 28 f/2, PANS. For future premier A.S. MacMillan's deployment of a very similar notion of "cashing in on antiquity," see A.S. MacMillan Papers, MG 2, 876A, file 3/26, PANS: "Nova Scotia being the oldest Province in Canada arms were granted to her in 1621. The arms were achieved by grant of King James VI of Scotland and in 1625 by King Charles I. Nova Scotia is the only province who has an approved flag of her own. With the foregoing background I felt we were justified in going as far as we were financially able to place before the people of Canada and the United States all that Nova Scotia had to offer in the way of antiquities and attractions as well as her natural beauties of mountains, valleys, rivers and lakes as well as the ennumeral [*sic*; innumerable] sand beaches, the deep sea fishing off the Atlantic Shores and the Bay of Fundy having in mind that the Bay of Fundy tides are the highest in the world. Hence for these reason [*sic*] I persuaded the Premier and my colleagues to allow us to cash in on a policy of inducing Canadians and our friends from the United States to look over and enjoy Nova Scotia, the greatest vacation land on this continent."

57 *Yarmouth Light,* 26 November 1953.

58 C.B. Macpherson, *Property: Mainstream and Critical Positions* (Toronto: University of Toronto Press, 1978), 202.

59 Historic properties – the unintentionally revealing name of the waterfront heritage district in Halifax – here becomes a term of much more general application.

60 As Marx says, "capital is not a thing, but a social relation between persons which is

mediated through things." He immediately draws out the implications of this statement in a footnote: "A negro is a negro. In certain relations he becomes a slave. A mule is a machine for spinning cotton. Only in certain relations does it become capital. Outside these circumstances, it is no more capital than gold is intrinsically money, or sugar is the price of sugar." Karl Marx, *Capital: A Critique of Political Economy,* vol. 1, trans. Ben Fowkes (London: Penguin, 1990), 932.

61 Alfred W. Crosby, *Ecological Imperialism: The Biological Expansion of Europe, 900–1900* (Cambridge: Cambridge University Press, 1986). According to John Weaver, between 1.5 billion and 2 billion acres of arable land and productive pastures were newly exploited from 1750 to 1900. John C. Weaver, *The Great Land Rush and the Making of the Modern World, 1650–1900* (Montreal and Kingston: McGill-Queen's University Press, 2003), 89.

62 This figure is drawn from page 61 of Gail Bossenga, "Society," in William Doyle, ed., *The Short Oxford History of France: Old Regime France* (Oxford: Oxford University Press, 2001). Note again the necessity of social context to enabling such forms of property. It is not simply a matter of seeing an attractive object and slapping a price tag on it. As these words are being written in Chicago, the state governor is being fingerprinted by the police as part of an ongoing scandal in which he is alleged to have tried to clandestinely sell a U.S. Senate seat for a million dollars. Senatorial status would no doubt command a handsome price, in theory. But in context such an attempt amounts almost to a category mistake, insofar as American society rigorously excludes public office from the sphere of private property. Little about this aborted transaction would, however, have raised eyebrows in eighteenth-century France, where venality of office was a mainstay of public life.

63 Bird, *Thirteen Years,* 143 (see chap. 3, n.13).

64 Bird, *So Much to Record,* 134 (see chap. 3, n. 92).

65 For an excellent discussion, see Barbara Arneil, *John Locke and America: The Defence of English Colonialism* (Oxford: Clarendon Press, 1996); also of note as a rigorous critique of "Lockean property rights" as they have normally been construed is Gopal Sreenivasan, *The Limits of Lockean Rights in Property* (New York and Oxford: Oxford University Press, 1995).

66 Raddall, *Roger Sudden,* 223 (see chap. 4, n. 78).

67 Raddall, *Hangman's Beach,* 32–3 (see chap. 4, n. 16).

68 "The Day We Celebrate," Response to the toast by Col. Robert S. Henry at the two hundred and seventh anniversary dinner of the St Andrew's Society of Charleston, 30 November 1936, Macdonald Papers, MG 2, vol. 904, file 28/1/46, PANS.

69 Macdonald, *Task of Liberalism,* 3–4 (see chap. 5, n. 83).

70 Drawing upon the discussion in Philip Girard, "Land Law, Liberalism, and the Agrarian Ideal: British North America, 1750–1920," in John McLaren, A.R. Buck, and Nancy E. Wright, eds, *Despotic Dominion: Property Rights in British Settler Societies* (Vancouver: University of British Columbia Press, 2005), 120, 122.

71 Acquired in 1939, Uniacke House drew over twenty-seven thousand visitors a year by 1951, which (according to Bird) "proved that the average tourist is greatly interested in things historic, and we are doing all we can to show him the historic features of the oldest part of Canada." W.R. Bird to Don Snowden, 13 December 1952, HSACP, MG 20, vol. 934, PANS. Historic houses by the score would follow its lead.

72 W.R. Bird to R.L. Stanfield, 16 December 1960, HSACP, MG 10, vol. 934, PANS.

73 Nova Scotia, Royal Commission on Provincial Development and Rehabilitation, *Report*, sec. 12: "Report on the Tourist Industry" (Halifax, 1944), 13, 25.

74 D.C. Harvey to A.L. Macdonald, 10 October 1947, Macdonald Papers, MG 2, vol. 933, PANS.

75 D.C. Harvey to A.L. Macdonald, 9 September 1947, Macdonald Papers, MG 2, vol. 933, PANS.

76 Certified Copy of Order in Council, Macdonald Papers, MG 2, vol. 933, F.24-6/7, PANS.

77 See, for example, the Minutes of the Historic Sites Advisory Council, 13 September 1957, MG 20, vol. 934, PANS.

78 W.R. Bird to R.L. Stanfield, 30 June 1961, HSACP, MG 20, vol. 934, PANS.

79 W.R. Bird to R.L. Stanfield, 3 September 1958, HSACP, MG 20, vol. 933, PANS.

80 W.R. Bird to R.L. Stanfield, 22 April 1960, HSACP, MG 20, vol. 934, PANS.

81 W.R. Bird to Angus L. Macdonald, 11 February 1953, HSACP, MG 20, vol. 933, PANS.

82 W.R. Bird to Douglas R. Oliver, 5 July 1950, HSACP, MG 20, vol. 933, PANS.

83 W.R. Bird to A.L. Macdonald, 5 September 1950, HSACP, MG 20, vol. 933, PANS.

84 Merkel Papers, MS 2.326, J-1, Miscellaneous Notes, DUA.

85 G.K. Fielding, "Report on Ten Mile House," 24 November 1960, and "Confidential Report: Listing No. 276," HSACP, MG 20, vol. 934, PANS.

86 *Mail* (Halifax), 12 May 1948, letter of "Interested Citizen"; Martha B. Brookfield to A.L. Macdonald, 12 August 1952 (copy), Macdonald Papers, MG 2, vol. 972, PANS.

87 W.R. Bird to E.F.J. Flemming, 3 November 1953, HSACP, MG 20, vol. 933, PANS.

88 Phyllis Blakeley to Shirley Blakeley, 25 January 1952, MG 1, vol. 3045, PANS. Borrett was also a heritage activist, writing to Will Bird to urge the restoration of Prince's Lodge (a relic of the Duke of Kent's Lodge in Rockingham, and hence of the heroic age commemorated by Raddall and Bird). William Coates Borrett to W.R. Bird, 22 July 1949, HSACP, MG 20, vol. 933, PANS.

89 Bird, *Historic Nova Scotia*, 82; see also Nova Scotia, *Nova Scotia, Canada's Ocean Playground* (n.p. [Halifax], n.d. [1935]), 36.

90 W.R. Bird to R.L. Stanfield, 8 February 1963, HSACP, MG 20, vol. 933, PANS.

91 Mrs K.G.T. (Deborah) Webster to W.R. Bird, 26 July 1949, MG 20, vol. 933, PANS.

92 Margaret L. Pugsley to W.R. Bird, 1 February 1963, HSACP, MG 20, vol. 934, PANS.

93 There is no easy way of confirming this impression. Preservationists did not have to register with any sort of central agency whose records we could pull. However, we have not found any prominent individual arguing on behalf of historical reconstruction and preservation in the period 1935–64 who was not of the "middling classes" – that is, who was not a small businessperson, professional, person of independent means, or someone linked to these social positions by marriage. Such people, after all, had the leisure time for such things. It also seems relatively apparent that women exercised disproportionate influence in this sphere, at least on the local level. "The social origins of public history" merits further exploration in more detailed local case studies.

94 Mrs K.G.T. Webster to W.R. Bird, 26 July 1949, HSACP, MG 20, vol. 933, PANS.

95 James D. How to W.R. Bird and members of the Historic Sites Advisory Council of Nova Scotia, n.d., HSACP, MG 20, vol. 933, PANS. Williamsburg, Virginia, is of course home to Colonial Williamsburg – the eighteenth-century capital of the Common-

wealth of Virginia that, beginning in 1926, was substantially reconstructed under Rockefeller patronage and that to this day bills itself as "the world's largest living history museum" (http://www.history.org/foundation/mission.cfm [accessed 19 January 2009]). Later in this chapter, we shall hear more of its influence north of the border.

96 W.R. Bird to Members of the Historic Sites Advisory Council of Nova Scotia, date illegible [August 1956], MG 20, vol. 934 (citing a letter from Laura Lawson), PANS.

97 W.R. Bird to R.L. Stanfield, 2 October 1961, HSACP, MG 20, vol. 934, PANS.

98 Alfred E. Jamieson, Secretary Halifax Civic Improvement League, to D.C. Harvey, 12 July 1938, MG 1, vol. 1789, file 1/31, PANS.

99 It is now known as the Royal Nova Scotia Historical Society. A detailed monograph on the society's many activities has yet to appear. Invaluable insights into its work can be found in the extraordinary diaries of Harry Piers, MG 1, vol. 1046, PANS. The statistic comes from the concluding pages of Bird, *Historic Nova Scotia*, 108–14.

100 One of the society's leading figures – and a mighty champion of the Fletcher Stone – Robert B. Blauveldt, UE, LLB, described his activities on his 1960 letterhead as involving "Blauveldt Publicity. Publishers, Historical Research, Radio & Newspaper Service; Campaigns, Public Relations, Promotional Advertising." R.B. [Robert Blauveldt] to W.R. Bird, 20 May 1960, HSACP, MG 20, vol. 934, PANS.

101 Yarmouth County Historical Society, Quiz, 6 March 1959, HSACP, MG 20, vol. 934, PANS. The answer: "Mud Island." Tourists on the Main Street of Yarmouth still learn much from Historical Society signage alerting them to the site of the "[f]irst brick mercantile building in western Nova Scotia, opened October 11, 1856," the "[f]irst plank sidewalk in the town" (commemorated twice over, once by a stone set into the sidewalk, and again in a sign on the Young and Baker brick building), and the site of the "Royal Department Store opened … on April 2, 1927 [which] served as the retail and social heart of the downtown," etc.

102 There were other smaller, more specialized societies, such as the Association of VanCortlandt Grantees, a group organized by Blauveldt to commemorate the descendants of forty Loyalist officers who accompanied Major Philip VanCortlandt to Tusket in 1788.

103 Bird, *Historic Nova Scotia*, 7, 38, 40, 42.

104 On these themes, in addition to materials referenced earlier, the reader might also consult F.H.H. Williamson, "Report on Investigation of Historic Sites in Maritime Provinces," Memorandum, n.d. (copy), Harvey Papers, PANS; A.J.B. Johnston, "Preserving History: The Commemoration of 18th Century Louisbourg, 1895–1940," *Acadiensis* 12, no. 2 (Spring, 1983): 53–80; for the Cabot Trail, consult A.S. MacMillan, "A Dream Come True: Story of the Development of the Tourist Industry in Northern Inverness and Victoria Counties," n.d. [1952], Macdonald Papers, MG 2, vol. 967, file 11-1, PANS.

105 Many people kept calling it by the previously standard title, "Order of Good Cheer," because "Order of the Good Time" sounds odd in English. Officialdom had excised "cheer" because it carried unseemly alcoholic connotations. W.R. Bird to A.A. Dunphy, 14 July 1950, HSACP, MG 20, vol. 933, PANS.

106 *Tourism Report, Journals of the House of Assembly, Nova Scotia* [hereafter JHA], 1937: 23. In 1941, the period was shortened to seven days. JHA, 1942: 30.

107 Membership in the order entitled tourists to receive "Special Attention by Hotel Men,"

"Special Attention by Service Stations and Garages," "Special Attention by Local Information Bureaus," "Extra Service at Shops," "Travel Booklets," and "Official Courtesy" – "The Mounted Police and Motor Constables will be instructed to render any help requested by these members and to use the utmost courtesy in dealing with minor infractions by them of the Motor Vehicle Act." Nova Scotia, *Nova Scotia, Canada's Ocean Playground* (1935), insert between pp. 20 and 21.

108 JHA, 1949: 60.
109 Ibid., 1956: 50.
110 Taylor, *Negotiating the Past*, 118 (see chap. 1, n. 12). See also C.W. Jeffreys, "The Reconstruction of the Port Royal Habitation of 1605–13," *Canadian Historical Review* 20 (December 1939): 369–77.
111 "Order of the Good Time," vertical files, vol. 197, #24, PANS.
112 JHA, 1938: 55.
113 *Halifax Star,* 25 September 1937.
114 *Chronicle* (Halifax), 1 October 1937.
115 Marjorie Ayer, "Thoughts on 'Order of the Good Time,'" *Chronicle* (Halifax), 30 September 1937. As his name and his predilection for Burns might indicate, Tweedsmuir was not in fact English, despite what Ayer might say. Born in Perth, an alumnus of the University of Glasgow, a past president of the Scottish Historical Society, the former MP for the Scottish universities, and biographer of Montrose and Walter Scott, he was unmistakably a Scotsman.
116 Ella K. Cork, Memorandum to the Members of the Historical Committee of the Canadian Tourism Association, 21 June 1950, HSACP, MG 20, vol. 933, PANS.
117 L.B. Firth to W.R. Bird, 12 January 1960, HSACP, MG 20, vol. 934, PANS. Bird fretted that the wives of the brothers who owned the museum might have sold invaluable old ships blocks for a pittance to canny tourists who knew the value of the collection: W.R. Bird to R.L. Stanfield, 18 January 1960, HSACP, MG 20, vol. 934, PANS.
118 *Morning Chronicle*, 27 August 1921. Milner was, of course, a Cassandra.
119 W.R. Bird to R.L. Stanfield, 18 January 1960, HSACP, MG 20, vol. 934, PANS.
120 Cited in W.R. Bird to Members of the Historic Sites Advisory Council, August 1956, HSACP, MG 20, vol. 934, PANS.
121 W.R. Bird to R.L. Stanfield, 18 August 1959, HSACP, MG 20, vol. 934, PANS.
122 W.R. Bird to Mary P. Webster, 7 August 1959, HSACP, MG 20 vol. 933, PANS.
123 W.R. Bird to Angus L. Macdonald, 14 June 1951, HSACP, MG 20, vol. 933, PANS.
124 Taylor, *Negotiating the Past,* 20.
125 Mrs K.G.T. (Deborah) Webster to W.R. Bird, 26 July 1949, HSACP, MG 20, vol. 933, PANS. Webster lived in Milton, Mass.
126 *Evening News* (New Glasgow), 23 August 1951.
127 Crowdis and R. Macgregor Dawson, "Memorandum on Provincial Museum," 1944, Macdonald Papers, MG 2, vol. 904, file 28 f.6/3, PANS.
128 Michael Wallace, "Visiting the Past: History Museums in the United States," in Susan Porter Benson et al., eds, *Presenting the Past: Essays on History and the Public* (Philadelphia: Temple University Press, 1986), 137–61, citation at 147–8.
129 Mrs K.L. Dawson to W.R. Bird, 30 October 1950; Margaret L. Pugsley to W.R. Bird, 1 February 1963, HSACP, MG 20, vol. 933, PANS.

130 James D. How to W.R. Bird and members of the Historic Sites Advisory Council of Nova Scotia, n.d., HSACP, MG 20, vol. 933, PANS.

131 Miss K. McLennan to W.R. Bird, 19 January 1954, HSACP, MG 20, vol. 933, PANS. Katharine McLennan was daughter of J.S. McLennan, the historian and executive of the Dominion Iron and Steel Company, and an artist in her own right. See A.J.B. Johnston, "A Vanished Era: The Petersfield Estate of J.S. McLennan, 1900–1942," in Kenneth Donovan, ed., *Cape Breton at 200: Historical Essays in Honour of the Island's Bicentennial 1785–1985* (Sydney: University College of Cape Breton Press, 1985), 85–105.

132 C.H. Wright to W.R. Bird, with enclosure, 9 March 1951, HSACP, MG 20, vol. 933, PANS.

133 Lowenthal, *Heritage Crusade,* 146 (see Prologue, n. 13).

134 Dominion Atlantic Railway, *High Lights* (see chap. 2, n. 85).

135 John Quinpool [J.W. Regan], *First Things in Acadia, "The Birthplace of a Continent"* (Halifax: First Things Publishers, 1936), preface. Regan began his career as a journalist and later became the Associated Press's correspondent for the Maritimes. Later still, he served as deputy mayor of Halifax. He devoted the years of his retirement, from the 1930s until his death in 1945, to historical books and pamphlets on Halifax and Nova Scotia.

136 Lowenthal, *Heritage Crusade,* 174.

137 Quinpool [Regan], *First Things, passim.* The only Nova Scotians left out of this vast and often tendentious record of firsts were, ironically, those whose ancestors had actually come first: the Mi'kmaq. For a more recent contribution to this genre that makes room for the Mi'kmaq, see Dan Soucoup, *Maritime Firsts: Historic Events, Inventions & Achievements* (Lawrencetown Beach, N.S.: Pottersfield Press, 1996).

138 W. Kaye Lamb to C. Bruce Fergusson, 4 August 1964, C. Bruce Fergusson Papers, MG 1, vol. 1911, folder 11, no. 7, PANS.

139 W.R. Bird to N.J.P. Melnick, 26 October 1960, HSACP, MG 20, vol. 934, PANS.

140 J.C. Webster to Harvey, 2 January 1938, MG 1, vol. 1790, file 1/57, PANS. The claim was that J.D.B. Fraser of Pictou County applied chloroform to his wife as she delivered in 1848.

141 Bird, *This Is Nova Scotia,* 77. Annapolis Royal was not the only Town of First Things. In its 1959 quiz, the Yarmouth Historical Society asked visitors, "[W]hat Yarmouthian built Canada's first Mortuary Chapel?" HSACP, MG 20, vol. 934, PANS.

142 W.R. Bird to Members of the Historic Sites Advisory Council of Nova Scotia, 18 November 1955, MG 20, vol. 934, PANS. In the records of the council, a far higher percentage (24 per cent) of cases put forward by local historical societies succeeded, compared with the overall average of 10 per cent.

143 W.R. Bird to R.L. Stanfield, 16 December 1960, HSACP, MG 10, vol. 934, PANS.

144 W.R. Bird to F.G. Fuller, Town Clerk, Amherst, 3 March 1948, HSACP, MG 20, vol. 933, PANS.

145 W.R. Bird to R.L. Stanfield, 18 August 1959, HSACP, MG 20, vol. 934, PANS.

146 Report of the Historic Sites Advisory Council for the Period Ending March 31, 1960, JHA, 1961: 26.

147 W.R. Bird to R.L. Stanfield, 19 October 1960, HSACP, MG 20, vol. 934, PANS.

148 W.R. Bird to R.L. Stanfield, 21 February 1961, HSACP, MG 20, vol. 934, PANS.

149 W.R. Bird to R.L. Stanfield, 14 May 1959, HSACP, MG 20, vol. 934, PANS. Taking the tourist gaze into account (and in contrast with the Historic Sites and Monuments

Board), the council did not impose a uniform style of display because its members thought it more likely that tourists would photograph the monuments if each one looked distinctive. W.R. Bird to Mr Stephen McLellan, Spencer's Island, N.S., 15 June 1963, HSACP, MG 20, vol. 934, PANS.

150 W.R. Bird to R.S. Longley, 10 July 1961, HSACP, MG 20, vol. 933, PANS.

151 See Hardy, *The Evangeline Land* (see chap. 1, n. 84): "There are but few cities in Canada that can boast of natural and artificial beauties such as displayed at Mountain Cemetery. It should be visited by every visitor who reaches Yarmouth" (n.p.).

152 W.R. Bird to Robert Stanfield, 19 September 1957, HSACP, MG 20, vol. 933, PANS.

153 Historic Sites Advisory Council, Minutes, 26 October 1951, HSACP, MG 20, vol. 934, PANS.

154 W.R. Bird to Arthur B. Merry, 29 September 1961, HSACP, MG 20, vol. 934, PANS. In addition to the argument of economy, the council could make the no-less-liberal point that the state had no place in the presbyteries of the nation. Many congregations cordially shared this view. The parishioners of the Old Meeting House in Barrington, one of the most significant of Nova Scotia's early religious structures, rebuffed all official requests that they repair their heritage property. "It was as if I were appearing before a session of Presbyterian elders and reporting some moral lapse," Bird remarked. Elsewhere – Morden, Baddeck, Bridgeville – factionalism, intensified by religious division or based on "small jealousies regarding prestige," prevailed. W.R. Bird to R.L. Stanfield, 12 January 1960; W.R. Bird to R.L. Stanfield, 6 November, 1961, HSACP, MG 20, vol. 934, PANS.

155 W.R. Bird to R.L. Stanfield, 21 January 1958, HSACP, MG 20, vol. 933, PANS.

156 Phyllis Blakeley to Uncle Welton and Aunt Annie, 27 October 1949, MG 1, vol. 3045, no. 8, PANS.

157 Ibid.

158 Thomas Raddall, "An Address by Thomas H. Raddall to the Commercial Club, Halifax, N.S, on the subject 'Halifax and the Tourist Trade,'" November 15th, 1945, Macdonald Papers, MG 2, vol. 907, 37B, general correspondence, PANS.

159 Harold A. Ball, of the Halifax Chronicle and Halifax Daily Star, to Angus L. Macdonald, 24 November 1945, Macdonald Papers, MG 2, vol. 907, 37B, general correspondence, PANS.

160 Macdonald to Harold A. Ball, 15 December 1945, Macdonald Papers, MG 2, vol. 907, file 37B, PANS.

161 Memorandum for W.R. Bird, undated [1948], Macdonald Papers, MG 2, vol. 933, file 24-6/6, PANS.

162 Harold Connolly to Macdonald, 28 April 1948, Macdonald Papers, MG 2, vol. 933, file 24-6/5, PANS.

163 Unsigned [presumably Macdonald] to Harold Connolly, 14 May 1948, Macdonald Papers, MG 2, vol. 933, file 24-6/4, PANS.

164 W.R. Bird to D.R. Oliver, 5 July 1950, Minutes of the 3rd Meeting, Historic Sites Advisory Council, HSACP, MG 20, vol. 933, PANS.

165 Minutes of the 3rd Meeting, Historic Sites Advisory Council, HSACP, MG 20, vol. 934, PANS.

166 Ibid.

167 Ibid.

168 W.R. Bird to Tom [Thomas Raddall], 14 January 1955, HSACP, MG 20, vol. 933, PANS.

169 W.R. Bird to Henry D. Hicks, 22 August 1954, HSACP, MG 20, vol. 933, PANS.

170 W.R. Bird to R.L. Stanfield, 21 January 1958, HSACP, MG 20, vol. 933, PANS.

171 W.R. Bird to Arthur Kelsall, 9 August 1960, HSACP, MG 20, vol. 934, PANS; Halifax Pattern Works to Historic Sites Advisory Council, Invoice, 30 July 1963, HSACP, MG 20, vol. 934, PANS.

172 This neglect is mitigated to the extent that many events in the earlier period of Anglo-French conflict were already being commemorated by the federal Historic Sites and Monuments Board, which deemed them worthy of national significance.

173 All these statistics are based on the records of the Historic Sites Advisory Council.

174 W.R. Bird to Mrs K.G.T. Webster, 29 July 1949, HSACP, MG 20, vol. 933, PANS.

175 W.R. Bird to R.L. Stanfield, 16 December 1960, HSACP, MG 20, vol. 934, PANS.

176 Mrs K.L. Dawson to W.R. Bird, 30 October 1950, HSACP, MG 20, vol. 933, PANS.

177 W.R. Bird to R.L. Stanfield, 6 November 1961, HSACP, MG 20, vol. 934, PANS.

178 W.R. Bird to R.L. Stanfield, 21 February 1961, HSACP, MG 20, vol. 934, PANS.

179 W.R. Bird to R.L. Stanfield, 1 November 1962, HSACP, MG 20, vol. 934, PANS.

180 W.R. Bird to R.L. Stanfield, 29 December 1958, HSACP, MG 20, vol. 933, PANS. Nonetheless, the mansion was saved from the wrecking ball and now functions as part of the university.

181 W.R. Bird to R.L. Stanfield, 18 August 1959, HSACP, MG 20, vol. 934, PANS.

182 W.R. Bird to Willard F. Allen, 15 August 1956, HSACP, MG 20, vol. 933, PANS. This was not, however, an official council plaque.

183 W.R. Bird to R.L. Stanfield, 8 February 1963, HSACP, MG 20, vol. 934, PANS. Over the past two decades, writings on the transnational significance of the history of Nova Scotia's blacks have blossomed, with as-yet-unrealized implications for the province's tourism/history system. For an insightful overview of some major recent titles, see Harvey Amai Whitfield, "Reviewing Blackness in Atlantic Canada and the African Atlantic Canadian Diaspora," *Acadiensis* 37, no. 2 (Summer/Autumn 2008): 130–9. Significant recent books include Simon Schama, *Rough Crossings: Britain, the Slaves and the American Revolution* (London: BBC Books, 2005); Casandra Pybus, *Epic Journeys of Freedom: Runaway Slaves of the American Revolution and Their Global Quest for Liberty* (Boston: Beacon Press, 2006); Sylvia Frey, *Water from the Rock: Black Resistance in a Revolutionary Age* (Princeton: Princeton University Press, 1991). For imaginative new work that analyses the responses of British travellers to blacks in Nova Scotia and shows how perceptions of their economic conditions affected debates over abolition in Britain, see Jeffrey L. McNairn, "British Travellers, Nova Scotia's Black Communities and the Problem of Freedom to 1860," *Journal of the Canadian Historical Association*, n.s., 19, no. 1 (2008): 27–56.

184 This museum opened in 1941. It was ahead of its time in attempting to simulate nineteenth-century mining conditions in a replica of an 1887 working face at the Albion Colliery at Stellarton. *Weekly Cape Bretoner* (Sydney), 12 July 1958.

185 W.R. Bird to R.L. Stanfield, 16 May 1962; J.M. Murphy to W.R. Bird, 5 June 1961; W.R. Bird to J.M. Murphy, 23 May 1962, HSACP, MG 20, vol. 934, PANS.

186 On one occasion, Bird blocked the cooperatives' entry into history by going to Tignish, P.E.I., and getting "positive proof that operations at Tignish ... were commenced three years before such an effort in Nova Scotia." W.R. Bird to R.L. Stanfield, 11 July 1958, HSACP, MG 20, vol. 933, PANS.

187 W.R. Bird to the Historic Sites Advisory Council, 24 April 1963; Historic Sites Advisory Council, Minutes, 20 May 1960, HSACP, MG 20, vol. 934, PANS.

188 Historic Sites Advisory Council, 13 September 1957, HSACP, MG 20, vol. 934, PANS.

189 See, for example, Edward Williams, *Nova Scotia from Yarmouth to Halifax* (Yarmouth: Edward Williams, 1901), 19.

190 Untitled note on Shubenacadie [on stylistic grounds, probably written by Bird], 8 August 1949, HSACP, MG 20, vol. 933, PANS.

191 Arthur B. Merry to W.R. Bird, 23 September 1961, HSACP, MG 20, vol. 934, PANS.

192 W.R. Bird to Arthur B. Merry, 21 November 1961; W.R. Bird to R.L. Stanfield, 16 May 1962, HSACP, MG 20, vol. 934, PANS.

193 Thomas H. Raddall to "Edwin" [E.K. Ford], 25 January 1949; A.L. Macdonald to E.K. Ford, 3 February 1949, W.R. Bird to James P. Richards, 5 July 1950, HSACP, MG 20, vol. 933, PANS.

194 W.R. Bird to "Tom" [Thomas H. Raddall], 26 May 1951, HSACP, MG 20, vol. 933, PANS.

195 In an overview of Cabot historiography, Brian Cuthbertson remarks, "In our story of John Cabot and His Historians, 'race' will be an ever present factor." He identifies Rev. Moses Harvey in Newfoundland and Samuel Edward Dawson in Nova Scotia as the two commentators most responsible for making a British Columbus of Cabot as his quatercentenary approached. Brian Cuthbertson, "John Cabot and His Historians: 500 Years of Controversy," *Royal Nova Scotia Historical Society Journal* 1 (1998): 16–35, citation at 24.

196 Observers outside Canada, though, may be blissfully unaware of any vexation surrounding the event. For instance, in his prodigious history of Europe, the British historian Norman Davies passes over Cabot in a sentence that offhandedly accords him to Cape Breton – "which," he continues rather more relevantly, "he took to be part of China." Norman Davies, *Europe: A History* (Oxford: Oxford University Press, 1996), 511.

197 See Nova Scotia, *Nova Scotia: The Ocean Playground* (Halifax, 1930), 2–3.

198 See Peter F. Pope, *The Many Landfalls of John Cabot* (Toronto: University of Toronto Press, 1997).

199 Ibid., 82–9, citation at 89. Pope notes that the Cape Breton landfall "first received intensive scholarly attention in the years immediately preceding the Cabot quadcentenary of 1897, with the publication of a series of Samuel Edward Dawson in the receptive pages of the *Transactions of the Royal Society of Canada*" (83).

200 D.C. Harvey to A.S. MacMillan, 8 May 1935, Harvey Papers, MG 1, vol. 1783, file 1/3, PANS.

201 D.C. Harvey to A.L. Macdonald, 26 February 1940, Harvey Papers, MG 1, vol. 1783, file 1/16, PANS.

202 S.P. Whiteway, "Experts Agree on Cabot's Landfall," unidentified article, Harvey Papers, MG 1, vol. 1783, file 1/18, PANS.

203 G.R.F. Prowse, letter, *Chronicle* (Halifax), 18 November 1935.

204 G.R.F. Prowse to Harvey, 23 October 1940, Harvey Papers, MG 1, vol. 1783, file 1/22, PANS. Prowse's "Bonavista tradition" remains as strong as ever. The municipal homepage of Bonavista, Newfoundland, carries the proud banner "Landfall of John Cabot, A.D. 1497": "Bonavista is where modern North America began. On June 24th, 1497, [an] Italian explorer sailing under the British flag for King Henry VII, made landfall in the New World. 'O Buona Vista,' Giovani Caboto was said to exclaim after nearly two months at sea. Oh happy site!" http://www.bonavista.net/ (accessed 17 July 2009).

205 Harold Innis, "Recent Books on the American Arctic," *Canadian Historical Review* 22 (1941): 187, as cited in Pope, *Many Landfalls*, 81.

206 D.C. Harvey to A.L. Macdonald, 11 May 1940, Harvey Papers, MG 1, vol. 1783, file 1/19, PANS.

207 W.R. Bird to Henry Hicks, 6 December 1955, HSACP, MG 20, vol. 933, PANS.

208 In 1954, the Halifax *Herald* misled its readers by headlining news of a new archival publication devoted to old maps, "Chart Indicates Cabot Landed in Cape Breton"; the small print suggested that he might also have landed in Labrador (a claim that the reporter, Thomas Dunhalun, airily dismisses). *Herald,* 28 May 1954. As Peter Pope remarks, all claims to certainty on the issue must be treated skeptically, in the absence of new evidence (*Many Landfalls,* 5).

209 *Chronicle* (Halifax), 19 April 1940.

210 For an example of the letterhead, see Mae Munro to W.R. Bird, 23 May 1959, HSACP, MG 20, vol. 934, PANS.

211 W.R. Bird to Members of the Historic Sites Advisory Council of Nova Scotia, 18 November 1955, HSACP, MG 20, vol. 934, PANS.

212 Mrs Maie Munro, Cape Breton Historical Society, Open Letter to the National Historic Sites and Monuments Board, 14 April 1953, HSACP, MG 20, vol. 933, PANS.

213 Maie Munro to W.R. Bird, 24 January 1953, HSACP, MG 20, vol. 933, PANS.

214 W.R. Bird to Maie Munro, 4 February 1953, HSACP, MG 20, vol. 933, PANS.

215 Emily E. Brown, Open Letter (mimeo), 17 April 1952, HSACP, MG 20, vol. 933, PANS.

216 W.R. Bird to Henry Hicks, 6 December 1955, HSACP, MG 20, vol. 933, PANS.

217 W.R. Bird to Members of the Historic Sites Advisory Council, 18 November 1955, HSACP, MG 20, vol. 934, PANS.

218 Bird, mark well, urged the society to make a further request – even telling Mrs Munro which points would make the greatest impact with his council. He clearly sympathized with her movement.

219 Historic Sites Advisory Council Minutes, 9 May 1958, MG 20, vol. 934, PANS.

220 W.R. Bird to R.L. Stanfield, 14 May 1958, HSACP, MG 20, vol. 933, PANS.

221 "Bust of Cabot to Be Unveiled," *Cape Breton Post,* 19 June 1959. The hopeful *Post* forecast Bird's attendance, with a parade of dignitaries, C. Bruce Fergusson (Nova Scotia archivist), E.A. Manson (Nova Scotia minister of trade and industry), and Fitzroy Chamberlain (lord mayor of Bristol) also included.

222 One can follow the imbroglio of the statue in W.R. Bird to R.L. Stanfield, 1 April 1959 and 1 June 1959, HSACP, MG 20, vol. 934, PANS.

223 Frank Keating, "An Argument Rages to Beat the Band, Swallow-Tail Whiskers, Where Did He Land?" *Weekly Cape Bretoner,* 21 June 1958.

224 C.B. Fergusson (Harvey's successor at the PANS) and Bird himself both thought it most likely that Cabot landed at Cape Breton, the easternmost extremity of Cape Breton Island, not Cape North.

225 The 1997 quincentennial inspired Heritage Canada to sponsor a symposium on "Cabot and His World," held at St John's and Bonavista (the favoured landfall of Newfoundland patriots). A panel convened to answer the inevitable question "Where did John Cabot make his landfall," ecumenically including ex-Newfoundland lieutenant-governor Fabian O'Dea, former head of Heritage Nova Scotia Brian Cuthbertson, and the Bristol-based historical geographer Alan F. Williams. This trio opined that the question admitted of no definitive answer. Williams said any possible response would only "balance probabilities" rather than proclaim certainties. O'Dea found all the relevant maps irredeemably dubious. Cuthbertson concluded, "All that can be said, without too great a fear of contradiction, is that Cabot … found land somewhere between Labrador and the Gulf of Maine, landed once and took possession." However, so inescapable had the conventions of the debate become that they compelled all three to answer the unanswerable. In southern Labrador, said Williams; on Cape Bonavista, said O'Dea; at Cape North, said Cuthbertson. Williams, for one, had felt himself under a great deal of pressure. When the president of the Newfoundland Historical Society had asked Williams (former head of geography at the Memorial University of Newfoundland) to write a commemorative volume on Cabot, "We both knew that the province's Cabot 500 Committee would brook nothing but Bonavista for a landfall." See Iona Bulgin, ed., *Cabot and His World Symposium, June 1997: Papers and Presentations* (St John's: Newfoundland Historical Society, 1999), 85–104.

CONCLUSION

1 Cited in Wolfgang Schivelbusch, *The Railway Journey: The Industrialization of Time and Space in the 19th Century* (Berkeley and Los Angeles: University of California Press, 1986), 52.

2 Ibid., 55; Karl Marx, *Outlines of the Critique of Political Economy* (The Grundrisse), in Karl Marx and Friedrich Engels, *Collected Works,* vol. 28 (New York: International Publishers, 1986), 448: "The more production comes to be based on exchange value, and thus on exchange, the more important for production do the physical conditions of exchange become – the means of communication and transport. By its very nature, capital strives to go beyond every spatial limitation. Hence the creation of physical conditions of exchange – of the means of communication and transport – becomes a necessity for it to an incomparably greater degree: space must be annihilated by time."

3 Schivelbusch, *Railway Journey,* 60–1.

4 Thomas C. Holt discusses liberal ideology this way in *The Problem of Freedom: Race, Labor and Politics in Jamaica and Britain, 1832–1938* (Baltimore: Johns Hopkins University Press, 1992), 25.

5 Stan Rogers, "Pharisee," on the posthumous recording *from coffee house to concert hall*

(2000). He varies this phrase as "I know this must sound different, but to us it's always been the same" and "We know this must sound different, but for us it always stays the same."

6 To reference Patrick Wright, *On Living in an Old Country* (see chap. 8, n. 1), whose inspiration in turn was the work of Agnes Heller.

7 Robert Graves, *Good-bye to All That: An Autobiography,* ed. Paul Fussell (New York: Anchor Books, 1998; first published 1926), 34.

Index

Abenaki people, 23–4

aboiteaux, 47, 74, 75

Aboriginal peoples. *See* First Nations

abstraction, 17, 154

Acadia, 77, 165, 259, 348, 358; Arcadian, 73; as "Cajuns," 32; complexity of, 26; dearth of visual evidence about, 79; erasure of, 95; fights for possession over, 24–8; as jurisdiction of New France, 25; liminal status of, 93; Longfellow and, 73–108; as Normans, 95; as *paradis perdu*, 78, 126; primitive Christianity and, 88; repositioned, 32; romanticized rendition of, 88; as site of therapeutic renewal, 77; as storybook land, 80; tourism and, 101; transformation of understanding of, 48

Acadian Convention, 100

Acadian Recorder, 60

Acadians, 11, 12, 15, 30, 118–19, 166, 282, 329, 362, 372, 378; as "awkward" people, 25; Bird's portrayal of, 176–9, 339–40, 362–3; Brebner's portrayal of, 42–3, 47–8; British and, 50; Catholicism and, 117; citizenship for, 411n157; deportation/expulsion of, 32–3, 35–6, 38, 42–5, 78, 92–3, 97–100, 111, 121–4, 165, 176–9, 180, 182, 184, 220, 339–41, 352–3, 358, 362, 372; elite, 47; as enemies, 26–7; *Evangeline* and, 74–5, 78–84, 86–9, 91–

102; as God's chosen people, 88; "helplessness" of, 47; Herbin and, 117–18; "litigiousness of," 40, 75; marginality of, 96, 221; morality of, 84–5; as nation, 94; oppression of, 96; Parkman's portrayal of, 39–40, 42, 47–8; poverty of, 36; as prestigious white race of Nova Scotia, 94–5; racist denigration of, 95; Raddall's portrayal of, 216, 220–1, 226, 329, 333–4; religiosity of, 102; resistance by, 33; standards of living of, 36; as "tourists of their own culture," 126; as warriors, 47

accumulation, 76, 375

Action catholique jeunesse, 119

Action française, 119

active neutrality, 25, 29, 32, 36, 75

Act of Union (1707), 26

adulthood vs childhood, 162–4, 195

Adventure, 202, 204, 422n149

aesthetic experiences, 16

aesthetics, primitivist, 65

Africville, 218

Afro–Nova Scotians, 11, 15, 180, 216, 217–19, 360–1. *See also* blacks

agency: historical, 234, 237, 339; human, 195

Akins, Thomas Beamish, 97–100, 179; *Selections from the Public Documents of the Province of Nova Scotia*, 98

Alexander, William, 258–60, 265, 267–8, 377; *Doomes-Day, or, the Great Day of the Lords Judgement*, 258; *An Elegie on the Death of Prince Henrie*, 258; *An encouragement to colonies*, 258; the Younger, 260
Alexander Keith's beer, advertisements for, 371
Alger, Horatio, 251
alienation, 374
Allen, Willard F., 325
American Bus Association, 305
American Revolution, 26, 33, 34, 43, 44, 207, 235, 243, 358
American War of Independence, 237
Amherst, 162, 291
analysis, Bird and, 144, 154, 164, 170, 197, 250
Anderson, Benedict, 92
Anglicanism, 149
anglicization, 88
Anglo-Celtic civilization, superiority of, 216
Anglo-Celtic males, character and, 148
Anglo-Mi'kmaw War, 31
anglophones vs francophones, 89, 266
Annapolis Royal, 25–8, 36, 75, 115, 265, 337, 350, 354
Annapolis Valley, 109, 115, 243, 323
Anne of Green Gables, 84
anti-Acadian sentiment, 100
anti-British sentiment, 100
Antiburghers vs Kirkmen, 262
anti-Catholic sentiment, 100, 177, 179
Antigonish, 264, 286
Antigonish County, 260; Highland Society of, 260, 289, 426n21
anti-history, 51, 252, 374
antimodernism, 67, 271, 337, 377–8; British imperialism and, 268; Canadian nationalism and, 393n111; "Golden Age," 47; Longfellow and, 73–4; Macdonald and, 281, 286, 297; as new language of tourism, 281; Scottish Myth/tartanism and, 255, 284, 309, 313, 315

anti-Protestant sentiment, 100
antiquarianism, 46
antiquity: cashing in on, 21, 54, 62, 327; lack of, 62
appropriation, 374
Arbuckle, Franklin, 369, *370*, 373
Argall, Samuel, 25
Armstrong, Lawrence, 30
Ashworth, G.J., 20, 59
Association of VanCortlandt Grantees, 448n102
Assomption Vie, 118
Austrian Succession, War of, 30
automobile transportation, tourism and, 63, 65, 125, 162
Ayer, Marjorie, 345

back-to-Africa movement, 48
back-to-the-land movements, 65
Baddeck, 103
Baker, L.E., 103
Ball, Harold, 353–4
Bannockburn, Battle of, 265, 266
Basque, Maurice, 47
Basque, runic stone and, 326
battalion histories, 132, 136–7
battlefield restorations, 50
battlefield travel writing, 152–3
Bauchman, Rosemary, 181
Bay of Fundy, 24, 26
"Bay View Stone," 319
Beau, Henry: *La dispersion des Acadiens*, 92
Beaubassin, 118
Beauséjour, 31–2
Beck, Murray, 280
Beinn Bhreagh, 103
Belcher, Jonathan, 98, 122
Belgium, 138, 145, 151–3
Bell, Alexander Graham, 103
Belliveau, Pierre, 121
Belliveau, W.J., 355
Benham, Jane E., 84
Bennet, C.L. "Ben," 244
Bentley, D.M.R., 112
Berman, Marshall, 156

Beveridge, Sir William, 278

bias, reduction vs strengthening of, 19

bioethics, 333, 378; Raddall and, 201, 212, 254

Birchtown, 361

Bird, Augusta, 130

Bird, Stephen, 130

Bird, Steve, 130, 133, 146, 150–1

Bird, Will R., 130–99, 287, 289, 310, 312, 323, *361*, 371, 378; Acadians, 176–9, 339–40, 362–3; alcohol and, 186–7, 195, 199; amorphous concept of progress of, 155; analysis and, 144, 154, 164, 170, 197, 250; *And We Go On*, 131, 132, 134–5, 137, 139, 141–3, 146, 149, 154, 156, 157, 161, 252; anti-heroism of, 171; anti-historicalism of, 252; as anti-intellectual intellectual, 132; artfulness of artlessness of, 132; attitudes of toward war, 136–42; audience of, 158; bioethical fitness and, 254; blacks in, 179–81; Black Watch, 134, 269; Bureau of Information, 156, 168; Canadian Authors Association, 157; *A Century at Chignecto*, 131, 167, 179, 182–3; character and, 145–8, 155, 170, 187; childlike simplicity of, 132, 136–7, 162–3; *The Communication Trench*, 131, 148; contravention of sexual order and, 147; as cultural cartographer, 250; cultural criticism of, 162; *Despite the Distance*, 132, 171, 176, 186, 190, 191, 192; *Done at Grand Pré*, 121, 178, 179; *An Earl Must Have a Wife*, 132, 157, 180, 192; egalitarianism of, 145; enhancing state-supported service sector, 169; fact and fiction, 157, 167, 170; faith and, 149; First Nations in, 175, 181–6, 339; Frenchmen in, 175–6; gender and, 147–8, 163; *Ghosts Have Warm Hands*, 132, 147, 150, 151; goodness and, 193–5; gothic romanticism of, 179; Great War and, 131, 133–55, 279; *Here Stays Good Yorkshire*, 131, 158, 170–3, 174–5, 193–5, 359; *Historic Nova Scotia*, 131–2, 164, 339–41, 346; Historic Sites Advisory Council, 331–40, 350–3, 354, 356–60, 367; histories of, 164–8, 180, 183; history as not historicized, 170; human condition and, 195; imagined Nova Scotia of, 199; inborn moral dispositions and, 170, 187, 250, 252; individualism and, 147, 154, 156, 187, 252, 289; Innocence of, 132–3, 156, 162, 164, 195–7, 250, 373; as intellectual and promoter of tourism/ history, 16, 69, 375; irrationalism of, 151; *Judgment Glen*, 131, 158, 180, 183, 185, 186, 191; "Keep Your Powder Dry," 168; liberalism of, 250–2, 277, 333; Maritime tourism and, 131, 155–70; as master of historical fiction, 170; men vs women in, 186, 188; Methodism of, 149; as "Mr Great War," 133; as "Mr Nova Scotia," 133, 156, 163, 169; moralism and, 193, 250; Mount Allison University honorary degree, 158, 169–70; naive sincerity and, 197; *The North Shore Regiment*, 132; *The Nova Scotia Highlanders*, 132; objectivity vs bias in, 179; *Off-Trail in Nova Scotia*, 132, 175, 409n90; optimism of, 142; "The Original Nova Scotians," 181; Parkman and, 39; parlour organ and, 162–3; *The Passionate Pilgrim*, 132, 170, 180, 184–5, 187, 188, 189–90; physical force and, 193; political and philosophical commitments of, 132; politics and, 195; positive thinking and, 199, 250; predetermination and, 151; *Private Timothy Fergus Clancy*, 147–8; property and, 329; provincial propaganda campaigns and, 250; as public-relations man, 168; as "quintessential articulator of Canada's war," 142; race and, 148, 310, 339; vs Raddall, 200–1, 207, 250–2; realism and, 137, 154, 170, 181, 252; resistance of to corrosive and destabilizing memory of war, 136; resistance of to negativity and realism, 136; Ryerson Press All-Canada Fiction Award, 158, 170; Scottishness and, 275; sex and sexuality, 192–3, 195–7; short stories, 131; *The Shy Yorkshireman*, 132, 171, 173–4, 405n1; slavery and, 180–1; *So Much to Record*, 132, 159, 164, 187–8, 191, 192–3, 359; supernatural and, 149–51; *Telephone Lines*, 168; *These Are the Maritimes*, 132; *Thirteen Years After*, 131, 145, 152; *This Is Nova Scotia*, 132, 158–9, 164, 167–8, 170, 179; *To Love and to Cherish*, 132, 193, 194, 195–9; as tourism professional, 164; as tourism promoter, 156, 168; tourism writing of, 155–68; touristic sensibility of, 159; as travel writer, 156; trench warfare and, 143, 146–7, 149, 151, 156, 159, 186, 250; *Tristram's Salvation*, 171; University of Alberta Award for Literature, 158; women and, 146, 188–93; writing as therapy, 156; Yorkshire emigrants and, 131, 170–5, 181

Black, Mary, 300

Black, Percy C., 164

blacks, 11, 34, 48, 95, 256, 360–1, 378; free, 217; marginalization of, 179, 439n226; portrayal of as casualties of war, 148; portrayal of by Bird, 179–81; portrayal of by Raddall, 216, 217–19. *See also* Afro–Nova Scotians

Black Watch of Canada, 133, 269, 290, 429n58

Blackwood, George, 227

Blackwood's Magazine, 202, 294

Blakeley, Phyllis, 121, 131, 203, 244–5, 275, 336

Blauveldt, Robert, 325, 448n100

Bluenose, 67

Bolles, Frank, 110–11

bonne ententisme, 92, 96

Bonnie Prince Charlie, 280, 287, 360, 427n31, 435n146

Borrett, William Coates, 336

Boston, 103

Boston and Yarmouth Steamship Company, 110

Boston Public Library, 102

Boudreau, Michael, 270, 272

Boulton, Henry, 435n146

Bourassa, Henri, 90, 119

Bourne Whaling Museum (New Bedford), 347

Brebner, J.B., 24, 26, 27, 40–8, 92, 95, 170; continentalism of, 389n60; critiques of, 46–8; *The Neutral Yankees of Nova Scotia*, 43, 45; *New England's Outpost: Acadia before the Conquest of Canada*, 40–1, 92; *The North Atlantic Triangle*, 389n60; portrayal of Acadians, 42–3, 47–8, 122, 177; romanticism and, 66; stereotypes of savages, 47; Trotsky and, 77

Bridgetown, 160

Brigadoon, 291

Brinley, Gordon: *Away to Cape Breton*, 284

British: colonial rule of in Acadia, 24–34, 36–7, 39, 46; hegemony of, 48

British Empire, 33, 49, 52, 72, 255, 296; Black Watch celebration of, 269; civilizing mission of, 38, 92, 235; decline of, 64; greatness of, 65; liberation from, 36

British Empire Steel Corporation, 265

British vs French: conflict between over Acadia, 24–34, 39, 49, 75; war between, 30, 131

Brock, Isaac, 248

Brotherhood of Locomotive Engineers, 362

Broussard, Joseph ("Beausoleil"), 75, 398n56

Brown, Dona, 63

Brown, Emily E., 266

brutalization, of soldiers, 136

Buchan, John (Lord Tweedsmuir), 203, 270, 344–5, 348

Buchanan, George, 428n49

Bumsted, J.M., 235

Burns, Robert, 263, 264, 273, 345, 432n113, 439n214

Butterworth, Hezekiah, 111; "Baptism of Indians at Port Royal," 41; *Zigzag Journeys in Acadia and New France*, 101

Cabot, John, 162, 349, 364–8
Caie, Clara, 337–8
"Cajuns," 32
Calendar Stone (Mexico City), 326
Callaghan, Morley, 203
Calvinism, 66
Camp Aldershot, 138
Campbell, A.J., 271, 273, 344, 423n155
Campbell, Thomas: "Ye Mariners of England," 428n52
Campbell, Wilfred, 285, 426n28
"Canada's Myth," 134–5, 137, 140–1, 143, 149, 154, 155
Canadian-American Gael, 301, 309, 311
Canadian Authors Association, 68, 131, 157, 158, 203, 228, 281
"Canadian Boat-Song, The," 294–5
Canadian Broadcasting Corporation, 124; Cotter's Saturday Night, 298; Gaelic broadcasts, 433n126
Canadian Corps, 138
Canadian Corps of Commissionaires, 336
Canadian Countryman, 131
Canadian Geographic Magazine, 168
Canadian Government Travel Bureau, 66
Canadianism, 255
Canadian Magazine, 112
"Canadian Mosaic," 119
Canadian National Railways, 64; magazine of, 131
Canadian Pacific Railway, 64, 65
Canadian School of Telegraphy, 202
Canadian Tourist Association, 345; Historical and Cultural Committee, 21
Cannon, Mary, 33
Canso, 27, 29, 30, 350
Canso Causeway, 316
Cape Blomidon, 115
Cape Breton Highlands, 275, 284, 285; National Park, 276, 284, 290, 292, 295, 311, 328
Cape Breton Historical Society, 365–7
Cape Breton Island, 32, 33, 281–4, 306, 309, 323; Baleine colony, 259; Cabot and, 364–7; Cabot Trail, 282; "Es-

quimaux" in, 95; French presence in, 28, 121; Gaelic in, 298, 301, 303–4; geography of, 284, 291; as Île Royale, 26, 27, 259; immigrants in, 11; Mi'kmaq in, 23; Scots in, 38, 259–60, 262–6, 269, 281, 293, 302, 316
Cape North, 162
capital, labour and, 265
capital accumulation, 127, 211, 278, 315
capitalism, 67, 77–8, 164, 219, 360, 368, 375, 377; colonialism and, 24; consumer, 19; core vs periphery of, 77; fin-de-siècle, 103; industrial, 77, 110; liberal, 7, 219, 236, 238, 241, 376
capitalist development, 238
capitalist social relations, 7
Carman, Bliss, 402n96
carnality, faith as safeguard against, 85
Carr, David, 382n3
Carter, Bob, 14
Cartier, Jacques, 23
Casgrain, Abbé H.R., 85, 87, 88, 99–100; Un Pèlerinage au pays d'Évangéline, 99
Castle Frederick, 33
categorization, 154
Catholic Church, 28, 86, 96; mission civilisatrice of, 96
Catholicism, 24, 25, 32, 77, 86, 88–90
Celtic motif, tartanist, 283
censorship, 227–8
centralization, 308
Chamberlain, Fitzroy, 454n221
Chambrun, Jacques, 422n149
Champion, Helen, 303
Champlain, Samuel de, 95, 165, 267, 342, 343, 345
chance, role of in war, 148
Chapdelaine, Maria, 89
Chapman House, 359
character, Will R. Bird and, 145–8, 155, 170, 187
Charles I, King, 258–9
Chase, Elizabeth B.: Over the Border, 113
Chester, 103
Chezzetcook, 101

Chiasson, Paulette, 95
Chignecto, Isthmus of, 31, 165–7, 359
"Childe ballads," 65, 296
childhood vs adulthood, 162–4, 195
childlike innocence, Will R. Bird and,
  132, 136–7, 162–3
Chinese, 256
Christianity, 149; Great War and, 141
Christie, Norm, 133
Chronicle (Halifax), 64, 267, 275, 278, 296,
  345
Chronicle-Herald (Halifax), 353
Church, Benjamin, 102
citizenry, folk vs, 64
civility, primitivism vs, 35
civilization: advance of, 237, 312; British,
  53, 57, 59, 219, 221; individual and, 237;
  narrative of, 37; Raddall and, 215, 223;
  Scots and, 262; superiority of Anglo-
  Celtic, 216; whiteness and, 37
clan gatherings, 270, 275, 331, 375
Clan MacLeod festivities, 303
clan system, 308
class, Raddall and, 210–11, 214
clergymen, in Great War, 141
coal industry, 7, 64, 77, 128, 276, 285–6,
  350
Cody, H.J., 121
coercion, 46
Cold War, 278
collective bargaining rights, 276
collectivism, 308
Collins, Enos, 360
colonialism, 24, 223–4; French, 226; sexuality and, 223; undoing of, 235
colonization, 216, 223, 258, 312, 350; English vs French, 224, 226; European, 48,
  124, 217, 318; French, 105–7, 224, 339,
  362; myth of white, 327
Comité de l'Église-Souvenir, 118
commemoration, 50–1, 206, 321, 328, 334,
  356–63, 364; of decontextualized moments and experiences, 17; Evangeline
  Phenomenon and, 120–2; of Expulsion,
  92; of Grand Pré, 117; Great War, 134,

136; Hector, 270–5, 393n111, 439n226;
  mnemonic apparatus and, 342; responsibility for, 51; rituals of, 69–70
commercialization, 280
commodification, 9, 20, 219, 255, 271, 315,
  327–30, 333, 368, 373; of culture, 169; of
  daily life, 107; heritage and, 15–16; logic
  of, 126, 327; Macdonald and, 315; universality and totalization of, 375
commodity exchange, 327, 368
communal therapy, writing as, 156
Communism, 376
Compagnie des Cent-Associés, 259
Confederation, Canadian, 20, 34, 52, 96
Congrès mondial acadien, 123
Connolly, Harold, 300, 303, 327; Historic
  Sites Advisory Council, 355; "Let's
  Cash In on Antiquity," 253, 327; on
  Macdonald, 277, 316, 376; MacKenzie
  and, 302; tartanism and, 253–4, 257
Conolly, Lorenzo, 71–2
Conquest of 1710, 27, 45
Conrad, Joseph, 213, 214
conscription, 266, 275
consent, 46
conservatism, 308–9
consumer capitalism, 19
consumerism, 17, 128
consumption, 160, 164, 247, 369, 373, 374;
  objects of, 12
consumption (disease), 210
contraception, 84
Cork, Ella K., 345
Cornwallis, Edward, 30
corruption, 46
cosmopolitanism, 52
Costain, Thomas, 203, 220, 226, 418n72,
  422n149; The Black Rose, 418n72; For
  My Great Folly, 418n72
Council of New England, 258
Cozzens, Frederic S., 60, 79, 80–1, 91,
  100–1, 262; Acadia; or, A Month with the
  Blue Noses, 100–1
Creighton, Helen, 131, 135, 203, 219, 296
Crerar, T.A., 295

critical realism, 46

Crosskill, Herbert, 62; *Nova Scotia: Its Climate, Resources and Advantages*, 54

Culler, Jonathan, 255

Culloden, Battle of, 265, 269, 427n31

cultural geography, 284

cultural history, 72; rise of, 44

cultural identity, 11, 22

cultural intervention, 169

cultural nostalgia, 74

cultural politics, 16, 254, 363, 379

cultural purity, 296

cultural register, 14

cultural selection, 16, 377

cultural tradition, manipulation of, 281

culture: commodification of, 169; savagery vs, 35; tourism and, 111

Currier & Ives, 80, *82–3*

Cuthbertson, Brian, 97, 455n225

Daigle, Jean, 47

Daily Star (Halifax), 266

Dalhousie University, 281

d'Anville, duc (Jean-Baptiste-Louis Frédéric de la Rochefoucauld de Roye), 31, 33, 35

Dartmouth, 31

Darwin, Charles, 14

Dashwood, Richard, 95, 261–2; *Chiploquorgan*, 54

Dawson, R.M.: *Report of the Royal Commission on Provincial Development and Rehabilitation*, 331

Dawson, Samuel Edward, 453n195

Deane, Albert: "How to See Scotland without Crossing the Atlantic," 292–4

de Beauvoir, Simone, 420n102

decolonization, 124, 235, 333

decontextualization: of elements of the past, 16–17; of images, 9

DeGarthe, William E., 339

degeneration, 213, 238

dehumanization, of soldiers, 136

de-industrialization, 40, 276

de la Durantaye, Morel, 84, 85

de la Tour, Charles, 259

del Rio, Dolores, 80–1, 115

democracy, 134, 308

Dennis, William, 66

d'Entremont, H. Leander, 322

"Deportation Cross," 119

Depression, 64, 202, 241, 306, 308

de Razilly, Isaac, 25

DesBarres, J.F.W., 33, 157

despotism, monstrous, 154

determinism, 49

Devoir, Le, 119, 266

Diamond Dick novels, 157

Dickens, Charles: *A Tale of Two Cities*, 421n133

Diefenbaker, John, 360

Digby, 103

Digby Gap, 352

dirigisme, 277

distributive justice, 351

Doers' and Dreamers' 2007 Guide, 314

Dolan, Leo, 118, 282–3

Dominion Archives, 338

Dominion Atlantic Railway (DAR), 109, 117, 121, 369, *370*, 371; *Evangeline Land in Nova Scotia*, 105, *106*; Evangeline Phenomenon and, 104–7, 114–15, 126; *High Lights of Nova Scotia History*, *106*, 348; SMA and, 118–19

Drummond, Robert, 260

Drummond, William Henry, 399n63

Dugua, Pierre, Sieur de Monts, 95, 399n66

du Maurier, Daphne, 230

Dumbrille, Dorothy, 170

Duncan, Dorothy: *Bluenose*, 280, 284–5

Eastern Automobile Company, 264–5

economic development, 77, 154, 234, 271, 278

Edinburgh Castle, 258, 287

egalitarianism, 145, 146; native, 23

elites, manipulation by, 134

elitism, 21, 140, 148

Ells, Margaret, 204; 221, 417n63

Emerson, H.P., 92

Emerson, Ralph Waldo, 371

Engels, Friedrich, 79

English Canadian fiction, history of, 231

Enlightenment: French, 74; modernity, 74

entrepreneurial mnemonic apparatus, 16

entrepreneurs: Evangeline Phenomenon and, 76, 103, 126; state and private, 16, 328

entrepreneurship, heritage, 328

entropy, 17

Erikson, Leif, 321–3

Erik the Red, 320

essentialism: ahistorical, 372; ethnic, 313, 379; racial, 379; Scottish, 306–9

Established Church, 37

"estrangement," 252, 424n167

ethnic cleansing, 127, 372

ethnic hierarchies, 309

ethnicity, 170; cohesive Nova Scotian, 244; ecumenical representation of, 254; homogeneous, 286; Macdonald's representation of, 280; reconstructed, 255

ethnic jokes, 254, 256

ethnic minorities, 311

ethno-cultural diversity, 285

ethno-racial re-description, 254, 379

Europeans: conflict between over territory, 23–34; non-British, Raddall on, 216

Evangeline: A Tale of Acadie, 72, 73–6, 78–87, 89–129, 188, 220, 243; bicentennial celebrations of, 121–2; feminist rereading of, 125; French-Canadian nationalism and, 89; futures offered by, 90; group cohesion of, 94; inaccuracies in, 74, 111, 117; misattribution of to Wordsworth, 122; nationalism and, 90–4; as paean to Innocence, 76

Evangeline (film), 115

Évangéline, L', 93

Evangeline, Land of, 43, 62, 72, 76–8, 103–7, 115, 117, 123, 125, 128–9, 165, 176, 256, 362, 370, 372, 374, 377; apotheosis of, 122; branding as, 76; depiction in films, 80; as early theme park, 77; Gateway to, 166; as "New England's outpost," 77, 103; Route of, 110; tourists, 111

Evangeline Phenomenon, 38, 69, 71–129, 130, 256, 266, 342, 371–2, 374, 375; apex of, 121; Brebner and, 77; initial iteration of, 96; paradoxes of, 77; political vs economic investment in, 113; Raddall's contempt for, 224–6; second iteration of, 111; third period of, 115; transformation of, 103; Trotsky and, 77

Everest, Robert, 59

evolution/evolutionary theory. See Raddall

exchange, 75, 374; units of, 9

exchange value, 9, 327

exclusion, 14, 16

exoticism, 148

Faed, James, 85, 119

Faed, Thomas, 85, 107, 115, 119

faith: in Acadia, 85–8, 128; Bird and, 149, 151

Family Herald, 131

family trees, 8

Farish, Henry G., 442n12

Farquhar, George, 275

fascism, 307

Fasolt, Constantin, 382n3

fatalism, 298–9; Lamarckian, 213

Fergusson, C. Bruce, 355, 454n221

film production, 70

Fingard, Judith, 388n40

First Nations, 23, 363; consciousness of, 124; cultural essence of, 247; demonization of, 182; as historical agents, 217; historical interest in, 178; portrayal of by Bird, 175, 181–6, 339; portrayal of by Raddall, 206, 216–17, 223, 224, 231, 245–7, 323, 329–30, 333; recovery of voices of, 46–8; "squaws," 185–6; subordination of, 312; treaties, 46. See also Mi'kmaq

First Things Publishers, 348

Firth, L.B., 346
Fleming, Sir Sandford, 57–8
Fletcher, Richard, 317
Fletcher Stone, *318*, 319–27; racial significance of, 319
Flinn, Timothy, 147
Flora Macdonald College, 280–1, 287
folk: vs citizenry, 64; rise of, 65
folk culture, 65
folk discourse, 67
folklore, 77, 219
folk romanticism, 167
Forbes, Ernest, 308–9
Fordism, 240
Foreign Protestants, 16, 38, 382n15, 430n86
Forest and Stream, 63
Forest, Stream and Seashore (Intercolonial Railway), 263
Fort Anne, 344
Fort Beauséjour, 31–2, 98
Fort Cumberland, 32, 165, 180. *See also* Fort Beauséjour
Fort Gaspereau, 32
Fort Lawrence, 31, 32
Fort Monckton, as "Gateway to the Land of Evangeline," 166–7
Fort Morris, 243
Fortress Louisbourg, 27–8, *39*, 121, 331, 347
Fort Ticonderoga, 347
framing the past, 7–8, 15
France, 24, 138, 145, 328; magistracies in, 328; Old Regime in, 328; settlers from, 15
francophones vs anglophones, 266
Frank, David, 265, 388n40
Fraser, A.D., 323
Fraser, Dawn, 167
Fraser, L.W., 164
Fraser, Thomas: "The Spirit of the Maritimes," 269
fratricide, reassurance of, 92–3
Fredericton, 163
free enterprise, as human right, 345

French: colonial control by, 25–8, 30, 36
French Canadians, portrayal of, 148, 175–6, 219–23, 224, 226–7
French/English duality, as key to history, 38–40, 42, 44, 75
French Guiana, 388n38
French language, disestablishment of on prairies, 89
French Revolution, 235
French vs British: conflict between, 24–34, 39, 49, 75; war between, 30, 131
frontier narratives, 36
Frost, C. Sydney, 360, *361*
Fukuyama, Francis, 239
Fussell, Paul, 156

Gaelic College, 257, 283, 299, 300–4, 306, 316, 376
Gaelic Foundation of Cape Breton, 297, 302
Gaelic language, 253, 257, 260, 265, 291, 296–306, 376; broadcasting in, 298; defence of, 297–9; in education system, 297–8; exploitation of, 296; fluency in, 15; Macdonald and, 296–306, 351; maintenance of, 66; racialization of, 297; wartime censor and, 298, 300
Gaelic Mod, 288, 291, 296, 302–3, 305; tourism promotion and, 303
Gàidhealtachd, 297
Garland, Edward J., 271
Gaspé Peninsula, 23, 24
"Gatherings of the Clans," 270, 275, 331, 375
Gazette (Montreal), 170
gender, 170; character and, 147–8, 163; Raddall and, 201, 207–10. *See also* women
gender roles, Victorian, 125
gender typologies, 67
geographical determinism, 45
Germans, views on, 141
Germany, 16
Gerrard, G.H., 113
Gibbon, Edward, 38, 99

Gibbon, J. Murray, 119
Ginzburg, Carlo, 424n167
Gobineau, Joseph Arthur de, 391n82
"Golden Age," 52, 78, 126, 156, 243, 287, 337, 357, 373, 389n48; of Acadia, 74; antimodernism, 47; Herbin and, 118; Raddall and, 237–8; of the Scot, 378
Golden Age of Sail, 64, 66, 159–60, 201, 236–8, 351
Gorsebrook, 359
Gouzenko Affair, 439n214
Gramsci, Antonio, 21, 46, 382n16
Grand Anse, 169
Grand Banks schooners, 66–7
Grand Pré, 76, 79–81, 93, 107, 109–10, 114–15, 124, 126, 266, 362; Acadian renaissance and, 94; Cozzens and, 91, 101; deportation and, 32, 71; destruction of, 76; Edenic qualities of, 102–3; French incursions at, 98; Herbin and, 74, 117–19; holism and, 102; Longfellow and, 80, 127; Memorial Church at, 118, 124; nationalization of, 121; as terrain of memory, 119
Grand Pré Massacre, 121
Grand-Pré National Historic Park, 122
Graves, Robert, 122, 379; Good-bye to All That, 379
Gray, John, 248–9
Great Disruption, 288
Great Soviet Encyclopedia, 324
Great War, 10, 266, 279; alcoholism and, 145; Bird and, 131, 133–55; as crusade for decency and humanity, 141; egalitarianism and, 146; as euphemism for Prussianism or militarism, 138; existential crisis of, 154; fraternity of, 146; horror, 142–3; irrational autocracy of organizers of, 154; medals in, 140; morality of, 138; mystique of, 134; public history of, 134
Griffiths, Naomi, 75, 76, 89, 127
group identity, 19
Guadeloupe, 388n38

Guevara, Che, 398n56
Guysborough, 355

habitants, French-Canadian, 226
Haddeland, Knute, 321, 323
haggis, 430n73
Haiti/Haitian Revolution, 232–5, 388n38
"Haki," 320
Haliburton, Mrs George Mordaunt, 71
Haliburton, R.G., 179
Haliburton, Thomas Chandler, 52, 92, 107, 262, 267, 337, 379; An Historical and Statistical Account of Nova Scotia, 38, 74, 76, 97, 101–2
Halifax, 32–6, 49, 67–8, 103, 176, 217, 268, 329, 353; Acacia Cottage, 359; Citadel, 338; as city of glamour, 68; critiques of, 53–61; as disappointment, 59; establishment of, 30, 31, 38, 43, 44, 97; Explosion, 202; freed blacks in, 180; Memorial Tower in, 57–9, 64, 348; North British Society of, 426n21; Raddall and, 201–2, 203, 206, 207–8, 229; rebuttals to critiques of, 61–2; representations of in travel literature and tourism brochures, 53–62; South End of, 61, 131, 279, 281, 332; as therapeutic space, 53; tourist trade in, 353–4
Halifax Hotel, 68
Hall, William, 361
Hallock, Charles: The Fishing Tourist, 63
handicrafts, 65, 69
Hannibal (Missouri), 401n95
Hanoverians, 12, 15, 256, 269; as a race, 16
Hardy, A.L.: The Evangeline Land, 114–17
Harper's Weekly, 60
Harrison, Charles Yale: Generals Die in Bed, 135
Harvey, D.C., 40, 170, 259, 350, 356; Cabot and, 364–5; Dawson Report and, 331–2; Historic Nova Scotia, 339, 341; on Norse settlement, 321–2
Harvey, Moses, 453n195
Haskell, Thomas, 382n3

Hautecoeur, Jean-Paul, 88; *L'Acadie du discours*, 123

Hawthorne, Nathaniel, 71–2, 84

Hayek, F.A.: *The Road to Serfdom*, 278

Hayhurst, Tom, 423n154

heather, 291–2, 311

Heatherington, Alexander, 61

Hébert, Henri, 119

Hébert, Louis-Philippe, 119

Hébert, Philippe, 119

Hector commemoration, 270–5, 393n111, 439n226

hegemony, 27, 46, 49, 306, 330, 377; politics and, 136; public history as, 51

Henderson, T. Stephen, 68–9

Herald (Halifax), 55, 59, 279, 287

Herbin, John (Sr), 117

Herbin, John Frederic, 74, 117–18; *History of Grand-Pré*, 117; *The Land of Evangeline*, 117

heritage, 50, 346, 371, 375; activism, 40, 325, 337; besieging of, 286; elite, 97; entrepreneurship, 328; explosion of, 19; history vs, 15, 18–20, 255, 257; liminal space of, 326; objects of, 244, 249, 255, 327, 329, 348, 375; politics and, 20; preservation of, 243, 337–8; provincial bureaucracy, 324; racialized, 256; selectivity and, 20; sites of, 76, 121, 329, 342; state investment in, 166; tartanism and, 256; tourism/history as forerunner of, 15

"Heritage Moments," 124

Hicks, Henry, 277, 366

Highland Association (Glasgow), 296

Highland Clearances, 265, 289

Highland games, 275

historical fiction: Bird as master of, 170; Raddall and, 204–6, 238, 363; romantic, 156, 157, 166, 238

historical objectivity, 221

historical romance, 36, 72, 101

historical sentimentality, 219

historical societies, 8, 338–9, 347, 350–1

historic assets, 331

historicity, active, 379

historicization, reification vs, 372

Historic Nova Scotia, 313, 323–4, 339–41, 344, 346

historic properties, 328; homogenization and commodification of, 328

historic sites, 69, 275, 281, 342

Historic Sites Advisory Council, 69, 287–8, 325, 363, 366; Bird and, 334, 354; establishment of, 331–2; Macdonald and, 354–5; Raddall and, 201

Historic Sites and Monuments Board of Canada (HSMBC), 325, 338, 341, 362, 365, 411n157, 450n149; Harvey and, 321–2, 331–2, 356

historiography, Nova Scotia, 365; changes in, 122; three periods of, 37–50

history: anti-historical, 374; as circumstances to rise above, 154; commodification of, 19, 330, 333; commodity vs remembrance, 119; as contact with personal experiences, 154; as disciplined knowledge, 372; eradication of, 235; as a generative mechanism, 328; ghosts of, 152; as healthful tonic for reality, 156; heritage vs, 15, 18–20, 255; as morally ambiguous, 176; objectification of, 17; philosophy of, 17, 372; as progressive, 378; pursuit of profit and, 337; Raddall's views on, 204–7; as resource for marketable purposes, 329; as romance, 176, 369–80; romance of, 102, 111, 176, 236; as struggle, 149; and survival of positive thinking, 151; teleology of, 252; as therapy, 144, 378; ultra-empiricist definition of, 205; writing of, 37–50

Hitlerism, 212

Holland. *See* Netherlands

homosexuality, 147

Hoskins, George R., 319

How, Edward, 178

How, James D., 337, 347

Howe, C.D., 316

Howe, Joseph, 34, 52, 54, 58, 61, 262, 275
Hume, David, 271
Huntington, Richard, 442n17
hybridity, 223–4
hypercriticism, 21

identity: cultural, 11, 22; engineered, 368; essentialist national, 379; group, 19; legitimation of, 8; marginalization of, 52; Nova Scotian, 17, 132, 200, 219, 244, 256; Scottish, 268, 309
ideology, hegemonic constellation of, 372
ignorance, knowledge vs, 35
Île Royale, 26, 27, 259. See also Cape Breton Island
Île St Jean, 118
images, decontextualized, 9
"imaginary Indian," 245
immigration: Europe, 11; menace of, 273; Newfoundland, 11
imperial beneficence, 124
imperialism: British, 38, 62, 64–5, 75, 89, 142, 235, 268, 270, 333; English Canadian, 235; flaws of, 135; French, 36, 142; in Haiti, 234; historically specific accounts of, 175; identification with, 64–5; race and, 333; Scottish, 387n25; social, 252; subordination to, 222
imperial mercantilism, 36
imperial tranquility, 11
individual: civilization and, 237; ontological and epistemological primacy of, 133
individualism/individuality, 7, 44, 333, 374; Bird and, 147, 154, 156, 187, 252, 289; liberal, 145, 201, 237, 239, 373, 374; Macdonald and, 276–7, 282, 289, 306, 309; male, 229; possessive, 52; Raddall and, 201, 213–15, 231, 239, 240–2, 251–2; Scottish, 288, 306–7, 309
individualist voluntarism, 45
industrialization, 72, 265
inequality, 140
injustice, 140, 142
Innis, Harold, 365

Innocence, 8–9, 64, 69, 129, 287, 306, 374; cultural politics of, 379; Evangeline as paean to, 76; tourism/history and, 17; Will R. Bird and, 132–3, 156, 162, 164, 195–7, 252, 373
innocence, analytical reasoning as compromising, 149
Intercolonial Railway: Forest, Stream and Seashore, 263
intermarriage, 313, 387n35
International Fishermen's Races, 67
invented tradition, 427n43
Inverness County, 15, 161
Irish, 95
Irmscher, Christopher, 72, 122
Iroquois, power of, 24
Island of St John, 33. See also Prince Edward Island

Jacobite rebellion (1745), 289
Jacques et Marie (Bourassa), 119
Jamaica, 217
James I/VI, King, 258–9, 265, 268
Jefferson, Thomas, 398n56
Jenkins, Keith, 382n3
Jesuit Estates, 100
Jesuits, 177
jingoism, 46
Jobb, Dean, 388n40
Johnny Belinda, 303
Johnston, A.J.B., 80
Johnston, J.L., 322
Johnston, Wayne, 414n2
Jones, Charles Hugh Le Pailleur: The Markland Sagas, 203, 319–20, 423n154
Jones, James, 87
Jones, Leonard, 304

Keating, Frank, 367
Kejimkujik Park, 363
Keltic Lodge, 282, 292, 293
Kensington (Minnesota), 319, 325
Kentville, 114–15
Kerr, Alexander, 303

Keynes, John Maynard, 278
Keynesianism, 307
kilts, 265, 270
King, William Lyon Mackenzie, 135, 275, 306
Kinnear, Muriel, 170
Kipling, Rudyard, 214; *Captains Courageous*, 263
Kirke, Brothers, 259
Kirkmen vs Antiburghers, 262
knights-baronetcies, 258, 265, 268, 287
Knox, John, 288
Ku Klux Klan, 273

labour movement, 276, 306, 308, 362
labour process, Raddall and, 211
Lamb, W. Kaye, 349
Land of Evangeline. *See* Evangeline
Landry, Valentin, 93
landscapes: public, 69; Raddall and, 231–2; reorganization of, 72; symbolic, transformation of, 65; thematization of, 105
La Tour, Charles, 224
Lawrence, Charles, 32, 42, 122
Lawrence, T.E., 122
Lawson, Laura, 337–8, 346
League of Norsemen in Canada, 321, 322
Lears, Jackson, 86, 268
Le Blanc, Barbara, 93, 126
LeBlanc, Dudley J., 120, 125
LeBourdais, Isabel, 228, 229
Leif Erikson National Park, 323
Le Loutre, Abbé, 47, 86, 87, 166, 216, 339–40, 363; Acadia, Expulsion, and, 177–9; Mi'kmaq and, 31–2, 75, 95; as "terrorist," 177–9
Lemay, Pamphile, 89–90, 93; *Essais poétiques*, 89
Le Moine, James MacPherson: *Picturesque Quebec*, 102
Lent, William, 443n24
Lesage, Jean, 121
Leslie, Kenneth, 433n126
Lewis, Gordon T.: *The Cruise of the Knorr:*

An Account of Early Norse Exploration in America, 322–3
Lewis, Grace S., 325–6
liberal epistemology and ontology, 45
liberal improvement, 52
liberalism, 16, 54, 133, 136, 146, 164, 178, 330, 353, 372–5; British, 34, 176; classical, 155; crisis of, 155; death of, 241; embedded vs facilitative, 330; infrastructure, 69; Macdonald and, 276–9, 286, 297, 306, 308, 333, 351, 353; new, 68, 333; Raddall and, 200–52; triumph of, 241; Victorian, 240
liberal order, 15, 219, 223, 239
Liberal Party, 68
liberty, 7
lightness vs darkness, metaphors of, 37
Litchfield (Connecticut), 63
literary tourism, 246
literary travel, interwar, 156
Liverpool, 243, 414n2
local culture, tourist subversion of, 21
locality, ties of, 9, 11
Locke, John, 386n18; *Second Treatise of Government*, 329–30
London, Jack, 213, 214; *Sea Wolf*, 214
London Board of Trade, 42
Lone Shieling, 295
Longfellow, Henry Wadsworth, 71–4, 89, 91–3, 100–1, 125, 243, 369; Acadia and, 76, 78, 80–1, 87, 94, 95, 97, 176, 179, 220; changing fortunes of, 122; *The Courtship of Miles Standish*, 72; cultural influence of, 72; enthusiasts of, 100; Herbin and, 117–18; Land of Evangeline and, 76, 80–1, 86, 110; nostalgia of, 73; Parkman on, 99; skeptics of, 100; *The Song of Hiawatha*, 72; *Tales of a Wayside Inn*, 72; tourism and, 107, 112–14; utopia of, 79. See also *Evangeline: A Tale of Acadie*
Longley, R.S., 355
Lorde, Audre, 96
Louisbourg, 30–2, 35, 36, *39*, 78, 118, 177, 265, 362

Louisiana: Acadian memorial in, 398n56; cult of remembrance in, 91; deportation of Acadians to, 32–3; "New Acadia" in, 75; slavery in, 396n39

Lowenthal, David, 15, 18–20, 255, 312, 348; *The Heritage Crusade and the Spoils of History*, 18

Lower, Arthur, 277, 439n214

Loyalists, 48, 193, 216, 339; influx of, 23; refugees, 33–4, 43; Shelburne, 38

Lunenburg, 32, 36, *314*, 430n86; "Foreign Protestants" from, 16

MacAskill, W.R., 309, 313

MacCannell, Dean, 255

McCurdy, J.A.D., 366

Macdonald, Angus L., 3, 164, 253–4, 306, 341, 345, 360, 372–3, 375, 378, 426n21; antimodernism of, 297; background of, 280; conservatism of, 308–9; ethnic essentialism of, 308; ethnicity and, 256–7; Gaelic language and, 296–306, 351; government involvement in tourism/history, 353–6; Historic Sites Advisory Council, 331–5; individualism of, 276–7, 282, 289, 306, 309; as intellectual and promoter of tourism/history, 16, 69; labour movement and, 306, 308; leadership of, 276–7; liberalism of, 276–9, 286, 297, 306, 308, 333, 351, 353; micromanagement of, 277, 353; modernity/antimodernism of, 280–1, 286; nightwatchman state and, 282; Norse settlement and, 321–2; as Nova Scotia's answer to FDR, 276; property rights and, 330; racialization of, 310; reinterpretation of history, 286–7, 289; Scots and, 117; Scottish myth and, 260, 275–95, 308–16; speeches of, 306; state-building activities of, 278; tartanism and, 275–95; tourism development and, 278, 280–2; and winning consent, 306

Macdonald, Flora, 287–9, 360, 435n146

Macdonald, I.A., 283, 292

Macdonald, John A., 58

MacDonald, Ramsay, 296

McGee, Thomas D'Arcy, 286

Macgillivray, Dougald, 59

Machiavelli, Niccolò, 252, 424n168

MacIntosh, Donald S., bequest of, 294

MacKenzie, Angus William Rugg, 299–304, 316, 376

Mackenzie, Ian, 289

MacKenzie, Simon, 300

MacKinnon, A.E., 271–2

MacKinnon, J.A., 290–1, 311

MacKinnon, James G., 436n160

McLachlan, J.B., 260, 264

Maclean Highlanders, 140

Maclean's, 131, 133, 155, 202, 418n72

MacLennan, Donald, 298

MacLennan, Hugh, 265, 280; *Barometer Rising*, 227

McLennan, J.S., 347

McLennan, Katharine, 347, 356

MacLeod, Agnes, 303

MacLeod, Alistair, 414n2

MacLeod, Calum Iain, 298–9

MacLeod, Flora, 295

McLeod, Norman, 288, 300, 309

McLeod, R.R., 52

MacLeod Pulp and Paper Company, 202

MacMechan, Archibald, 67, 203, 266–7, 278

MacMillan, A.S., 3, 282, 327, 364

MacMillan, Somerled, 304, 376

MacNeil, James, 297–8, 376

MacNeil, Neil, 291; *The Highland Heart in Nova Scotia*, 283–4, 432n109

MacNeil, Robert: *Wordstruck*, 313–15

McNeill, D.H., 289

MacNutt, W.S., 389n49

MacPhail, Agnes, 135

Macphail, Andrew, 273

Macpherson, C.B., 328

McPherson, James, 271

Mah, Harold, 406n7

Maillet, Antonine: *La Sagouine*, 123

Mail-Star (Halifax), 275, 288

Maine, 24, 348

Malecite, 217

Mancke, Elizabeth, 24

manhood, formulation of Western, 219

Manitoba Schools, 100

Manson, E.A., 454n221

Marconi, Guglielmo, 202

Margaret, Princess, 326

marginalization, 16, 96; of Acadians, 221; of blacks, 179; by "Canadianism," 255; of competing identities, 52; by Highland motif, 271; regional, 163

Mariners' Museum (Newport News), 347

Maritime Labour Herald, 265

Maritime Telegraph and Telephone Company (MT&T), 168–9; "New Halifax–Saint John Radio System," 169; *Telephone Lines*, 168

Maritime tourism, Will R. Bird and, 131, 155–70

"maritimicity," 66, *314*

marketing, of race, 253–316

Maroons, 217

Marquis, Gregory, 92

Marshall, T.H., 278

Martell, Jim, 45, 170, 204, 220–1, 226, 389n48

Martinique, 388n38

Marx, Karl, 211; *Communist Manifesto*, 79; modernity and, 156

Marxism, 77

Massachusetts, 26, 30, 45, 347; Evangeline Phenomenon and, 79, 90

mass communications, 296

mass consumption, 296

mass media, 70

"Master Race," Scots as, 253–4

Mather, Cotton, 27

Mathew, 366–7

Maurras, Charles, 119

Mayan people, runic stone and, 326

Mayflower, 270, 272

Meagher, Patrick, 253

medievalism, simplified, 268

memoirs, writing of, 8, 136

memory: collective, 94; contested, 154; public, 135, 281; shapers of, 99; sites of, 50, 118–19, 132, 324, 327, 330, 342, 353

mercantilism, imperial, 36

Merkel, Andrew, 244, 335

Merry, Arthur, 363

Methodism, 149

Métis, 89, 95, 226

Meuse, Francis, 75

Mi'kma'ki, 22–4, 29, 46

Mi'kmaq, 11, 15, 20, 50, 95, 124, 166, 176, 245, 256, 259, 350, 376, 378, 450n137; arrival of after Vikings, 319; Bird and, 182–5, 339, 363; bounty for scalps of, 31; force of, 23; imperial rivalry, 22–33; intermarriage with, 94–5, 226; Le Loutre and, 75, 86–7, 363; linguistic and political unity of, 23; military power of, 178; Raddall and, 216, 329, 363; trade with Europeans, 23

militarism, Prussian, 138

Mill, John Stuart, 263

Milner, W.C., 346

Minudie, 33, 176, 350

Missaguash River. *See* Missiquash

missionaries, 24

Missiquash River, 166

"mnemonic apparatus," 16, 328–9, 342, 349–50, 364

modernism, 142, 155

modernity, 8, 64, 236, 239, 350, 375–7; antimodernism and, 377; capitalist, 328, 337; denial of, 9; deracinated, 376; exemption from, 64; innocence from, 67; Marx and, 156

Moncrieff, George, 440n239

mongrelization, 285

Moniteur Acadien, Le, 93

Mons, capture of, 133

Monterey (California), 401n95

monuments, erection of, 8

Moody, Barry, 28, 45, 216, 238

Moore, H. Napier, 155

Moorsom, William, 262

moral choices, 157

moral excellence, 81

morality, 272–3; Acadian, 84–6, 88; Bird and, 132, 137, 149, 170–2; of Expulsion, 111; Raddall and, 212, 215–16, 227, 232

moral qualities, 12, 145; physical attractiveness and, 81–5

Morley, Margaret, 61

Morris, Charles, 32

Mount Allison University, 131

Muir, W. Bruce, 267–8, 377–8

multiculturalism, 50, 256

Munro, Maie, 366, 367

Munroe, Fred W., 167

Murdoch, Beamish, 97–9, 179; *History of Nova-Scotia*, 98

Murolo, Priscilla, 195

Murphy, J.M., 362

Murray, Alexander D., 299, 302–3

Murray, George, 267

Murray, James, 92

mutual coexistence, pragmatics of, 46

myths and symbols, privileging of, 20

myth-symbol complex, 94, 328, 372, 384n5

Nantucket (Massachusetts), 63

narratives, 19; of barbarism vs civilization, 35; English Canadian imperialist/ nationalist, 235; of European civilizing, 37; frontier, 36; of good vs evil, 35–6; of key events in Nova Scotia history, 35–7; of national liberation, 36–7

nationalism, 37, 48, 66, 67, 88, 90–4, 232; Acadian, 123; Anglo-Canadian, 123; antimodernism and, 393n111; clerical, 90, 123; French-Canadian, 117, 119–20, 123, 226, 266; myth-symbols of, 328; pan-Canadian, 255; "reassurance of fratricide," 92–3; romantic, 93, 287; U.S., 91

national liberation, 36

National Mod, 298

national park. *See* Cape Breton Highlands National Park

nation-building, 52

nationhood, 259

nation-states, 37, 48, 49–50

Native peoples. *See* First Nations

"Native Types," 10, 11–12, 14, 20, 51

native/white reconciliation, 183

Nelles, Viv, 92

neo-Europes, 328

neo-Jacobitism, 289

neo-liberalism, 315

Netherlands, 24

neutralism, 134–5

neutrality: active, 25, 29, 32, 36, 75; Bird and, 179

New, W.H., 231

New Brunswick, 23, 32, 33, 161, 202, 348; dismantling of Catholic separate school systems in, 89

New Deal, 68, 276

New England, 50, 66; Brebner and, 45–6, 77; British/French conflict and, 30, 41–4, 165; expansion of, 26–7; Expulsion and, 122; historical record preservation in, 98; as origin of Nova Scotians, 20, 27, 47–8, 216; "Planters" from, 33; therapeutic frontier of, 103; tourism in, 63; trade with, 25

New Englanders, 28–9, 35, 38, 50, 91, 179

Newfoundland, 348, 364–5

Newfoundland Historical Society, 364–5

New France, 25, 28, 259; end of, 31

New Hampshire, 63, 69

New Scotland. *See* Nova Scotia

New York Times, 122

New Zealand, McLeod migration to, 288

Nickerson, Moses H., 318

"nigger," use of by Raddall, 218–19

"Noble Savages," 184, 247

non-whites, ridicule of, 148

Norge Canada, 322

Norse: people and sagas of, 317–27, 339; Scots and, 327

nostalgia: antimodern cultural, 74; generalized, 111; objects of, 223; pseudo-Gaelic, 378

Nova Scotia: Anglo ascendancy in history of, 175; anglophone definition of, 95;

annexation of to Canada, 34; anomalies of history of, 319; apocrypha of, 327; Assembly of, 98; attitudes of Scots in, 264–6; attitudes toward Scots in, 261–4; branding of, 70, 76, 107, 255, 281; British civilization of, 57, 218, 255; as "Canada's Ocean Playground," 66; Celtic essence of, 291; "celtic motif" of, 292; challenges to tourism promotion in, 54, 76; coat of arms of, 311–12, *313*; Commission on Post-war Development and Rehabilitation, 243; controversy and awkwardness, cleansing of, 255; as cradle of British civilization, 221; cultural history, 72; cultural purity of, 296; Department of Industry and Publicity, 282, 331, 356, 377; economic marginality of, 377; education system of, 297–8; ethnic groups in, 256; first tourists in, 63; first white settlers in, 319; five founding white races of, 254, 311, 342; flag of, 266–8, 312; "forest primeval" in, 80–1, 101, 112, 114; framing history of, 7–8, 15; geopolitical location of, 20; Haiti as negation of, 235; heather in, 291–2, 311; Highland Heart of, 256, 320; Highland village historic site proposal, 266; as "historic land," 232; as "Home of the Happy," 73, 75, 93, 107, 126, 369, 371; identity of, 132, 200, 219, 244, 256; intellectual awakening of, 40; interpretive dilemmas in, 92; interwar-era collapse, 276; legendry of, 327; Ministry of Highways, 342; Ministry of the Interior, 112; motto of, 257, 296, 311–12; naming of, 26, 43, 256, 259; Norse pedigree of, 321; as novel, 70; as Old World province, 67, 127, 374; origins of population of, 261; out-migration from, 40, 128, 270, 288, 309; patriots in, 92; piper welcoming visitors, 69, 253, 254, 257, 275, 291, 315; as pre-industrial and romantic, 160; as Province of Longfellow, 100; as Province of Parkman, 100; Provincial

Economic Inquiry (Jones Commission), 276; racial purity of, 296; re-description of, 303; reshaping of culture of, 282; rocky coastline of, 64–5; as Scotland of New World, 253; Scottish-Norse, 320; Scottish origins of, 257–61; shifts in representational strategies, 19; speculative histories of, 320; tartan, 69, *314*, 315; tertiary economy in, 77–8; as therapeutic outpost of New England, 72, 77, 374; topography of, imaginative framework and, 112; tourism as answer to economic depression, 64, 128; as tourism Mecca, 353; underdevelopment of, 238, 241; as "vacationland," 272

Nova Scotia Bureau of Information, 156, 168

Nova Scotia by the Sea, 68

Nova Scotia Canada: Fertile, Productive Lands ... (Ministry of the Interior), 61

Nova Scotia Canada: The Country and Its People ... (Ministry of the Interior), 61

Nova Scotia, Canada's Ocean Playground, 3, *4, 10, 55*, 122, 282, *293, 343*

Nova Scotia Highlanders: 193rd Battalion of, 133; *Songbook of the 85th Battalion*, 269

Nova Scotia Historical Society, 67, 100, 266–7, 281, 322, 338

Nova Scotia Motor League, 64

Nova Scotiana, romantic, 155–6

"Nova Scotianness," 203, 261, 266, 278

Nova Scotians: archetypal, in Raddall, 216; as Britons across the sea, 57; cultural and historical distinctiveness of, 235; cultural identity of, 244

Nova Scotia Publicity Bureau, 64, 392n96

Nova Scotia, the Atlantic Pier of America (Halifax *Herald*), 59

Nova Scotia, The Ocean Playground (Department of Highways), *108*, 265

Nova Scotia Tourist Advisory Council, 278

Nova Scotia Tourist Association, 62, 64, 270–2, 392n96

Numismatic and Antiquarian Society of Philadelphia, 317

occupational therapy, writing as, 156
O'Dea, Fabian, 455n225
"Old Home Summer" campaign, 270
Old Sturbridge Village (Massachusetts), 347
Olsen, Magnus, 317
Ontario: elimination of French from dismantling of Catholic separate school systems in, 89; Regulation 17 in, 100; Scots in, 261
Order of the Good Time, 342–5
organic intellectuals, 51, 65, 69, 133, 144, 169, 254, 382n16
otherness, 223, 281; primitive, 296
out-migration, 40, 309

pacifism, secular, 135
Palmer, Frances Flora (Bond), 80, 82–3
pan-Canadian developments, 45
pan-Canadian reality, 52
pan-Celticism, 280, 283, 376
Parade of Sail, 375
paradis perdu, 78, 126
Parkman, Francis, 38–40, 39, 41, 50, 53, 70, 99–102, 177, 231, 375; Bird and, 177; Brebner and, 42, 46–8; France and England in North America, 38; on Le Loutre, 411n153; on Longfellow, 99; on Missiquash, 410n108; Montcalm and Wolfe, 99; Nova Scotia as province of, 100; portrayal of Acadians, 39–40, 42, 47–8, 99; power of over public history, 39
Parks Canada, 124
parliamentarianism, 52
Parrsboro, 159
Parsons, Talcott, 21
partisans, nineteenth-century historians as, 51–2
Passchendale, 139, 143, 147, 151
past: eclecticism and bricolage in creation of public, 377; framing of, 7–9, 51; golden, 287, 333; homogenized, 162;

imagined, 163, 352; public, 16, 21, 51–2, 62, 72, 132; public history as politics of, 21; public vs private nature of, 51; reification of readings of, 17
pastness, 16, 111
pastoralism, 78–81, 115, 156
paternalism, 307
patriarchy, 210
patriotism, 140–1, 212, 244, 322
patriots, nineteenth-century historians as, 51–2
Patterson, George, 428n45
Pearl, James, 338
Peggy's Cove, 65
People's History of Canada, 124
Phillips, Jr, Henry, 317
physical attractiveness, morality and, 81–5
Picard, Claude, 124
Pictou, 270–5
Pictou Academy, 270
Pictou County, 34, 260, 288; Green Hill Museum, 336, 346
"Pictou Product," 272
Piers, Harry, 318
Pioneers' Museum (Green Hill), 336
Plains of Abraham, 28
Plank, Geoffrey, 23, 26, 29
"Planters." See New England
"Planter Studies," 45
pluralism, 22
Pohl, Frederick J., 442n12
Poirier, Pascal, 100
political economy, liberal, 16, 273
population displacement, 154
populism, 138
Port Joli Harbour, 414n2
Port Royal, 124, 259, 349; fall of, 25, 29; first settlement at, 165, 236, 358; French settlers at, 119; Habitation, 335, 342, 344; New Englanders and, 26; Scottish primacy at, 267; Siege of, 29
Portugal, 24
possessive individualism, 52
Post (Cape Breton), 433n126
post-liberalism, 45–6

Post-Record (Sydney), 297
Pothier, Bernard, 87, 94
Pound, Ezra, 122
poverty, 40
power relations, 19
Pratt, Mary Louise, 22
Presbyterianism, 260, 273
preservationism, 51, 286, 337–8, 346, 353;
   Bird and, 353, 354, 356–8, 360, 362–3;
   Macdonald and, 286; Raddall and, 353,
   355, 357, 360, 362–3
primacy, 401n94; of individual, 133; Scottish, 267
primitivism, civility vs, 35, 37
Prince Edward, 104
Prince Edward Island, 23, 32, 33, 281, 348;
   dismantling of Catholic separate school
   systems in, 89; Scots in, 261
Prince George, 104
progress, 7, 10, 124, 155, 261, 264, 329; of
   British Empire, 92; Gaelic poems and,
   265; liberalism and, 213, 241; paeans to,
   52, 348–9; Raddall and, 238–9; Scots
   and, 262; story of, vs story of people, 8
promoters, nineteenth-century historians
   as, 51–2
property, 328–30; ownership of, 330;
   rights of, 329–30, 374
"prostitution," tourism as, 280
Protestant heretics, campaign against, 100
Protestantism, 178
Prowse, G.R.F., 365
Prussianism, 138
Public Archives of Canada, 341
Public Archives of Nova Scotia (PANS),
   40, 54, 98, 204, 331, 336, 341
public culture, 65
public history, 21, 95, 132, 368; of Great
   War, 134; as hegemony, 51; politicization
   of, 366; tourist economy and, 64
public memory, 135
public past. *See* past: public
Pugsley, Margaret, 336–7, 350

Quebec, 348; Archbishop of, 87; Bishop

of, 30; Catholic Church in, 25; conquest
in, 78; extra-provincial outrages and,
89; *habitants* of, 23; nationalism and, 88,
117, 119–20, 123; Quiet Revolution in,
121; religious authorities in, 86–7; self-
determination of, 123
Queens County Historical Society, 243,
   414n2
Queenston Heights, Battle of, 248
Quest of the Folk, The, 6, 8
Quinpool, John. *See* J.W. Regan

race, 11–17, 37, 170, 279–80; as bioethical
vs conceptual reality, 381n3; as biological fact, 13; Bird and, 148, 310, 339;
character and, 148; colonialism and, 224;
as cultural phenomenon, 310; distinct,
11; folk and, 66; hierarchy of, 14–15, 38;
idealized characteristics of, 280; marketing of, 253–316; ontological and epistemological reality of, 378; "pride of,"
284; Raddall and, 201, 224; riots, 256;
runic stone and, 319; "scientific" accounts of, 223; Scottish, 279; as tourism
promotion, 280
race science, 14
"racial aggrandizement," 311
racial antagonism, 266
racial continence, 222
racial discrimination, 309
racial division, 256
racial failure, 153
racial hierarchies, 234, 309, 311, 378
racialism, 13
racialization, 13–14, 283, 310, 327, 364, 378
racial minorities, 311
racial purity, 296
racial segregation, 256
racial separateness, 15
racial superiority, 216
racial theory, European, 223
racism, 13–14, 95, 100, 285, 309–10, 339
Raddall, Thomas H., 131, 176, 179, 200–
52, 270, 277, 310, 331, 341, 353–4, 357,
372–3; Acadians, views on, 216, 220–1,

226, 329, 333–4; African Americans, views on, 216, 217–19; alien and historic lands in, 232–5; anti-heroism in, 171; anti-historicalism of, 252; archival research of, 203–4, 206; *At the Tide's Turn, and Other Stories*, 202; "Bald Eagle," 245–7; bioethical fitness and, 254; biological dispositions and, 207; vs Bird, 200–1, 207; "Blind MacNair," 219, 237–8, 243–4; British partisanship of, 220, 244; Canadian Authors Association, 68; class and, 210–11, 214; colonialism and, 223–4; creative freedom of, 220; criticism of, 227; as cultural cartographer, 250; as culture hero, 244; degeneration in, 213, 238, 333; *The Dreamers*, 202, 236; eloquence of, 248–9; eroticism of, 228; Europeans, non-British, views on, 216; Evangeline Phenomenon and, 224–6; evolution and, 201, 213, 214, 216, 218, 222, 226, 228, 240, 249, 251–2, 333; fact and fiction in, 206, 208, 220, 248; fatalism of, 213; fate and, 240; First Nations people, views on, 206, 216–17, 223, 224, 231, 245–7, 323, 329–30, 333; *Footsteps on Old Floors: True Tales of Mystery*, 202; French Canadians, views on, 219–23, 224; gender and, 201, 207–10; Governor-General's Award, 203; *The Governor's Lady*, 202, 205, 206, 207, 208, 210, 216, 217, 229, 230; *Halifax, Warden of the North*, 200, 203, 205–6, 207, 208–9, 216, 229, 248, 412n163; *Hangman's Beach*, 202, 204, 229, 329; heritage preservation and, 243; *His Majesty's Yankees*, 202, 218, 237, 419n90; as historian, 200–1; historical accuracy of, 231; historical progression in, 201; Historic Sites Advisory Council, 332–4, 355; history, views on, 203–7; hybridity and, 223–4; imagined female perspective of, 209; impossible liberalism of, 200–52, 333; individualism and, 201, 213–15, 231, 240–2, 251–2; *In My Time*, 203; as intellectual and promoter of tourism/history, 16, 69; labour and, 211; Le Loutre and, 363; lieutenant-governorship, 203; Macdonald and, 280, 375–6; *The Markland Sagas*, 203, 319–20, 423n154; masculinity and, 237; "The Miracle," 238; miscegenation and, 256; misogyny of, 229; modernity and, 246; moral development/morality and, 212, 215–16, 232; *A Muster of Arms and Other Stories*, 202, 212, 249; narration of, 206; nationalism of, 232, 235; nature and, 238; "nigger," use of by, 218–19; Norse and Scots and, 327; Nova Scotia history and, 235–7, 251; Nova Scotia identity and, 244; *The Nymph and the Lamp*, 202, 208, 211, 217, 227–8, 229, 230, 252; *Ogomkegea: The Story of Liverpool, Nova Scotia*, 203; Parkman and, 39; *The Path of Destiny*, 203, 216, 236; *The Pied Piper of Dipper Creek and Other Tales*, 202, 203; popular history and, 244; "preciseness" of, 248–9; *Pride's Fancy*, 202, 218–19, 232–5, 237, 249, 418n72; as progressive thinker, 228; promotional books for Nova Scotia government, 203; race and, 201, 224; racial superiority, views on, 216, 378; realism of, 228, 231, 248, 251–2; regionalism, 235; "Reunion at Grand Pre," 224–6; *Roger Sudden*, 202, 204, 220, 222–4, 227, 329, 334, 417n55; romanticism and, 204, 244; *The Rover: The Story of a Canadian Privateer*, 202; *The Saga of the 'Rover,'* 202, 423n154; Scottishness and, 275; self-essentialization and, 246; self-mastery and self-sufficiency in, 213; sex/sexuality and, 207, 214, 223, 227–31; sex-trade workers and, 228–31; *Tambour, and Other Stories*, 202, 244; *This Is Nova Scotia: Canada's Ocean Playground*, 203; "Three Wise Men," 202; *Tidefall*, 202, 209, 214–16, 239–42, 360; "Tit for Tat," 216; Toronto and, 241–2; tourism bureaucracy and, 247; *The Wedding Gift and Other Stories*, 202; *West Novas: A History of the West Nova Scotia Regiment*,

202–3; *The Wings of Night*, 202, 209–10, 212–13, 238–9, 241; women and, 207–10, 230–1; working class and, 211, 213

Radforth, Ian, 60

Rawlyk, George, 26, 27, 45

Raymond, Francis, 75

Raynal, Abbé, 98, 107; *L'Histoire philosophique et politique des établissements et du commerce des Européens dans les deux Indes*, 73

readings of the past, reification of, 17

realism: Bird and, 134, 136–7, 154, 170, 181, 250; in English Canadian fiction, 231; Herbin and, 117; Machiavellian, 252; Raddall and, 228, 231, 248, 251

reductionism, 21

Regan, J.W., 131, 348–9, 362; *First Things in Acadia*, 348

regional underdevelopment, 238, 241

Reid, John, 23, 24, 33, 46–7, 48, 75, 124, 259; "*Pax Britannica* or *Pax Indigena*?," 46

reification, historicization vs, 372

religious zealotry, 288

remembrance: cult of, in Louisiana, 91; history as, 119; sites of, 92

Renan, Ernest, 92

republicanism, 87

retail therapy, 373, 377

revolution, 164

Richards, David Adams, 414n2

Richardson, Evelyn, 324–5

Richelieu, Cardinal, 259

Riel, Louis, 89, 100

Roberts, Charles G.D., 166, 391n82, 402n96; DAR and, 104; on Land of Evangeline, 103, 112, 114; on Longfellow, 84–5

Robert the Bruce, 93

Robichaud, Marie-Marguerite, 117

Robichaud, Prudent, 30

Rob Roy, 291

Rockefeller, Jr, John D., 347

Rogers, Norman McLeod, 177, 276

Rogers, Stan, 67, 379

romance, 81, 166, 346, 370; of the Gael, 279, 289; historical, 36, 72, 101; of history, 102, 111, 176, 236; Raddall and, 247

romantic history: medieval warfare, 151; tourism-oriented, 130

romanticism, 303, 337; of Acadian history, 88; antimodernist, 337; folk, 167; Gaelic, 299; gothic, 179; Raddall and, 220; Scottishness and, 313

romantic nationalism, 93

Ross-Thomson House, 336–7, 347, 358

Roy, Gabrielle, 203

Roy, Wally, 291. *See also* Nova Scotia: piper

Royal Nova Scotia Historical Society, 448n99. *See also* Historic Sites and Monuments Board of Canada

Royal Society of Canada, 99, 318

Rudin, Robert, 92

Rumilly, Robert, 89, 90

Runic Stone Committee, 325

runic stones, 317–27, 328, 330, 368, 372; readings of, 326

Sable Island, 202

St Andrew, Cross of, 312

Saint Andrew's Society of Glasgow, 267

St Ann's. *See* Gaelic College

Saint-Domingue. *See* Haiti

St Francis Xavier University, 257, 264, 281, 286, 299

St Lawrence colony, 24, 25

St Lawrence River system, 123

St Martinville (Louisiana), 115, 397n46

St Mary's University, 359–60

Saint Pierre et Miquelon, 388n38

Salverson, Laura, 325

Saturday Evening Post, 202, 418n72, 421n124

Saturday Night, 135

Saunders, Margaret Marshall, 124, 186, 402n96

Sauvageau, Robert, 47

savagery, culture vs, 35

scientific improvement, 7

Scotland, 24, 93, 253–316; autonomy of, 66; clan system of, 260, 268; Highlands of, 77, 78; immigration from, 260; monarchy of, 26; Scottish Myth in, 287

Scots, 20, 26, 33, 34, 48, 95; attitudes of, 264–6; attitudes toward, 261–4; essence of, 306–9; Golden Age of, 378; Highland, 11, 12, 15, 38, 182, 260, 263, 265, 269, 271; individualism of, 307; literary landscape and, 401n95; Lowland, 15, 38, 260; Norse and, 327; prestige and title of, 312; virtues of, 307

Scots Gaelic College, 253

Scott, Walter, 264

Scottish Catholic Society: *Mosgladh*, 265

Scottish Enlightenment, 35, 271, 308

Scottish independence, 308

Scottish Myth, 270, 273, 275, 291–2, 313, 315, 327, 376; individualism and, 309; Lone Shieling and, 295; A.L. Macdonald and, 260, 279–81, 283, 289, 355; F. Macdonald and, 287–9; Muir and, 268; race/whiteness and, 273, 284–5, 309–11; Scotland and, 287

Scottish National Party, 289

Scottishness, 64, 66, 254, 255, 257–61, 265, 292, 307, *314*, 315, 323; Antigonish and, 264; as brand name of Nova Scotia, 281; Canadian nationalism and, 66; Gaelic College and, 304; *Hector* commemoration and, 270; Macdonald and, 280–1, 283, 296, 306, 308, 333; as persuasive commonsense, 281; provincial tartan and, 315; romanticized, 313; white dominance and, 311

Scottish Privy Council, 258

Scottish Reformation, 308

Sea-Conditioned Nova Scotia, 109, *293*, *305*

Seaman, Amos "King," 336, 350

Sea Stories, 202

segregation, 14, 256

self-government, Canadian, 64

Seven Years' War, 31, 33

Sewell, Bill, 49, 382n3

sex-trade workers, Raddall on, 228–31

sexual politics, 125, 214

Shag Harbour, UFO sighting at, 327

Shelburne, 34, 38

Shirley, William, 30–1, 98

Shubenacadie, 31, 363

Sierra Leone, 217

Sigogne, Abbé Jean-Mandé, 86–7, 92, 94

Silliboy, Gabriel, 345

Silver, A.I., 88, 114

sites of memory, 50, 118–19, 132, 324, 327, 330, 342, 353

slavery, 48, 164, 180–1, 217, 234, 361, 396n39

Smith, Adam, 263, 271, 330

Smith, John A., 300

Smith, Sidney E., 360

Smith, Susan, 13

social control, 21, 134

social Darwinism, 373

social democracy, 308

social hierarchy, 135

social history, rise of, 44

socialism, 155, 277, 307, 330

social relations, 7, 64, 77, 240, 328, 372

Société mutuelle l'Assomption (SMA), 118–19, 121

Société nationale l'Assomption, 121

socio-economic transformation, 34

solidarity, remembered, 141

South Shore, 63, 65, 114, 187, 231, 237, 243–4, 247, 357

Spain, 24

spectaculars, mass, 69

Spedon, Andrew Learmont, 54

Spencer, Herbert, 212, 240

spiritualism, 136, 149, 151

Springfield Republican, 168

Squier, Emma-Lindsay, 68

Stallabrass, Julian, 295

Stallybrass, Peter, 223

Stanfield, Robert, 168, 331, 334, 352, 356, 359, 361, 362, 367

state intervention, accommodation of, 278

statism, 278, 282

Statue of Liberty, 268, 377; Halifax Memorial Tower as, 58–9

steel industry, 7, 64, 77, 128, 276

Stein, Harve, 415n14

Stellarton, 362

stereotypes: of savages, 47

Stewart, Gordon, 45

Strandwold, Olaf, 320, 321, 325–6; *The Runic Stone*, 326

structures, centrality of, 46

Sunday Leader (Halifax), 130, 131, 181

supernatural, 148–51

Sutherland, David, 388n40

Swan, Anna, 336

Swan, J. Wesley: *Through the Maritime Provinces*, 39, 56

Sweetheart Stories, 131

Switzerland, 93

Sydney, 159, 365

Sydney Post-Record, 68

tartan, 69

tartanism, 253–316, 372, 374, 375; language of, 66; naturalized, 279; twenty-first-century, *314*

Taunton River (Massachusetts), 319

Taylor, C.J., 342

Taylor, M. Brook, 38, 51–2, 97

teleology, 49, 378; of history, 252

Tell, William, 93

Ten Mile House, 359

Thackeray, William Makepeace: *Vanity Fair*, 416n30

"Third Acadie," 47

Thirteen Colonies, American, 26

Thomas Head Raddall Atlantic Fiction Prize, 414n2

Thomas Raddall Provincial Park, 414n2

Thornley, Betty D., 68, 113

Time, 303

Times (London), 58, 60

Titanic commemoration, 375

Toronto, 241–2

tourism: active, 113; advent of, 19, 63, 65; American, 243, 299; anatomical, 284; antimodernism as new vocabulary of, 281; artificial world of, 371; automobile, 65, 162; battlefields, 136, 152–3; Bird and, 155–70; challenges for promotion of, 54; as consequence of *Evangeline*, 80, 96, 101, 103–5, 107; culture and, 111, 279; culture of, 21; as domesticating history, 371; as economic nationalism, 66; economy, development of, 114, 128; historical, 154; historiography of, 393n101; and history in Raddall, 200, 201–2; instability of, 160; international patterns of, 255; Jones Commission and, 276; Lake District, 401n94; literary, 246; Macdonald and, 278, 280–4; mass, debut of, 63–9, 265; political economy of, 318, 327; popularization of, 168; postwar, 350; primitive otherness in, 296; promotion of, 15, 54, 126, 254–5, 270–2, 273, 280, 303, 331–2, 336, 342; as "prostitution," 280; race and, 280; Raddall and, 243, 247; redemptive role of, 279; romance and, 167; runic stone and, 319; state's role in, 282; structuring patterns of, 154; tertiary economy of, 77–8; trade vs industry of, 16, 128; war and, 149; Warner's influence on, 263

tourism/history, 9, 15, 16, 20, 68–9, 154, 346–7, 359, 368, 371–2, 374–80; in Annapolis Valley, 62; bias and, 19; Bird and, 144, 250; Britishness and, 333; British progressive, 67; characteristics of, 76; as closed commercial sphere, 51; conflicts with, 374; "credulous allegiance" and, 19; critical historiography and, 37; DAR and, 115; development of, 271, 278; Duncan and, 285; economic dimension of, 328; Evangeline phenomenon and, 71–129; facilitative liberalism and, 330; fact vs fiction in, 22, 377; as forerunner of heritage, 15; frontier narratives and, 36; government role in, 339, 353; Haliburton's impact on, 38; Harvey and, 356; Hector commemoration and, 273;

heritage objects and, 327–8; historical assets and, 350–1; historiography and, 365; Innocence and, 17; insider vs outsider in, 22; insulation of from historical knowledge and critique, 50–1; intellectuals, 68; Macdonald and, 353, 355; mnemonic complex and, 342; negotiated language of, 367; Order of the Good Time and, 343; organic intellectuals of, 68–9, 254; origins of, 71–129; political/economic development and, 77; promoters of, 68–9; Raddall and, 250; radicalism of, 21; romantic notions of, 49; runic stone and, 324, 327–8

tourist frame, 371

tourist gaze, 62, 113, 165, 292, 351, 371

tourist propaganda, 132

tourists: Acadians and, 101, 103; active, 113; American, 63, 66, 161, 164, 299, 346; automobile, 63, 65, 393n103; Canadian vs American, proportion of, 393n103; commodities for, 16; connotations of word, 63, 392n96; as credulous foreigners, 63; DAR and, 104, 107, 118; Erikson museum and, 321; Evangeline and, 85, 96, 117, 126; genealogy of word, 392n96; numbers of, 63–6; as readers, 159; as subverting local culture, 21; as summer visitors, 63; tartanism and, 283, 291, 305

tourist trade, 131, 243; vs industry, 128

trade unions, 362

tradition, invented, 280–1

transatlanticism, 389n60

travel writing, 156; battlefield, 152

Treaty of Aix-la-Chapelle, 31

Treaty of Breda, 387n21

Treaty of Ryswick, 387n21

Treaty of Saint-Germain-en-Laye, 259, 387n21

Treaty of Utrecht, 25, 26, 28–32, 94

trench warfare, 143, 146–7, 149, 151, 156, 159, 186, 250

Trevor-Roper, Hugh, 265

Trotsky, Leon, 77, 324

Tunbridge, J.E., 20, 59

Tupper, Charles, 275

Turner, Frederick Jackson, 36

Tweedsmuir, Lord. See John Buchan

typhus, 211

unemployment, 40

Union of 1707, 265

Unitarianism, 73

United Kingdom, relations with U.S., 91

United States: ascent of, 64; blacks and whites in, 13; nationalism, 91; relations with Britain, 91; tourism from, 63, 66, 105, 161, 164, 299, 346; War of Independence, 91

urban progressivism, 309

use value, 327

utopianism, 79, 237

Vacation Days in Nova Scotia, 120

Vance, Jonathan, 134–8, 140, 142

Vernon, C.W., 263–4

veterans, Great War, 133; alienation, 143

Victoria County, 15, 298, 299

Victoria Crosses, 140

"Viking National Park," 328

Vikings, 317, 319–20, 325

Villers-au-Bois, 139

Vimy Ridge, 133, 140, 154

Vinland, 327

violence, ethnic, 256

voluntarism, 337, 342

voyeurism, 85

Wabanaki Confederacy, 23

Walters, Angus, 67

war: Anglicanization of, 155; chance and, 148; decline of human civilization and, 149; futility of, 134, 144; preconditions of, 149; views on, 133–55; as wrong, 149. See also Great War; War of 1812

Warner, Charles Dudley: Baddeck, and That Sort of Thing, 262–3, 426n30

War of 1812, 216, 217, 236, 248

Webster, Daniel, 91

Webster, J.C., 170, 177, 350

Webster, K.G.T., 318, 336, 337, 347, 358

welfare state, 278, 308

Wells, H.G., 138

Western Home Monthly, 131

West Indies, 218–19

Wetmore, Don, 432n105

Whisky Galore!, 291

White, Allon, 223

White, Hayden, 382n3

White, Kenneth, 204, 422n149

whiteness, 11–12, 50, 117, 378; civilization and, 37; culture politics of, 253–316; "native type" and, 12

white races, 223, 279, 311, 312, 318, 327, 342, 378; local romance of, 320

Whiteway, S.P., 365

Whitton, Charlotte, 303

Wicken, William, 23, 29

Williams, Alan F., 455n225

Williams, Catherine A., 91, 93

Williams, Paul, 57–9

Williamsburg (Virginia), 347

Willson, Beckles, 52, 61; *Nova Scotia: The Province That Has Been Passed By*, 54–5, 263

Wilson, Daniel: "The Vinland of the Northmen," 317–18

Wilson, W.C., 291

Winant, Howard, 310

Windsor and Annapolis Railway, 103–4

Winnipeg General Strike, 145

Winnipeg Tribune, 158

Winslow, John, 76, 98

Winsor, Justin: *Narrative and Critical History of America*, 98–9

Winter, Jay, 136, 149

Wolfville, 102

Wolin, Sheldon, 424n168

women: attitudes of Bird toward, 145–6, 186, 188–92, 194, 196, 199; as blends of purity and beauty, 84; as temptresses in Raddall, 207–10, 218, 228–30

Woods, Nathan, 60

Woodstock (New Brunswick), 164

Woodsworth, J.S., 135

Woodworth, Margaret, 104

Wordsworth, William, 122, 401n94

work ethic, 273

Wright, C.H., 347

Writers' Federation of Nova Scotia, 414n2

Wulstukwik, 46

Wynn, Graeme, 114

Yarmouth, 59, 103, 115, 317–19, 325–6, 328, 352; Frost Monument, 360–1; Leif Erikson and, 321–3; Rock Cottage, 338; runic stone in, 317–19, 368

Yarmouth County Historical Society, 338

Yarmouth Light, 322

Yarmouth, Nova Scotia, Canada, 326

Yarmouth Public Library, 319, 325

Yarmouth Steamship Company, 103–4

Yarmouth Vanguard, 326, 327

Yorkshire emigrants, Will R. Bird and, 131, 170–5

Yorkshiremen, 33, 171, 333

Young, Robert J.C., 223

Zeno, Niccolò, 442n12